A TOUR THROUGH THE WHOLE ISLAND OF GREAT BRITAIN

DANIEL DEFOE

A TOUR
Through the
WHOLE ISLAND
of
GREAT BRITAIN

Abridged and Edited by
P.N. FURBANK AND W.R. OWENS

Picture Research by
A.J. COULSON

YALE UNIVERSITY PRESS
NEW HAVEN AND LONDON

Designed by Gillian Malpass

Set in Linotron Bembo by
Excel Typesetters Company, Hong Kong
Printed in Hong Kong by
Kwong Fat Offset Printing Co. Ltd

Library of Congress Cataloging-in-Publication Data

Defoe, Daniel, 1661?–1731.
 A tour through the whole island of Great Britain/Daniel Defoe;
edited and abridged by P.N. Furbank, W.R. Owens, and Anthony J.
Coulson.
  p. cm.
 Includes Index.
 ISBN 0-300-04980-3
   1. Great Britain—Description and travel—1701–1800. I. Furbank.
Philip Nicholas. II. Owens, W.R. III. Coulson, Anthony J.
IV. Title.
DA620.D31 1991
914.104′7—dc20   90-48710
                                                          CIP

Plate I (frontispiece): Detail from pl. XXXI
Endpapers: Map of England and Wales.
          From Herman Moll, *A Set of fifty new and correct maps of England and Wales* (1724).
          Bodleian Library, Oxford, c.17.e.2.
          Map of 'The North Part of Great Britain called Scotland'.
          From Thomas Taylor, *England exactly described* (1715).
          Bodleian Library, Oxford, Gough Maps 115.

CONTENTS

INTRODUCTION

ANIEL DEFOE ONCE WROTE that his novel *Robinson Crusoe* was allegorical. It is not exactly clear what he was implying or if he meant it was an allegory of his own life. There is no doubt, though, that, in trying to come to a judgement on Defoe and his career, one keeps thinking of Crusoe, a man with such a dedication to tranquillity, security and solid and prosaic goods, but an unrivalled capacity for mislaying them or throwing them away.

Defoe was born in 1660, the son of a London tallow chandler and merchant named James Foe, and was educated at a Dissenting Academy in Newington Green. There was some thought, soon abandoned, of his entering the Presbyterian ministry, and instead he went into business, first as a 'hose-factor' (or whole-sale haberdasher) and subsequently in various other branches of trade and manufacturing, marrying in 1684 the daughter of a well-to-do Dissenting merchant. He seems, indeed, and this may always have been his trouble, to have been over-ambitious; at all events, in 1692 he was bankrupted for a very considerable sum, and for the rest of his life he would be hounded by bailiffs and creditors, sometimes set on by his political enemies.

His ambitions were not limited to business. He rather rashly joined the forces of the Protestant Duke of Monmouth's army during his unsuccessful rebellion in 1685. He was also, or learned to be, a poet, a political thinker and economic theorist, and, as we know–but this happened quite late in his career–he became a novelist. His first substantial publication was a verse satire, *A New Discovery of an Old Intreague* (1691), and in 1698 he produced an important prose-work, entitled *An Essay on Projects*, in which he put forward schemes for a whole range of national improvements: road-making, insurance, pension offices, academies for women and so on. Then, early in 1701, angered by the chauvinistic cant levelled at England's foreign saviour William III, he published another verse-satire, *The True-Born Englishman*, genially complimenting the English on being the mongrels of

Europe. It won a great reputation and, so it would appear, it secured him the favour of King William. It also made him a host of enemies, among them some influential City magnates; and when, at the end of the following year, he published an anonymous pamphlet, *The Shortest Way with the Dissenters*, an impersonation of High-Church fanaticism so brilliant as to earn warm praise from High-Churchmen themselves, some of those enemies became his judges, and he was sent to Newgate for it and made to stand in the pillory.

It was then that a leading politician, Robert Harley, saw the use that might be made of such a talented pen and such a fertile-minded and reckless man, with a gift for disguise. Harley secured his release from Newgate, offered him employment as a pamphleteer and encouraged him to launch his famous *Review*, a twice- or thrice-weekly periodical of Whiggish tendency.[1] In this, for nine years, Defoe would lecture and tease the British public and become an influential opinion-maker on trade, politics, foreign policy and manners. Harley also engaged Defoe as his own confidential intelligence-agent, in which role Defoe made extensive fact-finding tours through England and Scotland.

By 1710 Harley had moved towards the Tories and had joined a Tory administration, but Defoe continued in his service. No doubt he did so partly out of self-interest. His enemies certainly said this, with great virulence. It could also be, though, that he did it partly out of conviction and loyalty. Defoe seems, indeed, to have been a loyal man; when, with the death of Queen Anne, the Tories were disgraced and Harley sent to the Tower, Defoe appears to have gone to some lengths, in anonymous pamphlets, to protect Harley and his reputation.

This period, the opening years of the reign of George I, was a low point in Defoe's career, and, though soon reconciled with the now-dominant Whigs, he was reduced to a humiliating role, that of masquerading as a Tory and insinuating himself into the management of Tory journals, to take the sting out of their attacks on the Whig government. He was, meanwhile, still busy as a pamphleteer on many topics, and in April 1719 he published—as usual with him, anonymously—*The Life and Strange Surprizing Adventures of Robinson Crusoe*. It is a matter of taste whether we regard this, or Bunyan's *Pilgrim's Progress*, as the first great English novel. At all events, Defoe's novel became and remained an enormous best-seller, rivalled only by Bunyan's; and, directly or indirectly (for conceivably he profited more from subsequent novels) it seems to have given him financial security.

During the mid-1720s he was living in some style in 'a very handsome house' at Stoke Newington. At this time, no doubt because less involved in day-to-day journalism, he began a series of lengthy and systematic prose treatises. Among them was the work we are here introducing, *A Tour Through the Whole Island of Great Britain*, which appeared in three volumes between 1724 and 1726. It was a work written in a vein of patriotic optimism, not to nag the British, as he was apt to do, but to encourage them and to offer them a vision of their own grandeur and resources.

His prosperity was not long-lasting. 'No man has tasted differing fortunes more,/ And thirteen times I have been rich and poor', once wrote Defoe,[2] and in this brief sketch we have hardly begun to suggest the vicissitudes of his career. He himself had theories about Providence and how one might learn its designs, but in the long run they did not help him, and this extraordinary man ended his no less extraordinary life once more in calamitous straits: he died in April 1731, alone, in hiding from his creditors and estranged from his family.

*   *   *

Defoe may be said to have been preparing all through his life, whether consciously or unconsciously, to compose *A Tour Through Great Britain*. He tells how as a young man he made a journey round England with an 'ancient friend', of great knowledgeableness and wisdom, and, if we are to believe him, he once contemplated a sea journey along the entire coastline of the British Isles, emulating the Roman general Agricola.[3] In 1705, as Harley's political emissary, he went on a fact-finding tour that took him through the whole West Country, and in the following year he made another long journey to Scotland, where he spent a year as Harley's spy and an unofficial agent in the Union negotiations. 'I have, within these twenty years past', he writes in the *Review* in 1711, 'travelled, I think I may say, to every Nook and Corner of that part of the Island, call'd *England*, either upon Publick Affairs, when I had the Honour to serve his late Majesty King *William*, of Glorious, (tho' forgotten) Memory—or upon my private Affairs; I have been in

every County, one excepted, and in every Considerable Town in every County, with very few Exceptions; I have not, I hope, been an idle Spectator, or a careless unobserving Passenger in any Place, and believe I can give some Account of my Travels if need were.'

As for his direct preparations for writing the *Tour*, he speaks of having taken 'seventeen very large circuits, or journeys . . . through divers parts separately, and three general tours over almost the whole English part of the Island' (p. 5), and in addition, of having 'travelled critically over a great part of Scotland' (p. 5). When, in the *Tour*, he goes on to tell us such things as that he 'set out, the 3d of April, 1722, going first eastward' (p. 7), it would be dull of us to take him literally, for the book is, after all, a work of art. But what are we to think of those 'seventeen very large circuits', or of the tour of Scotland? Are we, for one thing, meant to believe them all recent, and if so, to believe that they happened, roughly anyway, in the manner described in the *Tour*? Or were only some of them recent, or perhaps none? (After all, there is evidence to show that Defoe possessed a phenomenal and wonderfully well-organised memory.) Then, shall we believe him, and if so to what extent, when he claims to give 'but very few accounts of things, but what he has been an eye-witness of himself' (p. 5)? The questions multiply, and the answers we come to cannot be conclusive.

To take first the question of when his actual, as opposed to his pretended, travelling was done, opinion has differed widely. James Sutherland, in his *Defoe* (1937), wrote that 'Defoe was only working up materials which he had collected in almost forty years of travelling',[4] with the implication, evidently, that the *Tour* was out-of-date when it appeared and a most unreliable guide to the Britain of the 1720s. Recently, however, Pat Rogers has argued, with a good deal of persuasive evidence, that, on the contrary, the *Tour* is 'chock-full of recent information' and that the actual planning of the book, or parts of it, had been done quite recently. He has shown that it is up-to-date not merely on casual or incidental facts but in certain of its leading themes, such as the after-effects of the South Sea Bubble or the continuing rebuilding of London.[5]

But of course this leaves a further question to answer: to what extent was Defoe writing from first-hand knowledge and observation? Or, to put it more brutally, had he ever been to half the places that he describes? Several possibilities need considering here. One has to remember, for instance, that, in the course of his journeys for Harley, Defoe had set up his own private intelligence network, and vestiges of this might have been surviving twenty years later and have been of great service to him in gathering information. Then, unquestionably, he drew heavily on books, with or without acknowledgement (and passing comments, sometimes gracious, sometimes very rude, on their authors). He quotes continually, and with high approval though also some banter, from William Camden's *Britannia* (1586), in its great new edition of 1695 by Edmund Gibson; most of his church history comes from William Dugdale's *Monasticon*, in its edition of 1717; and, without actually naming it, he makes several unkind side-swipes at (but also takes some hints from) John Macky's *Journey Through England* of 1714–23.

Unlike these earlier works, however, Defoe's *Tour* is neither a guide book nor a collection of antiquarian lore. His book has a dominating theme, which is clearly stated in his preface. His subject is to be not simply the British Isles in general, but specifically Britain's wealth, prosperity and 'increase'. By corollary the book is to deal with the present time and with recent developments. The state of things in Britain is to be described 'not as they have been, but as they are; the improvements in the soil, the product of the earth, the labour of the poor, the improvement in manufactures, in merchandizes, in navigation, all respects the present time, not the time past' (p. 5). Every day, he writes, 'the face of things' is altering in Britain, commerce is taking a new turn, 'fine houses' and new undertakings are appearing on the scene. It is all an addition to the glory of Britain, but it complicates the job of an author, who can scarcely keep up with developments and can never hope to call his account complete.

We may put the matter even more simply. The ruling concern of the *Tour* is trade, trade in all its ramifications, and in particular the inland trade that has made Britain 'the most flourishing and opulent country in the world' (p. 3). Thus, if we want to understand the *Tour*, it may help to look at a work that Defoe published almost concurrently with it: his *Complete English Tradesman*. It stands to the *Tour*, one might say, as theory to practice. The *Tour* can be read as an illustration and practical exemplification of what is argued in *The Complete English Tradesman* as instruction and polemic.

There is, writes Defoe in *The Complete English Tradesman*, a 'peculiar circumstance' affecting Britain, which gives her an advantage over other countries. It is that, for geographical and other reasons, hardly any two of her manufactures are made in the same place. Thus if one considers—to take an example—the clothes of a country shopkeeper's wife, we find, says Defoe,

that she gets her silk gown from Spitalfields, the lining of it from Bristol or Norwich, her under-petticoat of black clamanco from Norwich, her inner petticoats of flannel or swan-skin from Salisbury or Wales, her stockings from Tewkesbury, her gloves from Scotland, etc., etc. The same would be true of her furniture: the hangings might come from Kidderminster and be painted in London; the cane chairs come from London; the bedding, from Taunton or Exeter; the ticking, from the west country; the brass kitchen utensils, from Birmingham; and the glassware, from Worcester.[6] It is the sort of knowledgeable demonstration that Defoe loves, and in the *Tour* all this is made to come true. We are asked to see Bristol and Norwich, Kidderminster and Birmingham, when the narrative reaches them, as knots in a web of connections, of which London is the cenre and nexus. Defoe's book is much concerned with networks—land-routes and sea-routes, rivers, canals, bridges, mountain passes and the like—and it pauses at about its mid-point for a lengthy excursus upon roads.

The Complete English Tradesman insists, with much force of argument, on the supremely significant role of London. It was essentially a matter of size, for, as Defoe rightly implies (though he exaggerates the actual figure both here and in the *Tour*), the population of London had by 1700 swollen out of all proportion to that of its English rivals or of most of its continental ones: half a million or more, as compared with the thirty thousand of Norwich, the second town in England, or the sixty thousand of Seville. Here, according to Defoe, lies a great difference between England and a country like Spain, which has ten substantial cities and no 'great and capital' one. Those ten Spanish cities are remote and isolated entities; supplies come to them directly and with ease, without the need for 'a multitude of hands to be employed in raising, procuring, fetching, or carrying them'. Thus the commercial influence of each city remains separate and limited, extending perhaps no more than thirty or forty miles; it does not give employment, as the giant metropolis London does, to a nationwide host of middlemen. The role of London is, in a sense, almost the opposite of theirs and of the normal role of cities. 'It is not the kingdom makes London rich, but the city of London makes all the country rich.'[7] London and its uniqueness is central to Defoe's economic vision. The manufacturing towns of Britain, each with their own speciality, are dedicated to the production of goods for exchange rather than use, and this kind of production, Defoe insists, requires a single central market such as only London is equipped to provide. It is with great fittingness, then, that London is equally central to the design, both topographic and artistic, of the *Tour*. It is Defoe's intention in the *Tour*, as indeed he often reminds us, that, at any stage in the book's circuits, the reader shall feel the tug, the extended presence, of London.

Nor is it just in economic, but also social, philosophy, that these two books illuminate each other. The reader of the *Tour*, accustomed to a matter-of-fact Defoe, is taken aback when he grows lyrical, and even more perhaps by what occasions it. It is a shock to a post-Wordsworthian to read that the 'distant glory' of suburban mansions, those summer retreats of well-heeled tradesmen and gentlemen, constitutes 'the most glorious sight without exception, that the whole world at present can show, or perhaps ever could show since the sacking of Rome in the European, and the burning of the Temple of Jerusalem in the Asian part of the world' (p. 68). The whole rapturous passage can be read as an acting-out of the social doctrines of *The Complete English Tradesman*, which argues that the terms 'citizens', 'gentry' and 'nobility' express real distinctions but not in the very least impassable barriers. The successful 'citizen' or tradesman, upon retirement, 'commences gentleman' in the most easy and natural way; his son, or at worst his grandson, may become a bishop or a lord, and as good a lord as any other. For here is another providential uniqueness in Britain: 'Trade is so far here from being inconsistent with a gentleman, that, in short, trade in England makes gentlemen, and has peopled this nation with gentlemen.' For Defoe, as against the Tories of his day and later, the wish to rise in the world is 'a noble emulation'; and all the cant of aristocratic 'blood', all affected contempt for wealth, which is the source of Britain's greatness, are as dishonest as they are unpatriotic.[8]

'Unpatriotic' is a word to cling on to. In all his writings Defoe adopted the stance of a patriot–the thing, if not the word, which was in bad odour at that period. Patriotism, nevertheless, had not deflected him from criticism; and in his pamphlets and his journal, the *Review*, he had been the nagging or sardonic scourge of his country: its chauvinism, its bigotry, its indolence, muddled thinking and neglect of its own providential advantages. Indeed, in the Preface to the *Tour*, he says that he could easily have written a satire on the English; 'but they are ill friends to England, who strive to write a history of her nudities' (p. 3). Thus, in the *Tour*, though the critic is by no means entirely silenced, the emphasis is essentially on Britain's glory. What he is essaying is not so much a dispassionate account, as a patriotic celebration or panegyric.

It was partly a matter of loyalty. For certain foreigners, he says, have 'pretended to travel into England' and, in their accounts, 'have treated us after a very indifferent manner' (p. 5). One of the ill-disposed foreigners that Defoe has in mind, we need not doubt, was Samuel de Sorbière. Sorbière was Historiographer Royal to Louis XIV and a convert from Protestantism to Catholicism. He had come to England in 1663 on the strength of some funds from the French King and had reported the English as being–among other regrettable things–insular, arrogant, envious, idle, greedy, cowardly, fierce and capricious, inclined to melancholy, prone to simony and congenitally schismatic. This was quite a list, especially from a man who had been so cordially welcomed by the Royal Society; and when a translation of his *Voyage to England* came out in 1709, the publishers appended to it some indignant 'Observations' by the historian of the Royal Society, Thomas Sprat.

In his picture of England in the *Tour*, what is inspiring to Defoe and grips his imagination is the spectacle of *plenty*: the plenty that nature offers and almost seems to thrust into mankind's hands, and the plenty which arises from the creativity and mutual dependence of human beings. Those rich mansions surrounding London, when the eye unfocusses and dwells on them '*en passant*, and in perspective', acquire an extra beauty from their own sheer abundance and the sense that they 'reflect beauty, and magnificence upon the whole country' (p. 68). We seem to have here Defoe's formula for beauty. It is a spectacle of overflowing, a vivid image or reminder of the very attributes he associates with trade. 'An estate's a pond, but trade's a spring', he writes, contrasting the expanding resources of the tradesman with the confined ones of the 'middling gentry'. Trade 'is an inexhausted current, which not only fills the pond, and keeps it full, but is continually running over, and fills all the lower ponds and places about it'.[9]

The same concept is at work in another lyrical and rhapsodic passage, which comes immediately after the horrors of his journey over Blackstone Edge. As Defoe and his companions approach Halifax, they begin to find the whole hillside covered with cottages; and as the sun comes out, the gleaming–and as it were, heavenly–spectacle of white cloth drying on tenters provides the explanation for all this concourse of humans. Providence or the bounty of nature has provided this 'otherwise frightful country' with two essentials for cloth-workers, coal and running water, right up to the summit of the hills. It is thus a spectacle of the most exemplary industry, a succession of cloth-manufactures, fed by a criss-cross of water-channels for their cleaning and dyeing processes, and, between them, innumerable cottages of piece-workers, 'always carding, spinning, etc., so that, no hand being unemployed, all can gain their bread, even from the youngest to the ancient'.

> I thought it was the most agreeable sight that I ever saw, for the hills, as I say, rising and falling so thick, and the vallies opening sometimes one way, sometimes another, so that sometimes we could see two or three miles this way, sometimes as far another; sometimes like the streets near St. Giles's, called the Seven Dials; we could see through the glades almost every way round us, yet look which way we would, high to the tops, and low to the bottoms, it was all the same; innumerable houses and tenters, and a white piece upon every tenter. [p. 257]

It is not what the modern reader exactly relishes, this finding of sublimity in pre-industrial capitalism and child labour. ('Hardly any thing above four years old, but its hands are sufficient to itself' writes Defoe approvingly. He was an enthusiast for child labour.) Nevertheless, sublime in a way the passage is, and we can agree with John McVeagh, who has written of the 'distinct and unsordid quality of Defoe's materialism' and of the 'sustaining awe which humanizes his commercial writings'.[10]

The *Tour* was written at the beginning of the Walpole era, and the moment is significant. For this was an era, in intention anyway, dedicated to peace, a truce to faction, and sound finance, and these were by this time Defoe's priorities also. We can see it in a striking passage in *The Complete English Tradesman*. Why, he asks there, does the English tradesman stand so high in the eyes of the world and is 'allowed to rank with the best gentlemen in Europe'?

> War has not done it; no, nor so much as helped or assisted to it; it is not by any martial exploits; we have made no conquests abroad, added no new kingdoms to the British empire, reduced no neighbouring nations, or extended the possession of our monarchs into the properties of others; we have gained nothing by war and encroachment; we are butted and bounded just where we were in Queen Elizabeth's time; the Dutch, the Flemings, the French, are in view of us, just as they were then . . . instead of being enriched by war and victory, on the contrary, we have been torn in pieces by civil wars and rebellions . . . and at last, the late rebellion in England, in which the monarch fell a sacrifice to the fury of the people, and monarchy itself gave way to tyranny and usurpation, for almost twenty years.

> These things prove abundantly that the greatness

of the British nation is not owing to war and conquests . . . but it is all owing to trade, to the increase of our commerce at home, and the extending it abroad.[11]

What the attentive reader of the *Tour* begins to sense is that, in Defoe's vision of history, the 'past', an unending succession of wars and civil tumults, really *is* past: it is so definitely concluded, albeit so recently, as already to seem far removed. A gentle and remote sympathy enters Defoe's voice when he mentions the civil-war battlefield of Marston Moor: 'I came back extremely well pleased with the view of Marston Moor, and the account my friend had given of the battle; 'twas none of our business to concern our passions in the cause, or regret the misfortunes of that day; the thing was over beyond our ken; time had levelled the victors with the vanquished . . .'. Of Dumbarton Castle he writes that it is 'the most antient, as well as the most important castle in Scotland' and often called the gate of the Highlands, but 'It is now not much regarded, the whole country being, as it were, buried in peace' (p. 376). He speaks, in a striking phrase, of a 'reserved secret pleasantness' in the sight of demolished fortifications at York (p. 273). His whole analysis of Edinburgh, and his defence of its citizens against the reproach of dirtiness, turns upon the same consideration: the dismal necessities imposed by an irrational warlike way of life, now happily dead and gone.

> It is easy to conclude, that such a situation as this [i.e., that of Edinburgh] could never be picked out for a city or town, upon any other consideration than that of strength to defend themselves from the sudden surprises and assaults of enemies . . . If this was not the reason, what should have hindered them from building the city in a pleasant, delightful valley, with the sea flowing up one side, and a fresh water river running through the middle of it; such as is all that space of ground between the city, as it now stands, and the sea, or Firth, and on the south shore, whereon the town of Leith now stands? . . .

> These things they did not foresee, or understand in those days; but, regarding immediate safety, fixed on the place as above as a sure strength, formed by Nature, and ready at their hand. [p. 311]

This heightened and politically coloured emphasis on the present, as a distinguishable historical epoch, may help to explain Defoe's insistence (it becomes an absolute *tic* with him) that he will not do the work of Camden over again or be tempted to 'straggle into antiquity'. The preceding half century had been a great age for antiquaries and for the exhumation of the British past: Dugdale's *Monasticon*, Hearne's edition of Leland's *Itinerary*, Strype's updating of Stow's *Survey of London* and the new edition of Camden were all products of this period. To rival them may indeed have been a temptation to Defoe, for he claims to have 'many times repented' of his boycott on antiquarianism, and he promises one day 'to travel through all these northern countries upon this very errand, and to please, nay, satiate myself with a strict search into every thing that is curious in nature and antiquity' (p. 285). At all events he was not lacking in feeling for the past. Pat Rogers speaks of his sense of it as 'Virgilian' and 'elegiac',[12] and one may perhaps allow 'Virgilian'; but what is important to note is that his response to the past contains not the least whiff of nostalgia. Not for Defoe any attachment to ruins and the relics of ancient militarism and popery, not even the ambivalent and Whiggish response, half gleeful, half nostalgic, to Gothic ruins of a Horace Walpole. He refers to the immemorial ruins of Launceston, disrepectfully, as being 'only in their old cloaths' (p. 111).

It is one of those little surprises for the present-day reader that, in Defoe's *Tour*, farming and landowning are considered entirely from a trading and industrial angle and in terms of the logistic problems of wholesale clothiers, cheese-exporters and large-scale brewers. As readers of Fielding and Addison we expect a different scene. We ask, where are the ignorant and good-hearted country landlords, dispensing rough justice; the loyal tenantry or 'yeomen'; the port-drinking parsons? Defoe's, it may be supposed, is the more literal truth, and Fielding and Addison's (or Richardson's and Goldsmith's) the, equally significant, mythology. We may put the point more precisely: where, in Defoe's *Tour*, is the fox-hunter? The fox-hunting 'squire' was already a real and important feature of the English scene. 'Your true country squire lives in boots all the winter', writes Shadwell as early as 1689, 'never talks or thinks of anything but sports, as he calls 'em, and if an ill day comes, saunters about his house, lolls upon couches; sighs and groans as if he were a prisoner in the Fleet'.[13] Equally the fox-hunter was already (though soon to be much more so) a highly influential political symbol or ideological construction. (The 'Squire' and fox-hunting seem to have come upon the scene at about the same time.) Now, Defoe approved of some sports: he approved of deer-hunting, as a fitting and picturesque occupation for the aristocracy; and he favoured the 'manly noble diversions of racings', which put him in mind of the Circus Maximus, as warmly as he disliked the sharping which went with them; he also has praise for the plebeian, but 'manly

and generous' (p. 111), sport of Cornish wrestling. For hurling, on the other hand, he has nothing good to say, finding it 'a rude violent play among the boors, or country people; brutish and furious, and a sort of an evidence, that they were, once, a kind of barbarians' (p. 110). His criterion is fairly clear and concerns what will add to the dignity of the British and the figure that they will cut in foreign eyes. As for fox-hunting, though he tells us that his grandfather kept a pack of hounds,[14] one may guess he would have thought it a low and useless pursuit and would not have understood, or wished to understand, its appeal and its significance.

* * *

Defoe's *Tour* is by far the most often quoted source for early eighteenth-century English social and economic history. Nevertheless, it is also a very personal book. There is a famous passage in his letters in which, writing from Scotland, he describes to Harley, with the utmost zest, his own skills as a secret agent:

> I am perfectly unsuspected as corresponding with anybody in England. I converse with Presbyterian, Episcopal-Dissenter, papist and Non-Juror, and I hope with equall circumspection. I flatter myself you will have no complaints of my conduct. I have faithfull emissaries in every company and I talk to everybody in their own way. To the merchants I am about to settle here in trade, building ships etc. With the lawyers I want to purchase a house and land to bring my family and live upon it (God knows where the money is to pay for it). Today I am going into partnership with a Member of Parliament in a glass house, tomorrow with another in a salt work . . . I am all to everyone that I may gain some.[15]

One tends to remember this passage, as a revelation of what Defoe, not on the whole a great enjoyer of life, really got pleasure from—indeed, not just as that, but as an important insight into his imaginative life. Thus, it should not have puzzled us, though we own that for a moment it did, why it seemed to us that one passage in the *Tour* had, at all costs, to be included. We refer to the wonderful little excursus on decoy ducks—those clever feathered English secret-agents who learn to kidnap the dull-witted ducks of the Netherlands and, with smooth duck-talk, lure them across the sea to their doom in the Lincolnshire fens.

> the decoy ducks . . . calling their foreign guests, seem to tell them, that now they may find their words good, and how well the ducks live in

England; so inviting or rather wheedling them forward, 'till by degrees they are all gotten under the arch or sweep of the net, which is on the trees, and which by degrees, imperceptibly to them, declines lower and lower, and also narrower and narrower, 'till at the farther end it comes to a point like a purse. [p. 220]

It seems to have wandered out of a novel, a novel by Defoe. How his imagination is fired up, very properly in a disciple of the Royal Society, by the challenge of patient description—could one be more scientifically precise than in that delineation of a net?—and how that elusive, cynical, faintly menacing humour of his is aroused with it!

*   *   *

The full text of Defoe's *Tour* runs to over 400,000 words. The problem of reducing it to somewhat under half that length is a difficult one, and it is worth saying a word about our principles of selection. The first, and most important, decision that we took was to retain Defoe's original arrangement of a series of consecutive tours, or 'Letters'. This seemed to us essential, since the admirably rational and practical organisation of the *Tour* strikes us as one of its leading virtues. (A glance at the sloppy construction of rival 'Tours', for instance John Macky's *Journey Through England*, brings this home to one forcibly.)

Secondly we decided to make substantial cuts where Defoe quotes from other authors, or copies out documents, at length; where he supplies standard detailed historical or archeological information (for instance about Oxford or Cambridge colleges) readily available elsewhere; where he repeats himself, for example in his accounts of various technical processes; and, but here very reluctantly, where he digresses from his journey to give an extended discussion of some general topic— for example, his lengthy and valuable appendix on the British road system at the end of Letter VII. We have noted a few of these major cuts in our notes to the text. The bulk of the remaining excisions relate to detail about small towns and villages of which, according to our judgement, he had relatively less of interest to say.

Defoe's *Tour* was an extraordinarily popular work throughout the eighteenth century, reaching its ninth edition by 1779. All editions after the first contained alterations and new matter designed to keep the book up to date; by 1742 it had been extended to four volumes. The present edition is based entirely upon the first edition of 1724–6, the only one to appear in Defoe's lifetime, but we have largely ignored the original three-volume structure (though retaining the

Introductions to the first and third volumes). Typographical features of the original such as use of initial capitals and italics have been modernised, but we have left Defoe's punctuation and spelling largely unaltered. In preparing our edition we have benefited greatly from two important twentieth-century editions of the *Tour*: the complete reprint edited by G.D.H. Cole, published in two volumes in 1927, and the admirable Penguin Books edition, abridged and annotated by Pat Rogers, which was published in 1971.

In selecting illustrations to Defoe's *Tour* our ambition has been that they should be informative as well as decorative and should provide genuine illumination of specific passages and allusions in his text. A fair number of the pictures chosen—for instance some of the Buck and Stukeley drawings and the Vertue drawings of Wilton House—have, so far as we know, never been reproduced before. Readers should note that the captions to illustrations are often closely tied to and supplemented by the Notes to Defoe's *Tour* at the end of the volume.

We have tried always to use illustrative material that is broadly contemporary in sense, if not always strictly in time. The visual records of the early eighteenth century that have survived are patchy and frequently incomplete and so we have on occasion had to use images from a little later than Defoe's lifetime; but they show buildings, views, conditions and processes that are substantially as Defoe may have seen them. As well as paintings and prints specifically commissioned to illustrate places and people for exhibition and publication, we have drawn on materials created by other travellers who have used pen, pencil and paint to document less ambitious itineraries for their own enjoyment or professional purposes. These range from the working notebooks and preliminary works of the eminent, such as the painters Sir James Thornhill and Paul Sandby, the prolific topographical artists Samuel and Nathaniel Buck, and the antiquarian William Stukeley, to enthusiastic individual travellers, such as Francis Place, Thomas Lodge and Edmund Prideaux. (Information on some of the artists is given in the Artists' Biographies and the List of Illustrations.)

*   *   *

We have received valuable assistance from many sources in the preparation of this edition but would like to express particular gratitude to John Bryon, Aubrey Manning and Maureen Piper for suggestions and information; to Douglas Matthews, our indexer, for his very knowledgeable advice and criticisms; and to our editors Gillian Malpass and Robert Baldock for their unfailing help and encouragement.

To the
Right Honourable
the Lords Commissioners
for Executing the Office of
Lord High Admiral of
Great Britain, Ireland &c.
This CHART, is with the
Greatest Submission
Presented
By Their LORDSHIP'S
Most Obedient
Humble Servant
Lewis Morris.

1. Industries: woollen manufactury, ship building, husbandry, mining, timber felling, fishery. Cartouche of Lewis Morris Chart of the Welsh Coast, 1748.

A TOUR

Thro' the whole ISLAND of

GREAT BRITAIN,

Divided into

Circuits *or* Journies.

GIVING

A Particular and Diverting ACCOUNT of Whatever is CURIOUS and worth OBSERVATION, *Viz.*

I. A DESCRIPTION of the Principal Cities and Towns, their Situation, Magnitude, Government, and Commerce.

II. The Customs, Manners, Speech, as also the Exercises, Diversions, and Employment of the People.

III. The Produce and Improvement of the Lands, the Trade, and Manufactures.

IV. The Sea Ports and Fortifications, the Course of Rivers, and the Inland Navigation.

V. The Publick Edifices, Seats, and Palaces of the NOBILITY and GENTRY.

With Useful OBSERVATIONS *upon the Whole.*

Particularly fitted for the Reading of such as desire to Travel over the ISLAND.

By a GENTLEMAN.   *De Foe*

LONDON:

Printed, and Sold by G. STRAHAN, in *Cornhill.*
W. MEARS, at the *Lamb* without *Temple-Bar.*
R. FRANCKLIN, under *Tom's* Coffee-house, *Covent-Garden,*
S. CHAPMAN, at the *Angel* in *Pall-Mall.*
R. STAGG, in *Westminster-Hall,* and
J. GRAVES, in St. *James's-Street.* MDCCXXIV.

Title-page of *A Tour thro' the Whole Island of Great Britain . . . By a gentleman* (1724). British Library.

III. Peter Tillemans, *From my Turit in Blackfriers Lambeth* (after 1708). View from open ground to the southwest across the Thames to Lambeth marsh. Lambeth Palace is in the distance to the right.

THE AUTHOR'S PREFACE

IF THIS WORK is not both pleasant and profitable to the reader, the author most freely and openly declares the fault must be in his performance, and it cannot be any deficiency in the subject.

As the work itself is a description of the most flourishing and opulent country in the world, so there is a flowing variety of materials; all the particulars are fruitful of instructing and diverting objects.

If novelty pleases, here is the present state of the country describ'd, the improvement, as well in culture, as in commerce, the encrease of people, and employment for them: also here you have an account of the encrease of buildings, as well in great cities and towns, as in the new seats and dwellings of the nobility and gentry; also the encrease of wealth, in many eminent particulars.

If antiquity takes with you, tho' the looking back into remote things is studiously avoided, yet it is not wholly omitted, nor any useful observations neglected; the learned writers on the subject of antiquity[1] in Great Britain have so well discharg'd themselves, that we can never over-value their labours, yet there are daily farther discoveries made, which give future ages room, perhaps not to mend, yet at least to add to what has been already done.

In travelling thro' England, a luxuriance of objects presents it self to our view: where-ever we come, and which way soever we look, we see something new, something significant, something well worth the traveller's stay, and the writer's care; nor is it any check to our design, or obstruction to its acceptance in the world, to say the like has been done already, or to panegyrick upon the labours and value of those authors who have gone before, in this work: a compleat account of Great Britain will be the work of many years, I might say ages, and may employ many hands: whoever has travell'd Great Britain before us, and whatever they have written, tho' they may have had a harvest, yet they have always, either by necessity, ignorance or negligence pass'd over so much, that others may come and glean after them by large handfuls.

Nor cou'd it be otherwise, had the diligence and capacities of all who have gone before been greater than they are; for the face of things so often alters, and the situation of affairs in this Great British empire gives such new turns, even to nature itself, that there is matter of new observation every day presented to the traveller's eye.

The fate of things gives a new face to things, produces changes in low life, and innumerable incidents; plants and supplants families, raises and sinks towns, removes manufactures, and trade; great towns decay, and small towns rise; new towns, new palaces, new seats are built every day; great rivers and good harbours dry up, and grow useless; again, new ports are open'd, brooks are made rivers, small rivers, navigable ports and harbours are made where none were before, and the like.

Several towns, which antiquity speaks of as considerable, are now lost and swallow'd up by the sea, as Dunwich in Suffolk for one; and others, which antiquity knew nothing of, are now grown considerable: In a word, new matter offers to new observation, and they who write next, may perhaps find as much room for enlarging upon us, as we do upon those that have gone before.

The author says, that indeed he might have given his pen a loose here, to have complain'd how much the conduct of the people diminishes the reputation of the island, on many modern occasions, and so we could have made his historical account a satyr upon the country, as well as upon the people; but they are ill friends to England, who strive to write a history of her nudities, and expose, much less recommend her wicked part to posterity; he has rather endeavour'd to do her justice in those things which recommend her, and humbly to move a reformation of those, which he thinks do not; In this he thinks he shall best pay the debt of a just and native writer, who, in regard to the reader, should conceal nothing which ought to be known, and in regard to his country, expose nothing which ought to be conceal'd.

A description of the country is the business here, not

discanting upon the errors of the people; and yet, without boasting, we may venture to say, we are at least upon a level with the best of our neighbours, perhaps above them in morals, whatever we are in their pride; but let that stand as it does, till times mend; 'tis not, I say, the present business.

The observations here made, as they principally regard the present state of things, so, as near as can be, they are adapted to the present taste of the times: the situation of things is given not as they have been, but as they are; the improvements in the soil, the product of the earth, the labour of the poor, the improvement in manufactures, in merchandizes, in navigation, all respects the present time, not the time past.

In every county something of the people is said, as well as of the place, of their customs, speech, employments, the product of their labour, and the manner of their living, the circumstances as well as situation of the towns; their trade and government; of the rarities of art, or nature; the rivers, of the inland, and river navigation; also of the lakes and medicinal springs, not forgetting the general dependance of the whole country upon the City of London, as well for the consumption of its produce, as the circulation of its trade.

The preparations for this work[2] have been suitable to the author's earnest concern for its usefulness; seventeen very large circuits, or journeys have been taken thro' divers parts separately, and three general tours over almost the whole English part of the Island; in all which the author has not been wanting to treasure up just remarks upon particular places and things, so that he is very little in debt to other men's labours, and gives but very few accounts of things, but what he has been an eye-witness of himself.

Besides these several journeys in England, he has also lived some time in Scotland, and has travell'd critically over great part of it; he has viewed the north part of England, and the south part of Scotland five several times over; all which is hinted here, to let the readers know what reason they will have to be satisfy'd with the authority of the relation, and that the accounts here given are not the produce of a cursory view, or rais'd upon the borrow'd lights of other observers.

It must be acknowledged, that some foreigners, who have pretended to travel into England, and to give account of things when they come home, have treated us after a very indifferent manner: as they viewed us with envy, so they have made their account rather equal to what they wish'd we should be, than to what we are; and wrote as if they were afraid the country they wrote to should be in love with us, and come away to live among us: In short, speaking of England, they have, like the Israelitish spies,[3] carried abroad a very ill report of the land. It is worth no man's while to examine and confute foreign authors, whose errors are their ignorance. Our business is to give just ideas of our country to our readers, by which foreigners may be rightly inform'd, if they please to judge impartially; if any man will not be inform'd, we must write on that blindness, *let him be ignorant.*

But after all that has been said by others, or can be said here, no description of Great Britain can be what we call a finished account, as no cloaths can be made to fit a growing child; no picture carry the likeness of a living face; the size of one, and the countenance of the other always altering with time, so no account of a kingdom thus daily altering its countenance, can be perfect.

Even while the sheets are in the press, new beauties appear in several places, and almost to every part we are oblig'd to add appendixes, and supplemental accounts of fine houses, new undertakings, buildings, &c. and thus posterity will be continually adding; every age will find an encrease of glory. And may it do so, till Great Britain as much exceeds the finest country in Europe, as that country now fancies they exceed her.

2. Detail from pl. 101.

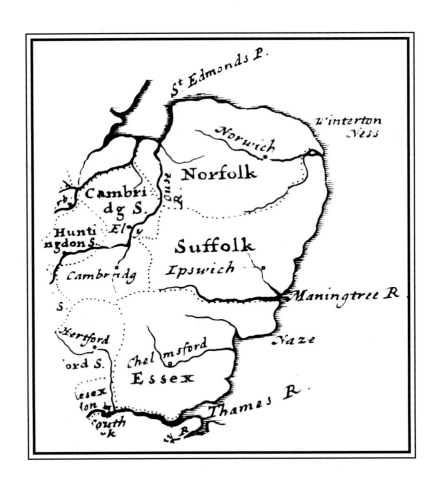

LETTER I

Containing a Description of the Sea-Coasts of the Counties of Essex, Suffolk, Norfolk, &c. as also of Part of Cambridge-shire

I BEGAN my travels, where I purpose to end them, viz. at the city of London, and therefore my account of the city itself will come last, that is to say, at the latter end of my southern progress; and as in the course of this journey I shall have many occasions to call it a circuit, if not a circle, so I chose to give it the title of circuits, in the plural, because I do not pretend to have travelled it all in one journey, but in many, and some of them many times over; the better to inform myself of every thing I could find worth taking notice of.

I hope it will appear that I am not the less, but the more capable of giving a full account of things, by how much the more deliberation I have taken in the view of them, and by how much the oftner I have had opportunity to see them.

I set out, the 3d of April, 1722, going first eastward, and took what I think, I may very honestly call a circuit in the very letter of it; for I went down by the coast of the Thames thro' the marshes or hundreds, on the south-side of the county of Essex, till I came to Malden, Colchester, and Harwich, thence continuing on the coast of Suffolk to Yarmouth; thence round by the edge of the sea, on the north and west-side of Norfolk, to Lynn, Wisbich, and the Wash; thence back again on the north-side of Suffolk and Essex, to the west, ending it in Middlesex, near the place where I began it, reserving the middle or center of the several counties to some little excursions, which I made by themselves.

Passing Bow-Bridge, where the county of Essex begins, the first observation I made was, that all the villages which may be called the neighbourhood of the city of London on this, as well as on the other sides thereof, which I shall speak to in their order; I say, all those villages are increased in buildings to a strange degree, within the compass of about 20 or 30 years past at the most.

The village of **Stratford**, the first in this county from London, is not only increased, but, I believe, more than doubled in that time; every vacancy filled up with new houses, and two little towns or hamlets, as they may be called, on the forest side of the town, entirely new, namely, Mary-land-Point, and the Gravel-Pits, one facing the road to Woodford, and Epping, and the other facing the road to Illford: and as for the hitherpart, it is almost joined to Bow, in spite of rivers, canals, marshy-grounds, &c. Nor is this increase of building the case only, in this and all the other villages round London; but the increase of the value and rent of the houses formerly standing, has, in that compass of years above-mentioned, advanced to a very great degree, and I may venture to say at least a fifth part; some think a third part, above what they were before.

This is indeed most visible, speaking of Stratford in Essex; but it is the same thing in proportion in other villages adjacent, especially on the forest-side; as at Low-Layton, Layton-stone, Walthamstow, Woodford, Wansted, and the towns of West-Ham, Plaistow, Upton, &c. In all which places, or near them, (as the inhabitants say) above a thousand new foundations have been erected, besides old houses repaired, all since the Revolution: And this is not to be forgotten too, that this increase is, generally speaking, of handsom large houses, from 20 l. a year to 60 l., very few under 20 l. a year; being chiefly for the habitations of the richest citizens, such as either are able to keep two houses, one in the country, and one in the city; or for such citizens as being rich, and having left off trade, live altogether in these neighbouring villages, for the pleasure and health of the latter part of their days.

The truth of this may at least appear, in that they tell me there are no less than two hundred coaches kept by the inhabitants within the circumference of these few village named above, besides such as are kept by accidental lodgers.

This increase of the inhabitants, and the cause of it, I shall inlarge upon when I come to speak of the like in the counties of Middlesex, Surrey, &c. where it is the same, only in a much greater degree: But this I must take notice of here, that this increase causes those villages to be much pleasanter and more sociable than formerly, for now people go to them, not for retirement into the country, but for good company; of which, that I may speak to the ladies as well as other authors do, there are in these villages, nay, in all, three or four excepted, excellent conversation, and a great deal of it, and that without the mixture of assemblées, gaming houses, and publick foundations of vice and debauchery; and particularly I find none of those incentives kept up on this side the country.

According to my first intention of effectually viewing the sea-coast of these three counties, I went from Stratford to **Barking**, a large market-town, but chiefly inhabited by fishermen, whose smacks ride in the Thames, at the mouth of their river, from whence their fish is sent up to London to the market at Billingsgate, by small boats, of which I shall speak by itself in my description of London.

3a and b. Dutch sloop and a dogger. From Robert C. Leslie, *Old Sea Wings, Ways and World* (1890).

One thing I cannot omit in the mention of these Barking fisher-smacks, viz. That one of those fishermen, a very substantial and experienced man, convinced me, that all the pretences to bringing fish alive to London market from the North Seas, and other remote places on the coast of Great Britain, by the new-built sloops called fish-pools,[1] have not been able to do any thing, but what their fishing-smacks are able on the same occasion to perform. These fishing-smacks are very useful vessels to the publick upon many occasions; as particularly, in time of war they are used as press-smacks, running to all the northern and western coasts to pick up seamen to man the navy, when any expedition is at hand that requires

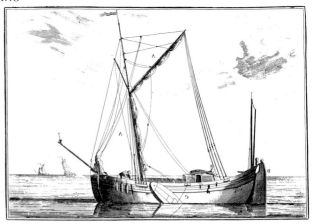

4. Dutch hoy or bilandre. From *Spectacle de la Nature* (1740).

5. Dutch schuyt. From Edward W. Hobbs, *Sailing ships at a glance* (1925).

a sudden equipment: at other times, being excellent sailors, they are tenders[2] to particular men of war; and on an expedition they have been made use of as machines, for the blowing up fortified ports and havens; as at Calais, St. Maloes,[3] and other places.

This side of the county is rather rich in land, than in inhabitants, occasioned chiefly by the unhealthiness of the air; for these low marsh grounds, which, with all the south-side of the county, have been saved out of the river Thames, and out of the sea, where the river is wide enough to be call'd so, begin here, or rather begin at West-Ham, by Stratford, and continue to extend themselves. From hence eastward, growing wider and wider, till we come beyond Tilbury, when the flat country lyes six, seven, or eight miles broad, and is justly said to be both unhealthy, and unpleasant.

However the lands are rich, and, as is observable, it is very good farming in the marshes, because the landlords let good penny-worths,[4] for it being a place where every body cannot live, those that venture it,

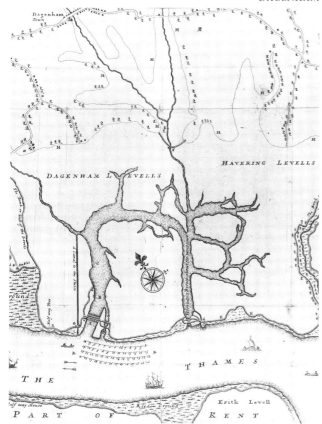

6. 'A plan of the late breach in the levells of Havering and Dagenham' by Herman Moll (1721).

will have encouragement, and indeed it is but reasonable they should.

Several little observations I made in this part of the county of Essex.

1. We saw passing from Barking to **Dagenham**, the famous breach,[5] made by an inundation of the Thames, which was so great, as that it laid near 5000 acres of land under water, but which after near ten years lying under water, and being several times blown up has been at last effectually stopped by the application of Captain Perry;[6] the gentleman, who for several years had been employed, in the Czar of Muscovy's works, at Veronitza, on the river Don. This breach appeared now effectually made up, and they assured us, that the new work, where the breach was, is by much esteemed the strongest of all the sea walls in that level.

2. It was observable that great part of the lands in these levels, especially those on this side East **Tilbury**, are held by the farmers, cow-keepers, and grasing butchers who live in and near London, and that they are generally stocked (all the winter half year) with large fat sheep, (viz.) Lincolnshire and Leicestershire wethers, which they buy in Smithfield in September and October, when the Lincolnshire and Leicestershire grasiers sell off their stock, and are kept here till Christmas, or Candlemas, or thereabouts, and tho' they are not made at all fatter here, than they were when bought in, yet the farmer, or butcher finds very good advantage in it, by the difference of the price of mutton between Michaelmas, when 'tis cheapest, and Candlemas when 'tis dearest; this is what the butchers value themselves upon, when they tell us at the market, that it is right marsh-mutton.

3. In the bottom of these marshes, and close to the edge of the rivers stands the strong fortress of Tilbury, called Tilbury Fort, which may justly be looked upon, as the key of the river of Thames, and consequently the key of the city of London: it is a regular fortification, the design of it, was a pentagon, but the water bastion as it would have been call'd, was never built; the plan was laid out by Sir Martin Beckman, chief engineer to King Charles II who also designed the works at Sheerness. The esplanade of the fort is very large, and the bastions, the largest of any in England, the foundation is laid so deep, and piles

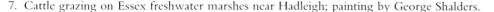

7. Cattle grazing on Essex freshwater marshes near Hadleigh; painting by George Shalders.

8. Tilbury fort; engraving, late eighteenth century.

under that, driven down two on end of one another, so far, till they were assur'd they were below the channel of the river, and that the piles, which were shod with iron, entered into the solid chalk rock adjoyning to, or reaching from the chalk-hills on the other side. These bastions settled considerably at first, as did also part of the curtain, the great quantity of earth that was brought to fill them up, necessarily, requiring to be made solid by time; but they are now firm as the rocks of chalk which they came from, and the filling up one of these bastions, as I have been told by good hands, cost the government 6000 l. being filled with chalk-rubbish fetched from the chalk-pits at North-Fleet, just above Gravesend.

From hence, there is nothing for many miles together remarkable, but a continued level of unhealthy marshes, called, the Three Hundreds, till we come before Leigh, and to the mouth of the river Chelmer, and Black-water. These rivers united make a large firth, or inlet of the sea, which by Mr. Camden is called *Idumanum Fluvium*; but by our fishermen and seamen, who use it as a port, 'tis called Malden-Water.

In this inlet of the sea is **Osey** or **Osyth** Island, commonly called Oosy Island, so well known by our London men of pleasure, for the infinite number of wild-fowl, that is to say, duck, mallard, teal and widgeon, of which there are such vast flights, that they tell us the island, namely the creek, seems covered with them, at certain times of the year, and they go from London on purpose for the pleasure of shooting; and indeed often come home very well loaden with game. But it must be remembered too, that those gentlemen who are such lovers of the sport, and go so far for it, often return with an Essex ague on their backs, which they find a heavier load than the fowls they have shot.

'Tis on this shoar, and near this creek, that the

greatest quantity of fresh fish is caught, which supplies not this country only, but London markets also: on the shoar beginning a little below Candy Island, or rather below Leigh road, there lies a great shoal or sand called the Black Tayl, which runs out near three leagues into the sea due east; at the end of it, stands a pole or mast, set up by the Trinity-House Men of London, whose business is, to lay buoys, and set up sea marks for the direction of the sailors; this is called Shoo-Bacon, from the point of land where this sand begins, which is call'd **Shooberry-Ness**, and that from the town of Shooberry, which stands by it. From this sand, and on the edge of Shooberry, before it, or south-west of it, all along, to the mouth of Colchester water, the shoar is full of shoals and sands, with some deep channels between; all which are so full of fish, that not only the Barking fishing-smacks come hither to fish, but the whole shoar is full of small fisher-boats in very great numbers, belonging to the villages and towns on the coast, who come in every tide with what they take; and selling the smaller fish in the country, send the best and largest away upon horses, which go night and day to London market.

On this shoar also are taken the best and nicest, tho' not the largest oysters in England; the spot from whence they have their common appellation is a little bank called Woelfleet, scarce to be called an island, in the mouth of the river Crouch, now called Crooksea Water; but the chief place where the said oysters are now had, is from **Wyvenhoo** and the shoars adjacent whither they are brought by the fishermen, who take them at the mouth of, that they call, Colchester water, and about the sand they call the Spits, and carry them up to Wyvenhoo, where they are laid in beds or pits on the shoar to feed, as they call it; and then being barrelled up, and carried to Colchester, which is but three miles off, they are sent to London by land, and are, from thence, called Colchester oysters.

In the several creeks and openings, as above, on this shoar, there are also other islands, but of no particular note, except Mersey, which lies in the middle of the two openings, between Malden water and Colchester water; being of the most difficult access, so that 'tis thought a thousand men well provided, might keep possession of it against a great force, whether by land or sea; on this account, and because if possessed by an enemy, it would shut up all the navigation and fishery on that side: The government formerly built a fort on the South-East point of it: and generally in case of Dutch war,[7] there is a strong body of troops kept there to defend it.

At this place may be said to end what we call the hundreds of Essex; that is to say, the three hundreds or divisions, which include the marshy country, viz. Barnstable hundred, Rochford hundred, and Dengy hundred.

I have one remark more, before I leave this damp part of the world, and which I cannot omit on the women's account; namely, that I took notice of a strange decay of the sex here; insomuch, that all along this county it was very frequent to meet with men that had had from five or six, to fourteen or fifteen wives; nay, and some more; and I was inform'd that in the marshes on the other side the river over-against Candy Island, there was a farmer, who was then living with the five and twentieth wife, and that his son who was but about 35 years old, had already had about fourteen; indeed this part of the story, I only had by report, tho' from good hands too; but the other is well known, and easie to be inquired in to, about Fobbing, Curringham, Thundersly, Benfleet, Prittlewell, Wakering, Great Stambridge, Cricksea, Burnham, Dengy, and other towns of the like situation: The reason, as a merry fellow told me, who said he had had about a dozen and half of wives, (tho' I found afterwards he fibb'd a little) was this; that they being bred in the marshes themselves, and season'd to the place, did pretty well with it; but that they always went up into the hilly country, or to speak their own language into the uplands for a wife: That when they took the young lasses out of the wholesome and fresh air, they were healthy, fresh, and clear, and well; but when they came out of their native air into the marshes among the fogs and damps, there they presently chang'd their complexion, got an ague or two, and seldom held it above half a year, or a year at most; and then, said he, we go to the uplands again, and fetch another; so that marrying of wives was reckon'd a kind of good farm[8] to them.

From the marshes, and low grounds, being not able to travel without many windings, and indentures, by reason of the creeks, and waters, I came up to the town of *Malden*, a noted market town situate at the conflux or joyning of two principal rivers in this country, the Chelm or Chelmer, and the Black-water, and where they enter into the sea. The channel, as I have noted, is call'd by the sailors Malden-Water, and is navigable up to the town, where, by that means, is a great trade for carrying corn by water to London; the county of Essex being (especially on all that side) a great corn country.

Nearer Chelmsford, hard by Boreham, lives the Lord Viscount Barrington,[9] who tho' not born to the title, or estate, or name which he now possesses, had the honour to be twice made heir to the estates of gentlemen, not at all related to him, at least one of them, as is very much to his honour mention'd in his patent of creation. His name was Shute, his uncle a linnen draper in London, and serv'd Sheriff of the said city, in very troublesome times. He chang'd the name of Shute, for that of Barrington, by an Act of Parliament, obtain'd for that purpose, and had the dignity of a baron of the Kingdom of Ireland conferr'd on him by the favour of King George. His Lordship is a Dissenter, and seems to love retirement. He was a Member of Parliament for the town of Berwick upon Tweed.

On the other side of Witham, at Fauburn, an antient mansion house, built by the Romans, lives Mr. Bullock, whose father married the daughter of that eminent citizen, Sir Josiah Child[10] of Wansted, by whom she had three sons; the eldest enjoys the estate, which is considerable.

It is observable, that in this part of the country, there are several very considerable estates purchas'd, and now enjoy'd by citizens of London, merchants, and tradesmen, as Mr. Western an iron merchant, near Kelvedon, Mr. Cresnor, a wholesale grocer, who was, a little before he died, nam'd for Sheriff at Earls Coln, Mr. Olemus, a merchant at Braintree, Mr. Westcomb, near Malden, Sir Thomas Webster at Copthall, near Waltham, and several others.

The product of all this part of the country is corn, as that of the marshy feeding grounds mention'd above, is grass, where their chief business is breeding of calves, which I need not say are the best and fattest, and the largest veal in England, if not in the world; and as an instance, I eat part of a veal or calf, fed by the late Sir Josiah Child at Wansted, the loyn of which weigh'd above 30 l. and the flesh exceeding white and fat.

Colchester is an antient Corporation; the town is large, very populous; the streets fair and beautiful; and tho' it may not be said to be finely built, yet there are abundance of very good and well-built houses in it: It still mourns, in the ruins of a civil war; during which, or rather after the heat of the war was over, it suffer'd a severe siege;[11] which, the garrison making a resolute defence, was turn'd into a blockade, in which the garrison and inhabitants also, suffer'd the utmost extremity of hunger, and were at last oblig'd to surrender at discretion, when their two chief officers, Sir Charles Lucas, and Sir George Lisle,[12] were shot to death under the castle-wall. The inhabitants had a tradition, that no grass would grow upon the spot where the blood of those two gallant gentlemen was spilt; and they shew'd the place bare of grass for many years, but whether for this reason, I will not affirm; the story is now dropp'd, and the grass, I suppose, grows there as in other places.

9. 'A New and Exact Prospect of Colchester taken from ye north part'; engraving by John Pryer (1724).

However, the batter'd walls, the breaches in the turrets, and the ruin'd churches still remain, except that the church of St. Mary's (where they had the royal fort) is rebuilt; but the steeple, which was two thirds batter'd down, because the besieged had a large culverine[13] upon it, that did much execution, remains still in that condition.

There is another church which bears the marks of those times, namely, on the south-side of the town, in the way to the Hithe, of which more hereafter.

The lines of contravallation, with the forts built by the besiegers, and which surrounded the whole town, remain very visible in many places; but the chief of them are demolish'd.

The river Coln, which passes through this town, compasses it on the north and east-sides, and serv'd in those times for a compleat defence on those sides. They have three bridges over it, one called North-Bridge, at the north gate, by which the road leads into Suffolk; one call'd East-Bridge, at the foot of the high

10a and b. Details of castle and abbey gate from 'A New and Exact Prospect of Colchester...' (see pl. 9).

street, over which lies the road to Harwich, and one at the Hithe, as above.

The river is navigable within three miles of the town for ships of large burthen; a little lower it may receive even a royal navy: and up to that part called the Hithe, close to the houses, it is navigable for hoys and small barks.[14] This Hithe is a long street, passing from west to east, on the south-side of the town; at the west-end of it, there is a small intermission of the buildings, but not much; and towards the river it is very populous; (it may be call'd the Wapping of Colchester;) there is one church in that part of the town, a large key by the river, and a good custom-house.

The town may be said chiefly to subsist by the trade of making bays,[15] which is known over most of the trading parts of Europe, by the name of Colchester bays, tho' indeed all the towns round carry on the same trade, namely, Kelvedon, Wittham, Coggshall, Braintree, Bocking, &c. and the whole county, large as it is, may be said to be employ'd, and in part maintain'd, by the spinning of wool for the bay trade of Colchester, and its adjacent towns.

The town of Colchester has been suppos'd to contain about 40000 people, including the out-villages which are within its liberty, of which there are a great many, the liberty of the town being of a great extent: one sad testimony of the town being so populous is, that they bury'd upwards of 5259 people in the plague year, 1665. But the town was severely visited indeed, even more in proportion than any of its neighbours, or than the City of London.

The government of the town is by a Mayor, High Steward, a Recorder, or his Deputy, eleven Aldermen, a Chamberlain, a Town-Clerk, Assistants, and eighteen Common-Council-Men.

Publick Edifices are,

1. Bay-Hall, an ancient society kept up for ascertaining the manufactures of bays; which are, or ought

to be, all brought to this hall, to be viewed and sealed according to their goodness, by the masters; and to this practice has been owing the great reputation of the Colchester bays in foreign markets; where to open the side of a bale and shew the seal, has been enough to give the buyer a character of the value of the goods without any farther search; and so far as they abate the integrity and exactness of their method, which, I am told, of late is much omitted; I say, so far, that reputation will certainly abate in the markets they go to, which are principally in Portugal and Italy. This corporation is govern'd by a particular set of men who are call'd Governors of the Dutch Bay Hall. And in the same building is the Dutch church.

2. The Guild Hall of the town, called by them the Moot Hall; to which is annex'd the town Goal.

3. The Work-house, being lately enlarg'd, and to which belongs a corporation, or a body of the inhabitants, consisting of sixty persons incorporated by Act of Parliament anno 1698, for taking care of the poor: they are incorporated by the name and title of the Governor, Deputy Governor, Assistants, and Guardians, of the poor of the town of Colchester. They are in number eight and forty; to whom are added the Mayor and Aldermen for the time being, who are always Guardians by the same Charter: these make the number of sixty, as above.

There is also a Grammar Free-School, with a good allowance to the master, who is chosen by the town.

4. The castle of Colchester is now become only a monument shewing the antiquity of the place, it being built as the walls of the town also are, with Roman bricks; and the Roman coins dug up here, and ploughed up in the fields adjoining, confirm it.

There are two CHARITY SCHOOLS set up here, and carried on by a generous subscription, with very good success.

From Colchester, I took another step down to the coast, the land running out a great way into the sea, south, and S. E. makes that promontory of land called the **Nase**, and well known to sea-men, using the northern trade. Here one sees a sea open as an ocean, without any opposite shore, tho' it be no more than the mouth of the Thames. This point call'd the Nase, and the N. E. point of Kent, near Margate, call'd the North Foreland, making (what they call) the mouth of the river, and the port of London, tho' it be here above 60 miles over.

At Walton, under the Nase, they find on the shoar, copperas-stone in great quantities; and there are several large works call'd copperas houses, where they make it with great expence.

On this promontory is a new sea mark,[16] erected by the Trinity-House Men, and at the publick expence, being a round brick tower, near 80 foot high. The sea gains so much upon the land here, by the continual winds at S. W. that within the memory of some of the inhabitants there, they have lost above 30 acres of land in one place.

From hence we go back into the country about four miles, because of the creeks which lie between; and then turning east again, come to Harwich, on the utmost eastern point of this large country.

Harwich is a town so well known, and so perfectly describ'd by many writers, I need say little of it: 'tis strong by situation, and may be made more so by art. But 'tis many years since the Government of England have had any occasion to fortify towns to the land-ward; 'tis enough that the harbour or road, which is one of the best and securest in England, is cover'd at the entrance by a strong fort, and a battery of guns to the seaward, just as at Tilbury, and which sufficiently defend the mouth of the river: And there is a particular felicity in this fortification, viz. that tho' the entrance or opening of the river into the sea, is very wide, especially at high-water, at least two miles, if not three

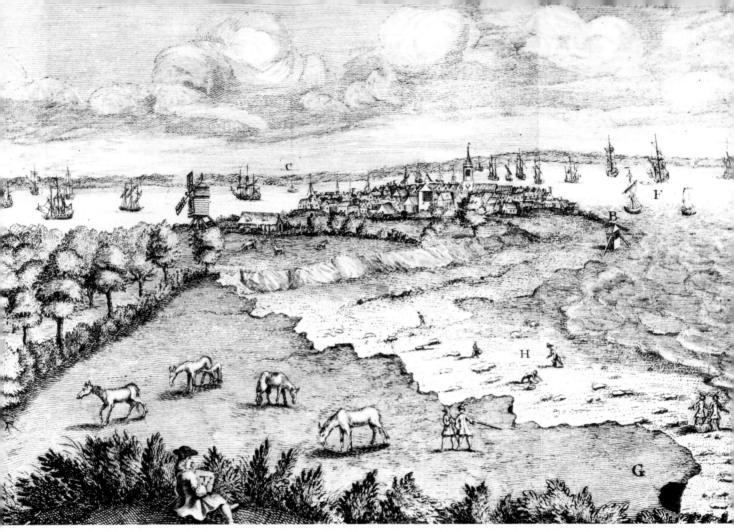

11. Harwich; engraving by R. Sheppard. From Silas Taylor, *History and Antiquities of Harwich and Dovercourt, topographical, dynastical and political . . . now much enlarged by Samuel Dale* (1730).

over; yet the channel, which is deep, and in which the ships must keep and come to the harbour, is narrow, and lies only on the side of the fort; so that all the ships which come in, or go out, must come close under the guns of the fort; that is to say, under the command of their shot.

The fort is on the Suffolk side of the bay, or entrance, but stands so far into the sea upon the point of a sand or shoal, which runs out toward the Essex side, as it were, laps over the mouth of that haven like a blind[17] to it; and our surveyors of the country affirm it to be in the county of Essex. The making this place, which was formerly no other than a sand in the sea, solid enough for the foundation of so good a fortification, has not been done but by many years labour, often repairs, and an infinite expence of money, but 'tis now so firm, that nothing of storms and high tides, or such things, as make the sea dangerous to these kind of works, can affect it.

The harbour is of a vast extent; for, as two rivers empty themselves here, viz. Stour from Mainingtree, and the Orwel from Ipswich; the channels of both are large and deep, and safe for all weathers, so where they joyn they make a large bay or road, able to receive the biggest ships, and the greatest number that ever the world saw together; I mean, ships of war. In the old Dutch war, great use has been made of this harbour; and I have known that there has been 100 sail of Men of War and their attendants, and between three and four hundred sail of collier ships, all in this harbour at a time, and yet none of them crowding, or riding in danger of one another.

Harwich is known for being the port where the packet-boats between England and Holland, go out and come in: the inhabitants are far from being fam'd for good usage to strangers, but on the contrary, are blamed for being extravagant in their reckonings, in the publick houses, which has not a little encourag'd the setting up of sloops, which they now call passage-boats, to Holland, to go directly from the river of Thames; this, tho' it may be something the longer passage, yet as they are said to be more obliging to

14

passengers, and more reasonable in the expence, and as some say also the vessels are better sea-boats, has been the reason why so many passengers do not go or come by the way of Harwich, as formerly were wont to do; insomuch, that the stage-coaches, between this place and London, which ordinarily went twice or three times a week, are now entirely laid down, and the passengers are left to hire coaches on purpose, take post-horses, or hire horses to Colchester, as they find most convenient.

The account of a petrifying quality in the earth here, tho' some will have it to be in the water of a spring hard by, is very strange: they boast that their town is wall'd, and their streets pav'd with clay, and yet, that one is as strong, and the other as clean as those that are built or pav'd with stone: the fact is indeed true, for there is a sort of clay in the cliff, between the town and the beacon-hill adjoining, which when it falls down into the sea, where it is beaten with the waves and the weather, turns gradually into stone: but the chief reason assign'd, is from the water of a certain spring or well, which rising in the said cliff, runs down into the sea among those pieces of clay, and petrifies them as it runs; and the force of the sea often stirring, and perhaps, turning the lumps of clay, when storms of wind may give force enough to the water, causes them to harden every where alike; otherwise those which were not quite sunk in the water of the spring, would be petrify'd but in part. These stones are gathered up to pave the streets, and build the houses, and are indeed very hard: 'Tis also remarkable, that some of them taken up before they are thoroughly petrify'd, will, upon breaking them, appear to be hard as a stone without, and soft as clay in the middle; whereas others, that have layn a due time, shall be thorough stone to the center, and as exceeding hard within, as without: The same spring is said to turn wood into iron: but this I take to be no more or less than the quality, which as I mention'd of the shoar at the Ness, is found to be in much of the stone, all along this shoar, (viz.) of the copperas kind; and 'tis certain, that the copperas stone (so call'd) is found in all that cliff, and even where the water of this spring has run; and I presume, that those who call the harden'd pieces of wood, which they take out of this well by the name of iron, never try'd the quality of it with the fire or hammer; if they had, perhaps they would have given some other account of it.

Harwich is a town of hurry and business, not much of gaiety and pleasure; yet the inhabitants seem warm in their nests, and some of them are very wealthy: there are not many (if any) gentlemen or families of note, either in the town, or very near it. They send two members to parliament; the present are, Sir Peter Parker, and Humphrey Parsons, Esq.[18]

From Harwich therefore, having a mind to view the harbour, I sent my horses round by Maningtree, where there is a timber bridge over the Stour, called Cataway Bridge, and took a boat up the river Orwell, for Ipswich; a traveller will hardly understand me, especially a seaman, when I speak of the river Stour and the river Orwell at Harwich, for they know them by no other names than those of Maningtree-Water, and Ipswich-Water; so while I am on salt water, I must speak as those who use the sea may understand me, and when I am up in the country among the in-land towns again, I shall call them out of their names no more.

It is twelve miles from Harwich up the water to **Ipswich**: before I come to the town, I must say something of it, because speaking of the river requires it: in former times, that is to say, since the writer of this remembers the place very well, and particularly just before the late Dutch Wars, Ipswich was a town of very good business; particularly it was the greatest town in England for large colliers or coal-ships, employed between New Castle and London: also they built the biggest ships and the best, for the said fetching of coals of any that were employ'd in that trade: they built also there so prodigious strong, that it was an ordinary thing for an Ipswich collier, if no disaster happen'd to him, to reign (as seamen call it) forty or fifty years, and more.

In the town of Ipswich the masters of these ships generally dwelt, and there were, as they then told me, above a hundred sail of them, belonging to the town at one time, the least of which carried fifteen-score, as

12. Detail of boys collecting stones for copperas ink making from pl. 11.

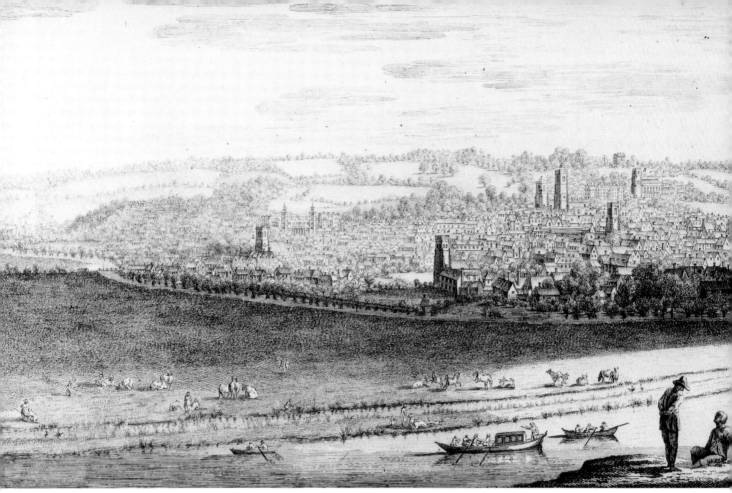

13. 'The South-West prospect of Ipswich in the County of Suffolk'; engraving by Samuel and Nathaniel Buck (1741).

they compute it, that is, 300 chaldron[19] of coals; this was about the year 1668 (when I first knew the place). This made the town be at that time so populous, for those masters, as they had good ships at sea, so they had large families, who liv'd plentifully, and in very good houses in the town, and several streets were chiefly inhabited by such.

The loss or decay of this trade, accounts for the present pretended decay of the town of Ipswich, of which I shall speak more presently: the ships wore out, the masters died off, the trade took a new turn; Dutch flyboats taken in the war, and made free ships by Act of Parliament, thrust themselves into the coal-trade for the interest of the captors, such as the Yarmouth and London merchants, and others; and the Ipswich men dropt gradually out of it, being discouraged by those Dutch flyboats:[20] these Dutch vessels which cost nothing but the caption,[21] were bought cheap, carried great burthens, and the Ipswich building fell of for want of price, and so the trade decay'd, and the town with it; I believe this will be own'd for the true beginning of their decay.

But to return to my passage up the river. In the winter time those great collier-ships, abovemention'd, are always laid up, as they call it: that is to say, the coal trade abates at London, the citizens are generally furnish'd, their stores taken in, and the demand is over; so that the great ships, the northern seas and coast being also dangerous, the nights long, and the voyage hazardous, go to sea no more, but lie by, the ships are unrigg'd, the sails, &c. carry'd a shore, the top-masts struck, and they ride moor'd in the river, under the advantages and security of sound ground, and a high woody shore, where they lie as safe as in a wet dock; and it was a very agreeable sight to see, perhaps two hundred sail of ships, of all sizes lye in that posture every winter: all this while, which was usually from Michaelmas to Lady day, the masters liv'd calm and secure with their families in Ipswich; and enjoying plentifully, what in the summer they got laboriously at sea, and this made the town of Ipswich very populous in the winter; for as the masters, so most of the men, especially their mates, boatswains, carpenters, &c. were of the same place, and liv'd in their proportions, just as the masters did: so that in the winter there might be perhaps a thousand men in the town more than in the summer.

Ipswich is seated, at the distance of 12 miles from

16

Harwich, upon the edge of the river, which taking a short turn to the west, the town forms, there, a kind of semi-circle, or half moon upon the bank of the river: It is very remarkable, that tho' ships of 500 tun may upon a spring tide come up very near this town, and many ships of that burthen have been built there; yet the river is not navigable any farther than the town itself, or but very little; no not for the smallest boats, nor does the tide, which rises sometimes 13 or 14 foot, and gives them 24 foot water very near the town, flow much farther up the river than the town, or not so much as to make it worth speaking of.

I am much mistaken too, if since the Revolution,[22] some very good ships have not been built at this town, and particularly the *Melford* or *Milford-Gally*, a ship of 40 guns; as the *Greyhound Frigate*, a Man of War of 36 to 40 guns, was at John's Ness. And why then is not Ipswich capable of building and receiving the greatest ships in the navy, seeing they may be built and brought up again loaden, within a mile and half of the town?

But the neighbourhood of London, which sucks the vitals of trade in this island to itself, is the chief reason of any decay of business in this place; and I shall in the course of these observations, hint at it, where many good sea-ports and large towns, tho' farther off than Ipswich, and as well fitted for commerce, are yet swallow'd up by the immense indraft of trade to the city of London; and more decay'd beyond all comparison, than Ipswich is suppos'd to be; as Southampton, Weymouth, Dartmouth, and several others which I shall speak to in their order: and if it be otherwise at this time, with some other towns, which are lately encreas'd in trade and navigation, wealth, and people, while their neighbours decay, it is because they have some particular trade or accident to trade, which is a kind of nostrum to them, inseparable to the place, and which fixes there by the nature of the thing; as the herring-fishery to Yarmouth; the coal trade to New-Castle; the Leeds cloathing-trade; the export of butter and lead, and the great corn trade for Holland, is to Hull; the Virginia and West-India trade at Liverpool; the Irish trade at Bristol, and the like; thus the war has brought a flux of business and people, and consequently of wealth, to several places, as well as to Portsmouth, Chatham, Plymouth, Falmouth, and others; and were any wars like those, to continue 20 years with the Dutch, or any nation whose fleets lay

14. The Market Cross at Ipswich. From Sir James Thornhill, *Sketchbook travel journal of 1711.*

something very solid and entertaining in their society: This may happen, perhaps, by their frequent conversing with those who have been abroad, and by their having a remnant of gentlemen and masters of ships among them, who have seen more of the world than the people of an inland town are likely to have seen. I take this town to be one of the most agreeable places in England, for families who have liv'd well, but may have suffered in our late calamities of stocks and bubbles,[23] to retreat to, where they may live within their own compass; and several things indeed recommend it to such;

1. Good houses, at very easie rents.

2. An airy, clean, and well govern'd town.

3. Very agreeable and improving company almost of every kind.

4. A wonderful plenty of all manner of provisions, whether flesh or fish, and very good of the kind.

5. Those provisions very cheap; so that a family may live cheaper here, than in any town in England of its bigness, within such a small distance from London.

6. Easie passage to London, either by land or water, the coach going through to London in a day.

From Ipswich I took a turn into the country to Hadley, principally to satisfy my curiosity, and see the place where that famous martyr, and pattern of charity and religious zeal in Queen Mary's time, Dr. Rowland Taylor,[24] was put to death; the inhabitants, who have a wonderful veneration for his memory, shew the very place where the stake which he was bound to, was set up, and they have put a stone upon it, which no body will remove; but it is a more lasting monument to him that he lives in the hearts of the people; I say more lasting than a tomb of marble would be, for the memory of that good man will certainly never be out of the poor people's minds, as long as this island shall retain the protestant religion among them; how long that may be, as things are going, and if the detestable conspiracy of the Papists[25] now on foot, should succeed, I will not pretend to say.

A little to the left is **Sudbury**, which stands upon the river Stour, mentioned above; a river which parts the counties of Suffolk and Essex, and which is within these few years made navigable to this town, tho' the navigation does not (it seems) answer the charge, at least not to advantage.

I know nothing for which this town is remarkable, except for being very populous and very poor. They have a great manufacture of says[26] and perpetuana's;[27] and multitudes of poor people are employ'd in working them; but the number of the poor is almost ready to eat up the rich: however this town sends two members to Parliament, tho' it is under no form of govern-

that way, as the Dutch do, it would be the like perhaps at Ipswich in a few years, and at other places on the same coast.

The country round Ipswich, as are all the counties so near the coast, is applied chiefly to corn, of which a very great quantity is continually shipped off for London; and sometimes they load corn here for Holland, especially if the market abroad is encouraging. They have 12 parish-churches in this town, with three or four meetings; but there are not so many Quakers here as at Colchester, and no Anabaptists, or Antipœdo Baptists, that I could hear of, at least there is no meeting-house of that denomination: there is one meeting-house for the Presbyterians, one for the Independants, and one for the Quakers; the first is as large and as fine a building of that kind as most on this side of England, and the inside the best finished of any I have seen, London not excepted; that for the Independants is a handsome new-built building, but not so gay or so large as the other.

There is a great deal of very good company in this town; and tho' there are not so many of the gentry here as at Bury, yet there are more here than in any other town in the county; and I observ'd particularly, that the company you meet with here, are generally persons well informed of the world, and who have

IV. Unknown painter, *Market square, Bury St Edmunds* (*c*.1700).

ment particularly to itself, other than as a village, the head magistrate whereof is a constable.

Near adjoining to it, is a village call'd **Long-Melfort**, and a very long one it is, from which I suppose it had that addition to its name; it is full of very good houses, and, as they told me, is richer, and has more wealthy masters of the manufacture in it than in Sudbury itself.

From this part of the country I return'd north-west by Lenham, to visit **St. Edmund's Bury**, a town of which other writers have talk'd very largely, and perhaps a little too much: It is a town fam'd for its pleasant situation and wholsome air, the Montpelier of Suffolk,[28] and perhaps of England; this must be attributed to the skill of the monks of those times, who chose so beautiful a situation for the seat of their retirement; and who built here the greatest and in its time, the most flourishing monastery in all these parts of England, I mean the monastery of St. Edmund the Martyr: It was, if we believe antiquity, a house of pleasure in more antient times; or to speak more properly, a court of some of the Saxon or East-Angle

kings; and, as Mr. Camden says, was even then call'd a royal village; tho' it much better merits that name now; it being the town of all this part of England, in proportion to its bigness, most thronged with gentry, people of the best fashion, and the most polite conversation: this beauty and healthiness of its situation, was no doubt the occasion which drew the clergy to settle here, for they always chose the best places in the country to build in, either for richness of soil, or for health and pleasure in the situation of their religious houses.

The abbey is demolish'd; its ruins are all that is to be seen of its glory: out of the old building, two very beautiful churches are built, and serve the two parishes, into which the town is divided, and they stand both in one church-yard. Here it was, in the path-way between these two churches, that a tragical and almost unheard of act of barbarity[29] was committed, which made the place less pleasant for some time, than it us'd to be, when Arundel Coke, Esq; a barrister at law, of a very antient family, attempted, with the assistance

19

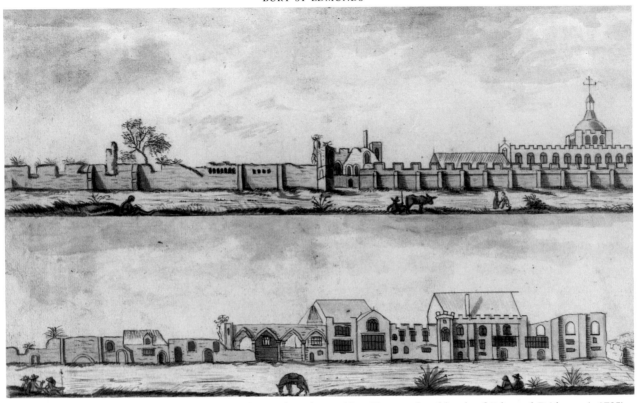

15. Bury St Edmunds. Ruins of the abbey on the north and east sides. From a sketchbook of Edmund Prideaux (*c*.1725).

of a barbarous assassin, to murther in cold blood, and in the arms of hospitality, Edward Crisp, Esq; his brother-in-law, leading him out from his own house, where he had invited him, his wife and children, to supper; I say, leading him out in the night, on pretence of going to see some friend that was known to them both; but in this church-yard, giving a signal to the assassin he had hir'd, he attack'd him with a hedge bill, and cut him, as one might say, almost in pieces; and when they did not doubt of his being dead, they left him: His head and face was so mangled, that it may be said to be next to a miracle that he was not quite killed: yet so providence directed for the exemplary punishment of the assassins, that the gentleman recover'd to detect them, who, (tho' he out-lived the assault) were both executed as they deserv'd, and Mr. Crisp is yet alive. They were condemned on the statute for defacing and dismembring, called the Coventry Act.[30]

But this accident does not at all lessen the pleasure and agreeable delightful shew of the town of Bury; it is crouded with nobility and gentry, and all sorts of the most agreeable company; and as the company invites, so there is the appearance of pleasure upon the very situation; and they that live at Bury, are supposed to live there for the sake of it.

Here is no manufacturing in this town, or but very little, except spinning; the chief trade of the place depending upon the gentry who live there, or near it, and who cannot fail to cause trade enough by the expence of their families and equipages, among the people of county town. They have but a very small river, or rather but a very small branch of a small river, at this town, which runs from hence to Milden-Hall, on the edge of the fens. However, the town and gentlemen about, have been at the charge, or have so encourag'd the engineer who was at the charge, that they have made this river navigable to the said Milden-Hall, from whence there is a navigable dyke, call'd Milden-Hall Dreyn, which goes into the river Ouse, and so to Lynn; so that all their coal and wine, iron, lead, and other heavy goods, are brought by water from Lynn, or from London, by the way of Lynn, to the great ease of the tradesmen.

From St. Edmund's Bury I returned by Stow-Market and Needham, to Ipswich, that I might keep as near the coast as was proper to my design'd circuit or journey; and from Ipswich, to visit the sea again, I went to Woodbridge, and from thence to Orford, on the sea-side.

Woodbridge has nothing remarkable, but that it is a

considerable market for butter and corn to be exported to London; for now begins that part which is ordinarily called High-Suffolk; which being a rich soil, is for a long tract of ground, wholly employed in dayries; and they again famous for the best butter, and perhaps the worst cheese, in England: The butter is barrelled, or often pickled up in small casks, and sold, not in London only, but I have known a firkin of Suffolk butter sent to the West-Indies, and brought back to England again, and has been perfectly good and sweet, as at first.

The port for the shipping off their Suffolk butter is chiefly Woodbridge, which for that reason is full of corn-factors, and butter-factors, some of whom are very considerable merchants.

From hence turning down to the shore, we see Orford Ness, a noted point of land for the guide of the colliers and coasters, and a good shelter for them to ride under, when a strong north-east wind blows and makes a foul shore on the coast.

South of the Ness is Orford Haven, being the mouth of two little rivers meeting together; 'tis a very good harbour for small vessels, but not capable of receiving a ship of burthen.

Orford was once a good town, but is decay'd, and as it stands on the land-side of the river, the sea daily throws up more land to it, and falls off itself from it, as if it was resolved to disown the place, and that it should be a sea port no longer.

A little farther lies Albro', as thriving, tho' without a port, as the other is decaying, with a good river in the front of it.

There are some gentlemen's seats up farther from the sea, but very few upon the coast.

From Albro' to *Dunwich*, there are no towns of note; even this town seems to be in danger of being swallowed up; for fame reports, that once they had fifty churches in the town; I saw but one left, and that not half full of people.

This town is a testimony of the decay of publick things, things of the most durable nature; and as the old poet[31] expresses it,

> By numerous Examples we may see,
> That Towns and Cities Die, as well as we.

The ruins of Carthage, of the great city of Jerusalem, or of antient Rome, are not at all wonderful to me; the ruins of Nineveh, which are so entirely sunk, as that 'tis doubtful where the city stood; the ruins of Babylon, or the great Persepolis, and many capital cities, which time and the change of monarchies have overthrown; these, I say, are not at all wonderful, because being the capitals of great and flourishing kingdoms, where those kingdoms were overthrown, the capital cities necessarily fell with them; but for a private town, a sea-port, and a town of commerce, to decay, as it were of itself (for we never read of Dunwich being plundered, or ruin'd, by any disaster, at least not of late years); this I must confess, seems owing to nothing but the fate of things, by which we see that towns, kings, countries, families and persons, have all their elevation, their medium, their declination, and even their destruction in the womb of time, and the course of nature. It is true, this town is manifestly decayed by the invasion of the waters, and as other towns seem sufferers by the sea, or the tide withdrawing from their ports, such as Orford, just now named; Winchelsea in Kent, and the like: so this town is, as it were, eaten up by the sea, as above; and the still encroaching ocean seems to threaten it with a fatal immersion in a few years more.

Yet Dunwich, however ruin'd, retains some share of trade, as particularly for the shipping off butter, cheese, and corn, which is so great a business in this county, that it employs a great many people and ships also; and this port lies right against the particular part of the county for butter, as Framlingham, Halsted, &c. Also a very great quantity of corn is bought up hereabout for the London market; for I shall still touch that point, how all the counties in England contribute something towards the subsistence of the great city of London, of which the butter here is a very considerable article; as also coarse cheese, which I mention'd before, us'd chiefly for the King's ships.

Hereabouts they begin to talk of herrings, and the fishery; and we find in the antient records, that this town, which was then equal to a large city; paid, among other tribute to the Government, 50000 of herrings. Here also, and at Swole, or Southole, the next sea-port, they cure sprats in the same manner as they do herrings at Yarmouth; that is to say, speaking in their own language, they make red sprats; or to speak good English, they make sprats red.

It is remarkable, that this town is now so much washed away by the sea, that what little trade they have, is carry'd on by *Walderswick*, a little town near Swole, the vessels coming in there, because the ruines of Dunwich make the shore there unsafe and uneasie to the boats; from whence the northern coasting seamen a rude verse of their own using, and I suppose of their own making; as follows,

> Swoul and Dunwich, and Walderswick,
> All go in at one lousie Creek.

This lousie creek, in short, is a little river at Swoul, which our late famous atlas-maker calls a good

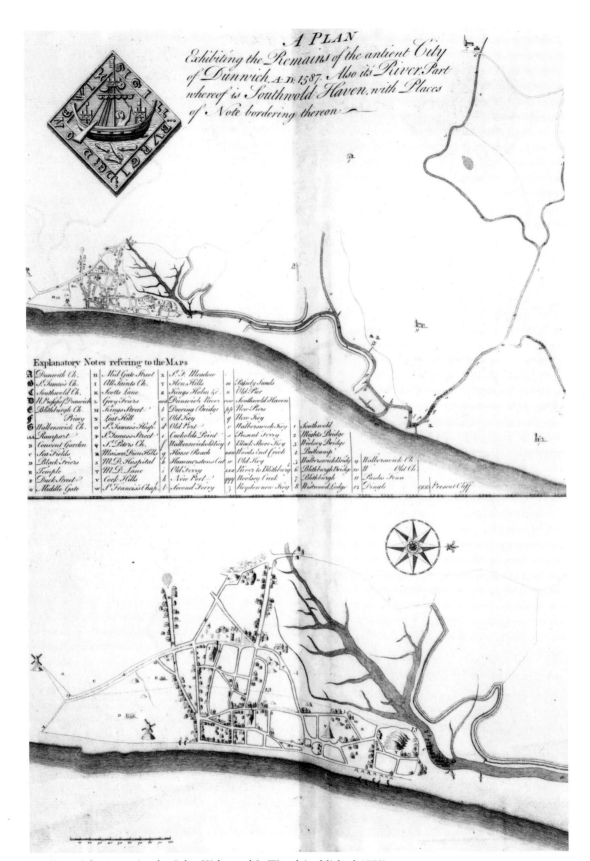

16. Dunwich; engraving by John Kirby and I. Wood (published 1753).

harbour for ships, and rendezvous of the Royal Navy; but that by the bye; the author it seems knew no better.

From Dunwich, we came to **Southwold**, the town above-named; this is a small port-town upon the coast, at the mouth of a little river call'd the Blith: I found no business the people here were employ'd in, but the fishery, as above, for herrings and sprats; which they cure by the help of smoak, as they do at Yarmouth.

There is but one church in this town, but it is a very large one and well-built, as most of the churches in this county are, and of impenetrable flint; indeed there is no occasion for its being so large, for staying there one sabbath-day, I was surprized to see an extraordinary large church, capable of receiving five or six thousand people, and but twenty-seven in it besides the parson and the clerk; but at the same time the meeting-house of the Dissenters was full to the very doors, having, as I guess'd from 6 to 800 people in it.

I find very little remarkable on this side of Suffolk, but what is on the sea shore as above; the inland country is that which they properly call High-Suffolk, and is full of rich feeding-grounds and large farms, mostly employ'd in dayries for making the Suffolk butter and cheese, of which I have spoken already.

This part of England is also remarkable for being the first where the feeding and fattening of cattle, both sheep as well as black cattle with turnips,[32] was first practis'd in England, which is made a very great part of the improvement of their lands to this day; and from whence the practice is spread over most of the east and south parts of England, to the great enriching of the farmers, and encrease of fat cattle: and tho' some have objected against the goodness of the flesh thus fed with turnips, and have fansied it would taste of the root; yet upon experience 'tis found, that at market there is no diference nor can they that buy, single out one joynt of mutton from another by the taste: so that the complaint which our nice palates at first made, begins to cease of itself; and a very great quantity of beef, and mutton also, is brought every year, and every week to London, from this side of England, and much more than was formerly known to be fed there.

I can't omit, however little it may seem, that this county of Suffolk is particularly famous for furnishing the City of London, and all the counties round, with turkeys; and that 'tis thought, there are more turkeys bred in this county, and the part of Norfolk that adjoins to it, than in all the rest of England, especially for sale. I receiv'd an account of from a person living on the place, (viz.) That they have counted 300 droves of turkeys (for they drive them all in droves on foot) pass in one season over Stratford-Bridge on the river Stour, which parts Suffolk from Essex, about six miles from Colchester on the road from Ipswich to London. These droves, as they say, generally contain from three hundred to a thousand each drove; so that one may suppose them to contain 500 one with another, which is 150000 in all.

For the further supplies of the markets of London with poultry, of which these countries particularly abound: they have within these few years found it practicable to make the geese travel on foot too, as well as the turkeys; and a prodigious number are brought up to London in droves from the farthest parts of Norfolk; even from the fenn-country, about Lynn, Downham, Wisbich, and the Washes; as also from all the east-side of Norfolk and Suffolk, of whom 'tis very frequent now to meet droves, with a thousand, sometimes two thousand in a drove: they begin to drive them generally in August, by which time the harvest is almost over, and the geese may feed in the stubbles as they go. Thus they hold on to the end of October, when the roads begin to be too stiff and deep for their broad feet and short leggs to march in.

Besides these methods of driving these creatures on foot, they have of late also invented a new method of carriage, being carts form'd on purpose, with four stories or stages, to put the creatures in one above another, by which invention one cart will carry a very great number; and for the smoother going, they drive with two horses a-breast, like a coach, so quartering the road for the ease of the gentry that thus ride; changing horses they travel night and day; so that they bring the fowls 70, 80, or 100 miles in two days and one night: the horses in this new-fashion'd voiture[33] go two a-breast, as above, but no perch[34] below as in a coach, but they are fasten'd together by a piece of wood lying cross-wise upon their necks, by which they are kept even and together, and the driver sits on the top of the cart, like as in the publick carriages for the army, &c.

When we come into Norfolk, we see a face of diligence spread over the whole country; the vast manufactures carry'd on (in chief) by the Norwich weavers, employs all the country round in spinning yarn for them; besides many thousand packs of yarn which they receive from other countries, even from as far as Yorkshire, and Westmoreland, of which I shall speak in its place.

This side of Norfolk is very populous, and throng'd with great and spacious market-towns, more and larger than any other part of England so far from London, except Devonshire, and the west-riding of Yorkshire; for example, between the frontiers of

17. 'The North East Prospect of the city of Norwich'; engraving by J. Kirkall (1724).

Suffolk and the city of Norwich on this side, which is not above 22 miles in breadth, are the following market-towns, viz.

Thetford,	Attleboro',
Dis,	Windham,
Harling,	Harleston,
Bucknam,	E. Deerham,
Hingham,	Watton,
West Deerham,	Loddon, &c.

Most of these towns are very populous and large; but that which is most remarkable is, that the whole country round them is so interspers'd with villages, and those villages so large, and so full of people, that they are equal to market-towns in other counties; in a word, they render this eastern part of Norfolk exceeding full of inhabitants.

An eminent weaver of Norwich, gave me a scheme of their trade on this occasion, by which, calculating from the number of looms at that time employ'd in the city of Norwich only, besides those employ'd in other towns in the same county, he made it appear very plain, that there were 120000 people employ'd in the woollen and silk and wool manufactures of that city only; not that the people all lived in the city, tho' Norwich is a very large and populous city too: but I say, they were employ'd for spinning the yarn used for such goods as were all made in that city. This account is curious enough, and very exact, but it is too long for the compass of this work.

This throng of villages continues thro' all the east part of the county, which is of the greatest extent, and where the manufacture is chiefly carry'd on: if any part of it be waste and thin of inhabitants, it is the west part, drawing a line from about Brand, or Brandon, south, to Walsingham, north. This part of the country indeed is full of open plains, and somewhat sandy and

barren, and feeds great flocks of good sheep: but put it all together, the county of Norfolk has the most people in the least tract of land of any county in England, except about London, and Exon, and the West-Riding of Yorkshire, as above.

Add to this, that there is no single county in England, except as above, that can boast of three towns so populous, so rich, and so famous for trade and navigation, as in this county: by these three towns, I mean the city of Norwich, the towns of Yarmouth and Lynn; besides, that it has several other sea-ports of very good trade, as Wisbich, Wells, Burnham, Clye, &c.

Norwich is the capital of all the county, and the center of all the trade and manufactures which I have just mention'd; an antient, large, rich, and populous city: If a stranger was only to ride thro' or view the city of Norwich for a day, he would have much more reason to think there was a town without inhabitants, than there is really to say so of Ipswich; but on the contrary, if he was to view the city, either on a sabbath-day, or on any publick occasion, he would wonder where all the people could dwell, the multitude is so great: But the case is this; the inhabitants being all busie at their manufactures, dwell in their garrets at their looms, and in their combing-shops, so they call them, twisting-mills,[35] and other work-houses; almost all the works they are employ'd in, being done within doors. There are in this city thirty-two parishes besides the cathedral, and a great many meeting-houses of Dissenters of all denominations. The publick edifices are chiefly the castle, antient and decayed, and now for many years past made use of for a jayl. The Duke of Norfolk's[36] house was formerly kept well, and the gardens preserved for the pleasure and diversion of the citizens, but since feeling too sensibly the sinking circumstances of that once glorious

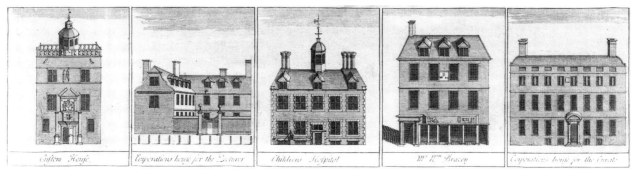

18a and b (below). Details of the Custom House and of some merchants' houses from pl. 19.

family, who were the first peers and hereditary Earl-Marshals of England.

The walls of this city are reckon'd three miles in circumference, taking in more ground than the City of London; but much of that ground lying open in pasture-fields and gardens; nor does it seem to be, like some antient places, a decayed declining town, and that the walls mark out its antient dimensions; for we do not see room to suppose that it was ever larger or more populous than it is now: but the walls seem to be placed, as if they expected that the city would in time encrease sufficiently to fill them up with buildings.

The cathedral of this city is a fine fabrick, and the spire-steeple very high and beautiful; it is not antient, the bishop's see having been first at Thetford; from whence it was not translated hither till the twelfth century; yet the church has so many antiquities in it, that our late great scholar and physician, Sir Tho. Brown,[37] thought it worth his while to write a whole book to collect the monuments and inscriptions in this church, to which I refer the reader.

The river Yare runs through this city, and is navigable thus far without the help of any art, (that is so say, without locks or stops) and being encreas'd by other waters, passes afterwards thro' a long tract of the richest meadows, and the largest, take them all together, that are any where in England, lying for thirty miles in length, from this city to Yarmouth, including the return of the said meadows on the bank of the Waveney south, and on the river Thyrn, north.

In this vast tract of meadows are fed a prodigious number of black cattle, which are said to be fed up for the fattest beef, tho' not the largest in England; and the quantity is so great, as that they not only supply the city of Norwich, the town of Yarmouth, and county adjacent, but send great quantities of them weekly in all the winter season, to London.

And this in particular is worthy remark, that the gross[38] of all the Scots cattle which come yearly into England, are brought hither, being brought to a small village lying north of the city of Norwich, call'd St. Faiths, where the Norfolk grasiers go and buy them.

These Scots runts, so they call them, coming out of the cold and barren mountains of the highlands in Scotland, feed so eagerly on the rich pasture in these marshes, that they thrive in an unusual manner, and grow monstrously fat; and the beef is so delicious for taste, that the inhabitants prefer 'em to the English cattle, which are much larger and fairer to look at, and they may very well do so: Some have told me, and I believe with good judgement, that there are above 40,000 of these Scots cattle fed in this county every year, and most of them in the said marshes between Norwich, Beccles, and Yarmouth.

Yarmouth is an antient town, much older than Norwich; and at present, tho' not standing on so much ground, yet better built; much more compleat; for number of inhabitants, not much inferior; and for wealth, trade, and advantage of its situation, infinitely superior to Norwich.

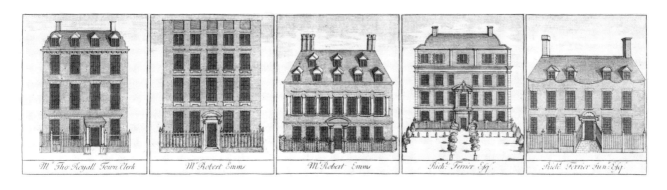

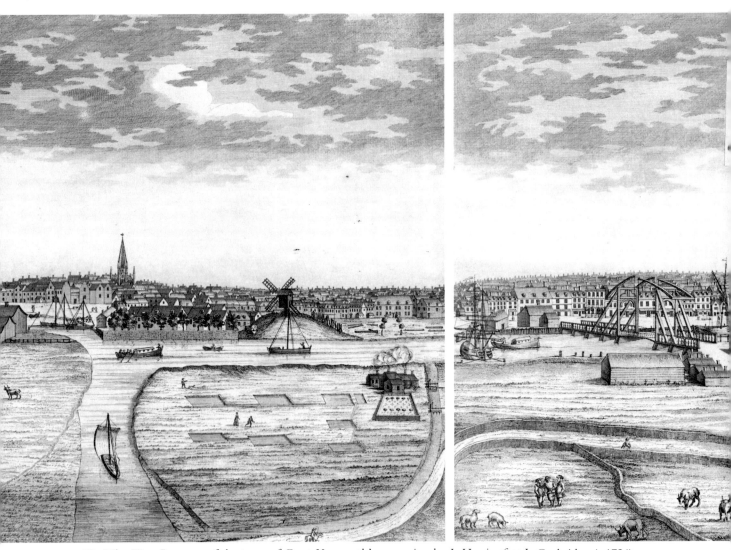

19. 'The West Prospect of the town of Great Yarmouth'; engraving by J. Harris after J. Corbridge (*c*.1724).

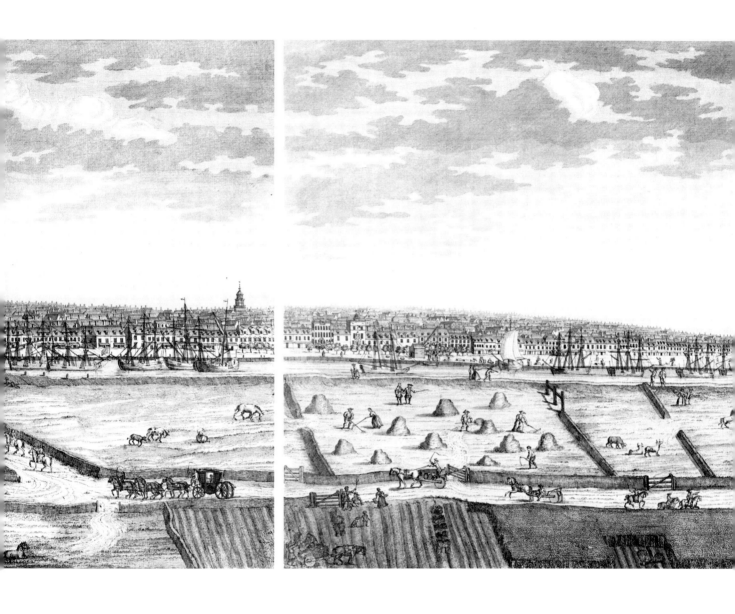

It is plac'd on a peninsula between the river Yare and the sea; the two last lying parallel to one another, and the town in the middle: the river lies on the west-side of the town, and being grown very large and deep, by a conflux of all the rivers on this side the county, forms the haven; and the town facing to the west also, and open to the river, makes the finest key[39] in England, if not in Europe, not inferior even to that of Marseilles itself.

The ships ride here so close, and as it were, keeping up one another, with their head-fasts[40] on shore, that for half a mile together, they go cross the stream with their bolsprits over the land, their bowes, or heads, touching the very wharf; so that one may walk from ship to ship as on a floating bridge, all along by the shore-side: the key reaching from the draw-bridge almost to the South-Gate, is so spacious and wide, that in some places 'tis near one hundred yards from the houses to the wharf. In this pleasant and agreeable range of houses are some very magnificent buildings, and among the rest, the Custom-House and Town-Hall, and some merchants houses, which look like little palaces, rather than the dwelling-houses of private men.

The greatest defect of this beautiful town, seems to be, that tho' it is very rich and encreasing in wealth and trade, and consequently in people, there is not room to enlarge the town by building; which would be certainly done much more than it is, but that the river on the land-side prescribes them, except at the north end without the gate; and even there the land is not very agreeable: But had they had a larger space within the gates, there would before now, have been many spacious streets of noble fine buildings erected, as we see is done in some other thriving towns in England, as at Liverpool, Manchester, Bristol, Frome, &c.

The key and the harbour of this town during the fishing-fair, as they call it, which is every Michaelmas, one sees the land cover'd with people, and the river with barks and boats, busy day and night, landing and carrying off the herrings, which they catch here in such prodigious quantities, that it is incredible. I happen'd to be there during their fishing-fair, when I told, in one tide, one hundred and ten barks and fishing vessels coming up the river, all loaden with herrings, and all taken the night before; and this was besides what was brought on shore on the dean, (that is the seaside of the town) by open boats, which they call (a) *cobles*, and which often bring in two or three

(b) *last* of fish at a time. The (c) *barks* often bring in ten last a piece.

This fishing-fair begins on Michaelmas day, and lasts all the month of October, by which time the herrings draw off to sea, shoot their spawn, and are no more fit for the merchants' business; at least not those that are taken thereabouts.

The quantity of herrings that are catch'd in this season are diversly accounted for; some have said, that the towns of Yarmouth and Leostof only, have taken forty thousand last in a season: I will not venture to confirm that report; but this I have heard the merchants themselves say, (viz.) That they have cur'd, that is to say, hang'd and dry'd in the smoak, 40,000 barrels of merchantable redherrings in one season, which is in itself (tho' far short of the other) yet a very considerable article; and it is to be added, that this is besides all the herrings consum'd in the country towns of both those populous counties, for thirty miles from the sea, whither very great quantities are carry'd every tide during the whole season.

But this is only one branch of the great trade carry'd on in this town; another part of this commerce, is in the exporting these herrings after they are cur'd; and for this their merchants have a great trade to Genoa, Leghorn, Naples, Messina, and Venice; as also to Spain and Portugal, also exporting with their herring very great quantities of worsted stuffs, and stuffs made of silk and worsted; camblets,[41] &c. the manufactures of the neighbouring city of Norwich, and of the places adjacent.

Besides this, they carry on a very considerable trade with Holland, whose opposite neighbours they are; and a vast quantity of woollen manufactures they export to the Dutch every year. Also they have a fishing trade to North-Seas for white fish, which from the place are called the North-Sea cod.

They have also a considerable trade to Norway, and to the Baltick, from whence they bring back deals, and fir-timber, oaken plank, baulks, sparrs, oars, pitch, tar, hemp, flax, spruce canvas, and sail-cloth; with all manner of naval stores, which they generally have a consumption for in their own port, where they build a very great number of ships every year, besides refitting and repairing the old.

Add to this the coal trade between Newcastle and the river of Thames, in which they are so improv'd of

(a) The cobles are open boats, which come from the north, from Scarbro', Whitby, &c. and come to Yarmouth to let themselves out to fish for the merchants during the fair-time.

(b) Note, a last is ten barrels, each barrel containing a thousand herrings.
(c) The barks come from the coast of Kent and Sussex, as from Foulkston, Dover, and Rye in Kent, and from Brithelmston in Sussex, and let themselves out to fish for the merchants during the said fair, as the cobles do from the north.

20. Details of herring fishing (*c.*1720). *Above*: herring busses under sail; *below*: pickling and barrelling herrings. Engravings by Sieuwert van der Meulen.

late years, that they have now a greater share of it than any other town in England; and have quite work'd the Ipswich men out of it, who had formerly the chief share of the colliery in their hands.

For the carrying on all these trades, they must have a very great number of ships, either of their own, or employ'd by them; and it may in some measure be judg'd of by this, that in the year 1697, I had an account from the town register, that there was then 1123 sail of ships using the sea, and belong'd to the town, besides such ships as the merchants of Yarmouth might be concern'd in, and be part-owners of, belonging to any other ports.

Here is one of the finest market-places, and the best serv'd with provisions, in England, London excepted, and the inhabitants are so multiplied in a few years, that they seem to want room in their town, rather than people to fill it, as I have observ'd above.

The streets are all exactly strait from north to south, with lanes or alleys, which they call Rows, crossing them in strait lines also from east to west; so that it is the most regular built town in England, and seems to have been built all at once; or, that the dimensions of the houses, and extent of the streets, were laid out by consent.

They have particular privileges in this town, and a jurisdiction by which they can try, condemn, and execute in especial cases, without waiting for a warrant from above; and this they exerted once very smartly, in executing a captain of one of the King's ships of war in the reign of King Charles II, for a murther committed in the street, the circumstance of which did indeed call for justice; but some thought they would not have ventur'd to exert their power as they did; however, I never heard that the government resented it, or blamed them for it.

It is also a very well govern'd town; and I have no where in England observed the sabbath-day so exactly kept, or the breach so continually punished as in this place, which I name to their honour.

Among all these regularities, it is no wonder if we do not find abundance of revelling, or that there is little encouragement to assemblies, plays, and gaming-meetings at Yarmouth, as in some other places; and yet I do not see that the ladies here come behind any of the neighbouring counties, either in beauty, breeding, or behaviour; to which may be added too, not at all to their disadvantage, that they generally go beyond them in fortunes.

Cromer is a market town close to the shoar of this dangerous coast, I know nothing it is famous for (besides it's being thus the terror of the sailors) except good lobsters, which are taken on that coast in great numbers, and carryed to Norwich, and in such quantities sometimes too, as to be convey'd by sea to London.

From Cromer, we ride on the strand or open shoar to Weyburn Hope, the shoar so flat that in some places the tide ebbs out near two miles: from Weyburn West lyes Clye, where there are large salt-works, and very good salt made, which is sold all over the county, and sometimes sent to Holland, and to the Baltick: From Clye, we go to Masham, and to Wells, all towns on the coast, in each whereof there is a very considerable trade cary'd on with Holland for corn, which that part of the county is very full of: I say nothing of the great trade driven here from Holland, back again to England, because I take it to be a trade carryed on with much less honesty than advantage; especially while the clandestine trade, or the art of smuggling was so much in practice; what it is now, is not to my present purpose.

From hence we turn to the S. W. to **Castle-Rising**, an old decay'd burrough town with perhaps not ten families in it, which yet (to the scandal of our prescription right)[42] sends two members to the British Parliament, being as many as the city of Norwich itself, or any town in the kingdom, London excepted can do.

On our left we see **Walsingham**, an antient town, famous for the old ruins of a monastery of note there, and the shrine of our Lady, as noted as that of St. Thomas-a-Becket at Canterbury, and for little else.

Near this place are the seats of the two ally'd families of the Lord Viscount Townsend,[43] and Robert Walpole,[44] Esq; the latter at this time one of the Lords Commissioners of the Treasury, and Minister of State, and the former one of the principal Secretaries of State to King George, of which again.

From hence we went to **Lyn**, another rich and populous thriving port-town. It stands on more ground than the town of Yarmouth, and has I think parishes, yet I cannot allow that it has more people than Yarmouth, if so many. It is a beautiful well built, and well situated town, at the mouth of the river Ouse, and has this particular attending it, which gives it a vast advantage in trade; namely, that there is the greatest extent of inland navigation here, of any port in England, London excepted. The reason whereof is this, that there are more navigable rivers empty themselves here into the sea, including the Washes, which are branches of the same port, than at any one mouth of waters in England, except the Thames and the Humber. By these navigable rivers the merchants of Lynn supply about six counties wholly, and three counties in part, with their goods, especially wine, and

21. 'Tuesday Market Place. Kings Lynn'; engraving ascribed to H. Bell.

coals, (viz.) By the little Ouse, they send their goods to Brandon, and Thetford, by the lake to Mildenhall, Barton-Mills, and St. Edmunds-Bury; by the river Grant to Cambridge, by the Great Ouse itself to Ely, to St. Ives, to St. Neots, to Barford-Bridge, and to Bedford; by the river Nyne, to Peterboro'; by the Dreyns and Washes to Wysbich, to Spalding, Market-Deeping, and Stamford; besides the several counties, into which these goods are carryed by land carriage, from the places where the navigation of those rivers ends; which has given rise to this observation on the town of Lynn, that they bring in more coals, than any sea-port between London and Newcastle; and import more wines than any port in England, except London and Bristol; their trade to Norway, and to the Baltick Sea is also great in proportion, and of late years they have extended their trade farther to the southward.

Here are more gentry, and consequently is more gayety in this town than in Yarmouth, or even in Norwich itself; the place abounding in very good company.

The situation of this town renders it capable of being made very strong, and in the late wars it was so; a line of fortification being drawn round it at a distance from the walls; the ruins, or rather remains of which works appear very fair to this day; nor would it be a hard matter to restore the bastions, with the ravelins and counterscarp, upon any sudden emergency, to a good state of defence; and that in a little time, a sufficient number of workmen being employed; especially be-

cause they are able to fill all their ditches with water from the sea, in such a manner as that it cannot be drawn off.

There is, in the market-place of this town, a very fine statue of King William on horseback,[45] erected at the charge of the town. The Owse is mighty large and deep, close to the very town itself, and ships of good burthen may come up to the key; but there is no bridge, the stream being too strong, and the bottom moorish[46] and unsound: nor for the same reason is the anchorage computed the best in the world; but there are good roads farther down.

They pass over here in boats into the fenn-country, and over the famous washes into Lincolnshire, but the passage is very dangerous and uneasy, and where passengers often miscarry and are lost; but then it is usually on their venturing at improper times, and without the guides, which if they would be perswaded not to do, they would very rarely fail of going or coming safe.

From Lynn, I bent my course to **Downham**, where is an ugly wooden bridge over the Ouse; from whence we pass'd the Fenn country to **Wisbich**, but saw nothing that way to tempt our curiosity but deep roads, in-numerable dreyns and dykes of water, all navigable, and a rich soil, the land bearing a vast quantity of good hemp; but a base unwholsome air; so we came back to Ely, whose cathedral, standing in a level flat country, is seen far and wide; and of which town, when the minster, so they call it, is describ'd, every thing re-

22. John Wootton, *Warren Hill* (*c*.1715).

markable is said that there is room to say; and of the minster this is the most remarkable thing that I could hear, namely, that some of it is so antient, totters so much with every gust of wind, looks so like a decay, and seems so near it, that when ever it does fall, all that 'tis likely will be thought strange in it, will be that it did not fall a hundred years sooner.

From hence we came over the Ouse, and in a few miles to Newmarket. Being come to **Newmarket** in the month of October, I had the opportunity to see the horse-races; and a great concourse of the nobility and gentry, as well from London as from all parts of England; but they were all so intent, so eager, so busy upon the sharping[47] part of the sport, their wagers and bets, that to me they seem'd just as so many horse-coursers in Smithfield[48], descending (the greatest of them) from their high dignity and quality, to picking one another's pockets, and biting[49] one another as much as possible, and that with such eagerness, as that it might be said they acted without respect to faith, honour, or good manners.

There was Mr. Frampton,[50] the oldest, and as some

say, the cunningest jockey in England, one day he lost 1000 guineas, the next he won two thousand; and so alternately he made as light of throwing away five hundred or one thousand pounds at a time, as other men do of their pocket-money, and as perfectly calm, cheerful, and unconcern'd, when he had lost one thousand pounds, as when he had won it. On the other side, there was Sir R—— Fagg,[51] of Sussex, of whom fame says he has the most in him and the least to shew for it, relating to jockeyship, of any man there; yet he often carry'd the prize; his horses, they said, were all cheats, how honest soever their master was; for he scarce ever produc'd a horse but he look'd like what he was not, and was what no body cou'd expect him to be: if he was as light as the wind, and could fly like a meteor, he was sure to look as clumsie, and as dirty, and as much like a cart-horse as all the cunning of his master and the grooms could make him; and just in this manner he bit some of the greatest gamesters in the field.

I was so sick of the jockeying part, that I left the crowd about the posts, and pleased myself with ob-

V. John Wootton, *Newmarket scene* (1737).

serving the horses; how the creatures yielded to all the arts and managements of their masters; how they took their airings in sport, and play'd with the daily heats which they ran over the course before the grand day; but how! as knowing the difference equally with their riders, would they exert their utmost strength at the time of the race itself; and that to such an extremity, that one or two of them died in the stable when they came to be rubb'd after the first heat.

Here I fansy'd myself in the Circus Maximus at Rome, seeing the antient games, and the racings of the chariots and horsemen; and in this warmth of my imagination I pleas'd and diverted myself more and in a more noble manner, than I could possibly do in the crowds of gentlemen at the weighing and starting posts, and at their coming in; or at their meetings at the coffee-houses and gaming-tables after the races were over, where there was little or nothing to be seen, but what was the subject of just reproach to them, and reproof from every wise man that look'd upon them. N.B. Pray take it with you as you go, you see no ladies at New-Market, except a few of the neighbouring gentlemen's families who come in their coaches on any particular day to see a race and so go home again directly.

I had still the county of Cambridge to visit, to compleat this tour of the eastern part of England, and of that I come now to speak.

We enter Cambridgeshire out of Suffolk with all the advantage in the world; the county beginning upon those pleasant and agreeable plains call'd New Market-Heath, where passing the Devil's Ditch, which has nothing worth notice but its name, and that but fabulous too, from the hills call'd Gogmagog, we see a rich and pleasant vale westward, cover'd with cornfields, gentlemen's seats, villages, and at a distance, to crown all the rest, that antient and truly famous town and university of Cambridge.

As my business is not to lay out the geographical situation of places, I say nothing of the buttings and boundings of this county: it lies on the edge of the great level, call'd by the people here the fenn-country; and great part, if not all, the Isle of Ely, lies in this county and Norfolk: The rest of Cambridgeshire is

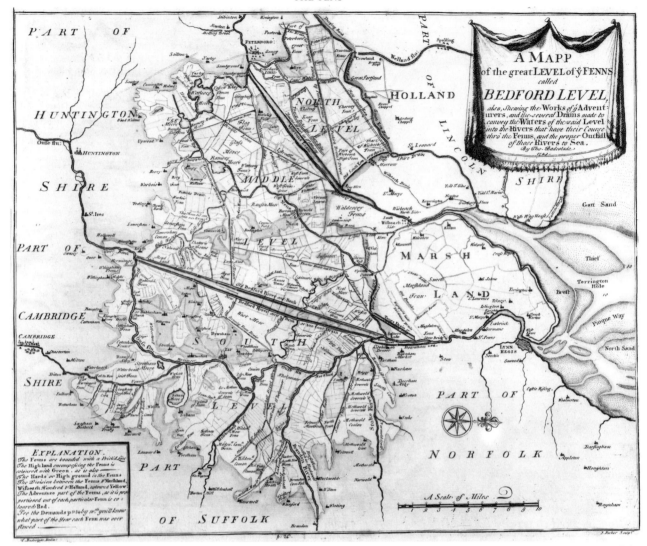

23. 'Map of the Great Level of the Fenns, called Bedford Level' (1723). From *The History of the ancient and present state of the navigation of. . .Kings Lynn* (1724).

almost wholly a corn country; and of that corn five parts in six of all they sow, is barly, which is generally sold to Ware and Royston, and other great malting-towns in Hertfordshire, and is the fund from whence that vast quantity of malt, call'd Hertfordshire malt, is made, which is esteem'd the best in England. As Essex, Suffolk, and Norfolk, are taken up in manufactures, and fam'd for industry, this county has no manufacture at all; nor are the poor, except the husband-men, fam'd for any thing so much as idleness and sloth, to their scandal be it spoken; what the reason of it is, I know not.

As I said, I first had a view of Cambridge from Gogmagog Hills: I am to add, that there appears on the mountain that goes by this name, an antient camp, or fortification, that lies on the top of the hill, with a double or rather treble rampart and ditch, which most of our writers say was neither Roman nor Saxon, but British: I am to add, that King James II caused a spacious stable to be built in the area of this camp, for his running-horses, and made old Mr. Frampton, whom I mention'd above, master or inspector of them: the stables remain still there, tho' they are not often made use of. As we descended westward, we saw the fenn country on our right, almost all cover'd with water like a sea, the Michaelmas rains having been very great that year, they had sent down great floods of water from the upland countries, and those fenns being, as may be very properly said, the sink of no less than thirteen counties; that is to say, that all the water, or most part of the water of thirteen counties, falls into them, they are often thus overflow'd.

24. Detail from pl. 19.

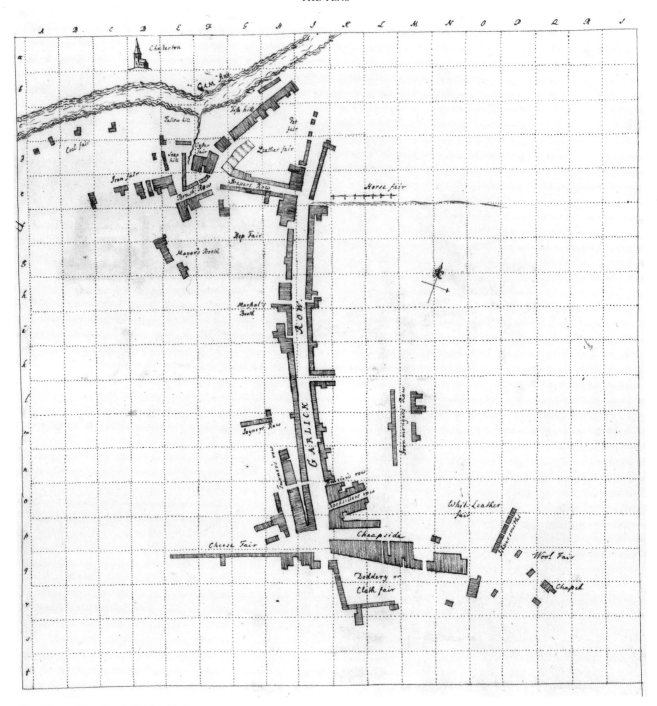

25. 'Plan of Sturbock Fair' (1725).

In these fenns are abundance of those admirable pieces of art call'd duckoys; that is to say, places so adapted for the harbour and shelter of wild-fowl, and then furnish'd with a breed of those they call decoy-ducks, who are taught to allure and entice their kind to the places they belong to, that it is incredible what quantities of wild-fowl of all sorts, duck, mallard, teal, widgeon, &c. they take in those duckoys every week, during the season; it may indeed be guess'd at a little by this, that there is a duckoy not far from Ely, which pays to the landlord, Sir Tho. Hare 500 l. a year rent, besides the charge of maintaining a great number of servants for the management; and from which duckoy alone they assured me at St. Ives, (a town on the Ouse, where the fowl they took was always brought to be sent to London;) that they generally sent up three thousand couple a week.

As these fenns appear cover'd with water, so I observ'd too, that they generally at this latter part of the year appear also cover'd with foggs, so that when the downs and higher grounds of the adjacent country were gilded with the beams of the sun, the Isle of Ely look'd as if wrapp'd up in blankets, and nothing to be seen, but now and then, the lanthorn or cupola of Ely Minster.

One could hardly see this from the hills and not pity the many thousands of families that were bound to or confin'd in those foggs, and had no other breath to draw than what must be mix'd with those vapours, and that steam which so universally overspread the country: but notwithstanding this, the people, especially those that are used to it, live unconcern'd, and as healthy as other folks, except now and then an ague, which they make light of, and there are great numbers of very antient people among them.

I now draw near to Cambridge, to which I fancy I look as if I was afraid to come, having made so many circumlocutions beforehand; but I must yet make another digression before I enter the town; (for in my way, and as I came in from New Market, about the beginning of September;) I cannot omit, that I came necessarily through Sturbridge Fair, which was then in its height.

If it is a diversion worthy a book to treat of trifles, such as the gayety of Bury fair, it cannot be very unpleasant, especially to the trading part of the world, to say something of this fair, which is not only the greatest in the whole nation, but in the world; nor, if I may believe those who have seen them all, is the fair at Leipsick in Saxony, the Mart at Frankfort on the Main, or the fairs at Neuremberg, or Ausburg, any way to compare to this fair at Sturbridge.

It is kept in a large corn-field, near Casterton, extending from the side of the river Cam, towards the road, for about half a mile square.

It is impossible to describe all the parts and circumstances of this fair exactly; the shops are placed in rows like streets, whereof one is call'd Cheapside; and here, as in several other streets, are all sorts of trades, who sell by retale, and who come principally from London with their goods; scarce any trades are omitted, goldsmiths, toyshops, brasiers, turners, milleners, haberdashers, hatters, mercers, drapers, pewtrers, chinawarehouses, and in a word all trades that can be named in London; with coffee-houses, taverns, brandy-shops, and eating-houses, innumerable, and all in tents, and booths, as above.

This great street reaches from the road, which as I said goes from Cambridge to New-Market, turning short out of it to the right towards the river, and holds in a line near half a mile quite down to the river-side: in another street parallel with the road are like rows of booths, but larger, and more intermingled with wholesale dealers, and one side, passing out of this last street to the left hand, is a formal great square, form'd by the largest booths, built in that form, and which they call the Duddery; whence the name is deriv'd, and what its signification is, I could never yet learn, tho' I made all possible search into it. The area of this square is about 80 to a 100 yards, where the dealers have room before every booth to take down, and open their packs, and to bring in waggons to load and unload.

26. A stall at Stourbridge Fair; engraving. From W. Hone, *Yearbook of Early Recreation* (1835).

This place is separated, and peculiar to the wholesale dealers in the woollen manufacture. Here the booths, or tents are of a vast extent, have different apartments, and the quantities of goods they bring are so great, that the insides of them look like another Blackwell-Hall,[52] being as vast ware-houses pil'd up with goods to the top. In this Duddery, as I have been inform'd, there have been sold one hundred thousand pounds worth of woollen manufactures in less than a week's time, besides the prodigious trade carry'd on here, by wholesale-men, from London, and all parts of England, who transact their business wholly in their pocket-books, and meeting their chapmen from all parts, make up their accounts, receive money chiefly in bills, and take orders: these they say exceed by far the sales of goods actually brought to the fair, and deliver'd in kind; it being frequent for the London wholesale men to carry back orders fom their dealers for ten thousand pounds

27. 'The North-East view of Cambridge Castle'; engraving by Samuel and Nathaniel Buck (1730).

worth of goods a man, and some much more. This especially respects those people, who deal in heavy goods, as wholesale grocers, salters, brasiers, iron-merchants, wine-merchants, and the like; but does not exclude the dealers in woollen manufactures, and especially in mercery goods of all sorts, the dealers in which generally manage their business in this manner.

Here are clothiers from Hallifax, Leeds, Wakefield and Huthersfield in Yorkshire, and from Rochdale, Bury, &c. in Lancashire, with vast quantities of Yorkshire cloths, kerseyes, pennistons,[53] cottons, &c. with all sorts of Manchester ware, fustians, and things made of cotton wool; of which the quantity is so great, that they told me there were near a thousand horse-packs of such goods from that side of the country, and these took up a side and half of the Duddery at least; also a part of a street of booths were taken up with upholsterer's ware, such as tickings, sackings, Kidder-minster stuffs, blankets, rugs, quilts, &c.

In the Duddery I saw one ware-house, or booth with six apartments in it, all belonging to a dealer in Norwich stuffs only, and who they said had there above twenty thousand pounds value, in those goods, and no other.

Western goods had their share here also, and several booths were fill'd as full with serges,[54] du-roys,[55] druggets,[56] shalloons,[57] cantaloons,[58] Devonshire kersies,[59] &c. from Exeter, Taunton, Bristol, and other parts west, and some from London also.

But all this is still out done, at least in show, by two articles, which are the peculiars of this fair, and do not begin till the other part of the fair, that is to say for the woollen manufacture, begins to draw to a close: These are the Wooll, and the Hops; as for the hops, there is scarce any price fix'd for hops in England, till they

know how they sell at Sturbridge fair; the quantity that appears in the fair is indeed prodigious, and they, as it were, possess a large part of the field on which the fair is kept, to themselves; they are brought directly from Chelmsford in Essex, from Canterbury and Maidstone in Kent, and from Farnham in Surrey, besides what are brought from London, the growth of those, and other places.

I might go on here to speak of several other sorts of English manufactures, which are brought hither to be sold; as all sorts of wrought iron, and brass ware from Birmingham; edg'd tools, knives, &c. from Sheffield; glass wares, and stockings, from Nottingham, and Leicester; and an infinite throng of other things of smaller value, every morning.

To attend this fair, and the prodigious conflux of people, which come to it, there are sometimes no less than fifty hackney coaches, which come from London, and ply night and morning to carry the people to and from Cambridge; for there the gross of the people lodge; nay, which is still more strange, there are wherries brought from London on waggons to plye upon the little river Cam, and to row people up and down from the town, and from the fair as occasion presents.

Towards the latter end of the fair, and when the great hurry of wholesale business begins to be over, the gentry come in, from all parts of the county round; and tho' they come for their diversion; yet 'tis not a little money they lay out; which generally falls to the share of the retailers, such as toy-shops,[60] goldsmiths, brasiers, ironmongers, turners, milleners, mercers, &c. and some loose coins, they reserve for the puppet-shows, drolls, rope-dancers, and such like; of which there is no want, though not considerable like the rest:

38

The last day of the fair is the horse-fair, where the whole is clos'd with both horse and foot-races, to divert the meaner sort of people only, for nothing considerable is offer'd of that kind: thus ends the whole fair, and in less than a week more, there is scarce any sign left that there has been such a thing there; except by the heaps of dung and straw, and other rubbish which is left behind, trod into the earth, and which is as good as a summer's fallow for dunging to the land; and as I have said above, pays the husband-man well for the use of it.

I should have mention'd, that here is a court of justice always open, and held every day in a shed built on purpose in the fair; this is for keeping the peace, and deciding controversies in matters deriving from the business of the fair: the magistrates of the town of Cambridge are judges in this court, as being in their jurisdiction, or they holding it by special priviledge: here they determine matters in a summary way, as is practis'd in those we call Pye-Powder courts[61] in other places, or as a court of conscience; and they have a final authority without appeal.

I come now to the town, and university of **Cambridge**; I say the town and university, for tho' they are blended together in the situation, and the colleges, halls, and houses for literature are promiscuously scatter'd up and down among the other parts, and some even among the meanest of the other buildings; as Magdalen College over the bridge, is in particular; yet they are all encorporated together, by the name of the university, and are govern'd apart, and distinct from the town, which they are so intermix'd with.

As their authority is distinct from the town, so are their priviledges, customs, and government; they choose representatives, or Members of Parliament for themselves, and the town does the like for themselves, also apart.

The town is govern'd by a Mayor, and Aldermen. The University by a Chancellor, and Vice-Chancellor, &c. Tho' their dwellings are mix'd, and seem a little confus'd, their authority is not so; in some cases the Vice-Chancellor may concern himself in the town, as in searching houses for the scholars at improper hours, removing scandalous women, and the like.

But as the colleges are many, and the gentlemen entertain'd in them are a very great number, the trade of the town very much depends upon them, and the tradesmen may justly be said to get their bread by the colleges; and this is the surest hold the university may be said to have of the townsmen, and by which they secure the dependence of the town upon them, and consequently their submission.

As to the antiquity of the university in this town, the originals and founders of the several colleges, their revenues, laws, government and governors, they are so effectually and so largely treated by other authors and are so foreign to the familiar design of these letters, that I refer my readers to Mr. Camden's *Britannia*, and the author of the Antiquities of Cambridge,[62] and other such learned writers, by whom they may be fully informed.

From Cambridge, my design obliging me, and the direct road, in part concurring, I came back thro' the west part of the country of Essex, and at **Saffron Walden** I saw the ruins of the once largest and most magnificent pile in all this part of England, (viz.) Audley End;[63] built by, and decaying with the noble Dukes and Earls of Suffolk.

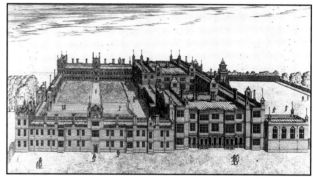

28. 'A General Prospect of the Royal Palace of Audlyene seen from the Mount Garden'; engraving by Henry Winstanley and Littleby.

A little north of this part of the country rises the river Stour, which for a course of fifty miles or more, parts the two counties of Suffolk and Essex; passing thro' or near Haveril, Clare, Cavendish, Halsted, Sudbury, Buers, Nayland, Stretford, Dedham, Manningtree, and into the sea at Harwich; assisting by its waters to make one of the best harbours for shipping that is in Great-Britain; I mean Orwell Haven, or Harwich, of which I have spoken largely already.

As we came on this side we saw at a distance Braintree and Bocking, two towns, large, rich and populous, and made so originally by the bay trade, of which I have spoken at large at Colchester, and which flourishes still among them.

Near to this is the Priory of Lees, a delicious seat of the late Dukes of Manchester, but sold by the present Duke to the Dutchess Dowager of Bucks; his Grace the Duke of Manchester removing to his yet finer seat of Kimbolton in Northamptonshire, the antient mansion of the family. From hence keeping the London road I came to Chelmsford, mention'd before, and Ingerstone, five miles west, which I mention again; because in the parish-church of this town are to be seen the antient monuments of the noble family of Petre;[64] whose seat, and a large estate, lie in the neighbourhood; and whose whole family, by a constant series of beneficent actions to the poor, and bounty upon all charitable occasions, have gain'd an affectionate esteem thro' all that part of the country, such as no prejudice of religion could wear out, or perhaps ever may; and I must confess, I think, need not; for good and great actions command our respect, let the opinions of the persons be otherwise what they will.

From hence we cross'd the country to the great forest, called **Epping Forest**, reaching almost to London. The country on that side of Essex is called the Roodings, I suppose, because there are no less than ten towns almost together, called by the name of Roding, and is famous for good land, good malt, and dirty roads; the latter indeed in the winter are scarce passable for horse or man. In the midst of this we see Chipping Onger, Hatfield Broad-Oak, Epping, and many forest-towns, fam'd, as I have said, for husbandry and good malt; but of no other note. On the south-side of the county is Waltham-Abby; the ruins of the abby remain; and tho' antiquity is not my proper business, I cou'd not but observe, that King Harold, slain in the great battle in Sussex[65] against William the conqueror, lies buried here; his body being begg'd by his mother, the Conqueror allow'd it to be carried hither; but no monument was, as I can find, built for him, only a flat grave-stone, on which was engraven, *Harold Infælix*.

From hence I came over the forest again, that is to say, over the lower or western part of it, where it is spangled with fine villages, and these villages fill'd with fine seats, most of them built by the citizens of London, as I observed before; but the lustre of them seems to be entirely swallow'd up in the magnificent palace of the Lord Castlemain,[66] whose father, Sir Josiah Child, as it were, prepar'd it in his life for the design of his son, tho' altogether unforeseen; by adding to the advantage of its situation innumerable rows of trees, planted in curious order for avenues and

29. Wanstead (bird's-eye view from the east); engraving by J. Kip after a drawing by L. Knyff (*c*.1710).

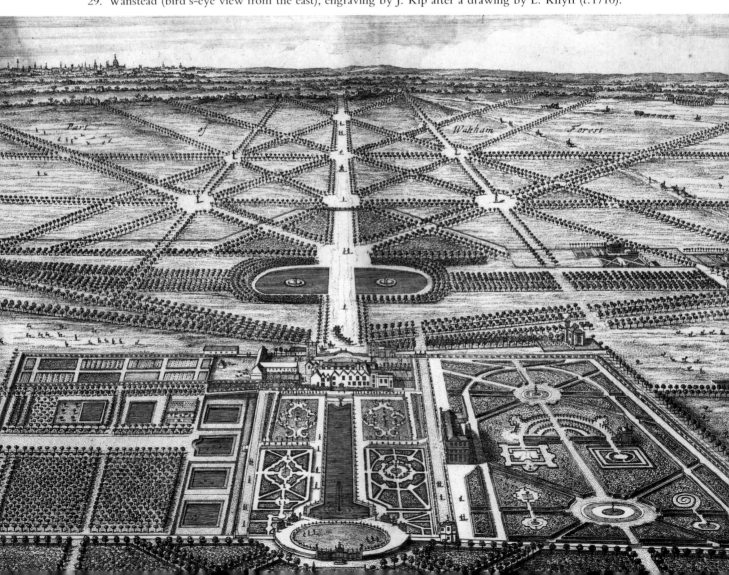

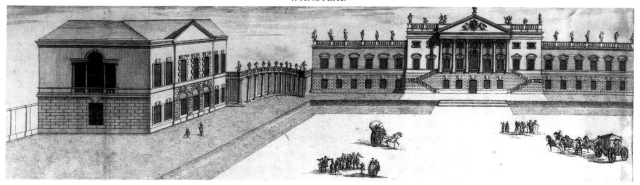

30. Detail of Wanstead House: the entrance from the west; engraving by J. Rocque (c.1735).

vistos, to the house, all leading up to the place where the old house stood, as to a center.

In the place adjoining, his Lordship, while he was yet Sir Richard Child only, and some years before he began the foundation of his new house, laid out the most delicious as well as most spacious pieces of ground for gardens that is to be seen in all this part of England. The house is built since these gardens have been finish'd: The building is all of Portland stone in the front, which makes it look extremely glorious and magnificent at a distance; it being the particular property of that stone, except in the streets of London, where it is tainted and ting'd with the smoak of the city, to grow whiter and whiter the longer it stands in the open air.

As the front of the house opens to a long row of trees, reaching to the great road at Leighton Stone; so the back-face, or front, if that be proper, respects the gardens, and with an easy descent lands you upon the terras, from whence is a most beautiful prospect to the river, which is all form'd into canals and openings, to answer the views from above, and beyond the river, the walks and wildernesses go on to such a distance, and in such a manner up the hill, as they before went down, that the sight is lost in the woods adjoining, and it looks all like one planted garden as far as the eye can see.

I shall cover as much as possible the melancholy part of a story, which touches too sensibly, many, if not most of the great and flourishing families in England: pity and matter of grief is it to think that families, by

estate, able to appear in such a glorious posture as this, should ever be vulnerable by so mean a disaster as that of stock-jobbing: But the general infatuation of the day is a plea for it; so that men are not now blamed on that account: South-Sea was a general possession; and if my Lord Castlemain was wounded by that arrow shot in the dark, 'twas a misfortune: But 'tis so much a happiness, that it was not a mortal wound, as it was to some men, who once seem'd as much out of the reach of it; and that blow, be it what it will, is not remember'd for joy of the escape; for we see this noble family, by prudence and management rise out of all that cloud, if it may be allow'd such a name, and shining in the same full lustre as before.

From my Lord Castlemain's house, and the rest of the fine dwellings on that side of the forest, for there are several very good houses at Wanstead, only that they seem all swallow'd up in the lustre of his lordship's palace; I say, from thence I went South, towards the great road over that part of the forest call'd the Flatts, where we see a very beautiful, but retired and rural Seat of Mr. Lethulier's, eldest Son of the late Sir John Lethulier, of Lusum in Kent, of whose family I shall speak when I come on that side.

By this turn I came necessarily on to Stratford, where I set out: and thus having finished my first circuit, I conclude my first letter; and am,

> Sir,
> Your Most Humble,
> And Obedient Servant.

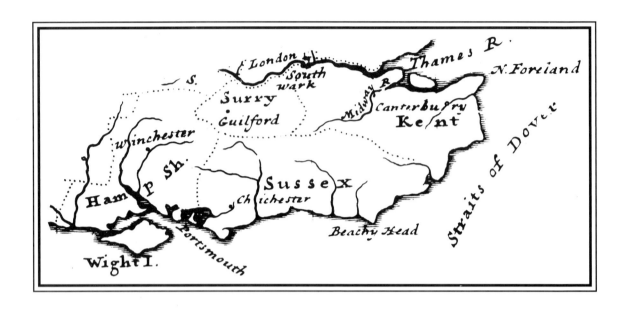

LETTER II

Containing a Description of the Sea-Coasts of Kent, Sussex, Hampshire, and of Part of Surrey.

Sir,

As in my first journey I went over the eastern counties of England, viz. Essex, Suffolk, Norfolk, and Cambridge, and took my course on that side the River Thames, to view the sea-coasts, harbours, &c. so being now to traverse the southern counties, I begin with the other side of the Thames, and shall surround the sea-coast of Kent, as I did that of Norfolk and Suffolk, and perhaps it is as fruitful of instructing and diverting observations as any of the other.

I took boat at Tower-Wharf, sending my horses round by land to meet me at **Greenwich**, that I might begin my journey at the beginning of the county, and here I had the advantage of making my first step into the county of Kent, at a place which is the most delightful spot of ground in Great-Britain; pleasant by situation, those pleasures encreas'd by art, and all made compleatly agreeable by the accident of fine buildings, the continual passing of fleets of ships up and down the most beautiful river in Europe; the best air, best prospect, and the best conversation in England.

The Royal Hospital for Seamen,[1] though not yet finished; the park, the Queen's House,[2] the Observatory on the hill, commonly call'd Flamstead-House,[3] are all things so well known, they need no particular description.

The ground, part of this hospital now stands upon, and is to stand upon, is the same on which formerly stood the royal palace of our Kings. Here Henry VIII held his royal feasts with justs and tournaments, and the ground which was call'd the tilt-yard, is the spot on which the eastermost wing of the hospital is built; the park, (for it was even then a park also) was enlarg'd, wall'd about, and planted with beautiful rows, or walks of trees by King Charles II soon after the

Restoration; and the design or plan of a royal palace was then lay'd out, one wing of which was finished and covered in a most magnificent manner, and makes now the first wing of the hospital as you come to it from London: The building is regular, the lower part a strong Dorick, the middle part a most beautiful Corinthian, with an Attick above all, to compleat the height; the front to the water-side is extreamly magnificent and graceful; embellish'd with rich carv'd work and fine devices, such as will hardly be outdone in this, or any age for beauty or art.

The river of Thames is here very broad, and the channel deep, and the water at some very high spring-tides is salt; but in ordinary tides, is very sweet and fresh, especially at the tide of ebb.

The country behind Greenwich adds to the pleasure of the place: **Black-Heath**, both for beauty of situation, and an excellent air, is not out-done by any spot of ground so near the river and so near land in England.

On the other side of the heath, north, is **Charleton**, a village famous, or rather infamous for that yearly collected rabble of mad-people, at Horn-Fair;[4] the rudeness of which I cannot but think, is such as ought to be suppress'd, and indeed in a civiliz'd well govern'd nation, it may well be said to be unsufferable. The mob indeed at that time take all kinds of liberties, and the women are especially impudent for that day; as if it was a day that justify'd the giving themselves a loose to all manner of indecency and immodesty, without any reproach, or without suffering the censure which such behaviour would deserve at another time.

Thro' this town lies the road to **Woolwich**, a town on the bank of the same river, wholly taken up by, and in a manner rais'd from, the yards, and publick works, erected there for the publick service; here, when the

VI. Samuel Scott, *Greenwich Hospital* (*c.*1750).

business of the Royal Navy encreased, and Queen Elizabeth built larger and greater ships of war than were usually employ'd before, new docks, and launches were erected, and places prepared for the building and repairing ships of the largest size; because, as here was a greater depth of water and a freer channel, than at Deptford, (where the chief yard in the river of Thames was before) so there was less hazard in the great ships going up and down; the croud of merchant-ships at Deptford, being always such, as that it could not be so safe to come up thither, as to put in at Woolwich.

The docks, yards, and all the buildings belonging to it, are encompassed with a high wall, and are exceeding spacious and convenient; and are also prodigious full of all manner of stores of timber, plank, masts, pitch, tar, and all manner of naval provisions to such a degree, as is scarce to be calculated.

Besides the building-yards, here is a large rope-walk[5] where the biggest cables are made for the men of war; and on the east or lower part of the town is the gun-yard, or place set apart for the great guns belonging to the ships, commonly call'd the Park, or the Gun-Park; where is a prodigious quantity of all manner of ordnance-stores, such as are fit for sea-service, that is to say, cannon of all sorts for the ships of war, every ship's guns by themselves; heavy cannon for batteries, and mortars of all sorts and sizes; insomuch, that, as I was inform'd here has been sometimes laid up at one time between seven and eight thousand pieces of ordnance, besides mortars and shells without number.

From this town there is little remarkable upon the river, till we come to Gravesend, the whole shore being low, and spread with marshes and unhealthy grounds, except with small intervals, where the land bends inward as at Erith, Greenwich, North-Fleet, &c. in which places the chalk hills come close to the river, and from thence the city of London, the adjacent coun-

31. London from Greenwich Park; painting by Jan Griffier the Elder (*c*.1710–15). Charlton Horn Fair is in the foreground.

tries, and, even Holland and Flanders, are supply'd with lime, for their building, or chalk to make lime, and for other uses.

From these chalky cliffs on the river side, the rubbish of the chalk, which crumbles away when they dig the larger chalk for lime, or (as we might call it) the chips of the chalk, and which they must be at the charge of removing to be out of their way, is bought and fetch'd away by lighters and hoys, and carry'd to all the ports and creeks in the opposite county of Essex, and even to Suffolk and Norfolk, and sold there to the country farmers to lay upon their land, and that in prodigious quantities; and so is it valued by the farmers of those counties, that they not only give from two shillings and six pence, to four shillings a load for it, according to the distance the place is from the said chalk-cliffs, but they fetch it by land-carriage ten miles, nay fifteen miles, up into the country.

On the back-side of these marshy grounds in Kent at

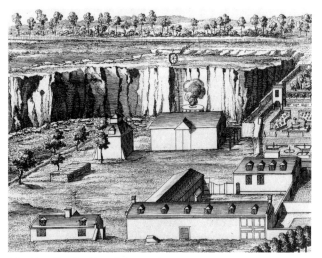

32. Detail of a lime kiln in the grounds of Ingries, Greenhythe, seat of Jonathan Smith, from an engraving by J. Kip after a drawing by Thomas Badeslade. From John Harris *The History of Kent* (1719).

33. A wagon (1709). From a *Table of Fares issued by the Sheriffs' court*.

a small distance, lies the road from London to Dover, and on that highway, or near it, several good towns; for example, **Eltham**, formerly a royal palace when the court was kept at Greenwich; and Queen Elizabeth, who (as before) was born at Greenwich, was often carry'd, as they say, to Eltham by her nurses to suck in the wholesome air of that agreable place; but at present there are few or no signs of the old palace to be seen.

From this side of the country all pleasant and gay, we go over **Shooter's Hill**, where the face of the world seems quite alter'd; for here we have but a chalky soil, and indifferently fruitful, far from rich; much overgrown with wood, especially coppice-wood, which is cut for faggots and bavins, and sent up by water to London. Here they make those faggots which the wood-mongers call ostrey wood, and here in particular those small light bavins[6] which are used in taverns in London to light their faggots, and are call'd in the taverns a brush, the woodmen call them pimps; 'tis incredible what vast quantities of these are lay'd up at Woolwich, Erith, and Dartford; but since the taverns in London are come to make coal fires in their upper rooms; that cheat of a trade declines.

As I passed, I saw **Gravesend** from the hills, but having been often in the town, I know enough to be able to say, that there is nothing considerable in it;

except first that it is the town where the great ferry, (as they call it) is kept up between London and East-Kent, it is hardly credible what numbers of people pass here every tide, as well by night as by day, between this town and London: almost all the people of East-Kent, when they go for London, go no farther by land than this town; and then for six-pence in the tilt-boat,[7] or one shilling in a small boat or wherry, are carry'd to London by water.

The other thing for which this town is worth notice, is, that all the ships which go to sea from London, take, as we say, their departure from hence; for here all outward-bound ships must stop, come to an anchor, and suffer what they call a second clearing, (viz.) here a searcher of the customs comes on board, looks over all the coquets[8] or entries of the cargo, and may, if he pleases, rummage the whole loading, to see if there are no more goods than are enter'd; which however they seldom do, tho' they forget not to take a compliment for their civility, and besides being well treated on board, have generally three or five guns fir'd in honour to them when they go off.

From Gravesend we see nothing remarkable on the road but **Gad's-Hill**, a noted place for robbing of seamen after they have receiv'd their pay at Chatham. From Gad's Hll we come to Rochester Bridge, the largest, highest, and the strongest built of all the bridges in England, except London-Bridge.

There's little remarkable in **Rochester**, except the ruins of a very old castle, and an antient but not extraordinary cathedral; but the river, and its appendices are the most considerable of the kind in the world. This being the chief arsenal of the Royal Navy of Great-Britain. The buildings here are indeed like the ships

VII. Unknown painter, *Rochester Bridge* (probably early eighteenth century).

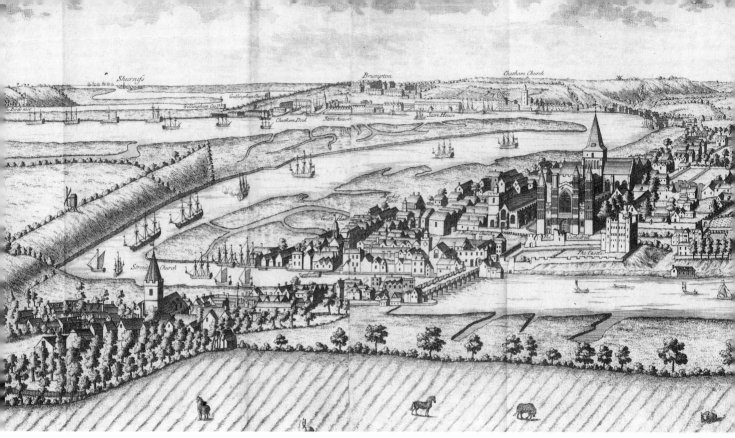

34. Bird's-eye view of Rochester and the Medway as far as Sheerness from the Strood side of the river; engraving by J. Kip after a drawing by Thomas Badeslade. From John Harris *The History of Kent* (1719).

themselves, surprisingly large, and in their several kinds beautiful: the ware-houses, or rather streets of warehouses, and store-houses for laying up the naval treasure are the largest in dimension, and the most in number, that are any where to be seen in the world: the rope-walks for making cables, and the forges for anchors and other iron-work, bear a proportion to the rest; as also the wet-dock for keeping masts, and yards of the greatest size, where they lye sunk in the water to preserve them, the boat-yard, the anchor yard; all like the whole, monstrously great and extensive, and are not easily describ'd.

It is about sixteen or eighteen miles from Rochester Bridge to **Sheerness** fort by water on the river Medway, of this it is about fourteen miles to Black-Stakes, the channel is so deep all the way, the banks soft, and the reaches of the river so short, that in a word, 'tis the safest and best harbour in the world; and we saw two ships of eighty guns, each riding a float at low water within musquet-shot of Rochester Bridge. The ships ride as in a mill-pond, or a wet-dock, except that being moor'd at the chains, they swing up and down with the tide; but as there is room enough, so they are moor'd in such manner, that they cannot swing foul of one another; 'tis as safe (I say) as in a wet-dock, nor did I ever hear of any accident that befel any of the king's ships here, I mean by storms and

weather; except in that dreadful tempest in 1703,[9] when one ship, (viz.) the *Royal Catherine* was driven on shoar, and receiving some damage sunk, and the ship also being old, could not be weigh'd again; but this was such a storm as never was known before, and 'tis hoped the like may never be known again.

There are two castles on the shore of this river, the one at Upnore, where there is a good platform of guns, and which guards two reaches of the river, and is supposed to defend all the ships which ride above, between that and the bridge; also on the other shore is Gillingham Castle, form'd for the same purpose, and well furnish'd with guns which command the river, besides which there is a fort or platform of guns at

35. Detail of Rochester cathedral from the bird's-eye view of Rochester (see pl. 34).

47

36. 'The West prospect of His Majesty's Dockyard at Chatham;' engraving by Samuel and Nathaniel Buck (1738).

a place call'd the swamp and another at Cockham Wood. But all these are added, or at least additions made to them, since the time that the Dutch made that memorable attempt upon the Royal Navy in this river (viz.) on the 22d of June, in the year 1667. This al-larm gave England such a sense of the consequence of the river Medway, and of the docks and yards at Chatham, and of the danger the Royal Navy lay exposed to there, that all these doors which were open then, are lock'd up and sufficiently barr'd since that time; and 'tis not now in the power of any nation under heaven, no, tho' they should be masters at sea, unless they were masters at land too at the same time, to give us such another affront; for besides all the castles, lines of guns, and platforms on each side the river Medway, as we go up, as above; there is now a royal fort built at the point of the Isle of Shepey, call'd Sheerness, which guards that entrance into the river: this is a regular, and so compleat a fortification, and has such a line of heavy cannon commanding the mouth of the river, that no man of war, or fleet of men of war, would attempt to pass by as the Dutch did; or at least cou'd not effect without hazard of being torn to pieces by those batteries.

At the south-west point of the Isle of Shepey, where the East-Swale parts from the West, and passes on, as above, stands a town memorable for nothing, but that which is rather a dishonour to our country than otherwise: namely, **Queenborough**, a miserable dirty, decay'd, poor, pitiful, fishing town; yet vested with corporation priviledges, has a mayor, aldermen, &c. and his worship the mayor has his mace carry'd before

him to church, and attended in as much state and ceremony as the mayor of a town twenty times as good: I remember when I was there, Mr. Mayor was a butcher, and brought us a shoulder of mutton to our inn himself in person, which we bespoke for our dinner, and afterwards he sat down and drank a bottle of wine with us.

But that which is still worse, and which I meant in what I said before, is, that this town sends two burgesses to Parliament, as many as the borough of Southwark, or the city of Westminster: tho' it may be presumed all the inhabitants are not possess'd of estates answerable to the rent of one good house in either of those places I last mentioned: the chief business of this town, as I could understand, consists in ale-houses, and oyster-catchers.

From hence following the coast, and the great road together, for they are still within view of one another, we come to **Feversham**, a large populous, and as some say, a rich town: tho' here is no particular remarkable trade, either for manufacture or navigation; the princi-pal business we found among them, was fishing for oysters, which the Dutch fetch hence in such extra-ordinary quantities, that when I was there, we found twelve large Dutch hoys and doggers[10] lying there to load oysters; and sometimes, as they told us, there are many more: this is greatly to the advantage of the place, as it employs abundance of men and boats in drudging for the oysters, which they catch in great plenty, in the mouth of the East-Swale; which, as I said above, enters in this part of the country into the sea, and opens very wide.

It was at the mouth of this Swale, namely, at **Shell-Ness**, so call'd from the abundance of oyster-shells always lying there, that the smack in which the late King James II was embark'd for his escape into France,[11] ran on shoar, and being boarded by the fishermen, the king was taken prisoner; and I must mention it to the reproach of the people of Feversham, let the conduct of that unfortunate prince be what it will, that the fishermen and rabble can never be excus'd, who treated the king, even after they were told who he was, with the utmost indecency, using his majesty; (for he was then their Sovereign, even in the acknowledged sense of his enemies) I say, using him with such indignity in his person, such insolence in their behaviour, and giving him such opprobrious and abusive language, and searching him in the rudest and most indecent manner, and indeed rifling him; that the king himself said, he was never more apprehensive of his life than at that time.

This leads me to cross the hills from Milton to **Maidstone**, about ten miles distant. This is a considerable town, very populous, and the inhabitants generally wealthy; 'tis the county town, and the river Medway is navigable to it by large hoys, of fifty to sixty tons burthen, the tide flowing quite up to the town. Round this town are the largest cherry orchards, and the most of them that are in any part of England; and the gross of the quantity of cherries, and the best of them which supply the whole city of London come from hence, and are therefore called Kentish cherries.

Maidstone is eminent for the plenty of provisions, and richness of lands in the country all round it, and for the best market in the county, not Rochester, no not Canterbury excepted.

From this town, and the neighbouring parts, London is supplied with more particulars than from any single market town in England; which I mention in pursuance of my first resolution of observing, how every part of England furnishes something to the city of London.

1. From the Wild of Kent, which begins but about six miles off, and particularly from that part which lyes this way; they bring the large Kentish bullocks, fam'd for being generally all red, and with their horns crooked inward, the two points standing one directly against the other, they are counted the largest breed in England.

2. From the same country are brought great quantities of the largest timber for supply of the king's yards at Chattham, and often to London; most of which comes by land carriage to Maidstone.

3. From the country adjoining to Maidstone also, is a very great quantity of corn brought up to London, besides hops and cherries, as above.

4. Also a kind of paving stone, about eight to ten inches square, so durable that it scarce ever wears out; 'tis used to pave court-yards, and passages to gentlemen's houses, being the same the Royal Exchange at London is pav'd with, which has never yet wanted the least repair.

5. Also fine white sand for the glass-houses,[12] esteem'd the best in England for melting into flint-glass, and looking glass-plates; and for the stationer's use also, vulgarly call'd writing-sand.[13]

6. Also very great quantities of fruit, such as Kentish pipins, runetts, &c. which come up as the cherries do, whole hoy-loads at a time to the wharf, call'd the Three Cranes,[14] in London; which is the greatest pipin market perhaps in the world.

At Maidstone you begin to converse with gentlemen, and persons of rank of both sexes, and some of

37. 'View of the Down from Wye to Ayslford'...This is taken from the land above Aylsford'. Drawing by William Stukeley (5 June 1725). Downs and agricultural area just north of Maidstone.

38. 'The South West prospect of the city of Canterbury'; engraving by Samuel and Nathaniel Buck (1738).

quality: all that side of the county which I have mentioned already, as it is marshy, and unhealthy, by its situation among the waters; so is it embarass'd with business, and inhabited chiefly by men of business, such as ship-builders, fisher-men, seafaring-men, and husband-men, or such as depend upon them, and very few families of note are found among them. But as soon as we come down Boxley Hill from Rochester, or Hollingbourn-Hill, from Milton, and descend from the poor chalky downs, and deep foggy marshes, to the wholesome rich soil, the well wooded, and well water'd plain on the banks of the Medway, we find the country every where spangl'd with populous villages, and delicious seats of the nobility and gentry.

There is not much manufacturing in this county; what is left, is chiefly at Canterbury, and in this town of Maidstone, and the neighbourhood; the manufacture of this town is principally in thread, that is to say, linen thread, which they make to pretty good perfection, tho' not extraordinary fine. At Cranbrook, Tenterden, Goudhurst, and other villages there-about, which are also in the neighbourhood of this part, on the other side the Medway, there was once a very considerable cloathing trade carry'd on, and the yeomen of Kent,[15] of which so much has been fam'd, were generally the inhabitants on that side, and who were much enrich'd by that clothing trade; but that trade is now quite decay'd, and scarce ten clothiers left in all the county.

These clothiers and farmers, and the remains of them, upon the general elections of Members of Parliament for the county, show themselves still there, being ordinarily 14 or 1500 freeholders brought from this side of the county; and who for the plainness of their appearance, are call'd the Gray Coats of Kent; but are so considerable, that whoever they vote for is always sure to carry it, and therefore the gentlemen are very careful to preserve their interest among them.

In prosecution of my journey East, I went from hence to **Canterbury**; of which town and its antiquities so much has been said, and so accurately, that I need do no more than mention it by recapitulation. The church is a noble pile of building indeed, and looks venerable and majestick at a distance, as well as when we come nearer to it. The old monastery of all, with the church there, dedicated to St. Augustine, and in the porch of which St. Augustine himself, with the six bishops lye buried, stands at, or rather stood at a distance, and the ruins of it shew the place sufficiently; what remains of the old buildings about Christ-Church, or the cathedral, are principally the cloyster, and the bishop's palace, which however is rather to be call'd a building raised from the old house, than a part of it.

The close or circumvallation, where the houses of the prebendaries, and other persons belonging to this cathedral stand, is very spacious and fair, and a great many very good houses are built in it, and some with good gardens; where those gentlemen live at large, and among whom a very good neighbourhood is kept up; as for the town, its antiquity seems to be its greatest beauty: the houses are truly antient, and the many ruins of churches, chapels, oratories, and smaller cells of religious people, makes the place look like a general ruin a little recover'd.

The city will scarce bear being call'd populous, were

it not for two or three thousand French Protestants, which, including men, women and children, they say there are in it, and yet they tell me the number of these decreases daily.

But the great wealth and encrease of the city of Canterbury, is from the surprizing encrease of the hop-grounds all round the place; it is within the memory of many of the inhabitants now living, and that none of the oldest neither, that there was not an acre of ground planted with hops in the whole neighbourhood, or so few as not to be worth naming; whereas I was assured that there are at this time near six thousand acres of ground so planted, within a very few miles of the city; I do not vouch the number, and I confess it seems incredible, but I deliver it as I receiv'd it.

It is observ'd that the ground round this city proves more particularly fruitful for the growth of hops than of any other production, which was not at first known; but which, upon its being discover'd, set all the world, speaking in the language of a neighbourhood, a digging up their grounds and planting; so that now they may say without boasting, there is at Canterbury the greatest plantation of hops in the whole island.

The shore from Whitstable, and the East-Swale, affords nothing remarkable but sea-marks, and small towns on the coast, till we come to Margate and the North Foreland. As soon as any vessels pass this foreland from London, they are properly said to be in the open sea; if to the north, they enter the German Ocean, if to the south, the Chanel, as 'tis call'd, that is the narrow seas between England and France; and all the towns or harbours before we come this length, whether on the Kentish or Essex shoar, are call'd members of the port of London.

From this point westward, the first town of note is **Ramsgate**, a small port, the inhabitants are mighty fond of having us call it Roman's Gate; pretending that the Romans under Julius Cæsar made their first attempt to land here, when he was driven back by a storm; but soon return'd, and coming on shore, with a good body of troops beat back the Britains, and fortify'd his camp, just at the entrance of the creek, where the town now stands.

Sandwich is the next town, lying in the bottom of a

39. Paul Sandby, *The West Gate, Canterbury*; gouache.

VIII. Richard Wilson, *Dover* (*c*.1746–7).

bay, at the mouth of the river Stour, an old, decay'd, poor, miserable town, of which when I have said that it is an antient town, one of the Cinque Ports, and sends two Members to Parliament; I have said all that I think can be worth any bodies reading of the town of Sandwich.

From hence to **Deal** is about —— miles.[16] This place is famous for the road for shipping, so well known all over the trading world, by the name of the Downs, and where almost all ships which arrive from foreign parts for London, or go from London to foreign parts, and who pass the Channel, generally stop; the home-ward-bound to dispatch letters, send their merchants and owners the good news of their arrival, and set their passengers on shoar, and the like; and the outward-bound to receive their last orders, letters, and farewells from owners, and friends, take in fresh provisions, &c.

From hence we pass over a pleasant champian[17] country, with the sea, and the coast of France, clear in your view; and by the very gates of the antient castle (to the town) of **Dover**: As we go, we pass by Deal Castle, and Sandown Castle, two small works, of no strength by land, and not of much use by sea; but however maintain'd by the government for the ordinary services of salutes, and protecting small vessels, which can lye safe under their cannon from picaroons, privateers, &c. in time of war.

Neither Dover nor its castle has any thing of note to be said of them, but what is in common with their neighbours; the castle is old, useless, decay'd, and serves for little; but to give the title and honour of government to men of quality, with a salary, and sometimes to those that want one.

The town, is one of the Cinque Ports, sends Members to Parliament, who are call'd barons, and has itself an ill repair'd, dangerous, and good for little harbour and peir, very chargeable and little worth: the packets for France go off here, as also those for Nieuport, with the mails for Flanders, and all those ships which carry freights from New-York to Holland, and from Virginia to Holland, come generally hither, and unlade their goods, enter them with, and show them to the custom-house-officers, pay the duties, and then enter them again by certificate, reload them, and draw back the duty by debenture, and so they go away for Holland.

As I rode along this coast, I perceiv'd several dragoons riding, officers, and others arm'd and on horseback, riding always about as if they were huntsmen beating up their game; upon inquiry I found their diligence was employ'd in quest of the Owlers,[18] as they call them, and sometimes they catch some of them; but when I came to enquire farther, I found too, that often times these are attack'd in the night, with such numbers, that they dare not resist, or if they do, they are wounded and beaten, and sometimes kill'd; and at other times are oblig'd, as it were, to stand still, and see the wool carry'd off before their faces, not daring to meddle; and the boats taking it in from the very horses backs, go immediately off, and are on the coast of France before any notice can be given of them, while the other are as nimble to return with their horses to their haunts and retreats, where they are not easily found out.

From the beginning of **Rumney Marsh**, that is to say, at Sandgate, or Sandfoot Castle near Hith, to this place, the country is a rich fertile soil, full of feeding grounds, and where an infinite number of large sheep are fed every year, and sent up to London market; these Rumney Marsh sheep, are counted rather larger than the Leicester-shire and Lincolnshire sheep, of which so much is said elsewhere.

Besides the vast quantity of sheep as above, abundance of large bullocks are fed in this part of the country; and especially those they call stall'd oxen, that is, house fed, and kept within the farmers' sheds or yards, all the latter season, where they are fed for the winter market. This I noted, because these oxen are generally the largest beef in England.

From hence it was that, turning north, and traversing the deep, dirty, but rich part of these two counties, I had the curiosity to see the great foundaries, or iron-works, which are in this county, and where they are carry'd on at such a prodigious expence of wood, that even in a country almost all over-run with timber, they begin to complain of the consuming it for those furnaces, and leaving the next age to want timber for building their navies: I must own however, that I found that complaint perfectly groundless, the three counties of Kent, Sussex, and Hampshire, (all which lye contiguous to one another) being one inexhaustible store-house of timber never to be destroy'd, but by a general conflagration, and able at this time to supply timber to rebuild all the royal navies in Europe, if they were all to be destroy'd, and set about the building them together.

After I had fatigued myself in passing this deep and heavy part of the country, I thought it would not be foreign to my design, if I refresh'd myself with a view of **Tunbridge-Wells**, which were not then above twelve miles out of my way.

The ladies that appear here, are indeed the glory of the place; the coming to the Wells to drink the water is a meer matter of custom; some drink, more do not, and few drink physically:[19] but company and diversion is in short the main business of the place; and those people who have nothing to do any where else, seem to be the only people who have any thing to do at Tunbridge.

After the appearance is over at the Wells, (where the ladies are all undress'd) and at the chapel, the company go home; and as if it was another species of people, or a collection from another place, you are surpriz'd to see the walks covered with ladies compleatly dress'd and gay to profusion; where rich cloths, jewels, and beauty not to be set out by (but infinitely above) ornament, dazzles the eyes from one end of the range to the other.

Here you have all the liberty of conversation in the world, and any thing that looks like a gentleman, has an address agreeable, and behaves with decency and

40. 'The Description of Romney Marsh . . . with the divisions of their waterings, their heads, Arms, principall sewers and their gutts for serving of the fresh waters that fall into the same . . . with marshes adjoining;' engraved by S. Parker, from William Dugdale, *History of Imbanking and Draining*, reproduced in John Harris, *The History of Kent* (1719).

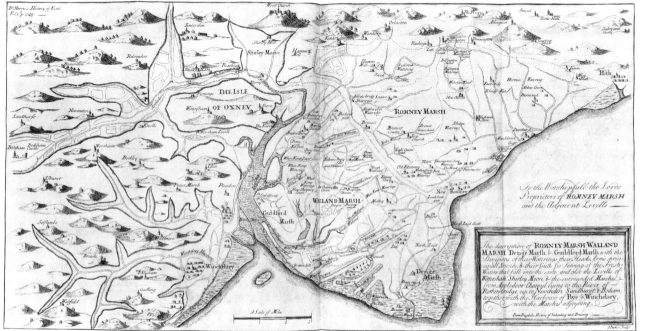

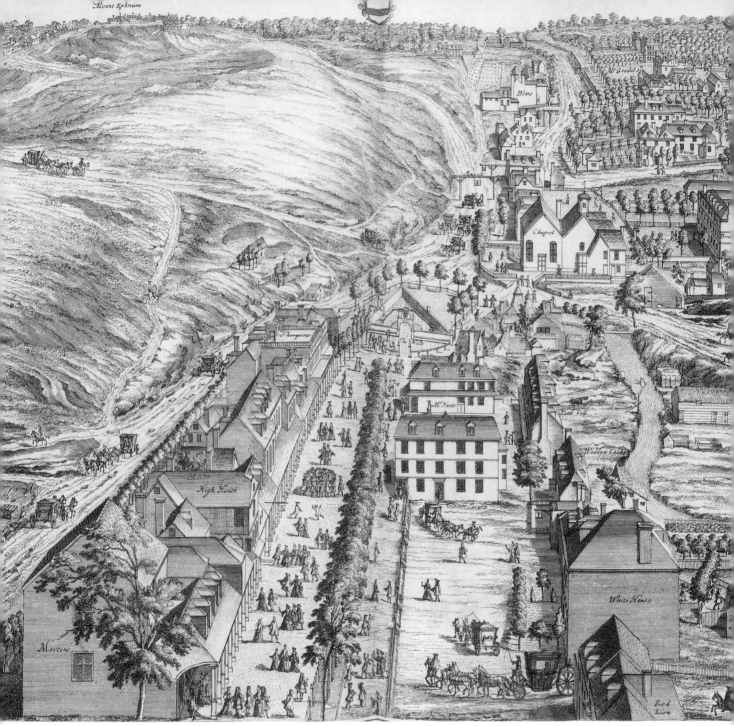

41. Tunbridge Wells; engraving by J. Kip after a drawing by Thomas Badeslade. From John Harris, *The History of Kent* (1719).

good manners, may single out whom he pleases, that does not appear engag'd, and may talk, rally, be merry, and say any decent thing to them; but all this makes no acquaintance, nor is it taken so, or understood to mean so; if a gentleman desires to be more intimate, and enter into any acquaintance particular, he must do it by proper application, not by the ordinary meeting on the walks, for the ladies will ask no gentleman there, to go off of the walk, or invite any one to their lodgings, except it be a sort of ladies of whom I am not now speaking.

As for gaming, sharping, intrieguing; as also fops, fools, beaus, and the like, Tunbridge is as full of these, as can be desired, and it takes off much of the diversion of those persons of honour and virtue, who go there to be innocently recreated: however a man of character, and good behaviour cannot be there any time, but he may single out such company as may be suitable to him, and with whom he may be as merry as heart can wish.

In a word, Tunbridge wants nothing that can add to the felicities of life, or that can make a man or woman compleatly happy, always provided they have money; for without money a man is no-body at Tunbridge, any more than at any other place; and when any man finds his pockets low, he has nothing left to think of, but to be gone, for he will have no diversion in staying there any longer.

I left Tunbridge, for the same reason that I give, why others should leave it, when they are in my condition; namely that I found my money almost gone; and tho' I had bills of credit to supply myself in the course of my intended journey; yet I had none there: so I came away, or as they call it there, I retir'd; and came to *Lewes*, through the deepest, dirtiest, but many ways the richest, and most profitable country in all that part of England.

The timber I saw here was prodigious, as well in quantity as in bigness, and seem'd in some places to be suffer'd to grow, only because it was so far off of any navigation, that it was not worth cutting down and carrying away; in dry summers, indeed a great deal is carry'd away to Maidstone, and other places on the Medway; and sometimes I have seen one tree on a carriage, which they call there a tug, drawn by two and twenty oxen, and even then, 'tis carry'd so little a way, and then thrown down, and left for other tugs to take up and carry on, that sometimes 'tis two or three year before it gets to Chatham; for if once the rains come in, it stirs no more that year, and sometimes a whole summer is not dry enough to make the roads passable: here I had a sight, which indeed I never saw in any other part of England: namely, that going to church at a country village, not far from Lewis, I saw an ancient lady, and a lady of very good quality, I assure you, drawn to church in her coach with six oxen; nor was it done in frolick or humour, but meer necessity, the way being so stiff and deep, that no horses could go in it.

From this town, following still the range of the South Downs, west; we ride in view of the sea, and on a fine carpet ground, for about twelve miles to **Bright Helmston**,[20] commonly call'd Bredhemston, a poor fishing town, old built, and on the very edge of the sea: here again, as I mention'd at Folkstone and Dover, the fisher-men having large barks go away to Yarmouth, on the coast of Norfolk, to the fishing fair there, and hire themselves for the season to catch herrings for the merchants; and they tell us, that these make a very good business of it.

From hence, still keeping the coast close on the left,

we come to **Shoreham**, a sea-faring town, and chiefly inhabited by ship-carpenters, ship-chandlers, and all the several trades depending upon the building and fitting up of ships, which is their chief business.

Here in the compass of about six miles are three burrough towns, sending Members to Parliament, (viz.) Shoreham, Bramber, and Stenning: and Shoreham, Stenning are tolerable little market-towns; but Bramber, (a little ruin of an old castle excepted) hardly deserves the name of a town, having not above fifteen or sixteen families in it, and of them not many above asking you an alms as you ride by; the chiefest house in the town is a tavern, and here, as I have been told, the vintner, or ale-house-keeper rather, for he hardly deserv'd the name of a vintner, boasted, that upon an election, just then over, he had made 300 l. of one pipe of canary.

From hence we come to **Arundel**, a decay'd town also; but standing near the mouth of a good river, call'd Arun, which signifies, says Mr. Cambden, the swift, tho' the river itself is not such a rapid current as merits that name; at least it did not seem to be so to me.

To the north of Arundel, and at the bottom of the hills, and consequently in the Wild, is the town of **Petworth**, a large handsome country market-town, and very populous, and as it stands upon an ascent, and is dry and healthy, it is full of gentlemen's families, and good well built houses both in the town and neighbourhood; but the beauty of Petworth, is the antient seat of the old family of Peircy, Earls of Northumberland now extinct; whose daughter, the sole heiress of all his vast estates, marry'd the present Duke of Somerset; of the noble and antient family of Seymour, and among other noble seats brought his Grace this of Petworth.

The Duke's house at Petworth, is certainly a compleat building in itself, and the apartments are very noble, well contriv'd, and richly furnish'd; but it cannot be said, that the situation of the house is equally design'd, or with equal judgment as the rest; the avenues to the front want space, the house stands as it were with its elbow to the town, its front has no visto answerable, and the west front look'd not to the parks or fine gardens, but to the old stables.

From Petworth west, the country is a little less woody than the Wild, and there begin to show their heads above the trees, a great many fine seats of the nobility and gentlemen of the country, as the Duke of Richmond's seat at Goodwood, near Chichester, the seats of the late Earl of Tankerville, and the Earl of Scarborough, the antient house of the Lord Montacute at Midhurst, an antient family of the sirname of

Brown, the eldest branch of the house: these and a great many more lying so near together, make the country hereabout much more sociable and pleasant than the rest of the woody country, call'd the Wild, of which I have made mention so often; and yet I cannot say much for the city of **Chichester**, in which, if six or seven good families were removed, there would not be much conversation, except what is to be found among the canons, and dignitaries of the cathedral.

This city is not a place of much trade, nor is it very populous; but they are lately fallen into a very particular way of managing the corn trade here, which it is said turns very well to account; the country round it is very fruitful, and particularly in good wheat, and the farmers generally speaking, carry'd all their wheat to Farnham, to market, which is very near forty miles by land-carriage, and from some parts of the country more than forty miles.

But some money'd men of Chichester, Emsworth, and other places adjacent, have join'd their stocks together, built large granaries near the Crook, where the vessels come up, and here they buy and lay up all the corn which the country on that side can spare; and having good mills in the neighbourhood, they grind and dress the corn, and send it to London in the meal about by Long Sea, as they call it; nor now the war is over do they make the voyage so tedious as to do the meal any hurt, as at first in the time of war was sometimes the case for want of convoys.

It is true, this is a great lessening to Farnham Market, but that is of no consideration in the case; for, if the market at London is supply'd, the coming by sea from Chichester is every jot as much a publick good, as the encouraging of Farnham Market, which is of itself the greatest corn-market in England, London excepted. Notwithstanding all the decrease from this side of the country, this carrying of meal by sea met with so just an encouragement from hence, that it is now practised from several other places on this coast, even as far as Shampton.

From hence we descend gradually to **Portsmouth**, the largest fortification, beyond comparison, that we have in England. The situation of this place is such, that it is chosen, as may well be said, for the best security to the navy above all the places in Britain; the entrance into the harbour is safe, but very narrow, guarded on both sides by terrible platforms of cannon, particularly on the Point; which is a suburb of Portsmouth properly so call'd, where there is a brick platform built with two tire of guns, one over another, and which can fire so in cover, that the gunners cannot be beaten from their guns, or their guns easily dismounted; the other is from the point of land on the side of Gosport, which they call Gilkicker, where also they have two batteries.

As to the strength of the town by land, the works are very large and numerous, and besides the battery at the Point aforesaid, there is a large hornwork on the south-side, running out towards South-Sea Castle; there is also a good counterscarp, and double mote, with ravelins in the ditch, and double pallisadoes, and advanc'd works to cover the place from any approach, where it may be practicable.

These docks and yards are now like a town by them-

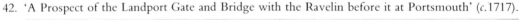

42. 'A Prospect of the Landport Gate and Bridge with the Ravelin before it at Portsmouth' (*c.*1717).

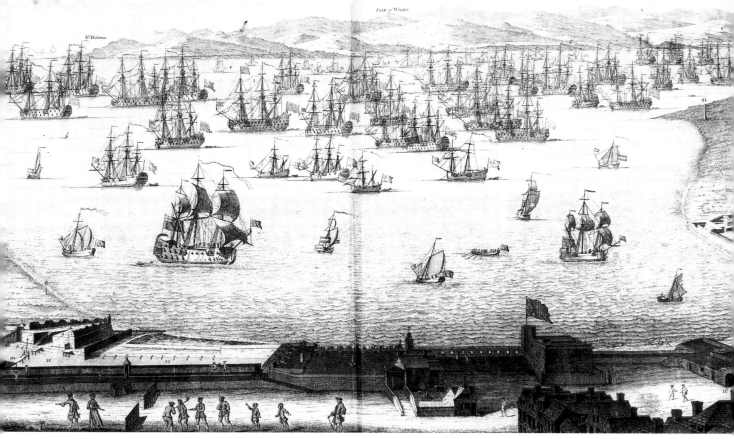

43. 'Prospect of the United British and Dutch fleets as they lay at Spit-head in the year 1729'.

selves and are a kind of marine corporation, or a government of their own kind within themselves; there being particular large rows of dwellings, built at the publick charge, within the new works, for all the principal officers of the place; especially the commissioner, the agent of the victualling, and such as these; the tradesmen likewise have houses here, and many of the labourers are allow'd to live in the bounds as they can get lodging.

From Portsmouth West, the country lyes low and flat, and is full of creeks and inlets of the sea and rivers, all the way to Southampton, so that we ferry over three times in about eighteen miles; besides going over one bridge, namely, at Tichfield. When we come opposite to Southampton, we pass another creek, being the mouth of the River Itchen which comes down from Winchester, and is both very broad and deep, and the ferry men having a very sorry boat, we found it dangerous enough passing it: on the other bank stands the antient town of Southampton, and on the other side of Southampton comes down another large river, entring Southampton Water by Red-Bridge; so that the town of Southampton stands upon a point running out into the sea, between two very fine rivers, both navigable, up some length into the country, and particularly useful for the bringing down timber out of one of the best wooded counties in Britain.

Southampton is a truly antient town, for 'tis in a manner dying with age; the decay of the trade is the real decay of the town; and all the business of moment that is transacted there, is the trade between us and the Islands of Jersey and Guernsey, with a little of the wine trade, and much smuggling: the building of ships also is much stop'd of late; however, the town is large, has many people in it, a noble fair high-street, a spacious key; and if its trade should revive, is able to entertain great numbers of people: there is a French Church, and no inconsiderable congregation, which was a help to the town, and there are still some merchants who trade to Newfoundland, and to the Streights[21] with fish; but for all other trade, it may be said of as of other towns, London has eaten it up.

I was now at the extent of my intended journey west, and thought of looking no farther this way for the present, so I came away North East, leaving Winchester a little on the left, and came into the Portsmouth road at *Petersfield*, a town eminent for little, but its being full of good inns, and standing in the middle of a country, still over-grown with a prodigious quantity of oak-timber. From hence we came to *Alton*, and in the road thither, began a little to taste the pleasure of the Western Downs, which reach from Winchester almost to Alton.

From Alton we came to *Farnham*, of which I can only say, that it is a large populous market-town, the farthest that way in the county of Surrey, and without

IX. Unknown painter, *Castle Street, Farnham, Surrey* (1761).

exception the greatest corn-market in England, London excepted; that is to say, particularly for wheat, of which so vast a quantity is brought every market-day to this market, that a gentleman told me, he once counted on a market-day eleven hundred teams of horse, all drawing waggons, or carts, loaden with wheat at this market; every team of which is supposed to bring what they call a load, that is to say, forty bushel of wheat to market; which is in the whole, four and forty thousand bushel; but I do not take upon me to affirm this relation, or to say whether it be a probable opinion or not.

From Farnham, that I might take in the whole county of Surrey, I took the coach-road, over **Bagshot-Heath**, and that great forest, as 'tis call'd, of Windsor: those that despise Scotland, and the north part of England, for being full of wast and barren land, may take a view of this part of Surrey, and look upon it as a foil to the beauty of the rest of England; or a mark of the just resentment shew'd by heaven upon the Englishmen's

pride; I mean the pride they shew in boasting of their country, its fruitfulness, pleasantness, richness, the fertility of the soil, &c. whereas here is a vast tract of land, some of it within seventeen or eighteen miles of

44. Squatter's hovel on Bagshot Heath; photograph, midnineteenth century.

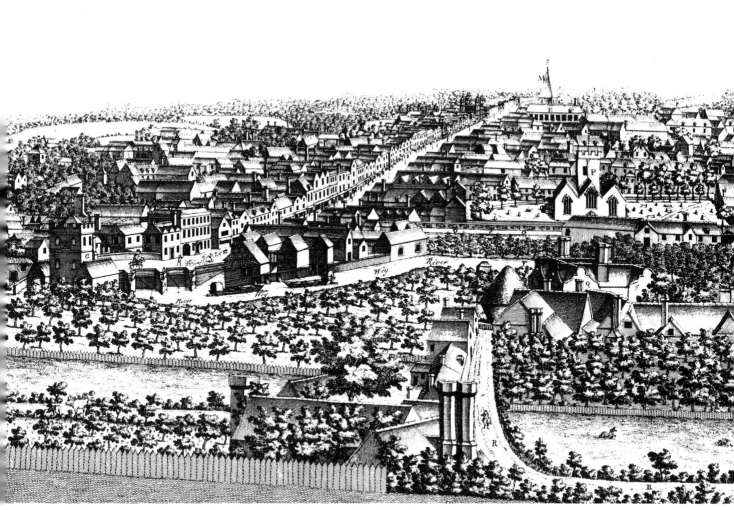

45. Detail showing the High Street from 'South West Prospect of Guildford'; engraving by John Harris (1738).

the capital city; which is not only poor, but even quite steril, given up to barrenness, horrid and frightful to look on, not only good for little, but good for nothing; much of it is a sandy desert, and one may frequently be put in mind here of Arabia Deserta, where the winds raise the sands, so as to overwhelm whole caravans of travellers, cattle and people together.

Thro' this desert, for I can call it no less, we come into the great western road, leading from London to Salisbury, Exeter, &c. and pass the Thames at Stanes; and here I could not but call to mind, upon viewing the beautiful prospect of the river, and of the meadows, on the banks of the river, on the left hand of the road, I say, I cou'd not but call to mind those two excellent lines of Sir John Denham, in his poem, call'd *Cooper's Hill*, viz.

Tho' Deep, yet Clear, tho' Gentle, yet not Dull,
Strong without Rage, without o'erflowing full.

From Stanes I turn'd S. and S. E. to **Chertsey**, another market-town, and where there is a bridge over the Thames: this town was made famous, by being the burial place of Henry VI till his bones were after removed to Windsor by Henry VII; also by being the retreat of the incomparable Cowley,[22] where he liv'd withdrawn from the hurries of the court and town, and where he dy'd so much a recluse, as to be almost wholly taken up in country business, farming and husbandry, for his diversion, not for bread, according to the publick flight of his own fancy.

From hence we came to **Guilford**, a well known and considerable market-town: it has the name of being the county town, tho' it cannot properly be call'd so; neither the county goal being here, or the assizes, any more than in common with other towns: but the election indeed for Parliament men for the county is always held here.

Here is a small remainder of an old manufacture, that is to say, of the clothing trade, and it extends itself to Godalming, Haselmeer, and the vale country, on

59

the side of the Holmwood, quite to Darking: these cloths of a middling price, have formerly been in great repute, and then again were almost quite decay'd, but by the application and skill of the clothiers, maintain'd the credit of their make, and are encourag'd, and indeed revived in reputation of late years, when the clothiers of Cranbrook and Tenterden in Kent, whose goods are of the same kind, are almost sunk to nothing.

This clothing trade, however small, is very assistant to the poor of this part of the country, where the lands, as I have noted, are but indifferent; except just above the great towns, and where abundance of the inhabitants are what we call cottagers,[23] and live chiefly by the benefit of the large commons and heath ground, of which the quantity is so very great.

From this town of Guilford, the road to Farnham is very remarkable, for it runs along west from Guilford, upon the ridge of a high chalky hill, so narrow that the breadth of the road takes up the breadth of the hill, and the declivity begins on either hand, at the very hedge that bounds the highway, and is very steep, as well as very high; from this hill is a prospect either way, so far that 'tis surprising; and one sees to the north or N. W. over the great black desart, call'd Bagshot-Heath, mentioned above, one way, and the other way south east into Sussex, almost to the South Downs, and west to an unbounded length, the horizon only restraining the eyes: this hill being all chalk, a traveller feels the effect of it in a hot summer's day, being scorch'd by the reflection of the sun from the chalk, so as to make the heat almost insupportable; and this I speak by my own experience: this hill reaches from Guilford town's end to within a mile and half of Farnham.

The ten miles from Guilford to Leatherhead make one continued line of gentlemen's houses, lying all, or most of them, on the west side of the road, and their parks, or gardens almost touching one another: here are pleasantly seated several very considerable persons, as the posterity of Sir Tho. Bludworth,[24] once Lord Mayor of London, a person famous for the implacable passion he put the people of London in, by one rash expression, at the time of the Great Fire: (viz.) *that it was nothing, and they might piss it out.*

At the north east end of this range of fine seats, is **Letherhead**, a little thorough-fare town, with a stone-bridge over the river Mole; this river is called the Mole, from its remarkable sinking into the earth, at the foot of box-Hill, near a village call'd Mickleham, and working its way under ground like a mole, rising again at or near this town of Leatherhead, where its wandering streams are united again, and form a pretty large river, as they were before, running together

under Leatherhead Bridge, and from thence to Cobham, and so it pursues its course to the Thames, which it joins at Molesy, which takes its name to be sure from the name of the river Mole.

The town of **Darking** is eminent for several little things worth observation; as first, for the great Roman highway, call'd Stonny-street, which Mr. Cambden says, passes through the very church-yard of this town: secondly, for a little common or heath, call'd the Cottman Dean, or the dean or heath of poor cottagers, for so the word signifies, belonging to the town; and where their alms-house stands; which some learned physicians have singled out for the best air in England: thirdly, for Mr. Howard's[25] house and garden, call'd Deaden, the garden is so naturally mounded with hills, that it makes a compleat amphitheatre, being an oblong square, the area about eighty yards by forty, and the hills unpassably steep, serve instead of walls, and are handsomely planted with trees, whose tops rising above one another gradually, as the hill rises at their roots, make a most beautiful green wall, of perhaps fifty or sixty foot high; at the north end, which is the entrance, is the house, which closes it wholly; and at the south end, the antient possessor, Mr. Howard, by what we call perforation, caused a vault or cave to be made quite through the hill, which came out again into a fine vineyard, which he planted the same year, on the south side, or slope of the hill, and which they say has produced since most excellent good wines, and a very great quantity of them.

The market of Darking is of all the markets in Eng-

46. Dorking capon (with extra claw); engraving by K.M. Dodson.

John Wootton, *Landscape from Box Hill, Surrey.*

land famous for poultry; and particularly for the fattest geese, and the largest capons, the name of a Darking Capon being well known among the poulterers in Leaden-Hall Market; in a word, they are brought to this market from as far as Horsham in Sussex; and 'tis the business of all the country, on that side for many miles, to breed and fatten them up, insomuch, that 'tis like a manufacture to the country people; and some of these capons are so large, as that they are little inferior to turkeys; and I have seen them sold for 4 s. to 4 s. 6 d. each, and weighing from 4 l. to 5 or 6 l. a piece.

On the top of **Box-Hill**, and in view of this town, grows a very great beech-tree, which by way of distinction is call'd the great beech, and a very great tree it is; but I mention it on the following account: under the shade of this tree, was a little vault or cave, and here every Sunday, during the summer season, there used to be a rendezvous of coaches and horsemen, with abundance of gentlemen and ladies from Epsome to take the air, and walk in the box-woods; and in a word, divert, or debauch, or perhaps both, as they thought fit, and the game encreased so much, that it began almost on a sudden, to make a great noise in the country.

A vintner who kept the King's-Arms-Inn, at Darking, taking notice of the constant and unusual flux of company thither, took the hint from the prospect of his advantage, which offer'd, and obtaining leave of Sir Adam Brown,[26] whose mannor and land it was, furnish'd this little cellar or vault with tables, chairs, &c. and with wine and eatables to entertain the ladies and gentlemen on Sunday nights, as above; and this was so agreeable to them as that it encreased the company exceedingly; in a word, by these means, the concourse of gentry, and in consequence of the country people, became so great, that the place was like a little fair; so that at length the country began to take notice of it, and it was very offensive, especially to the best governed people; this lasted some years, I think two or three, and tho' complaint was made of it to Sir Adam Brown, and the neighbouring justices; alledging the revelling, and the indecent mirth that was among them, and on the Sabbath Day too, yet it did not obtain a suitable redress: whereupon a certain set of young men, of the town of Darking, and perhaps prompted by some others, resenting the thing also, made an unwelcome visit to the place once on a Saturday night, just before the usual time of their wicked mirth, and behold when the coaches and ladies, &c. from Epsome appear'd the next afternoon, they found the cellar or vault, and all that was in it, blown up with gun-powder; and so secret was it kept, that upon the utmost enquiry it cou'd never be heard, or found out who were the persons that did it: that action put an end to their revels for a great while; nor was the place ever repair'd that I heard of, at least it was not put to the same wicked use that it was employ'd in before.

From this hill, and particularly from this part of it, is a fair view in clear weather quite over the Wild of Sussex, to the South-Downs; and by the help of glasses, those who know where things are scituated, may plainly see the town of Horsham, Ashdown-Forest, the Duke of Somerset's house at Petworth, and the South-Downs, as they range between Brighthelm-ston and Arundel; besides an unbounded prospect into Kent.

Here travelling east at the foot of the hills, we came to **Rygate**, a large market-town with a castle, and a mansion-house, inhabited for some years by Sir John Parsons,[27] once Lord Mayor of London, and whose son is in a fair way to be so also; being one of the aldermen and sheriffs of the said city at the writing these sheets.

At Nutfield, between Rygate and Bleechingly, is another branch of the family of Evelyn, who have flourish'd there many years, tho' in a kind of retreat, and are often chosen representatives for the town of Bleechingly, which is just at their door.

From hence, crossing still all the roads leading from London into Sussex, we come to a village call'd **Godstone**, which lyes on the road from London to Lewis; and keeping on (East) we come to **Westerham**, the first market town in Kent on that side: this is a neat handsome well built market-town, and is full of gentry, and consequently of good company. The late Earl of Jersey[28] built, or rather finished, for it was begun by a private gentleman, a very noble house here, which still remains in the family, and is every year made finer and finer.

All this part of the country is very agreeably pleasant, wholesome and fruitful, I mean quite from Guildford to this place; and is accordingly overspread with good towns, gentlemen's houses, populous vill-ages, abundance of fruit, with hop-grounds and cherry orchards, and the lands well cultivated; but all on the right-hand, that is to say, south, is exceedingly grown with timber, has abundance of waste and wild grounds, and forests, and woods, with many large iron-works, at which they cast great quantities of iron caldrons, chimney-backs, furnaces, retorts, boiling pots, and all such necessary things of iron; besides iron cannon, bomb-shells, stink-pots,[29] hand-grenadoes, and cannon ball, &c. in an infinite quantity, and which turn to very great account.

From hence going forward east, we come to **River-head**, a town on the road from London to Tunbridge; and then having little to speak of in Kent, except some petty market-towns, such as Wrotham, commonly call'd Rootham, Town-Mailing, Cranbrook, and the like; as I travell'd forward, in the beginning of this circuit, I turn'd north, and came to **Bromley**, a market-town, made famous by an hospital, lately built there by Dr. Warner, Lord Bishop of Rochester, for the relief of the widows of clergy-men.

Near this town we turn'd away by Beckenham, and thro' Norwood to Croydon; in the way we saw **Dullige** or Sydenham Wells, where great crouds of people throng every summer from London to drink the waters, as at Epsome and Tunbridge; only with this difference, that as at Epsome and Tunbridge, they go more for the diversion of the season, for the mirth and the company; for gaming, or intrigueing, and the like, here they go for meer physick, and this causes another difference; namely, that as the nobility and gentry go to Tunbridge, the merchants and rich citizens to Epsome; so the common people go chiefly to Dullwich and Stretham; and the rather also, because it lyes so near London, that they can walk to it in the morning, and return at night; which abundance do; that is to say, especially of a Sunday, or on holi-days, which makes the better sort also decline the place; the croud on those days being both unruly and unmannerly.

Banstead Downs need no description other than this, that their being so near London, and surrounded as they are with pleasant villages, and being in them-selves perfectly agreeable, the ground smooth, soft, level and dry; (even in but a few hours after rain) they conspire to make the most delightful spot of ground, of that kind in all this part of Britain.

When on the publick race days they are cover'd with coaches and ladies, and an innumerable company of horsemen, as well gentlemen as citizens, attending the sport; and then adding to the beauty of the sight, the racers flying over the course, as if they either touch'd not, or felt not the ground they run upon; I think no sight, except that of a victorious army, under the command of a Protestant King of Great Britain could exceed it.

About four miles, over those delicious Downs, brings us to **Epsome**, and if you will suppose me to come there in the month of July, or thereabouts, you may think me to come in the middle of the season, when the town is full of company, and all disposed to mirth and pleasantry; for abating one unhappy stock jobbing year,[30] when England took leave to act the frantick, for a little while; and when every body's

47. Edward Hassell, *Epsom High Street* (1830); watercolour. The building to the right is the old Assembly Rooms which still survives and in which Defoe is thought to have stayed.

heads were turn'd with projects and stocks, I say, except this year, we see nothing of business in the whole conversation of Epsome; even the men of business, who are really so when in London; whether it be at the Exchange, the Alley, or the Treasury-Offices, and the Court; yet here they look as if they had left all their London thoughts behind them, and had separated themselves to mirth and good company; as if they came hither to unbend the bow of the mind, and to give themselves a loose to their innocent pleasures; I say, innocent, for such they may enjoy here, and such any man may make his being here, if he pleases.

As, I say, this place seems adapted wholly to pleasure, so the town is suited to it; 'tis all rural, the houses are built at large, not many together, with gardens and ground about them; that the people who come out of their confin'd dwellings in London, may have air and liberty, suited to the design of country lodgings.

You have no sooner taken lodgings, and enter'd the apartments, but if you are any thing known, you walk out, to see who and who's together; for 'tis the general language of the place, *Come let's go see the town, Folks don't come to Epsome to stay within doors.*

The next morning you are welcom'd with the musick under your chamber window; but for a shilling or two you get rid of them, and prepare for going to the Wells.

Here you have the compliment of the place, are enter'd into the list of the pleasant company, so you become a citizen of Epsome for that summer; and this costs you another shilling, or if you please, half a crown: then you drink the waters, or walk about as if you did; dance with the ladies, tho' it be in your gown and slippers; have musick and company of what kind you like, for every man may sort himself as he pleases; the grave with the grave, and the gay with the gay, the bright, and the wicked; all may be match'd if they seek for it, and perhaps some of the last may be over-match'd, if they are not upon their guard.

After the morning diversions are over, and every one are walk'd home to their lodgings, the town is perfectly quiet again; nothing is to be seen, the Green, the Great Room, the raffling-shops[31] all are (as if it was a trading town on a holiday) shut up; there's little stirring, except footmen, and maid servants, going to and fro of errands, and higglers[32] and butchers, carrying provisions to people's lodgings.

This takes up the town till dinner is over, and the company have repos'd for two or three hours in the heat of the day; then the first thing you observe is, that the ladies come to the shady seats, at their doors, and to the benches in the groves, and cover'd walks; (of which, every house that can have them, is generally supply'd with several). Here they refresh with cooling liquors, agreeable conversation, and innocent mirth.

Those that have coaches, or horses (as soon as the sun declines) take the air on the Downs, and those that have not, content themselves with staying a little later, and when the air grows cool, and the sun low, they walk out under the shade of the hedges and trees, as they find it for their diversion: in the mean time, towards evening the Bowling-Green begins to fill, the musick strikes up in the Great Room, and company draws together a-pace: and here they never fail of abundance of mirth, every night being a kind of ball; the gentlemen bowl, the ladies dance, others raffle, and some rattle;[33] conversation is the general pleasure of the place, till it grows late, and then the company draws off; and, generally speaking, they are pretty

well as to keeping good hours; so that by eleven a clock the dancing generally ends, and the day closes with good wishes, and appointments to meet the next morning at the Wells, or somewhere else.

The retir'd part of the world, of which also there are very many here, have the waters brought home to their apartments in the morning, where they drink and walk about a little, for assisting the physical operation, till near noon, then dress dinner, and repose for the heat as others do; after which they visit, drink tea, walk abroad, come to their lodgings to supper, then walk again till it grows dark, and then to bed: the greatest part of the men, I mean of this grave sort, may be supposed to be men of business, who are at London upon business all the day, and thronging to their lodgings at night, make the families, generally speaking, rather provide suppers than dinners; for 'tis very frequent for the trading part of the company to place their families here, and take their horses every morning to London, to the Exchange, to the Alley, or to the warehouse, and be at Epsome again at night; and I know one citizen that practis'd it for several years together, and scarce ever lay a night in London during the whole season.

From hence we came to **Richmond**, the delightful retreat of their royal highnesses, the Prince and Princess of Wales, and where they have spent the fine season every summer for some years: The Prince's court[34] being so near must needs have fill'd Richmond, which was before a most agreeable retreat for the first and second rate gentry, with a great deal of the best

XI. Peter Tillemans, *The Thames from Richmond Hill* (*The Thames between Twickenham and Ham*) (1720–23).

company in England: This town and the country adjacent, encrease daily in buildings, many noble houses for the accommodation of such, being lately rais'd and more in prospect: but 'tis fear'd should the prince come, for any cause that may happen, to quit that side of the country, those numerous buildings must abate in the value which is now set upon them: the company however, at Richmond, is very great in the winter, when the Prince's court is not there; because of the neighbourhood of so many gentlemen, who live constantly there, and thereabouts; and of its nearness to London also; and in this it has the advantage both of Epsome and Tunbridge.

From Richmond to London, the river sides are full of villages, and those villages so full of beautiful buildings, charming gardens, and rich habitations of gentlemen of quality, that nothing in the world can imitate it; no, not the country for twenty miles round Paris, tho' that indeed is a kind of prodigy.

To enumerate the gentlemen's houses in their view, would be too long for this work to describe them, would fill a large folio; it shall suffice to observe something concerning the original of the strange passion, for fine gardens, which has so commendably possess'd the English gentlemen of late years, for 'tis evident it is but of late years.

It is since the Revolution that our English gentlemen, began so universally, to adorn their gardens with those plants, we call ever greens, which leads me to a particular obervation that may not be improper in this place; King William and Queen Mary introduced each of them two customs, which by the people's imitating them became the two idols of the town, and indeed of the whole kingdom; the Queen brought in (1.) the love of fine East-India callicoes, such as were then call'd masslapatan chints,[35] atlasses,[36] and fine painted callicoes,[37] which afterwards descended into the humours of the common people so much, as to make them greivous to our trade, and ruining to our manufactures and the poor; so that the Parliament were oblig'd to make two acts at several times to restrain, and at last prohibit the use of them: (2.) The Queen brought in the custom or humour, as I may call it, of furnishing houses with china-ware, which increased to a strange degree afterwards, piling their china upon the tops of cabinets, scrutores,[38] and every chymney-piece, to the tops of the ceilings, and even setting up shelves for their china-ware, where they wanted such places, till it became a grievance in the expence of it, and even injurious to their families and estates.

The good Queen far from designing any injury to the country where she was so entirely belov'd, little thought she was in either of these laying a foundation for such fatal excesses, and would no doubt have been the first to have reform'd them had she lived to see it.

The King on his part introduc'd (1.) the love of gardening; and (2.) of painting: in the first his majesty was particularly delighted with the decoration of ever greens, as the greatest addition to the beauty of a garden, preserving the figure of the place, even in the roughest part of an inclement and tempestuous winter.

With the particular judgement of the King, all the gentlemen in England began to fall in; and in a few years fine gardens, and fine houses began to grow up in every corner; the King began with the gardens at Hampton-Court and Kensington, and the gentlemen follow'd every where, with such a gust that the alteration is indeed wonderful thro' the whole kingdom; but no where more than in the two counties of Middlesex and Surrey, as they border on the river Thames; the beauty and expence of which are only to be wonder'd at, not describ'd; they may indeed be guess'd at, by what is seen in one or two such as these nam'd: but I think to enter into a particular of them would be an intollerable task, and tedious to the reader.

That these houses and gardens are admirably beautiful in their kind, and in their separate, and distinct beauties, such as their scituation, decoration, architect, furniture, and the like, must be granted; and many descriptions have been accurately given of them, as of Ham-House, Qew-Green, the Prince's House, Sir William Temple's, Sir Charles Hedges, Sion-House, Osterly, Lord Ranelagh's at Chelsea-Hospital; the many noble seats in Istleworth, Twittenham, Hamersmith, Fullham, Puttney, Chelsea, Battersea, and the like.

But I find none has spoken of what I call the distant glory of all these buildings: there is a beauty in these

48. Evergreen topiary arcades, garden view of Hartwell House by Balthasar Nebot.

XII. Peter Tillemans, *The Thames at Twickenham* (1720–25). View to the west across the river just south of Eel Pie Island, showing Alexander Pope's house left of centre and Lady Ferrer's domed summer house centre.

things at a distance, taking them *en passant*, and in perspective, which few people value, and fewer understand; and yet here they are more truly great, than in all their private beauties whatsoever; here they reflect beauty, and magnificence upon the whole country, and give a kind of a character to the island of Great Britain in general. The banks of the Sein are not thus adorn'd from Paris to Roan,[39] or from Paris to the Loign[40] above the city: the Danube can show nothing like it above and below Vienna, or the Po above and below Turin; the whole country here shines with a lustre not to be describ'd; take them in a remote view, the fine seats shine among the trees as jewels shine in a rich coronet; in a near sight they are meer pictures and paintings; at a distance they are all nature, near hand all art; but both in the extreamest beauty.

In a word, nothing can be more beautiful; here is a plain and pleasant country, a rich fertile soil, cultivated and enclosed to the utmost perfection of husbandry, then bespangled with villages; those villages fill'd with these houses, and the houses surrounded with gardens, walks, vistas, avenues, representing all the beauties of building, and all the pleasures of planting: It is impos-

sible to view these countries from any rising ground, and not be ravish'd with the delightful prospect: for example, suppose you take your view from the little rising hills about Clapham, there you see the pleasant villages of Peckham and Camberwell, with some of the finest dwellings about London; looking north, behold, to crown all, a fair prospect of the whole city of London it self; the most glorious sight without exception, that the whole world at present can show, or perhaps ever cou'd show since the sacking of Rome in the European, and the burning the Temple of Jerusalem in the Asian part of the world.

Add to all this, that these fine houses and innumerable more, which cannot be spoken of here, are not, at least very few of them, the mansion houses of families, the antient residences of ancestors, the capital messuages[41] of the estates; nor have the rich possessors any lands to a considerable value about them; but these are all houses of retreat, like the Bastides[42] of Marseilles, gentlemen's meer summer-houses, or citizen's country houses; whither they retire from the hurries of business, and from getting money, to draw their breath in a clear air, and to divert themselves and

49. Peter Andreas Rysbrack the Younger, *A View on the Thames at Deptford with shipping.*

II. After Jan Griffier the Elder, *The Thames at Horseferry, with Lambeth Palace and a distant view of the city* (*c*.1706–10).

families in the hot weather; and that they are shut up, and as it were strip'd of their inhabitants in the winter, who return to smoke and dirt, sin and seacoal, (as it was coursly express'd) in the busy city; so that in short all this variety, this beauty, this glorious show of wealth and plenty, is really a view of the luxuriant age which we live in, and of the overflowing riches of the citizens, who in their abundance make these gay excursions, and live thus deliciously all the summer retiring within themselves in the winter, the better to lay up for the next summer's expence.

If this then is produc'd from the gay part of the town only, what must be the immense wealth of the city itself, where such a produce is brought forth? where such prodigious estates are raised in one man's age; instances of which we have seen in those of Sir Josiah Child,[43] Sir John Lethulier,[44] Sir James Bateman,[45] Sir Robert Clayton,[46] Sir William Scawen,[47] and hundreds more; whose beginnings were small, or but small compar'd, and who have exceeded even the greatest part of the nobility of England in wealth, at their death, and all of their own getting.

I am come now to **Southwark**, a suburb to, rather than a part of London; but of which this may be said with justice.

A royal city were not London by.

To give you a brief description of Southwark, it might be call'd a long street, of about nine miles in length, as it is now built on eastward; reaching from Vaux-Hall to London-Bridge, and from the bridge to Deptford, and up to Deptford-Bridge, which parts it from Greenwich, all the way winding and turning as the river winds and turns; except only in that part, which reaches from Cuckold's-Point to Deptford, which indeed winds more than the river does.

In the center, which is opposite to the bridge, it is thicken'd with buildings, and may be reckon'd near a mile broad; (viz.) from the bridge to the end of Kent-street and Blackman-street, and about the Mint;[48] but else the whole building is but narrow, nor indeed can it be otherwise; considering the length of it.

A farther description of Southwark, I refer till I come to speak of London, as one general appellation for the two cities of London and Westminster; and all the burrough of Southwark, and all the buildings and villages included within the bills of mortallity,[49] make but one London, in the general appellation, of which in its order. I am, &c.

The End of the Second Letter

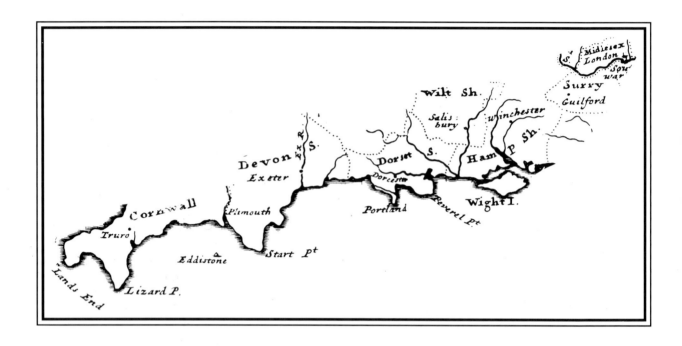

LETTER III

Containing a Description of the South Coasts of Hampshire, Wilts, Dorsetshire, Somersetshire, Devonshire, and Cornwall

SIR,

I find so much left to speak of, and so many things to say in every part of England, that my journey cannot be barren of intelligence, which way soever I turn; no, tho' I were to oblige myself to say nothing of any thing that had been spoken of before.

As I came down from Kingston, in my last circuit, by the south bank of the Thames, on the Surrey side of the river; so I go up to Hampton Court, now, on the north bank, and on the Middlesex side.

Hampton Court lyes on the north bank of the river Thames, about two small miles from Kingston, and on the road from Stanes to Kingston Bridge; so that the road straightening the parks a little they were obliged to part the parks, and leave the paddock, and the great park, part on the other side the road; a testimony of that just regard that the kings of England always had, and still have, to the common good, and to the service of the country, that they would not interrupt the course of the road, or cause the poor people to go out of the way of their business, to or from the markets and fairs, for any pleasure of their own whatsoever.

The palace of Hampton-Court was first founded, and built from the ground, by that great statesman, and favourite of King Henry VIII, Cardinal Wolsey; and if it be a just observation any where, as is made from the situation of the old abbies and monasteries, the clergy were excellent judges of the beauty and pleasantness of the country, and chose always to plant in the best; I say, if it was a just observation in any case, it was in this; for if there be a situation on the whole river between Stanes-bridge and Windsor-bridge, pleasanter than another, it is this of Hampton; close to the river, yet not offended by the rising of its

waters in floods, or storms, near to the reflux of the tides, but not quite so near as to be affected with any foulness of the water, which the flowing of the tides generally is the occasion of.

I shall sing you no songs here of the river in the first person of a water nymph, a goddess, (and I know not what) according to the humour of the ancient poets. I shall talk nothing of the marriage of old Isis,[1] the male river, with the beautiful Thame, the female river, a whimsy as simple as the subject was empty, but I shall speak of the river as occasion presents, as it really is made glorious by the splendor of its shores, gilded with noble palaces, strong fortifications, large hospitals, and publick buildings; with the greatest bridge, and the greatest city in the world, made famous by the opulence of its merchants, the encrease and extensiveness of its commerce; by its invincible navies, and by the innumerable fleets of ships sailing upon it, to and from all parts of the world.

Whoever knew Hampton-Court before it was begun to be rebuilt, or alter'd, by the late King William, must acknowledge it was a very compleat palace before, and fit for a King; and tho' it might not, according to the modern method of building, or of gardening, pass for a thing exquisitely fine; yet it had this remaining to itself, and perhaps peculiar; namely, that it shewed a situation exceedingly capable of improvement, and of being made one of the most delightful palaces in Europe.

This Her Majesty Queen Mary was so sensible of, that while the King had order'd the pulling down the old apartments, and building it up in that most beautiful form, which we see them now appear in, her Majesty, impatient of enjoying so agreeable a retreat, fix'd upon a building formerly made use of chiefly for landing from the river, and therefore call'd the Water Gallery; and here, as if she had been conscious that she had but a few years to enjoy it, she order'd all the little neat curious things to be done, which suited her own conveniences, and made it the pleasantest little thing within doors that could possibly be made, tho' its situation being such, as it could not be allowed to stand after the great building was finish'd; we now see no remains of it.

The Queen had here her gallery of beauties, being the pictures, at full length, of the principal ladies attending upon her majesty, or who were frequently in her retinue; and this was the more beautiful sight, because the originals were all in being, and often to be compar'd with their pictures. Her majesty had here a fine apartment, with a sett of lodgings, for her private retreat only, but most exquisitely furnish'd; particularly a fine chints bed,[2] then a great curiosity; another of her own work, while in Holland, very magnificent, and several others; and here was also her majesty's fine collection of Delft ware, which indeed was very large and fine; and here was also a vast stock of fine china ware, the like whereof was not then to be seen in England; the long gallery, as above, was fill'd with this china, and every other place, where it could be plac'd, with advantage.

The Queen had here also a small bathing-room, made very fine, suited either to hot or cold bathing, as the season should invite; also a dairy, with all its conveniencies, in which her majesty took great delight: all these things were finish'd with expedition, that here their majesties might repose while they saw the main building go forward. While this was doing, the gardens were laid out, the plan of them devised by the King himself; and especially the amendments and alterations were made by the King, or the Queen's particular special command, or by both; for their majesties agreed so well in their fancy, and had both so good judgment in the just proportions of things, which are the principal beauties of a garden, that it may be said they both order'd every thing that was done.

Here the fine parcel of limes, which form the semi-circle on the south front of the house, by the iron gates, looking into the park, were, by the dextrous hand of the head gardener, remov'd, after some of them had been almost thirty years planted in other places, tho' not far of. I know the King of France, in the decoration of the gardens of Versailles, had oaks remov'd, which, by their dimensions, must have been above an hundred years old, and yet were taken up with so much art, and by the strength of such engines, by which such a monsterous quantity of earth was raised with them, that the trees could not feel their remove; that is to say, their growth was not at all hinder'd. This I confess, makes the wonder much the less in those trees at Hampton-Court Gardens; but the performance was not the less difficult or nice, however, in these, and they thrive perfectly well.

While the gardens were thus laid out, the King also directed the laying the pipes for the fountain and jette d'eau's; and particularly the dimensions of them, and what quantity of water they should cast up, and encreas'd the number of them after the first design.

The ground on the side of the other front, has receiv'd some alterations since the taking down the water gallery; but not that part immediately next the lodgings: the orange trees, and fine Dutch bays, are plac'd within the arches of the building under the first floor: so that the lower part of the house was all one as a green house for some time: here stands advanced, on two pedestals of stone, two marble vases, or flower pots, of most exquisite workmanship; the one done by an Englishman, and the other by a German: 'tis hard to say which is the best performance, tho' the doing of it was a kind of tryal of skill between them; but it gives us room, without partiality, to say they were both masters of their art.

The parterre on that side descends from the terrass walk by steps, and on the left a terrass goes down to the water-side, from which the garden on the eastward front is overlook'd, and gives a most pleasant prospect.

The fine scrolls and bordure of these gardens were at first edg'd with box; but on the Queen's disliking the smell, those edgings were taken up, but have since been planted again, at least in many places, nothing making so fair and regular an edging as box, or is so soon brought to its perfection.

On the north side of the house, where the gardens seem'd to want skreening from the weather, or the view of the Chapel, and some part of the old building requir'd to be cover'd from the eye; the vacant ground, which was large, is very happily cast into a wilderness, with a labyrinth, and espaliers so high, that they effectually take off all that part of the old building, which would have been offensive to the sight. This labyrinth and wilderness is not only well design'd, and compleatly finish'd, but is perfectly well kept, and the espaliers fill'd exactly, at bottom to the very ground, and are led up to proportion'd heights on the top; so that nothing of that kind can be more beautiful.

I hinted in my last that King William brought into England the love of fine paintings, as well as that of fine gardens; and you have an example of it in the cartoons,[3] as they are call'd, being five pieces of such paintings, as, if you will believe men of nice judgment

XIV. Leonard Knyff, *Hampton Court Palace, Middlesex, Bird's-eye view from the east* (c.1702).

and great travelling, are not to be match'd in Europe: The stories are known, but especially two of them, viz. that of St. Paul preaching on Mars-Hill to the self-wise Athenians, and that of St. Peter passing sentence of death on Ananias; I say, these two strike the mind with the utmost surprize; the passions are so drawn to the life, astonishment, terror and death in the face of Ananias; zeal and a sacred fire in the eyes of the blessed apostle; fright and surprize upon the countenances of the beholders in the piece of Ananias; all these describe themselves so naturally, that you cannot but seem to discover something of the like passions, even in seeing them.

In the other, there is the boldness and courage with which St. Paul undertook to talk to a sett of men, who he knew despis'd all the world, as thinking themselves able to teach them any thing: in the audience, there is anticipating pride and conceit in some, a smile or fleer of contempt in others, but a kind of sensible conviction, tho' crush'd in its beginning, on the faces of the rest; and all together appear confounded, but have little to say, and know nothing at all of it, they gravely put him off to hear him another time; all these are seen here in the very dress of the face; that is, the very countenances which they hold while they listen to the new doctrine, which the apostle preached to a people at that time ignorant of it.

From Hampton Court I directed my course for a journey into the south west part of England; and, to take up my beginning where I concluded my last, I cross'd to Chertsey on the Thames, a town I mention'd before; from whence crossing the Black Desert, as I call'd it, of Bagshot-Heath, I directed my course for Hampshire, or Hantshire, and particularly for Basingstoke; that is to say, that a little before I pass'd into the great western road upon the heath, somewhat west of Bagshot, at a village call'd Blackwater, and enter'd Hampshire, near Hartleroe.

Before we reach Basingstoke, we get rid of that unpleasant country, which I so often call a desart, and enter into a pleasant fertile country, enclosed and cultivated like the rest of England; and passing a village or two, we enter Basingstoke, in the midst of woods and pastures, rich and fertile, and the country accordingly spread with the houses of the nobility and gentry, as in other places: on the right hand, a little before we come to the town, we pass at a small distance the famous fortress, so it was then, of Basing, being a house belonging then to the Marquis of Winchester, the great ancestor of the present family of the Dukes of Bolton.

Basingstoke is a large populous market town, has a good market for corn, and lately, within a very few years, is fallen into a manufacture, viz. of making druggets and shalloons, and such slight goods, which, however, employs a good number of the poor people, and enables them to get their bread, which knew not how to get it before.

From hence the great western road goes on to *Whitchurch* and *Andover*, two market towns, and sending members to Parliament; at the last of which, the Downs, or open country, begins, which we in general, tho' falsly, call Salisbury-Plain: But my resolution being to take in my view what I had pass'd by before; I was oblig'd to go off to the left hand, to Alresford and Winchester.

Alresford was a flourishing market town, and remarkable for this; that tho' it had no great trade, and particularly very little, if any manufactures, yet there was no collection in the town for the poor, nor any poor low enough to take alms of the parish, which is what I do not think can be said of any town in England besides.

But this happy circumstance, which so distinguish'd Alresford from all her neighbours, was brought to an end in the year ———, when, by a sudden and surprizing fire,[4] the whole town, with both the church and the market-house, was reduc'd to a heap of rubbish; and, except a few poor hutts at the remotest ends of the town, not a house left standing: the town is since that very handsomely rebuilt, and the neighbouring gentlemen contributed largely to the relief of the people, especially, by sending in timber towards their building; also their market-house is handsomely built; but the church not yet, tho' we hear there is a fund raising likewise for that.

Here is a very large pond, or lake of water, kept up to a head, by a strong batterd'eau,[5] or dam, which the people tell us was made by the Romans; and that it is to this day part of the great Roman highway, which leads from Winchester to Alton, and, as 'tis supposed, went on to London, tho' we no where see any remains of it, except between Winchester and Alton, and chiefly between this town and Alton.

From hence, at the end of seven miles over the Downs, we come to the very ancient city of *Winchester*; not only the great church, which is so famous all over Europe, and has been so much talk'd of, but even the whole city has, at a distance, the face of venerable, and looks ancient a far off; and yet here are many modern buildings too, and some very handsome; as the college schools; with the bishop's palace, built by Bishop Morley,[6] since the late wars; the old palace of the bishop having been ruin'd by that known church incendiary, Sir William Waller,[7] and his crew of plunderers; who, if my information is not wrong,

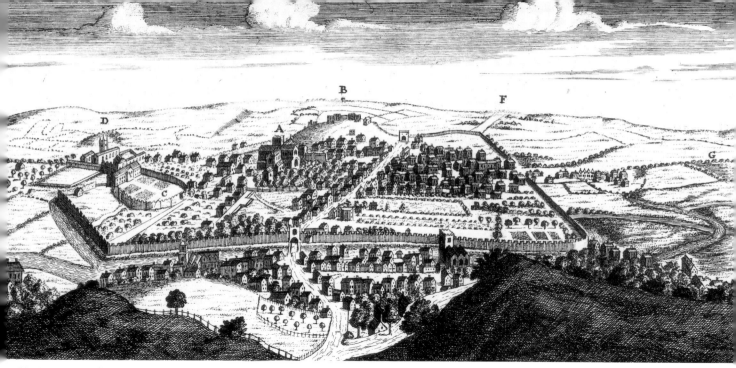

50. 'Prospect of Winchester from the south, 9 September 1723'; engraving after a drawing by William Stukeley. From his *Itinerarium Curiosum* (1724).

as I believe it is not, destroy'd more monuments of the dead, and defac'd more churches, than all the Round-heads in England beside.

This church, and the schools, also are accurately describ'd by several writers, especially by the *Monasticon*,[8] where their antiquity and original is fully set forth: the outside of the church is as plain and course, as if the founders had abhor'd ornaments, or that William of Wickham[9] had been a Quaker, or at least a Quietist:[10] There is neither statue, or a nich for a statue, to be seen on all the outside; no carv'd work, no spires, towers, pinacles, balustrades, or any thing; but meer walls, buttresses, windows, and coins, necessary to the support and order of the building: it has no steeple, but a short tower cover'd flat, as if the top of it had fallen down, and it had been cover'd in haste to keep the rain out, till they had time to build it up again.

But the inside of the church has many very good things in it, and worth observation; it was for some ages the burying place of the English Saxon kings; whose reliques, at the repair of the church, were collected by Bishop Fox,[11] and, being put together into large wooden chests, lin'd with lead, were again interr'd at the foot of the great wall in the choir, three on one side, and three on the other; with an account whose bones are in each chest, whether the division of the reliques might be depended upon, has been doubted, but is not thought material, so that we do but believe they are all there.

The choir of the church appears very magnificent; the roof is very high, and the gothick work in the arch'd part is very fine, tho' very old; the painting in the windows is admirably good, and easy to be distinguish'd by those that understand those things: the steps ascending to the choir make a very fine show, having the statues of King James, and his son[12] King Charles, in copper, finely cast; the first on the right hand, and the other on the left, as you go up to the choir.

The choir is said to be the longest in England; and as the number of prebendaries, canons, &c. are many, it requir'd such a length. The ornaments of the choir are the effects of the bounty of several bishops; the fine altar, (the noblest in England by much) was done by Bishop Morley; the roof, and the coat of arms of the Saxon and Norman kings, were done by Bishop Fox; and the fine throne, for the bishop in the choir, was given by Bishop Mew,[13] in his life-time; and it was well it was; for if he had order'd it by will, there is reason to believe it had never been done. That reverend prelate, notwithstanding he enjoy'd so rich a bishoprick, scarce leaving money enough behind him, to pay for his coffin.

As the city itself stands in a vale on the bank, and at the conjunction of two small rivers, so the country rising every way, but just as the course of the water keeps the valley open, you must necessarily, as you go out of the gates, go up hill every way: but when once ascended, you come to the most charming plains, and most pleasant country of that kind in England; which continues, with very small intersections of rivers and valleys, for above fifty miles, as shall appear in the sequel of this journey.

I cannot omit that there are several publick edifices in this city, and in the neighbourhood; as the hospitals, and the building adjoining near the east gate; and towards the north, a piece of an old monastry[14] un-demolish'd, and which is still preserv'd to the religion, being the residence of some private Roman Catholick gentlemen, where they have an oratory, and, as they say, live still according to the rules of St. Benedict. This building is call'd Hide-House; and, as they live very usefully and, to the highest degree, obliging among their neighbours, they meet with no obstruction or disturbance from any body.

Winchester is a place of no trade, other than is naturally occasion'd by the inhabitants of the city and neighbouring villages, one with another: here is no manufacture, no navigation; there was indeed an attempt to make the river navigable from Southampton; and it was once made practicable, but it never answer'd the expence, so as to give encouragement to the undertakers.

Here is a great deal of good company; and abundance of gentry being in the neighbourhood, it adds to the sociableness of the place: The clergy also here are, generally speaking, very rich, and very numerous.

As there is such good company, so they are gotten into that new-fashion'd way of conversing by assemblies: I shall do no more than mention them here; they are pleasant and agreeable to the young people, and some times fatal to them, of which, in its place: Winchester has its share of the mirth: may it escape the ill consequences.

The hospital[15] on the south of this city, at a mile's distance on the road to Southampton, is worth notice: 'Tis said to be founded by King William Rufus, but was not endow'd or appointed till later times by Cardinal Beaufort.[16] Every traveller that knocks at the door of this house, in his way, and asks for it, claims the relief of a piece of white bread and a cup of beer; and this donation is still continued; a quantity of good beer is set apart every day to be given away; and what is left, is distributed to other poor, but none of it kept to the next day.

How the revenues of this hospital, which should maintain the master and thirty private gentlemen, who they call Fellows, but ought to call Brothers, is now reduc'd to maintain only fourteen, while the Master lives in a figure equal to the best gentleman in the country, would be well worth the enquiry of a proper visitor, if such can be nam'd: 'tis a thing worthy of complaint, when publick charaties, design'd for the relief of the poor, are embezzel'd and depredated by the rich, and turn'd to the support of luxury and pride.

From Winchester, is about 25 miles, and over the most charming plains that can any where be seen, (far in my opinion) excelling the plains of Mecca, we come to Salisbury; the vast flocks of sheep, which one every where sees upon these Downs, and the great number of those flocks, is a sight truly worth observation; 'tis ordinary for these flocks to contain from 3 to 5000 in a flock; and several private farmers hereabouts have two or three such flocks.

But 'tis more remarkable still; how a great part of these Downs comes by a new method of husbandry, to be not only made arable, which they never were in former days, but to bear excellent wheat, and great crops too, tho' otherwise poor barren land, and never known to our ancestors to be capable of any such thing; nay, they would perhaps have laugh'd at any one that would have gone about to plough up the wild downs and hills, where the sheep were wont to go: but experience has made the present age wiser, and more skilful in husbandry; for by only folding the sheep upon the plow'd lands, those lands, which otherwise are barren, and where the plow goes within three or four inches of the solid rock of chalk, are made fruitful, and bear very good wheat, as well as rye and barley: I shall say more of this when I come to speak of the same practice farther in the country.

This plain country continues in length from Winchester to Salisbury 25 miles, from thence to Dorchester 22 miles, thence to Weymouth 6 miles, so that they lye near 50 miles in length, and breadth; they

51. Old Sarum; drawing by George Vertue (*c*.1730).

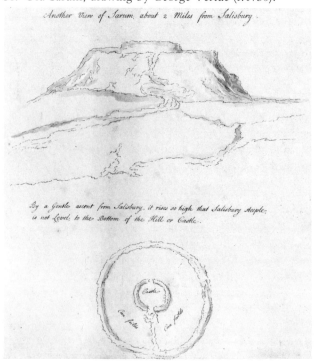

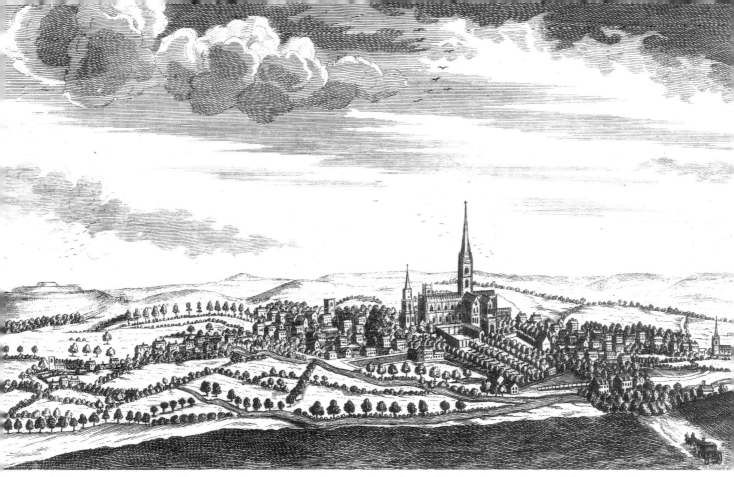

52. Salisbury, view from Harnham Hill (26 August 1723); engraving after a drawing by William Stukeley. From his *Itinerarium Curiosum* (1724).

reach also in some places 35 to 40 miles: They who would make any practicable guess at the number of sheep usually fed on these downs, may take it from a calculation made, as I was told, at Dorchester, that there were 600000 sheep fed within 6 miles of that town, measuring every way round, and the town in the center.

As we pass'd this plain country, we saw a great many old camps, as well Roman as British, and several remains of the ancient inhabitants of this kingdom, and of their wars, battles, entrenchments, encampments, buildings, and other fortifications, which are indeed very agreeable to a traveller, that has read any thing of the history of the country. Old Sarum is as remarkable as any of these, where there is a double entrenchment, with a deep graffe, or ditch, to either of them; the area about 100 yards in diameter, taking in the whole crown of the hill, and thereby rendering the ascent very difficult: near this, there is one farm house, which is all the remains I could see of any town in or near the place, for the encampment has no resemblance of a town; and yet this is call'd the borough of old Sarum, and sends two members to Parliament: who those members can justly say they represent, would be hard for them to answer.

Salisbury itself is indeed a large and pleasant city; tho' I do not think it at all the pleasanter for that which they boast so much of; namely, the water running thro' the middle of every street, or that it adds any thing to the beauty of the place, but just the contrary; it keeps the streets always dirty, full of wet and filth, and weeds, even in the middle of summer.

As the city of Winchester is a city without trade, that is to say, without any particular manufactures; so this city of Salisbury, and all the county of Wilts, of which it is the capital, are full of a great variety of manufactures; and those some of the most considerable in England; namely, the cloathing trade, and the trade of flannels, drugets, and several other sorts of manufactures, of which in their order.

The city of Salisbury has two remarkable manufactures carried on in it, and which employ the poor of great part of the country round; namely, fine flannels, and long cloths for the Turkey trade, call'd Salisbury whites:[17] The people of Salisbury are gay and rich, and have a flourishing trade; and there is a great deal of good manners and good company among them; I mean, among the citizens, besides what is found among the gentlemen; for there are many good families in Salisbury, besides the citizens.

53. 'Lord Pembroke's Garden at Wilton 20 August'; drawing by William Stukeley. From his *Drawings in a journey with Mr Roger Gale* (1721).

This society has a great addition from the closs, that is to say, the circles of ground wall'd in adjacent to the cathedral; in which the families of the prebendaries and commons, and others of the clergy belonging to the cathedral have their houses, as is usual in all cities where there are cathedral churches. These are so considerable here, and the place so large, that it is (as it is call'd in general) like another city.

The cathedral is famous for the height of its spire, which is without exception the highest, and the handsomest in England, being from the ground 410 foot, and yet the walls so exceeding thin, that at the upper part of the spire upon a view made by the late Sir Christopher Wren, the wall was found to be less than five inches thick; upon which a consultation was had, whether the spire, or at least the upper part of it should be taken down, it being suppos'd to have receiv'd some damage by the great storm in the year 1703; but it was resolv'd in the negative, and Sir Christopher order'd it to be so strengthen'd with bands of iron plates, as has effectually secur'd it; and I have heard some of the best architects say, it is stronger now than when it was first built.

They tell us here long stories of the great art us'd in laying the first foundation of this church; the ground being marshy and wet, occasion'd by the channels of the rivers; that it was laid upon piles according to some, and upon woolpacks according to others; but this is not suppos'd by those who know, that the whole country is one rock of chalk, even from the tops of the highest hills, to the bottom of the deepest rivers.

They tell us, this church was 40 years a building, and cost an immense sum of money, but it must be acknowledged that the inside of the work is not answerable in the decoration of things, to the workmanship without; the painting in the choir is mean, and more like the ordinary method of common drawing room, or tavern painting, than that of a church; the carving is good, but very little of it, and it is rather a fine church than finely set off.

The cloyster, and the chapter-house adjoyning to the church, are the finest here of any I have seen in England; the latter is octogon, or eight square, and is 150 foot in its circumference; the roof bearing all upon one small marble pillar in the center, which you may shake with your hand; and it is hardly to be imagin'd it can be any great support to the roof, which makes it the more curious, it is not indeed to be match'd I believe in Europe.

From hence directing my course to the sea-side in pursuit of my first design, viz. of viewing the whole coast of England, I left the great road, and went down the east side of the river towards New-Forest, and Lymington; and here I saw the antient house and seat of Clarendon the mansion of the antient family of Hide, ancestors of the great Earl of Clarendon, and from whence his lordship was honour'd with that title, or the house erected into an honour in favour of his family.

I have mention'd that this county is generally a vast continu'd body of high chalky hills, whose tops spread themselves into fruitful and pleasant downs and plains, upon which great flocks of sheep are fed, &c. But the reader is desir'd to observe these hills and plains are most beautifully intersected, and cut thro' by the course of divers pleasant and profitable rivers; in the course, and near the banks, of which there always is a chain of fruitful meadows, and rich pastures, and those interspers'd with innumerable pleasant towns, villages, and houses, and among them many of considerable magnitude; so that while you view the downs, and think the country wild and uninhabited; yet when you come to descend into these vales you are surpris'd with the most pleasant and fertile country in England.

One cannot be said to have seen any thing that a man of curiosity would think worth seeing in this county, and not have been at Wilton House; but not the beautiful building, not the antient trophy of a great family, not the noble scituation, not all the pleasures of the gardens, parks, fountains, hare-warren, or of whatever is rare either in art or nature are equal to, that yet more glorious sight, of a noble princely palace, constantly filled with its noble and proper inhabitants; viz. the Lord and proprietor, who is indeed a true patriarchal monarch, reigns here with an authority agreeable to all his subjects (family); and his reign is made agreeable, by his first practising the most exquisite government of himself, and then guiding all under him by the rules of honour and vertue; being also himself perfectly master of all the needful arts of family government; I mean needful to make that government, both easy, and pleasant to those who are under it, and who therefore willingly, and by choice conform to it.

Here an exhaulted genius is the instructor, a glorious example the guide, and a gentle well directed hand the governour and law-giver to the whole; and the family like a well govern'd city appears happy, flourishing and regular, groaning under no grievance, pleas'd with what they enjoy, and enjoying every thing which they ought to be pleas'd with.

Nor is the blessing of this noble resident extended to the family only, but even to all the country round, who in their degree feel the effects of the general beneficence; and where the neighbourhood, however

poor receive all the good they can expect, and are sure to have no injury, or oppression.

The canal before the house lyes parallel with the road, and receives into it the whole river Willey, or at least is able to do so; it may indeed be said, that the river is made into a canal; when we come into the court-yards before the house there are several peices of antiquity to entertain the curious; as particularly, a noble column of porphyry, with a marble statue of Venus on the top of it. In Italy, and especially at Rome and Naples, we see a great variety of fine columns, and some of them of excellent workmanship, and antiquity, and at some of the courts of the princes of Italy the like is seen; as especially at the court of Florence; but in England I do not remember to have seen any thing like this, which as they told me is two and thirty foot high and of excellent workmanship, and that it came last from Candia, but formerly from Alexandria; what may belong to the history of it any further, I suppose is not known, at least they could tell me no more of it, who shew'd it me.

As the present Earl of Pembroke,[18] the lord of this fine palace, is a nobleman of great personal merit, many other ways; so he is a man of learning, and reading, beyond most men of his lordship's high rank in this nation, if not in the world; and as his reading has made him a master of antiquity, and judge of such peices of antiquity, as he has had opportunity to meet with in his own travels, and otherwise in the world; so it has given him a love of the study, and made him a collector of valuable things, as well in painting as in sculpture, and other excellencies of art, as also of nature; in so much that Wilton-House is now a meer musæum, or a chamber of rarities, and we meet with several things there, which are to be found no where else in the world.

You ascend the great stair case, at the upper end of the hall, which is very large; at the foot of the stair-case you have a Bacchus large as the life, done in fine Peloponesian marble; carrying a young Bacchus on his arm, the young one eating grapes, and letting you see by his countenance, that he is pleas'd with the tast of them; nothing can be done finer, or more lively represent the thing intended; namely, the gust of the appetite, which if it be not a passion, 'tis an affection, which is as much seen in the countenance, perhaps more than any other: one ought to stop every two steps of this stair-case, as we go up, to contemplate the vast variety of pictures, that cover the walls, and of some of the best masters in Europe, and yet this is but an introduction to what is beyond them.

When you are enter'd the appartments, such variety seizes you every way, that you scarce know to which

54. View of the Great Room at Wilton; drawing by George Vertue (c.1730).

55. View of the family pictures, painted by Van Dyke, at the other end of the Great Room; drawing by George Vertue (c.1730).

hand to turn your self: First, on one side you see several rooms fill'd with paintings, as before, all so curious, and the variety such, that 'tis with reluctance, that you can turn from them; while looking another way, you are call'd off by a vast collection of busto's, and peices of the greatest antiquity of the kind, both Greek, and Romans; among these, there is one of the Roman emperor, Marcus Aurelius in *basso relievo*; I never saw any thing like what appears here, except in the chamber of rarieties at Munick[19] in Bavaria.

Passing these, you come into several large rooms, as if contriv'd for the reception of the beautiful guests that take them up; one of these is near 70 foot long and the ceiling 26 foot high, with another adjoyning of the same height, and breadth, but not so long: those together might be call'd the Great Gallery of Wilton, and might vie for paintings with the gallery of Luxemburg[20] in the Fauxbourg of Paris.

These two rooms are fill'd with the family peices of the house of Herbert, most of them by Lilly, or Vandyke, and one in particularly, out does all that ever I met with, either at home, or abroad, 'tis done, as was the mode of painting at that time, after the manner of a family peice of King Charles I[21] with his Queen, and children, which before the burning of White-Hall, I remember to hang at the east end of the Long Gallery in the palace.

After we have seen this fine range of beauties, for such indeed they are; far from being at an end of your surprize, you have three or four rooms still upon the same floor, fill'd with wonders, as before: nothing can be finer than the pictures themselves, nothing more surprising than the number of them; at length you descend the back-stairs, which are in themselves large, tho' not like the other: however, not a hand's breadth is left to crowd a picture in of the smallest size, and even the upper rooms, which might be call'd garrets, are not naked, but have some very good peices in them.

The gardens are on the south of the house, and extend themselves beyond the river, a branch of which runs thro' one part of them, and still south of the gardens in the great park, which extending beyond the vale, mounts the hill opening at the last to the Great Down, which is properly call'd by way of distinction, Salisbury-Plain, and leads from the city of Salisbury, to Shaftsbury; here also his lordship has a hare-warren (as 'tis call'd) tho' improperly; it has indeed been a sanctuary for the hares for many years; but the gentlemen complain that it marrs their game, for that as soon as they put up a hare for their sport, if it be any where within two or three miles, away she runs for the warren, and there is an end of their pursuit; on the other hand, it makes all the countrymen turn poachers, and destroy the hares, by what means they can; but this is a smaller matter, and of no great import one way or other.

From this pleasant and agreeable day's work, I return'd to Clarendon, and the next day took another short tour to the hills, to see that celebrated peice of antiquity, the wonderful Stone-Henge, being six miles from Salisbury, north, and upon the side of the river Avon, near the town of Amesbury: 'tis needless, that I should enter here into any part of the dispute about which our learned antiquaries have so puzzl'd themselves that several books, and one of them, in folio,

56. The central stones, Stonehenge; drawing by William Stukeley. From his *Drawings in a journey with Mr Roger Gale* (1721).

has been publish'd about it; some alledging it to be a heathen, or pagan temple, and altar, or place of sacrifice, as Mr. Jones;[22] others, a monument, or trophy of victory; others a monument for the dead, as Mr. Aubury,[23] and the like: again, some will have it be British, some Danish, some Saxon, some Roman, and some before them all, Phenician.

I shall suppose it, as the majority of all writers do, to be a monument for the dead, and the rather, because men's bones have been frequently dug up in the ground near them. The common opinion that no man could ever count them, that a baker carry'd a basket of bread, and laid a loaf upon every stone, and yet could never make out the same number twice; this, I take, as a meer country fiction, and a ridiculous one too; the reason why they cannot easily be told, is, that many of them lye half, or part buryed in the ground, and a peice here, and a peice there, only appearing above the grass, it cannot be known easily, which belong to one stone, and which to another, or which are separate stones, and which are joyned under ground to one another.

The form of this monument is not only describ'd but delineated in most authors, and indeed 'tis hard to know the first, but by the last; the figure was at first circular, and there were at least four rows or circles, within one another; the main stones were placed upright, and they were joyn'd on the top by cross stones, laid from one to another, and fastn'd with vast mortices and tenants: length of time has so decay'd them, that not only most of the cross stones which lay on the top are fallen down, but many of the upright also, notwithstanding the weight of them is so prodigious great: how they came thither, or from whence, no stones of that kind being now to be found in any part of England near it, is still the mistery, for they are of such immense bulk that no engines, or carriages which we have in use in this age could stir them.

The downs and plains in this part of England being so open, and the surface so little subject to alteration, there are more remains of antiquity to be seen upon them, than in other places; for example, I think they tell us there are three and fifty antient encampments, or fortifications to be seen in this one county, some whereof are exceeding plain to be seen, some of one form, some of another; some of one nation, some of another, British, Danish, Saxon, Roman, as at Ebbdown, Burywood, Oldburgh-Hill, Cummerford, Roundway-Down, St. Ann's-Hill, Bratton-Castle, Clay-Hill, Stournton-Park, Whitecole-Hill, Battlebury, Scrathbury, Yanesbury, Frippsbury, Suthbury-Hill, Amesbury, Great Bodwyn, Easterley, Merdon, Aubery, Martensoil-Hill, Barbury-Castle, and many more.

Also the barrows,[24] as we all agree to call them, are very many in number in this county, and very obvious, having suffer'd very little decay, these are large hillocks of earth cast up, as the antients agree, by the soldiers over the bodies of their dead comrades slain in battle; several hundreds of these are to be seen, especially in the north part of this county, about Marlbro' and the downs, from thence to St. Ann's-Hill, and even every way, the downs are full of them.

I am now to pursue my first design, and shall take the west part of Wiltshire in my return, where are several things still to be taken notice of, and some very well worth our stay. In the mean time I went on to Langbro' a fine seat of my Lord Colerain, which is very well kept, tho' the family it seems is not much in this country, having another estate, and dwelling at Tottenham-High-Cross near London.

From hence in my way to the sea-side I came to New-Forest, of which I have said something already with relation to the great extent of ground, which lyes wast, and in which there is so great a quantity of large timber, as I have spoken of already.

This wast and wild part of the country was, as some record, lay'd open, and wast for a forest, and for game, by that violent tyrant William the Conqueror, and for which purpose he un-peopled the country, pull'd down the houses, and which was worse, the churches of several parishes or towns, and of abundance of villages, turning the poor people out of their habitations, and possessions, and laying all open for his deer: The same histories likewise record that two of his own blood and posterity, and particularly his immediate successor William Rufus lost their lives in this forest: one (viz.) the said William Rufus being shot with an arrow directed at a deer, which the King, and his company were hunting, and the arrow glancing on a tree, chang'd his course and struck the King full on the breast, and kill'd him; this they relate as a just judgment of God on the cruel devastation made here by the Conqueror; be it so or not, as Heaven pleases; but that the King was so kill'd, is certain, and they show the tree, on which the arrow glanc'd to this day; in King Charles II time, it was ordered to be surrounded with a pale, but as great part of the paleing is down with age; whether the tree be really so old, or not, is to me a great question; the action being near 700 year ago.

I cannot omit to mention here a proposal made a few years ago to the late Lord Treasurer, Godolphin,[25] for re-peopling this forest, which for some reasons I can be more particular in, than any man now left alive, because I had the honour to draw up the scheme, and argue it before that noble lord, and some others who were principally concern'd at that time in bringing over, or rather providing for when they were come over, the poor inhabitants of the Palatinate;[26] a thing in itself commendable, but as it was manag'd, made scandalous to England, and miserable to those poor people.

I pass'd in this journey over the very spot where the design was laid out; namely, near Lindhurst, in the road from Rumsey to Limington, whither I now directed my course.

Limington is a little, but populous sea port, standing opposite to the Isle of Wight, in the narrow part of the streight, which ships some times pass thro', in fair weather, call'd, the Needles; and right against an ancient town of that island call'd Yarmouth, and which, in distinction from the great town of Yarmouth in Norfolk, is call'd South Yarmouth: this town of Limington is chiefly noted for making fine salt, which is indeed excellent good; and from whence all these south parts of England are supply'd, as well by water as by land carriage; and sometimes, tho' not often, they send salt to London, when contrary winds having kept the northern fleets back, the price at London has been very high; but this is very seldom and uncertain. Limington sends two members to Parliament, and this and her salt trade is all I can say to her; for tho' she is very well situated, as to the convenience of shipping, I do not find they have any foreign commerce, except it be what we call smugling, and roguing; which, I may say, is the reigning commerce of all this part of the English coast, from the mouth of the Thames to the Land's End of Cornwall.

From hence there are but few towns on the sea coast west, tho' there are several considerable rivers empty themselves into the sea, nor are there any harbours, or sea ports of any note, except Pool: As for **Christ Church**, tho' it stands at the mouth of the Avon,

which, as I have said, comes down from Salisbury, and brings with it all the waters of the south and east parts of Wiltshire; and receives also the Stour and Piddle, two Dorsetshire rivers, which bring with them all the waters of the north part of Dorsetshire; yet it is a very inconsiderable poor place, scarce worth seeing, and less worth mentioning in this account; only, that it sends two members to Parliament, which many poor towns in this part of England do, as well as that.

From hence I stept up into the country north-west, to see the ancient town of **Wimburn**, or Wimburnminster; there I found nothing remarkable, but the church, which is indeed a very great one, ancient, and yet very well built, with a very firm strong square tower, considerably high; but was, without doubt, much finer, when on the top of it, stood a most exquisite spire, finer and taller, if fame lyes not, than that at Salisbury, and, by its situation, in a plainer, flatter country, visible, no question, much farther: But this most beautiful ornament was blown down by a sudden tempest of wind, as they tell us, in the year 1622.

Having said this of the church, I have said all that is worth naming of the town; except that the inhabitants, who are many, and poor, are chiefly maintain'd by the manufacture of knitting stockings, which employs great part indeed of the county of Dorset, of which this is the first town eastward.

South of this town, over a sandy wild and barren country, we came to **Pool**, a considerable sea-port, and indeed the most considerable in all this part of England; for here I found some ships, some merchants, and some trade; especially, here were a good number of ships fitted out every year to the Newfoundland fishing, in which the Pool men were said to have been particularly successful for many years past.

The town sits in the bottom of a great bay, or inlet of the sea, which entring at one narrow mouth opens to a very great breadth within the entrance, and comes up to the very shoar of this town; it runs also west up almost to the town of Wareham, a little below which, it receives the rivers Froom and Piddle, the two principle rivers of the county.

This place is famous for the best, and biggest oysters in all this part of England, which the people of Pool pretend to be famous for pickling, and they are barrell'd up here, and sent not only to London, but to the West Indies, and to Spain, and Italy, and other parts. 'Tis observ'd more pearl are found in the Pool oysters, and larger than in any other oysters about England.

As the entrance into this large bay is narrow, so it is

57. 'South View of Corfe Castle'; engraving by Samuel and Nathaniel Buck (1733).

made narrower by an island, call'd Branksey, which lying in the very mouth of the passage, divides it into two, and where there is an old castle, call'd Branksey Castle built to defend the entrance, and this strength was very great advantage to the trade of this port, in the time of the late war with France.

Wareham is a neat town, and full of people, having a share of trade with Pool itself, it shows the ruins of a large town, and 'tis apparent has had eight churches, of which they have three remaining.

South of Wareham, and between the bay I have mention'd and the sea, lyes a large tract of land, which being surrounded by the sea, except on one side is call'd an island, tho' it is really what should be call'd a peninsula; this tract of land is better inhabited than the sea coast of this west end of Dorsetshire generally is, and the manufacture of stockings is carry'd on there also; it is called the Isle of Purbeck, and has in the middle of it a large market-town, call'd Corf, and from the famous castle there, the whole town is now call'd Corf-Castle, it is a corporation, sending members to Parliaments.

This part of the country is eminent for vast quarreys of stone, which is cut out flat, and us'd in London in great quantities for paving court-yards, alleys, avenues to houses, kitchins, foot-ways on the sides of the high-streets, and the like; and is very profitable to the place, as also in the number of shipping employ'd in bringing it to London. There are also several rocks of very good marble, only that the veins in the stone are not black and white, as the Italian, but grey, red, and other colours.

From hence to Weymouth, which is — miles[27] we rode in view of the sea; the country is open, and in

some respects pleasant, but not like the northern parts of the county, which are all fine carpet ground, soft as velvet, and the herbage, sweet as garden herbs, which makes their sheep be the best in England, if not in the world, and their wool fine to an extream.

I cannot omit here a small adventure, which was very surprizing to me on this journey; passing this plain country, we came to an open peice of ground where a neighbouring gentleman had at a great ex-pence laid out a proper peice of land for a Decoy, or Duck-coy, as some call it; the works were but newly done, the planting young, the ponds very large, and well made; but the proper places for shelter of the fowl not cover'd, the trees not being grown, and men were still at work improving, and enlarging, and planting on the adjoyning heath, or common: near the decoy keeper's house, were some places where young decoy-ducks were hatch'd, or otherwise kept to fit them for their work; to preserve them from vermin, polecats, kites, and such like, they had set traps, as is usual in such cases, and a gibbet by it, where abundance of such creatures as were taken were hang'd up for show.

While the decoy man was busy showing the new-works, he was alarm'd with a great cry about this house for help, help, and away he run, like the wind, guessing, as we suppos'd, that something was catch'd in the trap.

It was a good big boy about 13 or 14 year old, that cry'd out, for coming to the place, he found a great fowl catch'd by the leg in the trap, which yet was so strong, and so outrageous, that the boy going too near him, he flew at him, and frighted him, bit him, and beat him with his wings, for he was too strong for the boy; as the master ran from the decoy, so another

58. Dorchester; engraving by John Boydell (1750).

man-servant ran from the house, and finding a strange creature fast in the trap, not knowing what it was, laid at him with a great stick; the creature fought him a good while, but at length he struck him an unlucky blow, which quieted him; after this we all came up to see what was the matter, and found a monstruous eagle caught by the leg in the trap, and kill'd by the fellow's cudgel, as above.

When the master came to know what it was, and that his man had kill'd it, he was ready to kill the fellow for his pains, for it was a noble creature indeed, and would have been worth a great deal to the man to have it shown about the country, or to have sold to any gentleman curious in such things; but the eagle was dead, and there we left it: 'tis probable this eagle had flown over the sea from France, either there, or at the Isle of Weight, where the Channel is not so wide; for we do not find that any eagles are known to breed in those parts of Britain.

From hence we turn'd up to **Dorchester**, the county town, tho' not the largest town in the county; Dorchester is indeed a pleasant agreeable town to live in, and where I thought the people seem'd less divided into factions and parties, than in other places; for though here are divisions and the people are not all of one mind, either as to religion, or politicks, yet they

did not seem to separate with so much animosity as in other places: here I saw the Church of England clergymen, and the Dissenting minister, or preacher drinking tea together, and conversing with civility and good neighbourhood, like catholick Christians, and men of a catholick, and extensive charity: the town is populous, tho' not large, the streets broad, but the buildings old, and low; however, there is good company and a good deal of it; and a man that coveted a retreat in this world might as agreeably spend his time, and as well in Dorchester, as in any town I know in England.

The downs round this town are exceeding pleasant, and come up on every side, even to the very street's end; and here it was that they told me, that there were 600 thousand sheep fed on the downs, within six miles of the town; that is, six miles every way, which is twelve miles in diameter, and thirty six miles in circumference. This I say, I was told, I do not affirm it to be true; but when I viewed the country round, I confess I could not but incline to believe it.

It is observable of these sheep, that they are exceeding fruitful, and the ewes generally bringing two lambs, and they are for that reason bought by all the farmers thro' the east part of England, who come to Burford Fair in this country to buy them, and carry them into Kent and Surry eastward, and into Bucking-

59. 'South View of Portland Castle'; drawing for an engraving by Samuel and Nathaniel Buck (1733).

hamshire, and Bedfordshire, and Oxfordshire north, even our Bansted Downs in Surrey, so fam'd for good mutton, is supply'd from this place: the grass, or herbage of these downs is full of the sweetest, and the most aromatick plants, such as nourish the sheep to a strange degree, and the sheep's dung again nourishes that herbage to a strange degree; so that the valleys are render'd extreamly fruitful, by the washing of the water in hasty showers from off these hills.

From Dorchester it is six miles to the sea side south, and the ocean in view almost all the way: the first town you come to is **Weymouth**, or Weymouth and Melcomb, two towns lying at the mouth of a little rivulet, which they call the Wey, but scarce claims the name of a river; however, the entrance makes a very good, tho' small harbour, and they are joyn'd by a wooden bridge; so that nothing but the harbour parts them; yet they are seperate corporations, and choose each of them two Members of Parliament, just as London and Southwark.

The Isle of **Portland**, on which the castle I mention'd stands, lies right against this port of Weymouth: hence it is, that our best and whitest free stone comes, with which the cathedral of St. Paul's, the Monument, and all the publick edifices in the city of London, are chiefly built; and 'tis wonderful, and well worth the observation of a traveller to see the quarries in the rocks, from whence they are cut out, what stones, and of what prodigious a size are cut out there.

The island is indeed little more than one continued rock of free stone, and the height of the land is such, that from this island they see, in clear weather, above half over the Channel to France, tho' the Channel here is very broad; the sea off of this island, and especially

to the west of it, is counted the most dangerous part of the British Channel: due south, there is almost a continued disturbance in the waters, by reason of what they call two tides meeting, which I take to be no more than the setts of the currents from the French coast, and from the English shore meeting: this they call Portland Race; and several ships, not aware of these currents, have been embay'd to the west of Portland, and been driven on shore on the beach, (of which I shall speak presently) and there lost.

To prevent this danger, and guide the mariner in these distresses, they have, within these few months, set up two light-houses on the two points of that island; and they had not been many months set up, with the directions given to the publick for their bearings, but we found three outward-bound East-India ships which were in distress in the night, in a hard extream gale of wind, were so directed by those lights, that they avoided going on shore by it, which, if the lights had not been there, would inevitably happen'd to their destruction.

This island, tho' seemingly miserable, and thinly inhabited, yet the inhabitants being almost all stone-cutters, we found there was no very poor people among them; and when they collected money for the rebuilding St. Paul's, they got more in this island than in the great town of Dorchester, as we were told.

Tho' Portland stands a league off from the main land of Britain, yet it is almost joyn'd by a prodigious riffe[28] of beach, that is to say, of small stones cast up by the sea, which runs from the island so near the shore of England, that they ferry over with a boat and a rope, the water not being above half a stone's throw over; and the said riffe of beach ending, as it were, at

60. 'North view of Abbotesbury Abby'; engraving by Samuel and Nathaniel Buck (1733).

that inlet of water, turns away west, and runs parallel with the shore quite to Abbotsbury, which is a town about seven miles beyond Weymouth.

On the inside of this beach, and between it, and the land, there is, as I have said, an inlet of water, which they ferry over, as above, to pass and repass to and from Portland: this inlet opens at about two miles west, and grows very broad, and makes a kind of lake within the land of a mile and a half broad, and near three miles in length, the breadth unequal. At the farthest end west of this water is a large duck-coy, and the verge of the water well grown with wood, and proper groves of trees for cover for the foul; in the open lake, or broad part, is a continual assembly of swans: here they live, feed and breed, and the number of them is such, that, I believe, I did not see so few as 7 or 8000. Here they are protected, and here they breed in abundance; we saw several of them upon the wing, very high in the air, whence we supposed, that they flew over the riffe of beach, which parts the lake from the sea to feed on the shores as they thought fit, and so came home again at their leisure.

From this duck-coy west, the lake narrows, and at last almost closes, till the beach joyns the shore; and so Portland may be said not to be an island, but part of the continent; and now we came to **Abbotsbury**, a town anciently famous for a great monastery, and now eminent for nothing but its ruins.

From hence we went on to **Bridport**, a pretty large

corporation town on the sea shore, tho' without a harbour: here we saw boats all the way on the shore fishing for mackerell, which they take in the easiest manner imaginable; for they fix one end of the net to a pole, set deep into the sand, then the net being in a boat, they row right out into the water some length, then turn, and row parallel with the shore, vering out the net all the while, till they have let go all the net, except the line at the end, and then the boat rows on shore, when the men haling the net to the shore at both ends, bring to shore with it such fish, as they surrounded in the little way they rowed; this, at that time, proved to be an incredible number, insomuch, that the men could hardly draw them on shore: as soon as the boats had brought their fish on shore, we observed a guard, or watch, placed on the shore in several places, who we found had their eye not on the fishermen, but on the country people, who came down to the shore to buy their fish; and very sharp we found they were; and some that came with small carts were obliged to go back empty, without any fish. When we came to enquire into the particulars of this, we found, that these were officers placed on the shore by the justices and magistrates of the towns about, who were order'd to prevent the country farmers buying the mackerell to dung their land with them, which was thought to be dangerous, as to infection: In short, such was the plenty of fish that year, that the mackerell, the finest and largest I ever saw, were sold at the sea side a hundred for a penny.

From Bridport, a town in which we see nothing remarkable, we came to **Lime**, the town particularly made famous by the landing of the Duke of Monmouth, and his unfortunate troop, in the time of King James II of which I need say nothing, the history of it being so recent in the memory of so many living.

This is a town of good figure, and has in it several eminent merchants, who carry on a considerable trade to France, Spain, Newfoundland, and the Streights; and tho' they have neither creek or bay, road, or river, they have a good harbour; but 'tis such a one as is not in all Britain besides, if there is such a one in any part of the world.

It is a massy pile of building, consisting of high and thick walls of stone, rais'd, at first, with all the methods that skill and art could devise, but maintain'd now with very little difficulty: The walls are rais'd in the main sea, at a good distance from the shore; it consists of one main and solid wall of stone, large enough for carts and carriages to pass on the top, and to admit houses and ware houses to be built on it; so that it is broad as a street; opposite to this, but farther into the sea, is another wall of the same workmanship,

61. 'Prospect of Lyme 21 August 1723'; engraving after a drawing by William Stukeley. From his *Itinerarium Curiosum* (1724).

which crosses the end of the first wall, and comes about with a tail, parallel to the first wall.

Between the point of the first or main wall, is the entrance into the port, and the second, or opposite wall, breaking the violence of the sea from the entrance, the ships go into the basin, as into a peer, or harbour, and ride there as secure as in a mill pond, or as in a wet dock.

This work is call'd the Cobb: the custom-house officers have a lodge and warehouse upon it, and there were several ships of very good force, and rich in value, in the basin of it when I was there: it might be strengthen'd with a fort, and the walls themselves are firm enough to carry what guns they please to plant upon it; but they did not seem to think it needful; and as the shore is convenient for batteries, they have some guns planted in proper places, both for the defence of the Cobb, and the town also.

This town is under the government of a mayor and aldermen, and may pass for a place of wealth, considering the bigness of it: here we found the merchants began to trade in the pitchard fishing, tho' not to so considerable a degree as they do farther west; the pitchards seldom coming up so high eastward as Portland, and not very often so high as Lime.

While we stay'd here some time viewing this town and coast, we had opportunity to observe the pleasant way of conversation, as it is manag'd among the gentlemen of this county, and their families, which are without reflection some of the most polite and well bred people in the isle of Britain: as their hospitality is very great, and their bounty to the poor remarkable, so their generous friendly way of living with, visiting, and associating one with another is as hard to be describ'd, as it is really to be admir'd; they seem to have a mutual confidence in, and friendship with one another, as if they were all relations; nor did I observe the sharping tricking temper, which is too much crept in among the gameing and horse-racing gentry in some parts of England, to be so much known among them, any otherwise than to be abhorr'd; and yet they sometimes play too, and make matches, and horse-races, as they see occasion.

The ladies here do not want the help of assemblies to assist in match-making; or half-pay officers[29] to run away with their daughters, which the meetings, call'd assemblies in some other parts of England, are recommended for: here's no Bury Fair, where the women are scandalously said to carry themselves to market, and where every night they meet at the play, or at the assembly for intreague, and yet I observ'd that the women do not seem to stick on hand so much in this country, as in those countries, where those assemblies are so lately set up; the reason of which I cannot help saying, if my opinion may bear any weight, is, that the Dorsetshire ladies are equal in beauty, and may be superiour in reputation; in a word, their reputation seems here to be better kept; guarded by better conduct, and manag'd with more prudence, and yet the Dorsetshire ladies, I assure you, are not nuns, they do not go vail'd about streets, or hide themselves when visited; but a general freedom of conversation, agreeable, mannerly, kind, and good runs thro' the whole body of the gentry of both sexes, mix'd with the best of behaviour, and yet govern'd by prudence and modesty; such as I no where see better in all my observation, thro' the whole isle of Britain. In this little interval also I visited some of the biggest towns in the north-west part of this county, as *Blandford*, a town on the river Stour in the road between Salisbury and Dorchester, a handsome well built town, but chiefly famous for making the finest bonelace in England, and where they shew'd me some so exquisitely fine; as I think I never saw better in Flanders, France or Italy, and which they said, they rated at above 30 l. sterling a yard; but I suppose there was not much of this to be had, but 'tis most certain, that they make exceeding rich lace in that county, such as no part of England can equal.

From thence I went west to *Stourbridge*, vulgarly call'd Strabridge; the town, and the country round is employ'd in the manufacture of stockings, and which was once famous for making the finest, best, and highest priz'd knit stockings in England; but that trade now is much decay'd by the encrease of the knitting-stocking engine,[30] or frame, which has destroyed the hand knitting-trade for fine stockings thro' the whole kingdom, of which I shall speak more in its place.

From hence I came to *Shireburn*, a large and populous town, with one collegiate, or conventual church, and may properly claim to have more inhabitants in it than any town in Dorsetshire, tho' it is neither the county town, or does it send members to Parliament; the church is still a reverend pile, and shews the face of great antiquity.

Shaftsbury is also on the edge of this county, adjoyning to Wiltshire and Dorsetshire, being 14 miles from Salisbury, over that fine down or carpet ground, which they call particularly, or properly Salisbury Plain. It has neither house or town in view all the way, and the road which often lyes very broad, and branches off insensibly, might easily cause a traveller to loose his way, but there is a certain never failing

assistance upon all these downs for telling a stranger his way, and that is the number of shepherds feeding, or keeping their vast flocks of sheep, which are every where in the way, and who, with a very little pains, a traveller may always speak with. Nothing can be like it, the Arcadians' plains of which we read so much pastoral trumpery in the poets, could be nothing to them.

This Shaftsbury is now a sorry town, upon the top of a high hill, and which closes the plain, or downs, and whence nature presents you a new scene or prospect, (viz.) of Somerset and Wiltshire, where 'tis all enclosed, and grown with woods, forests, and planted hedge-rows: The county rich, fertile and populous, the towns and houses standing thick, and being large and full of inhabitants, and those inhabitants fully employ'd in the richest and most valuable manufacture in the world, (viz.) the English cloathing, as well, the medley, or mixt clothing, as whites; as well for the home trade, as the foreign trade.

In my return to my western progress, I pass'd some little part of Somersetshire, as thro' Evil, or *Yeovil*, upon the river Ivil, in going to which we go down a long steep hill, which they call Babylon-Hill; but from what original I could find none of the country people to inform me.

It cannot pass my observation here, that when we are come this length from London, the dialect of the English tongue, or the country way of expressing themselves is not easily understood, it is so strangely altered; it is true, that it is so in many parts of England besides, but in none in so gross a degree as in this part; this way of boorish country speech, as in Ireland, it is call'd the brogue upon the tongue; so here 'tis call'd *jouring*,[31] and 'tis certain, that tho' the tongue be all meer natural English, yet those that are but a little acquainted with them, cannot understand one half of what they say: it is not possible to explain this fully by writing, because the difference is not so much in the orthography of words, as in the tone, and diction; their abridging the speech, *cham* for *I am*, *chil* for *I will*, *don*, for *put on*, and *doff*, for *put off*, and the like. And I cannot omit a short story here on this subject; coming to a relation's house,[32] who was a schoolmaster at Martock in Somersetshire, I went into his school to beg the boys a play day, as is usual in such cases; I should have said to beg the Master a play day, but that by the way; coming into the school, I observ'd one of the lowest scholars was reading his lesson to the usher, which lesson it seems was a chapter in the Bible, so I sat down by the master, till the boy had read out his chapter: I observ'd the boy read a little oddly in the tone of the country, which made me the more atten-

XV. Painted wooden panel depicting expulsion of Adam and Eve, Abraham and Isaac and an angel by an unknown artist of the sixteenth century. Discovered in the kitchen of the Angel Inn, Yeovil, when it was demolished. It was probably the inn sign used in Defoe's time.

tive, because on enquiry, I found that the words were the same, and the orthography the same as in all our Bibles. I observ'd also the boy read it out with his eyes still on the book, and his head like a meer boy, moving from side to side, as the lines reach'd cross the columns of the book; his lesson was in the *Cant.* 5. 3. of which the words are these,

"I have put off my coat, how shall I put it on, I have "wash'd my feet, how shall I defile them?

The boy read thus, with his eyes, as I say full on the text.

"Chav a doffed my cooat, how shall I don't, chav a "wash'd. my veet, how shall I moil'em?

How the dexterous dunce could form his mouth to express so readily the words, (which stood right printed in the book) in his country jargon, I could not but admire; I shall add to this another peice as diverting, which also happen'd in my knowledge at this very town of Yeovil, tho' some years ago.

There liv'd a good substantial family in the town, not far from the Angel Inn, a well known house, which was then, and I suppose is still the chief inn of the town. This family had a dog, which among his other good qualities, for which they kept him (for he was a rare house dog) had this bad one, that he was a most notorious thief; but withal, so cunning a dog, and managed himself so warily, that he preserved a mighty good reputation among the neighbourhood; as the family was well beloved in the town, so was the

dog; he was known to be a very useful servant to them, especially in the night, when he was fierce as a lion, but in the day the gentlest, lovingest creature that could be, and as they said, all the neighbours had a good word for this dog.

It happen'd that the good wife, or mistress at the Angel Inn, had frequently missed several peices of meat out of the pail, as they say, or powdering-tub,[33] as we call it; and that some very large peices; 'tis also to be observ'd the dog did not stay to eat (what he took) upon the spot, in which case some peices, or bones, or fragments might be left, and so it might be discover'd to be a dog; but he made cleaner work, and when he fasten'd upon a peice of meat he was sure to carry it quite away, to such retreats as he knew he could be safe in, and so feast upon it at leisure.

It happen'd at last, as with most thieves it does, that the inn-keeper was too cunning for him, and the poor dog was nabb'd, taken in the fact, and could make no defence.

Having found the thief, and got him in custody, the master of the house, a good humour'd fellow, and loth to disoblige the dog's master, by executing the criminal, as the dog-law directs; mitigates his sentence, and handled him as follows; first taking out his knife, he cut off both his ears, and then bringing him to the threshold, he chop'd off his tail; and having thus effectually dishonour'd the poor cur among his neighbours, he tyed a string about his neck, and a peice of paper to the string directed to his master, and with these witty west country verses on it.

62. 'The South West Prospect of the City of Exeter'; engraving by Samuel and Nathaniel Buck (1736).

To my Honour'd Master —— Esq;

Hail Master a cham a' com hoam
So cut as an ape, and tail have I noan,
For stealing of beef, and pork, out of the pail,
For thease they'v cut my ears, for th' wother
    my tail;
Nea Measter, and us tell thee more nor that
And's come there again, my brains will be flat.

From Evil we came to Crookorn, thence to Chard, and from thence into the same road I was in before at **Honiton**.

This is a large and beautiful market-town, very populous, and well built, and is so very remarkably pav'd with small pebbles, that on either sides the way a little channel is left shouldered up on the sides of it; so that it holds a small stream of fine clear running water with a little square dipping place left at every door, so that every family in the town has a clear clean running river, (as it may be call'd) just at their own door, and this so much finer, so much pleasanter, and agreeable to look on, then that at Salisbury, which they boast so much of, that in my opinion, there is no comparison.

Here we see the first, of the great serge manufacture of Devonshire, a trade too great to be describ'd in miniature, as it must be, if I undertake it here; and which takes up this whole county, which is the largest

and most populous in England, Yorkshire excepted, (which ought to be esteem'd three counties, and is indeed divided as such into the East, West and North Riding;) but Devonshire one entire county, is so full of great towns, and those towns so full of people, and those people so universally employ'd in trade, and manufactures, that not only it cannot be equall'd in England, but perhaps not in Europe.

In my travel thro' Dorsetshire, I ought to have observ'd that the biggest towns in that county sent no members to Parliament, and that the smallest did; that is to say, that Sherborn, Blandford, Winbornminster, Sturmister, and several other towns choose no members, whereas Weymouth, Melcom, and Bridport, were all burgess towns; but now we come to Devonshire, we find almost all the great towns, and some smaller choosing members also.

From Honiton the country is exceeding pleasant still, and on the road they have a beautiful prospect almost all the way to Exeter, which is twelve miles; on the left hand of this road lyes that part of the county, which they call the South Hams, and which is famous for the best cyder in that part of England; also the town of **St. Mary Oterey**, commonly call'd St. Mary Autree: They tell us the name is deriv'd from the River Ottery, and that, from the multitude of otters found always in that river, which however to me seems

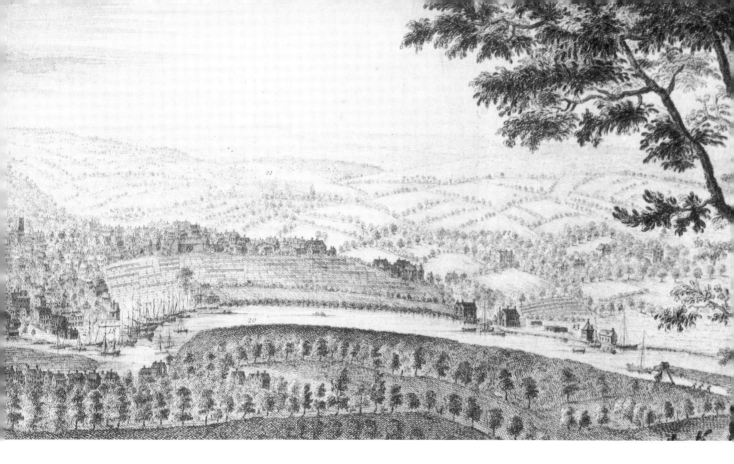

fabulous; nor does there appear to be any such great number of otters in that water, or in the county about, more than is usual in other counties, or in other parts of the county about them; they tell us they send 20000 hogsheds of cyder hence every year to London, and which is still worse, that it is most of it bought there by the merchants to mix with their wines, which if true, is not much to the reputation of the London vintners; but that by the by.

From hence we came to **Exeter**, a city famous for two things, which we seldom find unite in the same town, (viz.) that 'tis full of gentry, and good company, and yet full of trade and manufactures also; the serge market held here every week is very well worth a stranger's seeing, and next to the Brigg-Market at Leeds in Yorkshire, is the greatest in England. The people assur'd me that at this market is generally sold from 60 to 70 to 80, and sometimes a hundred thousand pounds value in serges in a week. I think 'tis kept on Mondays.

They have the river Esk here, a very considerable river, and principal in the whole county; and within three miles, or thereabouts, it receives ships of any ordinary burthen, the port there being call'd Topsham; but now by the application, and at the expence of the citizens, the channel of the river is so widened, deepen'd, and cleans'd from the shoal, which would

otherwise interrupt the navigation, that the ships come now quite up to the city, and there with ease both deliver and take in their lading.

This city drives a very great correspondence with Holland, as also directly to Portugal, Spain and Italy; shipping off vast quantities of their woollen-manufactures, especially, to Holland, the Dutch giving very large commissions here for the buying of serges, perpetuanas, and such goods; which are made not only in and about Exeter, but at Crediton, Honiton, Culliton, St. Mary Autry, Newton-Bushell, Ashburton and especially at Tiverton, Cullumbton, Bampton, and all the north east part of the county.

Excester is a large rich, beautiful, populous, and was once a very strong city; but as to the last, as the castle, the walls, and all the old works are demolish'd, so were they standing, the way of managing seiges, and attacks of towns is such now, and so alter'd from what it was in those days, that Excester in the utmost strength it could ever boast, would not now hold out five days open trenches; nay, would hardly put an army to the trouble of opening trenches against it at all.

About 22 miles from Excester we go to **Totness**, on the river Dart. This is a very good town; of some trade, but has more gentlemen in it than tradesmen of note; they have a very fine stone-bridge here over the river, which being within seven or eight mile of the

63. Detail from 'South East view of Totnes Castle'; watercolour by Samuel Buck (1734). The mill described by Defoe is situated to the left of the bridge.

XVI. George Lambert with, traditionally, William Hogarth, *Landscape with haymakers* (*c.*1730–40).

64. 'The South East View of Dartmouth Castle'; engraving by Samuel and Nathaniel Buck (1734).

sea, is very large, and the tide flows 10 or 12 foot at the bridge. Here we had the diversion of seeing them catch fish, with the assistance of a dog. The case is this, on the south side of the river, and on a slip, or narrow cut or channel made on purpose for a mill, there stands a corn-mill; the mill tayl, or floor for the water below the wheels is wharft up on either side with stone, above high-water mark, and for above 20 or 30 foot in length below it, on that part of the river towards the sea; at the end of this wharfing is a grating of wood, the cross-bars of which stand bearing inward, sharp at the end, and pointing inward towards one another, as the wyers of a mouse-trap.

When the tide flows up, the fish can with ease go in between the points of these cross-bars, but the mill being shut down they can go no farther upwards; and when the water ebbs again, they are left behind, not being able to pass the points of the grating, as above, outwards; which like a mouse-trap keeps them in, so that they are left at the bottom with about a foot, or a foot and half water. We were carryed hither at low water, where we saw about 50 or 60 small salmon, about 17 to 20 inches long, which the country people call salmon peal,[34] and to catch these, the person who went with us, who was our landlord at a great inn next the bridge, put in a net on a hoop at the end of a pole, the pole going cross the hoop, which we call in this country a shove net: the net being fix'd at one end of the place they put in a dog, who was taught his trade before hand, at the other end of the place, and he

drives all the fish into the net, so that only holding the net still in its place, the man took up two or three and thirty salmon peal at the first time.

Of these we took six for our dinner, for which they ask'd a shilling, (viz.) two pence a peice, and for such fish not at all bigger, and not so fresh, I have seen 6s. 6d. each given at a London fish-market, whither they are some time brought from Chichester by land carriage.

From hence we went still south about seven miles, (all in view of this river) to **Dartmouth**, a town of note, seated at the mouth of the river Dart, and where it enters into the sea at a very narrow, but safe entrance; The opening into Dartmouth Harbour is not broad, but the channel deep enough for the biggest ship in the Royal Navy; the sides of the entrance are high mounded with rocks; without which just at the first narrowing of the passage, stands a good strong fort without a platform of guns, which commands the port.

The narrow entrance is not much above half a mile, when it opens and makes a basin, or harbour able to receive 500 sail of ships of any size, and where they may ride with the greatest safety, even as in a mill-pond, or wet-dock: I had the curiosity here with the assistance of a merchant of the town to go out to the mouth of the haven in a boat to see the entrance, and castle, or fort that commands it; and coming back with the tide of flood, I observ'd some small fish to skip, and play upon the surface of the water, upon which I ask'd my friend what fish they were; immediately one of the rowers or seamen starts up in the boat, and throwing his arms abroad, as if he had been bet-witch'd, cryes out as loud as he could baul, a scool, a scool. The word was taken to the shore as hastily as it would have been on land if he had cry'd fire; and by that time we reach'd the keys, the town was all in a kind of an uproar.

The matter was, that a great shoal, or as they call it a scool of pilchards came swimming with the tide of flood directly, out of the sea into the harbour. My friend whose boat we were in, told me this was a surprize which he would have been very glad of, if he could but have had a day's or two's warning, for he might have taken 200 tun of them, and the like was the case of other merchants in town; for in short, no body was ready for them, except a small fishing boat, or two; one of which went out into the middle of the harbour, and at two or three hawls, took about forty thousand of them. We sent our servant to the key to buy some, who for a half-penny, brought us seven-teen, and if he would have taken them, might have had as many more for the same money; with these we went to dinner; the cook at the inn broil'd them for us, which is their way of dressing them, with pepper and salt, which cost us about a farthing; so that two of us, and a servant din'd, and at a tavern too; for three farthings, dressing and all, and this is the reason of telling the tale; what drink, wine, or beer we had, I do not remember, but whatever it was, that we paid for by itself; but for our food we really din'd for three farthings, and very well too: Our friend treated us the next day with a dish of large lobsters, and I being curious to know the value of such things, and having freedom enough with him to enquire; I found that for 6d. or 8d. they bought as good lobsters there, as would have cost in London 3s. to 3s. 6d. each.

In observing the coming in of those pilchards, as above, we found that out at sea, in the offing, beyond the mouth of the harbour there was a whole army of porpuses, which as they told us pursued the pilchards, and 'tis probable drove them into the harbour, as above. The scool it seems drove up the river a great way, even as high as Totness bridge, as we heard afterwards; so that the country people who had boats, and nets, catch'd as many as they knew what to do with, and perhaps liv'd upon pilchards for several days; but as to the merchants and trade, their coming was so suddain, that it was no advantage to them.

A little to the southward of this town, and to the east of the port, is **Torbay**, of which I know nothing proper to my observation, more than that it is a very good road for ships, tho' sometimes, especially with a southerly, or S.E. wind, ships have been oblig'd to quit the bay, and put out to sea, or run into Dartmouth for shelter.

This town as most of the towns of Devonshire are, is full of Dissenters, and a very large meeting-house they have here; how they act here with respect to the great dispute about the doctrine of the Trinity,[35] which has caus'd such a breach among those people at Excester, and other parts of the county, I cannot give any account of. This town sends two members to Parliament.

From hence we went to Plympton, a poor and thinly inhabited town, tho' blest with the like privilege of sending members to the Parliament; of which I have little more to say, but that from thence the road lyes to Plymouth, distance about six miles.

Plymouth, is indeed a town of consideration, and of great importance to the publick. The situation of it between two very large inlets of the sea, and in the bottom of a large bay, which is very remarkable for the advantage of navigation. The sound, or bay is compass'd on every side with hills, and the shoar generally steep and rocky, tho' the anchorage is good, and it is pretty safe riding: In the entrance to this bay, lyes a large and most dangerous rock, which at high-water is cover'd, but at low-tide lyes bare, where many a good ship has been lost, even in the view of safety, and many a ship's crew drown'd in the night, before help could be had for them.

Upon this rock, which was call'd the Edystone, from its situation, the famous Mr. Winstanley[36] under-took to build a light-house for the direction of sailors, and with great art, and expedition finish'd it; which work considering its height, the magnitude of its building, and the little hold there was, by which it was possible to fasten it to the rock, stood to admiration, and bore out many a bitter storm.

Mr. Winstanly often visited, and frequently strength-en'd the building, by new works, and was so confident of its firmness, and stability, that he usually said, he only desir'd to be in it when a storm should happen, for many people had told him, it would certainly fall, if it came to blow a little harder than ordinary.

But he happen'd at last to be in it once too often; namely, when that dreadful tempest blew, Nov. the 27, 1703. This tempest began on the Wednesday be-fore, and blew with such violence, and shook the light-house so much, that as they told me there, Mr. Winstanly would fain have been on shoar, and made signals for help, but no boats durst go off to him; and to finish the tragedy, on the Friday, Nov. 26, when the tempest was so redoubled, that it became a terror to the whole nation; the first sight there seaward, that the

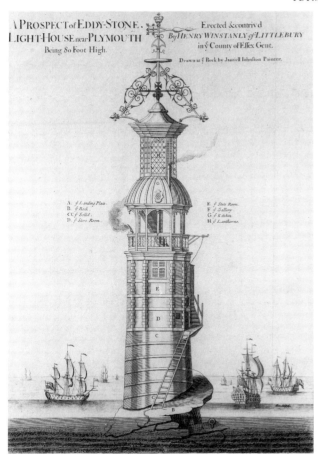

EDDYSTONE LIGHTHOUSE

The first lighthouse designed by Henry Winstanley and made of timber was destroyed in a storm in 1703. The second lighthouse designed in 1708 and constructed of timber and iron by John Rudyerd was destroyed by fire in 1755.

65 (left). 'A Prospect of Eddystone Lighthouse, near Plymouth, being 80 foot high, erected and contrivd by Henry Winstanly...'; engraving by I. Sturt after a drawing by Jaaziell Johnston (*c.*1700).

66. 'Edystone Lighthouse, being 90 foot high' (1725). Published by Joseph Smyth.

people of Plymouth, were presented with in the morning after the storm, was the bare Eddystone, the lighthouse being gone; in which Mr. Winstantly, and all that were with him perish'd, and were never seen, or heard of since: but that which was a worse loss still, was, that a few days after a merchant's ship call'd the *Winchelsea* homeward bound from Virginia, not knowing the Eddystone light-house was down; for want of the light that should have been seen run foul of the rock itself, and was lost with all her lading, and most of her men; but there is now another light-house built on the same rock.

One thing, which I was a witness too, on a former journey to this place, I cannot omit: It was the next year after that great storm, and but a little sooner in the year, being in August, I was at Plymouth, and walking on the Hoo, which is a plain on the edge of the sea, looking to the road, I observ'd the evening so serene, so calm, so bright, and the sea so smooth, that a finer sight, I think, I never saw; there was very little wind, but what was, seem'd to be westerly; and, about an hour after, it blew a little breeze at south west, with which wind there came into the sound, that night, and the next morning, a fleet of fourteen sail of ships, from Barbadoes; richly loaden, for London: Having been long at sea, most of the captains and passengers came on shore to refresh themselves, as is usual, after such tedious voyages, and the ships rode all in the sound on that side next to Catwater: as is customary, upon safe arriving to their native country, there was a general joy and rejoycing, both on board and on shore.

The next day the wind began to freshen, especially in the afternoon, and the sea to be disturb'd, and very hard it blew at night, but all was well for that time; but the night after it blew a dreadful storm, not much inferior, for the time it lasted, to the storm mention'd above, which blew down the light-house on the Eddy Stone; about midnight the noise indeed was very dreadful, what with the roaring of the sea, and of the wind, intermix'd with the firing of guns for help from the ships, the cries of the seamen and people on shore, and, which was worse, the cries of those, which were driven on shore by the tempest, and dash'd in pieces. In a word, all the fleet, except three, or thereabouts, were dash'd to pieces against the rocks, and sunk in the sea, most of the men being drowned: those three, who were sav'd, receiv'd so much damage, that their lading was almost all spoil'd: one ship in the dark of the night, the men not knowing where they were, run into Catwater, and run on shore there, by which she was however sav'd from shipwreck, and the lives of her crew were saved also.

This was a melancholly morning indeed; nothing was to be seen but wrecks of the ships, and a foaming furious sea, in that very place where they rode all in joy and triumph, but the evening before: The captains, passengers and officers who were, as I have said, gone on shoar, between the joy of saving their lives, and the affliction of having lost their ships, their cargoes, and their friends, were objects indeed worth our compassion and observation; and there were a great variety of the passions to be observ'd in them: now lamenting their losses, then giving thanks for their deliverance; the various cases were indeed very affecting, and, in many things, very instructing.

As, I say, Plymouth lyes in the bottom of this Sound, in the center between the two waters, so there lies against it, in the same position, an island, which they call St. Nicholas, on which there is a castle, which commands the entrance into Ham-Oze, and indeed that also into Catwater in some degree: in this island the famous General Lambert, one of Cromwell's great agents, or officers in the rebellion was imprison'd for life, and liv'd many years there.

On the shore, over-against this island, is the citadel of Plymouth, a small, but regular fortification, inaccessible by sea, but not exceeding strong by land, except that they say the works are of a stone, hard as marble, and would not soon yield to the batteries of an enemy: but that is a language our modern engineers[37] now laugh at.

The town stands above this, upon the same rock, and lyes sloping on the side of it, towards the east; the

67. The Citadel of Plymouth; copper engraving by C. Mosley after S. Mace (1737).

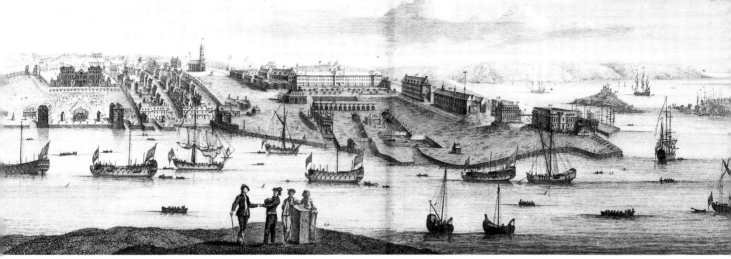

68. 'The West Prospect of His Majesties Dock-Yard, near Plymouth'; engraving by Samuel and Nathaniel Buck (1736).

inlet of the sea, which is call'd Catwater, and which is a harbour, capable of receiving any number of ships, and of any size, washing the eastern shore of the town.

The other inlet of the sea, as I term it, is on the other side of the town, and is call'd Ham-Oze, being the mouth of the river Tamar, a considerable river, which parts the two counties of Devon and Cornwall: here the war with France making it necessary that the ships of war should have a retreat nearer hand than at Portsmouth, the late King William order'd a wet dock, with yards, dry docks, launches, and conveniencies of all kinds for building, and repairing of ships to be built; and with these follow'd necessarily the building of store-houses and ware-houses, for the rigging, sails, naval and military stores, &c. of such ships as may be appointed to be laid up there, as now several are, with very handsome houses for the Commissioners, clerks, and officers of all kinds usual in the king's yards, to dwell in: it is in short, now become as compleat an arsenal, or yard, for building and fitting men of war as any the government are masters of, and perhaps much more convenient than some of them, tho' not so large.

From Plymouth we pass the Tamar, over a ferry to **Saltash**, a little poor shatter'd town, the first we sat foot on in the county of Cornwall. The Tamar here is very wide, and the ferry boats bad, so that I thought myself escap'd, when I got safe on shore in Cornwall.

Saltash seems to be the ruins of a larger place, and we saw many houses as it were falling down, and I doubt not but the mice and rats have abandoned many more, as they say they will, when they are likely to fall; yet this town is govern'd by a mayor and aldermen, has many privileges, sends members to Parliament, takes toll of all vessels that pass the river, and have the sole oyster fishing in the whole river, which is considerable.

This town has a kind of jurisdiction upon the river Tamar down to the mouth of the port, so that they claim anchorage of all small ships that enter the river, their coroner sits upon all dead bodies that are found drown'd in the river, and the like, but they make not much profit of them.

They talk of some merchants beginning to trade here, and they have some ships that use the Newfoundland fishery; but I could not hear of any thing considerable they do in it, there is no other considerable town up the Tamar, till we come to Lanceston, the county town, which I shall take in my return, so I turn'd west, keeping the south shore of the county, to the Lands End.

From Saltash I went to **Liskard**, about 7 miles. This is a considerable town, well built, has people of fashion in it, and a very great market; it also sends two members to Parliament, and is one of the five towns, call'd Stannary towns, that is to say, where the blocks of tinn are brought to the coinage, of which by itself; this coinage of tinn is an article very much to the advantage of the towns where it is settled, tho' the money paid goes another way.

This town of Liskard was once eminent, had a good castle, and a large house, where the antient Dukes of Cornwall kept their court in those days; also it enjoy'd

69. The Tamar, near Cothele, Cornwall; drawing by Edmund Prideaux (c.1727).

several privileges, especially by the favour of the Black Prince, who, as Prince of Wales, and Duke of Cornwall resided here; and in return, they say this town, and the country round it, rais'd a great body of stout young fellows, who entered into his service, and followed his fortunes in his wars in France, as also in Spain; but these buildings are so decay'd, that there are now scarce any of the ruins of the castle, or of the prince's court remaining.

The only publick edifices they have now to show, are the Guild, or Town-Hall, on which there is a turret with a fine clock; a very good free-school, well provided; a very fine conduit in the market-place; an antient large church, and which is something rare, for the county of Cornwall, a large new built meeting-house for the Dissenters, which I name, because they assur'd me there was but three more, and those very inconsiderable in all the county of Cornwall; whereas in Devonshire, which is the next county, there are reckon'd about seventy, some of which are exceeding large and fine.

This town is also remarkable for a very great trade in all manufactures of leather, such as boots, shoes, gloves, purses, breeches, &c. and some spinning of late years is set up here, encourag'd by the woollen manufacturers of Devonshire.

Between these two towns of Saltash and Liskard, is **St. Germans**, now a village, decay'd, and without any market, but the largest parish in the whole county; in the bounds of which is contained, as they report, 17 villages, and the town of Saltash among them, for Saltash has no parish church, it seems of itself but as a chappel of ease to St. Germans: in the neighbourhood of these towns are many pleasant seats of the Cornish gentry, who are indeed very numerous, tho' their estates may not be so large, as is usual in England; yet neither are they despicable in that part, and in particular this may be said of them, that as they generally live cheap, and are more at home than in other counties, so they live more like gentlemen, and keep more within bounds of their estates than the English generally do, take them altogether.

Add to this, that they are the most sociable, generous, and to one another, the kindest neighbours that are to be found; and as they generally live, as we may say, together, for they are almost always at one another's houses, so they generally intermarry among themselves, the gentlemen seldom going out of the county for a wife, or the ladies for a husband, from whence they say, that proverb upon them was rais'd (viz.) *That all the Cornish gentlemen are cousins.*

On the hills north of Liskard, and in the way between Liskard and Lanceston, there are many tinn

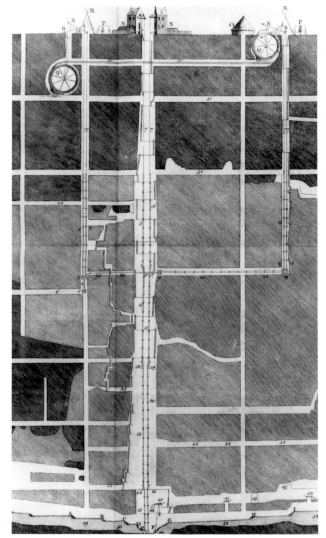

70. Bullen Garden tin mine, Cambourne; engraving by J. Barber and T. Kitchin From William Pryce, *Mineralogia Cornubiensis* (1778).

mines, and as they told us some of the richest veins of that metal are found there, that are in the whole county; the metal when cast at the blowing houses into blocks, being as above, carry'd to Liskard to be coin'd.

From Liskard, in our course west, we are necessarily carry'd to the sea coast, because of the river Fowey, or Fowath, which empties itself into the sea, at a very large mouth, and hereby this river rising in the middle of the breadth of the county, and running south, and the river Camel rising not far from it, and running north, with a like large channel, the land from Bodmyn to the western part of the county is almost made an island, and in a manner cut off from the eastern part, the peninsula, or neck of land between, being not above twelve miles over.

On this south side we came to **Foy**, or Fowey, an

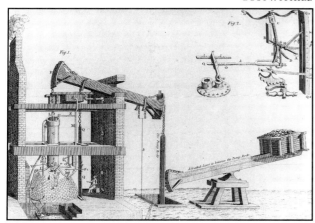

71. Steam fire engine used to provide power in tin mines; engraving. From William Pryce, *Mineralogia Cornubiensis* (1778).

antient town, and formerly very large; nay, not large only, but powerful and potent, for the Foyens, as they were then call'd, were able to fit out large fleets, not only for merchant's ships, but even of men of war; and with these not only fought with, but several times vanquished, and routed the squadron of the Cinque Port men, who in those days were thought very powerful.

The river Fowey, which is very broad and deep here, was formerly navigable by ships of good burthen as high as **Lestwithiel** an antient, and once a flourishing, but now a decay'd town, and as to trade and navigation quite destitute, which is occasioned by the river being fill'd up with sands. This town of Lestwithiel, retains however several advantages, which support its figure, as first, that it is one of the Coinage Towns, as I call them, or Stannary Towns, as others call them. (2.) The common goal for the whole Stannary is here, as are also the county courts for the whole county of Cornwall.

Behind Foye, and nearer to the coast at the mouth of a small river, which some call Lowe, tho' without any authority, there stand two towns opposite to one another, bearing the name of the river Loe, that is to say, distinguish'd by the addition of East Loe, and West Loe. These are both good trading towns, and especially fishing towns and which is very particular, are like Weymouth and Melcomb, in Dorsetshire, seperated only by the creek, or river; and yet each of them send members to Parliaments: these towns are joyn'd together by a very beautiful and stately stone bridge having fifteen arches.

East Loo, was the antienter corporation of the two, and for some ages ago the greater and more consuderable town; but now they tell us West Loo is the richest, and has the most ships belonging to it: were they put together, they would make a very handsome seaport town. They have a great fishing trade here, as well for supply of the country, as for merchandize, and the towns are not dispisable; but as to sending four members to the British Parliament, which is as many as the city of London chooses, that I confess seems a little scandalous, but to who, is none of my business to enquire.

Passing from hence, and ferrying over Foy river, or the river Foweth, call it as ye please, we come into a large country without many towns in it of note, but very well furnished with gentlemen's seats, and a little higher up with tinn works.

The sea making several deep bays here, they who travel by land are oblig'd to go higher into the country to pass above the water, especially at Trewardreth Bay, which lyes very broad, above ten miles within the country, which passing at Trewardreth, a town of no great note, tho' the bay takes its name from it, the next inlet of the sea, is the famous firth, or inlet, call'd Falmouth Haven. It is certainly next to Milford Haven in South Wales, the fairest and best road for shipping that is in the whole Isle of Britain, when there be considered the depth of water for above twenty miles within land; the safety of riding, shelter'd from all kind of winds or storms, the good anchorage, and the many creeks, all navigable, where ships may run in and be safe, so that the like is no where to be found.

St. Mawes and Pendennis are two fortifications placed at the points, or enterance of this Haven, opposite to one another, tho' not with a communication, or view; they are very strong; the first principally by sea, having a good platform of guns, pointing thwart the Channel, and planted on a level with the water; but Pendennis Castle is strong by land as well as by water, is regularly fortified, has good out works, and generally a strong garrison; St. Mawes, otherwise call'd St. Mary's has a town annex'd to the castle, and is a borough, sending members to the Parliament. Pendennis is a meer fortress, tho' there are some habitations in it too, and some at a small distance near the sea side, but not of any great consideration.

The town of **Falmouth** is by much the richest, and best trading town in this county, tho' not so antient as its neighbour town of Truro; and indeed, is in some things oblig'd to acknowledge the seigniorty; namely, that in the corporation of Truro, the person who they choose to be their mayor of Truro, is also mayor of Falmouth of course. How the jurisdiction is manag'd, is an account too long for this place; the Truro men also receive several duties collected in Falmouth, particularly wharfage for the merchandizes landed, or shipp'd off.

72. 'Pendennis and St Mawes castles, October 9, 1727'; drawing by Edmund Prideaux.

73. Falmouth; map. From Greenvile Collins, *Great Britain's Coasting Pilot* (1693).

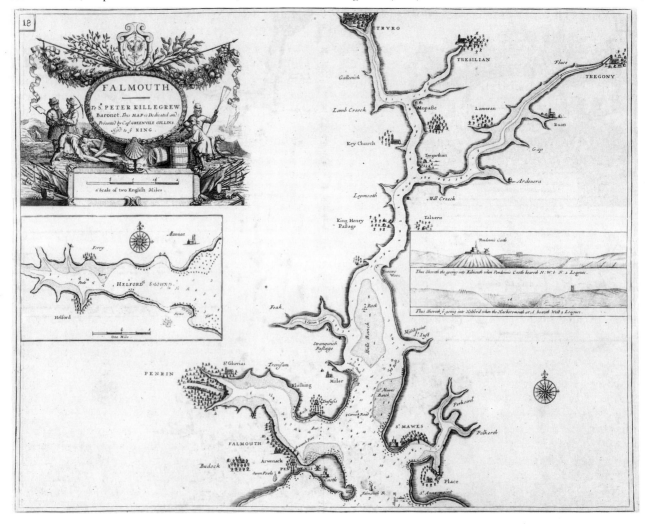

But let this be as it will, the trade is now in a manner wholly gone to Falmouth, the trade at Truro, being now chiefly if not only for the shipping off of block tinn and copper oar, the latter being lately found in large quantities in some of the mountains between Truro, and St. Michaels, and which is much improv'd since the several mills are erected at Bristol, and other parts, for the manufactures of battery ware or, as 'tis call'd, brass, which is made out of English copper, most of it dug in these parts; the oar itself also being found very rich and good.

Falmouth is well built, has abundance of shipping belonging to it, is full of rich merchants, and has a flourishing and encreasing trade. I say encreasing, because by the late setting up the English packets[38] between this port and Lisbon, there is a new commerce between Portugal and this town, carried on to a very great value.

It is true, part of this trade was founded in a clandestine commerce, carried on by the said packets at Lisbon, where being the king's ships, and claiming the privilege of not being searched, or visited by the custom-house officers, they found means to carry off great quantities of British manufactures, which they sold on board to the Portuguese merchants, and they convey'd them on shoar, as 'tis supposed without paying custom.

But the government there, getting intelligence of it, and complaint being made in England also, where it was found to be very prejudicial to the fair merchant, that trade has been effectually stopp'd; but the Falmouth merchants having by this means gotten a taste of the Portuguese trade, have maintain'd it ever since in ships of their own: these packets bring over such vast quantities of gold in specie, either in moidores, which is the Portugal coin, or in bars of gold, that I am very credible inform'd the carryer from Falmouth, brought by land from thence to London, at one time, in the month of January, 1722, or near it, eighty thousand moidores in gold, which came from Lisbon in the pacquet boats, for account of the merchants at London, and that it was attended with a guard of 12 horsemen well arm'd, for which the said carryer had half per cent. for his hazard.

Truro is however a very considerable town too; it stands up the water north and by east from Falmouth in the utmost extended branch of the haven, in the middle, between the conflux of two rivers, which tho' not of any long course, have a very good appearance for a port, and make a large wharf between them in the front of the town; and the water here makes a good port for small ships, tho' it be at the influx, but not for ships of burthen. This is the particular town where the

Lord Warden of the Stannaries always holds his famous Parliament of Miners, and for stamping of tinn. The town is well built, but shews that it has been much fuller, both of houses and inhabitants, than it is now; nor will it probably ever rise, while the town of Falmouth stands where it does, and while the trade is settled in it, as it is. There are at least three churches in it, but no Dissenter's meeting house, that I could hear of.

Penryn, is up the same branch of the Haven, as Falmouth, but stands four miles higher towards the west, yet ships come to it of as great a size, as can come to Truro itself; it is a very pleasant agreeable town, and for that reason has many merchants in it, who would perhaps otherwise live at Falmouth. The chief commerce of these towns, as to their sea affairs, is the pilchards, and Newfoundland fishing, which is very profitable to them all; it had formerly a conventual church, with a chantry, and a religious house, a cel to Kirton, but they are all demolish'd, and scarce the ruins of them distinguishable enough to know one part from another.

Quiting Falmouth Haven from Penryn west, we came to *Helsten*, about 7 Miles, and stands upon the little river Cober, which however, admits the sea so into its bosom as to make a tolerable good harbour for ships a little below the town. It is the fifth town, allow'd for the coining tinn, and several of the ships call'd tinn ships are loaden here.

This town is large and populous, and has four spacious streets, a handsome church, and a good trade: this town also sends members to Parliament. Beyond this is a market town tho' of no resort for trade, call'd

74. Details of tin miners and fishermen from a cartouche of the map of Falmouth in Greenvile Collins, *Great Britain's Coasting Pilot* (1693).

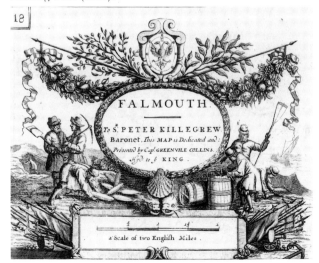

75. 'North East Prospect of Penzance'; wash drawing by R. Scadden (1747).

Market Jew, it lyes indeed on the sea-side, but has no harbour or safe road for shipping.

Pensance, is the farthest town of any note west, being 254 miles from London, and within about ten miles of the promontory, call'd the Lands End; so that this promontory is from London 264 miles, or there-abouts: this town of Pensance is a place of good business, well built and populous, has a good trade, and a great many ships belonging to it, notwithstanding it is so remote. Here are also a great many good families of gentlemen, tho' in this utmost angle of the nation; and, which is yet more strange, the veins of lead, tinn, and copper oar, are said to be seen, even to the utmost extent of land at low water mark, and in the very sea; so rich, so valuable a treasure is contain'd in these parts of Great Britain, tho' they are suppos'd to be so poor, because so very remote from London, which is the center of our wealth.

Between this town and St. Burien, a town midway

between it and the Land's End, stands a circle of great stones,[39] not unlike those at Stonehenge in Wiltshire, with one bigger than the rest in the middle; they stand about 12 foot asunder, but have no inscription, neither does tradition offer to leave any part of their history upon record; as whether it was a trophy, or a monument of burial, or an altar for worship, or what else; so that all that can be learn'd of them, is, that *here they are*: the parish where they stand is call'd Boscawone, from whence the ancient and honourable family of Boscawen derive their names.

Near Pensance, but open to the sea, is that gulph they call Mounts Bay, nam'd so from a high hill standing in the water, which they call St. Michael's Mount; the seamen call it only, the Cornish Mount; it has been fortify'd, tho' the situation of it makes it so difficult of access, that like the Bass in Scotland, there needs no fortification; like the Bass too, it was once made a prison for prisoners of state, but now it is wholly

102

76. 'South West Prospect of St Michael's Mount'; engraving by Samuel and Nathaniel Buck (1739).

neglected; there is a very good road here for shipping, which makes the town of Pensance be a place of good report.

A little up in the county towards the north west is Goodolchan, which tho' a hill, rather than a town, gives name to the noble and ancient family of Godolphin; and nearer on the northern coast is Royalton, which since the late Sydney Godolphin, Esq; a younger brother of the family, was created Earl of Godolphin, gave title of Lord to his eldest son, who was call'd Lord Royalton during the life of his father. This place also is infinitely rich in tinn mines.

I am now at my journey's end; as to the islands of Scilly, which lye beyond the Land's End, I shall say something of them presently: I must now return *sur mes pas*, as the French call it; tho' not literally so, for I shall not come back the same way I went; but as I have coasted the south shore to the Land's End, I shall come back by the north coast, and my observations in my return will furnish very well materials for a fourth letter.

I am, &c.

The End of the Third Letter

APPENDIX TO LETTER III

I HAVE ENDED THIS account at the utmost extent of the island of Great Britain west, without visiting those excrescences of the island, as I think I may call them, (viz.) the Rocks of Scilly, of which, what is most famous, is their infamy, or reproach; namely, how many good ships are, almost continually dash'd in pieces there, and how many brave lives lost, in spight of the mariners' best skill, or the light-houses, and other sea-marks best notice.

These islands lye so in the middle between the two vast openings of the north and south narrow seas, or as the sailors call them, the Bristol Channel, and The Channel, (so call'd by way of eminence) that it cannot, or perhaps never will be avoided, but that several ships in the dark of the night, and in stress of weather may by being out in their reckonings, or other unavoidable accidents mistake, and if they do, they are sure, as the sailors call it, to run *bump a shore* upon Scilly, where they find no quarter among the breakers, but are beat to pieces, without any possibility of escape.

One can hardly mention the Bishop and his Clerks, as they are call'd, or the Rocks of Scilly, without letting fall a tear to the memory of Sir Cloudesly Shovel,[40] and all the gallant spirits that were with him at one blow, and without a moment's warning dash'd into a state of immortality; the admiral with three men of war, and all their men (running upon these Rocks, right afore the wind, and in a dark night) being lost there, and not a man sav'd. But all our annals and histories are full of this, so I need say no more.

They tell us of eleven sail of merchant ships home-ward-bound, and richly laden from the southward, who had the like fate, in the same place, a great many years ago; and that some of them coming from Spain, and having a great quantity of bullion, or pieces of eight on board, the money frequently drives on shore still, and that in good quantities, especially after stormy weather.

This may be the reason why, as we observed during our short stay here, several mornings after, it had blown something hard in the night, the sands were cover'd with country people running too and fro' to see if the sea had cast up any thing of value. This the seamen call *going a shoring*; and it seems they do often find good purchase: sometimes also dead bodies are cast up here, the consequence of shipwrecks among those fatal rocks and islands; as also broken pieces of ships, casks, chests, and almost every thing that will float, or roll on shore by the surges of the sea.

Nor is it seldom that the voracious country people scuffle and fight about the right to what they find, and that in a desperate manner, so that this part of Corn-wall may truly be said to be inhabited by a fierce and ravenous people; for they are so greedy, and eager for the prey, that they are charg'd with strange, bloody, and cruel dealings, even sometimes with one another; but especially with poor distress'd seamen when they come on shore by force of a tempest, and seek help for their lives, and where they find the rocks themselves not more merciless than the people who range about them for their prey.

78. 'Sir Cloudesly Shovel in the Association with the Eagle, Rummny and the Firebrand lost on the rocks of Scilly, October 22, 1707'; contemporary engraving.

Here also, as a farther testimony of the immense riches which have been lost at several times upon this coast, we found several engineers, and projectors; some with one sort of diving engine,[41] and some with another; some claiming such a wreck, and some such and such others; where they alledg'd, they were assur'd there were great quantities of money; and strange unprecedented ways were us'd by them to come at it; some, I say, with one kind of engine, and some another; and tho' we thought several of them very strange impracticable methods, yet, I was assur'd by the country people, that they had done wonders with them under water, and that some of them had taken up things of great weight, and in a great depth of water; others had split open the wrecks they had found, in a manner one would have thought not possible to be done, so far under water, and had taken out things from the very holds of the ships; but we could not learn, that they had come at any pieces of eight, which was the thing they seem'd most to aim at, and depend upon; at least they had not found any great quantity, as they said they expected.

However, we left them as busy as we found them, and far from being discouraged; and if half the golden mountains, or silver mountains either, which they promise themselves, should appear, they will be very well paid for their labour.

From the tops of the hills, on this extremity of the land, you may see out into that they call the *Chops of the Channel*, which, as it is the greatest inlet of commerce, and the most frequented by merchant-ships of any place in the world; so one seldom looks out to seaward, but something new presents; that is to say, of ships passing, or repassing, either on the great or lesser Channel.

This point of the Lizard, which runs out to the south-ward, and the other promontory mention'd above, make the two angles, or horns, as they are call'd, from whence 'tis suppos'd this county receiv'd its first name of Cornwall, or as Mr. Cambden says, *Cornubia* in the Latin, and in the British *Kernaw*, as running out in two vastly extended horns; and indeed it seems as if nature had form'd this situation for the direction of mariners, as foreknowing of what importance it should be, and how in future ages these seas should be thus throng'd with merchant ships, the protection of whose wealth, and the safety of the people navigating them, was so much her early care, that she stretched out the land so very many ways, and extended the points and pro-montories so far, and in so many different places into

79. 'The Lands End'; engraving by E. Harding. From Richard Polwhele, *The History of Cornwall* (1803).

the sea, that the land might be more easily discover'd at a due distance, which way soever the ships should come.

Nor is the Lizard point less useful (tho' not so far west) than the other, which is more properly call'd the Land's End; but if we may credit our mariners, it is more frequently, first discover'd from the sea; for as our mariners knowing by the soundings when they are in the mouth of the Channel, do then most naturally stand to the southward, to avoid mistaking the Channel, and to shun the Severn Sea, or Bristol Channel, but still more to avoid running upon Scilly, and the rocks about it, as is observ'd before: I say, as they carefully keep to the south-ward, till they think they are fair with the Channel, and then stand to the northward again, or north east, to make the land; this is the reason why the Lizard is generally speaking, the first land they make, and not the Land's End.

Then having made the Lizard, they either (first) run in for Falmouth, which is the next port, if they are taken short with easterly winds, or are in want of provisions and refreshment, or have any thing out of order, so that they care not to keep the sea or; (2dly) stand away for the Ram Head, and Plymouth-Sound, or (3dly) keep an offing to run up the Channel.

Upon this remote part of the island we saw great numbers of that famous kind of crows, which is known by the name of the Cornish cough, or chough, so the country people call them: they are the same kind, which are found in Switzerland among the Alps, and which Pliny pretended, were peculiar to those mountains, and calls the *pyrrhocorax*; the body is black, the legs, feet, and bill of a deep yellow, almost to a red; I could not find that it was affected for any good quality it had, nor is the flesh good to eat, for it feeds much on fish and carrion; it is counted little better than a kite, for it is of ravenous quality, and is very mis-

XVII. *The Cornish Chough.* From Eleazar Albin, *A Natural History of Birds* (1738).

chievous; it will steal and carry away any thing it finds about the house, that is not too heavy, tho' not fit for its food; as knives, forks, spoons and linnen cloths, or whatever it can fly away with, sometimes they say it has stolen bits of firebrands, or lighted candles and lodged them in the stacks of corn, and the thatch of barns and houses, and set them on fire; but this I only had by oral tradition.

I might take up many sheets in describing the valuable curiosities of this little *cherosonese*,[42] or neck land, call'd the Land's End, in which there lyes an immense treasure, and many things worth notice, I mean besides those to be found upon the surface: but I am too near the end of this letter. If I have opportunity, I shall take notice of some part of what I omit here, in my return by the northern shore of the county.

The End of the Third Letter

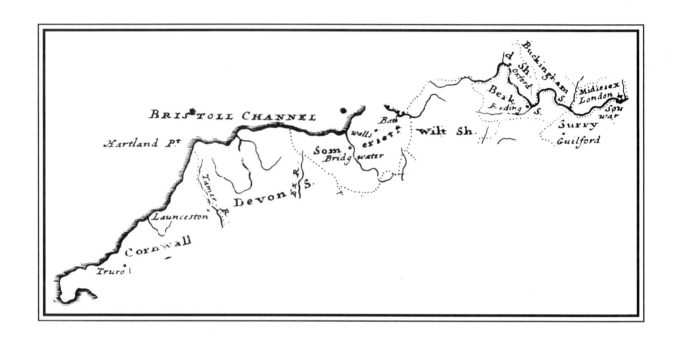

LETTER IV

Containing a Description of the North Shore
of the Counties of Cornwall, and Devon,
and some Parts of Somersetshire, Wiltshire,
Dorsetshire, Gloucestershire,
Buckinghamshire and Berkshire

SIR,

MY LAST LETTER ended the account of my travels, where nature ended her account, when she meeted out the island, and where she fix'd the utmost western bounds of Britain; and, being resolved to see the very extremity of it, I set my foot into the sea, as it were, beyond the farthest inch of dry land west, as I had done before near the town of Dover, at the foot of the rocks of the South-Foreland in Kent, which, I think, is the farthest point east in a line; and as I had done, also, at Leostoff in Suffolk, which is another promontory on the eastern coast, and is reckon'd the farthest land eastward of the island in general: likewise, I had used the same ceremony at Selsy near Chichester, which I take to be the farthest land south, except at Portland only, which, as it is not really an island, may be called, the farthest land south; so, in its place, I shall give you an account of the same curiosity at John a Grot's house in Caithness, the farthest piece of ground in Great Britain, north.

I had once, indeed, resolved to have coasted the whole circuit of Britain by sea, as 'tis said, Agricola[1] the Roman general, did; and in this voyage I would have gone about every promontory, and into the bottom of every bay, and had provided myself a good yacht, and an able commander for that purpose; but I found it would be too hazardous an undertaking for any man to justify himself in the doing it upon the meer foundation of curiosity, and having no other business at all; so I gave it over.

I now turned about to the east, and as, when I went west, I kept to the southern coast of this long county of Cornwall, and of Devonshire also, so in going east, I shall keep the north-shore on board. The first place, of any note, we came to, is **St. Ives**, a pretty good town, and grown rich by the fishing-trade; it is situated on the west side of a deep bay, called St. Ives Bay, from the name of the town. This bay is opposite, on the land side, to Mount's Bay, which I spoke of in my last, in my account of Pensance.

It is a very pleasant view we have at Madern Hills, and the plain by them, in the way from the Land's End to St. Ives, where, at one sight, there is a prospect of the ocean at the Land's-End west; of the British Channel at Mount's Bay south; and the Bristol Channel, or Severn Sea, north; at St. Ives, the land between the two bays being not above four or five miles over, is so situated, that upon the hill, neither of the two seas are above three miles off, and very plain to be seen; and also, in a clear day, the islands of Scilly, though above thirty miles off.

From this town and port of St. Ives, we have no town of any note on the coast; no, not a market town, except Redruth, which is of no consideration, 'till we come to Padstow-Haven, which is near thirty miles: The country is, indeed, both fruitful and pleasant, and several houses of gentlemen are seen as we pass; the sands, also, are very pleasant to the eye, and to travel upon; among the gentlemen's houses, is, Lanhidrock, the seat of the earls of Radnor, who are barons of Truro, and were so, long before they obtained the title of Radnor; also a good house belonging to the ancient family of Trefusis.

In viewing these things, we observ'd the hills fruit-

80. Pentire Point and Padstow Haven; drawing by Edmund Prideaux (2 October 1727).

81. 'The Hurlers near the Cheeswring said by ye country people to be men turned into stones for hurling on a Sunday'; drawing by Edmund Prideaux (21 September 1727).

ful of tin, copper, and lead, all the way on our right hand, the product of which, is carried all to the other shore; so that we shall have little to say of it here. The chief business on this shore, is the herring fishing; the herrings, about October, come driving up the Severn Sea, and from the coast of Ireland, in prodigious shoals, and beat all upon this coast as high as Biddeford, and Barnstable, in Devonshire, and are caught in great quantities by the fishermen, chiefly on account of the merchants of Falmouth, Foy, and Plymouth, and other ports on the south.

XVIII. Unknown painter, possibly Edmund Prideaux, *Padstow harbour and Prideaux Place (c.1730)*.

Padstow is a large town, and stands on a very good harbour for such shipping as use that coast, that is to say, for the Irish trade: the harbour is the mouth of the river Camel, or Camal, which rising at Camelford, runs down by Bodmyn to Wodbridge, or Wardbridge, a large stone bridge of eight arches, or thereabouts, built by the general good will of the country gentlemen; but at the motion of a religious man, named Lovibond, moved in mere charity; the passage over the river there, before, being very dangerous, and having been the loss of some lives, as well as goods.

Higher within the land, lies the town of **Bodmyn**, once one of the coining towns for tin, but lost it to Lestwithyel: however, this town enjoys several privileges, some of which are also tokens of its antiquity.

The coinage towns[2] were, in Queen Elizabeth's time, four; namely,

$$\left.\begin{array}{l}\text{Leskard,}\\\text{Lestwithyel,}\end{array}\right\}\quad\left\{\begin{array}{l}\text{Truro,}\\\text{Helston.}\end{array}\right.$$

Since that, in King James's time, was added,

Pensance.

We have nothing more of note in this county, that I could see, or hear of, but a set of monumental stones, found standing not far from Bodmyn, called The Hurlers,[3] of which the country, nor all the writers of the country, can give us no good account; so I must leave them as I found them.

The game called the hurlers,[4] is a thing the Cornish men value themselves much upon; I confess, I see nothing in it, but that it is a rude violent play among the boors, or country people; brutish and furious, and a sort of an evidence, that they were, once, a kind of barbarians: It seems to me, something to resemble the old way of play, as it was then called, with whirlebats,[5] with which Hercules slew the gyant, when he undertook to clean the Augean stable.

The wrestling in Cornwall, is, indeed, a much more manly and generous exercise, and that closure, which they call the Cornish Hug, has made them eminent in the wrestling rings all over England, as the Norfolk, and Suffolk men, are for their dexterity at the hand and foot, and throwing up the heels of their adversary, without taking hold of him.

I came out of Cornwall by passing the river Tamar at **Launceston**, the last, or rather, the first, town in the county, the town shewing little else, but marks of its antiquity; for great part of it is so old, as it may, in a manner pass for an old, ragged, decay'd place, in general. It stands at a distance, almost two miles from the river, over which, there is a very good bridge; the town is eminent, however, for being as we call it, the county town, where the assizes are always kept.

In the time when Richard, Earl of Cornwall,[6] had the absolute government of this county, and was, we might say, king of the country, it was a frontier town, walled about, and well fortified, and had, also, a strong castle to defend it; but these are seen, now, only in their old cloaths, and lie all in ruins and heaps of rubbish.

It is a principal gain to the people of this town, that they let lodgings to the gentlemen, who attend here in the time of the assizes, and other publick meetings; as particularly, that of electing Knights of the Shire, and at the county sessions, which are held here; for which purposes, the town's people have their rooms better furnished than in other places of this country, though their houses are but low; nor do they fail to make a good price to their lodgers, for the conveniences they afford them.

The town sends two members to Parliament, and so does Newport, a little village adjoining, and which, indeed, is but a part of Launceston itself; so that the town may be said, almost, to choose four Members of Parliament. There is a fine image, or figure of Mary Magdalen, upon the tower of the church, which the Catholicks fail not to pay their reverences to, as they pass by. There is no tin, or copper, or lead, found hereabouts, as I could find, nor any manufacture in the place; there are a pretty many attorneys here, who manage business for the rest of their fraternity at the assizes: As to trade, it has not much to boast of, and yet there are people enough in it to excuse those who call it a populous place. Passing the river Tamar, as above, about two miles from Launceston, we enter the great county of Devon, and as we enter Devonshire, in the most wild and barren part of the county, and where, formerly, tin mines were found, though now they are either quite exhausted, or not to be found without more charge than the purchase, if found,

82. Launceston castle and town; drawing by Edmund Prideaux (20 September 1727).

83. Calstock on the Tamar, drawing by Edmund Prideaux.

would be worth; so we must expect it a little to resemble its neighbour country for a while.

The river Tamar, here, is so full of fresh salmon, and those so exceeding fat, and good, that they are esteemed, in both counties, above the fish, of the same kind, found in other places; and the quantity is so great, as supplies the country in abundance, which is occasioned by the mouth of the river being so very large, and the water so deep for two leagues before it opens into Plymouth Sound, so that the fish have a secure retreat in the salt water for their harbour and shelter, and from thence they shoot up into the fresh water, in such vast numbers to cast their spawn, that the country people cannot take too many.

As we are just entered Devonshire, as I said above, it seems, at first sight, a wild, barren, poor country; but we ride but a few miles, 'till we find an alteration in several things: 1. More people; 2. Larger towns; 3. The people all busy, and in full employ upon their manufactures.

At the uppermost, and extreme part of the county, N. W. there runs a huge promontory, a mountain like proboscis, into the sea, beyond all the land on either side, whether of Devonshire, or of Cornwall. This they would fain have called Hercules's Promontory, and Mr. Cambden, in his writing, and his mapmaker also, calls it Herculis Promontorium; but the honest sailers, and after them, the plain country people, call it, in down-right modern English, Hartland Point, or, Hearty Point, from the town of Hartland, which stands just within the shore, and is on the very utmost edge of the county of Devon: It is a market town, though so remote, and of good resort too, the people coming to it out of Cornwall, as well as out of Devonshire; and particularly the fisher-boats of Barnstaple, Bidiford, and other towns on the coast, lying often under the lee, as they call it, of these rocks, for shelter from the S. W. or S. E. winds; the seamen go on shore here, and supply themselves with provisions; nor is the town unconcerned in that gainful fishing trade, which is carried on for the herrings on this coast, many seamen and fishing vessels belonging to the town.

From this point or promontory, the land, falling away for some miles, makes a gulph or bay, which, reaching to the head land, or point of Barnstable River or Haven, is called from thence, Barnstable Bay; into this bay, or at the W. end of this bay, the Rivers Taw and Tower empty themselves at one mouth, that is to say, in one channel; and it is very particular, that as two rivers join in one channel, so here are two great trading towns in one port, a thing which as it is not usual, so I cannot say 'tis any advantage to either of them; for it naturally follows, that they rival one another, and lessen both; whereas, had they been join'd together in one town, or were it possible to join them, they would make the most considerable town, or city rather, in all this part of England.

These are the towns of Barnstable and Biddiford, or, as some write it, Bediford; the first of these is the most antient, the last the most flourishing; the harbour or river is in its entrance the same to both, and when they part, the Tower turning to the right, or south west, and the Taw to the S. E. yet they seem to be both so safe, so easy in the channel, so equally good with respect to shipping, so equi-distant from the sea, and so equally advantageous, that neither town complains of the bounty of the sea to them, or their situation by land; and yet, of late years, the town of Biddiford has flourished, and the town of Barnstable rather declin'd.

Biddiford is a pleasant, clean, well-built town; the more antient street which lies next the river, is very pleasant, where is the bridge, a very noble key, and the custom-house; this part also is very well built and populous, and fronts the river for above three quarters of a mile: but besides this, there is a new spacious street, which runs N. and S. or rather N. W. and S. E. a great length, broad as the high street of Excester, well-built, and, which is more than all, well inhabited, with considerable and wealthy merchants, who trade to most parts of the trading world.

Here, as is to be seen in almost all the market towns of Devonshire, is a very large, well-built, and well-finish'd meeting-house, and, by the multitude of people which I saw come out of it, and the appearance of them, I thought all the town had gone thither, and began to enquire for the church: But when I came to the church, I found that also, large, spacious, and well filled too, and that with people of the best fashion. The person who officiates at the meeting-house in this town, I happened to have some conversation with, and found him to be not only a learned man, and master of good reading; but a most acceptable gentlemanly person, and one, who, contrary to our receiv'd opinion of those people, had not only good learning, and good sense, but abundance of good manners, and good humour; nothing soure, cynical, or morose in him, and, in a word, a very valuable man: and as such a character always recommends a man to men of sense and good breeding, so I found this gentleman was very well received in the place, even by those who he differ'd from in matters of religion, and those differences did not, as is usual, make any breach in their conversing with him: his name, as I remember, was Bartlet.[7] But this is a digression: I wish I could say the like of all the rest of his brethren.

84. Bideford Meeting House; print from the early nineteenth century before its destruction later in the century but showing its state soon after completion in 1696.

The trade of this town being very much in fish, as it is also of all the towns on this coast, I observed here, that several ships were employ'd to go to Leverpool, and up the river Mersey to Warrington, to fetch the rock salt, which is found in that county, (and of which I shall say more in my remarks on those parts) which rock salt they bring to Biddiford and Barnstable, and here they dissolve it into brine in the sea water, joyning the strength of two bodies into one, and then boil it up again into a new salt, as the Dutch do by the French and Portuguese salt: this is justly call'd salt upon salt, and with this they cure their herrings; and as this is a trade which can be but of a few years standing, because the rock itself has not been discover'd in England much above twenty years; so the difference in curing the fish has been such, and it has so recommended their herrings in foreign markets, that the demand for them has considerably increased, and consequently the trade.

Barnstable is a large, spacious, well built town, more populous than Biddiford, but not better built, and stands lower; insomuch, that at high water in spring tides, it is, as it were, surrounded with water; the bridge here, was built by the generous gift of one Stamford, a citizen and merchant of London, who, it seems, was not a native of this place, but by trading here to his gain, had kindness enough for the town, to offer such a benefaction to them as they enjoy the benefit of to this day.

A little above Barnstable, N. E. upon the coast, stands a good market and port town, call'd ***Ilfar-Comb***, a town of good trade, populous and rich, all which is owing to its having a very good harbour and road for ships, and where ships from Ireland often put in, when, in bad weather, they cannot, without the extremest hazard, run into the mouth of the Taw, which they call Barnstable Water; and this is one reason, which causes the merchants at Barnstable, to do much of their business at this port of Ilfar-comb.

Leaving the coast, we came, in our going southward, to the great river Ex, or Isca, which rises in the hills on this north side of the county, and that so far, as, like the Tamar, it begins within four or five miles of the Severn Sea; the country it rises in, is called Exmore, Cambden calls it a filthy, barren, ground, and, indeed, so it is; but as soon as the Ex comes off from the Moors, and hilly country, and descends into the lower grounds, we found the alteration; for then we saw Devonshire in its other countenance, viz. cultivated, populous, and fruitful; and continuing so 'till we came to ***Tiverton***, a town which I mentioned before, but did not fully describe.

Next to Excester, this is the greatest manufacturing town in the county, and, of all the inland towns, is next to it in wealth, and in numbers of people; it stands on the river Ex, and has over it, a very fine bridge, with another over the little river Loman, which, immediately after, falls into the Ex just below the town.

But the beauty of Tiverton is the Free-School, at the east entrance into the town, a noble building, but a much nobler foundation; it was erected by one Peter Blundel,[8] a clothier, and a lover of learning, who used the saying of William of Wickham to the king when he founded the Royal School at Winchester, viz. that if he was not himself a scholar, he would be the occasion of making more scholars, than any scholar in England; to which end he founded this school: he has endowed it with so liberal a maintenance, that, as I was informed, the school-master has, at least, sixty pounds per annum, besides a very good house to live in, and the advantage of scholars not on the foundation, and the usher in proportion; and to this he added two fellowships, and two scholarships, which he gave the maintenance for to Sydney-College in Cambridge, and one fellowship, and two scholarships, to Baliol-College in Oxford, all which are appointed for the scholars bred up in this school, and the present reverend master, was a scholar upon the foundation in the same school.

As this is a manufacturing country, as above, we found the people, here, all fully employ'd, and very few, if any, out of work, except such as need not be unemploy'd, but were so from mere sloth and idleness, of which, some will be found every where.

From this town, there is little belonging to Devonshire, but what has been spoken of, except what lies in

85. Blundell's Free Grammar School in Tiverton; engraving by W. Thomas (1784).

the road to Taunton, which we took next, where we meet with the river Columb, a river rising also in the utmost limits of the shire towards Somersetshire, and giving name to so many towns on its banks, as leaves no room to doubt of its own name being right, such as Columb David's, Ufcolumbe, Columstock, and Columbton; the last is a market town, and they are all full of manufacturers, depending much on the master manufacturers of Tiverton.

With this town, we leave the county of Devon, and entering Somersetshire, have really a taste of a different country from Devonshire; for entering Wellington, the first town we came at in Somersetshire, though partly employ'd in manufacturing too, we were immediately surrounded with beggars, to such a degree, that we had some difficulty to keep them from under our horse heels.

It was our misfortune at first, that we threw some farthings, and halfpence, such as we had, among them; for thinking by this to be rid of them, on the contrary, it brought out such a croud of them, as if the whole town was come out into the street, and they ran in this manner after us through the whole street, and a great way after we were quite out of the town; so that we were glad to ride as fast as we could through the town to get clear of them; I was, indeed, astonish'd at such a sight, in a country where the people were so generally full of work, as they were here; for in Cornwall, where there are hardly any manufacturers, and where there are, indeed, abundance of poor, yet we never found any thing like this.

I entered the county, as I observed above, by Wellington, where we had the entertainment of the beggars; from whence we came to *Taunton*, vulgarly called Taunton Dean upon the river Ton; this is a large, wealthy, and exceedingly populous, town: one of the chief manufacturers of the town told us, that there was at that time so good a trade in the town, that they had then eleven hundred looms going for the weaving of sagathies,[9] du roys, and such kind of stuffs, which are made there; and that which added to the thing very much, was, that not one of those looms wanted work: he farther added, that there was not a child in the town,[10] or in the villages round it, of above five years old, but, if it was not neglected by its parents, and untaught, could earn its own bread. This was what I never met with in any place in England, except at Colchester in Essex.

This town chooses two Members of Parliament, and their way of choosing is, by those who they call *Potwalloners*,[11] that is to say, every inhabitant, whether house-keeper or lodger, that dresses their own victuals; to make out which, several inmates, or lodgers, will,

sometime before the election, bring out their pots, and make fires in the street, and boil their victuals in the sight of their neighbours, that their votes may not be called in question.

There are two large parish churches in this town, and two or three meeting-houses, whereof one is said to be the largest in the county: the inhabitants have been noted for the number of Dissenters; for among them it was always counted a seminary of such: they suffered deeply in the Duke of Monmouth's rebellion, but paid King James home for the cruelty exercised by Jeffries[12] among them; for when the Prince of Orange arrived, the whole town ran in to him, with so universal a joy, that, 'twas thought, if he had wanted it, he might have raised a little army there, and in the adjacent part of the country.

There was, and, I suppose, is still, a private college, or academy, for the Dissenters in this town; the tutor, who then managed it, was named Warren,[13] who told me, that there were threescore and twelve ministers then preaching, whereof six had conformed to the Church, the rest were among the Dissenters, who had been his scholars, whereupon, one of his own sort had, it seems, stiled him the Father of the Faithful: the academy, since his death, is continued, but not kept up to the degree it was, in the days of the said Mr. Warren.

From this town of Taunton, which is by far the greatest in all this part of the country, and has more people in it, than the city of York, we went north to take a view of the coast. Exmore, of which mention was made above, where the river Ex rises, lies in the way, part of it in this country, and extending to the sea side: it gives, indeed, but a melancholy view, being a vast tract of barren, and desolate lands; yet on the coast, there are some very good sea-ports.

From hence the winding shore brings us to *Bridgewater*. This is an antient and very considerable town and port, it stands at the mouth of the river Parrat, or Perot, which comes from the south, after having received the river Tone from the west, which is made navigable up to Taunton, by a very fine new channel, cut at the expence of the people of Taunton, and which, by the navigation of it, is infinitely advantagious to that town, and well worth all their expence, first by bringing up coals, which are brought from Swanzy in Wales by sea to Bridgewater, and thence by barges up this river to Taunton; also for bringing all heavy goods and merchandizes from Bristol, such as iron, lead, oyl, wine, hemp, flax, pitch, tar, grocery, and dye stuffs, and the like; their tobacco they generally received from Barnstable by land, which is about sixteen miles west.

This town of Bridgewater, is a populous, trading town, is well built, and as well inhabited, and has many families of good fashion dwelling in it, besides merchants. The famous Admiral Blake,[14] was a native of this town. Here it was, that the Duke of Monmouth, finding himself defeated in his expectation of the city of Bristol, and repuls'd at the city of Bath, and press'd by the approach of the King's troops, who endeavour'd to surround him, made his retreat; where, finding the King's troops followed him, and seem'd resolved to attack him, he went up to the top of the steeple, with some of his officers, and viewing the situation of the King's army, by the help of perspectives, resolved to make an attempt upon them the same night, by way of prevention, and accordingly march'd out of the town in the dead of the night to attack them, and had he not, either by the treachery, or mistake of his guides, been brought to an unpassable ditch, where he could not get over, in the interval of which, the King's troops took the alarm, by the firing a pistol among the Duke's men, whether, also, by accident, or treachery, was not known; I say, had not those accidents, and his own fate, conspired to his defeat, he had certainly cut the Lord Feversham's army (for he commanded them) all to pieces; but by these

86. James Scott, Duke of Monmouth and Buccleuch (1649–85); painting after William Wissing.

87. Sheep and cattle; painting by Pieter Angillis (1729).

circumstances, he was brought to a battle on unequal terms, and defeated: the rest I need not mention.

This town was regularly fortified in the late Civil Wars, and sustained two sieges, if not more; the situation of it renders it easy to be fortified, the river and haven taking one chief part of the circumference; over the river, they have a very good bridge of stone, and the tide rises here, at high water, near six fathoms, whereof, sometimes it comes in with such furious haste, as to come two fathoms deep at a time, and when it does so, by surprize, it often does great damage to ships, driving them foul of one another, and oftentimes oversetting them. This sudden rage of the tide, is called, the Boar, and is frequent in all the rivers of this channel, especially in the Severn itself; 'tis also known in the north, particularly in the Trent, and the Ouse, at their entrance into Humber, and in several other places.

In this town of Bridgewater, besides a very large church, there is a fine new-built meeting-house, that is to say, built since the Toleration,[15] in which 'tis remarkable, that they have an advance'd seat for the mayor and aldermen, when any of the magistrates should be of their communion, as sometimes has happened. Here, also, is a college, or private academy, for the Dissenters to breed up their preaching youth.

As this country is all a grazing, rich, feeding soil, so a great number of large oxen are fed here, which are sent up to London; so that now we come into the reach of my former observation, viz. that every county furnishes something for the supply of London, and no county in England furnishes more effectual provisions, nor, in proportion, a greater value than this. These supplies are in three articles.

1. Fat oxen (as above) as large, and good, as any in England.

2. Large Cheddar cheese, the greatest, and best of the kind in England.

3. Colts bred in great numbers in the moors, and sold into the northern counties, where the horse copers, as they are called, in Staffordshire, and Leicestershire, buy them again, and sell them to London for cart horses, and coach horses, the breed being very large.

As the low part of this county is thus imployed in grazing and feeding cattle, so all the rest of this large extended country is imployed in the woollen manufactures, and in the best, and most profitable part of it, viz.

In Taunton } The serges, druggets, &c. and several other kinds of Stuffs.

In Wells, Shepton, Glastenbury, &c. } Knitting of stockings, principally for the Spanish trade.

In Bristol, and many towns on the Somersetshire side } Druggets, cantaloons, and other stuffs.

In Froom, Philips-Norton, and all the country bordering upon Wiltshire } Fine Spanish medley cloths, especially on that part of the county from Wincanton, and Meer, to Warminster, Bruton, Castlecary, Temple Comb, down to Gillingham, and Shaftsbury, in Dorsetshire.

I mention this at large, because this trade of fine Spanish medley cloth,[16] being the mix'd colours and cloths, with which all the gentlemen and persons of any fashion in England, are cloth'd, and vast quantities of which are exported to all parts of Europe, is so very considerable, so vast an advantage to England, maintains and supports so many poor families, and makes so many rich ones, that no man can be just in the description of things, and in a survey of this part of England, and not enter into a particular description of it; the above you may take as an introduction to it, only I shall add but a little more, concerning this county of Somerset, and shall, upon my entering into the north-west and west parts of Wiltshire, where the center of this prodigy of a trade is, sum it all up together, and shew you the extent of land which it spreads itself upon, and give you room, at least, to make some guess at the numbers of poor people, who are sustain'd and inrich'd by it.

Bus as I made a little trip from Bridgewater north, into the body of the county, I must take notice of what I observed in that part of it: the first place I came to was **Glastenbury**, where, indeed, the venerable marks of antiquity, however I have declin'd the observation of them, struck me with some unusual awe, and I resolved to hear all that could be told me upon that subject; and first they told me (for there are two pieces of antiquity, which were to be inquired of in this place) that King Arthur was buried here, and that his coffin had been found here.

88. 'Prospect of the ruins of Glasenbury Abbey, August 17, 1723'; engraving by E. Kirkall after William Stukeley. From William Stukeley, *Itinerarium Curiosum* (1745).

89. 'South view of Wells Palace in the county of Somerset'; engraving by Samuel and Nathaniel Buck (1733).

Secondly, that Joseph of Arimathea was here, and that when he fix'd his staff in the ground, which was on Christmas Day, it immediately took root, budded, put forth white-thorn leaves, and the next day, was in full blossom, white as a sheet, and that the plant is preserved, and blows every Christmas Day, as at first, to this very day.

I took all this ad referendum, but took guides afterward, to see what demonstrations there could be given of all these things; they went over the ruins of the place with me, telling me, which part every particular piece of building had been; and as for the White-thorn, they carried me to a gentleman's garden in the town, where it was preserved, and I brought a piece of it away in my hat, but took it upon their honour, that it really does blow in such manner, as above, on Christmas Day. However, it must be confess'd, that it is universally attested.

Four miles from Glastonbury, lies the little city of **Wells**, where is one of the neatest, and, in some respects, the most beautiful, cathedrals in England, particularly the west front of it, is one complete draught of imagery, very fine, and yet very antient.

This is a neat, clean city, and the clergy, in particular, live very handsomly; the closs, or part of the city, where the bishop's palace is, is very properly called so; for it is walled in, and lock'd up like a little fortification, and has a ditch round it.

The dignified clergy live in the inside of it, and the prebendaries, and canons, which are very numerous, have very agreeable dwellings, and live very pleasantly. Here are no less than seven-and-twenty prebends, and nineteen canons, belonging to this church, besides a dean, a chancellor, a precentor, and three arch deacons;

a number which very few cathedrals in England have, besides this.

The city lies just at the foot of the mountains called Mendip Hills, and is itself built on a stony foundation. Its manufacture is chiefly of stockings, as is mentioned already; 'tis well built, and populous, and has several good families in it; so that there is no want of good company there.

In the low country, on the other side Mendip Hills, lies **Chedder**, a village pleasantly situated under the very ridge of the mountains; before the village is a large green, or common, a piece of ground, in which the whole herd of the cows, belonging to the town, do feed; the ground is exceeding rich, and as the whole village are cowkeepers, they take care to keep up the goodness of the soil, by agreeing to lay on large quantities of dung for manuring, and inriching the land.

The milk of all the town cows, is brought together every day into a common room, where the persons appointed, or trusted for the management, measure every man's quantity, and set it down in a book; when the quantities are adjusted, the milk is all put together, and every meal's milk makes one cheese, and no more; so that the cheese is bigger, or less, as the cows yield more, or less, milk. By this method, the goodness of the cheese is preserved, and, without all dispute, it is the best cheese that England affords, if not, that the whole world affords.

As the cheeses are, by this means, very large, for they often weigh a hundred weight, sometimes much more, so the poorer inhabitants, who have but few cows, are obliged to stay the longer for the return of their milk; for no man has any such return, 'till his share comes to a whole cheese, and then he has it; and

90. Cheesemaking; engraving from Denis Diderot, *Encyclopédie*, vol. 6: *Addition à l'Economie Rustique* (*c*.1760).

if the quantity of his milk deliver'd in, comes to above a cheese, the overplus rests in account to his credit, 'till another cheese comes to his share; and thus every man has equal justice, and though he should have but one cow, he shall, in time, have one whole cheese. This cheese is often sold for six pence to eight pence per pound, when the Cheshire cheese is sold but for two pence to two pence halfpenny.

Here is a deep, frightful chasm[17] in the mountain, in the hollow of which, the road goes, by which they travel towards Bristol; and out of the same hollow, springs a little river, which flows with such a full stream, that, it is said, it drives twelve mills within a quarter of a mile of the spring.

I come now to that part of the country, which joins itself to Wiltshire, which I reserved, in particular, to this place, in order to give some account of the broadcloth manufacture, which I several times mentioned in my first journey, and which is carried on here, and that to such a degree, as deserves a place in all the descriptions, or histories, which shall be given of this country.

As the east, and south parts of Wiltshire are, as I have already observed, all hilly, spreading themselves far and wide, in plains, and grassy downs, for breeding, and feeding, vast flocks of sheep, and a prodigious number of them: and as the west and north parts of Somersetshire are, on the contrary, low, and marshy, or moorish, for feeding, and breeding, of black cattle, and horses, or for lead-mines, &c. So all the south west part of Wiltshire, and the east part of Somersetshire, are low and flat, being a rich, inclosed country, full of rivers and towns, and infinitely populous, insomuch, that some of the market towns are equal to cities in bigness, and superior to them in numbers of people.

This low, flat country, contains part of the three counties of Somerset, Wilts, and Gloucester, and that the extent of it may be the easier understood by those who know any thing of the situation of the country, it reaches from Cirencester in the north, to Sherburn on the edge of Dorsetshire south, and from the Devizes east, to Bristol west, which may take in about fifty miles in length where longest, and twenty in breadth where narrowest.

In this extent of country, we have the following

91. A view of Cheddar cliffs; engraving (c.1760).

market towns, which are principally employ'd in the clothing trade, that is to say, in that part of it, which I am now speaking of; namely, fine medley, or mix'd cloths, such as are usually worn in England by the better sort of people; and, also, exported in great quantities to Holland, Hamburgh, Sweden, Denmark, Spain, Italy, &c. The principal clothing towns in this part of the country, are these,

Somersetshire	Frome, Pensford, Philip's Norton, Bruton, Shepton Mallet, Castle Carey, and Wincanton.
Wiltshire	Malmsbury, Castlecomb, Chippenham, Caln, Devizes, Bradford, Trubridge, Westbury, Warminster, Meer.
Dorsetshire	Gillingham, Shaftsbury, Bemister, and Bere, Sturminster, Shireborn.
Gloucester	Cirencester, Tetbury, Marshfield, Minchinghampton, and Fairford.

These towns, as they stand thin, and at considerable distance from one another; for, except the two towns of Bradford and Trubridge, the other stand at an unusual distance; I say, these towns are interspers'd with a very great number of villages, I had almost said, innumerable villages, hamlets, and scattered houses, in which, generally speaking, the spinning work of all this manufacture is performed by the poor people; the master clothiers, who generally live in the greater towns, sending out the wool weekly to their houses, by their servants and horses, and, at the same time, bringing back the yarn that they have spun and finished, which then is fitted for the loom.

The increasing and flourishing circumstances of this trade, are happily visible by the great concourse of people to, and increase of buildings and inhabitants in

92. Sheep; frontispiece to Richard Bradley, *The Gentleman and Farmer's guide for the increase and improvement of cattle* (1739).

these principal clothing towns where this trade is carried on, and the wealth of the clothiers. The town of **Froom**, or, as it is written in our maps, Frome Sellwood, is a specimen of this, which is so prodigiously increased within these last twenty or thirty years, that they have built a new church, and so many new streets of houses, and those houses are so full of inhabitants, that Frome is now reckoned to have more people in it, than the city of Bath, and some say, than even Salisbury itself, and if their trade continues to increase for a few years more, as it has done for those past, it is very likely to be one of the greatest and wealthiest inland towns in England.

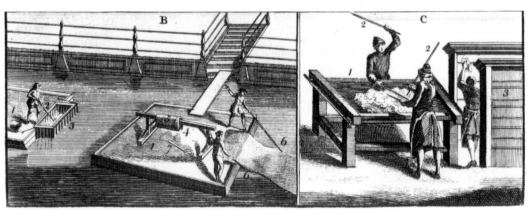

93a–c. Three plates depicting woollen manufacture, from the *Universal Magazine of Knowledge and Pleasure*, vol. 5 (August 1749) facing pl. 82; vol. 5 (October 1749) facing p. 180; vol. 7 (August 1750) facing p. 170.

The first plate shows shearing of sheep sometime after washing in clear water (A). The fleeces are then sold, scoured and washed (B), dried and beaten (C) to remove impurities and to soften the wool to make it easier to spin. Then (D) the wool is carded – fibres are separated out using heated iron combing tools called cards before being greased (oiled with one fourth of its weight if designed for the woof, one eighth of its weight if for the warp). The surplus grease left from the grease bath (5)is expelled with the aid of a windlass (6).

The second plate shows the spinning of thread on to a cone or coppin using a spinning wheel (A) which is then wound into skeins or hanks by the reel. The warp is wound on to wooden bobbins, the woof on to spools that will fit into the eye of the shuttle of the loom (B). The thread for the warp is then gathered on to the warping loom (C) after passage of the yarn over steam to strengthen the filaments. Meanwhile the thread for the woof is wound on to quills (three inch tubes that fit into the shuttle box of the loom)(D). The warp and weft are then woven together on the treadle operated loom (E).

The third plate shows the shearing or clearing the cloth of knots and impurities (A) before washing and teazling to make the fabric warmer (B) and pressing to give the textile a lustre and finish (C).

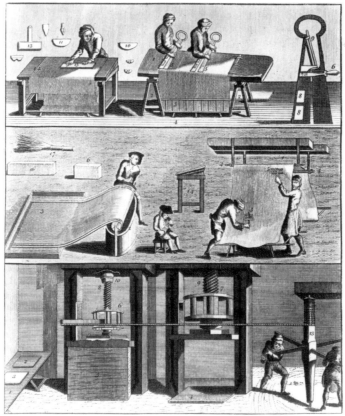

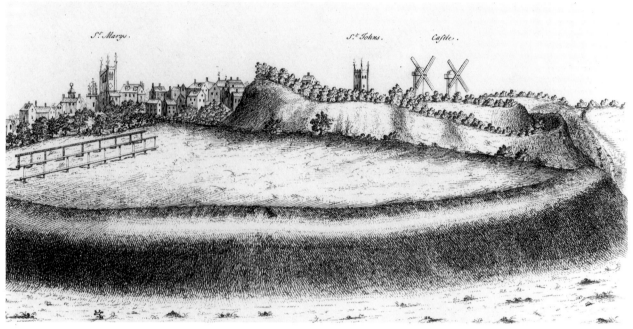

94. Devizes; engraving after William Stukeley (1723). From his *Itinerarium Curiosum* (1724).

I call it an inland town, because it is particularly distinguish'd as such, being, not only no sea–port, but not near any sea–port, having no manner of communication by water, no navigable river at it, or near it. Its trade is wholly clothing, and the cloths they make, are, generally speaking, all conveyed to London: Blackwell-Hall is their market, and thither they send up the gross of their clothing product; and, if we may believe common fame, there are above ten thousand people in Frome now, more than lived in it twenty years ago, and yet it was a considerable town then too.

The **Devizes** is, next to this, a large and important town, and full of wealthy clothiers; but this town has, lately, run pretty much into the drugget-making-trade; a business, which has made some invasion upon the broad-cloth[18] trade and great quantities of druggets are worn in England, as also, exported beyond the seas, even in the place of our broad-cloths, and where they usually were worn and exported; but this is much the same as to the trade still; for as it is all a woollen manufacture, and that the druggets may properly be called cloth, though narrow, and of a different make, so the makers are all called clothiers.

The river Avon, a noble and large fresh river, branching itself into many parts, and receiving almost all the rivers on that side the hills, waters this whole fruitful vale; and the water of this river seems particularly qualified for the use of the clothiers; that is to say, for dying the best colours, and for fulling[19] and dressing the cloth, so that the clothiers generally plant

themselves upon this river, but especially the dyers, as at Trubridge, and Bradford, which are the two most eminent cloathing towns in that part of the vale for the making fine Spanish cloths, and of the nicest mixtures.

From these towns South, to Westbury, and to Warminster, the same trade continues, and the finest medley Spanish cloths, not in England only, but in the whole world, are made in this part. They told me at Bradford, that it was no extraordinary thing to have clothiers in that country worth, from ten thousand, to forty thousand pounds a man, and many of the great families, who now pass for gentry in those counties, have been originally raised from, and built up by this truly noble manufacture.

It may be worth enquiry, by the curious, how the manufacturers, in so vast a consumption of the wooll, as such a trade must take up, can be supplied with wooll for their trade; and, indeed, it would be something strange, if the answer were not at hand.

1. We may reasonably conclude, that this manufacture was at first seated in this country, or, as we may say, planted itself here at first, because of the infinite numbers of sheep, which were fed at that time upon the downs and plains of Dorset, Wilts, and Hampshire, all adjoining, as a trading town is seated, or rises gradually upon some large river, because of the benefit of navigation; and as gentlemen place the mansion houses of their estates, and seats of their families, as near the pleasant rivers, woods, and fine prospects as possible, for the delight of their living; so the first

planters of the clothing manufacture, doubtless, chose this delightful vale for its seat, because of the neighbourhood of those plains, which might be supposed to be a fund of wooll for the carrying it on. Thus the manufacture of white cloth was planted in Stroud water in Gloucestershire, for the sake of the excellent water there for the dying scarlets, and all colours that are dyed in grain,[20] which are better dyed there, than in any other place of England, some towns near London excepted. Hence, therefore, we first observe, they are supplied yearly with the fleeces of two or three millions of sheep.

2. But as the number of sheep fed on these downs is lessened, rather than increased, because of the many thousand acres of the carpet ground[21] being, of late years, turned into arable land, and sowed with wheat; which, by the way, has made Warminster a market town, on the edge of Somersetshire, as it now is, without exception, the greatest market for wheat in England, with this exception only, viz. where none of it is bought to send to London.

I say, the number of sheep, and consequently the quantity of wooll, decreasing, and at the same time the manufacture, as has been said, prodigiously increasing, the manufacturers applied themselves to other parts for a supply, and hence began the influx of north-country wooll to come in from the counties of Northampton, Leicester, and Lincoln, the center of which trade, is about Tetbury and Cirencester, where are the markets for the north-country wooll, and where, as they say, several hundred packs of wooll are sold every week, for the supply of this prodigious consumption.

3. From London, they have great quantities of wooll, which is generally called Kentish wooll, in the fleece, which is brought up from thence by the farmers, since the late severe Acts[22] against their selling it within a certain number of miles of the sea, also fell-wooll[23] for the combers, bought of the woollstaplers in Barnabystreet, and sent back by the carriers, which bring up the cloths to market.

4. They have also, sometimes, large quantities of Irish wooll, by the way of Bristol, or of Mynhead, in Somersetshire; but this is uncertain, and only on extraordinary occasions. I omit the Spanish wooll, as being an article by itself.

All the lower part of this county, and also of Gloucestershire, adjoining, is full of large feeding farms, which we call dairies, and the cheese they make, as it is excellent good of its kind, so being a different kind from the Cheshire, being soft and thin, is eaten newer than that from Cheshire. Of this, a vast quantity is every week sent up to London, where, though it is called Gloucestershire cheese, yet a great part of it is made in Wiltshire, and the greatest part of that which comes to London, the Gloucestershire cheese being more generally carried to Bristol, and Bath, where a very great quantity is consumed, as well by the inhabitants of two populous cities, as also for the shipping off to our West-India colonies, and other places.

This Wiltshire cheese is carried to the river of Thames, which runs through part of the county, by land carriage, and so by barges to London.

Again, in the spring of the year, they make a vast quantity of that we call green cheese, which is a thin, and very soft cheese, resembling cream cheeses, only thicker, and very rich. These are brought to market new, and eaten so, and the quantity is so great, and this sort of cheese is so universally liked and accepted in London, that all the low, rich lands of this county, are little enough to supply the market; but then this holds only for the two first summer months of the year, May and June, or little more.

Besides this, the farmers in Wiltshire, and the part of Gloucestershire adjoining, send a very great quantity of bacon up to London, which is esteemed as the best bacon in England, Hampshire only excepted: this bacon is raised in such quantities here, by reason of the great dairies, as above, the hogs being fed with the vast quantity of whey, and skim'd milk, which so many farmers have to spare, and which must otherwise, be thrown away.

But this is not all, for as the north part of Wiltshire, as well the downs, as the vales, border upon the river Thames, and, in some places, comes up even to the banks of it; so most of that part of the county being arable land, they sow a very great quantity of barley, which is carried to the markets at Abingdon, at Farrington, and such places, where it is made into malt, and carried to London.

One thing here is worth while to mention, for the observation of those counties in England, where they are not yet arrived to that perfection of husbandry, as in this county, and I have purposely reserved it to this place: the case is this, the downs or plains, which are generally called Salisbury Plain; but, particularly, extend themselves over the counties of Southampton, Wilts, and Dorset, were formerly all left open to be fed by the large flocks of sheep so often mentioned; but now, so much of these downs are plowed up, as has increased the quantity of corn produced in this county, in a prodigious manner, and lessened their quantity of wooll, as above; all which has been done by folding their sheep upon the plow'd lands, removing the fold every night to a fresh place, 'till the whole piece of ground has been folden on; this, and this alone, has made these lands, which in themselves are poor, and where, in some places, the earth is not above six inches above the solid chalk rock, able to bear as good wheat, as any of the richer lands in the vales, though not quite so much: I say this alone; for many of these lands lie so remote from the farmers' houses, and up such high hills, for the farmers live always in the valleys, and by the rivers, that it could not be worth their while to carry dung from those farm-houses, to those remote lands; besides, the draught up hill would be so heavy, and the ways so bad, that it would kill all their cattle.

If this way of folding sheep upon the fallows, and plowed lands, were practised, in some parts of England, and especially in Scotland, they would find it turn to such account, and so effectually improve the waste lands, which now are useless and uncultivated, that the sheep would be more valuable, and lands turn to a better account than was ever yet known among them. In Wiltshire it appears to be so very significant, that if a farmer has a thousand of sheep, and no fallows to fold them on, his neighbours will give him ten shillings a night for every thousand.

At *Marlborough*, and in several villages near, as well as on the downs, there are several of those round rising mounts, which the country people call barrows, and which all our writers agree, were monuments of the dead, and particularly of soldiers slain in fight. This in Marlborough, stands in the Duke of Somerset's garden, and is, by that means, kept up to its due height. There is a winding way cut out of the mount, that goes several times round it, 'till insensibly it brings you to the top, where there is a seat, and a small pleasant green, from whence you look over great part of the town.

This is an antient town, and, at present, has a pretty good shop-keeping trade, but not much of the manufacturing part. The river Kennet, lately made navigable by Act of Parliament, rises just by this town, and running from hence to Hungerford, and Newbery, becomes a large stream, and passing by Reading, runs into the Thames near the town. This river is famous for craw-fish, which they help travellers to at Newbery; but they seldom want for price.

Between this town of Marlborough, and Abington, westward, is the Vale of White Horse: the inhabitants tell a great many fabulous stories of the original of its being so called; but there is nothing of foundation in them all, that I could see; the whole of the story is this; looking south from the vale, we see a trench cut on the side of a high green hill, this trench is cut in the shape of a horse, and not ill-shap'd I assure you. The trench is about two yards wide on the top, about a yard deep,

and filled almost up with chalk, so that at a distance, for it is seen many miles off, you see the exact shape of a White Horse; but so large, as to take up near an acre of ground, some say, almost two acres. From this figure the hill is called, in our maps, White Horse Hill, and the low, or flat country under it, the Vale of White Horse.

It is a very fertile and fruitful vale, and extends itself from Farrington almost to Abington, tho' not exactly in a line: some think 'twas done by the Saxons, whose device was a white horse, and is so still.

Having spoken of what is most remarkable, or at least, what most occurred to my observation from the Land's End to Newbery in Barkshire, I must here take the liberty to look round upon some passages in later times, which have made this part of the country more famous than before. On the hills on this side the Devizes, is Roundway Down, where the Lord Wilmot, and the king's forces, beat, and intirely routed, the famous Sir William Waller, in the late rebellion, or civil war; from whence the place is called, by some, Runaway Down to this day. At Newbery there was another, or rather a double scene of blood; for here were two obstinate, and hard fought, battles, at two several times, between the king's army, and the Parliament's, the king being present at them both, and both fought almost upon the same spot of ground.

But this is not my business: this town of *Newbery* is an antient cloathing town, though, now, little of that part remains to it; but it retains still a manufacturing genius, and the people are generally imployed in making shalloons, a kind of stuff, which, though it be used only for the lineing and insides of men's cloaths, for women use but little of it, nor the men for any thing but as above, yet it becomes so generally worn, both at home and abroad, that it is increased to a manufacture by itself, and is more considerable, than any single manufacture of stuffs in the nation. This imploys the town of Newbery, as also, Andover, another town on the side of Wiltshire, about twelve miles from it, and abundance of other towns, in other counties of England, of which I shall speak in their place.

And, having mentioned Andover, though out of the road that I was in, I must digress to tell you, that the town of *Andover* lies on the very edge of the downs which I have so often mentioned, and is in the road from Newbery to Salisbury, as it is from London to Taunton, and all the manufacturing part of Somersetshire; 'tis a handsom town, well built, populous, and much inrich'd by the manufacture, as above, and may be called a thriving town: it sends two members to Parliament, and is an antient corporation.

But the chief reason of my making this digression,

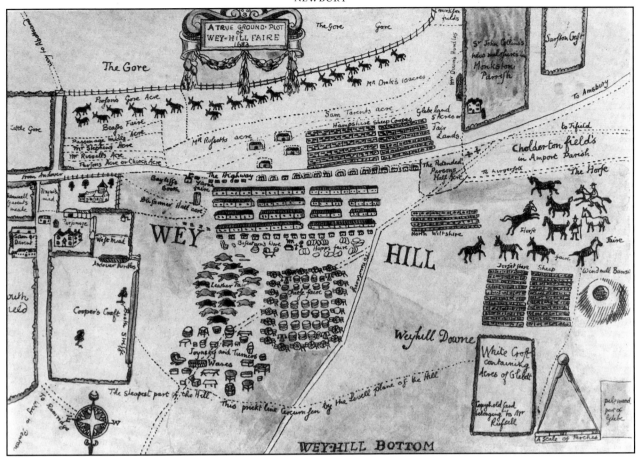

95. 'A true ground plot of Wey Hill Faire, 1683'.

is to mention, that within a mile, or thereabouts, of this town, at the place where the open down country begins, is Wey-Hill, where the greatest fair for sheep is kept, that this nation can shew.

The sheep sold here, are not for immediate killing, but are generally ewes for store sheep for the farmers, and they send for them from all the following counties, Berks, Oxford, Bucks, Bedford, Hertford, Middlesex, Kent, Surrey, and Sussex: the custom of these farmers, is, to send one farmer in behalf of (perhaps) twenty, and so the sheep come up together, and they part them when they come home. These ewes have also this property, that they generally bring two lambs at a time. What weathers are bought here, are carried off by the farmers, who have feeding grounds, in order to fat them for killing; but they are but few compared to the ewes.

But to go back to Newbery: not to insist upon the famous Jack of Newbery,[24] who was so great a clothier, that when King James met his waggons loaden with cloths going to London, and inquiring whose they were, was answered by them all, they were Jack of Newbery's, the King returned, if the story be true, that this Jack of Newbery was richer than he: but not to insist upon this man's story, which is almost grown fabulous, yet another story is fact, and to be proved, viz. that this is one of the two legatee towns (as they were called) in the will of the late famous Mr. Kenrick,[25] who being the son of a clothier of Newbery, and afterwards a merchant in London, left four thousand pounds to Newbery, and seven thousand five hundred pounds to Reading, to incourage the cloathing trade, and set the poor at work, besides other gifts of extraordinary value to the poor, as such. This gentleman I shall have occasion to mention again, and therefore I say no more now, only, that his effigie, or picture, was to be seen, before the fire, in S. Christopher's Church in Thread Needle Street, London, where he is buried, and where the benefaction he left for prayers every morning at six a clock, winter and summer, in that church, is still injoyed, and the prayers performed there accordingly: as likewise, it is at Reading, and at Newbery.

The next town of note, I say, is **Reading**, a very

96. 'South prospect of Reading in the county of Berks'; engraving for *London Magazine* (1734).

large and wealthy town, handsomly built, the inhabitants rich, and driving a very great trade. The town lies on the river Kennet, but so near the Thames, that the largest barges which they use, may come up to the town bridge, and there they have wharfs to load, and unload them. Their chief trade is by this water-navigation to and from London, though they have necessarily a great trade into the country, for the consumption of the goods which they bring by their barges from London, and particularly coals, salt, grocery wares, tobacco, oyls, and all heavy goods.

They send from hence to London by these barges, very great quantities of malt, and meal, and these are the two principal articles of their loadings, of which, so large are those barges, that some of them, as I was told, bring a thousand, or twelve hundred quarters of malt at a time, which, according to the ordinary

97. Detail of a barge carrying bulk cargo, from an anonymous painting of Windsor castle seen from the Thames (*c*.1700).

computation of tonnage in the freight of other vessels, is from a hundred, to an hundred and twenty ton, dead weight.

They also send very great quantities of timber from Reading; for Berkshire being a very-well wooded county, and the river Thames a convenient conveyance for the timber, they send most of it, and especially the largest and fairest of the timber, to London, which is generally bought by the shipwrights in the river, for the building merchant ships; as also, the like trade of timber is at Henley, another town on the Thames, and at Maidenhead, of which by itself.

Here was a large manufacture of sail-cloth set up in this town, by the late Sir Owen Buckingham,[26] Lord Mayor of London, and many of the poor people were, profitably (to them) imployed in it; but Sir Owen himself dying, and his son being unhappily killed in a duel, a little while after, that manufacture died also.

There are three churches, and two large meeting houses in this town, besides that of the Quakers; and the town, Cambden calls it a little city, is said to contain about eight thousand people, including a little hamlet at the bridge over the Thames.

It was here that the Dutch with two hundred and eighty horse and dragoons, attacked the forces of the late King James, in aid of the distress'd town's-men, who they threatened to murther and plunder that very day. It was on a Sunday morning, that the Irish dragoons had resolved on the design'd mischief, if they really intended it: in order to it, they posted a guard at the principal church in the piazza there, and might, indeed, easily have lock'd all the people in, and

126

have cut their throats; also they placed a company of foot in the church-yard of another church, over-against the Bear Inn; so that if they really did not intend to massacre the people, as their officers said they did not, yet that way of posting their men, joyn'd to the loud oaths and protestations, that they would do it, made it look as like such a design, as any thing unexecuted, or unattempted, could do.

In this posture things stood when the Dutch entered the town: the Irish had placed a centinel on the top of the steeple of the great church, with orders, if he saw any troops advance, to fire his piece, and ring the bell; the fellow, being surprized with the sight, for he discover'd the Dutch but a little before they reached the town, fired his musquet, but forgot to ring the bell, and came down. However, his firing gave the alarm sufficiently, and the troops in the town, who were all under arms before, whether for the design'd execution, or not, I will not determine; but, I say, being under arms before, they had little more to do, but to post their troops, which they did with skill enough, being commanded by Sir John Lanier,[27] an experienced officer, and colonel of a regiment of horse in King James's army; and had the men done their duty, they might easily have repuls'd the few troops that attacked them; but the Dutch entering the town in two places, one by the ordinary road from Newbery, and the other by the Broad Street near where the horse-fair is kept, forc'd both the posts, and entered the market place, where the main body of the Irish troops were drawn up.

The first party of the Dutch found a company of foot drawn up in the church-yard over-against the Bear Inn, and a troop of dragoons in the Bear Inn Yard; the dragoons hearing the Dutch were at hand, their officer bravely drew them out of the inn yard, and faced the Dutch in the open road, the churchyard wall being lined with musquetiers to flank the street; the Dutch, who came on full gallop, fell in upon the dragoons, sword in hand, and with such irresistable fury, that the Irish were immediately put into confusion, and after three or four minutes bearing the charge, they were driven clear out of the street. At the very same instant, another party of the Dutch dragoons, dismounting, entered the church-yard, and the whole body posted there, fled also, with little or no resistance, not sufficient, indeed, to be called resistance. After this, the dragoons, mounting again, forced their squadrons, and entered the market place.

Here, the troops being numerous, made two or three regular discharges; but finding themselves charged in the rear by the other Dutchmen, who had by this time entered the said Broad Street, they not knowing the strength, or weakness of their enemy, presently broke, and fled by all the ways possible. Sir John Lanier, having a calash and six horses, got away with the first, though he was twice headed by a Dutch trooper, who endeavoured to shoot one of the horses, but miss'd his shot, so the Colonel got away.

Thus the town of Reading was delivered from the danger they were threatened with, and which they as really expected, as they expected the sun would rise. It is true, the Irish officers denied afterwards, that there was any such design, or that they intended to offer the people any violence; but it is as true, that several of their soldiers confess'd it, and gave private intimations of it, to the people in the houses where they quartered, especially some that had been kindly treated in their quarters, and had a little more gratitude and humanity than the rest.

My next stage from Reading, was to **Great Marlow** in Buckinghamshire, which, though not in the direct road, yet lying on the banks of the river of Thames, is, in my course, proper enough to be spoken of, and is particularly worth notice for several things.

1. It is a town of very great embarkation on the Thames, not so much for goods wrought here, (for the trade of the town is chiefly in bone-lace) but for goods from the neighbouring towns, and particularly, a very great quantity of malt, and meal, is brought hither from High-Wickham, a large market town, about —— miles off, which is one of the greatest corn markets on this side of England, and lies on the road from London to Oxford.

2. Between High Wickham and Marlow, is a little river called the Loddon, on which are a great many mills, and particularly corn mills, and paper mills; the first of these, grind and dress the wheat, and then the meal is sent to Marlow, and loaded on board the barges for London: and the second makes great quantities of printing paper, and that, very good of its kind, and cheap, such as generally is made use of in printing our news papers, journals, &c. and smaller pamphlets; but not much fine, or large, for bound books, or writing.

3. On the river of Thames, just by the side of this town, though on the other bank, are three very remarkable mills, which are called the Temple-Mills, and are called also, the Brass-Mills, and are for making Bisham Abbey battery work, as they call it, viz. brass kettles, and pans, &c. of all sorts. They have first a foundary, where, by the help of *lapis caliminaris*,[28] they convert copper into brass, and then, having cast the brass in large broad plates, they beat them out by the force of great hammers, wrought by the water mills, into what shape they think fit for sale. Those mills went on by the strength of a good stock of

money in a company or partnership, and with very good success, 'till at last, they turned it into what they call a bubble, brought it to Exchange-Alley, set it a stock-jobbing in the days of our South Sea madness, and brought it up to be sold at one hundred pounds per share, whose intrinsick worth was perhaps ten pounds, 'till, with the fall of all those things together, it fell to nothing again. Their treasurer, a tradesman in London, failed, having misapply'd about thirty thousand pounds of their money, and then, as it is usual where want of success goes before, quarelling among themselves followed after, and so the whole affair sunk into a piece of mere confusion and loss, which otherwise was certainly a very beneficial undertaking.

4. Next to these are two mills, both extraordinary in themselves, one for making of thimbles, a work excellently well finished, and which performs to admiration, and another for pressing of oyl from rapeseed, and flax-seed, both which, as I was told, turn to very good account to the proprietors.

Here is also brought down a vast quantity of beech wood, which grows in the woods of Buckinghamshire more plentifully than in any other part of England. This is the most useful wood, for some uses, that grows, and without which, the city of London would be put to more difficulty, than for any thing of its kind in the nation.

1. For fellies[29] for the great carrs, as they are called, which ply in London streets for carrying of merchandizes, and for cole-carts, dust-carts, and such like sorts of voiture, which are not, by the city laws, allowed to draw with shod wheels, or wheels tyr'd with iron.

2. For billet wood[30] for the King's palaces, and for the plate and flint glass houses, and other such nice purposes.

3. Beech quarters for divers uses, particularly chair-makers, and turnery wares. The quantity of this, brought from hence, is almost incredible, and yet so is the country overgrown with beech in those parts, that it is bought very reasonable, nor is there like to be any scarcity of it for time to come.

And now I am, by just degrees, come to **Windsor**, where I must leave talking of trade, river, navigation, meal, and malt, and describe the most beautiful, and most pleasantly situated castle, and royal palace, in the whole isle of Britain.

Windsor Castle, founded, as some say, by William the Conqueror, if there was any thing in that part, was at least rebuilt, by Edward III. King Edward III took an extreme liking to the place, because of its beautiful situation, and pleasing prospect, which, indeed, is not to be out-done in any part of the kingdom: here, at length, the King resolved to fix his summer residence,

and himself laid out the plan of a most magnificent palace, the same, as to the outward form and building, as we now see it; for whatever has been done for beautifying, altering, or amending the inside and apartments, there has nothing been added to the building itself, except that noble terras, which runs under the north front, and leads to the green on the park, at the east side, or end of it, along which east end, the fine lodgings, and royal apartments, were at first built, all the north part being then taken up in rooms of state, and halls for publick balls, &c.

The house itself was, indeed, a palace, and without any appearance of a fortification; but when the building was brought on to the slope of the hill on the town side, the King added ditches, ramparts, the round tower, and several addenda of strength; and so it was immediately called a castle.

King Edward was the founder of the whole work, and the plan of it was much of his own contrivance; but he committed the overseeing, and direction of the works, to William of Wickham, or, if you please, William of Wickham was the Sir Christopher Wren of that court; for William was then a layman, not having had a liberal education, but had a good genius, a mighty lover of building, and had applied his head much that way; nor, indeed, does the building itself fail to do the head, or master-builder, a great deal of honour; for in all the decorations and ornaments, which have been made since by the princes who have liked Windsor best, they have found no occasion to alter any of the front, or to pull down, or build up, add, or diminish, except it be some small matter at the entrance to the great stair-case, the kitchen, and offices below stairs, and the like; but the great north, and east fronts, the square of the inner court, the great gates at the entering from the town, with the Round Tower, and the walls annexed, are all standing in the very form in which King Edward III left them.

On the outside was added, the Terrace Walk, built by Queen Elizabeth, and where she usually walked for an hour every day before her dinner, if not hindered by windy weather, which she had a peculiar aversion to; for as to rainy weather, it would not always hinder her; but she rather loved to walk in a mild, calm rain, with an umbrella over her head.

This noble walk is covered with fine gravel, and has cavities, with dreins, to carry off all the water; so that let it rain as it will, not a drop of it is seen to rest on the walk, but it is dry, hard, and fit to walk on immediately. The breadth of this walk is very spacious on the north side, on the east side it is narrower; but neither at Versailles, or at any of the royal palaces in France, or at Rome, or Naples, have I ever seen any thing like it. At

98. Windsor Castle, from Isherwood's Brewhouse, Datchet Lane, Windsor; pen, watercolour and gouache by Paul Sandby.

the north-east corner of this terrace, where it turns south, to run on by the east side of the castle, there are steps, by which you go off upon the plain of the park, which is kept smooth as a carpet, and on the edge of which, the prospect of the terrace is doubled by a vista, south over the park, and quite up to the great park, and towards the forest. Here also is a small seat, fit for one, or but two at the most, with a high back, and cover for the head, which turns so easily, the whole being fix'd on a pin of iron, or brass, of strength sufficient, that the persons who sit in it, may turn it from the wind, and which way soever the wind blows, or how hard soever, yet they may sit in a perfect tranquility, and enjoy a compleat calm. This is said also, to be Queen Elizabeth's own invention, who, though she delighted in being abroad in the air, yet hated to be ruffled with the wind. It is also an admirable contrivance for the person sitting in it, to shelter himself from the sun.

On that side of the building which looks out upon the terrace, are all the royal apartments, King Edward III's were on the east side. The east side is now allotted to great officers of state, who are obliged to attend whenever the court removes to Windsor, such as the Lord Treasurers, Secretaries of State, Lord High Chancellor, Lord Archbishop of Canterbury, and the like; and below they have proper offices for business, if they please to order any to be done there.

You mount into the royal apartments, by several back stairs; but the publick way is up a small ascent to a flat, or half pace[31] (for I love to make my account speak English) where there are two entries of state, by

two large stair-cases, one on the left hand to the royal apartments, and the other, on the right, to St. George's-Hall, and the Royal Chapel.

Before the enterance to these, on either side, you pass through the guard chambers, where you see the walls furnished with arms, and the King's Beef-eaters, as they call the Yeomen of the Guard, keep their station, or, as it may be called, their main guard. These rooms lead either way, towards the fine lodgings, or towards St. George's Hall, which you please.

It may be proper here to say something to the beauties and ornaments of St. George's Hall, though nothing can be said equal to what the eye would be witness to; 'tis surprizing, at the first entrance, to see at the upper end, the picture of King William on horseback, under him, an ascent with marble steps, a balustrade, and a half pace, which, formerly, was actually there, with room for a throne, or chair of state, for the sovereign to sit on, when on publick days he thought fit to appear in ceremony.

No man that had seen the former steps, or ascent, and had gone up to the balustrade and throne, as I had done, could avoid supposing, they were there still; and

99. Fragment of a wall painting of King William III by Sir Godfrey Kneller, from St George's Hall.

as on a casual view, having been absent some years out of the nation, I was going forward towards the end of the hall, intending to go up the steps, as I had done formerly, I was confounded, when I came nearer, to see that the ascent was taken down, the marble steps gone, the chair of state, or throne, quite away, and that all I saw, was only painted upon the wall[32] below the King and his horse; indeed it was so lively, so bright, so exquisitely performed, that I was perfectly deceived, though I had some pretensions to judgment in pictures too; nor was my eye alone deceived, others were under the same deception, who were then with me.

At the west end of the hall, is the Chapel Royal, the neatest and finest of the kind in England; the carv'd work is beyond any that can be seen in England, the altar-piece is that of the institution, or, as we may call it, our Lord's first supper. I remember, that going with some friends to shew them this magnificent palace, it chanced to be at the time when the Dissenters were a little uneasy at being obliged to kneel at the sacrament; one of my friends, who, as I said, I carried to see Windsor Castle, was a Dissenter, and when he came into the Chapel, he fix'd his eyes upon the altar-piece with such a fix'd, steady posture, and held it so long, that I could not but take notice of it, and asked him, whether it was not a fine piece? Yes, says he, it is; but, whispering to me, he added, how can your people prosecute us for refusing to kneel at the sacrament? Don't you see there, that though our Saviour himself officiates, they are all sitting about the table?

I cannot leave Windsor, without taking notice, that we crossed the Thames upon a wooden bridge, for all the bridges on the river, between London and Oxford, are of timber, for the conveniency of the barges: here we saw Eaton college, the finest school for what we call grammar learning, for it extends only to the humanity class, that is in Britain, or, perhaps, in Europe.

The building except the great school room, is antient, the chapel truly Gothick; but all has been repaired, at a very great expence, out of the college stock, within these few years.

The gardens are very fine, and extended from the College, down, almost, to the bank of the Thames; they are extremely well planted, and perfectly well kept.

This college was founded by King Henry VI, a prince munificent in his gifts, for the encouragement of learning, to profusion: witness, besides this noble foundation, that of King's College in Cambridge, to which the scholars of Eaton are annually removed.

This college has a settled revenue of about five thousand pounds per annum, and maintains as follows.

A Provost.

A Vice Provost, who is also a Fellow.

Seven Fellows, inclusive of the Vice Provost.

Seventy scholars on the foundation, besides a full choir for the chapel, with officers, and servants usual.

100. Eton College; watercolour attributed to Paul Sandby.

The school is divided into the upper and lower, and each into three classes.

Each school has one Master, and each Master four assistants, or ushers.

None are received into the upper school, 'till they can make Latin verse, and have a tolerable knowledge of the Greek.

In the lower school, the children are received very young, and are initiated into all school-learning.

Besides the seventy scholars upon the foundation, there are always abundance of children, generally speaking, of the best families, and of persons of distinction, who are boarded in the houses of the masters, and within the college.

The number of scholars instructed here, is from 400 to 500; but has not been under 400 for many years past.

The elections of scholars for the university out of this school, is worth taking notice of: it being a time of jubilee to the school.

The election is once every year, and is made on the first Tuesday in August. In order to the election, there are deputed from King's College in Cambridge, three persons, viz. the Provost of King's College for the time being, with one senior, and one junior poser, fellows of the same college. To these are joyn'd, on the part of Eaton College, the Provost, the Vice Provost, and the head Master.

These calling the scholars of the upper class, called the Sixth Class, before them, and examining them in

X. Leonard Knyff, *Windsor Castle. Prospect from the north* (*c.*1704–5).

the several parts of their learning, choose out twelve such as they think best qualified, and these are entered in a roll, or list, for the university. The youths thus chosen, are not immediately removed from the school, but must wait till vacancies fall in the said King's College, to make room to receive them; and as such vacancies happen, they are then called up, as they stand in seniority in the said list, or roll of election.

And now being come to the edge of Middlesex, which is a county too full of cities, towns, and palaces, to be brought in at the close of a letter, and with which I purpose to begin my next travels; I conclude this letter, and am,

Sir,

Your most humble servant.

The End of the Fourth Letter

LETTER V

*Containing a Description of the City of
London, as taking in the City of Westminster,
Borough of Southwark, and
the Buildings circumjacent*

Sir,

As I am now near the center of this work, so I am to describe the great center of England, the city of London, and parts adjacent. London, as a city only, and as its walls and liberties line it out, might, indeed, be viewed in a small compass; but, when I speak of London, now in the modern acceptation, you expect I shall take in all that vast mass of buildings, reaching from Black-Wall in the east, to Tot-Hill Fields[1] in the west; and extended in an unequal breadth, from the bridge, or river, in the south, to Islington north; and from Peterburgh House[2] on the bank side in Westminster, to Cavendish Square, and all the new buildings by, and beyond, Hannover Square, by which the city of London, for so it is still to be called, is extended to Hide Park Corner in the Brentford Road, and almost to Maribone in the Acton Road, and how much farther it may spread, who knows? New squares, and new streets rising up every day to such a prodigy of buildings, that nothing in the world does, or ever did, equal it, except old Rome in Trajan's time, when the walls were fifty miles in compass, and the number of inhabitants six millions eight hundred thousand souls.

It is the disaster of London, as to the beauty of its figure, that it is thus stretched out in buildings, just at the pleasure of every builder, or undertaker of buildings, and as the convenience of the people directs, whether for trade, or otherwise; and this has spread the face of it in a most straggling, confus'd manner, out of all shape, uncompact, and unequal; neither long or broad, round or square; whereas the city of Rome, though a monster for its greatness, yet was, in a manner, round, with very few irregularities in its shape.

At London, including the buildings on both sides the water, one sees it, in some places, three miles broad, as from St. George's in Southwark, to Shoreditch in Middlesex; or two miles, as from Peterburgh House to Montague House;[3] and in some places, not half a mile, as in Wapping; and much less, as in Redriff.

We see several villages, formerly standing, as it were, in the country, and at a great distance, now joyn'd to the streets by continued buildings, and more making haste to meet in the like manner; for example, Deptford, this town was formerly reckoned, at least two miles off from Redriff, and that over the marshes too, a place unlikely ever to be inhabited; and yet now, by the encrease of buildings in that town itself, and the many streets erected at Redriff, and by the docks and building-yards on the river side, which stand between both, the town of Deptford, and the streets of Redriff, or Rotherhith (as they write it) are effectually joyn'd, and the buildings daily increasing; so that Deptford is no more a separated town, but is become a part of the great mass, and infinitely full of people also; here they have, within the last two or three years, built a fine new church,[4] and were the town of Deptford now separated, and rated by itself, I believe it contains more people, and stands upon more ground, than the city of Wells.

The town of Islington, on the north side of the city, is in like manner joyn'd to the streets of London, excepting one small field, and which is in itself so small, that there is no doubt, but in a very few years, they will be intirely joyn'd, and the same may be said of Mile-End, on the east end of the town.

Newington, called Newington-Butts, in Surrey,

133

101. 'The East Prospect of London, Southwark and the Bridge... looking up the river'; engraving by Sutton Nicholls (1723).

reaches out her hand north, and is so near joining to Southwark, that it cannot now be properly called a town by itself, but a suburb to the Burrough,[5] and if, as they now tell us is undertaken, St. George's Fields[6] should be built into squares and streets, a very little time will shew us Newington, Lambeth, and the Burrough, all making but one Southwark.

That Westminster is in a fair way to shake hands with Chelsea, as St. Gyles's is with Marybone; and Great Russel Street by Montague House, with Tottenham-Court; all this is very evident, and yet all these put together, are still to be called London: whither will this monstrous city then extend? and where must a circumvallation or communication line of it be placed?

The government of this great mass of building, and of such a vast collected body of people, though it consists of various parts, is, perhaps, the most regular and well-ordered government, that any city, of above half its magnitude, can boast of.

The government of the city of London in particular, and abstractedly considered, is, by the Lord Mayor, twenty four Aldermen, two Sheriffs, the Recorder and Common Council; but the jurisdiction of these is confined to that part only, which they call the city and its liberties, which are marked out, except the Borough, by the walls and the bars, as they are called, and which the particular maps of the city have exactly lin'd out, to which I refer.

134

Besides this, the Lord Mayor and Aldermen of London have a right presidial, as above, in the Borough of Southwark, as conservators of the bridge, and the bridge itself is their particular jurisdiction.

Also the Lord Mayor, &c. is conservator of the river Thames, from Stanes Bridge in Surry and Middlesex, to the river Medway in Kent, and, as some insist, up the Medway to Rochester Bridge.

The government of the out parts, is by Justices of the Peace, and by the Sheriffs of London, who are, likewise, Sheriffs of Middlesex; and the government of Westminster is, by a High Bailiff, constituted by the Dean and Chapter, to whom the civil administration is so far committed.

The remaining part of Southwark side, when the city jurisdiction is considered, is govern'd, also, by a Bench of Justices, and their proper substituted Peace Officers; excepting out of this the privileges[7] of the Marshalseas, or of the Marshal's Court, the privilege of the Marshal of the King's Bench, the Mint, and the like.

To enter here, into a particular description of the city of London, its antiquities, monuments, &c. would be only to make an abridgment of Stow[8] and his continuators, and would make a volume by itself; but it will, I believe, be allowed to be agreeable and sufficient to touch at those things principally, which no other authors have yet mentioned, concerning this great and monstrous thing, called London.

* * *

A Brief Description of the New Buildings erected in and about the Cities of London and Westminster and Borough of Southwark, since the Year 1666

This account of new buildings is to be understood,

1. Of houses re-built after the great fires in London and Southwark, &c.

2. New foundations, on ground where never any buildings were erected before.

Take, then, the city and its adjacent buildings to stand, as described by Mr. Stow, or by any other author, who wrote before the Fire of London, and the difference between what it was then, and what it is now, may be observed thus:

It is true, that before the Fire of London, the streets were narrow, and publick edifices, as well as private, were more crowded, and built closer to one another; for soon after the fire, the King, by his proclamation, forbid all persons whatsoever, to go about to re-build for a certain time, viz. till the Parliament (which was soon to sit) might regulate and direct the manner of building, and establish rules for the adjusting every man's property, and yet might take order for a due inlarging of the streets, and appointing the manner of building, as well for the beauty as the conveniency of the city, and for safety, in case of any future accident; for though I shall not inquire, whether the city was burnt by accident, or by treachery,[9] yet nothing was more certain, than that as the city stood before, it was strangely exposed to the disaster which happen'd, and the buildings look'd as if they had been form'd to make one general bonefire, whenever any wicked party of incendiaries should think fit.

The streets were not only narrow, and the houses all built of timber, lath and plaister, or, as they were very properly call'd *paper work*, and one of the finest range of buildings in the Temple, are, to this day, called the Paper Buildings, from that usual expression.

But the manner of the building in those days, one story projecting out beyond another, was such, that in some narrow streets, the houses almost touch'd one another at the top, and it has been known, that men, in case of fire, have escaped on the tops of the houses, by leaping from one side of a street to another; this made it often, and almost always happen, that if a house was on fire, the opposite house was in more danger to be fired by it, according as the wind stood, than the houses next adjoining on either side.

But tho' by the new buildings after the fire, much ground was given up, and left unbuilt, to inlarge the streets, yet 'tis to be observed, that the old houses stood severally upon more ground, were much larger upon the flat, and in many places, gardens and large yards about them, all which, in the new buildings, are, at least, contracted, and the ground generally built up into other houses, so that notwithstanding all the ground given up for beautifying the streets, yet there are many more houses built than stood before upon the same ground; so that taking the whole city together, there are more inhabitants in the same compass, than there was before.

Another increase of buildings in the city, is to be taken from the inhabitants in the unburnt parts following the same example, of pulling down great old buildings, which took up large tracks of ground in some of the well inhabited places, and building on the same ground, not only several houses, but even whole streets of houses, which are since fully inhabited.

All those palaces of the nobility, formerly making a most beautiful range of buildings fronting the Strand, with their gardens reaching to the Thames, where they had their particular water-gates and stairs, one of which remains still, viz. Somerset House, have had the same fate, such as Essex, Norfolk, Salisbury, Worcester, Exceter, Hungerford, and York Houses; in the place of which, are now so many noble streets and beautiful houses, erected, as are, in themselves, equal to a large city, and extend from the Temple to Northumberland House; Somerset-House and the Savoy,[10] only intervening; and the latter of these may be said to be, not a house, but a little town, being parted into innumerable tenements and apartments.

Many other great houses have, by the example of these, been also built into streets, as Hatton-House[11] in Holborn, and the old Earl of Bedford's great garden, called New Convent Garden;[12] but those I omit, because built before the year 1666; but I may add the Lord Brook's house[13] in Holborn; the Duke of Bedford's last remaining house and garden in the Strand, and many others.

But all this is a small matter, compared to the new foundations raised within that time, in those which we justly call the out parts; and not to enter on a particular description of the buildings, I shall only take notice of the places where such enlargements are made; as, first, within the memory of the writer hereof, all those numberless ranges of building, called Spittle Fields, reaching from Spittle-yard, at Northern Fallgate, and from Artillery Lane in Bishopsgate-street, with all the new streets, beginning at Hoxton, and the back of Shoreditch church, north, and reaching to Brick-Lane, and to the end of Hare-street, on the way to Bethnal Green, east; then sloping away quite to White Chapel road, south east, containing, as some people say, who

102. Somerset House, the garden and the Folly (a large rivercraft adapted for pleasure in left foreground); engraving by J. Kip after L. Knyff (1714).

103. 'A view of the Savoy from the River Thames . . . as it appeared in 1736'; engraving after a plan by George Vertue (published 1750).

pretend to know, by good observation, above three hundred and twenty acres of ground, which are all now close built, and well inhabited with an infinite number of people, I say, all these have been built new from the ground, since the year 1666.

The lanes were deep, dirty, and unfrequented, that part now called Spittlefields-Market, was a field of grass with cows feeding on it, since the year 1670. The Old Artillery Ground (where the Parliament listed their first soldiers against the king) took up all those long streets, leading out of Artillery Lane to Spittle-yard-back-gate, and so on to the end of Wheeler-street.

Brick-Lane, which is now a long well-pav'd street, was a deep dirty road, frequented chiefly by carts fetching bricks that way into White-Chapel from brick-kilns in those fields, and had its name on that account; in a word, it is computed, that above two hundred thousand inhabitants dwell now in that part of London, where, within about fifty years past, there was not a house standing.

2. On the more eastern part, the same increase goes on in proportion, namely, all Goodman's Fields,[14] the name gives evidence for it, and the many streets between White-Chapel and Rosemary Lane, all built since the year 1678. Well Close, now called Marine Square, was so remote from houses, that it used to be a very dangerous place to go over after it was dark, and many people have been robbed and abused in passing it; a well standing in the middle, just where the Danish church is now built, there the mischief was generally done; beyond this, all the hither or west end of Ratcliff-high-way, from the corner of Gravel-Lane, to the east end of East Smithfield, was a road over the fields; likewise those buildings, now called Virginia-street, and all the streets on the side of Ratcliff-high-way to Gravel-Lane above named.

3. To come to the north side of the town, and beginning at Shoreditch, west, and Hoxton-Square, and Charles's-Square adjoining, and the streets intended for a market-place, those were all open fields, from Anniseed-clear to Hoxton Town, till the year 1689, or thereabouts; Pitfield-street was a bank, parting two pasture grounds, and Ask's Hospital was another open field: farther west, the like addition of buildings begins at the foot way, by the Pest-house, and includes the French Hospital, Old Street two squares, and several streets, extending from Brick-Lane to Mount-Mill, and the road to Islington, and from that road, still west, to Wood's Close, and to St. John's, and Clerkenwell, all which streets and squares are built since the year 1688 and 1689, and were before that, and some for a long time after, open fields or gardens, and never built on till after that time.

From hence we go on still west, and beginning at Gray's-Inn, and going on to those formerly called Red Lyon Fields, and Lamb's Conduit Fields, we see there a prodigious pile of buildings; it begins at Gray's-Inn Wall towards Red-Lyon Street, from whence, in a strait line, 'tis built quite to Lamb's Conduit Fields, north, including a great range of buildings yet unfinish'd, reaching to Bedford Row and the Cockpit, east, and including Red Lyon Square, Ormond Street,

and the great New Square at the west end of it, and all the streets between that square and King's Gate in Holbourn, where it goes out; this pile of buildings is very great, the houses so magnificent and large, that abundance of persons of quality, and some of the nobility are found among them particularly in Ormond Street, is the D— of Powis's house,[15] built at the expence of France, on account of the former house being burnt, while the Duke D'Aumont, the French ambassador extraordinary lived in it; it is now a very noble structure, tho' not large, built of free-stone, and in the most exact manner, according to the rules of architecture, and is said to be, next the Banquetting House, the most regular building in this part of England.

Here is also a very convenient church, built by the contribution of the gentry inhabitants of these buildings, tho' not yet made parochial, being called St. George's Chapel.[16]

Farther west, in the same line, is Southampton great Square, called Bloomsbury, with King-street on the east side of it, and all the numberless streets west of the square, to the market place, and through Great-Russel-street by Montague House,[17] quite into the Hamstead Road, all which buildings, except the old building of Southampton House and some of the square, has been form'd from the open fields, since the time above-mentioned, and must contain several thousands of houses; here is also a market, and a very handsome church new built.

From hence, let us view the two great parishes of

104. Powis House; engraving by H. Terasson (1714). The Gallic cocks on the capitals note the fact that the building was rebuilt at the cost of the French government.

XX. William Grimbaldson, *Hermes House, Islington, London. View from the garden with a prospect of London* (*c.*1725).

St. Giles's and St. Martin's in the Fields, the last so increased, as to be above thirty years ago formed into three parishes, and the other about now to be divided also.

The increase of the buildings here, is really a kind of prodigy; all the buildings north of Long Acre, up to the Seven Dials, all the streets, from Leicester-Fields and St. Martin's Lane, both north and west, to the Hay-Market and Soho, and from the Hay-Market to St. James's-street inclusive, and to the park wall; then all the buildings on the north side of the steet, called Pica-dilly, and the road to Knight's-Bridge, and between that and the south side of Tyburn Road, includ-ing Soho-Square, Golden-Square, and now Hanover-Square, and that new city on the north side of Tyburn Road, called Cavendish-Square, and all the streets about it.

This last addition, is, by calculation, more in bulk than the cities of Bristol, Exeter and York, if they were all put together; all which places were, within the time mentioned, meer fields of grass, and employ'd only to feed cattle as other fields are.

Hitherto I have been upon the figure and extent of the city and its out-parts; I come now to speak of the inside, the buildings, the inhabitants, the commerce, and the manner of its government, &c.

It should be observed, that the city being now re-built, has occasioned the building of some publick edifices, even in the place which was inhabited, which yet were not before, and the re-building others in a new and more magnificent manner than ever was done before.

1. That beautiful column, called the Monument,[18] erected at the charge of the city, to perpetuate the fatal burning of the whole, cannot be mentioned but with some due respect to the building itself, as well as to the city; it is two hundred and two feet high, and in its kind, out does all the obelisks and pillars of the ancients, at least that I have seen, having a most stupendous stair-case in the middle to mount up to the balcony, which is about thirty feet short of the top, and whence there are other steps made even to look out at the top of the whole building; the top is fashioned like an urn.

2. The canal or river, called Fleet-ditch, was a work of great magnificence and expence; but not answering the design, and being now very much neglected, and out of repair, is not much spoken of, yet it has three fine bridges over it, and a fourth, not so fine, yet useful as the rest, and the tide flowing up to the last, the canal is very useful for bringing of coals and timber, and other heavy goods; but the warehouses intended under the streets, on either side, to lay up such goods in, are

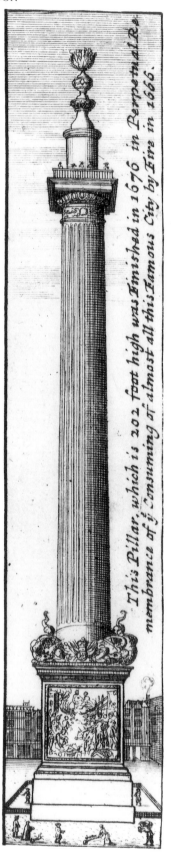

105. The Monument; vignette from *A new description of England and Wales with adjacent islands. . .* London (1724).

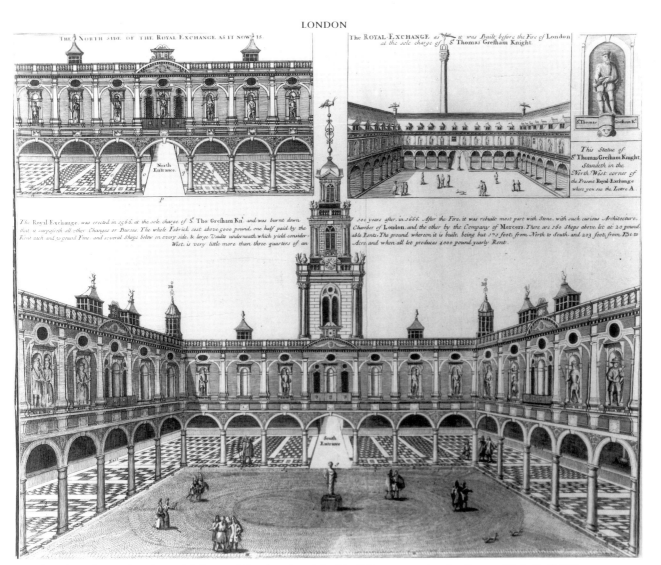

106. Royal Exchange interior, with inset of Gresham's original building; engraving by Sutton Nicholls (1712).

not made use of, and the wharfs in many places are decay'd and fallen in, which make it all look ruinous.

The Royal Exchange,[19] the greatest and finest of the kind in the world, is the next publick work of the citizens, the beauty of which answers for itself, and needs no description here; 'tis observable, that tho' this Exchange cost the citizens an immense sum of money re-building, some authors say, eighty thousand pounds, being finished and embellished in so exquisite a manner, yet it was so appropriated to the grand affair of business, that the rent or income of it for many years, fully answered the interest of the money laid out in building it: whether it does so still or not, I will not say, the trade for millenary goods, fine laces, &c. which was so great above stairs for many years, being since scattered and removed, and the shops, many of them, left empty; but those shops, of which there were eight double rows above, and the shops and offices round it below, with the vaults under the whole, did at, first, yield a very great sum.

Among other publick edifices, that of the hospital of Bethlehem, or Bedlam,[20] should not be forgot, which is at the very time of writing this, appointed to be inlarged with two new wings, and will then be the most magnificent thing of its kind in the world.

Likewise the Custom-House,[21] an accidental fire having demolished part of it, and given the commissioners opportunity to take in more ground, will, when it is finished, out-shine all the Custom-Houses in Europe.

The churches in London are rather convenient than fine, not adorned with pomp and pageantry as in Popish countries; but, like the true Protestant plainness, they have made very little of ornament either

107. Custom House as reconstructed to the designs of Ripley after the fire of 1718; engraving (published by J. Bowles, 1725).

within them or without, nor, excepting a few, are they famous for handsome steeples, a great many of them are very mean, and some that seem adorned, are rather deform'd than beautified by the heads that contrived, or by the hands that built them.

Some, however, hold up their heads with grandeur and magnificence, and are really ornaments to the whole, I mean by these, such as Bow, St. Brides, the new church in the Strand,[22] Rood-Lane church, or St. Margaret Pattons, St. Antholins, St. Clement Danes, and some others, and some of the fifty churches, now adding by the bounty and charity of the government, are like to be very well adorned.

Three or four Gothick towers have been rebuilt at the proper expences of the fund appointed, and are not the worst in all the city, namely St. Michael at Cornhill, St. Dunstan in the East, St. Christophers, St. Mary Aldermary, and at St. Sepulchre's.

But the beauty of all the churches in the city, and of all the Protestant churches in the world, is the cathedral of St. Paul's; a building exceeding beautiful and magnificent; tho' some authors are pleased to expose their ignorance, by pretending to find fault with it: 'tis easy to find fault with the works even of God himself, when we view them in the gross, without regard to the particular beauties of every part separately considered, and without searching into the reason and nature of the particulars; but when these are maturely inquired into, viewed with a just reverence, and considered with judgment, when we fly out in due admirations of the wisdom of the author from the excellency of his works.

The vast extent of the dome, that mighty arch, on which so great a weight is supported (meaning the upper towers or lanthorn of stone work seventy feet high) may well account for the strength of the pillars and butments below; yet those common observers of the superficial parts of the building, complain, that the columns are too gross, that the work looks heavy, and the lower figures near the eye are too large, as if the

108. North prospect of St Paul's; engraving by J. King.

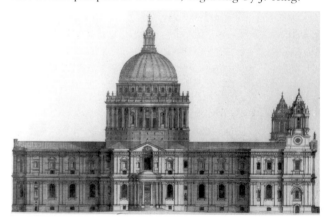

Dorick and the Attick were not each of them as beautiful in their place as the Corinthian.

The wise architect, like a compleat master of his
business, had the satisfaction, in his lifetime, of hearing those ignorant reprovers of his work confuted, by
the approbation of the best masters in Europe; and
the church of St. Peter's in Rome, which is owned to
be the most finished piece in the world, only exceeds
St. Paul's in the magnificence of its inside work; the
painting, the altars, the oratories, and the variety of its
imagery; things, which, in a Protestant church, however ornamental, are not allowed of.

If all the square columns, the great pillasters, and the
flat pannel work, as well within as without, which
they now alledge are too heavy and look too gross,
were filled with pictures, adorned with carved work
and gilding, and crowded with adorable images of the
saints and angels, the kneeling crowd would not complain of the grossness of the work; but 'tis the Protestant plainness, that divesting those columns, &c. of
their ornaments, makes the work, which in itself is not
so large and gross as that of St. Peter's, be called gross
and heavy; whereas, neither by the rules of order, or
by the necessity of the building, to be proportioned
and sufficient to the height and weight of the work,
could they have been less, or any otherwise than they
are.

When all these things are considered complexly, no
man that has the least judgment in building, that
knows any thing of the rules of proportion, and will
judge impartially, can find any fault in this church; on
the contrary, those excellent lines[23] of Mr. Dryden,
which were too meanly applied in allegory to the
praise of a paltry play, may be, with much more
honour to the author, and justice to this work, be
applied here to St. Paul's church.

> Strong Dorick Pillars form the Base,
> Corinthian fills the upper Space;
> So all below is Strength, and all above is Grace.

Sir Christopher's design was, indeed, very unhappily
baulked in several things at the beginning, as well in
the situation as in the conclusion of this work, which,
because very few may have heard of, I shall mention in
publick, from the mouth of its author.

1. In the situation: he would have had the situation
of the church removed a little to the north, that it
should have stood just on the spot of ground which is
taken up by the street called Pater-noster-Row, and
the buildings on either side; so that the north side of
the church should have stood open to the street now
called Newgate-street, and the south side, to the
ground on which the church now stands.

By this situation, the east end of the church, which
is very beautiful, would have looked directly down the
main street of the city, Cheapside; and for the west
end, Ludgate having been removed a little north, the
main street called Ludgate-street and Ludgate-Hill,
would only have sloped a little W.S.W. as they do
now irregularly two ways, one within, and the other
without the gate, and all the street beyond Fleet-
Bridge would have received no alteration at all.

By this situation, the common thorough-fare of the
city would have been removed at a little farther
distance from the work, and we should not then have
been obliged to walk just under the very wall as we do
now, which makes the work appear quite out of all
perspective, and is the chief reason of the objections
I speak of; whereas, had it been viewed at a little
distance, the building would have been seen infinitely
to more advantage.

Had Sir Christopher been allowed this situation, he
would then, also have had more room for the ornament of the west end, which, tho' it is a most beautiful
work, as it now appears, would have been much more
so then, and he would have added a circular piazza to
it, after the model of that at Rome, but much more
magnificent, and an obelisk of marble in the center of
the circle, exceeding any thing that the world can
now shew of its kind, I mean of modern work.

But the circumstance of things hindered this noble
design, and the city being almost rebuilt before he
obtained an order and provision for laying the foundation; he was prescribed to the narrow spot where we
see it now stands, in which the building, however
magnificent in itself, stands with infinite disadvantage
as to the prospect of it; the inconveniencies of which
was so apparent when the church was finished, that
leave was at length, tho' not without difficulty,
obtained, to pull down one whole row of houses on
the north side of the body of the church, to make way
for the ballister that surrounds the cimetry or church-
yard, and, indeed, to admit the light into the church,
as well as to preserve it from the danger of fire.

Another baulk which, as I said, Sir Christopher met
with, was in the conclusion of the work, namely, the
covering of the dome, which Sir Christopher would
have had been of copper double gilded with gold; but
he was over-ruled by party, and the city thereby,
deprived of the most glorious sight that the world ever
saw, since the temple of Solomon.

Yet with all these disadvantages, the church is a
most regular building, beautiful, magnificent, and
beyond all the modern works of its kind in Europe, St.
Peter's at Rome, as above, only excepted.

It is true, St. Peter's, besides its beauty in ornament

and imagery, is beyond St. Paul's in its dimensions, is every way larger; but it is the only church in the world that is so; and it was a merry hyperbole of Sir Christopher Wren's, who, when some gentlemen in discourse compared the two churches, and in compliment to him, pretended to prefer St. Paul's, and when they came to speak of the dimensions, suggested, that St. Paul's was the biggest: I tell you, says Sir Christopher, you might set it in St. Peter's, and look for it a good while, before you could find it.

Having thus spoken of the city and adjacent buildings of London, and of the particulars which I find chiefly omitted by other writers, I have not room here to enter into all the articles needful to a full description: however, I shall touch a little at the things most deserving a stranger's observation.

Supposing now, the whole body of this vast building to be considered as one city, London, and not concerning myself or the reader with the distinction of its several jurisdictions; we shall then observe it only as divided into three, viz. the city, the court, and the out-parts.

The city is the center of its commerce and wealth.

The court of its gallantry and splendor.

The out-parts of its numbers and mechanicks; and in all these, no city in the world can equal it.

Between the court and city, there is a constant communication of business to that degree, that nothing in the world can come up to it.

As the city is the center of business; there is the Custom-house, an article, which, as it brings in an immense revenue to the publick, so it cannot be removed from its place, all the vast import and export of goods being, of necessity, made there; nor can the merchants be removed, the river not admitting the ships to come any farther.

Here, also, is the Excise Office, the Navy Office, the Bank, and almost all the offices where those vast funds are fixed, in which so great a part of the nation are concerned, and on the security of which so many millions are advanced.

Here are the South Sea Company, the East India Company, the Bank, the African Company, &c. whose stocks support that prodigious paper commerce, called stock-jobbing; a trade, which once bewitched the nation almost to its ruin, and which, tho' reduced very much, and recover'd from that terrible infatuation which once overspread the whole body of the people, yet is still a negotiation, which is so vast in its extent, that almost all the men of substance in England are more or less concerned in it, and the property of which is so very often alienated, that even the tax upon the transfers of stock, tho' but

five shillings for each transfer, brings many thousand pounds a year to the government; and some have said, that there is not less than a hundred millions of stock transferred forward or backward from one hand to another every year, and this is one thing which makes such a constant daily intercourse between the court part of the town, and the city; and this is given as one of the principal causes of the prodigious conflux of the nobility and gentry from all parts of England to London, more than ever was known in former years, viz. that many thousands of families are so deeply concerned in those stocks, and find it so absolutely necessary to be at hand to take the advantage of buying and selling, as the sudden rise or fall of the price directs, and the loss they often sustain by their ignorance of things when absent, and the knavery of brokers and others, whom, in their absence, they are bound to trust, that they find themselves obliged to come up and live constantly here, or at least, most part of the year.

This is the reason why, notwithstanding the encrease of new buildings, and the addition of new cities, as they may be called, every year to the old, yet a house is no sooner built, but 'tis tenanted and inhabited, and every part is crouded with people, and that not only in the town, but in all the towns and villages round, as shall be taken notice of in its place.

There has formerly been a great emulation between the court end of the town, and the city; and it was once seriously proposed in a certain reign, how the court should humble the city; nor was it so impracticable a thing at that time, had the wicked scheme been carried on: indeed it was carried farther than consisted with the prudence of a good government, or of a wise people; for the court envy'd the city's greatness, and the citizens were ever jealous of the court's designs: the most fatal steps the court took to humble the city, and which, as I say, did not consist with the prudence of a good government, were, 1. the shutting up the Exchequer,[24] and, 2. the bringing a *quo warranto*[25] against their charter; but these things can but be touch'd at here; the city has outliv'd it all, and both the attempts turn'd to the discredit of the court party, who pushed them on: but the city, I say, has gained the ascendant, and is now made so necessary to the court (as before it was thought rather a grievance) that now we see the court itself the daily instrument to encourage and increase the opulence of the city, and the city again, by its real grandeur, made not a glory only, but an assistance and support to the court, on the greatest and most sudden emergencies.

Nor can a breach be now made on any terms, but the city will have the advantage; for while the stocks,

109. 'The Bubblers Medley'; engraving by Thomas Bowles (1720). Contemporary satire of the South Sea Bubble scandal.

and Bank, and trading companies remain in the city, the center of the money, as well as of the credit and trade of the kingdom, will be there.

Nor are these capital offices only necessarily kept in the city, but several offices belonging to the publick oeconomy of the administration, such as the Post Office, the Navy, the Victualling, and the Pay Offices, including the Ordnance Office, which is kept in the Tower. In a word, the offices may, indeed, be said to be equally divided.

The city has all those above-mentioned, and the court has the Admiralty, the Exchequer, and the Secretaries of State's Offices, with those of the Pay-Masters of the Army, &c.

Besides these, the Council, the Parliament, and the Courts of Justice, are all kept at the same part of the town; but as all suits among the citizens are, by virtue of their privileges, to be try'd within the liberty of the city, so the term is obliged to be (as it were) adjourned from Westminster-Hall to Guild-Hall, to try causes there; also criminal cases are in like manner tried monthly at the Old Baily, where a special commission is granted for that purpose to the judges; but the Lord Mayor always presides, and has the chair.

Besides the companies and publick offices, which are kept in the city, there are several particular offices and places, some built or repaired on purpose, and others hired and beautified for the particular business they carry on respectively: as,

Here are several great offices for several societies of ensurers; for here almost all hazards may be ensured; the four principal are called, 1. Royal Exchange Ensurance: 2. The London Ensurers: 3. The Hand in Hand Fire Office: 4. The Sun Fire Office.

In the two first of those, all hazards by sea are ensured, that is to say, of ships or goods, not lives; as also houses and goods are ensured from fire.

In the last, only houses and goods.

In all which offices, the *premio* is so small, and the recovery, in case of loss, so easy and certain, where no fraud is suspected, that nothing can be shewn like it in the whole world; especially that of ensuring houses from fire, which has now attained such an universal approbation, that I am told, there are above seventy thousand houses thus ensured in London, and the parts adjacent.

The East-India House is in Leadenhall-Street, an old, but spacious building; very convenient, though not beautiful, and I am told, it is under consultation to have it taken down, and rebuilt with additional buildings for warehouses and cellars for their goods, which at present are much wanted.

The African Company's house is in the same street,

a. The Sun Fire Office (1710–1959).

b. The Hand in Hand Fire Office (1696–1905).

c. The Royal Exchange Assurance Insurance (1720–1968).

d. The London Assurance (1720–1965).

110a–d. Contemporary Firemarks displayed on buildings to denote insurance cover by particular London Insurance companies.

a very handsome, well-built, and convenient house, and which fully serves for all the offices their business requires.

The Bank[26] is kept in Grocer's Hall, a very convenient place, and, considering its situation, so near the Exchange, a very spacious, commodious place.

Here business is dispatch'd with such exactness, and such expedition and so much of it too, that it is really prodigious; no confusion, nobody is either denied or delayed payment, the merchants who keep their cash there, are sure to have their bills always paid, and even advances made on easy terms, if they have occasion. No accounts in the world are more exactly kept, no place in the world has so much business done, with so much ease.

In the next street (the Old Jury) is the Excise Office, in a very large house, formerly the dwelling of Sir John Fredrick, and afterwards, of Sir Joseph Hern, very considerable merchants. In this one office is managed an immense weight of business, and they have in pay, as I am told, near four thousand officers: The whole kingdom is divided by them into proper districts, and to every district, a collector, a supervisor, and a certain number of gaugers, called, by the vulgar title excise men.

Nothing can be more regular, than the methods of this office, by which an account of the whole excise is transmitted from the remotest parts of the kingdom, once every six weeks, which is called a sitting, and the money received, or prosecutions commenced for it, in the next sitting.

Under the management of this office, are now brought, not only the excise upon beer, ale, and other liquors, as formerly, but also the duties on malt and candles, hops, soap, and leather, all which are managed in several and distinct classes, and the accounts kept in distinct books; but, in many places, are collected by the same officers, which makes the charge of the collection much easier to the government: nor is the like duty collected in any part of the world, with so little charge, or so few officers.

The South-Sea House is situate in a large spot of ground, between Broad-Street and Threadneedle-Street, two large houses having been taken in, to form the whole office; but, as they were, notwithstanding, straighten'd for room, and were obliged to summon their general courts in another place, viz. at Merchant-Taylors Hall; so they have now resolved to erect a new and compleat building for the whole business, which is to be exceeding fine and large, and to this end, the company has purchased several adjacent buildings, so that the ground is inlarged towards Threadneedle-Street; but, it seems, they could not be accommodated

to their minds on the side next Broad-Street, so we are told, they will not open a way that way, as before.

As the company are enlarging their trade to America, and have also engaged in a new trade, namely, that of the Greenland whale fishing, they are like to have an occasion to enlarge their offices. This building, they assure us, will cost the company from ten to twenty thousand pounds, that is to say, a very great sum.

The Post Office, a branch of the revenue formerly not much valued, but now, by the additional penny upon the letters,[27] and by the visible increase of business in the nation, is grown very considerable. This office maintains now, pacquet boats to Spain and Portugal, which never was done before: so the merchants' letters for Cadiz or Lisbonne, which were before two and twenty days in going over France and Spain to Lisbonne, often-times arrive there now, in nine or ten days from Falmouth.

Likewise, they have a pacquet from Marseilles to Port Mahone, in the Mediterranean, for the constant communication of letters with his majesty's garrison and people in the island of Minorca.

They have also a pacquet from England to the West-Indies; but I am not of opinion, that they will keep it up for much time longer, if it be not already let fall.

This office is kept in Lombard-Street, in a large house, formerly Sir Robert Viner's,[28] once a rich goldsmith; but ruined at the shutting up of the Exchequer, as above.

The Penny Post, a modern contrivance of a private person, one Mr. William Dockraw,[29] is now made a branch of the general revenue by the Post Office; and though, for a time, it was subject to miscarriages and mistakes, yet now it is come also into so exquisite a management, that nothing can be more exact, and 'tis

111. The General Post Office; engraving by Sutton Nicholls (1710).

with the utmost safety and dispatch, that letters are delivered at the remotest corners of the town, almost as soon as they could be sent by a messenger, and that from four, five, six, to eight times a day, according as the distance of the place makes it practicable; and you may send a letter from Ratcliff or Limehouse in the east, to the farthest part of West-minster for a penny, and that several times in the same day.

Nor are you tied up to a single piece of paper, as in the General Post-Office,[30] but any packet under a pound weight, goes at the same price.

I mention this the more particularly, because it is so manifest a testimony to the greatness of this city, and to the great extent of business and commerce in it, that this penny conveyance should raise so many thousand pounds in a year, and employ so many poor people in the diligence of it, as this office employs.

We see nothing of this at Paris, at Amsterdam, at Hamburgh, or any other city, that ever I have seen, or heard of.

The keys, or wharfs, next the river, fronting not the Custom House only, but the whole space from the Tower stairs, or dock, to the bridge, ought to be taken notice of as a publick building; nor are they less an ornament to the city, as they are a testimony of the vast trade carried on in it, than the Royal Exchange itself.

The revenue, or income, brought in by these wharfs, inclusive of the warehouses belonging to them, and the lighters they employ, is said to amount to a prodigious sum; and, as I am told, seldom so little as forty thousand pounds per annum: and abundance of porters, watchmen, wharfingers, and other officers, are maintained here by the business of the wharfs; in which, one thing is very remarkable, that here are porters, and poor working men, who, though themselves not worth, perhaps, twenty pounds in the world, are trusted with great quantities of valuable goods, sometimes to the value of several thousand pounds, and yet 'tis very rarely to be heard, that any loss or embezzlement is made. The number of these keys extending, as above, from the bridge to the Tower Dock, is seventeen.

From these publick places, I come next to the markets, which, in such a mass of building, and such a collection of people, and where such business is done, must be great, and very many. To take a view of them in particular;

First, Smithfield Market for living cattle, which is, without question, the greatest in the world; no description can be given of it, no calculation of the numbers of creatures sold there, can be made. This market is every Monday and Friday.

There is, indeed, a liberty taken by the butchers, to go up to Islington, and to Whitechapel, and buy of the country drovers, who bring cattle to town; but this is called forestalling the market, and is not allowed by law.

There is also a great market, or rather fair for horses, in Smithfield every Friday in the afternoon, where very great numbers of horses, and those of the highest price, are to be sold weekly.

The flesh markets are as follow.

Leaden-Hall, Honey-Lane, Newgate, Clare, Shadwell, Southwark, Westminster, Spittle Fields, Hoxton (forsaken) Brook, Bloomsbury, Newport, St. James's, Hungerford.

N. B. At all these markets, there is a part set by for a Fish Market, and a part for an Herb Market; so that when I say afterwards, there are Fish Markets, and Herb Markets, I am to be understood, such as are wholly for fish, or for herbs and fruit. For example,

Fish Markets	Billingsgate, Fishstreet Hill, and Old Fishstreet.
Herb Markets	Covent Garden, and Stocks Market.
N. B. Cherry Market, and Apple Market	At the Three Cranes.
Corn Markets	Bear Key, and Queen Hith.
Meal Markets	Queen Hith, Hungerford, Ditch-Side, and Whitecross-Street.
Hay Markets	Whitechapel, Smithfield, Southwark, the Hay-Market-Street, Westminster, and Bloomsbury.
Leather Market	Leaden Hall.
Hides and Skins	Leaden Hall, and Wood's Close.
Coal Markets	Billingsgate, Room Land.
Bay Market	Leaden Hall.
Broad Cloth Market	Blackwell Hall.

N. B. The last three are, without doubt, the greatest in the world of those kinds.

Bubble Market   Exchange Alley.[31]

Of the fourteen flesh markets, or markets for provisions, seven of them are of antient standing, time out of mind: but the other seven are erected since the enlargement of buildings mentioned above. The old ones are, Leaden-Hall, Honey-Lane, Newgate Market, Southwark, Clare, St. James's, and Westminster; and these are so considerable, such numbers of buyers, and such an infinite quantity of provisions of all sorts, flesh, fish, and fowl, that, especially of the first, no city in the world can equal them. 'Tis of the first of these markets, that a certain Spanish ambassador

XXI. Pieter Angillis, *Covent Garden* (*c*.1726).

said, there was as much meat sold in it in one month, as would suffice all Spain for a year.

This great market, called, Leaden-Hall, though standing in the middle of the city, contains three large squares, every square having several outlets into divers streets, and all into one another. The first, and chief, is called, the Beef Market, which has two large gates, one into Leaden Hall Street, one into Gracechurch Street, and two smaller, viz. one by a long pav'd

112. 'The Butcher'; satirical engraving by George Bickham (c.1737).

passage leading into Limestreet, and one under a gateway from the second square. In this square, every Wednesday is kept a market for raw hides, tann'd leather, and shoemakers' tools; and in the warehouses, up stairs on the east and south sides of the square, is the great market for Colechester bayes.

The second square is divided into two oblongs, in the first is the Fish Market, and in the other, a market for country higlers, who bring small things, such as pork, butter, eggs, pigs, country dress'd, with some fouls, and such like country fare.

The north part of the Fish Market, the place being too large for the fishmongers' use, are the stalls of the town butchers for mutton and veal, the best and largest of which, that England can produce, is to be bought there, and the east part is a Flesh Market for country butchers.

The third, and last square, which is also very large, is divided into three parts: round the circumference, is the Butter Market, with all the sorts of higglary goods,[32] as before: the south part is the Poultry Market, and the Bacon Market, and the center is an Herb Market.

All the other markets follow the same method in proportion to the room they have for it; and there is an Herb Market in every one; but the chief markets in the whole city for herbs and garden-stuff, are the Stocks and Covent Garden.

There are but two Corn Markets in the whole city and out parts; but they are monsters for magnitude, and not to be matched in the world. These are Bear Key, and Queen Hith: to the first comes all the vast quantity of corn that is brought into the city by sea, and here corn may be said, not to be sold by cart loads, or horse loads, but by ship loads, and, except the corn chambers and magazines in Holland, when the fleets come in from Dantzick and England, the whole world cannot equal the quantity bought and sold here.

This is the place whither all the corn is brought, which, as I have observed, is provided in all the counties of England, near the sea coast, and shipp'd for London, and no quantity can be wanted, either for home consumption, or for foreign exportation, but the corn factors, who are the managers of this market, are ready to supply it.

The other, which I call a Corn Market too, is at Queen Hith; but this market is chiefly, if not wholly, for malt; as to the whole corn, as the quantity of malt brought to this market is prodigious great, so I must observe too, that this place is the receiver of all the malt, the barley of which, takes up the ground of so many hundred thousand acres of land in the counties of Surrey, Bucks, Berks, Oxford, Southampton, and Wilts, and is called West Country malt.

It is true, there is a very great quantity of malt, and of other corn too, brought to some other places on the river, and sold there, viz. to Milford Lane, above the bridge, and the Hermitage, below the bridge; but this is but, in general, a branch of the trade of the other places.

It must not be omitted, that Queen Hith is also a very great market for meal, as well as malt, and, perhaps, the greatest in England.

The next market, which is more than ordinary remarkable, is the Coal Market at Billingsgate. This is kept every morning on the broad place just at the head of Billingsgate Dock, and the place is called Room Land; from what old forgotten original it has that name, history is silent. I need not, except for the sake of strangers, take notice, that the city of London, and parts adjacent, as also all the south of England, is supplied with coals, called therefore sea-coal, from Newcastle upon Tine, and from the coast of Durham, and Northumberland. This trade is so considerable, that it is esteemed the great nursery of our best sea-men, and of which I shall have occasion to say more in my account of the northern parts of England. The quantity of coals, which it is supposed are, *communibus annis*,[33] burnt and consumed in and about this city, is supposed to be about five hundred thousand chalder, every chalder containing thirty-six bushels, and generally weighing about thirty hundred weight.

All these coals are bought and sold on this little spot of Room Land, and, though sometimes, especially in case of a war, or of contrary winds, a fleet of five hundred to seven hundred sail of ships, comes up the river at a time, yet they never want a market: the brokers, or buyers of these coals, are called crimps, for what reason, or original, is likewise a mystery peculiar to this trade; for these people are noted for giving such dark names to the several parts of their trade; so the vessels they load their ships with at New Castle, are called keels, and the ships that bring them, are called cats, and hags, or hag boats, and fly boats, and the like. But of that hereafter.

It must be observed, that as the city of London occasions the consumption of so great a quantity of corn and coals, so the measurement of them is under the inspection of the Lord Mayor and Court of Aldermen, and for the direction of which, there are allowed a certain number of corn meeters,[34] and coal meeters, whose places are for life, and bring them in a very considerable income. These places are in the gift of the Lord Mayor for the time being, and are generally sold for three or four thousand pounds a piece, when they fall.

They have abundance of poor men employ'd under them, who are called, also, meeters, and are, or ought to be, Freemen of the city.

This is, indeed, a rent-charge upon the buyer, and is a kind of gabel,[35] as well upon the coals as the corn; but the buyer is abundantly recompensed, by being ascertained in his measure without any fraud; so that having bought his coals or corn, he is perfectly unconcerned about the measure, for the sworn meeters are so placed between the buyer and seller, that no injury can be offered, nor have I heard that any com-

113. 'The view and humours of Billingsgate'; engraving by Arnold Vanhaecken (1736).

plaint of injustice is ever made against the meeters, who are generally men of good character, are sworn to do right, and cannot easily do wrong without being detected; so many eyes being about them, and so many several persons concerned in the work, who have no dependance one upon another.

There is one great work yet behind, which, however, seems necessary to a full description of the city of London, and that is the shipping and the pool; but in what manner can any writer go about it, to bring it into any reasonable compass? The thing is a kind of infinite, and the parts to be separated from one another in such a description, are so many, that it is hard to know where to begin.

The whole river, in a word, from London-Bridge to Black Wall, is one great arsenal, nothing in the world can be like it: the great building-yards at Schedam near Amsterdam, are said to out-do them in the number of ships which are built there, and they tell us, that there are more ships generally seen at Amsterdam, than in the Thames.

As to the building part, I will not say, but that there may be more vessels built at Schedam, and the parts adjacent, than in the River Thames; but then it must be said;

1. That the English build for themselves only, the Dutch for all the world.

2. That almost all the ships the Dutch have, are built there, whereas, not one fifth part of our shipping is built in the Thames; but abundance of ships are built

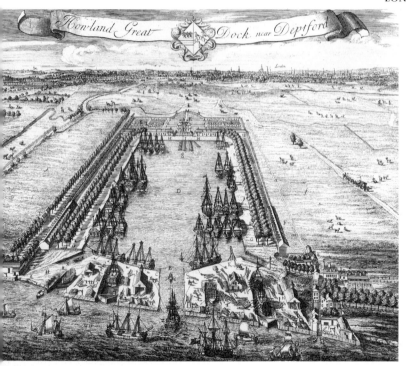

114. Howland Great Dock; engraving by J. Kip after Thomas Badeslade (1717).

To enter into any description of the great magazines of all manner of naval stores, for the furnishing those builders, would be endless, and I shall not attempt it; 'tis sufficient to add, that England, as I have said elsewhere, is an inexhaustible store-house of timber, and all the oak timber, and generally the plank also, used in the building these ships, is found in England only, nay, and which is more, it is not fetched from the remoter parts of England, but these southern counties near us are the places where 'tis generally found.

But I must land, lest this part of the account seems to smell of the tarr, and I should tire the gentlemen with leading them out of their knowledge.

I should mention, for the information of strangers, &c. that the buildings of this great city are chiefly of brick, as many ways found to be the safest, the cheapest, and the most commodious of all other materials; by safe, I mean from fire, and as by Act of Parliament, every builder is bound to have a partition wall of brick also, one brick and half thick between every house, it is found to be, indeed, very helpful in case of fire.

And as I am speaking of fire and burning of houses, it cannot be omitted, that no where in the world is so good care taken to quench fires as in London; I will not say the like care is taken to prevent them; for I must say, that I think the servants, nay, and masters too in London, are the most careless people in the world about fire, and this, no doubt, is the reason why there are frequently more fires in London and in the outparts, than there are in all the cities of Europe put them together; nor are they the more careful, as I can learn, either from observation or report, I say, they are not made more cautious, by the innumerable fires which continually happen among them.

And this leads me back to what I just now said, that no city in the world is so well furnished for the extinguishing fires when they happen.

1. By the great convenience of water which being every where laid in the streets in large timber pipes, as well from the Thames as the New-River, those pipes are furnished with a fire plug, which the parish officers have the key of, and when opened, let out not a pipe, but a river of water into the streets, so that making but a dam in the kennel,[37] the whole street is immediately under water to supply the engines.

2. By the great number of admirable engines, of which, almost, every parish has one, and some halls also, and some private citizens have them of their own, so that no sooner does a fire break out, but the house is surrounded with engines, and a flood of water poured upon it, 'till the fire is, as it were, not extinguished only, but drowned.

3. The several ensurance offices, of which I have

at all the sea-ports in England, such as at New-Castle, Sunderland, Stockton, Whitby, Hull, Gainsborough, Grimsby, Lynn, Yarmouth, Alborough, Walderswick, Ipswich and Harwich, upon the east coast; and at Shoram, Arundel, Brighthelmston, Portsmouth, Southampton, Pool, Weymouth, Dartmouth, Plymouth, besides other places, on the south coast.

3. That we see more vessels in less room at Amsterdam; but the setting aside their hoys, bilanders and schoots,[36] which are in great numbers always there, being vessels particular to their inland and coasting navigation; you do not see more ships, nor near so many ships of force, at Amsterdam as at London.

4. That you see more ships there in less room, but, perhaps, not so many ships in the whole.

In the river, as I have observed, there are from Battle-Bridge on the Southwark side, and the Hermitage-Bridge on the City-side, reckoning to Black-Wall, inclusive,

Three wet docks for laying up
Twenty two dry docks for repairing } merchants ships.
Thirty three yards for building

This is inclusive of the builders of lighters, hoys, &c. but exclusive of all boat-builders, wherry-builders, and above-bridge barge-builders.

XXII. Samuel Scott, *The So-called Custom House Quay* (c.1757).

115. 'The New Sucking Worm Fire Engine', dedicated to King George I by John Lofting, but patented in 1690.

116. Detail of watermills and mechanism for raising water from the Thames, from an engraving of the east and west side of London Bridge by Sutton Nicholls (*c.*1720). The upstream (west) view depicts the input with screening mesh and timbers together with a detail of watermill wheel to left used to raise water.

spoken above, have each of them a certain sett of men, who they keep in constant pay, and who they furnish with tools proper for the work, and to whom they give jack-caps of leather, able to keep them from hurt, if brick or timber, or any thing not of too great a bulk, should fall upon them; these men make it their business to be ready at call, all hours, and night or day, to assist in case of fire; and it must be acknowledged, they are very dextrous, bold, diligent and successful. These they call *fire-men*, but with an odd kind of contradiction in the title, for they are really most of them *water-men*.

Having mentioned, that the city is so well furnished with water, it cannot be omitted, that there are two great engines for the raising the Thames water, one at the bridge, and the other near Broken Wharf; these raise so great a quantity of water, that, as they tell us, they are able to supply the whole city in its utmost extent, and to supply every house also, with a running pipe of water up to the uppermost story.

However, the New-River,[38] which is brought by an aqueduct or artificial stream from Ware, continues to supply the greater part of the city with water, only with this addition by the way, that they have been obliged to dig a new head or basin at Islington on a higher ground than that which the natural stream of the river supplies, and this higher basin they fill from the lower, by a great engine worked formerly with six sails, now by many horses constantly working; so from that new elevation of the water, they supply the higher part of the town with the same advantage, and more ease than the Thames engines do it.

There were formerly several beautiful conduits of running-water in London, which water was very sweet and good, and was brought at an infinite expence, from several distant springs, in large leaden pipes to those conduits, and this was so lately, that several of those conduits were re-built since the fire, as one on Snow-Hill and one at Stocks-Market, which serves as a pedestal for the great equestrian statue of King Charles II[39] erected there at the charge of Sir Robert Viner, then Lord Mayor, and who was then an eminent banker in Lombard-street; but his loyalty could not preserve him from being ruined by the common calamity, when the King shut up the Exchequer.

They tell us a merry story of this statue, how true it may be, let those testify who saw it, if any such witnesses remain, viz. that a certain famous court lady, I do not say it was the D——ss of Portsmouth,[40] being brought to bed of a son late in the night, the next morning this glorious equestrian statue had a pillion[41] handsomely placed on it behind the body of the K——,

117. Equestrian statue of Charles II in the Stocks Market; engraving (published by Thomas Bowles, 1738).

with a paper pinned to the trapping of the pillion,[41] with words at length, *Gone for a midwife*.

The gates of the city are seven, besides posterns, and the posterns that remain are four, besides others that are demolished.

The gates are all remaining, two of them which were demolished at the Fire, being beautifully re-built: these are Ludgate and Newgate; the first a prison for debt for Freemen of the City only, the other a prison for criminals, both for London and Middlesex, and for debtors also for Middlesex, being the County Goal.

Moregate is also re-built, and is a very beautiful gateway, the arch being near twenty foot high, which was done to give room for the City train'd bands[42] to go through to the Artillery Ground, where they muster, and that they might march with their pikes advanc'd, for then they had pikemen in every regiment, as well in the army as in the militia, which since that, is quite left off; this makes the gate look a little

155

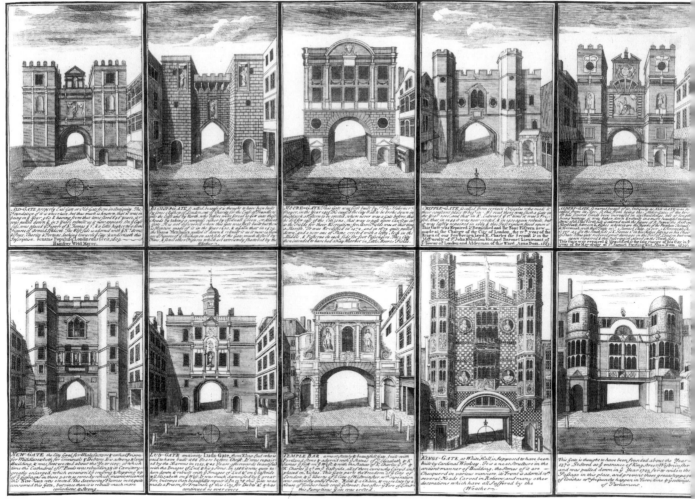

118. The City Gates of London; engraving by Sutton Nicholls (published by John Bowles, c.1720). *Top row (left to right):* Aldgate, Bishopsgate, Mooregate, Cripplegate, Aldersgate. *Botton row (left to right):* Newgate, Ludgate, Temple Bar, with Kings Gate (Whitehall), King Street Gate (Westminster).

out of shape, the occasion of it not being known. Cripplegate and Bishopsgate are very old, and make but a mean figure; Aldersgate is about one hundred and twenty years old, and yet being beautified, as I have said, on the occasion of King James's entry, looks very handsome.

Aldgate was very ancient and decay'd, so that *as old as Aldgate*, was a city proverb for many years; but this gate was re-built also, upon the triumphant entry of K. James I and looks still very well; on the east side of this gate are two statues in stone, representing two men, from the waste upward, and in armour, throwing down two great stones, supposing it to be on an enemy assaulting the gate, which I mention, because some time ago, one of these men in armour, whether tired with holding it so long, or dreaming of enemies assaulting the gate, our authors do not inform us; but he threw down the stone, or rather let it fall, after

having held it upwards of an hundred years; but, as it happened, it did no harm.

Most of these gates are given by the city to the chief of the officers of the city to live in, and the houses are very convenient dwellings.

Temple-Bar[43] is the only gate which is erected at the extent of the city liberties, and this was occasioned by some needful ceremonies at the proclaiming any King or Queen of England, at which time the gates are shut; the Herald at Arms knocks hard at the door, the Sheriffs of the city call back, asking who is there? Then the Herald answers, *I come to proclaim, &c.* according to the name of the prince who is to succeed to the crown, and repeating the titles of Great Britain, France and Ireland, &c. at which the Sheriffs open, and bid them welcome, and so they go on to the Exchange, where they make the last proclamation.

This gate is adorned with the figures of kings below,

and traytors above, the heads of several criminals executed for treason being set up there; the statues below are of Queen Elizabeth and King James I, King Charles I and II; and this is the fourth statue of King Charles II which is to be seen in the city of London, besides his picture nobly done at full length, which was set up formerly in the Guild-Hall.

There are in London, and the far extended bounds, which I now call so, notwithstanding we are a nation of liberty, more publick and private prisons, and houses of confinement, than any city in Europe, perhaps as many as in all the capital cities of Europe put together; for example:

PUBLIC GOALS

The Tower.
Newgate.
Ludgate.
King's Bench.
The Fleet.
Bridewell.
Marshalseas.
The Gatehouse.
Two Counters in the City.
One Counter in the Burrough.
St. Martin's le Grand.
The Clink, formerly the prison to the Stews.
Whitechapel.
Finsbury.
The Dutchy.
St. Katherines.
Bale-Dock.
Little-Ease.
New-Prison.
New-Bridewell.
Tottil-Fields Bridewell.
Five night prisons, called Round-houses, &c.

TOLERATED PRISONS

Bethlem or Bedlam.
One hundred and nineteen Spunging Houses.
Fifteen private Mad-Houses.
The King's Messengers-Houses.
The Serjeant at Arms's Officers Houses.
The Black Rod Officers-Houses.
Cum aliis.
Three Pest-houses.
The Admiralty Officers-Houses.
Tip-staffs Houses.
Chancery Officers Houses.

N. B. All these private houses of confinement, are pretended to be like little purgatories, between prison and liberty, places of advantage for the keeping prisoners at their own request, till they can get friends to deliver them, and so avoid going into publick prisons; tho' in some of them, the extortion is such, and the accommodation so bad, that men choose to be carried away directly.

This has often been complained of, and hopes had of redress; but the rudeness and avarice of the officers prevails, and the oppression is sometimes very great; but that by the way.

In a word; to sum up my description of London, take the following heads; there are in this great mass of buildings thus called London,

Two cathedrals.
Four choirs for musick-worship.
One hundred and thirty five parish churches.
Nine new churches unfinished, being part of fifty appointed to be built.
Sixty nine chapels where the Church of England service is perform'd.
Two churches at Deptford, taken into the limits now describ'd.
Twenty eight foreign churches.
Besides Dissenters' meetings of all persuasions;
Popish chapels; and
One Jews' synagogue.
There are also, thirteen hospitals, besides lesser charities, call'd alms-houses, of which they reckon above a hundred, many of which have chapels for divine service.
Three colleges.
Twenty-seven publick prisons.
Eight publick schools, called Free Schools.
Eighty three charity schools.
Fourteen markets for flesh.
Two for live cattle besides two herb-markets.
Twenty three other markets, as describ'd.
Fifteen inns of court.
Four fairs.
Twenty seven squares, besides those within any single building, as the Temple, Somerset House, &c.
Five publick bridges.
One town-house, or Guild-Hall.
One Royal Exchange.
Two other Exchanges only for shops.
One Custom-house.
Three Artillery Grounds.
Four Pest-houses.
Two bishop's palaces; and
Three royal palaces.

Having dwelt thus long in the city, I mean properly called so, I must be the shorter in my account of other things.

The court end of the town, now so prodigiously increased, as is said before, would take up a volume by itself, and, indeed, whole volumes are written on the subject.

The king's palace, tho' the receptacle of all the pomp and glory of Great Britain, is really mean, in comparison of the rich furniture within, I mean the living furniture, the glorious court of the King of Great Britain: the splendor of the nobility, the wealth and greatness of the attendants, the oeconomy of the house, and the real grandeur of the whole royal family, out-does all the courts of Europe, even that of France itself, as it is now managed since the death of Lewis the Great.

But the palace of St. James's is, I say, too mean, and only seems to be honoured with the court, while a more magnificent fabrick may be erected, where the King of England usually resided, I mean at White-Hall.[44]

The Parliament meets, as they ever did, while the court was at Westminster, in the King's old palace,[45] and there are the Courts of Justice also, and the officers of the Exchequer, nor can it be said, however convenient the place is made for them; but that it has a little an air of venerable, tho' ruin'd antiquity: what is the Court of Requests, the Court of Wards, and the Painted Chamber, tho' lately repair'd, but the corps of the old English grandeur laid in state?

The royal apartments, the prince's lodgings, the

119. Reception of King George I at St James's Palace on 20 September 1714; engraving by A. Allard.

great officers' apartments, what are they now, but little offices for clerks, rooms for coffee-houses, auctions of pictures, pamphlet and toy-shops?

Even St. Stephen's Chapel, formerly the royal chapel of the palace, but till lately beautify'd for the convenience of the House of Commons, was a very indifferent place, old and decay'd: The House of Lords is a venerable old place, indeed; but how mean, how incoherent, and how straitned are the several avenues to it, and rooms about it? the matted gallery, the lobby, the back ways the king goes to it, how short are they all of the dignity of the place, and the glory of a King of Great Britain with the Lords and Commons, that so often meet there?

Come we next to Westminster-Hall;[46] 'tis true, it is a very noble Gothick building, ancient, vastly large, and the finest roof of its kind in England, being one hundred feet wide; but what a wretched figure does it make without doors; the front, a vast pinacle or pedement, after the most ancient and almost forgotten part of the Gothick way of working; the building itself, resembles nothing so much as a great barn of three hundred feet long, and really looks like a barn at a distance.

Nay, if we view the whole building from without doors, 'tis like a great pile of something, but a stranger would be much at a loss to know what; and whether it was a house, or a church, or, indeed, a heap of churches; being huddled all together, with differing and distant roofs, some higher, some lower, some standing east and west, some north and south, and some one way, and some another.

The Abbey, or collegiate church of Westminster, stands next to this; a venerable old pile of building, it is indeed, but so old and weak, that had it not been taken in hand some years ago, and great cost bestowed in upholding and repairing it, we might, by this time, have called it a heap, not a pile, and not a church, but the ruins of a church.

But it begins to stand upon new legs now, and as they continue to work upon the repairs of it, the face of the whole building will, in a short while, be intirely new.

The monarchs of Great Britain are always crown'd here, even King James II submitted to it, and to have it perform'd by a Protestant bishop. It is observable, that our kings and queens make always two solemn visits to this church, and very rarely, if ever, come here any more, viz. to be *crown'd* and to be *buried*.

Two things I must observe here, and with that I close the account of it. 1. 'Tis very remarkable, that the royal vault, in which the English royal family was laid, was filled up with Queen Ann; so that just as the

120. Westminster Hall and adjoining buildings; anonymous watercolour(*c.*1720).

family was extinct above, there was no room to have buried any more below. 2. It is become such a piece of honour to be buried in Westminster-Abbey, that the body of the church begins to be crowded with the bodies of citizens, poets, seamen and parsons, nay, even with very mean persons, if they have but any way made themselves known in the world; so that in time, the royal ashes will be thus mingled with common dust, that it will leave no room either for king or common people, or at least not for their monuments, some of which also are rather pompously foolish, than solid and to the purpose.

Near to this church is the Royal Free-School, the best of its kind in England, not out-done either by Winchester or Eaton, for a number of eminent scholars.

There are three Chapels of Ease to St. Margaret's in this part of Westminster, besides that, great numbers of people go to the Abbey, so that there is no want of churches. There is but one meeting-house in this whole part, which is called Calamy's Meeting, and was formerly supplied by Mr. Stephen Lobb,[47] who, tho' a Dissenter, lived and died a Jacobite.

The Cottonian Library is kept here in an ancient building, near Westminster-Hall gate; we were told it would be removed to the royal library, and then, that it would be removed to a house to be built on purpose; but we see neither yet in hand. This is one of the most valuable collections in Britain, and, the Bodleian Library excepted, is, perhaps, the best: it has in it some books and manuscripts invaluable for their antiquity; but I have not room so much as to enter upon giving an account of the particulars.

121. Whitehall, view towards the King Street Gate with the Banqueting House to left, Horse Guards to right; engraving by J. Kip (1724).

This part of Westminster has but one street, which gives it a communication with London, and this is called King-street, a long, dark, dirty and very inconvenient passage; but there seems to be no remedy for it, for most passengers get out of it through the Privy Garden, and some by private passages into the park, as at Locket's,[48] at the Cock-Pit, and the new gate from Queen's-Square; but these are all upon sufferance.

From hence we come through two very handsome, tho' ancient gates, into the open palace before White-Hall and the Banqueting-house.

His Majesty resides, especially all the winter, at St. James's; but the business of the government, is chiefly carried on at the Cock-pit: this is a royal building, was once part of White-hall, first the Duke of Monmouth lived in it, then Prince George of Denmark and his Princess, afterwards Queen Ann, and since the fire at White-Hall, and Treasury, the Secretary's Office, the Council Chamber, the Board of Trade, and the Lord Chamberlain, hold all their particular offices here; and here there is also, a by-way out of Duke-street into the park.

From thence we come to the Horse Guards, a building commodious enough, built on purpose, as a barrack for a large detachment of the Horse-Guards, who keep their post here, while attending on duty; over it are offices for payment of the troops, and a large court of judicature, for holding councils of war, for tryal of deserters and others, according to the articles of war.

In the same range of buildings, stood the Admiralty Office, built by the late King William; but tho' in itself a spacious building, is found so much too narrow now the business is so much increased, and as there is a sufficient piece of spare ground behind it, to inlarge the building, we find a new and spacious office is now building in the same place, which shall be sufficient to all the uses required.

This office is, perhaps, of the most importance of any of the publick parts of the administration, the royal navy being the sinews of our strength, and the whole direction of it being in the hands of the commissioners for executing this office. The Navy and the Victualling Offices, are but branches of this administration, and receive their orders from hence, as likewise the docks and yards receive their orders from the navy: the whole being carried on with the most exquisite order and dispatch.

From this part of the town, we come into the publick streets, where nothing is more remarkable than

160

XXIII. Joseph Nickolls, *A view of Charing Cross and Northumberland House* (1746).

122. 'The Coffee House Mob'; engraving. From Edward Ward, *Vulgus Britannicus, or the British Hudibras*, London (1711).

the hurries of the people; Charing-Cross is a mixture of court and city; Man's coffee-house[49] is the Exchange-Alley of this part of the town, and 'tis perpetually throng'd with men of business, as the others are with men of play and pleasure.

From hence advancing a little, we see the great equestrian statue of King Charles[50] the First in brass, a costly, but a curious piece; however, it serves sufficiently, to let us know who it is, and why erected there. The circumstances are two, he faces the place where his enemies* triumph'd over him, and triumphs, that is, tramples in the place where his †murtherers were hang'd.

From this place due north, are the king's stables,

*The statue faces the broad place before White-Hall, where the king was beheaded.
†The gibet, where the regicides were executed, stood just where the statue now stands.

called the Meuse, where the king's horses, especially his coach-horses, are kept, and the coaches of state are set up.

On the right side of the street, coming from White-Hall, is Northumberland-House,[51] so called, because belonging to the Northumberland family for some ages; but descending to the Duke of Somerset in right of marriage, from the late Dutchess, heiress of the house of Piercy.

'Tis an ancient, but a very good house, the only misfortune of its situation is, its standing too near the street; the back part of the house is more modern and beautiful than the front, and when you enter the first gate, you come into a noble square fronting the fine lodgings: 'tis a large and very well design'd building, and fit to receive a retinue of one hundred in family; nor does the Duke's family come so far short of the number, as not very handsomely to fill the house.

Advancing hence to the Hay-Market, we see, first, the great new theatre,[52] a very magnificent building, and perfectly accommodated for the end for which it was built, tho' the entertainment there of late, has been chiefly operas and balls.

123. King's Theatre, Haymarket; watercolour by William Capon (*c*.1770). The building illustrated was designed by Sir John Vanbrugh, opened in 1705 as the Queen's Theatre and was destroyed by fire in 1789.

These meetings are called balls, the word *masquerade* not being so well relished by the English, who, tho' at first fond of the novelty, began to be sick of the thing on many accounts; however, as I cannot in justice say any thing to recommend them, and am by no means, to make this work be a satyr upon any thing; I choose to say no more; but go on.

The hospitals in and about the city of London,

deserve a little further observation, especially those more remarkable for their magnitude, as,

I. Bethlem or Bedlam: this and Bridewell, indeed, go together, for though they are two several houses, yet they are incorporated together, and have the same governors; also the president, treasurer, clerk, physician and apothecary are the same; but the stewards and the revenue are different, and so are the benefactions; but to both very great.

The orders for the government of the hospital of Bethlem are exceeding good, and a remarkable instance of the good disposition of the gentlemen concerned in it, especially these that follow;

1. That no person, except the proper officers who tend them, be allowed to see the lunaticks of a Sunday.

2. That no person be allowed to give the lunaticks strong drink, wine, tobacco or spirits, or to sell any such thing in the hospital.

3. That no servant of the house shall take any money given to any of the lunaticks to their own use; but that is shall be carefully kept for them till they are recovered, or laid out for them in such things as the committee approves.

4. That no officer or servant shall beat or abuse, or offer any force to any lunatick; but on absolute necessity. The rest of the orders are for the good government of the house.

This hospital was formerly in the street now called Old Bedlam, and was very ancient and ruinous: the new building was erected at the charge of the city in 1676, and is the most beautiful structure for such a use that is in the world, and was finished from its foundation in fifteen months; it was said to be taken ill at the court of France, that it was built after the fashion of one of the King of France's palaces.

The number of people who are generally under cure in this hospital, is from 130 to 150 at a time.

II. The hospital of Bridewell, as it is an hospital, so it is also a house of correction. The house was formerly the king's city palace; but granted to the city to be in the nature of what is now called a work-house, and has been so employed, ever since the year 1555.

As idle persons, vagrants, &c. are committed to this house for correction, so there are every year, several poor lads brought up to handicraft trades, as apprentices, and of these the care is in the governors, who maintain them out of the standing revenues of the house.

There are two other Bridewells, properly so called, that is to say, houses of correction; one at Clarkenwell, called New Prison, being the particular Bridewell for the county of Middlesex, and another in Tuttle-fields, for the City of Westminster.

The other city hospitals, are the Blue-coat Hospital[53] for poor freemen's orphan children, and the two hospitals for sick and maimed people, as St. Bartholomew's and St. Thomas's: these three are so well known by all people that have seen the city of London, and so universally mention'd by all who have written of it, that little can be needful to add; however I shall say something as an abridgment.

III. Christ's Hospital was originally constituted by King Edward VI who has the honour of being the founder of it, as also of Bridewell; but the original design was, and is owing to the Lord Mayor and Aldermen of London, and the christian endeavours of that glorious martyr, Dr. Ridley[54] then Bishop of London, who never ceased moving his charitable master, the king, till he brought him to join in the foundation. The design is for entertaining, educating, nourishing and bringing up the poor children of the citizens, such as, their parents being dead, or fathers, at least, have no way to be supported, but are reduced to poverty.

IV. St. Bartholomew's Hospital adjoyns to Christ Church, and St. Thomas's is in Southwark, both which, however, being the same in kind, their description may come under one head, tho' they are, indeed, two foundations, and differently incorporated: the first founder is esteem'd to be King Henry VIII whose statue in stone and very well done, is, for that very reason, lately erected in the new front, over the entrance to the cloyster in West-Smithfield: the king gave 500 marks a year, towards the support of the house, which was then founded for an hundred poor sick, and the city was obliged to add 500 marks a year more to it.

From this small beginning, this hospital rose to the greatness we now see it arrived at, of which take the following account for one year, viz. 1718;

Cur'd and discharg'd, of sick, maimed and wounded, from all parts	3088
Buried at the expence of the house	198
Remaining under cure	513

V. St. Thomas's Hospital in Southwark, has a different foundation, but to the same purpose; it is under the same government, viz. the Lord Mayor, Aldermen and Commonalty of the city of London, and had a revenue of about 2000 l. per annum, about 100 years ago.

This hospital has received greater benefactions than St. Bartholomew's; but then 'tis also said to have suffered greater losses, especially by several great fires in Southwark and elsewhere, as by the necessity of expensive buildings, which, notwithstanding the charitable gifts of divers great benefactors, has cost the hospital great sums. The state of this hospital is so advanced at this time, that in the same year as above, viz. 1718, the state of the house was as follows;

Cur'd and discharged of Sick, wounded and maimed, from all parts	3608
Buried at the expence of the house	216
Remaining under cure	566

Adjoining to this of St. Thomas's, is lately laid a noble foundation of a new hospital, by the charitable gift and single endowment of one person, and, perhaps, the greatest of its kind, next to that of Sutton's Hospital, that ever was founded in this nation by one person, whether private or publick, not excepting the kings themselves.

This will, I suppose, be called Guy's Hospital, being to be built and endowed at the sole charge of one Mr. Thomas Guy,[55] formerly a bookseller in Lombard street, who lived to see the said hospital not only design'd, the ground purchased and cleared, but the building begun, and a considerable progress made in it, and died while these sheets were in the press.

Next to these hospitals, whose foundations are so great and magnificent, is the work-house, or city work-house, properly so called, which being a late foundation, and founded upon meer charity, without any settled endowment, is the more remarkable, for here are a very great number of poor children taken in, and supported and maintained, fed, cloath'd, taught, and put out to trades, and that at an exceeding expence, and all this without one penny revenue.

It is establish'd, or rather the establishment of it, is supported by an old Act of Parliament, 13, 14. Car. II, impowering the citizens to raise contributions for the charge of employing the poor, and suppressing vagrants and beggars, and it is now, by the voluntary assistance and bounty of benefactors, become so considerable, that in the year 1715 they gave the following state of the house, viz.

Vagabonds, beggars, &c. taken into the house, including fifty-five which remained at the end of the preceding year	418
Discharged, including such as were put out to trades	356
Remaining in the house	62
Not one buried that whole year.	

124. Guy's Hospital for Incurables with eight views of the wards and other parts of the buildings; engraving (1725).

But the supplies and charities to this commendable work, have not of late come in so readily as they used to do, which has put the governors to some difficulties; upon which, *anno* 1614, the common council, by virtue of the powers above-mentioned, agreed to raise five thousand pounds upon the whole city, for the support of the house; but we do not find that any new demand has been made since that.

The hospital call'd the Charter House,[56] or Sutton's Hospital, is not by this supposed to be forgot, or the honour of it lessen'd. On the other hand, it must be recorded for ever, to be the greatest and noblest gift that ever was given for charity, by any one man, publick or private, in this nation, since history gives us any account of things.

I come now to an account of new edifices and publick buildings, erected or erecting in and about London, since the writing the foregoing account; and with this I conclude.

1. The fine new church of St. Martin's in the Fields,[57] with a very fine steeple, which they tell us is 215 feet high, all wholly built by the contribution of that great parish, and finished with the utmost expedition.

2. The new Admiralty Office near White-hall, being on the same ground where the old office stood; but much larger, being both longer in front and deeper backward, not yet finished.

3. Mr. Guy's new hospital for incurables, mentioned above, situated on ground purchased for that purpose, adjoyning to St. Thomas's Hospital in Southwark, being a most magnificent building not yet quite finished.

4. Two large wings to the hospital of Bedlam, appointed also for incurables; proposed first by the charitable disposition of Sir William Withers deceased; this also not yet finished.

5. A large new meeting-house in Spittle-fields, for the sect of Dissenters, call'd Baptists, or Antepædo Baptists.

6. The South-Sea house in Threadneedle-street, the old house being intirely pulled down, and several other houses adjoyning being purchased, the whole building will be new from the foundation; this not finished.

7. Several very fine new churches, being part of the fifty churches[58] appointed by Act of Parliament, viz. one in Spittle-fields, one in Radcliff-High-way, one in Old-street, one at Lime-house, with a very beautiful tower, and one in Bloomsbury, and five more not finished.

8. The parish church of St. Botolph without Bishopsgate, pulled down and re-building, by the contribution of the inhabitants, not as one of the fifty churches.

9. The Custom-house, which since the late fire in Thames-street, is ordered to be inlarged; but is not yet finished.

All these buildings are yet in building, and will all, in their several places, be very great ornaments to the city.

10. A new street or range of houses taken out of the south side of the Artillery Ground near Morefields, also an enlargement to the new burying ground as it was formerly called, on the north side of the same ground.

11. The iron ballustrade, or as others call it, balcony, on the lanthorn upon the cupolo of St. Paul's Church, gilded. It was done at the cost and as the gift of an Irish nobleman, who scarce lived to see it finished.

12. A new Bear-Garden, called Figg's Theater,[59] being a stage for the gladiators or prize-fighters, and is built on the Tyburn Road.

N.B. The gentlemen of the science, taking offence at its being called Tyburn Road, though it really is so, will have it called the Oxford Road; this publick edifice is fully finished, and in use.

I conclude this account of London, with mentioning something of the account of mortality, that is to say, the births and burials, from whence Sir William Petty[60] thought he might make some calculations of the numbers of the inhabitants, and I shall only take notice, that whereas, the general number of the burials in the year 1666, and farther back, were from 17000 to 19000 in a year, the last yearly bill for the year 1723, amounted as follows,

Christenings 19203.   Burials 29197.

Here is to be observed, that the number of burials exceeding so much the number of births, is, because as it is not the number born, but the number christened that are set down, which is taken from the parish register; so all the children of Dissenters of every sort, Protestant, Popish and Jewish are omitted, also all the children of foreigners, French, Dutch, &c. which are baptized in their own churches, and all the children of those who are so poor, that they cannot get them registred: so that if a due estimate be made, the births may be very well supposed to exceed the burials one year with another by many thousands.

It is not that I have no more to say of London, that I break off here; but that I have no room to say it.

I am, Sir,

Yours, &c.

The End of the Fifth Letter

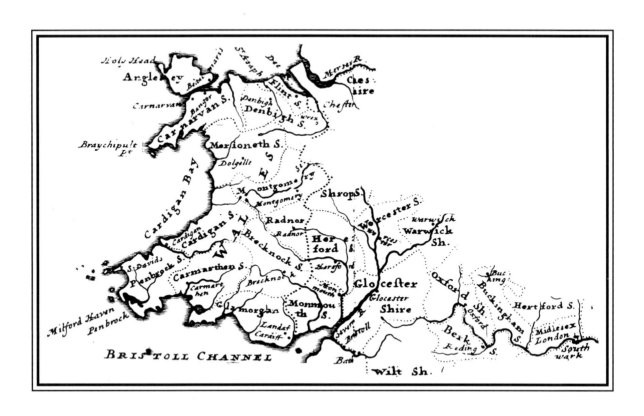

Holy Head

Angle ey

Beaumaris

Carnarvan

Bangor

Carnarvan S.

Braychipule Pt

Cardigan Bay

Dolgelle

Merioneth S.

St Asaph

Dee

Flint S.

Denbigh

Denbigh S.

wrex

Mersey R.

Che shire

Chester

Montgomery

Montgomery

Shrops.

Cardigan S.

Cardigan

Radnor

Radnor

Brecknock S.

Her ford

Worcester S.

West

Warwick
Sh.

warwick

St Davids

Penbrock S.

Carmarthen S.

Brecknock

Hereford

Mon
mouth

Gloucester

Oxford

Sh.

Oxford

Buc
king

Hertford S.

Milford Haven

Penbrock

Carmart
hen

Glamorgan

Landaf
Cardiff

Monmou
th
S.

Gloucester
Shire

Savern Bristoll

Berk

Reding S.

Midlesex
London

South
wark

BRISTOLL CHANNEL

Bath

Wilt Sh.

LETTER VI

*Containing a Description of Part of the
Counties of Middlesex, Hertford, Bucks,
Oxford, Wilts, Somerset, Gloucester,
Warwick, Worcester, Hereford, Monmouth,
and the several Counties of
South and North-Wales.*

I HAVE SPENT so much time, and taken up so much room in my description of London, and the adjacent parts, that I must be the more cautious, at least, as to needless excursions in the country near it.

The villages round London partake of the influence of London, so much, that it is observ'd as London is encreased, so they are all encreased also, and from the same causes.

Hackney and Bromley are the first villages which begin the county of Middlesex, east; for Bow as reckon'd to Stepney, is a part of the great mass. This town of **Hackney** is of a great extent, containing no less than 12 hamlets or separate villages, tho' some of them now join, viz.

Church-street,	Well-street,
Hummerton,	Cambridge-Heath,
Wyck-House,	Shacklewell,
Grove-street,	Dalstone,
Clapton,	Kingsland,
Mare-street,	Newington.

All these, tho' some of them are very large villages, make up but one parish (viz.) of Hackney.

All these, except the Wyck-House, are within a few years so encreas'd in buildings, and so fully inhabited, that there is no comparison to be made between their present and past state: every separate hamlet is encreas'd, and some of them more than treble as big as formerly; indeed as this whole town is included in the bills of mortality, tho' no where joining to London, it is in some respects to be call'd part of it.

This town is so remarkable for the retreat of wealthy citizens, that there is at this time near a hundred coaches kept in it; tho' I will not join with a certain satyrical author, who said of Hackney, that there were more coaches than Christians in it.

Newington, Tottenham, Edmonton, and Enfield stand all in a line N. from the city; the encrease of buildings is so great in them all, that they seem to a traveller to be one continu'd street; especially Tottenham and Edmonton, and in them all, the new buildings so far exceed the old, especially in the value of them, and figure of the inhabitants, that the fashion of the towns are quite altered.

The first thing we see in **Tottenham** is a small but beautiful house, built by one Mr. Wanly, formerly a goldsmith, near Temple Bar; it is a small house, but for the beauty of the building and the gardens, it is not outdone by any of the houses on this side the country.

There is not any thing more fine in their degree, than most of the buildings this way; only with this observation, that they are generally belonging to the middle sort of mankind, grown wealthy by trade, and who still taste of London; some of them live both in the city, and in the country at the same time: yet many of these are immensely rich.

High-gate and Hamstead are next on the north-side; at the first is a very beautiful house built by the late Sir William Ashurst,[1] on the very summit of the hill, and with a view from the very lowest windows over the whole vale, to the city: and that so eminently, that they see the very ships passing up and down the river for 12 or 15 miles below London. The Jews have par-

125. View of Hampstead from the top of Pond Street, engraving by J.B.C. Chatelain 1752.

ticularly fixt upon this town for their country retreats, and some of them are very wealthy; they live there in good figure, and have several trades particularly depending upon them, and especially, butchers of their own to supply them with provisions kill'd their own way; also, I am told, they have a private synagogue here.

Hampstead indeed is risen from a little country village, to a city, not upon the credit only of the waters,[2] tho' 'tis apparent, its growing greatness began there; but company increasing gradually, and the people liking both the place and the diversions together; it grew suddenly populous, and the concourse of people was incredible. This consequently raised the rate of lodgings, and that encreased buildings, till the town grew up from a little village, to a magnitude equal to some cities; nor could the uneven surface, inconvenient for building, uncompact, and unpleasant, check the humour of the town, for even on the very steep of the hill, where there's no walking twenty yards together, without tugging up a hill, or stradling down a hill, yet 'tis all one, the buildings encreased to that degree, that the town almost spreads the whole side of the hill.

On the top of the hill indeed, there is a very pleasant plain, called the heath, which on the very summit, is a plain of about a mile every way; and in good weather 'tis pleasant airing upon it, and some of the streets are extended so far, as that they begin to build, even on the highest part of the hill. But it must be confest, 'tis so near heaven, that I dare not say it can be a proper situation, for any but a race of mountaineers, whose lungs have been used to a rarify'd air, nearer the second region, than any ground for 30 miles round it.

It is true, this place may be said to be prepared for a summer dwelling, for in winter nothing that I know can recommend it: 'Tis true, a warm house, and good company, both which are to be had here, go a great way to make amends for storms, and severity of cold.

Here is a most beautiful prospect indeed, for we see here Hanslop steeple one way, which is within eight miles of Northampton, N. W. to Landown-Hill in Essex another way, east, at least 66 miles from one another; the prospect to London, and beyond it to Bansted Downs, south; Shooters-Hill, S. E. Red-Hill, S. W. and Windsor-Castle, W. is also uninterrupted: Indeed due north, we see no farther than to Barnet, which is not above six miles; but the rest is sufficient.

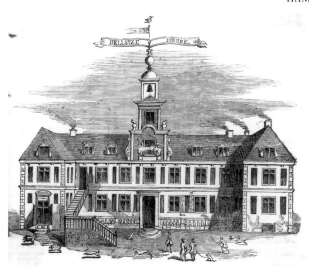

HESE are to give Notice, tnat *Bellfize* is now o pen'd for the whole Seafon, and that all Things are moft commodioufly concerted for the Reception of Gentlemen and Ladies; The *Park, Wildernefs,* and *Gardens,* being wonderfully Improv'd, and fill'd with variety of Birds which compofe a moft Melodious and Delightfome Harmony. Every Morning at Seven a Clock, the Mufick begins to play and continues the whole Day thro'; and any Perfons inclin'd to walk and divert themfelves in the Morning, may as cheaply break faft there, on *Tea* or *Coffee,* as in their own Chambers: And for the convenience of fingle Perfons or Families who refide at *Hampftead,* there are Coaches prepar'd to ply betwixt the 2 places; which, by the leaft Notice given, fhall attend at their Lodgings or Houfes for fixpence *per* Paffenger; and for the Security of his Guefts, there are 12 ftout Fellows compleatly Arm'd to patrole betwixt *London* and *Bellfize* to prevent the Infults of Highwaymen or Footpads which may infeft the Road.

126a and b. Bellsize House and the accompanying announcement of its reopening; engravings (*c.*1724).

At the foot of this hill is an old seat of the Earls of Chesterfields, called Bellsize;[3] which for many years had been neglected, and as it were forgotten: But being taken lately by a certain projector to get a penny, and who knew by what handle to take the gay part of the world, he has made it a true house of pleasure; here, in the gardens he entertained the company with all kind of sport, and in the house with all kinds of game, to say no more of it: this brought a wonderful concourse of people to the place, for they were so effectually gratified in all sorts of diversion, that the wicked part at length broke in, till it alarm'd the magistrates, and I am told it has been now in a manner suppress'd by the hand of justice.

Here was a great room fitted up with abundance of dexterity for their balls, and had it gone on to a degree of masquerading as I hear was actually begun, it would have bid fair to have had half the town run to it: one saw pictures and furniture there beyond what was to have been expected in a meer publick house; and 'tis hardly credible how it drew company to it; But it could not be, no British government could be supposed to bear long with the liberties taken on such publick occasions: so as I have said, they are reduc'd, at least restrain'd from liberties which they could not preserve by their prudence.

Yet Hampstead is not much the less frequented for this. But as there is (especially at the wells) a conflux of all sorts of company, even Hampstead itself has suffered in its good name; and you see sometimes more gallantry than modesty: so that the ladies who value their reputation, have of late more avoided the wells and walks at Hampstead, than they had formerly done.

I could not be at Hampstead, and not make an excursion to Edgworth, a little market town, on the road to St. Albans; I say to St. Albans, because 'tis certain, that this was formerly the only or the main road from London to St. Albans; being the famous high road, call'd Watling-street, which in former times reached from London to Shrewsbury, and on towards Wales.

The remains of this road are still to be seen here, and particularly in this, (viz.) that from Hide-Park Corner, just where Tyburn stands, the road makes one straight line without any turning, even to the very town of St. Albans. In this road lyes the town of Edgworth, some will have it that it was built by King Edgar the Saxon monarch, and called by his name, and so will have the town called Edgar, and that it was built as a garrison on the said Watling-street, to preserve the high-way from thieves: but all this I take to be fabulous, and without authority.

Near this town, and which is the reason of naming it, the present Duke of Chandos[4] has built a most magnificent palace or mansion house, I might say, the most magnificent in England: it is erected where formerly stood an old seat belonging to Sir Lancelot Lake, whose son and successor struggled hard to be chosen representative for the county, but lost it, and had a great interest and estate hereabouts.

This palace is so beautiful in its situation, so lofty, so majestick the appearance of it, that a pen can but ill describe it, the pencil not much better; 'tis only fit to be talk'd of upon the very spot, when the building is under view, to be consider'd in all its parts.

The fronts are all of freestone, the columns and pilasters are lofty and beautiful, the windows very high, with all possible ornaments: the pilasters running

127. South front of Cannons, seat of James, Duke of Chandos; engraving by H. Hulsbergh after a drawing by John Price (*c.* 1720).

flush up to the cornish and architrave, their capitals seem as so many supporters to the fine statues which stand on the top, and crown the whole; in a word, the whole structure is built with such a profusion of expence, and all finish'd with such a brightness of fancy, goodness of judgment; that I can assure you, we see many palaces of sovereign princes abroad, which do not equal it, which yet pass for very fine too either within or without. And as it is a noble and well con-triv'd building; so it is as well set out, and no ornament is wanting to make it the finest house in England. The plaistering and guilding is done by the famous Pargotti an Italian, said to be the finest artist in those particular works now in England. The great salon or hall is painted by Paolucci,[5] for the Duke spared no cost to have every thing as rich as possible. The pillars supporting the building are all of marble: the great staircase is the finest by far of any in England; and the steps are all of marble, every step being of one whole piece, about 22 foot in length.

It is in vain to attempt to describe the beauties of this building at Cannons; the whole is a beauty, and as the firmament is a glorious mantle filled with, or as it were made up of a concurrence of lesser glories the stars; so every part of this building adds to the beauty of the whole. The avenue is spacious and majestick, and as it gives you the view of two fronts, join'd as it were in one, the distance not admitting you to see the angle, which is in the centre; so you are agreeably drawn in, to think the front of the house almost twice as large as it really is.

And yet when you come nearer you are again sur-

prized, by seeing the winding passage opening as it were a new front to the eye, of near 120 feet wide, which you had not seen before, so that you are lost a while in looking near hand for what you so evidently saw a great way off. Tho' many of the palaces in Italy are very large fine buildings, yet I venture to say, not Italy itself can show such a building rais'd from the common surface, by one private hand, and in so little a time as this; for Cannons as I was inform'd, was not three years a building and bringing the gardens and all, to the most finish'd beauty we now see it in.

The inside of this house is as glorious, as the outside is fine; the lodgings are indeed most exquisitely finish'd, and if I may call it so, royally furnish'd; the chapel is a singularity, not only in its building, and the beauty of its workmanship, but in this also, that the Duke maintains there a full choir, and has the wor-ship perform'd there with the best musick, after the manner of the Chappel Royal, which is not done in any other noble man's chappel in Britain; no not the Prince of Wales's, though heir apparent to the crown.

Nor is the chapel only furnish'd with such excellent musick, but the Duke has a set of them to entertain him every day at dinner.

The avenues and vista's to this house are extreamly magnificent, the great walk or chief avenue is near a mile in length, planted with two double rows of trees, and the middle walk broad enough for a troop of horse to march in front; in the middle way there is a large basin or fountain of water, and the coaches drive round it on either side; there are three other avenues exceeding fine, but not so very large; the beauty of them all will double, with time, when the trees may be grown, like those of New-Hall,[6] in Essex.

Two miles from hence, we go up a small ascent by the great road, which for what reason I know not, is there call'd Crab Tree Orchard, when leaving the street way on the right, we enter a spacious heath or common call'd Bushy-Heath, where, again, we have a very agreeable prospect.

I cannot but remember, with some satisfaction, that having two foreign gentlemen in my company, in our passing over this heath, I say I could not but then observe, and now remember it with satisfaction, how they were surprized at the beauty of this prospect, and how they look'd at one another, and then again turning their eyes every way in a kind of wonder, one of them said to the other, that England was not like other country's, but it was all a planted garden.

They had there on the right hand, the town of St. Albans in their view; and all the spaces between, and further beyond it, look'd indeed like a garden. The inclos'd corn-fields made one grand parterre, the thick planted hedge rows, like a wilderness or labyrinth, divided in espaliers; the villages interspers'd, look'd like so many several noble seats of gentlemen at a distance. In a word, it was all nature, and yet look'd all like art; on the left hand we see the west-end of London, Westminster-Abbey, and the Parliament-House, but the body of the city was cut off by the hill, at which Hampstead intercepted the sight on that side.

More to the south we had Hampton Court, and S. W. Windsor, and between both, all those most beautiful parts of Middlesex and Surrey, on the bank of the Thames, of which I have already said so much, and which are indeed the most agreeable in the world.

St. Albans is the capital town, tho' not the county town of Hertfordshire, it has a great corn market, and is famous for its antient church, built on the ruins, or part of the ruins of the most famous abbey of Verulam; the greatness of which, is to be judg'd by the old walls, which one sees for a mile before we come to town.

But I must travel no farther this way, till I have taken a journey west from London, and seen what the country affords that way; the next towns adjacent to London, are, Kensington, Chelsea, Hammersmith, Fulham, Twickenham, &c. all of them near, or adjoyning to the river of Thames, and which, by the beauty of their buildings, make good the north shore of the river, answerable, to what I have already describ'd.

Kensington cannot be nam'd without mentioning

128. Kensington Palace and Garden; engraving by T. Bowles (1724).

The Royal Palace of KINGSINGTON.

XXIV. Peter Tillemans, *The Thames with Chelsea Hospital* (c.1725).

the King's palace there; a building which may now be call'd entirely new, tho' it was originally an old house of the Earl of Nottingham's of whom the late King William bought it, and then enlarg'd it as we see; some of the old building still remaining in the center of the house.

The house itself fronts to the garden three ways, the gardens being now made exceeding fine, and enlarged to such a degree, as to reach quite from the great road to Kensington town, to the Acton road north, more than a mile. The first laying out of these gardens was the design of the late Queen Mary, who finding the air agreed with, and was necessary to the health of the King, resolved to make it agreeable to herself too, and gave the first orders for enlarging the gardens: the author of this account, having had the honour to attend her majesty, when she first viewed the ground, and directed the doing it, speaks this with the more satisfaction.

The late Queen Anne completed what Queen Mary began, and delighted very much in the place; and often was pleased to make the green house which is very beautiful, her summer supper house.

But this house has lost much of its pleasantness on one account, namely, that all the princes that ever might be said to single it out for their delight, had the fate to dye in it; namely, King William, Prince George

of Denmark, and lastly, Queen Anne herself; since which it has not been so much in request, King George having generally kept his summer, when in England, at Hampton Court.

As this palace opens to the west, there are two great wings built, for lodgings for such as necessarily attend the court, and a large port cocher at the entrance, with a postern and a stone gallery on the south side of the court which leads to the great stair-case.

This south wing was burnt down by accident, the King and Queen being both there, the Queen was a little surprized at first, apprehending some treason, but King William a stranger to fears smil'd at the suggestion, chear'd her majesty up, and being soon dress'd, they both walked out into the garden, and stood there some hours till they perceived the fire by the help that came in, and by the diligence of the foot guards, was gotten under foot.

South of this town stands **Chelsea**, a town of palaces, and which by its new extended buildings seems to promise itself to be made one time or other a part of London.

Here is the noblest building, and the best foundation of its kind in the world, viz. for the entertainment of maimed and old soldiers. If we must except the hospital[7] call'd des Invalids at Paris, it must be only that the number is greater there, but I pretend to say that the oeconomy of the invalids there, is not to compare with this at Chelsea; and as for the provisions, the lodging, and attendance given, Chelsea infinitely exceeds that at Paris. Here the poor men are lodg'd, well cloathed, well furnish'd, and well fed, and I may say there are thousands of poor families in England who are said to live well too, and do not feed as the soldiers there are fed; and as for France, I may add, they know nothing there what it is to live so. The like may be said of the invalid sea men at the hospital of Greenwich.

Sir Stephen Fox's[8] house at **Chiswick** is the flower of all the private gentlemen's palaces in England. Here when the late King William, who was an allowed judge of fine buildings, and of gardening also, had seen the house and garden, he stood still on the terras for near half a quarter of an hour without speaking one word, when turning at last to the Earl of Portland, the King said, This place is perfectly fine, I could live here five days.

In the village of **Hammersmith**, which was formerly a long scattering place, full of gardeners' grounds, with here and there an old house of some bulk: I say, in this village we see now not only a wood of great houses and palaces, but a noble square built as it were in the middle of several handsome streets, as if the village seem'd enclin'd to grow up into a city.

Here we are told they design to obtain the grant of a market, tho' it be so near to London, and some talk also of building a fine stone bridge over the Thames; but these things are yet but in embryo, tho' it is not unlikely but they may be both accomplished in time, and also Hammersmith and Chiswick joyning thus, would in time be a city indeed.

On the right hand as we ride from London to Uxbridge, or to Colebrook, we see **Harrow**, a little town on a very high hill, and is therefore call'd Harrow on the Hill: the church of this town standing upon the summit of the hill, and having a very handsome and high spire, they tell us, King Charles II ridiculing the warm disputes among some critical scripturallists of those times, concerning the visible church of Christ upon earth; us'd to say of it, that if there was e'er a visible church upon earth, he believ'd this was one.

From hence, we proceeded on the road towards Oxford; but first turned to the right to visit **Aylesbury**. This is the principal market town in the county of Bucks; tho' Buckingham a much inferior place, is call'd the county town: here also is held the election for Members of Parliament, or Knights of the Shire for the county, and county goal, and the assizes. It is a large town, has a very noble market for corn, and is famous for a large tract of the richest land in England, extended for many miles round it, almost from Tame, on the edge of Oxfordshire, to Leighton in Bedfordshire, and is called from this very town, the Vale of Aylesbury. Here it was that conversing with some gentlemen, who understood counry affairs, for all the gentlemen hereabouts are graziers, tho' all the graziers are not gentlemen; they shew'd me one remarkable pasture-field, no way parted off or separated, one piece of it from another; I say, 'tis one enclosed field of pasture ground, which was let for 1400 l. per ann. to a grazier, and I knew the tenant very well, whose name was Houghton, and who confirm'd the truth of it.

We went on from Aylesbury to **Thame** or Tame, a large market town on the River Thames: this brings me to mention again the Vale of Aylesbury; which as I noted before, is eminent for the richest land, and perhaps the richest graziers in England: But it is more particularly famous for the head of the river Thame or Thames, which rises in this vale near a market town call'd Tring, and waters the whole vale either by itself or the several streams which run into it, and when it comes to the town of Tame, is a good large river.

At **Tring** abovenam'd is a most delicious house, built *à la moderne*, as the French call it, by the late Mr. Guy,[9] who was for many years Secretary of the Treasury, and continued it till near his death; when he was succeeded by the late Mr. Lowndes. The late King William did Mr. Guy the honour to dine at this house, when he set out on his expedition to Ireland, in the year 1690, the same year that he fought the battle of the Boyn; and tho' his majesty came from London that morning, and was resolv'd to lye that night at Northampton, yet he would not go away without taking a look at the fine gardens, which are perhaps the best finish'd in the worst situation of any in England. This house was afterwards bought by Sir William Gore, a

129. View of the Vale of Aylesbury from Whitchurch (published by Byrne and Cadell, 1803).

merchant of London; and left by him to his eldest son, who now enjoys it.

There was an eminent contest here between Mr. Guy, and the poor of the parish, about his enclosing part of the common to make him a park; Mr. Guy presuming upon his power, set up his pales, and took in a large parcel of open land, call'd Wiggington-Common; the cottagers and farmers oppos'd it, by their complaints a great while; but finding he went on with his work, and resolv'd to do it, they rose upon him, pull'd down his banks, and forced up his pales, and carried away the wood, or set it on a heap and burnt it; and this they did several times, till he was oblig'd to desist; after some time he began again, offering to treat with the people, and to give them any equivalent for it: but that not being satisfactory, they mobb'd him again. How they accommodated it at last, I know not; but I see that Mr. Gore has a park, and a very good one but not large: I mention this as an instance of the popular claim in England; which we call right of commonage, which the poor take to be as much their property, as a rich man's land is his own.

From hence I came to **Oxford**, a name known throughout the learned world; a city famous in our English history for several things, besides its being an University.

1. So eminent for the goodness of its air, and healthy situation; that our courts have no less than three times, if my information is right, retir'd hither, when London has been visited with the pestilence; and here they have been always safe.

2. It has also several times been the retreat of our princes, when the rest of the kingdom has been embroil'd in war and rebellion; and here they have found both safety and support; at least, as long as the loyal inhabitants were able to protect them.

3. It was famous for the noble defence of religion, which our first reformers and martyrs made here, in their learned and bold disputations against the Papists, in behalf of the Protestant religion; and their triumphant closing the debates, by laying down their lives for the truths which they asserted.

4. It was likewise famous for resisting the attacks of arbitrary power, in the affair of Magdalen College,[10] in King James's time; and the fellows laying down their fortunes, tho' not their lives, in defence of liberty and property.

This, to use a scripture elegance, is that city of Oxford; the greatest, (if not the most antient) university in this island of Great-Britain; and perhaps the most flourishing at this time, in men of polite learning, and in the most accomplish'd masters, in all sciences, and in all the parts of acquir'd knowledge in the world.

I know there is a long contest, and yet undetermin'd between the two English universities, about the antiquity of their foundation; and as they have not decided it themselves, who am I? and what is this work? that I should pretend to enter upon that important question, in so small a tract?

The city itself is large, strong, populous, and rich; and as it is adorn'd by the most beautiful buildings of the colleges, and halls, it makes the most noble figure of any city of its bigness in Europe.

The theatre at Oxford prepared for the publick exercises of the schools, and for the operations of the learned part of the English world only, is in its grandeur and magnificence, infinitely superior to any thing in the world of its kind; it is a finish'd peice, as to its building, the front is exquisitely fine, the columns and pilasters regular, and very beautiful; 'tis all built of free-stone: the model was approv'd by the best masters of architecture at that time, in the presence of K. Charles II who was himself a very curious observer, and a good judge; Sir Christopher Wren was the director of the work, as he was the the person that drew the model: Archbishop Sheldon,[11] they tell us, paid for it, and gave it to the University: there is a world of decoration in the front of it, and more beautiful additions, by way of ornament, besides the antient inscription, than is to be seen any where in Europe; at least, where I have been.

The Bodleian Library is an ornament in itself worthy of Oxford, where its station is fix'd, and where it had its birth. The history of it at large is found in Mr. Speed,[12] and several authors of good credit; containing in brief, that of the old library, the first publick one in Oxford, erected in Durham now Trinity College, by Richard Bishop of Durham, and Lord Treasurer to Ed. III, it was afterward joined to another, founded by Cobham Bishop of Worcester, and both enlarg'd by the bounty of Humphry Duke of Gloucester, founder of the divinity schools: I say, these libraries being lost, and the books embezzled by the many changes and hurries of the suppressions in the reign of Hen. VIII, the commissioners appointed by King Edw. VI to visit the universities, and establish the Reformation; found very few valuable books or manuscripts left in them.

In this state of things, one Sir Thomas Bodley,[13] a wealthy and learned knight, zealous for the encouragement both of learning and religion, resolv'd to apply, both his time, and estate, to the erecting and furnishing a new library for the publick use of the University.

In this good and charitable undertaking, he went on so successfully, for so many years, and with such a profusion of expence, and obtain'd such assistances

130. South prospect of the city of Oxford; engraving by Sutton Nicholls (1724).

from all the encouragers of learning in his time, that having collected books and manuscripts from all parts of the learned world; he got leave of the University, (and well they might grant it) to place them in the old library room, built as is said, by the good Duke Humphry.

To this great work, great additions have been since made in books, as well as contributions in money, and more are adding every day; and thus the work was brought to a head, the 8th of Nov. 1602, and has continued encreasing by the benefactions of great and learned men to this day: to remove the books once more and place them in beauty and splendor suitable to so glorious a collection, the late Dr. Radcliff[14] has left a legacy of 40000 l. say some, others say not quite so much, to the building a new repository or library for the use of the University: this work is not yet built, but I am told 'tis likely to be such a building as will be a greater ornament to the place than any yet standing in it.

Oxford, had for many ages the neighbourhood of the court, while their kings kept up the royal palace at Woodstock; which tho' perhaps it was much discontinu'd, for the fate of the fair Rosamond,[15] mistress to Henry Fitz Empress, or Henry II, of which history tells us something, and fable much more; yet we after find that several of the kings of England made the house and park at Woodstock, which was always fam'd for its pleasant situation, the place of their summer retreat for many years.

The old buildings are now no more, nor so much as the name, but the place is the same and the natural beauty of it indeed, is as great as ever.

It is still a most charming situation, and 'tis still disputable after all that has been laid out, whether the country round gives more lustre to the building, or the building to the country. It has now chang'd masters, 'tis no more a royal house or palace for the king; but a mark of royal bounty to a great, and at that time powerful subject, the late Duke of Marlborough.

The magnificence of the building does not here as at Canons, at Chatsworth, and at other palaces of the nobility, express the genius and the opulence of the possessor, but it represents the bounty, the gratitude, or what else posterity pleases to call it, of the English nation, to the man whom they delighted to honour: posterity when they view in this house the trophies of the Duke of Marlborough's fame, and the glories of his great achievements will not celebrate his name only; but will look on Blenheim[16] House, as a monument of the generous temper of the English nation; who in so glorious a manner rewarded the services of those who acted for them as he did: nor can any nation in Europe shew the like munificence to any general, no nor the greatest in the world.

The magnificent work then is a national building, and must for ever be call'd so. Nay, the dimensions of it will perhaps call upon us hereafter, to own it as such in order to vindicate the discretion of the builder, for making a palace too big for any British subject to fill, if he lives at his own expence.

Nothing else can justify the vast design, a bridge or

175

131. Unknown painter, *View of the harvesting field of James Higford's manor, Dixton, Gloucestershire* (*c.*1725–35).

XXV. a (below), b and c (facing page). Unknown painter, *Views of the harvesting field of James Higford's manor, Dixton, Gloucestershire* (*c.*1725–35). The scene looks eastwards to the Cotswold Hills with Alderton Hill on the left and Langley Hill on the right.

132. 'Rowldricht Stones from the West, Sept 11 1724;' engraving by William Stukeley. From his *Abury* (1740).

ryalto rather, of one arch costing 20000 l. and this, like the bridge at the Escurial in Spain, without a river. Gardens of near 100 acres of ground. Offices fit for 300 in family. Out-houses fit for the lodgings of a regiment of guards, rather than of livery servants. Also the extent of the fabrick, the avenues, the salons, galleries, and royal apartments; nothing below royalty and a prince, can support an equipage suitable to the living in such a house: and one may without a spirit of prophecy, say, it seems to intimate, that some time or other Blenheim may and will return to be as the old Woodstock once was, the palace of a king.

From Woodstock I could not refrain taking a turn a little northward as high as Banbury to the banks of the Charwell, to see the famous spot of ground where a vigorous rencounter happen'd between the Royalists in the grand Rebellion, and the Parliament's forces, under Sir William Waller; I mean at Croprady Bridge,[17] near Banbury. It was a vigorous action, and in which the King's forces may be said fairly to out-general their enemies, which really was not always their fate: I had the plan of that action before me, which I have had some years, and found out every step of the ground as it was disputed on both sides by inches, where the horse engaged and where the foot; where Waller lost his cannon, and where he retired; and it was evident to me the best thing Waller cou'd do, (tho' superiour in number) was to retreat as he did, having lost half his army.

From thence, being within eight miles of Edge-Hill,[18] where the first battle in that war happen'd, I had the like pleasure of viewing the ground about Keinton, where that bloody battle was fought; it was evident, and one could hardly think of it without regret, the King with his army had an infinite advantage by being posted on the top of the hill, that he

knew that the Parliament's army were under express orders to fight, and must attack him lest his majesty who had got two days march of them, should advance to London, where they were out of their wits for fear of him.

The King I say knowing this, 'tis plain he had no business but to have intrench'd, to fight upon the eminence where he was posted, or have detach'd 15000 men for London, while he had fortify'd himself with a strong body upon the hill: but on the contrary, his majesty scorning to be pursued by his subjects, his army excellently appointed, and full of courage, not only halted, but descended from his advantages and offer'd them battle in the plain field, which they accepted.

But to leave the war, 'tis the place only I am taking notice of. From hence I turn'd south, for I was here on the edge both of Warwickshire, and Gloucestershire: but I turned south, and coming down by and upon the west side of Oxfordshire, to Chipping-Norton, we were shew'd Roll-Richt-Stones,[19] a second Stone-Henge; being a ring of great stones standing upright, some of them from 5 to 7 foot high.

We were very merry at passing thro' a village call'd Bloxham, on the occasion of a meeting of servants for hire, which the people there call a Mop;[20] 'tis generally in other places vulgarly call'd a Statute, because founded upon a statute law in Q. Elizabeth's time for regulating of servants. This I christen'd by the name of a Jade-fair, at which some of the poor girls began to be angry, but we appeas'd them with better words.

I have observ'd at some of these fairs, that the poor servants distinguish themselves by holding something in their hands, to intimate what labour they are particularly qualify'd to undertake; as the carters a whip, the labourers a shovel, the wood men a bill, the manufacturers a wool comb, and the like. But since the ways and manners of servants[21] are advanc'd as we now find them to be, those Jade Fairs are not so much frequented as formerly, tho' we have them at several towns near London; as at Enfield, Waltham, Epping, &c.

Here we saw also the famous parish of Brightwell, of which it was observed, that there had not been an alehouse nor a dissenter from the church, nor any quarrel among the inhabitants that rise so high as to a suit of law within the memory of man. But they could not say it was so still, especially as to the alehouse part; tho' very much is still preserved, as to the unity and good neighbourhood of the parishioners, and their conformity to the church.

Being now on the side of Warwickshire, as is said before, I still went south, and passing by the four Shire stones, we saw where the counties of Oxford, Warwick, and Gloucester joyn all in a point; one stone standing in each county, and the fourth touching all three.

Hence we came to the famous Cotswold-Downs, so eminent for the best of sheep, and finest wool in England: it was of the breed of these sheep. And fame tells us that some were sent by King Rich. I into Spain, and that from thence the breed of their sheep was raised, which now produce so fine a wool, that we are oblig'd to fetch it from thence, for the making our finest broad cloaths; and which we buy at so great a price.

Upon these downs we had a clear view of the famous old Roman high-way, call'd the Fosse, which evidently crosses all the middle part of England, and is to be seen and known (tho' in no place plainer than here,) quite from the Bath to Warwick, and thence to Leicester, to Newark, to Lincoln, and on to Barton, upon the bank of Humber.

Here it is still the common road, and we follow'd it over the downs to Cirencester. We observ'd also how several cross roads as antient as itself, and perhaps more antient, joyn'd it, or branch'd out of it; some of which the people have by antient usage tho' corruptly call'd also Fosses, making the word Fosse as it were a common name for all roads. For example,

The Ackemanstreet which is an antient Saxon road leading from Buckinghamshire through Oxfordshire to the Fosse, and so to the Bath; this joyns the Fosse between Burford and Cirencester. It is worth observing how this is said to be call'd Ackeman's Street; namely, by the Saxon way of joyning their monysyllables into significant words, as thus, Ackman or Achman, a man of aching limbs, in English a cripple travelling to the Bath for cure: So Achmanstreet was

the road or street for diseased people going to the Bath; and the city of Bath was on the same account call'd Achmanchester, or the city of diseased people; or, *Urbs Ægrotorum hominum*. Thus much for antiquity.

There are other roads or fosses which joyn this grand high-way, viz. Grinnes Dike, from Oxfordshire, Wattle Bank, or Aves ditch from ditto, and the Would Way, call'd also the Fosse crossing from Gloucester to Cirencester.

In passing this way we very remarkably cross'd four rivers within the length of about 10 miles, and enquiring their names, the country people call'd them every one the Thames, which mov'd me a little to enquire the reason, which is no more than this; namely, that these rivers, which are, the Lech, the Coln, the Churn, and the Isis; all rising in the Cotswould Hills and joyning together and making a full stream at Lechlade near this place, they become one river there, and are all call'd Thames, or vulgarly Temms; also beginning there to be navigable, you see very large barges at the key, taking in goods for London, which makes the town of Lechlade a very populous large place.

On the Churne one of those rivers, stands ***Cirencester***, or Ciciter for brevity, a very good town, populous and rich, full of clothiers, and driving a great trade in wool; which as likewise at Tetbury, is brought from the midland counties of Leicester, Northampton, and Lincoln, where the largest sheep in England are found, and where are few manufactures; it is sold here in quantities, so great, that it almost exceeds belief: it is generally bought here by the clothiers of Wiltshire and Gloucestershire, for the supply of that great clothing trade; of which I have spoken already: they talk of 5000 packs in a year.

As we go on upon the Fosse, we see in the vale on the left hand, the antient town of Malmsbury, famous for a monastary, and a great church, built out of the ruins of it; and which I name in meer veneration to that excellent, and even best of our old historians *Gulielmus Malmsburiensis*,[22] to whom the world is so much oblig'd, for preserving the history and antiquities of this kingdom.

We next arriv'd at Marshfield, a Wiltshire clothing town, very flourishing and where we cross'd the great road from London to Bristol, as at Cirencester, we did that from London, to Gloucester; and in the evening keeping still the Fosse-Way, we arriv'd at ***Bath***.

My description of this city would be very short, and indeed it would have been a very small city, (if at all a city) were it not for the hot baths here, which give both name and fame to the place.

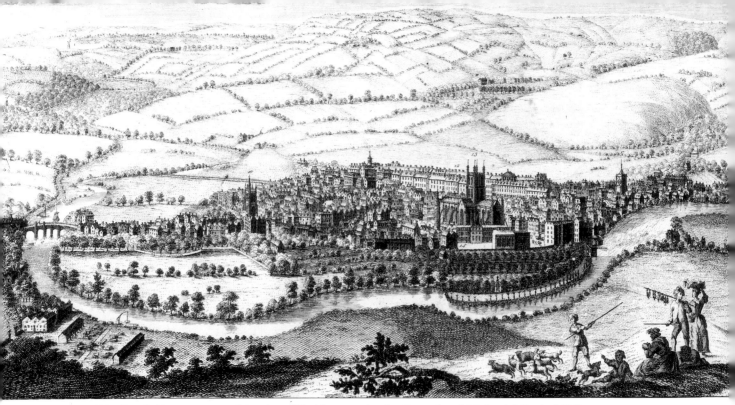

133. 'South East prospect of the city of Bath'; engraving by Samuel and Nathaniel Buck (1734).

The antiquity of this place, and of the baths here, is doubtless very great, tho' I cannot come in to the inscription under the figure, said to be of a Brittish king, placed in that call'd the King's Bath, which says that this King Bladud,[23] (Mr. Cambden calls him Blayden, or Blaydon Cloyth; that is, the South-sayer) found out the use of these baths, 300 years before our Saviour's time. I say, I cannot come into this, because even the discovery is ascribed to the magick of the day, not their judgment in the physical virtue of minerals, and mineral-waters.

It has been observ'd before, that in former times this was a resort hither for cripples, and the place was truly *Urbs Ægrotorum Hominum*: and we see the crutches hang up at the several baths, as the thank-offerings of those who have come hither lame, and gone away cur'd. But now we may say it is the resort of the sound, rather than the sick; the bathing is made more a sport and diversion, than a physical prescription for health; and the town is taken up in raffling, gameing, visiting, and in a world, all sorts of gallantry and levity.

The whole time indeed is a round of the utmost diversion. In the morning you (supposing you to be a young lady) are fetch'd in a close chair, dress'd in your bathing cloths, that is, stript to the smock, to the Cross-Bath. There the musick plays you into the bath, and the women that tend you, present you with a little floating wooden dish, like a bason; in which the lady puts a handkerchief, and a nosegay, of late the snuff-box is added, and some patches; tho' the bath occasioning a little perspiration, the patches do not stick so kindly as they should.

Here the ladies and the gentlemen pretend to keep some distance, and each to their proper side, but frequently mingle here too, as in the King and Queens Bath, tho' not so often; and the place being but narrow, they converse freely, and talk, rally, make vows, and sometimes love; and having thus amus'd themselves an hour, or two, they call their chairs and return to their lodgings.

The rest of the diversion here, is at the walks in the great church, and at the raffling shops, which are kept (like the cloyster at Bartholomew Fair,) in the church-yard, and ground adjoyning. In the afternoon there is generally a play, tho' the decorations are mean, and the performances accordingly; but it answers, for the company here (not the actors) make the play, to say no more. In the evening there is a ball, and dancing at least twice a week, which is commonly in the great Town Hall, over the Market-House; where there never fails in the season to be a great deal of very good company.

There is one thing very observable here, which tho' it brings abundance of company to the Bath, more than ever us'd to be there before; yet it seems to have quite inverted the use and virtue of the waters, (viz.) that whereas for seventeen hundred or two thousand years, if you believe King Bladud, the medicinal virtue of these waters had been useful to the diseased people

180

by bathing in them, now they are found to be useful also, taken into the body; and there are many more come to drink the waters, than to bathe in them; nor are the cures they perform this way, less valuable than the outward application; especially in colicks, ill digestion, and scorbutick distempers.

This discovery they say, is not yet above fifty years old, and is said to be owing to the famous Dr. Radcliff, but I think it must be older, for I have myself drank the waters of the Bath[24] above fifty years ago: but be it so, 'tis certain, 'tis a modern discovery, compar'd to the former use of these waters.

As to the usefulness of these waters to procure conception, and the known story of the late King James's Queen here, the famous monument in the Cross-Bath gives an account of it. Those that are enclin'd to give faith to such things, may know as much of it at the Santa Casa of Loretto, as here; and in Italy I believe it is much more credited.

There is nothing in the neighbourhood of this city worth notice, except it be Chipping-Norton-Lane, where was a fight between the forces of King James II and the Duke of Monmouth, in which the latter had plainly the better; and had they push'd their advantage, might have made it an entire victory. On the N. W. of this city up a very steep hill, is the King's Down, where sometimes persons of quality who have coaches go up for the air.

When one is upon King-Down, and has pass'd all the steeps and difficulties of the ascent, there is a plain and pleasant country for many miles, into Gloucestershire, and two very noble palaces, the one built by Mr.

134. Old town hall and High Street, Bath; watercolour by Edward Eyre (c.1776, from an earlier lost drawing).

135. The Cross Bath; engraving by John Fayram (1739).

Blathwait, late Secretary of War; and the other is call'd Badminton,[25] the mansion of the most noble family of the Dukes of Beaufort, the present Duke being under age. The lustre and magnificence of this palace is magnify'd by the surprise one is at, to see such a house in such a retreat, so difficult of access, at least this way, so near to so much company, and yet, so much alone.

Following the course of the river Avon, which runs thro' Bath, we come in ten miles to the city of **Bristol**, the greatest, the richest, and the best port of trade in Great Britain, London only excepted.

The merchants of this city not only have the greatest trade, but they trade with a more entire independency upon London, than any other town in Britain. And 'tis evident in this particular, (viz.) that whatsoever exportations they make to any part of the world, they are able to bring the full returns back to their own port, and can dispose of it there.

This is not the case in any other port in England. But they are often oblig'd either to ship part of the effects in the ports abroad, on the ships bound to London; or to consign their own ships to London, in order both to get freight, as also to dispose of their own cargoes.

But the Bristol merchants as they have a very great trade abroad, so they have always buyers at home, for

136. Hot wells, Bristol; engraving by W. Milton after S. Pye (1747).

their returns, and that such buyers that no cargo is too big for them. To this purpose, the shopkeepers in Bristol who in general are all wholesale men, have so great an inland trade among all the western counties, that they maintain carriers just as the London tradesmen do, to all the principal countries and towns from Southampton in the south, even to the banks of the Trent north; and tho' they have no navigable river that way, yet they drive a very great trade through all those counties.

Add to this, that, as well by sea, as by the navigation of two great rivers, the Wye, and the Severn, they have the whole trade of South-Wales, as it were, to themselves, and the greatest part of North-Wales; and as to their trade to Ireland, it is not only great in itself, but is prodigiously encreas'd in these last thirty years, since the Revolution, notwithstanding the great encrease and encroachment of the merchants at Liverpool, in the Irish trade, and the great devastations of the war; the Kingdom of Ireland itself being wonderfully encreas'd since that time.

The greatest inconveniences of Bristol, are, its situation, and the tenacious folly of its inhabitants; who by the general infatuation, the pretence of freedoms and priviledges, that corporation-tyranny, which prevents the flourishing and encrease of many a good town in

England, continue obstinately to forbid any, who are not subjects of their city soveraignty, (that is to say, freemen,) to trade within the chain of their own liberties; were it not for this, the city of Bristol, would before now, have swell'd and encreas'd in buildings and inhabitants, perhaps to double the magnitude it was formerly of.

This is evident by this one particular; there is one remarkable part of the city where the liberties extend not at all, or but very little without the city gate. Here and no where else, they have an accession of new inhabitants; and abundance of new houses, nay, some streets are built, and the like 'tis probable wou'd have been at all the rest of the gates, if liberty had been given. As for the city itself, there is hardly room to set another house in it, 'tis so close built, except in the great square, the ground about which is a little too subject to the hazard of inundations: so that people do not so freely enlarge that way.

The Hot Well, or, the water of St. Vincents Rock, is not in the city, but at the confluence of the two little rivers, and on the north side of the stream. It is but a few years since this spring lay open at the foot of the rock, and was covered by the salt water at every tide, and yet it preserved both its warmth and its mineral virtue entire.

XXVI. Unknown painter, *Broad Quay, Bristol* (early eighteenth century). The gabled houses had disappeared by 1780. The church in the background is St Michael's and, to the left, St Mark's.

The rock tho' hard to admiration, has since that been work'd down, partly by strength of art, and partly blown in pieces by gunpowder, and a plain foundation made for building a large house upon it, where they have good apartments for entertaining diseased persons. The Well is secur'd, and a good pump fix'd in it, so that they have the water pure and unmix'd from the spring itself.

The water of this Well posses'd its medicinal quality no doubt from its original, which may be as antient as the deluge. But what is strangest of all is, that it was never known before; it is now famous for being a specifick in that otherwise incurable disease the diabetes; and yet was never known to be so, 'till within these few years; namely, thirty years, or thereabout.

There are in Bristol 21 parish churches, many meeting-houses, especially Quakers', one (very mean) cathedral, the reason of which, may be, that it is but a very modern bishoprick. It is supposed they have an hundred thousand inhabitants in the city, and within three miles of its circumference; and they say above three thousand sail of ships belong to that port, but of the last I am not certain.

'Tis very remarkable, that this city is so plentifully supply'd with coals, tho' they are all brought by land carriage, that yet they are generally bought by the inhabitants, laid down at their doors, after the rate of from seven to nine shillings per chaldron.

The situation of the city is low, but on the side of a rising hill. The ground plat of it is said very much to resemble that of old Rome, being circular, with something greater diameter one way than another, but not enough to make it oval: and the river cutting off one small part, as it were, a sixth, or less from the rest.

They draw all their heavy goods here on sleds, or sledges without wheels, which kills a multitude of horses; and the pavement is worn so smooth by them, that in wet-weather the streets are very slippery, and in frosty-weather 'tis dangerous walking.

From Bristol West, you enter the county of Gloucester, and keeping the Avon in view, you see King Road, where the ships generally take their departure, as ours at London do from Graves-End; and Hung Road, where they notify their arrival, as ours for London do in the Downs: The one lyes within the Avon, the other, in the open sea or the Severn; which is there call'd the Severn Sea. Indeed great part of Bristol is in the bounds of Gloucestershire, tho' it be a county of itself. From hence going away a little north west, we come to the Pill, a convenient road for shipping, and where therefore they generally run back for Ireland or for Wales. There is also a little farther, an ugly, dangerous, and very inconvenient ferry over the Severn, to the mouth of Wye; namely, at Aust; the badness of the weather, and the sorry boats, at which, deterr'd us from crossing there.

As we turn north towards Gloucester, we lose the sight of the Avon, and in about two miles exchange it

137. Berkeley Castle from the east; drawing by L. Knyff (c.1676).

for an open view of the Severn Sea, which you see on the west side, and which is as broad as the ocean there; except, that you see two small islands in it, and that looking N. W. you see plainly the coast of South Wales; and particularly a little nearer hand, the shore of Monmouthshire. Then as you go on, the shores begin to draw towards one another, and the coasts to lye parallel; so that the Severn appears to be a plain river, or an *æstuarium*, somewhat like the Humber, or as the Thames is at the Nore, being 4 or 5 and 6 miles over; and to give it no more than its just due, a most raging, turbulent, furious place. This is occasion'd by those violent tides call'd the Bore, which flow here sometimes six or seven foot at once, rolling forward like a mighty wave: so that the stern of a vessel shall on a sudden be lifted up six or seven foot upon the water, when the head of it is fast a ground.

Hence we kept on north, passing by Dursley to Berkley-Castle;[26] the antient seat of the Earls of Berkley, a noble tho' antient building, and a very fine park about it. The castle gives title to the Earl, and the town of Dursly to the heir apparent; who during the life of his father, is call'd the Lord Dursley. I say nothing of the dark story of King Edward II of England; who, all our learned writers agree, was murther'd in this castle: as Richard II was in that of Pontefract, in Yorkshire; I say I take no more notice of it here, for history is not my present business: 'Tis true, they show the apartments where they say that king was kept a prisoner: but they do not admit that he was kill'd there. The place is rather antient, than pleasant or healthful, lying low, and near the water; but 'tis honour'd by its present owner, known to the world for his many services to his country, and for a fame, which our posterity will read of, in all the histories of our times.

From hence to Gloucester, we see nothing considerable, but a most fertile, rich country, and a fine river, but narrower as you go northward, 'till a little before we come to Gloucester it ceases to be navigable by ships of burthen, but continues to be so, by large barges, above an hundred miles farther; not reckoning the turnings and windings of the river: besides that, it receives several large and navigable rivers into it.

Gloucester is an antient middling city, tolerably built, but not fine; was fortify'd and stood out obstinately against its lord King Charles the 1st. who besieged it to his great loss in the late Rebellion, for which it had all its walls and works demolish'd; for it was then very strong: here is a large stone bridge over the Severn, the first next the sea; and this, and the cathedral is all I see worth recording of this place.

From Gloucester we kept the east shore of the Severn, and in twelve miles came to *Tewksbury*, a large and very populous town situate upon the river Avon, this is call'd the Warwickshire Avon, to distinguish it from the Avon at Bristol and others, for there are several rivers in England of this name; and some tell us that Avona was an old word in the British tongue signifying a river.

This town is famous for a great manufacture of stockings, as are also, the towns of Pershore, and Evesham, or Esham; on the same river.

The great old church at Tewksbury may indeed be call'd the largest private parish church in England; I mean, that is not a collegiate or cathedral chuch. This town is famous for the great, and as may be said, the last battle[27] fought between the two houses of Lancaster and York, in which Edward IV was conqueror; and in, or rather after which, Prince Edward the only surviving son of the house of Lancaster, was kill'd by the cruel hands of Richard the king's brother; the same afterwards Richard III or Crookback Richard. In this place begins that fruitful and plentiful country which was call'd the Vale of Esham, which runs all along the banks of the Avon, from Tewksbury to Pershore, and to Stratford upon Avon, and in the south part of Warwickshire; and so far, (viz. to Stratford,) the river Avon is navigable.

At this last town, going into the parish church, we saw the monument of old Shakespear, the famous poet, and whose dramatick performances so justly maintain his character among the British poets; and perhaps will do so to the end of time. The busto of his head is in the wall on the north side of the church, and a flat grave-stone covers the body, in the isle just under him. On which grave-stone these lines are written.

> Good Friend, for Jesus's sake, forbear
> To move the dust that resteth here.
> Blest be the man that spares these stones,
> And curst be he, that moves my bones.

The navigation of this river Avon is an exceeding advantage to all this part of the country, and also to the commerce of the city of Bristol. For by this river they drive a very great trade for sugar, oil, wine, tobacco, iron, lead, and in a word, all heavy goods which are carried by water almost as far as Warwick; and in return the corn, and especially the cheese, is brought back from Gloucestershire and Warwickshire, to Bristol.

This same vale continuing to extend itself in Warwickshire, and under the ridge of little mountains call'd Edge-Hill, is there call'd the vale of Red-Horse. All the grounds put together, make a most pleasant

138. The art of stocking frame work knitting. From the *Universal Magazine of Knowledge and Pleasure*, vol. 7 (1750), p. 49. A. The 'jack' for the bobbins to turn on; B. The 'sizer' to twist the threads; C. The 'rices' which wind the skeins; D. The 'winder'; E. The stocking frame.

corn country, especially remarkable for the goodness of the air, and fertility of the soil.

Gloucestershire must not be pass'd over, without some account of a most pleasant and fruitful vale which crosses part of the country, from east to west on that side of the Cotswold, and which is call'd Stroud-Water;[28] famous not for the finest cloths only, but for dying those cloths of the finest scarlets, and other grain colours that are any where in England; perhaps in any part of the world: Here I saw two pieces of broad cloth made, one scarlet, the other crimson in grain, on purpose to be presented, the one to His Majesty King George, and the other to the prince; when the former was Elector of Hanover, and the latter, Electoral Prince: and it was sent to Hanover, presented accordingly, and very graciously accepted. The cloth was valued including the colour, at 45 s. per yard, indeed it

was hardly to be valued, nothing so rich being ever made in England before, at least as I was informed.

The clothiers lye all along the banks of this river for near 20 miles, and in the town of Stroud, which lyes in the middle of it, as also at Paynswick, which is a market-town at a small distance north. The river makes its way to the Severn about 5 miles below Gloucester.

From Tewkesbury we went north 12 miles, to Worcester, all the way still on the bank of the Severn; and here we had the pleasing sight of the hedge-rows, being fill'd with apple trees and pear trees, and the fruit so common, that any passenger as they travel the road may gather and eat what they please; and here, as well as in Gloucestershire, you meet with cyder in the publick-houses sold as beer and ale is in the other parts of England, and as cheap.

139. East prospect of the city of Worcester (1742).

Worcester is a large, populous, old, tho' not a very well built city; I say not well built because the town is close and old, the houses standing too thick. The north part of the town is more extended and also better built. There is a good old stone bridge over the Severn, which stands exceeding high from the surface of the water. But as the stream of the Severn is contracted here by the buildings on either side, there is evident occasion sometimes for the height of the bridge, the waters rising to an incredible height in the winter-time.

The cathedral of this city is an antient, and indeed, a decay'd building; the body of the church is very mean in its aspect, nor did I see the least ornament about it, I mean in the outside. The tower is low, without any spire, only four very small pinnacles on the corners; and yet the tower has some little beauty in it more than the church itself, too; and the upper part has some images in it, but decay'd by time.

The inside of the church has several very antient monuments in it, particularly some royal ones; as that of King John, who lyes interr'd between two sainted bishops, namely, St. Oswald, and St. Woolstan. Whether he ordered his interment in that manner, believing that they should help him up at the last call, and be serviceable to him for his salvation I know not; it is true they say so, but I can hardly think the King himself so ignorant, whatever the people might be in those days of superstition; nor will I say but that it may be probable, they may all three go together at last (as it is) and yet, without being assistant to, or acquainted with one another at all.

Here is also a monument for that famous Countess of Salisbury, who dancing before, or with K. Edward III in his great hall at Windsor, dropt her garter, which the King taking up, honoured it so much as to make it the denominating ensign of his new order of knighthood, which is grown so famous, and is call'd the most Noble Order of the Garter: what honour, or that

any honour redounds to that most noble order, from its being so deriv'd from the garter of a —— for 'tis generally agreed, she was the King's mistress, I will not enquire.

This city is very full of people, and the people generally esteem'd very rich, being full of business, occasion'd chiefly by the cloathing trade, of which the city and the country round carries on a great share, as well for the Turkey trade as for the home trade.

The salt springs in this county which were formerly esteem'd as next to miraculous, have since the discovery of the mines of rock salt in Lancashire, Cheshire, &c. lost all of wonder that belong'd to them, and much of the use also; the salt made there being found to be much less valuable than what is now made of the other. So I need say little to them.

Near this city are the famous Maulvern Hills, or Mauvern Hills, seen so far every way. In particular, we saw them very plainly on the downs, between Marlborough and Malmsbury; and they say they are seen from the top of Salisbury steeple, which is above 50 miles.

There are three or four especial manufactures carried on in this country, which are peculiar to itself, or at least to this county with the two next adjoining; namely, Chester, and Warwick.

1. Monmouth cups[29] sold chiefly to the Dutch seamen, and made only at Beawdly.

2. Fine stone potts for the glass-makers melting their metal, of which they make their fine flint glass, glass plates, &c. not to be found any where but at Stourbridge in this county, the same clay makes crucibles and other melting pots.

3. The Birmingham iron works: The north indeed claims a share or part of this trade, but it is only a part.

4. Kidderminster stuff call'd lindsey woolseys,[30] they are very rarely made any where else.

As Stourbridge also they have a very great manufacture for glass of all sorts.

From Worcester I took a tour into Wales,[31] which tho' I mentioned above, it was not at the same time with the rest of my journey; my account I hope will be as effectual.

In passing from this part of the country to make a tour through Wales, we necessarily see the two counties of Hereford and Monmouth, and for that reason I reserv'd them to this place, as I shall the counties of Chester and Salop to my return.

A little below Worcester the Severn receives a river of a long course and deep chanel, call'd the Teme, and going from Worcester we past this river at a village call'd Broadways; from whence keeping a little to the north, we come to Ludlow-Castle, on the bank of the same river. On another journey I came from Stourbridge, famous for the clay for melting pots as above; thence to Kidderminster, and passing the Severn at Bewdley we came to Ludlow, on the side of Shropshire.

In this course we see two fine seats not very far from the Severn, (viz.) the Lord Foley's, and the Earl of Bradford's, as we had before a most delicious house, belonging to the Lord Conway, now in the family of the late famous Sir Edward Seymour. Indeed this part of the county, and all the county of Salop is fill'd with fine seats of the nobility and gentry, too many so much as to give a list of, and much less to describe.

The castle of Ludlow[32] shows in its decay, what it was in its flourishing estate: it is the palace of the Princes of Wales, that is, to speak more properly, it is annex'd to the principality of Wales; which is the appanage of the heir apparent, and this is his palace in right of his being made Prince of Wales.

The situation of this castle is most beautiful indeed; there is a most spacious plain or lawn in its front, which formerly continu'd near two miles; but much of it is now enclosed. The country round it is exceeding pleasant, fertile, populous, and the soil rich; nothing can be added by nature to make it a place fit for a royal palace: it only wants the residence of its princes, but that is not now to be expected.

The castle itself is in the very perfection of decay, all the fine courts, the royal apartments, halls, and rooms of state, lye open, abandoned and some of them falling down; for since the Courts of the President and Marches are taken away, here is nothing to do that requires the attendance of any publick people; so that time, the great devourer of the works of men, begins to eat into the very stone walls, and to spread the face of royal ruins upon the whole fabrick.

The town of **Ludlow** is a tolerable place, but it decays to be sure with the rest: it stands on the edge of the two counties, Shropshire, and Worcestershire, but is itself in the first; 'tis on the bank of the Teme, over which it has a good bridge, and it was formerly a town of good trade; the Welch call this town Lye Twysoe, which is in English, the Prince's court. Mr. Cambden calls the river Teme the Tem'd, and another river which joyns it just at this town, the Corve, whence the rich flat country below the town is call'd Corvesdale.

From Ludlow we took our course due south to Lemster, or **Leominster**, a large and good trading town on the river Lug. This river is lately made navigable by Act of Parliament, to the very great profit of the trading part of this country, who have now a very great trade for their corn, wool, and other products of this place, into the river Wye; and from the Wye, into the Severn, and so to Bristol.

Leominster has nothing very remarkable in it, but that it is a well built, well inhabited town: The church which is very large, has been in a manner rebuilt, and is now, especially in the inside, a very beautiful church. This town, besides the fine wool, is noted for the best wheat, and consequently the finest bread; whence Lemster bread, and Weobly ale, is become a proverbial saying.

The country on our right as we came from Ludlow is very fruitful and pleasant, and is call'd the Hundred of Wigmore, from which the late Earl of Oxford at his creation, took the title of Baron of Wigmore: and here we saw two antient castles, (viz.) Brampton-Brian,[33] and Wigmore-Castle,[34] both belonging to the Earl's father, Sir Edward Harley; Brampton is a stately pile, but not kept in full repair, the fate of that antient family not permitting the rebuilding it as we were told was intended. Yet it is not so far decay'd as Ludlow, nor is it abandoned, or like to be so, and the parts are still very fine, and full of large timber.

We were now on the borders of Wales, properly so call'd; for from the windows of Brampton-Castle, you have a fair prospect into the county of Radnor, which is, as it were, under its walls; nay, even this whole county of Hereford, was if we may believe antiquity, a part of Wales, and was so esteem'd for many ages. The people of this county too, boast that they were a part of the antient Silures, who for so many ages withstood the Roman arms, and who could never be entirely conquer'd. But that's an affair quite beyond my enquiry. I observ'd they are a diligent and laborious people, chiefly addicted to husbandry, and they boast, perhaps, not without reason, that they have the finest wool, the best hops, and the richest cyder in all Britain.

Indeed the wool about Leominster, and in the Hundred of Wigmore observ'd above, and the Golden Vale as 'tis call'd, for its richness on the banks of the

188

river Dove, (all in this county) is the finest without exception, of any in England, the South Down wool not excepted: As for hops, they plant abundance indeed all over this county, and they are very good. And as for cyder, here it was, that several times for 20 miles together, we could get no beer or ale in their publick houses, only cyder; and that so very good, so fine, and so cheap, that we never found fault with the exchange; great quantities of this cyder are sent to London, even by land carriage tho' so very remote, which is an evidence for the goodness of it, beyond contradiction.

140. Cidermaking using a handpress. From John Worlidge, *Vinetum Britannicum, or a treatise of cider* (1691).

One would hardly expect so pleasant, and fruitful a country as this, so near the barren mountains of Wales; but 'tis certain, that not any of our southern counties, the neighbourhood of London excepted, comes up to the fertility of this county. As Gloucester furnishes London with great quantities of cheese, so this county furnishes the same city with bacon in great quantities, and also with cyder as above.

From Lemster it is 10 miles to **Hereford**, the chief city, not of this county only, but of all the counties west of Severn: 'Tis a large and a populous city, and in the time of the late Rebellion, was very strong, and being well fortify'd, and as well defended, supported a tedious and very severe siege; for besides the Parliament's forces, who could never reduce it, the Scots army was call'd to the work, who lay before it, 'till they laid above 4000 of their bones there, and at last, it was rather taken by the fate of the war, than by the attack of the besiegers.

It is truly an old, mean built, and very dirty city, lying low, and on the bank of Wye, which sometimes

incommodes them very much, by the violent freshes that come down from the mountains of Wales; for all the rivers of this county, except the Diffin-Doe, come out of Wales.

The chief thing remarkable next to the cathedral, is the college, which still retains its foundation laws, and where the residentiaries are still oblig'd to celibacy, but otherwise, live a very happy, easy, and plentiful life; being furnish'd upon the foot of the foundation, besides their ecclesiastical stipends.

The great church is a magnificent building, however antient, the spire is not high, but handsome, and there is a fine tower at the west end, over the great door or entrance. The choir is very fine, tho' plain, and there is a very good organ: The revenues of this bishoprick are very considerable, but lye under some abatement at present, on account of necessary repairs.

From Hereford keeping the bank of Wye as near as we could, we came to **Ross**, a good old town, famous for good cyder, a great manufacture of iron ware, and a good trade on the river Wye; and nothing else as I remember, except it was a monstrous fat woman, who they would have had me gone to see. But I had enough of the relation, and so I suppose will the reader, for they told me she was more than three yards about her wast; that when she sat down, she was oblig'd to have a small stool plac'd before her, to rest her belly on, and the like.

From hence we came at about 8 miles more into Monmouthshire, and to the town of **Monmouth**. It is an old town situate at the conflux of the Wye and of Munnow, whence the town has its name; it stands in the angle where the rivers joyn, and has a bridge over each river, and a third over the river Trothy, which comes in just below the other.

This town shews by its reverend face, that it is a place of great antiquity, and by the remains of walls, lines, curtains, and bastions, that it has been very strong, and by its situation that it may be made so again: this place is made famous, by being the native place of one of our most antient historians Jeoffry of Monmouth.[35] At present 'tis rather a decay'd than a flourishing town, yet, it drives a considerable trade with the city of Bristol, by the navigation of the Wye.

This river having as I said, just received two large streams, the Mynevly or Munno, and the Trother, is grown a very noble river, and with a deep channel, and a full current hurries away towards the sea, carrying also vessels of a considerable burthen hereabouts.

Lower down upon the Wye stands **Chepstow**, the sea port for all the towns seated on the Wye and Lug, and where their commerce seems to center. Here is a noble bridge over the Wye: to this town ships of good burthen may come up, and the tide runs here with the same impetuous current as at Bristol; the flood rising from six fathom, to six and a half at Chepstow Bridge. This is a place of very good trade, as is also Newport, a town of the like import upon the river Uske, a great river, tho' not so big as Wye; which runs thro' the center of the county, and falls also into the Severn sea.

This county furnishes great quantities of corn for exportation, and the Bristol merchants frequently load ships here, to go to Portugal, and other foreign countries with wheat; considering the mountainous part of the west of this county, 'tis much they should have such good corn, and so much of it to spare; but the eastern side of the county, and the neighbourhood of Herefordshire, supplies them.

I am now at the utmost extent of England west, and here I must mount the Alps, traverse the mountains of Wales, (and indeed, they are well compar'd to the Alps in the inmost provinces;) but with this exception, that in abundance of places you have the most pleasant and beautiful valleys imaginable, and some of them, of very great extent, far exceeding the valleys so fam'd among the mountains of Savoy, and Piedmont.

The two first counties which border west upon Monmouthshire, are Brecknock, and Glamorgan, and as they are very mountainous, so that part of Monmouthshire which joyns them, begins the rising of the hills. Kyrton-Beacon, Tumberlow, Blorench, Penvail, and Skirridan, are some of the names of these horrid mountains, and are all in this shire; and I could not but fansy myself in view of Mount Brennus, Little Barnard, and Great Barnard, among the Alps. When I saw Plinlimmon Hill, and the sources of the Severn on one side of it, and the Wye and Rydall on the other: it put me in mind of the famous hill, call'd ———[36] in the cantons of Switzerland, out of which the Rhine rises on one side, and the Rhosne, and the Aa on the other. But I shall give you more of them presently.

We now entered South Wales: the provinces which bear the name of South Wales, are these, Glamorgan, Brecknock, Radnor, Caermarthen, Pembroke, and Cardigan. We began with Brecknock, being willing to see the highest of the mountains, which are said to be hereabouts; and indeed, except I had still an idea of the height of the Alps, and of those mighty mountains of America, the Andes, which we see very often in the

141. Chepstow castle and bridge; engraving by J. Kip (1705).

South-Seas, 20 leagues from the shore: I say except that I had still an idea of those countries on my mind, I should have been surprized at the sight of these hills; nay, (as it was) the Andes and the Alps, tho' immensly high, yet they stand together, and they are as mountains, pil'd upon mountains, and hills upon hills; whereas sometimes we see these mountains rising up at once, from the lowest valleys, to the highest summits which makes the height look horrid and frightful, even worse than those mountains abroad; which tho' much higher, rise as it were, one behind another: so that the ascent seems gradual, and consequently less surprizing.

Brecknockshire is a meer inland county, as Radnor is; the English jestingly (and I think not very improperly) call it Breakneckshire: 'tis mountainous to an extremity, except on the side of Radnor, where it is something more low and level. It is well watered by the Wye, and the Uske, two rivers mentioned before; upon the latter stands the town of Brecknock, the capital of the county: the most to be said of this town, is what indeed I have said of many places in Wales, (viz.) that it is very antient, and indeed to mention it here for all the rest, there are more tokens of antiquity to be seen every where in Wales, than in any particular part of England, except the counties of Cumberland, and Northumberland. Here we saw Brecknock-Mere, a large or long lake of water, two or three miles over; of which, they have a great many Welch fables, not worth relating: the best of them is, that a certain river call'd the Lheweni runs thro' it, and keeps its colour in mid-chanel distinguish'd from the water of the lake, and as they say, never mingles with it. They take abundance of good fish in this lake, so that as is said of the river Thysse in Hungary; they say this lake is two thirds water, and one third fish. The country people

142 Brecknock Mere; engraving by Thomas Jones of Pencerrig. From his *Six views in South Wales after nature* (1775).

affirm, there stood a city once here, but, that by the judgment of heaven, for the sin of its inhabitants, it sunk into the earth, and the water rose up in the place of it.

It was among the mountains of this county that the famous Glendower[37] shelter'd himself, and taking arms on the deposing Richard II proclaimed himself Prince of Wales; and they shew us several little refuges of his in the mountains, whither he retreated; and from whence, again, he made such bold excursions into England.

Tho' this county be so mountainous, provisions are exceeding plentiful, and also very good all over the county; nor are these mountains useless, even to the city of London, as I have noted of other counties; for from hence they send yearly, great herds of black cattle to England, and which are known to fill our fairs and markets, even that of Smithfield itself.

The yellow mountains of Radnorshire are the same, and their product of cattle is the same; nor did I meet with any thing new, and worth noticing, except monuments of antiquity, which are not the subject of my enquiry: the stories of Vortigern,[38] and Roger of Mortimer,[39] are in every old woman's mouth here. There is here a great cataract or water fall of the river Wye, at a place call'd Rhayadr Gwy in Welch, which signifies the cataract or water fall of the Wye, but we did not go to see it, by reason of a great flood at that time, which made the way dangerous: There is a kind of desart too, on that side, which is scarce habitable or passable, so we made it our north boundary for this part of our journey, and turn'd away to Glamorganshire.

Entring this shire, from Radnor and Brecknock, we were saluted with Monuchdenny-Hill on our left, and the Black-Mountain on the right, and all a ridge of horrid rocks and precipices between, over which, if we had not had trusty guides, we should never have found our way; and indeed, we began to repent our curiosity, as not having met with any thing worth the trouble; and a country looking so full of horror, that we thought to have given over the enterprise, and have left Wales out of our circuit: but after a day and a night conversing thus with rocks and mountains, our guide brought us down into a most agreeable vale, opening to the south, and a pleasant river running through it, call'd the Taaffe; and following the course of this river, we came in the evening to the antient city of Landaff, and Caerdiff, standing almost together.

Landaff is the seat of the episcopal see, and a city; but Cardiff which is lower on the river, is the port and town of trade; and has a very good harbour opening

143. Coal mine and horse gin near Neath; engraving (*c*.1778).

into the Severn Sea, about 4 miles below the town. The cathedral is a neat building, but very antient; they boast that this church was a house of religious worship many years before any church was founded in England, and that the Christian religion flourish'd here in its primitive purity, from the year 186, till the Pelagian heresy[40] overspread this country; which being afterwards rooted out by the care of the orthodox bishop, they plac'd St. Dobricius as the first bishop in this town of Landaff, then call'd Launton.

Neath is another port, where the coal trade is also considerable, tho' it stands farther within the land. Kynfig Castle, is now the seat and estate of the Lord Mansel,[41] who has here also a very royal income from the collieries; I say royal, because equal to the revenues of some sovereign princes, and which formerly denominated Sir Edward Mansel, one of the richest commoners in Wales; the family was enobled by Her late Majesty Queen Anne.

In this neighbourhood, near Margan Mynydd, we saw the famous monument[42] mentioned by Mr. Cambden, on a hill, with the inscription, which the people are so terrify'd at, that no body will care to read it; for they have a tradition from father to son, that whoever ventures to read it, will dye within a month. We did not scruple the adventure at all, but when we came to try, the letters were so defac'd by time, that we were effectually secur'd from the danger; the inscription not being any thing near so legible, as it seems it was in Cambden's time.

The stone pillar is about 4 or 5 foot high, and 1 foot thick, standing on the top of this hill; there are several

other such monuments in Radnorshire, and other counties in Wales, as likewise in Scotland we saw the like.

Having thus touch'd at what is most curious on this coast, we pass'd thro' the land of Gowre, and going still west, we came to **Caermarthen**, or Kaer-Vyrdhin, as the Welsh call it, the capital of the county of Kaermardhinshire.

This is an antient but not a decay'd town, pleasantly situated on the river Towy, or Tovy, which is navigable up to the town, for vessels of a moderate burthen. The town indeed is well built, and populous, and the country round it, is the most fruiful, of any part of all Wales, considering that it continues to be so for a great way; namely, thro' all the middle of the county, and a great way into the next; nor is this county so mountainous and wild, as the rest of this part of Wales: but it abounds in corn, and in fine flourishing meadows, as good as most are in Britain, and in which are fed, a very great number of good cattle.

The Chancery, and Exchequer of the Principality, was usually kept at this town, till the jurisdiction of the Court and Marches of Wales was taken away. This town was also famous for the birth of the old Brittish prophet Merlin, of whom so many things are fabled, that indeed nothing of its kind ever prevail'd so far, in the delusion of mankind, and who flourish'd in the year 480: And here also the old Britains often kept their Parliament or assemblies of their wise men, and made their laws. The town was fortify'd in former times, but the walls are scarcely to be seen now, only the ruins of them.

Here we saw near Kily-Maen Ibwyd,[43] on a great mountain, a circle of mighty stones, very much like Stone-henge in Wiltshire, or rather like the Rollrych Stones in Oxfordshire; and tho' the people call it Bruarth Arthur, or King Arthur's Throne, we see no reason to believe that King Arthur knew any thing of it, or that it had any relation to him.

We found the people of this county more civiliz'd and more curteous, than in the more mountainous parts, where the disposition of the inhabitants seems to be rough, like the country: But here as they seem to converse with the rest of the world, by their commerce, so they are more conversible than their neighbours.

The next county west, is Pembrokeshire, which is the most extreme part of Wales on this side, in a rich, fertile, and plentiful country, lying on the sea coast, where it has the benefit of Milford Haven, one of the greatest and best inlets of water in Britain. Mr. Cambden says it contains 16 creeks, 5 great bays, and 13 good roads for shipping, all distinguish'd as such by their names; and some say, a thousand sail of ships may ride

144. 'South East view of Carmarthen'; engraving by Samuel and Nathaniel Buck (1745).

in it, and not the topmast of one be seen from another; but this last, I think, merits confirmation.

Before we quitted the coast, we saw **Tenbigh**, the most agreeable town on all the sea coast of South Wales, except Pembroke, being a very good road for shipping, and well frequented: here is a great fishery for herring in its season, a great colliery, or rather export of coals, and they also drive a very considerable trade to Ireland.

From hence, the land bearing far into the sea, makes a promontory, call'd St. Govens Head or Point. But as we found nothing of moment was to be seen there, we cross'd over the isthmus to Pembroke, which stands on the E. shore of the great haven of **Milford**.

This is the largest and richest, and at this time, the most flourishing town of all S. Wales: here are a great many English merchants, and some of them men of good business; and they told us, there were near 200 sail of ships belong'd to the town, small and great; in a word, all this part of Wales is a rich and flourishing

county, but especially this part is so very pleasant, and fertile, and is so well cultivated, that 'tis call'd by distinction, Little England, beyond Wales.

This is the place also made particularly famous for the landing of King Henry VII, then Duke of Richmond: from hence, being resolv'd to see the utmost extent of the county west, we ferry'd over the haven and went to Haverford, or by some call'd Haverford-West; and from thence to St. Davids, or St. Taffys, as the Welch call it. Haverford is a better town than we expected to find, in this remote angle of Britain; 'tis strong, well built, clean, and populous.

From hence to St. Davids, the country begins to look like Wales again, dry, barren, and mountainous; St. Davids is not a bishop's see only, but was formerly an arch-bishop's, which they tell us, was by the Pope transferr'd to Dole in Britany, where it still remains.

The venerable aspect of this cathedral church, shews that it has been a beautiful building, but that is much decay'd. The west end or body of the church is toler-

145. Tenby; drawing by Francis Place (1678).

ably well; the choir is kept neat, and in tollerable repair, the S. isle without the choir, and the Virgin Mary's chappel, which makes the E. end of the church, are in a manner demolish'd, and the roofs of both fallen in.

From hence we turn'd N. keeping the sea in our W. prospect, and a rugged mountainous country on the E. where the hills even darken'd the air with their heighth; as we went on, we past by Newport, on the river Nevern, a town having a good harbour, and consequently a good trade with Ireland.

Here we left Pembrokeshire, and after about 22 miles, came to the town of **Cardigan**, an old and well inhabited town, on the river Tivy: 'tis a very noble river indeed, and famous for its plenty of the best and largest salmon in Britain.

The country people told us, that they had beavers[44] here, which bred in the lakes among the mountains, and came down the stream of Tivy to feed; that they

destroy'd the young frye of salmon, and therefore the country people destroy'd them; but they could shew us none of them, or any of their skins, neither could the countrymen describe them, or tell us that they had ever seen them; so that we concluded they only meant the otter, till I found after our return, that Mr. Cambden mentions also, that there were beavers seen here formerly.

The town is not large, has been well fortify'd, but that part is now wholly neglected. It has a good trade with Ireland, and is enrich'd very much, as is all this part of the country, by the famous lead mines, formerly discover'd by Sir Carbery Price, which are the greatest, and perhaps the richest in England; and particularly as they require so little labour and charge to come at the oar, which in many places lyes within a fathom or two of the surface, and in some, even bare to the very top.

Going N. from the Tyvy about 25 miles, we came

146. 'A Map of that Part of Cardiganshire wherein are the mines belonging to ye Governor and Company of Mine Adventurers of England'. From William Waller, *Report on lead and silver mines* (1709).

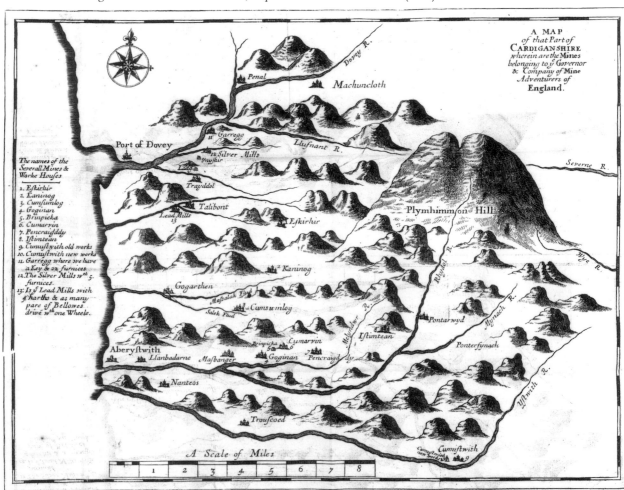

to Abrystwyth, that is to say, the town at the mouth of the river Ystwyth. This town is enrich'd by the coals and lead which is found in its neighbourhood, and is a populous, but a very dirty, black, smoaky place, and we fancy'd the people look'd as if they liv'd continually in the coal or lead mines. However, they are rich, and the place is very populous.

The whole county of Cardigan is so full of cattle, that 'tis said to be the nursery, or breeding-place for the whole kingdom of England, S. by Trent; but this is not a proof of its fertility, for tho' the feeding of cattle indeed requires a rich soil, the breeding them does not, the mountains and moors being as proper for that purpose as richer land.

Now we enter'd N. Wales, only I should add, that as we pass'd, we had a sight of the famous Plymlymon-Hill, out of the east side of which as I mentioned before, rises the Severn, and the Wye; and out of the west side of it, rises the Rydall and the Ystwyth. This mountain is exceeding high, and tho' it is hard to say which is the highest hill in Wales, yet I think this bids fair for it; nor is the county for 20 miles round it, any thing but a continued ridge of mountains: So that for almost a whole week's travel, we seem'd to be conversing with the upper regions; for we were often above the clouds, I'm sure, a very great way, and the names of some of these hills seem'd as barbarous to us, who spoke no Welch, as the hills themselves.

Passing these mountains, I say, we enter'd N. Wales, which contains the counties of Montgomery, Merionith, Caernarvon, Denbeigh, and Flint Shires, and the isle of Anglesea.

In passing Montgomery-shire, we were so tired with rocks and mountains, that we wish'd heartily we had kept close to the sea shore, but it not much mended the matter if we had, as I understood afterwards: the river Severn is the only beauty of this county, which rising I say, out of the Plymlymon mountain, receives instantly so many other rivers into its bosom, that it becomes navigable before it gets out of the county; namely, at Welch Pool, on the edge of Shropshire. This is a good fashionable place, and has many English dwelling in it, and some very good families; but we saw nothing farther worth remarking.

The vales and meadows upon the bank of the Severn, are the best of this county, I had almost said, the only good part of it; some are of opinion, that, the very water of the Severn, like that of Nile, impregnates the valleys, and when it overflows, leaves a vertue behind it, particularly to itself; and this they say is confirm'd, because all the country is so fruitful, wherever this river does overflow, and its water reach. The town, or rather as the natives call it, the city of **Montgomery**,

147. Merionethshire girl; aquatint by Paul Sandby (published 1776).

lyes not far from this river, on the outer edge of the country next to Herefordshire. This was, it seems, a great frontier town in the wars between the English and the Welch, and was beautify'd and fortify'd by King Henry III; the town is now much decay'd: It gives title to the eldest son of the Ducal house of Powis, who is call'd Lord Montgomery, and Marquiss of Powis; they have a noble seat at Troy, hard by this town on the other side the river: But the house of Pembroke also claims the title of Montgomery.

This county is noted for an excellent breed of Welch horses, which, though not very large, are exceeding valuable, and much esteem'd all over England; all the north and west part of the county is mountainous and stony.

Merionithshire, or Merionydshire, lyes west from Montgomeryshire; it lyes on the Irish sea, or rather the ocean; for St. George's Chanel does not begin till further north, and it is extended on the coast, for near 35 miles in length, all still mountainous and craggy. The principal river is the Tovy, which rises among the

148. Caernarvon castle; painting by Richard Wilson (c.1745–50).

unpassable mountains, which range along the center of this part of Wales, and which we call unpassable, for that even the people themselves called them so.

Here among innumerable summits, and rising peaks of nameless hills, we saw the famous Kader-Idricks, which some are of opinion, is the highest mountain in Britain, another called Rarauvaur, another call'd Mowylwynda, and still every hill we saw, we thought was higher than all that ever we saw before.

That side of the country of Carnarvon, which borders on the sea, is not so mountainous, and is both more fertile and more populous. The principal town in this part, is **Carnarvon**, a good town, with a castle built by Edward I to curb and reduce the wild people of the mountains, and secure the passage into Anglesea. As this city was built by Edward I so he kept his court often here, and honour'd it with his presence very much; and here his eldest son and successor, tho' unhappy, (Ed. II) was born, who was therefore call'd Edward of Caernarvon. This Edward was the first Prince of Wales; that is to say, the first of the Kings of England's sons, who was vested with the title of Prince of Wales: and here was kept the Chancery and Exchequer of the Prince's of Wales, for the N. part of the Principality, as it was at —— for the S. part. It is

a small, but strong town, clean and well built, and considering the place the people are very courteous and obliging to strangers. It is seated on the firth or inlet call'd Menai, parting the Isle of Anglesea, or Mona, from the main land; and here is a ferry over to the island called Abermenai Ferry.

Whoever travels critically over these mountains, I mean of S. Wales, and Merionithshire, will think Stone-henge in Wiltshire, and Roll-Rich stones. in Oxfordshire no more a wonder, seeing there are so many such, and such like, in these provinces; that they are not thought strange of at all, nor is it doubted, but they were generally monuments of the dead, as also are the single stones of immense bulk any other, of which we saw so many, that we gave over remarking them; some we saw from 7, 8, to 10, and one 16 foot high, being a whole stone, but so great, that the most of the wonder is, where they were found, and how dragg'd to the place; since, besides the steep ascents to some of the hills on which they stand, it would be impossible to move some of them, now, with 50 yoke of oxen. And yet a great many of these stones are found confusedly lying one upon another on the utmost summit or top of the Glyder, or other hills, in Merionith and Carnarvonshire; to which it is next to impossible,

196

149. Holyhead; drawing by Francis Place (1699).

that all the power of art, and strength of man and beast could carry them, and the people make no difficulty of saying the Devil set them up there.

There is nothing of note to be seen in the isle of Anglesea but the town, and the castle of Baumaris, which was also built by King Edward I and call'd Beau-Marsh, or the Fine Plain; for here the country is very level and plain, and the land is fruitful and pleasant. The castle was very large, as may be seen by its remains, and that it was strong; the situation will tell also, but 'tis now of no use.

As we went to Holly Head, by the S. part of the island from Newborough, and came back thro' the middle to Beaumaris, we saw the whole extent of it, and indeed, it is a much pleasanter country, than any part of N. Wales, that we had yet seen; and particularly is very fruitful for corn and cattle.

From hence, I say, we cross'd to Bangor, a town noted for its antiquity, its being a bishop's see, and an old, mean looking, and almost despicable cathedral church.

From Bangor we went north, (keeping the sea on our left hand) to Conway. This is the poorest but pleasantest town in all this county for the bigness of it; it is seated on the bank of a fine river, which is not only pleasant and beautiful, but is a noble harbour for ships, had they any occasion for them there; the stream is deep and safe, and the river broad, as the Thames at Deptford: it only wants a trade suitable to so good a port, for it infinitely out does Chester or Leverpool itself.

In this passage, we went over the famous precipice call'd Penmen-muir, which indeed fame has made abundance more frightful, than it really is; for tho' the rock is indeed very high, and if any one should fall

from it, it wou'd dash them in pieces, yet, on the other hand, there is no danger of their falling; and besides, there is now a wall built all the way, on the edge of the precipice, to secure them: those who have been at the hill or pass of Enterkin[45] in Scotland, know very well, the danger there is much greater, than what can be thought of here; as the frequent loss of lives, both of man and horse will testify.

We have but little remarkable in the road from Conway to Hollywell, but craggs and rocks all along the N. shore of Denbeigh, till we came to Denbeigh town. This is the county town, and is a large populous place, which carries something in its countenance of its neighbourhood to England, but that which was most surprizing, after such a tiresom and fatiguing journey, over the unhospitable mountains of Merioneth, and Carnarvonshire, was, that descending now from the hills, we came into a most pleasant, fruitful, populous, and delicious vale, full of villages and towns, the fields shining with corn, just ready for the reapers, the meadows green and flowery, and a fine river, with a mild and gentle stream running thro' it: Nor is it a small or casual intermission, but we had a prospect of the country open before us, for above 20 miles in length, and from 5 to 7 miles in breadth, all smiling with the same kind of complexion; which made us think ourselves in England again, all on a sudden.

In this pleasant vale, turning N. from Denbeigh, and following the stream of the river, we came to S. Asaph, a small city, with a cathedral, being a bishoprick of tolerable good value, though the church is old: It is but a poor town, and ill built, tho' the country is so pleasant and rich round it. There are some old monuments in this church, but none of any note, nor could we read the Welch inscriptions.

150. Conway castle; painting by Paul Sandby (1789).

XXVII. Peter Tempest after Francis Place, *St Winefrid's Well, called Holy Well, near Flint* (c.1735).

From hence we come to Holly-well:[46] the stories of this Well of S. Winifrid are, that the pious virgin, being ravished and murthered, this healing water sprung out of her body when buried; but this smells too much of the legend, to take up any of my time; the Romanists indeed believe it, as 'tis evident, from their thronging hither to receive the healing sanative virtue of the water, which they do not hope for as it is a medicinal water, but as it is a miraculous water, and heals them by virtue of the intercession and influence of this famous virgin, St. Winifrid; of which I believe as much as comes to my share.

Here is a fine chapel cut out of a solid rock, and was dedicated to this holy virgin; and numbers of pilgrims resort to it, with no less devotion than ignorance; under this chapel the water gushes out in a great stream, and the place where it breaks out, is form'd like a basin or cistern, in which they bathe: the water is intensely cold, and indeed there is no great miracle in that point, considering the rocks it flows from, where it is impregnated by divers minerals, the virtue of which, and not of the saint, I suppose, work the greatest part of the cures.

There is a little town near the well, which may, indeed, be said to have risen from the confluence of the people hither, for almost all the houses are either publick houses, or let into lodgings; and the priests that attend here, and are very numerous, appear in disguise: sometimes they are physicians, sometimes surgeons, sometimes gentlemen, and sometimes patients, or any thing as occasion presents. No body takes notice of them, as to their profession, tho' they know them well enough, no not the Roman Catholicks themselves; but in private, they have their proper oratory's in certain places, whither the votaries resort; and good manners has prevail'd so far, that however the Protestants know who and who's together; no body takes notice of it, or enquires where one another goes, or has been gone.

From hence we past by Flint-Castle, a known place, but of no significance; and then in a few hours we cross'd the river Dee, and arriv'd at the city of West Chester, from whence, I shall give a farther account of my journey in my next.

I am,

Sir,

Yours, &c.

The End of the Sixth Letter

LETTER VII

*Containing a Description of Part of
Cheshire, Shropshire, Wales, Staffordshire,
Warwickshire, Northamptonshire,
Leicestershire, Lincolnshire, Rutlandshire,
and Bedfordshire.*

Sir,

MY LAST FROM West Chester, gave you a full account of my progress thro' Wales, and my coming to Chester, at the end of that really fatiguing journey: I must confess, I that have seen the Alps, on so many occasions, have gone under so many of the most frightful passes in the country of the Grisons, and in the mountains of Tirol, never believ'd there was any thing in this island of Britain that came near, much less that exceeded those hills, in the terror of their aspect, or in the difficulty of access to them; but certainly, if they are out done any where in the world, it is here: even Hannibal himself wou'd have found it impossible to have march'd his army over Snowden, or over the rocks of Merioneth and Montgomery shires; no, not with all the help that fire and vinegar[1] could have yielded, to make way for him.

The only support we had in this heavy journey, was, (1.) that we generally found their provisions very good and cheap, and very good accommodations in the inns. And (2.) that the Welsh gentlemen are very civil, hospitable, and kind; the people very obliging and conversible, and especially to strangers; but when we let them know, we travell'd merely in curiosity to view the country, and be able to speak well of them to strangers, their civility was heightened to such a degree, that nothing could be more friendly, willing to tell us every thing that belong'd to their country, and to show us every thing that we desired to see.

They value themselves much upon their antiquity: the antient race of their houses, and families, and the like; and above all, upon their antient heroes: their King Caractacus, Owen ap Tudor, Prince Lewellin, and the like noblemen and princes of British extraction; and as they believe their country to be the pleasantest and most agreeable in the world, so you cannot oblige them more, than to make them think you believe so too.

I continued at Chester for some time, except that I made two or three excursions into the neighbouring country, and particularly into that part of Shropshire which I had not view'd as I went; as also into the north, and north west part of Cheshire.

As I am now at **Chester**,' tis proper to say something of it, being a city well worth describing: Chester has four things very remarkable in it. 1. It's walls, which are very firm, beautiful, and in good repair. 2. The castle, which is also kept up, and has a garrison always in it. 3. The cathedral. 4. The river Dee, and 5. the bridge over it.

It is a very antient city, and to this day, the buildings are very old; nor do the rows as they call them, add any thing, in my opinion, to the beauty of the city; but just the contrary, they serve to make the city look both old and ugly: these rows are certain long galleries, up one pair of stairs, which run along the side of the streets, before all the houses, tho' joined to them, and as is pretended, they are to keep the people dry in walking along. This they do indeed effectually, but then they take away all the view of the houses from the street, nor can a stranger, that was to ride thro' Chester, see any shops in the city; besides, they make the shops themselves dark, and the way in them is dark, dirty, and uneven.

151. An inside view of the Rows, Chester; engraving by J. Landseer after J. Webster (1810). This shows the Rows substantially in their eighteenth-century state before extensive alterations in the nineteenth century.

The best ornament of the city, is, that the streets are very broad and fair, and run through the whole city in strait lines, crossing in the middle of the city, as at Chichester: the walls as I have said, are in very good repair, and it is a very pleasant walk round the city, upon the walls, and within the battlements, from whence you may see the country round; and particularly on the side of the Roodee, which I mentioned before, which is a fine large low green, on the bank of the Dee. In the winter this green is often under water by the inundations of the river, and a little before I came there, they had such a terrible land flood, which flow'd 8 foot higher than usual so that it not only overflowed the said green, call'd the Roodee, but destroy'd a fine new wharf and landing-place for goods, a little below the town, bore down all the warehouses, and other buildings, which the merchants had erected for securing their goods, and carried all away goods and buildings together, to the irreparable loss of the persons concern'd: also beyond the Roodee, one sees from the walls of Chester the county of Flint, and the mountains of Wales, a prospect best indeed, at a distance.

The castle of Chester is a good firm building, and strong, tho' not fortify'd, with many out works: there is always a good garrison kept, and here the prisoners taken at Preston,[2] in the late time of Rebellion, were kept a great while, till compassion to their misery, mov'd the clemency of the conqueror to deliver them. They say this castle was built or at least repair'd by Hugh Lupus, the famous Earl of Chester, and brother to William the Conqueror as also was the church.

The great church here is a very magnificent building, but 'tis built of a red, sandy, ill looking stone, which takes much from the beauty of it, and which yielding to the weather, seems to crumble, and suffer by time, which much defaces the building.

There are 2 parishes in this city, and very good churches to them, and it is the largest city in all this side of England that is so remote from London. When I was formerly at this city,[3] about the year 1690, they had no water to supply their ordinary occasions, but what was carried from the river Dee upon horses, in great leather vessels, like a pair of baker's panyers; just the very same for shape and use, as they have to this day in the streets of Constantinople, and at Belgrade,

152. Chester and the Roodee; engraving after Peter Tillemans (1725).

in Hungary; to carry water about the streets to sell, for the people to drink. But at my coming there this time, I found a very good water-house in the river, and the city plentifully supply'd by pipes, just as London is from the Thames; tho' some parts of Chester stands very high from the river.

This county [i.e. Cheshire], however remote from London, is one of those which contributes most to its support, as well as to several other parts of England, and that is by its excellent cheese, which they make here in such quantities, and so exceeding good, that as I am told from very good authority, the city of London only takes off 14000 ton every year; besides 8000 ton which they say goes every year down the rivers Severn and Trent, the former to Bristol, and the latter to York; including all the towns on both these large rivers: and besides the quantity ship'd both here, and at Leverpool, to go to Ireland, and Scotland. So that the quantity of cheese made in this country, must be prodigious great. Indeed, the whole county is employ'd in it, and part of its neighbourhood too; for tho' 'tis all call'd by the name of Cheshire Cheese, yet great quantities of it are made in Shropshire, Staf-

fordshire and Lancashire, that is to say, in such parts of them as border upon Cheshire.

The soil is extraordinary good, and the grass they say, has a peculiar richness in it, which disposes the creatures to give a great quantity of milk, and that very sweet and good; and this cheese manufacture, for such it is, encreases every day, and greatly enriches all the county; raises the value of the lands, and encourages the farmers to the keeping vast stocks of cows; the very number of the cattle improving and enriching the land.

The east part of the county abounds in salt springs, from which they draw the brine, and boyl it into fine salt; and once it was a very considerable trade, which they carried on with this salt; but since the discovery of the rock salt, which they dig in great quantities, towards Warrington, the other salt is not in so much request.

I now resolv'd to direct my course east, and making the Wever and the Trent, my northern boundary in this circuit; I came forward to view the midland counties of England, I mean such as may be said to lye between the Thames and the Trent.

203

153. Refining common salt, from William Brownrigg, *The Art of making common salt* (1748). Screening and heating of salt in solution to remove impurities.

I had taken a little trip into the N. E. parts of Cheshire before, seen a fine old seat of the Lord Delamere's, and which is beyond it all, the fine forest, which bears the name of that noble family; intending to see the salt pits at Northwich, which are odd indeed, but not so very strange as we were made to believe; the thing is, they say, the salt spring is found to be just perpendicularly under the stream or chanel of a fresh water river, namely, the Wever, and it is so, for the spring is very deep indeed in the ground, but that very thing takes off the wonder; for as the earth under the river, is but as a gutter to carry the water, there is no difficulty that it should not penetrate through it, the soil being a strong clay. So we came away not extremely gratify'd in our curiosity.

From Northwich we turn'd S. and following the

stream of the river by Middle Wich, we cross'd the great London road at Nantwich, or as some write it Namptwych; these are the three salt making towns of this county; there is a fourth which is call'd Droitwych, in Worcestershire; the nature of the thing is this, they boil the brine into fine salt, which is much priz'd for the beauty of its colour, and fineness of the grain, but the salt is not so strong, as what we now make from the rock salt mentioned above, and therefore loses of its value.

Hence we turn'd a little W. to Whitchurch, in Shropshire. But before I leave Cheshire, I must note two things of it. (1.) That there is no part of England, where there are such a great number of families of gentry, and of such antient and noble extraction. (2.) That it is a County Palatine,[4] and has been for so many ages, that its government is distinct from any other and very particular; it is administred by a Chamberlain, a Judge special, two Barons of the Exchequer, three Serjeants at Law, a Sheriff, an Attorney, an Escheator, and all proper and useful subordinate officers; and the jurisdiction of all these offices are kept up, and preserv'd very strictly, only we are to note, that the Judge special as he is call'd, tries only civil causes, not criminal, which are left to the ordinary Judges of England, who go the circuits here, as in other places.

Whitchurch is a pleasant and populous town, and has a very good church, in which is the famous monument of the great Talbot, first Earl of Shrewsbury,[5] who, perhaps, and not unworthily, was call'd in this time, the English Achilles.

But the most to be said of this town now, is, that they have a good market, and a great many gentry near it, whereof some are Roman Catholicks. They tell us that this town when King Charles I remov'd his standard from Nottingham to Shrewsbury, raised a whole regiment for the king: nor has this town lost its old loyal principle, to this time; tho' now it may run a little another way.

From hence we went towards Wales again, and cross'd the Dee, at Bangor Bridge; I could not satisfy myself to omit seeing this famous town, which was once so remarkable, but was surpriz'd when I came there, to see there was a stone-bridge over the Dee, and indeed, a very fine one: but as for the town or monastery, scarce any of the ruins were to be seen, and as all the people spoke Welch, we could find no body that could give us any intelligence. So effectually had time in so few years, ras'd the very foundations of the place. I will not say, as some do, that this is miraculous, and that it is the particular judgment of God upon the place, for being the birth-place of that arch

heretick Pelagius,[6] who from hence also began to broach his heretical opinions, which afterwards so terribly overspread the church: I say I will not insist upon this: that Pelagius was a monk of Bungor, or Banchor, is not doubted; but for the rest I leave it where I find it.

The place is now (I say) a poor contemptible village, and has nothing to show but a fine stone bridge over Dee, by which we enter Denbighshire in Wales. From thence we visited **Wrexham**, having heard much of a fine church there, but we were greatly disappointed: there is indeed a very large tower steeple, if a tower may be call'd a steeple, and 'tis finely adorn'd with imagery; but far from fine: the work is mean, the statues seem all mean and in dejected postures, without any fancy or spirit in the workmanship, and as the stone is of a reddish crumbling kind, like the cathedral at Chester, time has made it look gross and rough.

This town is large, well built and populous, and

154. 'West view of Wrexham steeple, July 1712'; drawing by William Stukeley. From his *Pocket Sketchbook*.

The West View of Wrexam Steeple in Denbighshire & Wales.
july 1712.

besides the church there are two large meeting-houses, in one of which we were told they preach in Welch one part of the day, and in English the other. Here is a great market for Welch flannel which the factors buy up of the poor Welch people, who manufacture it; and thence it is sent to London; and it is a very considerable manufacture indeed thro' all this part of the country, by which the poor are very profitably employ'd.

From hence we turn'd south, and passing by Wem, the title given by King James II to the late Lord Chancellor Jefferies,[7] we saw the house where his father, then but a private gentleman liv'd, and in but middling circumstances. Thence we came to Ellsmere, famous for a great lake or mere, which gives the town its name, and which the people pretend has in some places no bottom. This place is remarkable for good fish. From hence we came the same night to **Shrewsbury**.

This is indeed a beautiful, large, pleasant, populous, and rich town; full of gentry and yet full of trade too; for here too, is a great manufacture, as well of flannel, as also of white broadcloth, which enriches all the country round it.

The Severn surrounds this town, just as the Thames does the Isle of Dogs; so that it makes the form of an horse-shoe, over which there are two fine stone bridges, upon one of which is built a very noble gate, and over the arch of the gate the statue of the great Lewellin,[8] the idol of the Welch, and their last Prince of Wales.

This is really a town of mirth and gallantry, something like Bury in Suffolk, or Durham in the north, but much bigger than either of them, or indeed than both together.

Over the market-house is kept a kind of hall for the manufactures, which are sold here weekly in very great quantities; they speak all English in the town, but on a market-day you would think you were in Wales.

Here is the greatest market, the greatest plenty of good provisions, and the cheapest that is to be met with in all the western part of England; the Severn supplies them here with excellent salmon, but 'tis also brought in great plenty from the river Dee, which is not far off, and which abounds with a very good kind, and is generally larger than that in the Severn; as an example of the cheapness of provisions, we paid here, in a publick inn, but a groat a night for hay, and sixpence a peck for oats for our horses, which is cheaper than we found it in the cheapest part of the north of England; all our other provisions were in proportion; and there is no doubt but the cheapness of provisions joined to the pleasantness and healthiness of the place, draws a great many families thither, who love to live within the compass of their estates.

This town will for ever be famous for the reception it gave to King Charles the I who, after setting up his standard at Nottingham, and finding no encouragement there, remov'd to Shrewsbury, being invited by the gentry of the town and country round, where he was receiv'd with such a general affection, and hearty zeal by all the people, that his majesty recover'd the discouragement of his first step at Nottingham, and raised and compleated a strong army in less time than could be imagin'd; insomuch that to the surprize of the Parliament, and indeed of all the world, he was in the field before them, and advanced upon them so fast, that he met them two thirds onward of his way to London, and gave them battle at Edge-hill near Banbury.

155. 'Prospect of South side of Shrewsbury taken from Coney Green'; engraved by J. Kip (*c*.1715).

But the fate of the war turning afterward against the king, the weight of it fell heavy upon this town also, and almost ruin'd them.

But they are now fully recover'd, and it is at this time one of the most flourishing towns in England: the walls and gates are yet standing, but useless, and the old castle is gone to ruin, as is the case of almost all the old castles in England.

Here I was shew'd a very visible and remarkable appearance of the great antient road or way call'd Watling-Street, which comes from London to this town, and goes on from hence to the utmost coast of Wales; where it cross'd the Severn, there are remains of a stone bridge to be seen in the bottom of the river, when the water is low. On this road we set out now for Litchfield in our way towards London; and I would gladly have kept to this old road, if it had been possible, because I knew several remarkable places stood directly upon it. But we were oblig'd to make many excursions, and sometimes quit the street for a great way together: and first we left it to go away south to the edge of Stafford-shire, to see the old house call'd White Ladies,[9] and the Royal Oak, the famous retreat of King Charles II after the Battle of Worcester. The tree is surrounded with a palisadoe, to preserve it from the fate which threatned it from curiosity; or almost every body that came to see it for several years, carry'd away a piece of it, so that the tree was litterally in danger not to dye of age, but to be pull'd *limb from limb*; but the veneration of that kind is much abated, and as the palisadoes are more decay'd than the tree, the latter seems likely to stand safe without them; as for the house, there is nothing remarkable in it; but it being a house always inhabited by Roman Catholicks, it had and perhaps has still some rooms so private in it, that in those times could not have been discover'd without pulling down the whole buildings.

Entring Stafford-shire we quitted the said Street-way, a little to the left, to see Stafford the county town, and the most considerable except Litchfield in the county. In the way we were surpriz'd in a most agreeable manner, passing thro' a small but ancient town call'd Penkrige, vulgarly Pankrage, where happen'd to be a fair. We expected nothing extraordinary; but was I say surpriz'd to see the prodigious number of horses brought hither, and those not ordinary and common draught-horses, and such kinds as we generally see at country-fairs remote from London: but here were really incredible numbers of the finest and most beautiful horses that can any where be seen; being brought hither from Yorkshire, the bishoprick of Durham, and all the horse-breeding countries: we were told that there were not less than an hundred

jockies and horse-kopers, as they call them there, from London, to buy horses for sale. Also an incredible number of gentlemen attended with their grooms to buy gallopers, or race-horses, for their Newmarket sport. In a word, I believe I may mark it for the greatest horse-fair in the world, for horses of value, and especially those we call saddle-horses. There are indeed greater fairs for coach-horses, and draught horses; though here were great numbers of fine large stone horses for coaches, &c. too. But for saddle-horses, for the light saddle, hunters, pads, and racers, I believe the world cannot match this fair.

We staid 3 days here to satisfy our curiosity, and indeed the sight was very agreeable, to see what vast stables of horses there were, which never were brought out or shewn in the fair. How dextrous the northern grooms and breeders are in their looking after them, and ordering them: those fellows take such indefatigable pains with them, that they bring them out like pictures of horses, not a hair amiss in them; they lye constantly in the stables with them, and feed them by weight and measure; keep them so clean, and so fine, I mean in their bodies, as well as their outsides, that, in short, nothing can be more nice. Here were several horses sold for 150 guineas a horse; but then they were such as were famous for the breed, and known by their race, almost as well as the Arabians know the genealogy of their horses.

From hence we came in two hours easy riding to **Stafford**, on the river Sow; 'tis an old and indeed antient town, and gives name to the county; but we thought to have found something more worth going so much out of the way in it.

The people of this county have been particularly famous, and more than any other county in England, for good footmanship, and there have been, and still are among them, some of the fleetest runners in England; which I do not grant to be occasion'd by any particular temperature of the air or soil, so much as to the hardy breed of the inhabitants, especially in the moorlands or northern part of the county, and to their exercising themselves to it from their child-hood; for running foot-races seems to be the general sport or diversion of the country.

Near Stafford we saw Ingestre,[10] where the late Walter Chetwynd, Esq; built or rather rebuilt a very fine church at his own charge, and where the late Lord Chetwynd has with a profusion of expence laid out the finest park and gardens that are in all this part of England, and which, if nothing else was to be seen this way, are very well worth a traveller's curiosity.

I am now at the utmost extent of my limits for this circuit; for Ingestre parks reach to the very banks of

156. 'East view of the cathedral church and close of Lichfield, taken from Stow pool'; engraving by John Wood after Richard Greene (1745).

the Trent, which I am not to pass; so I turn'd to the right and intending for Litchfield.

Litchfield is a fine, neat, well-built, and indifferent large city; there is a little lake[11] or lough of water in the middle of it, out of which runs a small stream of water, which soon becomes a little rivulet, and save that it has but 4 or 5 miles to the Trent, would soon become a river; this lake parts Litchfield, as it were, into two cities, one is call'd the town, and the other the close; in the first is the market-place, a fine school, and a very handsome hospital well-endow'd. This part is much the largest and most populous: but the other is the fairest, has the best buildings in it, and, among the rest, the cathedral-church, one of the finest and most beautiful in England, especially for the out-side, the form and figure of the building, the carv'd work'd, imagery, and the three beautiful spires; the like of which are not to be seen in one church, no not in Europe.

There are two fine causways which join the city and the close, with sluices to let the water pass, but those were cut thro' in the time of the late intestine wars in England; and the closs, which is wall'd about, and was then fortify'd for the king, was very strong, and stood out several vigorous attacks against Crom-well's men, and was not at last taken without great loss of blood on both sides, being gallantly defended to the last drop, and taken by storm.

There are in the close, besides the houses of the clergy residentiaries, a great many very well-built houses, and well inhabited too; which makes Litch-field a place of good conversation and good company, above all the towns in this county or the next, I mean Warwickshire or Darbyshire.

The church I say is indeed a most beautiful building; the west prospect of it is charming, the two spires on the corner towers being in themselves perfect beauties of architect, in the old Gothic way of building, but made still more shining and glorious by a third spire, which rising from the main tower in the body of the church, surmounts the other two, and shews itself exactly between them.

It is not easy to describe the beauty of the west end; you enter by three large doors in the porch or portico, which is as broad as the whole front; the spaces between the doors are fill'd with carv'd work and imagery, no place being void, where (by the rules of architect) any ornament could be plac'd.

Over the first cornish is a row of statues or images of all the kings which reign'd in Jerusalem from King David to the captivity; but I cannot say that they are all sufficiently distinguish'd one from another: above there are other images without number, whose names no account (I could meet with there) could explain.

The great window over the middle door is very large, and the pediment over it finely adorn'd, a large cross finishing the top of it; on either corner of the west front are two very fine towers, not unlike the two towers on the west end of St. Peter's church at Westminster, only infinitely finer: even with the battle-ment of the porch, and adjoining to the towers, are large pinnacles at the outer angles, and on the top of the towers are to each tower eight more, very beautiful and fine; between these pinnacles, on the top of each tower, rises a spire equal in height, in thickness, and in workmanship, but so beautiful no pen can describe them.

From Litchfield we came to **Tamworth**, a fine pleasant trading town, eminent for good ale and good company, of the middling sort; from whence we came into the great road again at Coleshill in Warwickshire.

From Coles-hill we came to **Coventry**, the sister city to Litchfield, and join'd in the title of the see, which was for some little time seated here, but afterwards return'd to Litchfield.

It was a very unhappy time when I first came to this city;[12] for their heats and animosities for election of members to serve in Parliament, were carry'd to such a hight, that all manner of method being laid aside, the inhabitants (in short) enraged at one another, met, and fought a pitch'd battle in the middle of the street, where they did not take up the breadth of the street, as two rabbles of people would generally do; in which case no more could engage, but so many as the breadth of the street would admit in the front; but, on the contrary, the two parties meeting in the street, one party kept to one side of the way, and one side to the other, the kennel in the middle only parting them, and so marching as if they intended to pass by one another, 'till the front of one party was come opposite to the reer of the other, and then suddenly facing to one another, and making a long front, where their flanks were before, upon a shout given, as the signal on both

157. 'The Ribbon weaver in his loom', from the *Universal Magazine* (July 1747).

sides, they fell on with such fury with clubs and staves, that in an instant the kennel was cover'd with them, not with slain, but with such as were knock'd down on both sides, and, in a word, they fought with such obstinacy that 'tis scarce credible.

Nor were these the scum and rabble of the town, but in short the burghers and chief inhabitants, nay even magistrates, aldermen, and the like.

Nor was this one skirmish a decision of the quarrel, but it held for several weeks, and they had many such fights; nor is the matter much better among them to this day, only that the occasion does not happen so often.

Coventry is a large and populous city, and drives a very great trade; the manufacture of tammies[13] is their chief employ, and next to that weaving of ribbons of the meanest kind, chiefly black. The buildings are very old, and in some places much decay'd; the city may be taken for the very picture of the city of London, on the south side of Cheapside before the great Fire; the timber-built houses, projecting forwards and towards one another, till in the narrow streets they were ready to touch one another at the top.

The tale of the Lady Godiva, who rode naked thro' the high street of the city to purchase her beloved city of Coventry exemption from taxes, is held for so certain a truth, that they will not have it question'd upon any account whatever; and the picture of the poor fellow that peep'd out of window to see her, is still kept up, looking out of a garret in the high street of the city: but Mr. Cambden says positively no body look'd at her at all.

From Coventry we could by no means pass the town of **Warwick**, the distance too being but about six miles, and a very pleasant way on the banks of the river Avon: 'tis famous for being the residence of the great Guy Earl of Warwick,[14] known now only by fame, which also has said so much more than the truth of him, that even what was true is become a kind of romance, and the real history of his actions is quite lost to the world.

As to the town of Warwick, it is really a fine town, pleasantly situated on the bank of the Avon, over which there is a large and stately bridge, the Avon being now grown a pretty large river. Warwick was ever esteem'd a handsome, well-built town, and there were several good houses in it, but the face of it is now quite alter'd; for having been almost wholly reduc'd to a heap of rubbish, by a terrible fire[15] about two and twenty years ago, it is now rebuilt in so noble and so beautiful a manner, that few towns in England make so fine an appearance. The new church also is a fine building, but all the old monuments, which were very

The Names of the Grand Iury, Returned by Thomas Chiſswell and Thomas = Smith Sheriffs, at the Aſsizes Held for this City & County, *Auguſt the .4 .1705.* who (upon the Evidence of William Bennion *Butcher,* Tom Dines *Iuni*., & Ioseph Charley Three Notorious Rioters, at the late Election of Members to ſerve in Parliament) ffound Bills of Indictment, for Riots, Aſsaults, & Batteries, &c. at the said Election, againſt **Samuel Billing** then Mayor, and several of the Aldermen &. other Citizens of this City, who then & there, Endeavoured to keep &. preſerve Her Majesties Peace, in Purſuance of the Queens Directions & Comands; Recei= ved from the Right Honourable Robert = Harley *Esq*. one of Her Majesties Principal Secretaries of State.

Note the Red Letter men only Agreed to Find y̆ Bills.

Samuel Walker,	Richard Lindley,
Thomas Wright *Sen*,	Thomas Hurt,
William Gullon,	Edward Hadesford,
Thomas Hollier,	Ioseph Norton,
Thomas Smith *Tanner*,	Ioseph Ash,
Clement Ruttur,	Thomas Holbech,
Thomas Graſcombe,	Iohn Lander,
Robert Bedſon,	William Bryan,
Henry Gravenor,	Matthew Neale, *of Exhall*,
Thomas Kernon,	Thomas Hall *of Stoke*

XXVIII. Painted notice of the names of the Grand Jury called to try rioters after disturbances in 1705.

many, are entirely defac'd, and lost by the fire: however the memory and even the figure of 'em are eminently preserv'd by Mr. Dugdale,[16] in his Antiquities of this County, to which I refer.

The castle is a fine building, beautiful both by situation and its decoration; it stands on a solid rock of free-stone, from whose bowels it may be said to be built, as likewise is the whole town; the terrass of the castle, like that of Windsor, overlooks a beautiful contry, and sees the Avon running at the foot of the precipice, at above 50 foot perpendicular hight: the building is old, but several times repair'd and beautify'd by its several owners, and 'tis now a very agreeable place both within and without: the apartments are very nicely contriv'd, and the communication of the remotest parts of the building, one with another, are so well preserved by galleries, and by the great hall, which is very magnificent, that one finds no irregularity in the whole place, notwithstanding its ancient plan, as it was a castle not a palace, and built for strength rather than pleasure.

Being at Warwick, I took a short circuit thro' the S. E. part of the county, resolving after viewing a little the places of note, that lay something out of my intended rout, to come back to the same place.

Three miles from Warwick we pass'd over the Foss Way, which goes on to Leicester; then we came by Southam to **Daventry**, a considerable market town, but which subsists chiefly by the great concourse of travellers on the old Watling-street Way, which lies near it; and the road being turned by modern usage, lies now thro' the town itself, then runs on to Dunsmore Heath, where it crosses the Foss, and one branch goes on to Coventry, the other joins the Foss, and goes on to a place call'd High-Cross, where it falls into the old Watling-street again, and both meet again near Litchfield.

It is a most pleasant curiosity to observe the course of these old famous highways; the Icknild Way, the Watling-street, and the Foss, in which one sees so lively a representation of the antient British, Roman and Saxon governments, that one cannot help reallizing those times to the imagination; and tho' I avoid meddling with antiquity as much as possible in this work, yet in this case a circuit or tour thro' England would be very imperfect, if I should take no notice of these ways, seeing in tracing them we necessarily come to the principal towns, either that are or have been in every county.

From Daventry we cross'd the country to **Northampton**, the handsomest and best built town in all this part of England; but here, as at Warwick, the beauty of it is owing to its own disasters, for it was so effectually and suddenly burnt down,[17] that very few houses were left standing, and this, tho' the fire began in the day-time; the flame also spread itself with such fury, and run on with such terrible speed, that they tell us a townsman being at Queen's Cross upon a hill, on the south side of the town, about two miles off, saw the fire at one end of the town then newly begun, and that before he could get to the town it was burning at the remotest end, opposite to that where he first saw it; 'tis now finely rebuilt with brick and stone, and the streets made spacious and wide.

The great new church, the town-hall, the jayl, and all their public buildings, are the finest in any country town in England, being all new built.

158. 'North-West prospect of All Saints church, Northampton, 28 June 1711'; drawing by William Stukeley. From his *Pocket Sketchbook.*

The great inn at the George, the corner of the high street, looks more like a palace than an inn, and cost above 2000 l. building; and so generous was the owner, that, as we were told, when he had built it, he gave it to the poor of the town.

This is counted the center of all the horse-markets and horse-fairs in England, there being here no less than four fairs in a year: here they buy horses of all sorts, as well for the saddle as for the coach and cart, but chiefly for the two latter.

Near this town is the ancient royal house of Holmby,[18] which was formerly in great esteem, and by its situation is capable of being made a royal palace indeed. But the melancholy reflection of the imprisonment of King Charles the First in this house, and his being violently taken hence again by the mutinous rebels, has cast a kind of odium upon the place, so that it has been, as it were, forsaken and uninhabited. The house and estate has been lately purchas'd by the Dutchess of Marlborough; but we do not see that the house is like to be built or repair'd, as was at first discours'd; on the contrary it goes daily to decay.

160. Ruins of Holdenby, 25 April 1709; drawing by William Stukeley. From his *Pocket Sketchbook*.

The Earl of Sunderland's house at Althorp,[19] on the other hand, has within these few years changed its face to the other extreme, and had the late Earl liv'd to make some new apartments, which, as we were told, were design'd as two large wings to the buildings, it would have been one of the most magnificent palaces in Europe. The gardens are exquisitely fine, and add, if it be possible, to the natural beauty of the situation.

From hence we went north to Harborough, and in the way, in the midst of the deep dismal roads, the dirtyest and worst in all that part of the country, we saw Boughton,[20] the noble seat of the Duke of Mountague, a house built at the cost and by the fancy of the late Duke, very much after the model of the palace of Versailles; the treble wings projecting and expanded, forming a court or space wider and wider, in proper stades,[21] answerable to the wings, the body of the house closing the whole view.

The pavillions are also after the manner of Versailles; the house itself is very large and magnificent, but the situation facing so beautiful a park adds to the glory of it; the park is wall'd round with brick, and so finely planted with trees, and in such an excellent order, as I saw nothing more beautiful, no not in Italy itself, except that the walks of trees were not orange and limon, and citron, as it is in Naples, and the Abruzzo, and other southern parts of Italy.

Being thus got a little out of our way, we went on with it, and turning into the great Watling-street way, at High Cross, where the Foss crosses it, and which I suppose occasioned the name, we kept on the street way to Non-Eaton, a manufacturing town on the River Anker, and then to **Atherstone**, a town famous for a great cheese fair on the 8th of September; from whence the great cheese factors carry the vast quantities of cheese they buy to Sturbridge Fair, which begins about the same time, but holds much longer; and here 'tis sold again for the supply of the counties of Essex, Suffolk, and Norfolk.

From Atherson we turn'd N. to see Bosworth-Field, famous for the great battle which put an end to the usurpation of Richard III and to the long and bloody contention between the red rose and the white, or the two royal houses of York and Lancaster, which, as fame tells us, had cost the lives of eleven princes, three and twenty earls and dukes, three thousand noblemen, knights, and gentlemen, and two hundred thousand of the common people: they shew'd us the spot of ground where the battle was fought, and at the town they shew'd us several pieces of swords, heads of lances, barbs of arrows, pieces of pole-axes, and such like instruments of death, which they said were found by the country people in the several grounds near the place of battle, as they had occasion to dig, or trench, or plough up the ground.

Having satisfy'd our curiousity in these points, we turn'd east towards **Leicester**.

Leicester is an ancient large and populous town, containing about five parishes, 'tis the capital of the county of Leicester, and stands on the river Soar, which rises not far from that High Cross I mention'd before: they have a considerable manufacture carry'd on here, and in several of the market towns round for weaving of stockings by frames;[22] and one would scarce think it possible so small an article of trade could employ such multitudes of people as it does; for the whole county seems to be employ'd in it: as also Nottingham and Darby, of which hereafter.

The sheep bred in this county and Lincolnshire, which joins to it, are, without comparison, the largest, and bear not only the greatest weight of flesh on their bones, but also the greatest fleeces of wool on their backs of any sheep of England: nor is the fineness of the wool abated for the quantity; but as 'tis the longest staple, (so the clothiers call it) so 'tis the finest wool in the whole island, some few places excepted, such as Lemster in Herefordshire, the South Downs in Sussex, and such little places, where the quantity is small and insignificant, compar'd to this part of the country; for the sheep-breeding country reaches from

159. Detail from 'South West prospect of Northampton'; engraving by Samuel and Nathaniel Buck (1731).

the river Anker on the border of Warwickshire to the Humber at the farthest end of Lincolnshire, which is near a hundred miles in length, and from the bank of Trent in Lincoln and Leicestershire, to the bank of Ouse bordering Bucks, Bedford, Cambridge, and Huntingdonshires, above sixty miles in breadth.

The horses produced here, or rather fed here, are the largest in England, being generally the great black coach horses and dray horses, of which so great a number are continually brought up to London, that one would think so little a spot as this of Leicestershire could not be able to supply them: nor indeed are they all bred in this county, the adjoining counties of Northampton and Bedford having of late come into the same business; but the chief supply is from this county, from whence the other counties rather buy them and feed them up, as jockeys and chapmen, than breed them up from their beginning.

The Foss Way leads us from hence through the eastern and north east part of the county, and particularly through the Vale of Belvoir, or, as it is commonly call'd, of Bever, to Newark in Nottinghamshire: in all this long tract we pass, a rich and fertile country,

fruitful fields, and the noble river Trent, for twenty miles together, often in our view; the towns of Mount Sorrel, Loughborough, Melton Mowbray, and Waltham in the Would, that is to say, on the Downs; all these are market towns, but of no great note.

At **Newark** one can hardly see without regret the ruins of that famous castle,[23] which maintain'd itself through the whole civil war in England, and keeping a strong garrison there for the king to the last, cut off the greatest pass into the north that is in the whole kingdom; nor was it ever taken, 'till the king, press'd by the calamity of his affairs, put himself into the hands of the Scots army, which lay before it, and then commanded the governor to deliver it up, after which it was demolish'd, that the great road might lye open and free; and it remains in rubbish to this day. Newark is a very handsome well-built town, the market place a noble square, and the chuch is large and spacious, with a curious spire, which, were not Grantham so near, might pass for the finest and highest in all this part of England: the Trent divides itself here, and makes an island, and the bridges lead just to the foot of the castle wall; so that while this place was in the

161. 'The Town of Leicester from the South, July 30, 1724'; drawing by Samuel Buck. From his *Sketchbook* (1724).

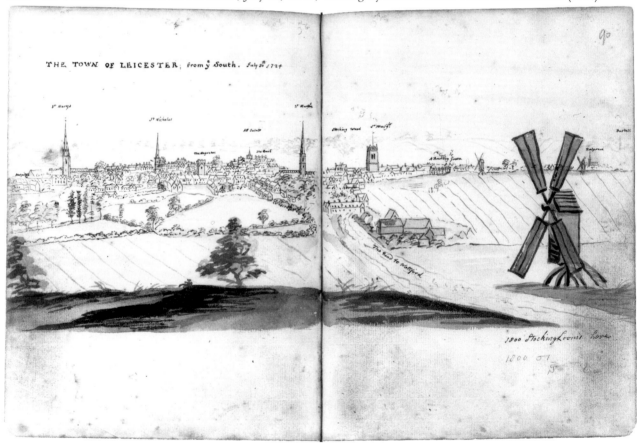

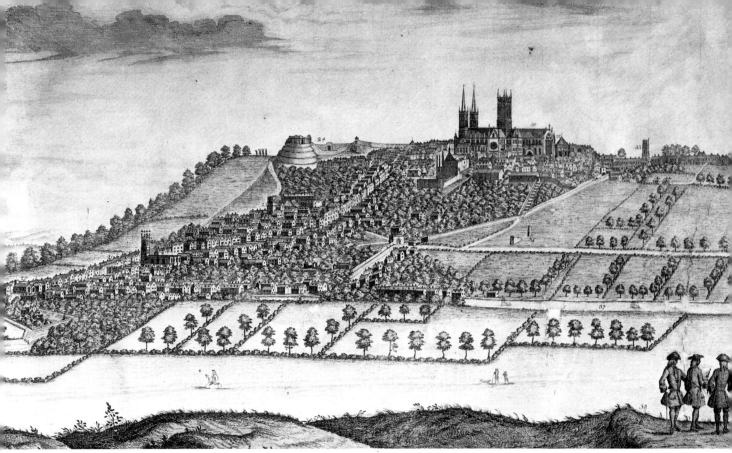

162. 'South view of the Antient city of Lincoln taken from Mr Dickinson's Summer House at Canwick'; engraving by Samuel Buck (*c*.1724–5).

hands of any party, there was no travelling but by their leave; but all the travelling into the north at that time was by Nottingham Bridge, of which by itself.

From Newark, still keeping the Foss Way, which lies as strait as a line can mark it out, we went on to Lincoln, having a view of the great church call'd the Minster all the way before us, the river Trent on the left, and the downs call'd Lincoln Heath on the right.

Lincoln is an antient, ragged, decay'd and still decaying city; it is so full of the ruins of monasteries and religious houses, that, in short, the very barns, stables, out-houses, and, as they shew'd me, some of the very hog-styes, were built church-fashion; that is to say, with stone walls and arch'd windows and doors. There are here 13 churches, but the meanest to look on that are any where to be seen; the cathedral indeed and the ruins of the old castle are very venerable pieces of antiquity.

The situation of the city is very particular; one part is on the flat and in a bottom, so that the Wittham, a little river that runs through the town, flows sometimes into the street, the other part lies upon the top of a high hill, where the cathedral stands, and the very steepest part of the ascent of the hill is the best part of the city for trade and business.

Nothing is more troublesome than the communi-cation of the upper and lower town, the street is so steep and so strait, the coaches and horses are oblig'd to fetch a compass another way, as well on one hand as on the other.

This [Lincoln's] cathedral is in itself a very noble structure, and is counted very fine, though I thought it not equal to some that I have already describ'd, particularly not to that at Litchfield: its situation indeed is infinitely more to advantage, than any cathedral in England, for it is seen far and wide; it stands upon an exceeding high hill, and is seen into five or six counties.

The building in general is very noble, and the church itself is very large; it has a double cross, one in the nave or center on which the great tower stands, and one at the east end of the choir, under which are several antient monuments; the length of the church is near 500 foot, the breadth 126; so that it is much larger than that at Litchfield; but the spires on the towers at the angles of the west end are mean, small, and low, and not to be nam'd with those at Litchfield: the tower also is very plain, and has only four very ill-proportion'd spires, or rather pinnacles, at the four corners small and very mean.

The city was a large and flourishing place at the time of the Norman Conquest, tho' neither the castle or the great church were then built; there were then three and fifty parish churches in it, of which I think only thirteen remain; the chief extent of the city then was from the foot of the hill south, and from the lake or lough which is call'd Swanpool east; and by the Domesday Book they tell us it must be one of the greatest cities in England, whence perhaps that old English proverbial line:

Lincoln was, London is, and York shall be.

It is certain William the Conqueror built the castle, and, as 'tis said, to curb the potent citizens; and the ruins show that it was a most magnificent work, well fortify'd, and capable of receiving a numerous garrison.

But all this relates to times past, and is an excursion, which I shall attone for by making no more. Such is the present state of Lincoln, that it is an old dying, decay'd, dirty city; and except that part, which, as above, lies between the castle and the church, on the top of the hill, it is scarce tolerable to call it a city.

Yet it stands in a most rich, pleasant, and agreeable country; for on the north, and again on the south east, the noble plain, call'd Lincoln Heath, extends itself, like the plains about Salisbury, for above fifty miles; namely, from Sleeford and Ancaster South to the bank of the Humber north, tho' not with a breadth equal to the vast stretch'd out length; for the plain is hardly any where above three or four miles broad.

On the west side of this plain, the Trent waters a pleasant and rich valley, running from Newark to Gainsborough, a town of good trade, as well foreign as home trade, thence to Burton, and so into the Humber.

As the middle of the country is all hilly, and the west side low, so the east side is the richest, most fruitful, and best cultivated of any county in England, so far from London; one part is all fen or marsh grounds, and extends itself south to the isle of Ely, and here it is that so vast a quantity of sheep are fed, as makes this county and that of Leicester an inexhaustible fountain of wool for all the manufacturing counties in England.

There are abundance of very good towns too in this part, especially on the sea coast, as Grimsby, in the utmost point of the country north east, facing the Humber and the ocean, and almost opposite to Hull: a little farther within Humber is Barton, a town noted for nothing that I know of, but an ill-favoured dangerous passage, or ferry, over the Humber to Hull; where in an open boat, in which we had about fifteen horses, and ten or twelve cows, mingled with about seventeen or eighteen passengers, call'd Christians; we were about four hours toss'd about on the Humber, before we could get into the harbour at Hull; whether I was sea-sick or not, is not worth notice, but that we were

all sick of the passage, any one may suppose, and particularly I was so uneasy at it, that I chose to go round by York, rather than return to Barton, at least for that time.

Grimsby is a good town, but I think 'tis but an indifferent road for shipping; and in the great storm, (ann. 1703) it was proved to be so, for almost all the ships that lay in Grimsby road were driven from their anchors, and many of them lost.

The Fen country begins about Wainfleet, which is within twenty miles of Grimsby, and extends itself to the Isle of Ely south, and to the grounds opposite to Lynn Regis in Norfolk east.

This part is indeed very properly call'd Holland, for 'tis a flat, level, and often drowned country, like Holland itself; here the very ditches are navigable, and the people pass from town to town in boats, as in Holland: here we had the uncouth musick of the bittern, a bird formerly counted ominous and presaging, and who, as fame tells us, (but as I believe no body knows) thrusts its bill into a reed, and then gives the dull, heavy groan or sound, like a sigh, which it does so loud, that with a deep base, like the sound of a gun at a great distance, 'tis heard two or three mile, (say the people) but perhaps not quite so far.

Here we first saw *Boston*, a handsome well-built sea port town, at the mouth of the river Wittham. The tower of this church is, without question, the largest and highest in England; and, as it stands in a country, which (they say) has no bottom, nothing is more strange, than that they should find a foundation for so noble and lofty a structure; it has no ornament, spire, or pinnacle on the top, but it is so very high, that few spires in England can match it, and is not only beautiful by land, but is very useful at sea to guide pilots into that port, and even into the mouth of the river Ouse;

163. Boston (29 August 1722); engraving by Thornton after William Stukeley. From William Stukeley *Itinerarium Curiosum* (1724).

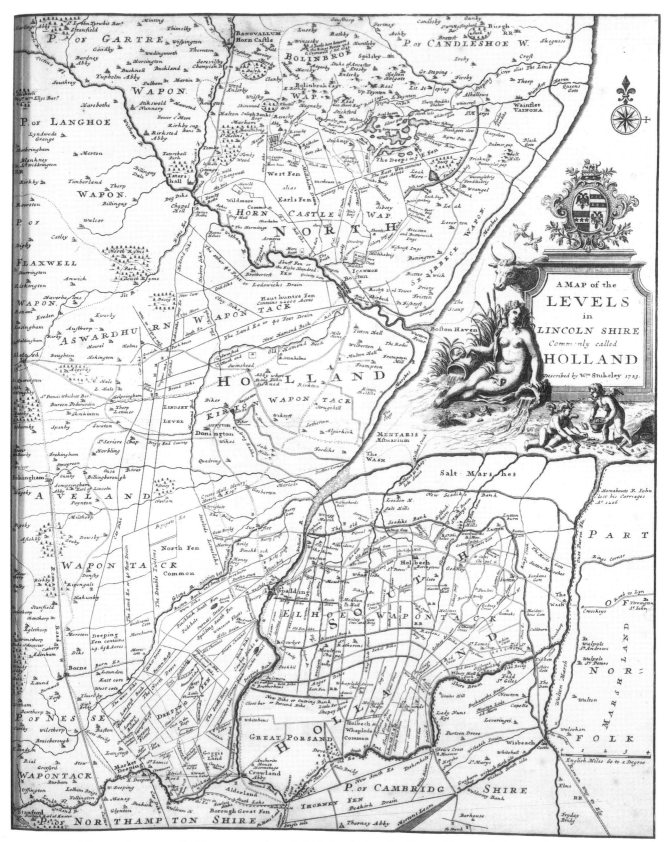

164. 'Map of the Levels in Lincolnshire commonly called Holland, described by William Stukeley 1723'.

for in clear weather 'tis seen quite out at sea to the entrance of those channels, which they call Lynn Deeps, and Boston Deeps, which are as difficult places as most upon the whole eastern shore of Britain.

The town of Boston is a large, populous, and well-built town, full of good merchants, and has a good share of foreign trade, as well as Lynn. Here is held one of those annual fairs, which preserve the antient title of a Mart, whereof I remember only four in England of any considerable note, viz. Lynn, Gainsborough, Beverly, and Boston.

The country round this place is all fenn and marsh grounds, the land very rich, and which feeds prodigious numbers of large sheep, and also oxen of the largest size, the overplus and best of which goes all to London market; and from this part, as also from the downs or heath above-mentioned, comes the greatest part of the wool, known, as a distinction for its credit, because of its fineness, by the name of Lincolnshire wool; which is sent in great quantities into Norfolk and Suffolk, for the manufacturers of those countries, and indeed to several other of the most trading counties in England.

These fens are indeed very considerable for their extent, for they reach in length in some places fifty miles, and in breadth above thirty: and as they are so level that there is no interruption to the sight, any building of extraordinary hight is seen a long way; for example, Boston steeple is seen upon Lincoln Heath near thirty miles, Petersborough and Ely ministers are seen almost throughout the whole level, so are the spires of Lynn, Whittlesea, and Crowland, seen at a very great distance, which adds a beauty to the country.

From Boston we came on through the fen country to **Spalding**, which is another sea port in the level, but standing far within the land on the river Welland. Here was nothing very remarkable to be seen as to antiquity, but the ruins of an old famous monastry, of which the *Monasticon* gives a particular description. There is a bridge over the Welland, and vessels of about fifty or sixty ton may come up to the town, and that is sufficient for the trade of Spalding, which is chiefly in corn and coal.

The town of Spalding is not large, but pretty well built and well inhabited; but for the healthyness or pleasantness of it, I have no more to say than this, that I was very glad when I got out of it, and out of the rest of the fen country; for 'tis a horrid air for a stranger to breathe in.

The history of the draining those fens, by a set of gentlemen call'd the Adventurers,[24] tho' it would be very useful and agreeable to have it fully and geo-graphically describ'd, yet it would take up so much room, and be so tedious here, where you are expecting a summary description of things, rather than the history and reasons of them, that I cannot think of entering any farther into it.

I have only to add, that these fens of Lincolnshire are of the same kind with, and contiguous to those already mentioned in the Isle of Ely, in the counties of Cambridge and Huntingdon, and that here, as well as there, we see innumerable numbers of cattle, which are fed up to an extraordinary size by the richness of the soil.

Here are also an infinite number of wild fowl, such as duck and mallard, teal and widgeon, brand geese, wild geese, &c. and for the taking of the four first kinds, here are a great number of decoys or duckoys, call them which you please, from all which the vast number of fowls they take are sent up to London; the quantity indeed is incredible, and the accounts which the country people give of the numbers they sometimes take, are such, that one scarce dares report it from them. But this I can say, of my certain knowledge, that some of these decoys are of so great an extent, and take such great quantities of fowl, that they are let for great sums of money by the year, viz. from 100 l. to 3, 4, and 500 l. a year rent.

The art of taking the fowls, and especially of breeding up a set of creatures, call'd decoy ducks, to entice and then betray their fellow-ducks into the several decoys, is very admirable indeed, and deserves a description; tho' 'tis not very easy to describe it, take it in as few words as I can.

The decoy ducks are first naturalized to the place, for they are hatch'd and bred up in the decoy ponds: there are in the ponds certain places where they are constantly fed, and where being made tame, they are used to come even to the decoy man's hand for their food.

When they fly abroad, or, as might be said, are sent abroad, they go none knows where; but 'tis believ'd by some they fly quite over the seas into Holland and Germany; there they meet with others of their acquaintance, that is to say, of their own kind, where sorting with them, and observing how poorly they live, how all the rivers are frozen up, and the lands cover'd with snow, and that they are almost starv'd, they fail not to let them know, (in language that they make one another understand) that in England, from whence they came, the case is quite alter'd; that the English ducks live much better than they do in those cold climates; that they have open lakes, and sea shores full of food, the tides flowing freely into every creek; that they have also within the land, large lakes, re-

XXIX. Francis Barlow, *The Decoy* (*c*.1680).

freshing springs of water, open ponds, covered and secured from human eyes, with large rows of grown trees and impenetrable groves; that the lands are full of food, the stubbles yielding constant supplies of corn, left by the negligent husbandmen, as it were on purpose for their use, that 'tis not once in a wild duck's age, that they have any long frosts or deep snows, and that when they have, yet the sea is never frozen, or the shores void of food; and that if they will please but to go with them into England, they shall share with them in all these good things.

By these representations, made in their own duck language, (or by whatever other arts which we know not) they draw together a vast number of the fowls, and, in a word, kidnap them from their own country; for being once brought out of their knowledge, they follow the decoys, as a dog follows the huntsman; and 'tis frequent to see these subtle creatures return with a vast flight of fowls with them, or at their heels, as we may say, after the said decoy ducks have been absent several weeks together.

When they have brought them over, the first thing they do is to settle with them in the decoy ponds, to which they (the decoy ducks) belong: here they chatter and gabble to them, in their own language, as if they were telling them, that these are the ponds they told them of, and here they should soon see how well they should live, how secure and how safe a retreat they had here.

When the decoy-men perceive they are come, and that they are gathering and encreasing, they fail not to go secretly to the pond's side, I say secretly, and under the cover which they have made with reeds, so that they cannot be seen, where they throw over the reeds handfuls of corn, in shallow places, such where the decoy ducks are usually fed, and where they are sure to come for it, and to bring their new guests with them for their entertainment.

This they do for two or three days together, and no harm follows, 'till throwing in this bait one time in an open wide place, another time in another open wide place, the third time it is thrown in a narrower place; that is to say, where the trees, which hang over the water and the banks, stand nearer, and then in another yet narrower, where the said trees are overhead like an arbour, though at a good hight from the water.

Here the boughs are so artfully managed, that a large net is spread near the tops of the trees among the branches, and fasten'd to hoops which reach from side to side: this is so high and so wide, and the room is so much below, and the water so open, that the fowls do not perceive the net above them at all.

Here the decoy-man keeping unseen, behind the hedges of reeds, which are made perfectly close, goes forward, throwing corn over the reeds into the water; the decoy ducks greedily fall upon it, and calling their foreign guests, seem to tell them, that now they may find their words good, and how well the ducks live in England; so inviting or rather wheedling them forward, 'till by degrees they are all gotten under the arch or sweep of the net, which is on the trees, and which by degrees, imperceptibly to them, declines lower and lower, and also narrower and narrower, 'till at the farther end it comes to a point like a purse; though this farther end is quite out of sight, and perhaps two or three hundred yards from the first entrance.

165. The form of the decoys in Lincolnshire with a diagram of a decoy pipe into which the ducks are driven to be captured; based on a drawing by William Stukeley (*c.*1722).

When the whole quantity are thus greedily following the leading ducks or decoys, and feeding plentifully as they go; and the decoy-man sees they are within the arch of the net, and so far within as not to be able to escape, on a sudden a dog, which 'till then he keeps close by him, and who is perfectly taught his business, rushes from behind the reeds, and jumps into the water, swimming directly after the ducks, and (terribly to them) barking as he swims.

Immediately the ducks (frighted to the last degree) rise upon the wing to make their escape, but to their great surprize, are beaten down again by the arched net, which is over their heads: being then forced into the water, they necessarily swim forward, for fear of that terrible creature the dog; and thus they crowd on, 'till by degrees the net growing lower and narrower, as is said, they are hurried to the very farther end, where another decoy-man stands ready to receive them, and who takes them out alive with his hands.

As for the traytors, that drew the poor ducks into this snare, they are taught to rise but a little way, and so not reaching to the net, they fly back to the ponds, and make their escape; or else being used to the decoy-man, they go to him fearless, and are taken out as the rest; but instead of being kill'd with them, are strok'd, made much of, and put into a little pond just by him, and fed and made much of for their services.

There are many particulars in the managing and draining these levels, throwing off the water by mills and engines, and cultivating the grounds in an unusual manner, which would be very useful to be describ'd; but the needful brevity of this work will not admit of it: yet something may be touch'd at.

1. That here are some wonderful engines for throwing up water, and such as are not to be seen any where else, whereof one in particular threw up, (as they assur'd us) twelve hundred ton of water in half an hour, and goes by wind-sails, 12 wings or sails to a mill: this I saw the model of, but I must own I did not see it perform.

2. Here are the greatest improvements by planting of hemp,[25] that, I think, is to be seen in England; particularly on the Norfolk and Cambridge side of the fens, as about Wisbech, Well, and several other places, where we saw many hundred acres of ground bearing great crops of hemp.

3. Here is a particular trade carry'd on with London, which is no where else practis'd in the whole kingdom, that I have met with, or heard of, (viz.) for carrying fish alive by land-carriage; this they do by carrying great buts fill'd with water in waggons, as the carriers draw other goods: the buts have a little square flap, instead of a bung, about ten, twelve, or fourteen inches square, which, being open'd, gives air to the fish, and every night, when they come to the inn, they draw off the water, and let more fresh and sweet water run into them again. In these carriages they chiefly carry tench and pike, pearch and eels, but especially tench and pike, of which here are some of the largest in England.

166. Beating hemp; engraving. From Denis Diderot *Encyclopédie*, vol. 6: *L'Economie Rustique* (*c*.1760).

Whittlesea and Ramsey meres are two lakes, made by the river Nyne or Nene, which runs through them; the first is between five and six miles long, and three or four miles broad, and is indeed full of excellent fish for this trade.

From the fenns, longing to the deliver'd from fogs and stagnate air, and the water of the colour of brew'd ale, like the rivers of the Peak, we first set foot on dry land, as I call'd it, at **Peterborough**.

This is a little city, and indeed 'tis the least in England; for Bath, or Wells, or Ely, or Carlisle, which are all call'd cities, are yet much bigger; yet Peterborough is no contemptible place neither; there are some good houses in it, and the streets are fair and well-built; but the glory of Peterborough is the cathedral, which is truly fine and beautiful; the building appears to be more modern, than the story of the raising this pile implies, and it wants only a fine tower steeple, and a spire on the top of it, as St. Paul's at London had, or as Salisbury still has; I say, it wants this only to make it the finest cathedral in Britain, except St. Paul's, which is quite new, and the church of St. Peter at York.

Coming to this little city landed us in Northamptonshire; but as great part of Lincolnshire, which is a vastly extended large county, remain'd yet unseen, we were oblig'd to turn north from Peterborough, and take a view of the fens again, though we kept them at some distance too. Here we pass'd the Welland at Market Deeping, an old, ill-built and dirty town; then we went thro' Bourn to Folkingham, near which we saw two pieces of decay'd magnificence; one was the old demolish'd monastry of Sempringham, the seat of the Gilbertine nuns,[26] so famous for austerity, and the severest rules, that any other religious order have yielded to, and the other was antient house of the Lord Clinton, Queen Elizabeth's admiral, where that great

and noble person once liv'd in the utmost splendor and magnificence; the house, tho' in its full decay, shows what it has been, and the plaister of the cielings and walls in some rooms is so fine, so firm, and so entire, that they break it off in large flakes, and it will bear writing on it with a pencil or steel pen, like the leaves of a table book. This sort of plaister I have not seen any where so very fine, except in the palace of Nonesuch in Surrey, near Epsom, before it was demolish'd by the Lord Berkeley.

From hence we cross'd part of the great heath mentioned before, and came into the high road again at **Ankaster**, a small but antient Roman village, and full of remnants of antiquity: this town gives now the title of duke to the ancient family of Lindsey, now Dukes of Ankaster, formerly only Earls of Lindsey, and hereditary Lords Chamberlains of England.

From hence we came to **Grantham**, famous for a very fine church and a spire steeple, so finely built, and so very high, that I do not know many higher and finer built in Britain. The vulgar opinion, that this steeple stands leaning, is certainly a vulgar error: I had no instrument indeed to judge it by, but, according to the strictest observation, I could not perceive it, or any thing like it, and am much of opinion with that excellent poet:

'Tis hight makes Grantham steeple stand awry.

This is a neat, pleasant, well-built and populous town, has a good market, and the inhabitants are said to have a very good trade, and are generally rich. There is also a very good free-school here. This town lying on the great northern road is famous, as well as Stamford, for abundance of very good inns, some of them fit to entertain persons of the greatest quality and their retinues, and it is a great advantage to the place.

Turning southward from hence we enter'd Rutlandshire, remarkable for being the least county in England, having but two market towns in it, viz. Okeham and Uppingham, but famous for abundance of fine seats of the gentlemen, and some of the first rank; as particularly the Earls of Gainsborough and Nottingham; the latter has at a very great expence, and some years labour, rebuilt the ancient seat of Burleigh on the Hill, near Okeham, and on the edge of the vale of Cathross.

From hence we came to **Stamford**; the town is placed in a kind of an angle of the county of Lincoln, just upon the edge of three counties, viz. Lincoln, Northampton, and Rutland: this town boasts greatly too of its antiquity, and indeed it has evident marks of its having been a very great place in former days.

It is at this time a very fair, well-built, considerable and wealthy town, consisting of six parishes, includ-

167. Grantham; drawing by William Stukeley. From his *Drawings in a journey with Mr Roger Gale* (1721).

168. 'Prospect of the town of Stamford from Worthrop Warren'; engraving by Thornton (1726).

ing that of St. Martin in Stamford-Baron; that is to say, in that part of the town which stands over the river, which, tho' it is not a part of the town, critically speaking, being not in the liberty, and in another county, yet 'tis all called Stamford, and is rated with it in the taxes, and the like.

But the beauty of Stamford is the neighbourhood of the noble palace of the Earl of Excester, call'd Burleigh House, built by the famous Sir William Cecil, Lord Burleigh, and Lord High Treasurer to Queen Elizabeth. This house, built all of free-stone, looks more like a town than a house, at which avenue soever you come to it; the towers and the pinnacles so high, and placed at such a distance from one another, look like so many distant parish-churches in a great town, and a large spire cover'd with lead, over the great clock in the center, looks like the cathedral, or chief church of the town.

The house stands on an eminence, which rises from the north entrance of the park, coming from Stamford: on the other side, viz. south and west, the country lies on a level with the house, and is a fine plain, with posts and other marks for horse-races; as the entrance looks towards the flat low grounds of Lincolnshire, it gives the house a most extraordinary prospect into the fens, so that you may see from thence twenty or near thirty miles, without any thing to intercept the sight.

As you mount the hill, you come to a fine esplanade, before the great gate or first entrance of the house, where there is a small but very handsome semi-circle, taken in with an iron balustrade, and from this, rising a few steps, you enter a most noble hall, but made infintely more noble by the invaluable paintings, with which it is so fill'd, that there is not room to place any thing between them.

The late Earl of Excester, father of his present lordship, had a great genius for painting and architecture,

and a superior judgment in both, as every part of this noble structure will testify; for he chang'd the whole face of the building; he pull'd down great part of the front next the garden, and turn'd the old Gothic windows into those spacious sashes which are now seen there; and tho' the founder or first builder, who had an exquisite fancy also, (as the manner of buildings then was) had so well ordered the situation and avenues of the whole fabrick, that nothing was wanting of that kind, and had also contriv'd the house itself in a most magnificent manner; the rooms spacious, well directed, the cielings lofty, and the decorations just, yet the late Earl found room for alterations, infinitely to the advantage of the whole; as particularly, a noble stair case, a whole set of fine apartments, with rooms of state, fitting for the entertainment of a prince, especially those on the garden side; tho' at present a little out of repair again.

As this admirable genius, the late Earl, lov'd paintings, so he had infinite advantage in procuring them; for he not only travell'd three times into Italy, and stay'd every time a considerable while at Florence, but he was so entertain'd at the court of Tuscany, and had, by his most princely deportment and excellent accomplishments, so far obtain'd upon the great Duke, that he might be said indeed to love him, and his highness shew'd the Earl many ways that esteem; and more particularly, in assisting him to purchase many excellent pieces at reasonable prices; and not only so, but his highness presented him with several pieces of great value.

Among the rest, there is, in the great hall, his lordship's picture, on horseback, done by the great Duke's principal painter, at his highness's charge, and given to his lordship, as a mark of the great Duke's special favour: there is also a fine piece of Seneca bleeding to death in the warm bath, and dictating his

169. South prospect of Burleigh House; engraving by J. Caldwall after P. Tillemans (*c.*1720).

last morals to his scholars; the passions are in so lively a manner described in the scholars, their eager attention, their generous regard to their master, their vigilant catching at his words, and some of them taking minutes, that it is indeed admirable and inexpressible. I have been told, that the King of France offer'd the Earl 6000 pistoles for it.

Besides the pictures, which, as above, were brought from abroad, the house itself, at least the new apartments may be said to be one entire picture. The stair-case, the cielings of all the fine lodgings, the chapel, the hall, the late Earl's closet, are all finely painted by Varrio,[27] of whose work I need say no more than this, that the Earl kept him twelve years in his family, wholly employ'd in painting those cielings and stair-cases, &c. and allow'd him a coach and horses, and equipage, a table, and servants, and a very considerable pension.

N.B. The character this gentleman left behind him at this town, is, that he deserv'd it all for his paintings; but for nothing else; his scandalous life, and his unpaid debts, it seems, causing him to be but very meanly spoken of in the town of Stamford.

As we pass by Burleigh Park wall, on the great road, we see on the west side, not above a mile from it, another house, built by the same Lord Burleigh, and which might pass for a very noble seat, were not Burleigh by. This is call'd Wathorp, and stands just on

the Great Roman Way; this is the house of which the old Earl said he built it to *remove to, and to be out of the dust, while Burleigh House was a sweeping.* This saying is indeed father'd upon the noble founder, but I must acknowledge, I think it too haughty an expression to come from so wise and great a man.

170. Verrio's ceiling decoration in the second George room, Burghley House (1688–98).

At Overton, now call'd Cherry Orton, a village near Gunworth Ferry, is an old mansion house, formerly belonging to a very antient and almost forgotten race, or family of great men, call'd Lovetoft, which I nam'd for a particular reason. The estate is now in the heirs of the late Duke of Newcastle, and the house lies neglected. On the other side of the river is a fine new-built house, all of free stone, posses'd by Sir Francis St. John, Bart. which affords a very beautiful prospect to travellers, as they pass from the hill beyond Stilton to Wansford Bridge. This Wansford has obtain'd an idle addition to its name, from a story so firmly believ'd by the country people, that they will hardly allow any room for contradiction; namely, that a great flood coming hastily down the river Nyne, in hay-making-time, a country fellow, having taken up his lodging on a cock of hay in the meadow, was driven down the stream in the night, while he was fast asleep; and the hay swimming, and the fellow sleeping, they drove together towards Wisbech in the fens, whence he was fairly going on the sea; when being wakened, he was seen and taken up by some fishermen, almost in the open sea; and being ask'd, who he was? he told them his name; and where he liv'd? he answer'd, *at Wansford in England*: from this story the town is called *Wansford* in *England*; and we see at the great inn, by the south end of the bridge, the sign of a man floating on a cock of hay, and over him written, *Wansford* in *England*.

Coming south from hence we pass'd **Stilton**,[28] a town famous for cheese, which is call'd our English Parmesan, and is brought to table with the mites, or maggots round it, so thick, that they bring a spoon with them for you to eat the mites with, as you do the cheese.

Hence we came through Sautrey Lane, a deep descent between two hills, in which is Stangate Hole, famous for being the most noted robbing-place in all this part of the country. Hence we pass'd to **Huntington**, the county town, otherwise not considerable; it is full of very good inns, is a strong pass upon the Ouse, and in the late times of rebellion it was esteemed so by both parties.

Here are the most beautiful meadows on the banks of the river Ouse, that I think are to be seen in any part of England; and to see them in the summer season, cover'd with such innumerable stocks of cattle and sheep, is one of the most agreeable sights of its kind in the world.

This town has nothing remarkable in it; 'tis a long continued street, pretty well built, has three parish churches, and a pretty good market-place; but the bridge, or bridges rather, and causway over the Ouse is a very great ornament to the place.

On the west side of this town, and in view of the plain lower side of the county, is a noble, tho' ancient seat, of the Earl of Sandwich; the gardens very fine and well kept; the situation seems a little obscur'd by the town of Huntington. In the same plain we saw Bugden, a small village, in which is remarkable a very pleasant, tho' ancient house or palace, of the bishops of Lincoln: the house and garden surrounded by a very large and deep moat of water; the house is old, but pleasant, the chappel very pretty, 'tho' small; there is an organ painted against the wall, but in a seeming organ-loft, and so properly placed and well painted, that we at first believed it really to be an organ.

Hence we went a little north to see Oundle, being told that the famous drum[29] was to be heard just at that time in the well; but when we came there, they shew'd us indeed the well and the town, but as for the drum, they could only tell us they heard of it, and that it did drum; but we could meet with no person of sufficient credit, that would say seriously they had heard it: so we came away dissatisfy'd.

From Oundle we cross'd the county of Northampton into Bedfordshire, and particularly to the town of **Bedford**, the chief town of the county; for this county has no city in it, tho' even this town is larger and more populous, than several cities in England, having five parish-churches, and a great many, and those wealthy and thriving inhabitants. This is one of the seven counties, which they say lie together, and have not one city among them; namely, Huntington, Bedford, Bucks, Berks, Hertford, Essex, and Suffolk.

Bedford, as I have said, is a large, populous, and thriving town, and a pleasant well-built place; it has five parish churches, a very fine stone bridge over the Ouse, and the high street, (especially) is a very handsome fair street, and very well-built; and tho' the town is not upon any of the great roads in England, yet it

171. Buckden Palace; engraving from the *Ladies Magazine* (1749–53).

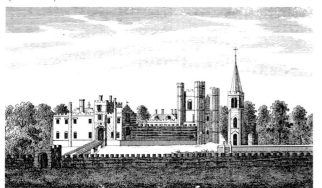

XXX. George Lambert, *Landscape near Woburn Abbey, Bedfordshire* (1733). Depicts view south towards Sharpenhoe.

172 (facing page). Two people carrying bundles; drawing by Samuel Buck. From his *Sketchbook* (1724).

is full of very good inns, and many of them; and in particular we found very good entertainment here.

Here is the best market for all sorts of provisions, that is to be seen at any country town in all these parts of England; and this occasions, that tho' it is so far from London, yet the higglers or carriers buy great quantities of provisions here for London markets; also here is a very good trade down the river to Lynn.

Here is also a great corn market, and great quantities of corn are bought here, and carry'd down by barges and other boats to Lynn, where it is again shipp'd, and carry'd by sea to Holland: the soil hereabouts is exceeding rich and fertile, and particularly produces great quantities of the best wheat in England, which is carry'd by waggons from hence, and from the north part of the county twenty miles beyond this, to the markets of Hitchin and Hertford, and bought again there, and ground and carry'd in the meal (still by land) to London.

Indeed the whole product of this county is corn, that is to say, wheat and malt for London; for here are very few manufactures, except that of straw-hats and bone-lace, of which by itself: there are but ten market towns in the whole county, and yet 'tis not a small county neither: the towns are,

Bedford,	Shefford,
Biggleswood,	Luton,
Leighton,	Potton,
Dunstable,	Tuddington,
Ampthill,	Wooburn.

The last of these was almost demolish'd by a terrible fire,[30] which happen'd here just before my writing this account; but as this town has the good luck to belong to a noble family, particularly eminent for being good landlords; that is to say, bountiful and munificent to their poor tenants, I mean the ducal house of Bedford; there is no doubt but that the trustees, tho' his grace the present Duke is in his minority, will preserve that good character to the family, and re-edify the town, which is almost all their own.

The Duke's house, call'd Wooburn Abbey,[31] is just by the town, a good old house, but very ancient, spacious and convenient rather than fine, but exceedingly pleasant by its situation; and for the great quantity of beach woods which surround the parks and cover the hills, and also for great woods of oak too, as rich and valuable, as they are great and magnificent.

Ampthill is grac'd like Wooburn; for tho' in itself, like the other, it is not a considerable town, and has no particular manufacture to enrich it, yet by the neighbourhood of that great and noble family of Bruce Earls of Ailesbury,[32] the very town is made both rich and honourable: it is however the misfortune of this noble family, that the present Earl lives abroad, being a Roman; but the next heirs are in view of recovering the grandeur of that ancient family. The old venerable seat of the family is near the town, and is a noble and magnificent palace, tho' not wholly re-built, as is the fortune of many of the seats of our nobility of this age.

From hence, thro' the whole south part of this county, as far as the border of Buckinghamshire and Hertfordshire, the people are taken up with the manufacture of bone-lace, in which they are wonderfully encreas'd and improv'd within these few years past.

Also the manufactures of straw-work, especially straw hats, spreads itself from Hertfordshire into this county, and is wonderfully encreased within a few years past.

Having thus viewed this county in all its most considerable towns, we came from Dunstable to St. Albans, and so into London, all which has been spoken of before; I therefore break off this circuit here, and subscribe,

Sir,

Your most obedient Servant.

The End of the Seventh Letter

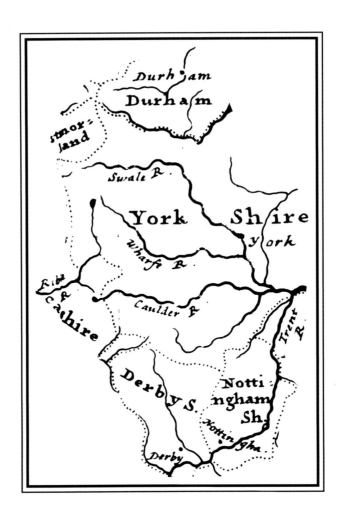

LETTER VIII

Introduction

S<small>IR</small>,

I HAVE NOW FINISHED my account of the several circuits which I took the last year, compleating the southern parts of the isle of Britain; my last brought me to the banks of the river Trent, and from thence back to London, where I first set out.

I have yet the largest, tho' not the most populous, part of Britain to give you an account of; nor is it less capable of satisfying the most curious traveller: though, as in some places things may stand more remote from one another, and there may, perhaps, be more waste ground to go over; yet 'tis certain a traveller spends no waste hours, if his genius will be satisfied with just observations. The widest part of the country is full of variety, the most mountainous places have their rarities to oblige the curious, and give constant employ to the enquiries of a diligent observer, making the passing over them more pleasant than the traveller cou'd expect, or than the reader perhaps at first sight will think possible.

The people in these northern climes will encrease the variety; their customs and genius differing so much from others, will add to our entertainment; the one part of them being, till now, a distinct nation, the inhabitants thereof will necessarily come in as a part of what we are to describe: Scotland is neither so considerable, that we should compliment her at the expence of England; or so inconsiderable, that we should think it below us to do her justice; I shall take the middle of both extremes.

I shall be tempted very often to make excursions here on account of the history and antiquities of persons and places, both private and publick. For the northern parts of Britain, especially of England, as they were long the seat of war between the several nations; such as the Britains, Scots, Picts, Romans, Saxons, and Danes, so there are innumerable remains of antiquity left behind them, and those more visible in those parts, and less defac'd by time, and other accidents than in any other part of the island.

He that travels through such a country, if he sees and knows the meaning of those monuments of antiquity, and has due memoirs of the historical part still in his head, must be inexcusable if he takes up his own time, or his reader's patience, in observing trifles, and recording things of no signification.

I knew two gentlemen who travelled over the greatest part of England in several journies together; the result of their observations were very different indeed; one of them took some minutes of things for his own satisfaction, but not much; but the other, as he said, took an exact journal; the case was thus:

He that took minutes only, those minutes were very critical, and upon some very significant things; but for the rest his memory was so good, and he took so good notice of every thing worth observing, that he wrote a very good and useful account of his whole journey after his return; that account I have seen, and had the advantage to look it over again upon this occasion, and by it correct and enlarge some of my own observations; it being as impossible any one man could see or observe every thing worth seeing in England, as it is to know every face he meets in a croud.

The other gentleman's papers, which I called an exact journal, contained the following very significant heads:

I. The day of the month when he set out.

II. The names of the towns where they din'd every day, and where they lodg'd at night.

III. The signs of the inns where they din'd and lodg'd, with the memorandums of which had good claret, which not.

IV. The day of the month when he return'd.

The moral of this brief story, which I insist that I know to be true, is very much to my purpose. The difference between these two gentlemen in their travelling, and in their remarks upon their journey, is a good emblem of the differing genius in readers, as well as authors, and may be a guide to both in the work now before us.

The north part of Great Britain, I mean Scotland, is a country which will afford a great variety to the observation, and to the pen of an itinerate; a kingdom so famous in the world for great and gallant men, as well states-men as soldiers, but especially the last, can never leave us barren of subject, or empty of somewhat to say of her.

The Union has seemed to secure her peace, and to encrease her commerce: but I cannot say she has raised her figure in the world at all since that time, I mean as a body; she was before considered as a nation, now she appears no more but as a province, or at best a dominion; she has not lost her name as a place; but as a state, she may be said to have lost it, and that she is now no more than a part of Great Britain in common with other parts of it, of which England itself is also no more. I might enlarge here upon the honour it is to Scotland to be a part of the British Empire, and to be incorporated with so powerful a people under the crown of so great a monarch; their being united in name as one, Britain, and their enjoying all the privileges of, and in common with, a nation who have the greatest privileges, and enjoy the most liberty of any people in the world. But I should be told, and perhaps justly too, that this was talking like an Englishman, rather than like a Briton; that I was gone from my declared impartiality, and that the Scots would perhaps talk a different stile when I came among them. Nor is it my business to enquire which nation have the better end of the staff in the late coalition, or how the articles on which it is established, are performed on one side or other.

My business is rather to give a true and impartial description of the place; a view of the country, its present state as to fertility, commerce, manufacture, and product; with the manners and usages of the people, as I have done in England; and to this I shall confine myself as strictly as the nature of a journey thro' the country requires.

SIR,

As I am to begin this circuit from the river Trent, and to confine my observations to that part of Britain which the Scots and Northumberlanders, and others on that side, call North by Trent, it seems necessary (at least it cannot be improper) to give some description of the river itself, and especially the course which it runs, by which, adding a little river call'd the Weaver, and a branch of it call'd the Dane in Staffordshire and Cheshire, the whole island of Britain is, as it were divided into two parts.

It rises in the hills or highlands of Staffordshire, called the Moorlands, receiving, from the edge of Cheshire, and towards Lancashire, a great many (some say thirty, and that thence it had its name) little rivulets into it, very near its head, all which may claim a share in being the originals of the Trent; thus it soon becomes one large river, and comes down from the hills with a violent current into the flat country; where, being encreased by several other little rivers, it carries a deeper channel, and a stiller current; and having given its name to Trentham, a small market town in the same county, it goes on to Stone, a considerable town on the great road to West-Chester.

One branch of the Trent rises within a quarter of a mile of the Dane, (viz.) from a moor adjoining to, or part of a little ridge of hills called Molecop Hill, near Congleton, and is within twenty two miles of the Irish Sea, or that arm or inlet of the sea which the Mersee makes from Frodsham to Liverpool and Hyle-lake; and as the Dane runs into the Weaver, and both into that arm of the sea, and the Trent into the Humber, which opens into the great German Ocean, those rivers may be said to cut the island across in the middle.

The Trent runs a course of near two hundred miles, through the four counties of Stafford, Derby, Nottingham, and Lincoln; it receives, besides lesser waters, the larger rivers of the Sowe from the west side of the county, and from the town of Stafford; the Tame from Birmingham and Tamworth; the Soar from Leicester; and the Dove and Derwent, two furiously rapid streams, from the Peak of Derby; the Idle, a gentle navigable stream from Rhetford and Nottinghamshire; with part of the Wittham, called the Fossdike from Lincoln, also navigable; and the greatest of them all, the Don, from Doncaster, Rothram, and Sheffield, after a long and rapid course through the moors called Stanecross on the edge of Derby, and the West-Riding of Yorkshire.

The Trent is navigable by ships of good burthen as high as Gainsbrough, which is near 40 miles from the Humber by the river. The barges without the help of locks or stops go as high as Nottingham, and farther by the help of art, to Burton upon Trent in Staffordshire. The stream is full, the channel deep and safe, and the tide flows up a great way between Gainsborough and Newark. This, and the navigation lately, reaching up to Burton and up the Derwent to Derby, is a great support to, and encrease of the trade of those counties which border upon it; especially for the cheese trade from Cheshire and Warwickshire, which have otherwise no navigation but about from West Chester to London; whereas by this river it is brought by water to Hull, and from thence to all the south and north coasts on the east side of Britain; 'tis calculated that there is about four thousand ton of Cheshire cheese only, brought down the Trent every year from those parts of England to Gainsborough and Hull; and especially in time of the late war, when the seas on the other side of England were too dangerous to bring it by long-sea.

As I am travelling now cross the island, and begin at the mouth of Trent, the first town of note that I meet with is **Nottingham**, the capital of that shire, and is the most considerable in all that part of England.

Nottingham is one of the most pleasant and beautiful towns in England. The situation makes it so, tho' the additions to it were not to be nam'd. It is seated on the side of a hill overlooking a fine range of meadows about a mile broad, a little rivulet running on the north side of the meadows, almost close to the town; and the noble river Trent parallel with both on the further or south side of the meadows.

The town of Nottingham is situated upon the steep ascent of a sandy rock; which is consequently remarkable, for that it is so soft that they easily work into it for making vaults and cellars, and yet so firm as to support the roofs of those cellars two or three under one another; the stairs into which, are all cut out of the solid, tho' crumbling rock; and we must not fail to have it be remember'd that the bountiful inhabitants generally keep these cellars well stock'd with excellent ale; nor are they uncommunicative in bestowing it among their friends, as some in our company experienc'd to a degree not fit to be made matter of history.

The beauties of Nottingham, next to its situation, are the castle[1], the market-place, and the gardens of Count Tallard;[2] who, in his confinement here as prisoner of war taken by the Duke of Marlborough at the great battle of Blenheim, amused himself with

173. 'South prospect of the town of Nottingham'; engraving. From George C. Deering, *Nottinghamia Vetus et Nova* (1750). The engraving shows river craft on the Trent after they have passed under Trent bridge.

making a small, but beautiful parterre, after the French fashion. But it does not gain by English keeping.

Nottingham, notwithstanding the navigation of the Trent, is not esteemed a town of very great trade, other than is usual to inland towns; the chief manufacture carried on here is frame-work knitting for stockings, the same as at Leicester, and some glass, and earthern ware-houses; the latter much increased since the increase of tea-drinking;[3] for the making fine stone-mugs, tea-pots, cups, &c. the glass-houses, I think, are of late rather decayed.

As there is a fine market-place, so is there a very good market, with a vast plenty of provisions, and those of the best sort, few towns in England exceeding it; to say nothing of their ale, as having reserved it to a place by itself.

As they brew very good liquor here, so they make the best malt, and the most of it of any town in this part of England, which they drive a great trade for, sending it by land-carriage to Derby, through all the Peak as far as Manchester, and to other towns in Lancashire, Cheshire, and even into Yorkshire itself; to which end all the lower lands of this county, and especially on the banks of Trent, yield prodigious crops of barley.

The government of Nottingham is in the Mayor, two Sheriffs, six Aldermen, Coroners and Chamberlains, twenty four Common-Council, whereof six are called Juniors; the rest of course, I suppose, may pass for Seniors.

From Nottingham, a little mile west on the road to Derby, we saw Woollaton Hall,[4] the noblest antient-built palace in this county, the mansion of the antient family of Willoughby, now Lord Middleton, created Baron in the late Queen Anne's time. The house, the gardens, the great hall, the monuments of the family in the church of Woollaton, and the pedigree of that noble family, are well worth a stranger's view.

This house, all of stone, was built by Sir Francis Willoughby, second son of the honourable —— Willoughby Esq; slain in the 4th of Edward VI in the rebellion or tumult at Norwich, anno 1546, and Dame Anne, daughter of the Marquiss of Dorchester; the first and eldest son, Sir Thomas Willoughby, dying unmarried. The stately fabrick shews the genius, as well as the wealth, of the founder; the hall, at the first entrance, is so high that a man on horseback might exercise a pike in it. The figure of building, as an artist said of it to me, was rather antick than antient; the architect is noble, and the order of building regular, except the four pavillions of the Dorick order on the top, which they alledge is inexcusable in architecture. Some, who excuse the design, will have it to be, that the upper building is an attick, and set on to grace the other. But I must be allowed to differ from that opinion too.

Having thus passed the Rubicon (Trent) and set my face northward, I scarce knew which way to set forward, in a country too so full of wonders, and on so great a journey, and yet to leave nothing behind me to call on as I came back, at least not to lead me out of my way in my return.

I resolved indeed first for the Peak, which lay on my left-hand north east; but, as I say, to leave as little behind me as possible, I was obliged to make a little excursion into the forest, where, in my way, I had the diversion of seeing the annual meeting of the gentry at the horse-races near Nottingham. I could give a long and agreeable account of the sport itself, how it brought into my thoughts the Olympick Games among the Greeks; and the Circus Maximus at Rome; where the racers made a great noise, and the victors

XXXI. Jan Siberechts, *Wollaton Hall and Park, Nottinghamshire* (1695).

174. Pierrepont House, Nottingham; painting by unknown artist (c.1708–13).

made great boasts and triumphs: but where they chiefly drove in chariots, not much unlike our chaises, and where nothing of the speed, or of skill in horsemanship could be shown, as is in our races.

It is true, in those races the young Roman and Grecian gentlemen rode, or rather drove themselves; whereas in our races the horses, not the riders, make the show; and they are generally ridden by grooms and boys, chiefly for lightness; sometimes indeed the gentlemen ride themselves, as I have often seen the Duke of Monmouth, natural son to King Charles II ride his own horses at a match, and win it too, though he was a large man, and must weigh heavy.

But the illustrious company at the Nottingham races was, in my opinion, the glory of the day; for there we saw, besides eleven or twelve noblemen, an infinite throng of gentlemen from all the countries round, nay, even out of Scotland itself; the appearance, in my opinion, greater, as it was really more numerous, than ever I saw at Newmarket, except when the King have

been there in ceremony; for I cannot but say, that in King Charles II's time, when his majesty used to be frequently at Newmarket, I have known the assembly there have been with far less company than this at Nottingham; and, if I might go back to one of these Nottingham meetings when the mareschal Duke de Tallard was there, I should say, that no occasions at Newmarket, in my memory, ever came up to it, except the first time that King William was there after the Peace of Ryswick.[5]

Nor is the appearance of the ladies to be omitted, as fine and without comparison more bright and gay, tho' they might a little fall short in number of the many thousands of nobility and gentry of the other sex; in short, the train of coaches filled with the beauties of the north was not to be described; except we were to speak of the garden of the Tulleries at Paris, or the Prado[6] at Mexico, where they tell us there are 4000 coaches with six horses each, every evening taking the air.

175. Detail from 'East prospect of Derby'; engraving by Samuel and Nathaniel Buck (1728). The silkmill illustrated in pl. 176 can be seen to the right of the church tower.

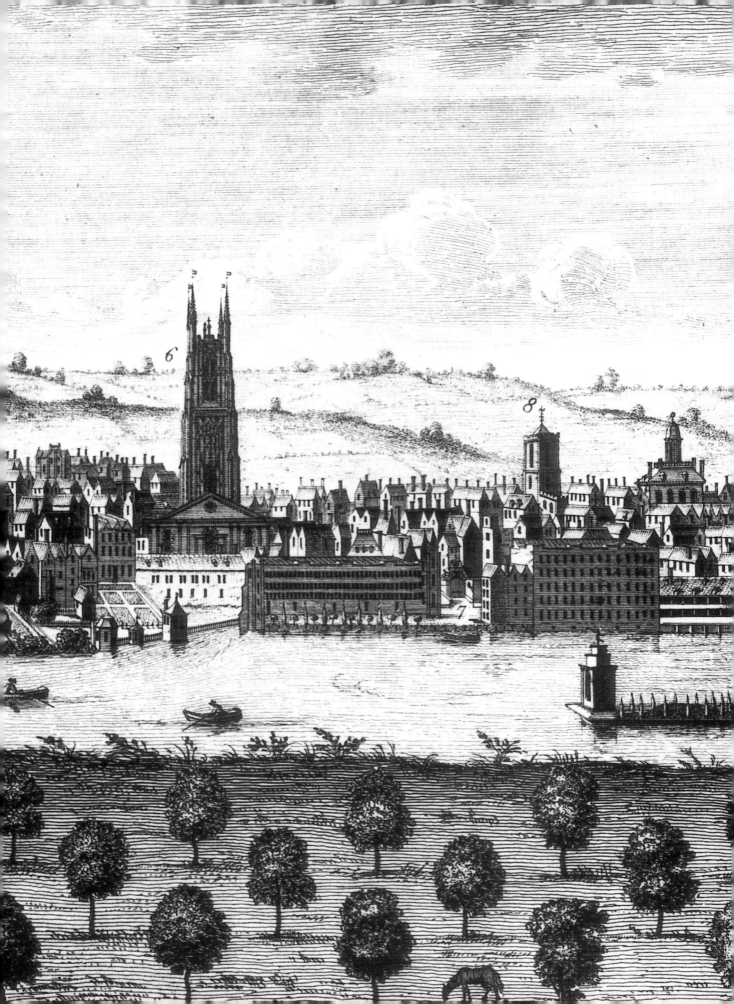

XXXIV. Jan Siberechts, *View of Nottingham and the Trent* (1695).

XXXII (facing page top). Jan Siberechts, *Crossing the Ford, Wollaton* (1695).

XXXIII (facing page bottom).? John Harris II, *Derbyshire landscape: view of Dovedale with figures fishing and cattle.*

176. Derby silk mill; engraving by Walker and Storer after an earlier drawing by J. Nixon (published 1798).

From hence I was going on to see Rugford Abbey, the fine seat of the late Marquiss of Hallifax, but was called aside to take a view of the most famous piece of church history in this part of the whole island, I mean the collegiate church of Southwell.

Paulinus,[7] Archbishop of York, was (so antient record supplies the tale) the founder of this church, having preached to the people of the country round, and baptized them in the river Trent; the antient word imports Christianized them, by dipping them in the river Trent.

The thing which makes this foundation the more remarkable, is, that though it was surrendered into the King's hands, with all the rest of the religious foundations, in the reign of King Henry VIII yet it was restored whole as it was before, in the 35th of the same reign.

Hence crossing the forest I came to Mansfield, a market town, but without any remarkables. In my way I visited the noble seat of the Duke of Kingston at Thoresby, of the Duke of Newcastle at Welbeck,[8] and the Marquiss of Hallifax at Rufford, or Rugeford

Abbey, all very noble seats, tho' antient, and that at Welbeck especially, beautify'd with large additions, fine apartments, and good gardens; but particularly the park, well stocked with large timber, and the finest kind, as well as the largest quantity of deer that are any where to be seen; for the late Duke's delight being chiefly on horseback and in the chace, it is not to be wondered if he rather made his parks fine than his gardens, and his stables than his mansion-house; yet the house is noble, large, and magnificent.

From hence leaving Nottinghamshire, the west part abounding with lead and coal, I cross'd over that fury of a river called the Derwent, and came to **Derby**, the capital of the county. This is a fine, beautiful, and pleasant town; it has more families of gentlemen in it than is usual in towns so remote, and therefore here is a great deal of good and some gay company: Perhaps the rather, because the Peak being so near, and taking up the larger part of the county, and being so inhospitable, so rugged and so wild a place, the gentry choose to reside at Derby, rather than upon their estates, as they do in other places.

177. Diagrams of basic manual operations of winding and twisting (or doubling) silk that Thomas Lombe (mill owner) and George Sorocold's innovations mechanised in possibly the first factory operation in Great Britain. From the *Universal Magazine*, vol. 1 (July 1747).

It must be allowed, that the twelve miles between Nottingham and this town, keeping the mid-way between the Trent on the left, and the mountains on the right, are as agreeable with respect to the situation, the soil, and the well planting of the country, as any spot of ground, at least that I have seen of that length, in England.

The town of Derby is situated on the west bank of the Derwent, over which it has a very fine bridge, well built, but antient, and a chapel upon the bridge, now converted into a dwelling-house. Here is a curiosity in trade worth observing, as being the only one of its kind in England, namely, a throwing or throwster's mill,[9] which performs by a wheel turn'd by the water; and though it cannot perform the doubling part of a throwster's work, which can only be done by a hand-wheel, yet it turns the other work, and performs the labour of many hands. Whether it answers the expence or not, that is not my business.

This work was erected by one Soracole,[10] a man expert in making mill-work, especially for raising water to supply towns for family use: but he made a very odd experiment at this place; for going to show some gentlemen the curiosity, as he called it, of his mill, and crossing the planks which lay just above the mill-wheel; regarding, it seems, what he was to show his friends more than the place where he was, and too

eager in describing things, keeping his eye rather upon what he pointed at with his fingers than what he stept upon with his feet, he stepp'd awry and slipt into the river.

He was so very close to the sluice which let the water out upon the wheel, and which was then pulled up, that tho' help was just at hand, there was no taking hold of him, till by the force of the water he was carried through, and pushed just under the large wheel, which was then going round at a great rate. The body being thus forc'd in between two of the plashers of the wheel, stopt the motion for a little while, till the water pushing hard to force its way, the plasher beyond him gave way and broke; upon which the wheel went again, and, like Jonah's whale, spewed him out, not upon dry land, but into that part they call the apron, and so to the mill-tail, where he was taken up, and received no hurt at all.

Derby, as I have said, is a town of gentry, rather than trade; yet it is populous, well built, has five parishes, a large market-place, a fine town-house, and very handsome streets.

In the church of Allhallows, or, as the Spaniards call it, *De Todos los Santos*, All Saints, is the Pantheon, or burial-place of the noble, now ducal family of Cavendish, now Devonshire, which was first erected by the Countess of Shrewsbury, who not only built the vault or sepulchre, but an hospital for eight poor men and four women, close by the church, and settled their maintenance, which is continued to this day: Here are very magnificent monuments for the family of Cavendish; and at this church is a famous tower or steeple, which for the heighth and beauty of its building, is not equalled in this county, or in any of those adjacent.

By an inscription upon this church, it was erected, or at least the steeple, at the charge of the maids and batchelors of the town; on which account, whenever a maid, native of the town, was marry'd, the bells were rung by batchelors: how long the custom lasted, we do not read; but I do not find that it is continued, at least not strictly.

The government of this town, for it is a corporation, and sends two burgesses to Parliament, is in a Mayor, High-Steward, nine Aldermen, a Recorder, fourteen Brothers, fourteen Capital Burgesses, and a Town-Clerk: the trade of the town is chiefly in good

178. Diagram of the basic waterpowered silk mill mechanism adapted by Thomas and John Lombe from Italian precedents and modified by George Sorocold for use in their mill. From Vittorio Zonca, *Novo Teatro di Machine et Edificii* (1607).

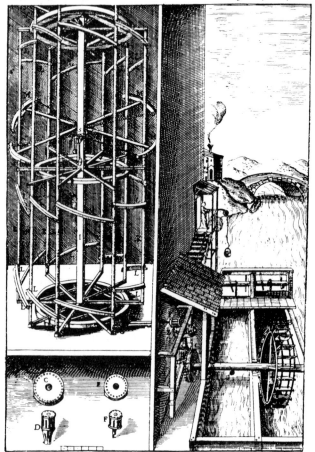

malt and good ale; nor is the quantity of the latter unreasonably small, which, as they say, they dispose of among themselves, though they spare some to their neighbours too.

It is observable, that as the Trent makes the frontier or bounds of the county of Derby south, so the Dove and the Erwash make the bounds east and west, and the Derwent runs through the center; all of them beginning and ending their course in the same county; for they rise in the Peak, and end in the Trent.

179. Cliff on one side of the castle above Castleton; drawing by Sir James Thornhill. From his *Sketchbook* (1699–1718).

I that had read Cotton's *Wonders of the Peak*,[11] in which I always wondered more at the poetry than at the Peak; and in which there was much good humour, tho' but little good verse, could not satisfy myself to be in Derbyshire, and not see the river Dove, which that gentleman has spent so much doggerel upon, and celebrated to such a degree for trout and grailing: so from Derby we went to Dove-Bridge, or, as the country people call it, Dowbridge, where we had the pleasure to see the river drowning the low-grounds by a sudden shower, and hastning to the Trent with a most outrageous stream, in which there being no great diversion, and travelling being not very safe in a rainy season on that side, we omitted seeing Ashbourn and Uttoxeter, the *Utocetum* of the antients, two market towns upon that river, and returning towards Derby, we went from thence directly up into the High Peak.

In our way we past an antient seat, large, but not very gay, of Sir Nathaniel Curson, a noted and (for wealth) over great family, for many ages inhabitants of this county. Hence we kept the Derwent on our right-hand, but kept our distance, the waters being out; for the Derwent is a frightful creature when the hills load her current with water; I say, we kept our distance, and contented ourselves with hearing the roaring of its waters, till we came to Quarn or Quarden, a little ragged, but noted village, where there is a famous chalybeat spring, to which abundance of people go in the season to drink the water, as also a cold bath. There are also several other mineral waters in this part of the counry, as another chalybeat near Quarden or Quarn, a hot bath at Matlock, and another at Buxton, of which in its place; besides these, there are hot springs in several places which run waste into the ditches and brooks, and are taken no notice of, being remote among the mountains, and out of the way of the common resort.

We found the wells, as custom bids us call them, pretty full of company, the waters good, and very physical, but wretched lodging and entertainment; so I resolved to stay till I came to the south, and make shift with Tunbridge or Epsom, of which I have spoken at large in the counties of Surrey and Kent.

From Quarden we advanc'd due north, and, mounting the hills gradually for four or five miles, we soon had a most frightful view indeed among the black mountains of the Pĕak; however, as they were yet at a distance, and a good town lay on our left called Wirksworth, we turned thither for refreshment; here indeed we found a specimen of what I had heard before, (viz.) that however rugged the hills were, the vales were every where fruitful, well inhabited, the markets well supplied, and the provisions extraordinary good; not forgetting the ale, which every where exceeded, if possible, what was pass'd, as if the farther north the better the liquor, and that the nearer we approach'd to Yorkshire, as the place for the best, so the ale advanc'd the nearer to its perfection.

Wirksworth is a large well-frequented market town, and market towns being very thin placed in this part of the county, they have the better trade, the people generally coming twelve or fifteen miles to a market, and sometimes much more; though there is no very great trade to this town but what relates to the lead works, and to the subterranean wretches, who they call Peakrills, who work in the mines, and who live all round this town every way.

The inhabitants are a rude boorish kind of people, but they are a bold, daring, and even desperate kind of fellows in their search into the bowels of the earth; for no people in the world out-do them; and therefore they are often entertained by our engineers in the wars to carry on the sap, and other such works, at the sieges of strong fortified places.

This town of Wirksworth is a kind of a market for lead, the like not known any where else that I know of, except it be at the custom-house keys in London. The Barmoot Court,[12] kept here to judge controversies among the miners, that is to say, to adjust subterranean quarrels and disputes, is very remarkable: Here they summon a Master and twenty-four Jurors, and they have power to set out the bounds of the works under ground, the terms are these, they are empowered to set off the meers (so they call them) of ground in a pipe and a flat, that is to say, twenty nine yards long in the first, and fourteen square in the last; when any man has found a vein of oar in another man's ground, except orchards and gardens; they may appoint the proprietor cartways and passage for timber, &c. This court also prescribes rules to the miners, and limits their proceedings in the works under ground; also they are judges of all their little quarrels and disputes in the mines, as well as out, and, in a word, keep the peace among them; which, by the way, may be called the greatest of all the wonders of the Peak, for they are of a strange, turbulent, quarrelsome temper, and very hard to be reconciled to one another in their subterraneous affairs.

And now I am come to this wonderful place, the Peak, where you will expect I should do as some others have, (I think, foolishly) done before me, viz. tell you strange long stories of wonders as (I must say) they are most weakly call'd; and that you may not think me arrogant in censuring so many wise men, who have wrote of these wonders, as if they were all fools, I shall give you four Latin lines out of Mr. Cambden, by which you will see there were some men of my mind above a hundred years ago.

Mira alto Pecc tria sunt, barathrum, specus, antrum;
　Commoda tot, Plumbum, Gramen, Ovile pecus.
Tot speciosa simul sunt, Castrum, Balnea, Chatsworth,
　Plura sed occurrunt, quæ speciosa minus.
Cambd. Brit. fol. 495.

Which, by the same hand, are englished thus:

Nine Things that please us at the Peak we see;
A cave, a den, a hole, the wonder be;
Lead, sheep and pasture, are the useful Three.
Chatsworth the Castle, and the Bath delight;
Much more you see; all little worth the sight.

Now to have so great a man as Mr. Hobbes,[13] and after him Mr. Cotton, celebrate the trifles here, the first in a fine Latin poem, the last in English verse, as if they were the most exalted wonders of the world; I cannot but, after wondering at their making wonders of them, desire you, my friend, to travel with me through this houling wilderness in your imagination, and you shall soon find all that is wonderful about it.

Near Wirksworth, and upon the very edge of Derwent, is, as above, a village called *Matlock*, where

180. Matlock Bath; engraving by John Boydell (1749).

there are several warm springs, lately one of these being secured by a stone wall on every side, by which the water is brought to rise to a due heighth, is made into a very convenient bath; with a house built over it, and room within the building to walk round the water or bath, and so by steps to go down gradually into it.

This bath would be much more frequented than it is, if two things did not hinder; namely, a base, stony, mountainous road to it, and no good accommodation when you are there: they are intending, as they tell us, to build a good house to entertain persons of quality, or such who would spend their money at it; but it was not so far concluded or directed when I was there, as to be any where begun: The bath is milk, or rather blood warm, very pleasant to go into, and very sanative, especially for rheumatick pains, bruises, &c.

For some miles before we come to Matlock, you pass over the hills by the very mouths of the lead-mines, and there are melting-houses for the preparing the oar, and melting or casting it into pigs; and so they carry it to Wirksworth to be sold at the market.

Over against this warm bath, and on the other, or east side of the Derwent, stands a high rock, which rises from the very bottom of the river (for the water washes the foot of it, and is there in dry weather very shallow); I say, it rises perpendicular as a wall, the precipice bare and smooth like one plain stone, to such a prodigious heighth, it is really surprising; yet what the people believed of it surmounted all my faith too, though I look'd upon it very curiously, for they told me it was above four hundred foot high, which is as high as two of our Monuments, one set upon another; that which adds most to my wonder in it is, that as the stone stands, it is smooth from the very bottom of the Derwent to the uppermost point, and nothing can be seen to grow upon it. The prodigious heighth of this Tor, (for it is called Matlock Tor) was to me more a wonder than any of the rest in the Peak, and, I think, it should be named among them, but it is not. So it must not be called one of the Wonders.

A little on the other side of Wirksworth, begins a long plain called Brassington Moor, which reaches full twelve miles in length another way, (viz.) from Brassington to Buxton. At the beginning of it on this side from Wirksworth, it is not quite so much. The Peak people, who are mighty fond of having strangers shewed every thing they can, and of calling everything a wonder, told us here of another high mountain, where a giant was buried, and which they called the Giant's Tomb.

This tempted our curiosity, and we presently rode up to the mountain in order to leave our horses, dragoon-like, with a servant, and to clamber up to the top of it, to see this Giant's Tomb: here we miss'd the imaginary wonder, and found a real one; the story of which I cannot but record, to shew the discontented part of the rich world how to value their own happiness, by looking below them, and seeing how others live, who yet are capable of being easie and content, which content goes a great way towards being happy, if it does not come quite up to happiness. The story is this:

"As we came near the hill, which seemed to be round, and a precipice almost on every side, we perceived a little parcel of ground hedg'd in, as if it were a garden, it was about twenty or thirty yards long, but not so much broad, parallel with the hill, and close to it; we saw no house, but, by a dog running out barking, we perceived some people were thereabout; and presently after we saw two little children, and then a third run out to see what was the matter. When we came close up we saw a small opening, not a door, but a natural opening into the rock, and the noise we had made brought a woman out with a child in her arms, and another at her foot. N. B. The biggest of these five was a girl, about eight or ten years old.

"We asked the woman some questions about the tomb of the giant upon the rock or mountain: She told us, there was a broad flat stone of a great size lay there, which, she said, the people call'd a gravestone; and, if it was, it might well be called a giant's, for she thought no ordinary man was ever so tall, and she describ'd it to us as well as she could, by which it must be at least sixteen or seventeen foot long; but she could not give any farther account of it, neither did she seem to lay any stress upon the tale of a giant being buried there, but said, if her husband had been at home he might have shown it to us. I snatch'd at the word, at home! says I, good wife, why, where do you live. Here, sir, says she, and points to the hole in the rock. Here! says I; and do all these children live here too? Yes, sir, says she; they were all born here. Pray how long have you dwelt here then? said I. My husband was born here, said she, and his father before him. Will you give me leave, says one of our company, as curious as I was, to come in and see your house, dame? If you please, sir, says she, but 'tis not a place fit for such as you are to come into, calling him, your worship, forsooth; but that by the by. I mention it, to shew that the good woman did not want manners, though she liv'd in a den like a wild body.

"However, we alighted and went in: there was a large hollow cave, which the poor people by two curtains hang'd cross, had parted into three rooms. On one side was the chimney, and the man, or perhaps his father, being miners, had found means to work a shaft or funnel through the rock to carry the smoke out at the top, where the giant's tombstone was. The habitation was poor, 'tis true but things within did not look so like misery as I expected. Every thing was clean and neat, tho' mean and ordinary: there were shelves with earthen ware, and some pewter and brass. There was, which I observed in particular, a whole flitch or side of bacon hanging up in the chimney, and by it a good piece of another. There was a sow and pigs running about at the door, and a little lean cow feeding upon a green place just before the door, and the little enclosed piece of ground I mentioned, was growing with good barley; it being then near harvest.

"To find out whence this appearance of substance came, I asked the poor woman, what trade her husband was? She said, he worked in the lead mines. I asked her, how much he could earn a day there? she said, if he had good luck he could earn about five pence a day, but that he worked by the dish (which was a term of art I did not understand, but supposed, as I afterward understood it was, by the great, in proportion to the oar, which they measure in a wooden bowl, which they call a dish). I then asked, what she did? She said, when she was able to work she washed the oar: but, looking down on her children, and shaking her head, she intimated, that they found her so much business she could do but little, which I easily granted must be true. But what can you get at washing the oar, said I, when you can work? She said, if she work'd hard she could gain three-pence a day. So that, in short, here was but eight-pence a day when they both worked hard, and that not always, and perhaps not often, and all this to maintain a man, his wife, and five small children, and yet they seemed to live very pleasantly, the children look'd plump and fat, ruddy and wholesome; and the woman was tall, well shap'd, clean, and (for the place) a very well looking, comely woman; nor was there any thing look'd like the dirt and nastiness of the miserable cottages of the poor; tho' many of them spend more money in strong drink than this poor woman had to maintain five children with.

"This moving sight so affected us all, that, upon a short conference at the door, we made up a little lump of money, and I had the honour to be almoner for the company; and though the sum was not great, being at most something within a crown, as I told it into the poor woman's hand, I could perceive such a surprize in her face, that, had she not given vent to her joy by a sudden flux of tears, I found she would have fainted away. She was some time before she could do any thing but cry; but after that was abated, she expressed herself very handsomely (for a poor body) and told me, she had not seen so much money together of her own for many months.

"We asked her, if she had a good husband; she smiled, and said, Yes, thanked God for it, and that she was very happy in that, for he worked very hard, and they wanted for nothing that he could do for them; and two or three times made mention of how contented they were: in a word, it was a lecture to us all, and that such, I assure you, as made the whole company very grave all the rest of the day: And if it has no effect of that kind upon the reader, the defect must be in my telling the story in a less moving manner than the poor woman told it herself.

From hence enquiring no farther after the giant, or his tomb, we went, by the direction of the poor woman, to a valley on the side of a rising hill, where there were several grooves, so they call the mouth of the shaft or pit by which they go down into a lead mine; and as we were standing still to look at one of them, admiring how small they were, and scarce believing a poor man that shew'd it us, when he told us, that they went down those narrow pits or holes to so great a depth in the earth; I say, while we were wondering, and scarce believing the fact, we were agreeably surprized with seeing a hand, and then an arm, and quickly after a head, thrust up out of the very groove we were looking at. It was the more surprizing as not we only, but not the man that we were talking to, knew any thing of it, or expected it.

Immediately we rode closer up to the place, where we see the poor wretch working and heaving himself up gradually, as we thought, with difficulty; but when he shewed us that it was by setting his feet upon pieces of wood fixt cross the angles of the groove like a ladder, we found that the difficulty was not much; and if the groove had been larger they could not either go up or down so easily, or with so much safety, for that now their elbows resting on those pieces as well as their feet, they went up and down with great ease and safety.

Those who would have a more perfect idea of those grooves, need do no more than go to the church of St. Paul's, and desire to see the square wells which they have there to go down from the top of the church into the very vaults under it, to place the leaden pipes which carry the rain water from the flat of the roof to the common-shore,[14] which wells are square, and have small iron bars placed cross the angles for the workmen to set their feet on, to go up and down to

repair the pipes; the manner of the steps are thus describ'd:

When this subterranean creature was come quite out, with all his furniture about him, we had as much variety to take us up as before, and our curiosity received full satisfaction without venturing down, as we were persuaded to by some people, and as two of our company were inclined to do.

First, the man was a most uncouth spectacle; he was cloathed all in leather, had a cap of the same without brims, some tools in a little basket which he drew up with him, not one of the names of which we could understand but by the help of an interpreter. Nor indeed could we understand any of the man's discourse so as to make out a whole sentence; and yet the man was pretty free of his tongue too.

For his person, he was lean as a skeleton, pale as a dead corps, his hair and beard a deep black, his flesh lank, and, as we thought, something of the colour of the lead itself, and being very tall and very lean he look'd, or we that saw him ascend *ab inferis*,[15] fancied he look'd like an inhabitant of the dark regions below, and who was just ascended into the world of light.

Besides his basket of tools, he brought up with him about three quarters of a hundred weight of oar, which we wondered at, for the man had no small load to bring, considering the manner of his coming up; and this indeed made him come heaving and struggling up, as I said at first, as if he had great difficulty to get out; wheras it was indeed the weight that he brought with him.

We asked him, how deep the mine lay which he came out of: he answered us in terms we did not understand; but our interpreter, as above, told us, it signified that he was at work 60 fathoms deep, but there were five men of his party, who were, two of them, eleven fathoms, and the other three, fifteen fathoms deeper: he seemed to regret that he was not at work with those three; for that they had a deeper vein of oar than that which he worked in, and had a way out at the side of the hill, where they pas'd without coming up so high as he was obliged to do.

If we blessed ourselves before, when we saw how the poor woman and her five children lived in the hole or cave in the mountain, with the Giant's Grave over their heads; we had much more room to reflect how much we had to acknowledge to our maker, that we were not appointed to get our bread thus, one hundred and fifty yards under ground, or in a hole as deep in

181. Pennine leadminer, from a lost painting of 'Old Curly', an old gang worthy (*c.* 1760). Although this miner comes from further north (Swaledale) the miner's costume and equipment will probably not have varied much throughout the Pennines.

182. Harborough Cave, suggested by local mining historians as a possible location for Defoe's miner's cave near Brassington.

the earth as the cross upon St. Paul's cupolo is high out of it: Nor was it possible to see these miserable people without such reflections, unless you will suppose a man as stupid and sensless as the horse he rides on. But to leave moralizing to the reader, I proceed.

We then look'd on the oar, and got the poor man's leave to bring every one a small piece of it away with us, for which we gave him two small pieces of better mettle, called shillings, which made his heart glad; and, as we understood by our interpreter, was more than he could gain at sixty fathoms under ground in three days; and we found soon after the money was so much, that it made him move off immediately towards the alehouse, to melt some of it into good Pale Derby; but, to his farther good luck, we were gotten to the same alehouse before him; where, when we saw him come, we gave him some liquor too, and made him keep his money, and promise us to carry it home to his family, which they told us lived hard by.

From hence entring upon Brassington Moor, mentioned above, we had eight mile smooth green riding to Buxton Bath, which they call one of the Wonders of the Peak; but is so far from being a wonder, that to us, who had been at Bath in Somersetshire, and at Aix la Chapelle in Germany, it was nothing at all; nor is it any thing but what is frequent in such mountainous countries as this is, in many parts of the world.

But though I shall not treat this warm spring as a wonder for such it is not; I must nevertheless give it the praise due to the medicinal virtue of its waters; for it is not to be deny'd, but that wonderful cures have been wrought by them, especially in rheumatick, scorbutick and scrofulous distempers, aches of the

joints, nervous pains, and also in scurfy and leprous maladies.

The waters are temperately hot, or rather warm, and operate rather as a cold bath, without that violent attack which the cold bath makes upon all nature at once; you feel a little chilness when you first dip or plunge into the water, but it is gone in a moment; and you find a kind of an equality in the warmth of your blood and that of the water, and that so very pleasant, that far from the fainting and weakening violence of the hot baths, which makes you ready to die away if you continue above an hour, or thereabouts, in them, and will shrivel up the fingers like those of women, who have been washing cloaths; on the contrary, here you are never tired, and can hardly be persuaded to come out of the bath when you are in.

The village where the principal springs are, is called **Buxton**; though there are several of them, for they rise unregarded in the banks of the enclosures, and on the sides of the hill, so that the number is hardly known; there is but one bath which is walled in with stone walls, and steps made to go down into it, and a house built over it, though not so close as is fit for winter bathing.

The Duke of Devonshire[16] is lord of the village, and consequently of the bath itself; and his grace has built a large handsome house at the bath, where there is convenient lodging, and very good provisions, and an ordinary well served for one shilling per head; but it is but one.

South west from hence, about a quarter of a mile, or not so much, on the side, or rather at the foot of a very high ridge of mountains, is a great cave or hole in the earth, called Poole's Hole, another of the wonder-

183. Buxton Bath; drawing by William Stukeley (July 1712). From his *Pocket sketchbook*.

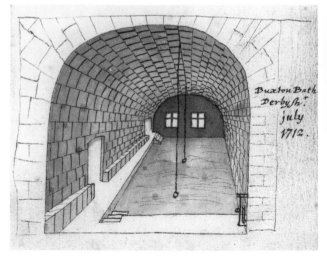

The Entrance into Pool's-Hole near Buxton in the County of Derby. The North View. July 3, 1727.

Alice Needham the Door keeper Ætat: 72

184. The entrance to Pool's Hole in Derbyshire with the doorkeeper, Alice Needham (3 July 1727); watercolour by an unknown artist.

less wonders of the Peak. The wit that has been spent upon this vault or cave in the earth, had been well enough to raise the expectation of strangers, and bring fools a great way to creep into it; but is ill bestowed upon all those that come to the place with a just curiosity, founded upon antient report; when these go in to see it, they generally go away, acknowledging that they have nothing suitable to their great expectation, or to the fame of the place.

It is a great cave, or natural vault, antient doubtless as the mountain itself, and occasioned by the fortuitous position of the rocks at the creation of all things, or perhaps at the great absorption or influx of the surface into the abyss at the great rupture of the earth's crust or shell, according to Mr. Burnet's theory;[17] and to me it seems a confirmation of that hypothesis of the breaking in of the surface. But that by the way:

It may be deepen'd and enlarged by streams and eruptions of subterraneous waters, of which here are several, as there generally are in all such cavities; as at Castleton in this country, at Wooky Hole in Somersetshire, which I have already spoken of; and at several like caves which are now to be seen among the mountains in Swisserland, in Norway, in Hungary, and other places.

The story of one Pole or Poole, a famous giant or robber, (they might as well have called him a man eater) who harboured in this vault, and whose kitchen and lodging, or bed-chamber, they show you on your right-hand, after you have crept about ten yards upon all-four; I say, this I leave to those who such stories are better suited to, than I expect of my readers.

Dr. Leigh[18] spends some time in admiring the spangled roof. Cotton and Hobbes are most ridiculously and outrageously witty upon it. Dr. Leigh calls it fret work, organ, and choir work. The whole of the matter is this, that the rock being every where moist and dropping, the drops are some fallen, those you see below; some falling, those you have glancing by you *en passant*; and others pendant in the roof. Now as you have guides before you and behind you, carrying every one a candle, the light of the candles reflected by the globular drops of water, dazle upon your eyes from every corner; like as the drops of dew in a sunny-bright morning reflect the rising light to the eye, and are as ten thousand rainbows in miniature; whereas were any part of the roof or arch of this vault to be seen by a clear light, there would be no more beauty on it than on the back of a chimney; for, in short, the stone is coarse, slimy, with the constant wet, dirty and dull; and were the little drops of water gone, or the candles gone, there would be none of these fine sights to be seen for wonders, or for the learned authors above to show themselves foolish about.

Let any person therefore, who goes into Poole's Hole for the future, and has a mind to try the experiment, take a long pole in his hand, with a cloth tied to the end of it, and mark any place of the shining pyramids below, if such there were, any thing but what is frequent and natural both to water and to stone, placed thus under ground, and seems to be the way by which even stone itself, like other vegetables, fructifies and grows.

So that, in short, there is nothing in Poole's Hole to make a wonder of, any more than as other things in nature, which are rare to be seen, however easily accounted for, may be called wonderful.

Having thus accounted for two of the seven things, called Wonders in this country, I pass by Elden Hole, which I shall take notice of by itself, and come to two more of them, as wonderless, and empty of every thing that may be called rare or strange, as the other; and indeed much more so.

The first of these is Mam Tor, or, as the word in the mountain jargon signifies, the Mother Rock, upon a suggestion that the soft crumbling earth, which falls from the summit of the one, breeds or begets several young mountains below. The sum of the whole wonder is this, that there is a very high hill, nay, I will add (that I may make the most of the story, and that it may appear as much like a wonder as I can) an exceeding high hill. But this in a country which is all over hills, cannot be much of a wonder, because also there are several higher hills in the Peak than that, only not just there.

The south side of this hill is a precipice, and very steep from the top to the bottom; and as the substance of this hill is not a solid stone, or rocky, as is the case of all the hills thereabouts, but a crumbling loose earth mingled with small stones, it is continually falling down in small quantities, as the force of hasty

185. Pool's Hole or cave and Elden Hole. From *The Genuine Poetical Works of Charles Cotton* (1741).

186. Mam Tor; drawing by Sir James Thornhill. From his *Sketchbook* (1699–1718).

spangled roof which his pole will reach to; and then, wiping the drops of water away, he shall see he will at once extinguish all those glories; then let him sit still and wait a little, till, by the nature of the thing, the drops swell out again, and he shall find the stars and spangles rise again by degrees, here one, and there one, till they shine with the same fraud, a meer *deceptio visus*,[19] as they did before.

As to the several stones called Mr. Cotton's, Haycock's, Poole's Chair, Flitches of Bacon, and the like, they are nothing but ordinary stones; and the shapes very little resemble the things they are said to represent; but the fruitful imagination of the country carls, who fancy to call them so, will have them to look like them; a stranger sees very little even of the similitude, any more than when people fancy they see faces and heads, castles and cities, armies, horses and men, in the clouds, in the fire, and the like.

Nor is the petrifying of the water, which appears in its pendant form like icecles in the roof aloft, or rising showers, or solid heavy rains, loosens and washes it off, or as frosts and thaws operate upon it in common with other parts of the earth; now as the great hill, which is thick, as well as high, parts with this loose stuff, without being sensibly diminished, yet the bottom which it falls into, is more easily perceived to swell with the quantity that falls down; the space where it is received being small, comparatively to the heighth and thickness of the mountain: here the pretended wonder is form'd, namely, that the little heap below, should grow up into a hill, and yet the great hill not be the less for all that is fallen down; which is not true in fact, any more than, as a great black cloud pouring down rain as it passes over our heads, appears still as great and as black as before, though it continues pouring down rain over all the country. But nothing is more certain than this, that the more water comes down from it, the less remains in it; and so it certainly is of Mam Tor, in spite of all the poetry of Mr. Cotton or Mr. Hobbes, and in spight of all the women's tales in the Peak.

This hill lies on the north side of the road from Buxton to Castleton, where we come to the so famed wonder call'd, saving our good manners, The Devil's A—e in the Peak; Now notwithstanding the grossness of the name given it, and that there is nothing of similitude or coherence either in form and figure, or any other thing between the thing signified and the thing signifying; yet we must search narrowly for any thing in it to make a Wonder, or even any thing so strange, or odd, or vulgar, as the name would seem to import.

The short of this story is; that on the steep side of a mountain there is a large opening very high, broad at bottom, and narrow, but rounding, on the top, almost the form of the old Gothick gates or arches, which come up, not to a half circle or half oval at the top, but to a point; though this being all wild and irregular, cannot be said to be an arch, but a meer chasme, entring horizontally; the opening being upwards of thirty foot perpendicular, and twice as much broad at the bottom at least.

The arch continues thus wide but a little way, yet far enough to have several small cottages built on either side of it within the entrance; so that 'tis like a little town in a vault: in the middle, (as it were a street) is a running stream of water; the poetical descriptions of it will have this be called a river, tho' they have not yet bestow'd a name upon it, nor indeed is it worthy a name.

The next wonder, which makes up number five, is called Tideswell, or a spring of water which ebbs and flows, as they will have it, as the sea does. A poor thing indeed to make a wonder of; and therefore most of the writers pass it over with little notice; only that they are at a loss to make up the number seven without it.

This well or spring is called Weeden Well; the basin or receiver for the water is about three foot square every way; the water seems to have some other receiver within the rock, which, when it fills by the force of the original stream, which is small, the air being contracted or pent in, forces the water out with a bubbling noise, and so fills the receiver without; but when the force is spent within, then it stops till the place is filled again; and, in the mean time, the water without runs off or ebbs, till the quantity within swells again, and then the same causes produce the same effects, as will always be while the world endures. So that all this wonder is owing only to the situation of the place, which is a meer accident in nature; and if any person were to dig into the place, and give vent to the air, which fills the contracted space within, they would

187. The Devil's Arse. From *The Genuine Poetical Works of Charles Cotton* (1741).

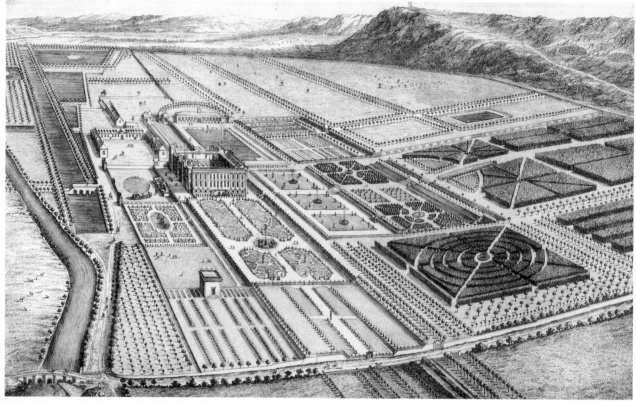

188. Chatsworth, house of the Duke of Devonshire; engraving by J. Kip after L. Knyff (*c*.1707).

soon see Tideswell turned into an ordinary running stream, and a very little one too.

So much for fictitious wonders, or indeed simple wonders. The two real wonders which remain, are first, Elden Hole, and secondly, the Duke of Devonshire's fine house at Chatsworth;[20] one a wonder of nature, the other of art. I begin with the last.

Chatsworth is indeed a most glorious and magnificent house, and, as it has had two or three founders, may well be said to be compleatly designed and finished. It was begun on a much narrower plan than it now takes up, by Sir William Cavendish, of Cavendish in Suffolk, who married the Countess Dowager of Shrewsbury, and with her came into a noble and plentiful fortune in this country.

Sir William died, having done little more than built one end of the fabrick, and laid out the plan, as I have said, or ichnography of the whole. But the lady, who, it seems, was the mover of the first design, finish'd the whole in the magnificent manner which it appeared, when it was first christen'd a Wonder, and ranked among the *Marvelleux* of the Peak.

The front to the garden is the most regular piece of architect I have seen in all the north part of England; the pilaster seventy two foot high to the foot of the ballaster on the top; the frize under the cornish is spacious, and has the motto of the family upon it, the letters so large (and gilded) as takes up the whole front, tho' the words are but these two:

Cavendo Tutus.[21]

The sashes of the second story we were told are seventeen foot high, the plates polish'd looking-glass, and the woodwork double gilded; which, I think, is no where else to be seen in England.

Under this front lye the gardens exquisitely fine, and, to make a clear vista or prospect beyond into the flat country, towards Hardwick, another seat of the same owner, the Duke, to whom what others thought impossible, was not only made practicable, but easy, removed, and perfectly carried away a great mountain that stood in the way, and which interrupted the prospect.

This was so entirely gone, that, having taken a strict view of the gardens at my first being there, and retaining an idea of them in my mind, I was perfectly confounded at coming there a second time, and not knowing what had been done; for I had lost the hill, and found a new country in view, which Chatsworth itself had never seen before.

250

First, 'tis to be observed that on the east side rises a very high mountain, on the top of which they dig mill-stones, and it begins so close to, and so overlooks the house, being prodigiously high that, should they roll down a pair of those stones coupled with a wooden axis, as is the way of drawing them, they would infallibly give a shock to the building; yet this mountain is so planted, and so covered with a wood of beautiful trees, that you see no hill, only a rising wood, as if the trees grew so much higher than one another, and was only a wall of trees, whose tops join into one another so close, as nothing is seen through them.

Upon the top of that mountain begins a vast extended moor or waste, which, for fifteen or sixteen miles together due north, presents you with neither hedge, house or tree, but a waste and houling wilderness, over which when strangers travel, they are obliged to take guides, or it would be next to impossible not to lose their way.

Nothing can be more surprising of its kind, than for a stranger coming from the north, suppose from Sheffield in Yorkshire, for that is the first town of note, and wandering or labouring to pass this difficult desart country, and seeing no end of it, and almost discouraged and beaten out with the fatigue of it, (just such was our case) on a sudden the guide brings him to this precipice, where he looks down from a frightful heighth, and a comfortless, barren, and, as he thought, endless moor, into the most delightful valley, with the most pleasant garden, and most beautiful palace in the world: if contraries illustrate, and the place can admit of any illustration, it must needs add to the splendor of the situation, and to the beauty of the building, and I must say (with which I will close my short observation) if there is any wonder in Chatsworth, it is, that any man who had a genius suitable to so magnificent a design, who could lay out the plan for such a house, and had a fund to support the charge, would build it in such a place where the mountains insult the clouds, intercept the sun, and would threaten, were earthquakes frequent here, to bury the very towns, much more the house, in their ruins.

On the top of that mountain, that is to say, on the plain which extends from it, is a large pond or basin for water, spreading, as I was told, near thirty acres of ground, which, from all the ascents round it, receives, as into a cistern, all the water that falls, and from which again by pipes, the cascades, waterworks, ponds, and canals in the gardens, are plentifully supplied.

On the west side, which is the front or entrance of the house, and where the first foundress built a very august portal or gate; I say, on the west side, runs the river Derwent, which, though not many miles from its source here, is yet a terrible river, when, by hasty rains, or by the melting of the snows, the hills are pleased to pour down their waters into its channel; for the current is so rapid, and it has so many contracted passages among the rocks, and so many little cataracts among the stones, of which sometimes we see some of an incredible bulk come rouling down its stream; I say, there are so many of these, that the river, on the least motion of its waters above their ordinary highth, roars like the breaches on the shores of the sea.

But I must dwell no longer here, however pleasant and agreeable the place. The remaining article, and which, I grant, we may justly call a wonder, is Elden Hole: the description of it, in brief, is thus: in the middle of a plain open field, gently descending to the south, there is a frightful chasme, or opening in the earth, or rather in the rock, for the country seems thereabouts to be all but one great rock; this opening goes directly down perpendicular into the earth, and perhaps to the center; it may be about twenty foot over one way, and fifty or sixty the other; it has no bottom, that is to say, none that can yet be heard of. Mr. Cotton says, he let down eight hundred fathoms of line into it, and that the plummet drew still; so that, in a word, he sounded about a mile perpendicular; for as we call a mile 1760 yards, and 884 is above half, then doubtless eight hundred fathoms must be 1600 yards, which is near a mile.

This I allow to be a wonder, and what the like of is not to be found in the world, that I have heard of, or believe.

What nature meant in leaving this window open into the infernal world, if the place lies that way, we cannot tell: but it must be said, there is something of horror upon the very imagination, when one does but look into it.

Having thus viewed the two counties of Nottingham and Derby, as beginning that part of England, which we call north by Trent, I resolved to go northward on the east side of the island, taking the western shore, or the Irish Sea in my return.

The Peak concludes the northern part of Derbyshire; nor are there any towns on that side worth noting.

So we left the Peak, and went to **Chesterfield**, a handsome market town at the northermost border of the county, north east from Chatsworth.

Chesterfield is a handsome populous town, well-built and well inhabited, notwithstanding it stands in the farthest part of this rocky country; for being on the north west side next to Yorkshire, it enters Scarsdale, which is a rich fruitful part of the country, though surrounded with barren moors and mountains, for such the name Scarsdale signifies, according to that master of etymologies, Mr. Cambden. Here is, however, nothing remarkable in this town but a free school, and a very good market, well stored with provisions; for here is little or no manufacture.

From hence (travelling still north) we entred the great county of York.

The county is divided into three Ridings; as I entred it from the south, it follows, I went in, by what they call the West Riding, which, as it is by much the largest, so it is the wealthiest and the most populous, has the greatest towns in it, and the greatest number of them; the greatest manufactures, and consequently the greatest share of wealth, as it has also of people.

Two eminent towns, tho' only meer market towns, and one of them no corporation, open the door into the west Riding of Yorkshire; these are Sheffield and Doncaster. It is true, there is a little market town, at the very first entrance into the county before we come to Doncaster, call'd *Bautry*, a town bless'd with two great conveniencies which assists to its support, and makes it a very well frequented place.

1. That it stands upon the great post highway, or road from London to Scotland; and this makes it be full of very good inns and houses of entertainment.

2. That the little but pleasant river Idle runs through, or rather just by, the side of it, which, contrary to the import of its name, is a full and quick, though not rapid and unsafe stream, with a deep channel, which carries hoys, lighters, barges, or flat-bottom'd vessels, out of its channel into the Trent, which comes within seven miles of it, to a place called Stockwith, and from thence to Burton, and from thence, in fair weather, quite to Hull; but if not, 'tis sufficient to go to Stockwith, where vessels of 200 ton burthen may come up to the town loaden as well as empty.

By this navigation, this town of Bautry becomes the center of all the exportation of this part of the country, especially for heavy goods, which they bring down hither from all the adjacent countries, such as lead, from the lead mines and smelting-houses in Derbyshire, wrought iron and edge-tools, of all sorts, from the forges at Sheffield, and from the country call'd Hallamshire, being adjacent to the towns of Sheffield and Rotherham, where an innumerable number of people are employed; as I shall speak more largely of in its place.

Also millstones and grindstones, in very great quantities, are brought down and shipped off here, and so carry'd by sea to Hull, and to London, and even to Holland also. This makes Bautry wharf be famous all over the south part of the West Riding of York-

shire, for it is the place whether all their heavy goods are carried, to be embarked and shipped off.

From hence to Doncaster is a pleasant road, and good ground, and never wants any repair, which is very hard to be said in any part of this lower side of the country.

Doncaster is a noble, large, spacious town, exceeding populous, and a great manufacturing town, principally for knitting; also as it stands upon the great northern post-road, it is very full of great inns; and here we found our landlord at the posthouse was mayor of the town as well as post-master, that he kept a pack of hounds, was company for the best gentlemen in the town or in the neighbourhood, and lived as great as any gentleman ordinarily did.

Here we saw the first remains or ruins of the great Roman highway, which, though we could not perceive it before, was eminent and remarkable here, just at the entrance into the town; and soon after appeared again in many places: Here are also two great, lofty, and very strong stone bridges over the Don, and a long causeway also beyond the bridges, which is not a little dangerous to passengers when the waters of the Don are restrained, and swell over its banks, as is sometimes the case.

Leaving Doncaster, we turned out of the road a little way to the left, where we had a fair view of that antient whittl-making,[22] cutlering town, called *Sheffield*; the antiquity, not of the town only, but of the trade also, is established by those famous lines of Geoffry Chaucer[23] on the Miller of Trumpington, which, however they vary from the print in Chaucer, as now extant, I give it you as I find it:

> At Trumpington, not far from Cambridge,
> There dwelt a miller upon a bridge;
> With a rizzl'd beard, and a hooked nose,
> And a Sheffield whittl in his hose.

This town of Sheffield is very populous and large, the streets narrow, and the houses dark and black, occasioned by the continued smoke of the forges, which are always at work: Here they make all sorts of cutlery-ware, but especially that of edged-tools, knives, razors, axes, &c. and nails; and here the only mill of the sort, which was in use in England for some time was set up, (viz.) for turning their grindstones, though now 'tis grown more common.

Here is a very spacious church, with a very handsome and high spire; and the town is said to have at least as many, if not more people in it than the city of York. Whether they have been exactly numbered one against the other, I cannot tell. The manufacture of hard ware, which has been so antient in this town,

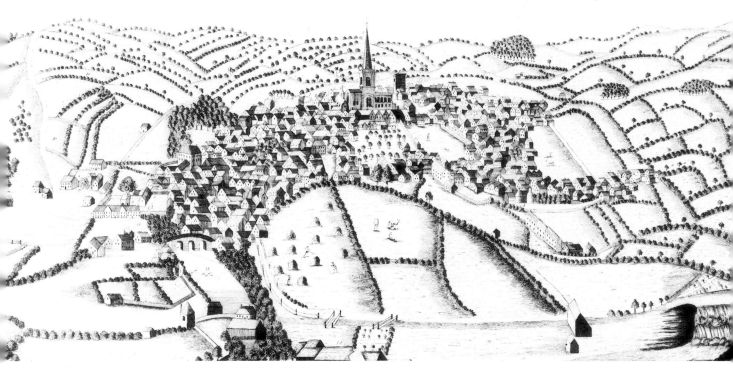

189. Sheffield; engraving by Thomas Outerbridge (1736).

is not only continued, but much encreased; insomuch that they told us there, the hands employed in it were a prodigious many more than ever dwelt, as well in the town, as in the bounds of that they call Hallamshire;[24] and they talked of 30000 men employed in the whole; but I leave it upon the credit of report.

Here is a fine engine or mill also for raising water to supply the town, which was done by Mr. Serocoal, the same who fell into the river at the throwing-mill at Derby, as is said in its place: here is also a very large and strong bridge over the Don, as there is another at **Rotherham**, a market town six miles lower. Here is also a very fine hospital, with the addition of a good revenue, settled at first by Gilbert, Earl of Shrewsbury, and confirmed afterwards by the family of Howard, Dukes of Norfolk.

From Rotherham we turned north west to Wentworth, on purpose to see the old seat of Tankersly,[25] and the park, where I saw the largest red deer that, I believe, are in this part of Europe: one of the hinds, I think, was larger than my horse, and he was not a very small pad of fourteen hands and half high. This was antiently the dwelling of the great Thomas Wentworth, Earl of Strafford, beheaded in King Charles the First's time, by a law, *ex post facto*, voted afterward not to be drawn into a precedent. The body lies interred in Wentworth church.

Thence over vast moors, I had almost said waste moors, we entred the most populous part of this county, I mean of the West Riding, only passing a town call'd Black Barnsley, eminent still for the working in iron and steel; and indeed the very town

looks as black and smoaky as if they were all smiths that lived in it; tho' it is not, I suppose, called Black Barnsley on that account, but for the black hue or colour of the moors, which, being covered with heath, (or heather, as 'tis called in that country) look all black, like Bagshot Heath, near Windsor; after, I say, we had pass'd these moors, we came to a most rich, pleasant and populous country, and the first town of note we came to in it was Wakefield, a large, handsome, rich clothing town, full of people, and full of trade.

Wakefield is a clean, large, well-built town, very populous and very rich; here is a very large church, and well filled it is, for here are very few Dissenters; the steeple is a very fine spire, and by far the highest in all this part of the country, except that at Sheffield. They tell us, there are here more people also than in the city of York, and yet it is no corporation town; and the highest magistrate, as I understand, was a constable.

Here also is a market every Friday for woollen cloaths, after the manner of that at Leeds, tho' not so great; yet as all the cloathing trade is encreasing in this country, so this market too flourishes with the rest; not but that sometimes, as foreign markets receive interruption either by wars, by a glut of the goods, or by any other incident, there are interruptions of the manufacture too, which, when it happen, the clothiers are sure to complain of loss of trade; but when the demand comes again they are not equally forward with their acknowledgments; and this, I observed, was the case every where else, as well as here.

The river Calder, of which I shall give an account

190. 'Wakefield as it appears from London Road'; engraving by William Lodge (1680). The Calder and the bridge with the chapel occupy the middle ground, with watermills right centre.

by and by, having trac'd it from its beginning, receiving a mighty confluence of rivers into it, is now, as I have said, become a large river, and the first town it comes near of note is Huthersfield, another large cloathing place; it passes also by Eland, where there is a very fine stone bridge. This was the original seat of the Earls or Marquisses of Hallifax, when the title went in the name of Saville. Huthersfield is one of the five towns which carry on that vast cloathing trade by which the wealth and opulence of this part of the country has been raised to what it now is, and where those woollen manufactures are made in such prodigious quantities, which are known by the name of Yorkshire kersies.[26] Whether the scandal rais'd upon this country be just or not, (viz.) shrinking cloth and sharping k——s, that I will not take upon me to determine; at this town there is a market for kersies every Tuesday.

Nor, as I speak of their manufactures, must I forget that most essential manufacture called Yorkshire ale, which indeed is in its perfection here, and in all this part of the county; of which I shall speak again in its place.

As the Calder runs by Hallifax, Huthersfield, and through Wakefield; so the Aire runs by Skippon, Bradforth and thorough Leeds, and then both join at Castleford Bridge, near Pontefract, so in an united stream forming that useful navigation from this trading part of Yorkshire to Hull; to the infinite advantage of the whole country.

It is not easie to take a view of this populous and wealthy part, called the West Riding, at one, no, nor at two journies, unless you should dwell upon it, and go cross the country backward and forward, on purpose to see this or that considerable place.

In my first journey I came only west from York to Wakefield, and then, turning south by Barnsley to Doncaster, went away still south to Rotherham, Sheffield, Chesterfield, Chatsworth, and the Peak, all which journey, except York, and the towns about it, and in the way to it, I have mentioned already.

The second journey, I came out of the western part of England, namely, from Cheshire thro' Lancashire, and, passing west over those Andes of England, called Blackstone Edge, and the mountains, which, as I hinted before, part Yorkshire and Lancashire, and reach from the High Peak to Scotland, I came to Hallifax, Bradforth, Huthersfield, Leeds, Wetherby, Pontefract and Burrow Bridge, and so went away into the East Riding, as you have heard.

The third journey, I went from the Peak in Derbyshire again, and, traversing the same country as I returned by in the first journey as far as Wakefield, went on again north to Leeds, and thence over Harwood Bridge to Knaresborough Spaw, thence to Rippon, and thro' that old Roman Street-way, called Leeming Lane, to Pier's Bridge, thence to Durham, and so into Scotland; of all which in their order.

In my second journey, as above, I came from Lancashire, where you are to note, that all this part of the country is so considerable for its trade, that the Post-Master General had thought fit to establish a cross-post[27] thro' all the western part of England into it, to maintain the correspondence of merchants and men of business, of which all this side of the island is so full; this is a confirmation of what I have so often repeated, and may still repeat many times on farther occasion, of the greatness of the trade carried on in this part of the island. This cross-post begins at Plymouth, in the south west part of England, and, leaving the great western post road of Excester behind, comes away north to Taunton, Bridgwater and Bristol; from thence goes on thro' all the great cities and towns up the Severn; such as Gloucester, Worcester, Bridgenorth and Shrewsbury, thence by West-Chester to Liverpool and Warrington, from whence it turns away east, and passes to Manchester, Bury, Rochdale, Hallifax, Leeds and York, and ends at Hull.

By this means the merchants at Hull have immediate advice of their ships which go out of the channel, and come in; by their letters from Plymouth, as readily as the merchants at London, and without the double charge of postage. The shopkeepers and manufacturers can correspond with their dealers at Manchester, Liverpool and Bristol, nay, even with Ireland directly; without the tedious interruption of sending their letters about by London, or employing people at London to forward their packets; and as the trade on this side is exceeding great, this correspondence is a mighty advantage; nor is the encrease of the revenue by it inconsiderable, the quantity of letters which pass and repass this way, being, as I was told, in all places very great.

I follow'd this post-road, from Liverpool to Bury and Rochdale, both manufacturing towns in Lanca-shire, and the last very considerable, for a sort of course goods, called half-thicks[28] and kersies, and the market for them is very great, tho' otherwise the town is situated so remote, so out of the way, and so at the very foot of the mountains, that we may suppose it would be but little frequented.

Here, for our great encouragement, though we were but at the middle of August, and in some places the harvest was hardly got in, we saw the mountains covered with snow, and felt the cold very acute and piercing; but even here we found, as in all those northern countries is the case, the people had an extraordinary way of mixing the warm and the cold very happily together; for the store of good ale which flows plentifully in the most mountainous part of this country, seems abundantly to make up for all the in-clemencies of the season, or difficulties of travelling, adding also the plenty of coals for firing, which all those hills are full of.

We mounted the hills, fortified with the same pre-caution, early in the morning, and though the snow which had fallen in the night lay a little upon the ground, yet we thought it was not much; and the morning being calm and clear, we had no appre-hension of an uneasy passage, neither did the people at Rochdale, who kindly directed us the way, and even offered to guide us over the first mountains, apprehend any difficulty for us; so we complimented ourselves out of their assistance, which we afterwards very much wanted.

It was, as I say, calm and clear, and the sun shone when we came out of the town of Rochdale; but when we began to mount the hills, which we did within a mile, or little more of the town, we found the wind began to rise, and the higher we went the more wind; by which I soon perceived that it had blown before, and perhaps all night upon the hills, tho' it was calm below; as we ascended higher it began to snow again, that is to say, we ascended into that part where it was snowing, and had, no doubt, been snowing all night, as we could easily see by the thickness of the snow.

It is not easy to express the consternation we were in when we came up near the top of the mountain; the wind blew exceeding hard, and blew the snow so directly in our faces, and that so thick, that it was impossible to keep our eyes open to see our way. The ground also was so covered with snow, that we could see no track, or when we were in the way, or when out; except when we were shewed it by a frightful precipice on one hand, and uneven ground on the other; even our horses discovered their uneasiness at it; and a poor spaniel dog that was my fellow traveller, and usually diverted us with giving us a mark for our gun, turn'd tail to it and cry'd.

In the middle of this difficulty, and as we began to call to one another to turn back again, not knowing what dangers might still be before us, came a surpriz-ing clap of thunder, the first that ever I heard in a storm of snow, or, I believe, ever shall; nor did we perceive any lightning to precede the thunder, as must naturally be the case; but we supposed the thick falling of the snow might prevent our sight.

I must confess I was very much surprized at this blow; and one of our company would not be persuaded that it was thunder, but that it was some blast of a coal-pit, things which do sometimes happen in the country, where there are many coal mines. But we were all against him in that, and were fully satisfied that it was thunder, and, as we fancy'd, at last we were confirmed in it, by hearing more of it at a distance from us.

Upon this we made a full stop, and coming al-together, for we were then three in company, with two servants, we began to talk seriously of going back again to Rochdale; but just then one of our men called out to us, and said, he was upon the top of the hill, and could see over into Yorkshire, and that there was a plain way down on the other side.

We rode all up to him, and found it as the fellow had said, all but that of a plain way; there was indeed the mark or face of a road on the side of the hill, a little turning to the left north; but it was so narrow, and so deep a hollow place on the right, whence the water descending from the hills made a channel at the bottom, and looked as the beginning of a river, that the depth of the precipice, and the narrowness of the way, look'd horrible to us; after going a little way in it, the way being blinded too by the snow, the hollow on the right appeared deeper and deeper, so we resolved to alight and lead our horses, which we did for about a mile, though the violence of the wind and snow continuing, it was both very troublesome and dangerous.

All this way the hollow on our right continued very deep, and just on the other side of it a parallel hill continued going on east, as that did which we rode on the side of; the main hill which we came down from, which is properly called Blackstone Edge,[29] or, by the country people, the Edge, without any sirname or addition, ran along due north, crossing and shutting up those hollow gulls and vallies between, which were certainly originally formed by the rain and snow water running into them, and forcing its way down, washing the earth gradually along with it, till, by length of time, it wore down the surface to such a depth.

We continued descending still, and as the weather was quieter, so the way seemed to mend and be broader, and, to our great satisfaction, enclining more to the hill on the left; the precipice and hollow part where the water run, as I have said, went a little off from us, and by and by, to our no small comfort, we saw an enclosed piece of ground that is enclosed with a stone wall, and soon after a house, where we asked our way, and found we were right.

Soon after this we came to the bottom, by another very steep descent, where we were obliged to alight again, and lead our horses. At the bottom, we found the hollow part, which I have so often mentioned as a precipice, was come to a level with us, that is to say, we were come down to a level with it, and it turning to the left toward us, we found a brook of water running from it, which cross'd our way to the north, you shall hear of it again presently; when we cross'd this brook, which, by reason of the snow on the hills which melted, was risen about knee deep, and run like a sluice for strength, we found a few poor houses, but saw no people, no not one; till we call'd at a door, to get directions of our way, and then we found, that though there was no body to be seen without doors, they were very full of people within, and so we found it on several occasions afterward, of which we shall speak again.

We thought now we were come into a Christian country again, and that our difficulties were over; but we soon found ourselves mistaken in the matter; for we had not gone fifty yards beyond the brook and houses adjacent, but we found the way began to ascend again; and soon after to go up very steep, till in about half a mile we found we had another mountain to ascend, in our apprehension as bad as the first, and

before we came to the top of it, we found it began to snow too, as it had done before.

From Blackstone Edge to Hallifax is eight miles, and all the way, except from Sorby to Hallifax, is thus up hill and down; so that, I suppose, we mounted to the clouds and descended to the water level about eight times, in that little part of the journey.

But now I must observe to you, that after having pass'd the second hill, and come down into the valley again, and so still the nearer we came to Hallifax, we found the houses thicker, and the villages greater in every bottom; and not only so, but the sides of the hills, which were very steep every way, were spread with houses, and that very thick; for the land being divided into small enclosures, that is to say, from two acres to six or seven acres each, seldom more; every three or four pieces of land had a house belonging to it.

Then it was I began to perceive the reason and nature of the thing, and found that this division of the land into small pieces, and scattering of the dwellings, was occasioned by, and done for the convenience of the business which the people were generally employ'd in, and that, as I said before, though we saw no people stirring without doors, yet they were all full within; for, in short, this whole country, however mountainous, and that no sooner we were down one hill but we mounted another, is yet infinitely full of people; those people all full of business; not a beggar, not an idle person to be seen, except here and there an alms-house, where people antient, decrepid, and past labour, might perhaps be found.

This business is the clothing trade, for the convenience of which the houses are thus scattered and spread upon the sides of the hills, as above, even from the bottom to the top; the reason is this; such has been the bounty of nature to this otherwise frightful country, that two things essential to the business, as well as to the ease of the people are found here, and that in a situation which I never saw the like of in any part of England; and, I believe, the like is not to be seen so contrived in any part of the world; I mean coals and running water upon the tops of the highest hills: this seems to have been directed by the wise hand of Providence for the very purpose which is now served by it, namely, the manufactures, which otherwise could not be carried on; neither indeed could one fifth part of the inhabitants be supported without them, for the land could not maintain them. After we had mounted the third hill, we found the country, in short, one continued village, tho' mountainous every way, as before; hardly a house standing out of a speaking distance from another, and (which soon told us their business) the day clearing up, and the sun shining, we could see that almost at every house there was a tenter,[30] and almost on every tenter a piece of cloth, or kersie, or shalloon, for they are the three articles of that country's labour; from which the sun glancing, and, as I may say, shining (the white reflecting its rays) to us, I thought it was the most agreeable sight that I ever saw, for the hills, as I say, rising and falling so thick, and the vallies opening sometimes one way, sometimes another, so that sometimes we could see two or three miles this way, sometimes as far another; sometimes like the streets near St. Giles's, called the Seven Dials;[31] we could see through the glades almost every way round us, yet look which way we would, high to the tops, and low to the bottoms, it was all the same; innumerable houses and tenters, and a white piece upon every tenter.

191. Tenters, detail from 'East prospect of the town of Leeds'; engraving by I. Harris after a drawing by Samuel Buck (1720).

But to return to the reason of dispersing the houses, as above; I found, as our road pass'd among them, for indeed no road could do otherwise, wherever we pass'd any house we found a little rill or gutter of running water, if the house was above the road, it came from it, and cross'd the way to run to another; if the house was below us, it cross'd us from some other distant house above it, and at every considerable house was a manufactury or work-house, and as they could not do their business without water, the little streams were so parted and guided by gutters or pipes, and by turning and dividing the streams; that none of those houses were without a river, if I may call it so, running into and through their work-houses.

Again, as the dying-houses, scouring-shops[32] and places where they used this water, emitted the water again, ting'd with the drugs of the dying fat, and with

the oil, the soap, the tallow, and other ingredients used by the clothiers in dressing and scouring, &c. which then runs away thro' the lands to the next, the grounds are not only universally watered, how dry soever the season, but that water so ting'd and so fatten'd enriches the lands they run through, that 'tis hardly to be imagined how fertile and rich the soil is made by it.

Then, as every clothier must keep a horse, perhaps two, to fetch and carry for the use of his manufacture, (viz.) to fetch home his wooll and his provisions from the market, to carry his yarn to the spinners, his manufacture to the fulling mill, and, when finished, to the market to be sold, and the like; so every manufacturer generally keeps a cow or two, or more, for his family, and this employs the two, or three, or four pieces of enclosed land about his house, for they scarce sow corn enough for their cocks and hens; and this feeding their grounds still adds by the dung of the cattle, to enrich the soil.

But now, to speak of the bounty of nature again, it is to be observed, that not only on the sides, but even to the very tops, there is scarce a hill but you find, on the highest part of it, a spring of water, and a coal-pit. Having thus fire and water at every dwelling, there is no need to enquire why they dwell thus dispers'd upon the highest hills, the convenience of the manufactures requiring it. Among the manufacturers' houses are likewise scattered an infinite number of cottages or small dwellings, in which dwell the workmen which are employed, the women and children of whom, are always busy carding, spinning, &c. so that no hands being unemploy'd, all can gain their bread, even from the youngest to the antient; hardly any thing above four years old, but its hands are sufficient to it self.

I must only say a word or two of the river Calder, to

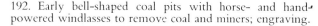

192. Early bell-shaped coal pits with horse- and hand-powered windlasses to remove coal and miners; engraving.

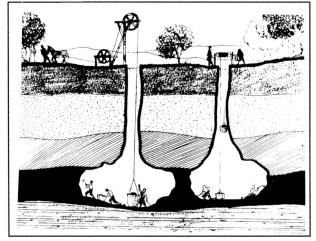

193. Eighteenth-century miner working underground.

compleat the description of the country I thus pass'd through. I hinted to you, that all the rills or brooks of water which we cross'd, one at least in every bottom, went away to the left or north side of us as we went forward east: I am to add, that following those little brooks with our eye, we could observe, that at some distance to the left there appeared a larger valley than the rest, into which not only all the brooks which we pass'd emptied themselves, but abundance more from the like hollow deep bottoms, among the hills on the north side of it, which emptied this way south, as those on our side run that way north, so that it was natural to conclude, that in this larger valley the waters of all those brooks joining, there must be some pretty large stream which received them all, and ran forward east, parallel to the way we were in.

After some time we found that great opening seemed to bend southward towards us, and that probably it would cross our road, or our road would rather cross the valley; and so it was natural to expect we should pass that larger water, either by a bridge or a ford; but we were soon convinced it was not the latter; for the snow, as is said, having poured down a quantity of water, we soon found at the next opening, that there was a considerable river in the larger valley, which, having received all those little brooks, was risen to a little flood; and at the next village we pass'd it over a stately stone bridge of several great arches. This village is called Sorby or Sowreby; and this was the main river Calder, which I mentioned at Wakefield, where it begins to be navigable, and which, without any spring or fountain, to be called the head or source of it, is formed on the declivity of these mountains, meerly by the continued fall of rains and snows, which the said mountains intercepting the clouds, are seldom free from; and this stream receiving the smaller gulls and hollows, I just now mentioned, like a common-shore, carries all away in the channel of a noble river.

This is the beginning of the Calder; and my reason for dwelling upon it, and giving so particular a description, is, because this may, once for all, shew you how all, or most of the great rivers in the north, take their rise.

Having passed the Calder at Sorby Bridge, I now began to approach the town of **Hallifax**; in the description of which, and its dependencies, all my account of the commerce will come in, for take Halli-fax, with all its dependencies, it is not to be equalled in England. First, the parish or vicaridge, for it is but a vicaridge; is, if not the largest, certainly is the most populous in England; in short, it is a monster, I mean, for a country parish, and a parish so far out of the way of foreign trade, courts, or sea ports.

The extent of the parish, they tell us, is almost circular, and is about twelve miles in diameter. There are in it twelve or thirteen chapels of ease, besides about sixteen meeting-houses, which they call also chapels, and are so, having bells to call the people, and burying grounds to most of them, or else they bury within them. I think they told me, the Quakers' meetings, of which there are several too, are not reckoned into the number. In a word, it is some years ago that a reverend clergyman of the town of Hallifax, told me, they reckoned that they had a hundred thousand communicants in the parish, besides children.

History tells us also, that in Queen Elizabeth's time, when the inhabitants of Hallifax addressed the Queen for some privileges, which I do not at present remember the particulars of, it was expressed in the petition as a moving argument, why the Queen should take them into her royal care, that they were zealous Protestants, and were so loyal to her Majesty, as well as so considerable, that no less than twelve thousand young men went out arm'd from this one parish, and, at her majesty's call, joined her troops to fight the Popish army,[33] then in rebellion under the Earl of Westmorland.

If they were so populous at that time, how much must they be encreased since? and especially since the late Revolution, the trade having been prodigiously encouraged and encreased by the great demand of their kersies for clothing the armies abroad, insomuch that it is the opinion of some that know the town, and its bounds very well, that the number of people in the vicaridge of Hallifax, is encreased one fourth, at least, within the last forty years, that is to say, since the late Revolution. Nor is it improbable at all, for besides the number of houses which are encreased, they have entered upon a new manufacture which was never made in those parts before, at least, not in any quantities, I mean, the manufactures of shalloons, of which they now make, if fame does not bely them, a hundred thousand pieces a year in this parish only, and yet do not make much fewer kersies than they did before.

The trade in kersies also was so great, that I was told by very creditable, honest men, when I was there, men not given to gasconading or boasting, and less to lying, that there was one dealer in the vicaridge, who traded, by commission, for three-score thousand pounds a year in kersies only, and all that to Holland and Hamburgh.

But I must not leave Hallifax yet, as the vicaridge is thus far extended, and the extent of it so peopled, what must the market be, and where must this vast number of people be supplied. For, as to corn, I have observed already, they sow little and hardly enough to feed their poultry, if they were to be corn fed; and as to beef and mutton, they feed little or none; and as they are surrounded with large, populous, manufacturing towns on every side, all of them employed as these are, in the cloathing trade, they must then necessarily have their provisions from other parts of the country.

This then is a subsistence to the other part of the country, and so it is for us, the West Riding is thus taken up, and the lands occupied by the manufacture; the consequence is plain, their corn comes up in great quantities out of Lincoln, Nottingham, and the East Riding, their black cattle and horses from the North Riding, their sheep and mutton from the adjacent counties every way, their butter from the East and North Riding, their cheese out of Cheshire and Warwickshire, more black cattle also from Lancashire. And here the breeders and feeders, the farmers and country people find money flowing in plenty from the manufacturers and commerce; so that at Hallifax, Leeds, and the other great manufacturing towns so often mentioned, and adjacent to these, for the two months of September and October, a prodigious quantity of black cattle is sold.

This demand for beef is occasioned thus, the usage of the people is to buy in at that season beef sufficient for the whole year, which they kill and salt, and hang up in the smoke to dry. This way of curing their beef keeps it all the winter, and they eat this smoak'd beef as a very great rarity.

Upon this foot, 'tis ordinary for a clothier that has a large family, to come to Hallifax on a market-day, and buy two or three large bullocks from eight to ten pounds a piece. These he carries home and kills for his store. And this is the reason that the markets at all those times of the year are thronged with black cattle, as Smithfield is on a Friday; whereas all the rest of the year there is little extraordinary sold there.

Thus this one trading, manufacturing part of the country supports all the countries round it, and the numbers of people settle here as bees about a hive.

But I must not quit Hallifax, till I give you some account of the famous course of justice antiently executed here, to prevent the stealing of cloth. Modern accounts pretend to say, it was for all sorts of felons; but I am well assured, it was first erected purely, or at least principally, for such thieves as were apprehended stealing cloth from the tenters; and it seems very reasonable to think it was so, because of the conditions of the trial. The case was thus:

The erecting the woollen manufacture here was about the year 1480, when King Henry VII by giving encouragement to foreigners to settle in England, and to set up woollen manufactures, caused an act to pass prohibiting the exportation of wooll into foreign parts, unwrought, and to encourage foreign manufacturers to come and settle here, of whom several coming over settled the manufactures of cloths in several parts of the kingdom, as they found the people tractable, and as the country best suited them; as the bays at Colchester, the says at Sudbury, the broadcloth in Wilts, and other counties; so the trade of kersies and narrow cloth fixed at this place, and other adjacent towns.

When this trade began to settle, nothing was more frequent than for young workmen to leave their cloths out all night upon the tenters, and the idle fellows would come in upon them, and tearing them off without notice, steal the cloth. Now as it was absolutely necessary to preserve the trade in its infancy, this severe law was made, giving the power of life and death so far into the hands of the magistrates of Hallifax, as to see the law executed upon them. As this law was particularly pointed against the stealing of cloth, and no other crime, so no others were capable of being punished by it, and the conditions of the law intimate as much; for the power was not given to the magistrates to give sentence, unless in one of these three plain cases:

1. Hand napping, that is, to be taken in the very fact, or, as the Scots call it in the case of murther, red hand.

2. Back bearing, that is, when the cloth was found on the person carrying it off.

3. Tongue confessing, that part needs no farther explanation.

This being the case, if the criminal was taken, he was brought before the magistrates of the town, who at that time were only a Baily and the Eoaldermen, how many we do not read, and these were to judge, and sentence, and execute the offender, or clear him, within so many days; I think it was three market days

194. 'Execution according to Halifax Law'; vignette from *A New description of England and Wales with adjacent islands. . .*, London (1724).

if the offence was committed out of the vicaridge, but within the bounds of the forest then there were Frith Borges[34] also to judge of the fact, who were to be summoned of the Forest Holders, as they are called, who were to hold of that frith, that is, of the forest; but those were to be good and sober men, and by the magistrates of the town to be approved as such; if those acquitted him of the fact he was immediately discharged; it those censured him, no body could reprieve him but the town. The country people were, it seems, so terrified at the severity of this proceeding, that hence came that proverbial saying, which was used all over Yorkshire, (viz.)

From Hell, Hull, and Hallifax,[35]
Good Lord, deliver us.

How Hull came to be included in this petition, I do not find; for they had no such law there, as I read of.

The manner of execution was very remarkable; the engine[36] indeed is carried away, but the scaffold on which it stood is there to this time, and may continue many ages; being not a frame of wood, but a square building of stone, with stone steps to go up.

They tell us of a custom which prevailed here, in the case of a criminal being to be executed, (viz.) that if after his head was laid down, and the signal given to pull out the pin, he could be so nimble as to snatch out his head between the pulling out the pin and the falling down of the ax, and could get up upon his feet, jump off of the scaffold, run down a hill that lies just before it, and get through the river before the executioner could overtake him, and seize upon him, he was to escape; and though the executioner did take him on the other side the river, he was not to bring him back, at least he was not to be executed.

This engine was removed, as we are told, in the year 1620, during the reign of King James the First, and the usage and custom of prosecution abolished, and criminals or felons left to the ordinary course of justice, as it is still; and yet they do not find the stealing cloth from the tenters is so frequent now as it was in those times.

But the manner of execution is preserv'd; for in the reign of the same prince, the Earl Morton, Regent or Prime Minister of Scotland, under King James, passing thro' Hallifax, and seeing one of their executions, was so pleased with the performance, that he caused a model to be taken and carried into Scotland, where it is preserved and constantly made use of for executions to this day. But one thing must not be forgotten in this part of the story, namely, that his Lordship's own head was the first that was cut off with it; and it being many years before that happened, the engine was called the

Maiden, as not having so long handsell'd,[37] and still retains the name, tho' it has cut off many a head since that.

We quitted Hallifax not without some astonishment at its situation, being so surrounded with hills, and those so high, as (except the entrance by the west) makes the coming in and going out of it exceeding troublesome, and indeed for carriages hardly practicable, and particularly the hill which they go up to come out of the town eastwards towards Leeds, and which the country people call Hallifax Bank, is so steep, so rugged, and sometimes too so slippery, that, to a town of so much business as this is, 'tis exceeding troublesome and dangerous.

From Hallifax it is twelve miles to Leeds north east, and about as many to Wakefield; due east, or a little southerly, between Hallifax and Leeds, is a little town called **Burstall**. Here the kersey and shalloon trade being, as it were, confined to Hallifax, and the towns already named, of Huthersfield and Bradforth, they begin to make broad cloth; I call it broad, in distinction from kersies and druggets, and such things, though the cloths in this country are called narrow, when they are spoken of in London, and compared with the broad cloths made in Wilts, Gloucester, Somerset and Devonshire, of which I have spoken in former letters.

This town is famed for dying, and they make a sort of cloths here in imitation of the Gloucester white cloths, bought for the Dutch and the Turkey trades; and though their cloths here may not be as fine, they told us their colours are as good. But that is not my business to dispute, the West Country clothiers deny it; and so I leave it as I find it.

From hence to **Leeds**, and every way to the right hand and the left, the country appears busy, diligent, and even in a hurry of work, they are not scattered and dispersed as in the vicaridge of Hallifax, where the houses stand one by one; but in villages, those villages large, full of houses, and those houses thronged with people, for the whole country is infinitely populous.

Leeds is a large, wealthy and populous town, it stands on the north bank of the river Aire, or rather on both sides the river, for there is a large suburb or part of the town on the south side of the river, and the whole is joined by a stately and prodigiously strong stone bridge, so large, and so wide, that formerly the cloth market was kept in neither part of the town, but on the very bridge itself; and therefore the refreshment given the clothiers by the inn-keepers, of which I shall speak presently, is called the Brigg-shot to this day.

The encrease of the manufacturers and of the trade, soon made the market too great to be confined to the brigg or bridge, and it is now kept in the high-street, beginning from the bridge, and running up north almost to the market-house, where the ordinary market for provisions begins, which also is the greatest of its kind in all the north of England, except Hallifax, of which I have spoken already, nay, the people at Leeds will not allow me to except Hallifax, but say, that theirs is the greatest market, and that not the greatest plenty only, but the best of all kinds of provisions are brought hither.

But this is not the case; it is the cloth market I am now to describe, which is indeed a prodigy of its kind, and is not to be equalled in the world. The market for serges at Exeter is indeed a wonderful thing, and the value sold there is very great; but then the market there is but once a week, here it is twice a week, and the quantity of goods vastly great too.

The market itself is worth describing, tho' no description can come up to the thing itself; however, take a sketch of it with its customs and usages as follows:

The street is a large, broad, fair and well-built street, beginning, as I have said, at the bridge, and ascending gently to the north.

Early in the morning, there are tressels placed in two rows in the street, sometimes two rows on a side, but always one row at least; then there are boards laid cross those tressels, so that the boards lie like long counters on either side, from one end of the street to the other.

The clothiers come early in the morning with their cloth; and as few clothiers bring more than one piece, the market being so frequent, they go into the inns and publick houses with it, and there set it down.

At seven a clock in the morning, the clothiers being supposed to be all come by that time, even in the winter, but the hour is varied as the seasons advance (in the summer earlier, in the depth of winter a little later) I take it, at a medium, and as it was when I was there, at six or seven, I say, the market bell rings; it would surprize a stranger to see in how few minutes, without hurry or noise, and not the least disorder, the whole market is fill'd; all the boards upon the tressels are covered with cloth, close to one another as the pieces can lie long ways by one another, and behind every piece of cloth, the clothier standing to sell it.

This indeed is not so difficult, when we consider that the whole quantity is brought into the market as soon as one piece, because as the clothiers stand ready in the inns and shops just behind, and that there is a clothier to every piece, they have no more to do, but, like a regiment drawn up in line, every one takes up his piece, and has about five steps to march to lay it upon the first row of boards, and perhaps ten to the second row; so that upon the market bell ringing, in half a quarter of an hour the whole market is fill'd, the rows of boards cover'd, and the clothiers stand ready.

As soon as the bell has done ringing, the merchants and factors, and buyers of all sorts, come down, and coming along the spaces between the rows of boards, they walk up the rows, and down as their occasions direct. Some of them have their foreign letters of orders, with patterns seal'd on them, in rows, in their hands; and with those they match colours, holding them to the cloths as they think they agree to: when they see any cloths to their colours, or that suit their occasions, they reach over to the clothier and whisper, and in the fewest words imaginable the price is stated; one asks, the other bids; and 'tis agree, or not agree, in a moment.

The merchants and buyers generally walk down and up twice on each side of the rows, and in little more than an hour all the business is done; in less than half an hour you will perceive the cloths begin to move off, the clothier taking it up upon his shoulder to carry it to the merchant's house; and by half an hour eight a clock the market bell rings again; immediately the buyers disappear, the cloth is all sold, or if here and there a piece happens not to be bought, 'tis carried back into the inn, and, in a quarter of an hour, there is not a piece of cloth to be seen in the market.

Thus, you see, ten or twenty thousand pounds value in cloth, and sometimes much more, bought and sold in little more than an hour, and the laws of the market the most strictly observed as ever I saw done in any market in England; for,

1. Before the market bell rings, no man shews a piece of cloth, nor can the clothiers sell any but in open market.

2. After the market bell rings again, no body stays a moment in the market, but carries his cloth back if it be not sold.

3. And that which is most admirable is, 'tis all managed with the most profound silence, and you cannot hear a word spoken in the whole market, I mean, by the persons buying and selling; 'tis all done in whisper.

The reason of this silence, is chiefly because the clothiers stand so near to one another; and 'tis always reasonable that one should not know what another does, for that would be discovering their business, and exposing it to one another.

If a merchant has bidden a clothier a price, and he will not take it, he may go after him to his house, and tell him he has considered of it, and is willing to let him have it; but they are not to make any new agree-ment for it, so as to remove the market from the street to the merchant's house.

By nine a clock the boards are taken down, the tressels are removed, and the street cleared, so that you see no market or goods any more than if there had been nothing to do; and this is done twice a week. By this quick return the clothiers are constantly supplied with money, their workmen are duly paid, and a pro-digious sum circulates thro' the county every week.

If you should ask upon all this, where all these goods, as well here as at Wakefield, and at Hallifax, are vented and disposed of? It would require a long treatise of commerce to enter into that part: But that I may not bring you into the labyrinth, and not show you the way out, I shall, in three short heads, describe the consumption, for there are three channels by which it goes:

1. For the home consumption; their goods being, as I may say, every where made use of, for the cloathing the ordinary people, who cannot go to the price of the fine medley cloths made, as I formerly gave you an account, in the western counties of England. There are for this purpose a set of travelling merchants in Leeds, who go all over England with droves of pack horses, and to all the fairs and market towns over the whole island, I think I may say none excepted. Here they supply not the common people by retail, which would denominate them pedlars indeed, but they supply the shops by wholesale or whole pieces; and not only so, but give large credit too, so that they are really travelling merchants, and as such they sell a very great quantity of goods; 'tis ordinary for one of these men to carry a thousand pounds value of cloth with them at a time, and having sold it at the fairs or towns where they go, they send their horses back for as much more, and this very often in a summer, for they chuse to travel in the summer, and perhaps towards the winter time, tho' as little in winter as they can, because of the badness of the roads.

2. Another sort of buyers are those who buy to send to London; either by commissions from London, or they give commissions to factors and warehouse-keepers in London to sell for them; and these drive also a very great trade: these factors and warehouse-keepers not only supply all the shop-keepers and wholesale men in London, but sell also very great quantities to the merchants, as well for exportation to the English colonies in America, which take off great quantities of those course goods, especially New England, New York, Virginia, &c. as also to the Russia merchants, who send an exceeding quantity to Petersburgh, Riga, Dantzic, Narva, and to Sweden and Pomerania.

3. The third sort of buyers, and who are not less

05. *A New and exact plan of the town of Leeds*; engraved by J. Cossins (1725). The location of the street cloth market is shown.

considerable than the other, are truly merchants, that is to say, such as receive commissions from abroad to buy cloth for the merchants chiefly in Hamburgh, and in Holland, and from several other parts; and these are not only many in number, but some of them are very considerable in their dealings, and correspond as far as Nuremberg, Frankfort, Leipsick, and even to Vienna and Ausburgh, in the farthest provinces of Germany.

On account of this trade it was, that some years ago[38] an Act of Parliament was obtained for making the rivers Aire and Calder navigable; by which a communication by water was opened from Leeds and Wakefield to Hull, and by which means all the woollen manufactures which those merchants now export by commission, as above, is carried by water to Hull, and there shipped for Holland, Bremen, Hamburgh, and the Baltick. And thus you have a brief account, by what methods this vast manufacture is carried off, and which way they find a vent for it.

There is another trade in this part of the country, which is now become very considerable since the opening the navigation of these rivers, and that is, that from hence they carry coals down from Wakefield (especially) and also from Leeds, at both which they have a very great quantity, and such, as they told me, could never be exhausted. These they carry quite down into the Humber, and then up the Ouse to York, and up the Trent, and other rivers, where there are abundance of large towns, who they supply with coals; with this advantage too, that whereas the Newcastle coals pay four shillings per chaldron duty to the publick; these being only called river borne coal, are exempted, and pay nothing; though, strictly speaking, they are carried on the sea too, for the Humber is properly the sea. But they have been hitherto exempted from the tax, and so they carry on the trade to their very great profit and advantage.

I need not add, that by the same navigation they receive all their heavy goods, as well such as are imported at Hull, as such as come from London, and such as other counties supply, as butter, cheese, lead, iron, salt; all sorts of grocery, as sugars, tobacco, fruit, spice, hops, &c. oyl, wine, brandy, spirits, and every sort of heavy or bulky goods.

The town of Leeds is very large, and, as above, there are abundance of wealthy merchants in it. Here are two churches, and two large meeting-houses of Dissenters, and six or seven chapels of ease, besides Dissenters' chapels, in the adjacent, depending villages; so that Leeds may not be much inferiour to Hallifax in numbers of people: It is really a surprising thing to see what numbers of people are thronged together in all the villages about these towns, and how busy they all are, being fully employed in this great manufacture.

I had no sooner pass'd out of the district of Leeds about four or five miles, and pass'd the wharfe, at a fine stone bridge of eleven arches at a little pretty town call'd Harwood; I say, I was no sooner gotten hither, but it was easie to see we were out of the manufacturing country. Now the black moorish lands, like Black Barnsley, shew'd dismal again and frightful, the towns were thin, and thin of people too; we saw but little enclosed ground, no tenters with the cloths shining upon them, nor people busied within doors, as before; but, as in the vicaridge, we saw inhabited mountains, here we saw waste and almost uninhabited vales.

In a word, the country look'd as if all the people were transplanted to Leeds and Hallifax, and that here was only a few just left at home to cultivate the land, manage the plough, and raise corn for the rest.

The river Warfe seemed very small, and the water low, at Harwood Bridge, so that I was surprised to see so fine a bridge over it, and was thinking of the great bridge at Madrid over the Mansanares, of which a Frenchman of quality looking upon it, said to the Spaniards that were about him, That the King of Spain ought either to buy them some water, or they should sell their bridge. But I was afterwards satisfied that was not the case here; for coming another time this way after a heavy rain, I was convinced the bridge was not at all too big, or too long, the water filling up to the very crown of the arches, and some of the arches not to be seen at all.

From the Wharfe we went directly north, over a continued waste of black, ill looking, desolate moors, over which travellers are guided, like race horses, by posts set up for fear of bogs and holes, to a town call'd Ripley, that stands upon another river called the Nud by some, by others the Nyd, smaller than the Wharfe, but furiously rapid, and very dangerous to pass in many places, especially upon sudden rains. Notwithstanding such lofty, high built bridges as are not to be seen over such small rivers in any other place; and, on this occasion, it may be observed here, once for all, that no part of England, I may say so because I can say I have seen the whole island, a very little excepted, I say, no part can shew such noble, large, lofty, and long stone bridges as this part of England, nor so many of them; nor do I remember to have seen any such thing as a timber bridge in all the northern part of England, no not from the Trent to the Tweed; whereas in the south parts of England there are abundance.

A little below Ripley, on the same river Nyd, and with a very fine bridge over it also, we saw *Knaresborough*; known among foreigners by the name of

196. 'South East prospect of Rippon'; engraving by Samuel and Nathaniel Buck (1745).

Knaresborough Spaw; in the south of England I have heard it call'd the Yorkshire Spaw.

The first thing recommended to me for a wonder, was that four springs, the waters of which are in themselves of so different a quality, should rise in so narrow a compass of ground; but I, who was surfeited with country wonders in my passing the Peak, was not so easily surprized at the wonderful strangeness of this part.

But now to speak of the other two springs, they are indeed valuable rarities, and not to be equalled in England.

197. Dropping Well, Knaresborough; drawing by Francis Place (1711). This was a petrifying well, not a medicinal spa as Defoe suggests.

1. The first is the sweet spaw, or a vitriolick water; it was discovered by one Mr. Slingsby, anno 1630. and all physicians acknowledge it to be a very sovereign medicine in several particular distempers. Vid. Dr. Leigh's Nat. Hist. of Lancashire.

198. 'Knaresborough Spa'; engraving of the building located at the Sweet Spa, Harrogate (probably early eighteenth century). Slingsby discovered the Spa in 1571, earlier than the date stated by Defoe.

2. The stinking spaw, or, if you will, according to the learned, the sulphur well. This water is clear as chrystal, but fœtid and nauseous to the smell, so that thos who drink it are obliged to hold their noses when they drink; yet it is a valuable medicine also in scorbutic, hypochondriac, and especially in hydropic distempers; as to its curing the gout, I take that, as in other cases, *ad referendum*.

The people formerly, and that for many years, only

199. 'South West prospect of Richmond'; engraving by Samuel and Nathaniel Buck (1749).

drank these waters, and used them no otherwise; but are now come into the use of bathing in them as a cold bath, and thus they must necessarily be very good for rheumatic pains, paralitic numbnesses, and many other distempers which afflict mankind.

We were surprised to find a great deal of good company here drinking the waters, and indeed, more than we found afterwards at Scarborough; though this seems to be a most desolate out-of-the-world place, and that men would only retire to it for religious mortifications, and to hate the world, but we found it was quite otherwise.

Rippon is a very neat, pleasant, well built town, and has not only an agreeable situation on a rising ground between two rivers, but the market place is the finest and most beautiful square that is to be seen of its kind in England.

In the middle of it stands a curious column of stone, imitating the obelisks of the antients, tho' not so high, but rather like the pillar in the middle of Covent-

Garden, or that in Lincoln's Inn, with dials also upon it.

A mile from this town, or less, is a stately beautiful seat,[39] built a few years since by Sir Edward Blacket; the park is extended to the bank of the river Eure, and is sometimes in part laid under water by the river, the water of which, they say, coming down from the western mountains, thro' a marly, loamy soil, fructifies the earth, as the river Nile does the Egyptian fields about Grand Cairo, tho' by their leave not quite so much.

As Sir Edward spared no cost in the building, and Sir Christopher Wren laid out the design, as well as chose the ground for him, you may believe me the better, when I add, that nothing can either add to the contrivance or the situation; the building is of brick, the avenues, now the trees are grown, are very fine, and the gardens not only well laid out, but well planted, and as well kept; the statues are neat, the parterre beautiful; but, as they want fine gravel, the

266

walks cannot shew themselves, as in this southern part of England they would. The house has a fine prospect over the country, almost to York, with the river in view most of the way; and it makes itself a very noble appearance to the great north road, which lies within two miles of it, at Burrow-bridge.

As you now begin to come into the North Riding, for the Eure parts the West Riding from it, so you are come into the place noted in the north of England for the best and largest oxen, and the finest galloping horses, I mean swift horses, horses bred, as we call it, for the light saddle, that is to say, for the race, the chace, for running or hunting. Sir Edward was a grazier, and took such delight in the breeding and feeding large siz'd black cattle, that he had two or three times an ox out of his park led about the country for a sight, and shewed as far as Newcastle, and even to Scotland, for the biggest bullock in England; nor was he very often, if ever, over-match'd.

From this town of Rippon, the north road and the Roman highway also, mentioned before, which comes from Castleford Bridge, parting at Abberforth, leads away to a town call'd Bedal, and, in a strait line (leaving Richmond about two miles on the west) call'd Leeming Lane, goes on to Piersbridge on the river Tees, which is the farthest boundary of the county of York.

But before I go forward I should mention Burrow Bridge, which is but three miles below Rippon, upon the same river Eure, and which I must take in my way, that I may not be obliged to go farther out of the way, on the next journey.

There is something very singular at this town, and which is not to be found in any other part of England or Scotland, namely, two borough towns in one parish, and each sending two members to Parliament, that is, Borough Brigg and Aldborough.

From the Eure entring the North Riding, and keeping the Roman causeway, as mentioned before, one part of which went by this *Isurium Brigantum* from

York, we came to Bedall, all the way from Hutton, or thereabout, this Roman way is plain to be seen, and is called now Leeming Lane, from Leeming Chapel, a village which it goes through.

I met with nothing at or about Bedall, that comes within the compass of my enquiry but this, that not this town only, but even all this country, is full of jockeys, that is to say, dealers in horses, and breeders of horses; and the breeds of their horses in this and the next country are so well known, that tho' they do not preserve the pedigree of their horses for a succession of ages, as they say they do in Arabia and in Barbary, yet they christen their stallions here, and know them, and will advance the price of a horse according to the reputation of the horse he came of.

They do indeed breed very fine horses here, and perhaps some of the best in the world, for let foreigners boast what they will of barbs[40] and Turkish horses, and, as we know five hundred pounds has been given for a horse brought out of Turkey, and of the Spanish jennets[41] from Cordova, for which also an extravagant price has been given, I do believe that some of the gallopers of this country, and of the bishoprick of Durham, which joins to it, will outdo for speed and strength the swiftest horse that was ever bred in Turkey, or Barbary, take them all together.

My reason for this opinion is founded upon those words altogether; that is to say, take their strength and their speed together; for example; match the two horses, and bring them to the race post, the barb may beat Yorkshire for a mile course, but Yorkshire shall distance him at the end of four miles; the barb shall beat Yorkshire upon a dry, soft carpet ground, but Yorkshire for a deep country; the reason is plain, the English horses have both the speed and the strength; the barb perhaps shall beat Yorkshire, and carry seven stone and a half; but Yorkshire for a twelve to fourteen stone weight; in a word, Yorkshire shall carry the man, and the barb a feather.

The reason is to be seen in the very make of the horses. The barb, or the jennet, is a fine delicate creature, of a beautiful shape, clean limbs, and a soft coat; but then he is long jointed, weak pastured, and under limb'd: whereas Yorkshire has as light a body, and stronger limbs, short joints, and well bon'd. This gives him not speed only but strength to hold it; and, I believe, I do not boast in their behalf, without good vouchers, when I say, that English horses, take them one with another, will beat all the world.

As this part of the country is so much employed in horses, the young fellows are naturally grooms, bred up in the stable, and used to lie among the horses; so that you cannot fail of a good servant here, for looking after horses is their particular delight; and this is the reason why, whatever part of England you go to, though the farthest counties west and south, and whatever inn you come at 'tis two to one but the hostler is a Yorkshire man; for as they are bred among horses, 'tis always the first business they recommend themselves to; and if you ask a Yorkshire man, at his first coming up to get a service, what he can do; his answer is, Sir, he can look after your horse, for he handles a curry-comb as naturally as a young scrivener does a pen and ink.

Besides their breeding of horses, they are also good grasiers over this whole country, and have a large, noble breed of oxen, as may be seen at North Allerton fairs, where there are an incredible quantity of them bought eight times every year, and brought southward as far as the fens in Lincolnshire, and the isle of Ely, where, being but, as it were, half fat before, they are fed up to the grossness of fat which we see in London markets. The market whither these north country cattle are generally brought is to St. Ives, a town between Huntingdon and Cambridge, upon the river Ouse, and where there is a very great number of fat cattle every Monday.

Richmond, which, as I said, is two or three miles wide of the Leeming Lane, is a large market town, and gives name to this part of the country, which is called after it Richmondshire, as another part of it east of this is call'd North Allertonshire.

Here you begin to find a manufacture on foot again, and, as before, all was cloathing, and all the people clothiers, here you see all the people, great and small, a knitting; and at Richmond you have a market for woollen or yarn stockings, which they make very coarse and ordinary, and they are sold accordingly for the smallest siz'd stockings for children are here sold at eighteen pence per dozen, or three half pence a pair, something less.

This trade extends itself also into Westmoreland, or rather comes from Westmoreland, extending itself hither, for at Kendal Kirkby Stephen, and such other places in this county as border upon Yorkshire; the chief manufacture of yarn stockings is carried on; it is indeed a very considerable manufacture in itself, and of late mightily encreased too, as all the manufactures of England indeed are.

The Swale is a noted river, though not extraordinary large for giving name to the lands which it runs through for some length, which are called Swale Dale, and to an antient family of that name, one of whom had the vanity, as I have heard to boast, that his family was so antient as not to receive that name from, but to give name to the river itself. One of the worthless

200. The great fall of the Tees, County Durham; painting by George Lambert (1761).

country round here are grooms, as is noted before; so here and hereabouts they have an excellent knack at dressing horses hides into leather, and thinking or making us think it is invulnerable, that is to say, that it will never wear out; in a word, they make the best bridle reins, belts broad or narrow, and all accoutrements for a compleat horse-master, as they do at Rippon for spurs and stirrups.

Barnard's Castle stands on the north side of the Tees, and so is in the bishoprick of Durham. 'Tis an antient town, and pretty well built, but not large; the manufacture of yarn stockings continues thus far, but not much farther; but the jockeys multiply that way; and here we saw some very fine horses indeed; but as they wanted no goodness, so they wanted no price, being valued for he stallion they came of, and the merit of the breed. One very beautiful stone-horse which they here kept, they asked two hundred guineas for; but, as I heard afterwards, tho' they carried him to London, which was no small addition to the charge of him, they sold him for much less money.

The length of the late war,[43] it seems, caused the breeders here to run into a race or kind of horses, differing much from what they were used to raise, that is to say, from fine fleet horses for galloping and hunting, to a larger breed of charging horses, for the use of the general officers, and colonels of horse, aids du camp, and the like, whose service required strong charging horses, and yet if they were fleet horses too, they had a vast advantage of the enemy; for that if the rider was conquered and forced to fly, there was no overtaking him; and if his enemies fled they could never get away from him. I saw some of this breed, and very noble creatures they were, fit for any business whatever; strong enough for charging, fleet enough for hunting, tempered enough for travelling; and indeed, there is one thing to be said for the horse breeders in this country, their horses are all well broke, perfectly brought to hand, and to be under command, which is a thing absolutely necessary in the army, and in the hunting field also.

I was come now to the extent of the county of York northward. But as I have kept all along to the west side of the country, even from the Peak of Darby hither; and that I have all the East Riding and the eastern part of the North and West Riding to go over, I shall break off here, and conclude my first circuit; and am, with due respect,

Sir,

Your most humble servant.

successors of this line, who had brought himself to the dignity of what they call in London, a Fleeter,[42] used to write himself, in his abundant vanity, Sir Solomon Swale, of Swale Hall, in Swale Dale, in the county of Swale in the North Riding of York.

Leaving Richmond, we continue through this long Leeming Lane, which holds for about the length of six mile to the bank of Tees, where we pass'd over the river Tees at Piersbridge; the Tees is a most terrible river, so rapid, that they tell us a story of a man who coming to the ferry place in the road to Darlington, and finding the water low began to pull off his hose and shoes to wade thro', the water not being deep enough to reach to his knees, but that while he was going over, the stream swell'd so fast as to carry him away and drown him.

This bridge leads into the bishoprick of Durham, and the road soon after turns into the great post road leading to the city of Durham. I shall dwell no longer upon the particulars found on this side except Barnard Castle, which is about four miles distant from the Tees Bank west, and there I may speak of it again; as all the

The End of the Eighth Letter

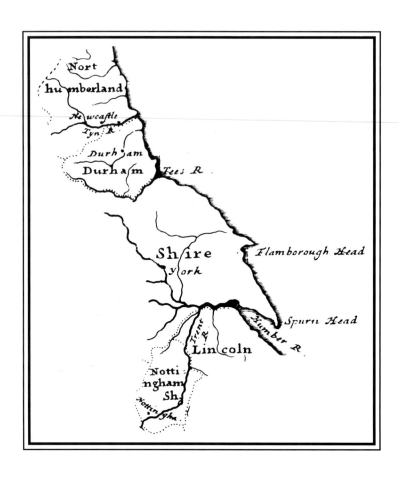

LETTER IX

Sir,

I BEGAN MY FIRST circuit at the bank of Trent, namely, at Nottingham Bridge, and keeping the middle of the island, travelled due north into the West Riding of Yorkshire, and to the farthest part of the county to the bank of Tees, as you have seen.

I am now come back, as the French say, *sur mes pas*, to the same bank of the Trent, though lower down, towards the east, and shall gather up some fragments of Nottinghamshire and the West Riding of Yorkshire, as I go, and then hasten to the sea side, where we have not cast our eye yet.

Passing Newark Bridge, we went through the lower side of Nottinghamshire, keeping within the river Idle. Here we saw Tuxford in the clays, that is to say, Tuxford in the dirt, and a little dirty market town it is, suitable to its name.

Then we saw **Rhetford**, a pretty little borough town of good trade, situate on the river Idle; the mayor treated us like gentlemen, though himself but a tradesman; he gave us a dish of fish from the river Idle, and another from the Trent, which I only note, to intimate that the salmon of the Trent is very valuable in this country, and is oftentimes brought to London, exceeding large and fine; at Newark they have it very large, and likewise at Nottingham.

Having found nothing in this low part of the coun-

201. 'A Prospect...on the Foss, September 7, 1722' (the banks of the Trent near Nottingham going North); engraving by E. Kirkall after a drawing by William Stukeley. From William Stukeley, *Itinerarium Curiosum* (1724).

202. 'The South East Prospect of the city of York'; engraving by Samuel and Nathaniel Buck, 1745.

try but a wonderful conflux of great rivers, all pouring down into the Humber, which receiving the Aire, the Ouse, the Don and the Trent, becomes rather a sea than a river, we left it on the right; and knowing we should necessarily visit its shores again, we turned up into the post road, where, as I said, I left it before near Brotherton, and went on for Tadcaster.

Tadcaster has nothing that we could see to testify the antiquity it boasts of, but some old Roman coins, which our landlord the post master shewed us, among which was one of Domitian, the same kind, I believe, with that Mr. Cambden gives an account of, but so very much defaced with age, that we could read but D O, and A V, at a distance. Here is the hospital and school, still remaining, founded by Dr. Oglethorp,[1] Bishop of Carlisle, who, for want of a Protestant archbishop, set the crown on the head of Queen Elizabeth.

From Tadcaster it is but twelve miles to York; the country is rich, fruitful and populous, but not like the western parts about Leeds, Wakefield, Hallifax, &c. which I described above; it bears good corn, and the city of York being so near, and having the navigation

of so many rivers also to carry it to Hull, they never want a good market for it.

The antiquity of **York**, though it was not the particular enquiry I proposed to make, yet shewed itself so visibly at a distance, that we could not but observe it before we came quite up to the city, I mean the mount and high hills, where the antient castle stood, which, when you come to the city, you scarcely see, at least not so as to judge of its antiquity.

The cathedral, or the minster, as they call it, is a fine building, but not so antient as some of the other churches in the city seem to be: that mount I mentioned above, and which, at a distance, I say was a mark of antiquity, is called the old Bale,[2] which was some ages ago fortified and made very strong; but time has eaten through not the timber and plank only, which they say it was first built with, but even the stones and mortar; for not the least footstep of it remains but the hill.

York is indeed a pleasant and beautiful city, and not at all the less beautiful for the works and lines about it being demolished, and the city, as it may be said, being laid open, for the beauty of peace is seen in the

rubbish; the lines and bastions and demolished fortifications, have a reserved secret pleasantness in them from the contemplation of the publick tranquility, that outshines all the beauty of advanced bastions, batteries, cavaliers, and all the hard named works of the engineers about a city.

The cathedral is a Gothick building, but with all the most modern addenda that order of building can admit; and with much more ornament of a singular kind, than we see any thing of that way of building grac'd with. I see nothing indeed of that kind of structure in England go beyond it, except it be the building we call King Henry VIIth's chapel, additional to the abbey church at Westminster, and that is not to be named with this, because it is but a chapel, and that but a small one neither.

The only deficiency I find at York minster, is the lowness of the great tower, or its want of a fine spire upon it, which, doubtless, was designed by the builders.

As then this church was so compleatly finished, and that so lately that it is not yet four hundred years old, it is the less to be wondered that the work continues so

firm and fine, that it is now the beautifullest church of the old building that is in Britain. In a word, the west end is a picture, and so is the building, the outsides of the quire especially, are not to be equall'd.

The chapter-house is a beauty indeed, and it has been always esteem'd so, witness the Latin verse which is written upon it in letters of gold.

Ut rosa flos florum, sic est domus ista domorum.[3]

But to return to the city itself; there is abundance of good company here, and abundance of good families live here, for the sake of the good company and cheap living; a man converses here with all the world as effectually as at London; the keeping up assemblies among the younger gentry was first set up here, a thing other writers recommend mightily as the character of a good country, and of a pleasant place; but which I look upon with a different view, and esteem it as a plan laid for the ruin of the nation's morals, and which, in time, threatens us with too much success that way.

However, to do the ladies of Yorkshire justice, I found they did not gain any great share of the just

203. 'Prospect of a noble terras walk...York'; engraving by C. Grignion after a drawing by Nathan Drake (1756).

reproach which in some other places has been due to their sex; nor has there been so many young fortunes carried off here by half-pay men,[4] as has been said to be in other towns, of merry fame, westward and southward.

No city in England is better furnished with provisions of every kind, nor any so cheap, in proportion to the goodness of things; the river being so navigable, and so near the sea, the merchants here trade directly to what part of the world they will; for ships of any burthen come up within thirty mile of the city, and small craft from sixty or eighty ton, and under, come up to the very city.

With these they carry on a considerable trade; they import their own wines from France and Portugal, and likewise their own deals and timber from Norway; and indeed what they please almost from where they please; they did also bring their own coals from Newcastle and Sunderland, but now have them down the Aire and Calder from Wakefield, and from Leeds, as I have said already.

The publick buildings erected here are very con-siderable, such as halls for their merchants and trades, a large townhouse or guild-hall, and the prison, which is spacious, and takes up all the ground within the walls of the old castle, and, in a building newly erected there, the assizes for the county are kept.

The old walls are standing, and the gates and posterns; but the old additional works which were cast up in the late rebellion, are slighted; so that York is not now defensible as it was then: but things lie so too, that a little time, and many hands, would put those works into their former condition, and make the city able to stand out a small siege. But as the ground seems capable by situation, so an ingenious head, in our company, taking a stricter view of it, told us, he would undertake to make it as strong as Tournay in Flanders, or as Namure, allowing him to add a citadel at that end next the river. But this is a speculation; and 'tis much better that we should have no need of forti-fied towns than that we should seek out good situa-tions to make them.

York, as I have said, is a spacious city, it stands upon a great deal of ground, perhaps more than any city in

274

England out of Middlesex, except Norwich; but then the buildings are not close and throng'd as at Bristol, or as at Durham; nor is York so populous as either Bristol or Norwich. But as York is full of gentry and persons of distinction, so they live at large, and have houses proportioned to their quality; and this makes the city lie so far extended on both sides the river. It is also very magnificent, and, as we say, makes a good figure every way in its appearance, even at a distance; for the cathedral is so noble and so august a pile, that 'tis a glory to all the rest.

There are very neat churches here besides the cathedral, and were not the minster standing, like the Capitol in the middle of the city of Rome, some of these would pass for extraordinary, as the churches of St. Mary's and Allhallows, and the steeples of Christ-Church, St. Mary's, St. Peg's, and Allhallows.

There are also two fine market-houses, with the town-hall upon the bridge, and abundance of other publick edifices, all which together makes this city, as I said, more stately and magnificent, though not more populous and wealthy, than any other city in the king's dominions, London and Dublin excepted. The reason of the difference is evidently for the want of trade.

Here is no trade indeed, except such as depends upon the confluence of the gentry: but the city, as to lodgings, good houses, and plenty of provisions, is able to receive the king, lords and commons, with the whole court, if there was occasion; and once they did entertain King Charles I[5] with his whole court, and with the assembly of peers, besides a vast confluence of the gentry from all parts to the king, and at the same time a great part of his army.

We went out in a double excursion from this city, first to see the Duke of Leed's house, and then the Earl of Carlisle's, and the Earl of Burlington's in the East Riding; Carlisle House is by far the finest design, but it is not finished, and may not, perhaps, in our time; they say his lordship sometimes observes noblemen should only design, and begin great palaces, and leave posterity to finish them gradually, as their estates will allow them; it is called Castle Howard.[6] The Earl of Burlington's[7] is an old built house, but stands deliciously, and has a noble prospect towards the Humber, as also towards the Woulds.

At Hambledon Down, near this city, are once a year very great races, appointed for the entertainment of the gentry, and they are the more frequented, because the king's plate of a hundred guineas is always run for there once a year; a gift designed to encourage the gentlemen to breed good horses.

Yorkshire is throng'd with curiosities, and two or

204. 'Bonny Black' at Hambleton race course. York; painting by John Wootton (c.1725). The dial stone on the right was one of the landmarks of the Hambleton race course.

three constantly attend these races, namely, first, that (as all horse matches do) it brings together abundance of noblemen and gentlemen of distinction, and a proportion of ladies; and, I assure you, the last make a very noble appearance here, and, if I may speak my thoughts without flattery, take the like number where you will, yet, in spite of the pretended reproach of country breeding, the ladies of the north are as handsome and as well dress'd as are to be seen either at the Court or the ball.

The river Derwent, contrary to the course of all the rivers in Yorkshire, (as I have observed) runs north and south, rising in that part of the country called Cleveland, and running through, or hard by, several market towns, as Pickering, Pocklington, North Malton, and others, and is, by the course, a good guide to those who would take a view of the whole country.

I observed the middle of this riding or division of Yorkshire is very thin of towns, and consequently of people, being overspread with woulds, that is to say, plains and downs, like those of Salisbury; on which they feed great numbers of sheep, and breed also a great many black cattle and horses; especially in the northern part, which runs more mountainous, and makes part of the North Riding of York. But the east and west part is populous and rich, and full of towns, the one lying on the sea coast, and the other upon the river Derwent, as above; the sea coast or west side, is call'd Holderness.

After passing the Derwent we saw little of moment, but keeping under the woulds or hills mentioned above, we came to your old acquaintance John a Beverley,[8] I mean the famous monastery at that town.

It is a large and populous town, though I find no considerable manufacture carried on there. The great collegiate church is the main thing which ever did, and still does, make the town known in the world. The famous story of John of Beverley, is, in short, this: that one John, Archbishop of York, a learned and devout man, out of meer pious zeal for religion, and contempt of the world, quitted or renounced his honours and superiority in the church, and, laying aside the pall, and the mitre, retired to Beverley, and liv'd here all the rest of his time a recluse.

This story will prompt you to enquire how long ago 'twas, for you know as well as I, and will naturally observe, that very few such bishops are to be found now; it was indeed a long time ago, for it is this very year just five year above a thousand year ago that this happened; for the good man died anno dom. 721, you may soon cast up the rest to 1726.

The memory of this extraordinary man has been much honoured; and had they gone no farther, I should have join'd with them most heartily. But as to sainting him, and praying to him, and offering at his shrine, and such things, that we Protestants must ask their leave to have nothing to say to.

The minster here is a very fair and neat structure; the roof is an arch of stone, in it there are several monuments of the Piercy's, Earls of Northumberland, who have added a little chapel to the choir, in the windows of which are the pictures of several of that family drawn in the glass at the upper end of the choir. On the right side of the altar-place stands the freed stool,[9] mentioned by our author,[10] made of one entire stone, and said to have been removed from Dunbar in Scotland, with a well of water behind it. At the upper end of the body of the church, next the choir, hangs an antient table with the picture of St. John (from whom the church is named) and of King Athelstan the founder of it, and between them this distich:

Als free make I thee,
As heart can wish, or egh can see.

Hence the inhabitants of **Beverley** pay no toll or custom in any port or town in England; to which immunity (I suppose) they owe, in a great measure, their riches and flourishing condition; for indeed, one is surprized to find so large and handsome a town within six miles of Hull: in the body of the church stands an antient monument, which they call the Virgins' Tomb, because two virgin sisters lay buried there who gave the town a piece of land, into which any freeman may put three milch kine from Ladyday to Michaelmas. At the lower end of the body of the church, stands a fair, large font of agat stone.

But to come to the present condition of the town, it is above a mile in length, being of late much improv'd in its buildings, and has pleasant springs running quite through its streets. It is more especially beautified with two stately churches, and has a free-school that is improved by two fellowships, six scholarships, and three exhibitions in St. John's College, in Cambridge, belonging to it; besides six alms-houses, the largest whereof was built lately by the executors of Michael Warton, Esq; who, by his last will, left one thousand pounds for that use; the mayor and aldermen having sometimes been deceived in their choice, admit none into their alms-houses but such as will give bond to leave their effects to the poor when they die; a good example to other places.

The principal trade of the town is making malt, oatmeal, and tann'd leather; but the poor people mostly support themselves by working bone-lace,[11] which of late has met with particular encouragement, the children being maintain'd at school to learn to read, and to work this sort of lace. The cloathing trade was formerly follow'd in this town, but Leland[12] tells us, that even in his time it was very much decay'd.

They have several fairs, but one more especially remarkable, called the Mart, beginning about nine days before Ascension Day, and kept in a street leading to the Minster Garth, called Londoners Street, for then the Londoners bring down their wares, and furnish the country tradesmen by wholesale.

About a mile from Beverley to the east, in a pasture belonging to the town, is a kind of spaw, though they say it cannot be judg'd by the taste whether or no it comes from any mineral; yet taken inwardly it is a great drier, and wash'd in, dries scorbutick scurf, and all sorts of scabs, and also very much helps the king's evil.

From Beverley I came to **Hull**, distance six miles. If you would expect me to give an account of the city of Hamburgh or Dantzick, or Rotterdam, or any of the second rate cities abroad, which are fam'd for their commerce, the town of Hull may be a specimen. The place is indeed not so large as those; but, in proportion to the dimensions of it, I believe there is more business done in Hull than in any town of its bigness in Europe; Leverpool indeed of late comes after it apace; but then Leverpool has not the London trade to add to it.

In the late war, the fleets from Hull to London were frequently a hundred sail, sometimes including the other creeks in the Humber, a hundred and fifty to a hundred and sixty sail at a time; and to Holland their trade is so considerable, that the Dutch always

205. 'South East prospect of Kingston upon Hull'; engraving by Samuel and Nathaniel Buck (1745).

employ'd two men of war to fetch and carry, that is, to convoy the trade, as they call'd it, to and from Hull, which was as many as they did to London.

In a word, all the trade at Leeds, Wakefield and Hallifax, of which I have spoken so justly and so largely, is transacted here, and the goods are ship'd here by the merchants of Hull; all the lead trade of Derbyshire and Nottinghamshire, from Bautry wharf, the butter of the East and North Riding, brought down the Ouse to York: the cheese brought down the Trent from Stafford, Warwick and Cheshire, and the corn from all the counties adjacent, are brought down and shipp'd off here.

Again, they supply all these countries in return with foreign goods of all kinds, for which they trade to all parts of the known world; nor have the merchants of any port in Britain a fairer credit, or fairer character, than the merchants of Hull, as well for the justice of their dealings as the greatness of their substance or funds for trade. They drive a great trade here to Norway, and to the Baltick, and an important trade to Dantzick, Riga, Narva and Petersburgh; from whence they make large returns in iron, copper, hemp, flax, canvas, pot-ashes, Muscovy linnen and yarn, and other things; all which they get vent for in the country to an exceeding quantity. They have also a great importation of wine, linen, oil, fruit, &c. trading to Holland, France and Spain; the trade of tobacco and sugars from the West-Indies, they chiefly manage by the way of London. But besides all this, their export of corn, as well to London as to Holland and France, exceeds all of the kind, that is or can be done at any port in England, London excepted.

Their shipping is a great article in which they outdo all the towns and ports on the coast except Yarmouth, only that their shipping consists chiefly in smaller vessels than the coal trade is supplied with, tho' they have a great many large vessels too, which are employed in their foreign trade.

The town is situated at the mouth of the river Hull, where it falls into the Humber, and where the Humber opens into the German ocean, so that one side of their town lies upon the sea, the other upon the land. This makes the situation naturally very strong; and, were there any occasion, it is capable of being made impregnable, by reason of the low situation of the grounds round it.

The town is exceeding close built, and should a fire ever be its fate, it might suffer deeply on that account; 'tis extraordinary populous, even to an inconvenience, having really no room to extend itself by buildings. There are but two churches, but one of them is very large, and there are two or three very large meeting-houses, and a market stored with an infinite plenty of all sorts of provision.

They shew us still in their town-hall the figure of a northern fisherman,[13] supposed to be of Greenland, that is to say, the real Greenland, being the continent of America to the north of those we call the north west passages; not of Spiltbergen, where our ships go a whale fishing, and which is, by mistake, called Greenland. He was taken up at sea in a leather boat, which he sate in, and was covered with skins, which drew together about his waste, so that the boat could not fill, and he could not sink; the creature would never feed nor speak, and so died.

They have a very handsome exchange here, where the merchants meet as at London, and, I assure you, it is wonderfully filled, and that with a confluence of real merchants, and many foreigners, and several from the country; for the navigation of all the great rivers which fall into the Humber centers here, such as the Trent, the Idle, the Don, the Aire and Calder, and the Ouse; and consequently the commerce of all the great towns on those rivers is managed here, from Gainsborough and Nottingham on the Trent, York and Selby on the Ouse, and so of the rest.

There is also a fine free school, over which is the merchant's hall. But the Trinity-House[14] here is the glory of the town: it is a corporation of itself, made up of society of merchants: it was begun by voluntary contribution for relief of distressed and aged seamen, and their wives or widows; but was afterwards approved by the government, and incorporated: they have a very good revenue, which encreases every day by charities, and bounties of pious minded people.

They maintain thirty sisters now actually in the house, widows of seamen; they have a government by twelve elder brethren and six assistants; out of the twelve they chuse annually two wardens, but the whole eighteen vote in electing them, and two stewards. These have a power to decide disputes between masters of ships and their crews, in matters relating to the sea affairs only; and with this limitation, that their judgment be not contrary to the laws of the land; and, even in trials at law, in such affairs they are often called to give their opinions.

They have a noble stone bridge here over the river Hull, consisting of fourteen arches. They had once set up a Greenland fishery, and it went on with success for a time; but it decayed in the time when the Dutch wars were so frequent, and the house built by the Greenland merchants is now turned into granaries for corn, and warehouses for other goods.

Farther east from Hull there is a little pleasant town call'd Headon, handsome, well built, and having a little haven from the sea, which threatens Hull, that it will in time grow up to be a great place, for it indeed increases daily; but I fear for them, that their haven will do nothing considerable for them, unless they can do something very considerable for that.

They tell us at Headon, that the sea encroaches upon the land on all that shore, and that there are many large fields quite eaten up; that several towns were formerly known to be there, which are now lost; from whence they may suppose, that as the sea by encroachment has damnified their harbour, so if it grows upon them a little more they shall stand open to the sea, and so need no harbour at all, or make a mole, as 'tis called abroad, and have a good road without it. But this is a view something remote.

The Spurn Head, a long promontory thrusting out into the sea, and making the north point of Humber, is a remarkable thing. But I leave that to the description of the sea coasts, which is none of my work; the most that I find remarkable here, is, that there is nothing remarkable upon this side for above thirty miles together; not a port, not a gentleman's seat, not a town of note; Bridlington or Burlington is the only place, and that is of no note, only for a bay or road for shipping, which is of use to the colliers on this coast to defend them, in case of extremity of weather.

The country people told us a long story here of gipsies which visit them often in a surprising manner. We were strangely amused with their discourse at first, forming our ideas from the word, which, in ordinary import with us, signifies a sort of strolling, fortune-telling, hen-roost-robbing, pocket-picking vagabonds, called by that name. But we were soon made to understand the people, as they understood themselves here, namely, that at some certain seasons, for none knows when it will happen, several streams of water gush out of the earth with great violence, spouting up a huge heighth, being really natural *jette d'eaus* or fountains; that they make a great noise, and, joining together, form little rivers, and so hasten to the sea. I had not time to examine into the particulars; and as the irruption was not just then to be seen, we could say little to it: that which was most observable to us, was, that the country people have a notion that whenever those *gipsies*, or, as some call 'em, *vipseys*, break out, there will certainly ensue either famine or plague. This put me in mind, that the very same thing is said to happen at Smitham Bottom in Surrey, beyond Croydon, and that the water gushing out of the chalky hills about eight miles from Croydon, on the road to Ryegate, fills the whole bottom, and makes a large river running just to the towns end of Croydon; and then turning to the left runs into the river which rises in the town, and runs to Cashalton; and I name it, because the country people here have exactly the same notion, that this water never breaks out but against a famine; and as I am sure it has not now broken out for more than fifty years, it may, for ought I know, be true.

Scarborough next presents itself, a place formerly famous for the strong castle, situate on a rock, as it were hanging over the sea, but now demolish'd, being ruined in the last wars. The town is well built, populous and pleasant, and we found a great deal of good company here drinking the waters, who came not only from all the north of England, but even from Scotland. It is hard to describe the taste of the waters; they are apparently ting'd with a collection of mineral salts, as of vitriol, allom, iron, and perhaps sulphur, and taste evidently of the allom. Here is such a plenty of all sorts of fish, that I have hardly seen the like, and, in particular, here we saw turbets of three quarters of a hundred weight, and yet their flesh eat exceeding fine when taken new.

206. View of Scarborough Well and Governor Dicky's house; drawing by George Vertue (*c.*1720–30).

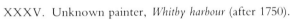

XXXV. Unknown painter, *Whitby harbour* (after 1750).

At the entrance of a little nameless river, scarce indeed worth a name, stands **Whitby**, which, however, is an excellent harbour, and where they built very good ships for the coal trade, and many of them too, which makes the town rich.

From hence the North Riding holds on to the bank of Tees, the northern bounds of Yorkshire, and where there are two good towns, (viz.) Stockton and Yarum, towns of no great note; but what they obtain by the river and adjacent sea, but are greatly encreased of late years, especially the first, by being the chiefest place in the North Riding of York, or in the county of Cumberland, for the shipping off lead, and butter for London.

I began now to consider the long journey I had to go, and that I must not stop at small matters: we went from Stockton to Durham. **North Allerton**, a town on the post road, is remarkable for the vast quantity of black cattle sold there, there being a fair once every fortnight for some months, where a prodigious quantity are sold.

I have not concern'd this work at all in the debate among us in England, as to Whig and Tory. But I must observe of this town, that, except a few Quakers, they boasted that they had not one Dissenter here, and yet at the same time not one Tory, which is what, I believe, cannot be said of any other town in Great Britain.

I must now leave Yorkshire, which indeed I might more fully have described, if I had had time; for there are abundance of rarities in nature spoken of in this North Riding, which I had not leisure to enquire into; as the allom mines or pits near Moultgrave or Musgrave, from whence the Lord Musgrave, now Duke of

Buckinghamshire, has his title, as he has also a great part of his estate from the allom works not far off. Next here are the snake stones, of which nothing can be said but as one observes of them, to see how nature sports herself to amuse us, as if snakes could grow in those stones. Then the glates or gargates, that is, in short jett, a black smooth stone found in Cleveland; also a piece of ground, which, if the wild geese attempt to fly over, they fall down dead. But I cannot dwell any longer here.

Darlington, a post town, has nothing remarkable but dirt, and a high stone bridge over little or no water, the town is eminent for good bleaching of linen, so that I have known cloth brought from Scotland to be bleached here. As to the Hell Kettles,[15] so much talked up for a wonder, which are to be seen as we ride from the Tees to Darlington, I had already seen so little of wonder in such country tales, that I was not hastily deluded again. 'Tis evident, they are nothing but old coal pits filled with water by the river Tees.

Durham is next, a little compact neatly contriv'd city, surrounded almost with the river Wear, which with the castle standing on an eminence, encloses the city in the middle of it; as the castle does also the cathedral, the bishop's palace, and the fine houses of the clergy, where they live in all the magnificence and splendor imaginable.

I need not tell you, that the Bishop of Durham is a temporal prince, that he keeps a court of equity, and also courts of justice in ordinary causes within himself. The county of Durham, like the country about Rome, is called St. Cuthbert's Patrimony. This church, they tell us, was founded by David, King of Scots; and afterward Zouch,[16] the valiant bishop, fought the Scots army at Nevil's Cross, where the Scots were terribly cut in pieces, and their king taken prisoner.

But what do I dip into antiquity for, here, which I have avoided as much as possible every where else? The church of Durham is eminent for its wealth; the bishoprick is esteemed the best in England; and the prebends and other church livings, in the gift of the bishop, are the richest in England. They told me there, that the bishop had thirteen livings in his gift, from five hundred pounds a year to thirteen hundred pounds a year; and the living of the little town of Sedgfield, a few miles south of the city, is said to be worth twelve hundred pounds a year, beside the small tithes, which maintain a curate, or might do so.

Going to see the church of Durham, they shewed us the old popish vestments of the clergy before the Reformation, and which, on high days, some of the residents put on still. They are so rich with em-

207. Durham cathedral and castle; painting once attributed to George Lambert.

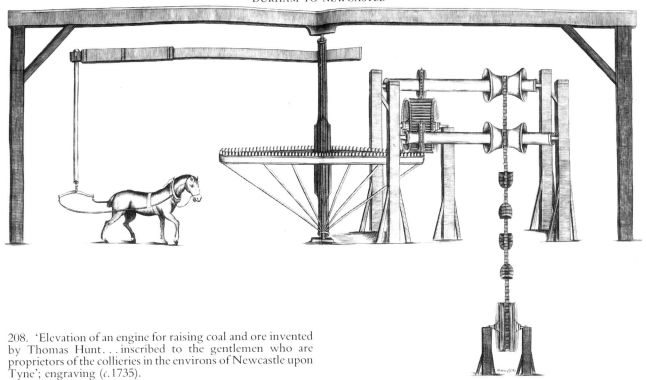

208. 'Elevation of an engine for raising coal and ore invented by Thomas Hunt...inscribed to the gentlemen who are proprietors of the collieries in the environs of Newcastle upon Tyne'; engraving (c.1735).

broidery and emboss'd work of silver, that indeed it was a kind of a load to stand under them.

The town is well built but old, full of Roman Catholicks, who live peaceably and disturb no body, and no body them; for we being there on a holiday, saw them going as publickly to mass as the Dissenters did on other days to their meeting-house.

From hence we kept the common road to **Chester in the Street**, an old, dirty, thorowfare town, empty of all remains of the greatness which antiquaries say it once had, when it was a Roman colony. Here is a stone bridge, but instead of riding over it we rode under it, and riding up the stream pass'd under or through one of the arches, not being over the horse hoofs in water; yet, on enquiry, we found, that sometimes they have use enough for a bridge.

Here we had an account of a melancholy accident, and in itself strange also, which happened in or near Lumley Park, not long before we pass'd through the town. A new coal pit being dug or digging, the workmen workt on in the vein of coals till they came to a cavity, which, as was supposed, had formerly been dug from some other pit; but be it what it will, as soon as upon the breaking into the hollow part, the pent up air got vent, it blew up like a mine of a thousand barrels of powder, and, getting vent at the shaft of the pit, burst out with such a terrible noise, as made the very earth tremble for some miles round, and terrify'd the whole country. There were near three score poor people lost their lives in the pit, and one or two, as we were told, who were at the bottom of the shaft, were blown quite out, though sixty fathom deep, and were found dead upon the ground.

Lumley Castle[17] is just on the side of the road as you pass between Durham and Chester, pleasantly seated in a fine park, and on the bank of the river Were. The park, besides the pleasantness of it, has this much better thing to recommend it, namely, that it is full of excellent veins of the best coal in the country, (for the Lumley coal are known for their goodness at London, as well as there). This, with the navigable river just at hand, by which the coals are carried down to Sunderland to the ships, makes Lumley Park an inexhaustible treasure to the family.

They tell us, that King James the First lodg'd in this castle, at his entrance into England to take possession of the crown, and seeing a fine picture of the antient pedigree of the family, which carried it very far beyond what his majesty thought credible, turn'd this good jest upon it to the Bishop of Durham, who shewed it him, viz. *That indeed he did not know that Adam's sirname was Lumley before.*

From hence the road to Newcastle gives a view of the inexhausted store of coals and coal pits, from whence not London only, but all the south part of England is continually supplied; and whereas when we

209. 'South East prospect of Newcastle upon Tyne'; engraving by Samuel and Nathaniel Buck (1743).

are at London, and see the prodigious fleets of ships which come constantly in with coals for this encreasing city, we are apt to wonder whence they come, and that they do not bring the whole country away; so, on the contrary, when in this country we see the prodigious heaps, I might say mountains, of coals, which are dug up at every pit, and how many of those pits there are; we are filled with equal wonder to consider where the people should live that can consume them.

Newcastle is a spacious, extended, infinitely populous place; 'tis seated upon the river Tyne, which is here a noble, large and deep river, and ships of any reasonable burthen may come safely up to the very town. As the town lies on both sides the river, the parts are join'd by a very strong and stately stone bridge of seven very great arches, rather larger than the arches of London Bridge; and the bridge is built into a street of houses also, as London Bridge is.

The town itself, or liberty, as it is a corporation, extends but to part of the bridge, where there is a noble gate built all of stone, not much unlike that upon London Bridge, which so lately was a safeguard to the whole bridge, by stopping a terrible fire which otherwise had endangered burning the whole street of houses on the city side of the bridge, as it did those beyond it.

There is also a very noble building here, called the Exchange: and as the wall of the town runs parallel from it with the river, leaving a spacious piece of ground before it between the water and the wall, that ground, being well wharf'd up, and fac'd with freestone, makes the longest and largest key for landing and lading goods that is to be seen in England, except that at Yarmouth in Norfolk, and much longer than that at Bristol.

Here is a large hospital built by contribution of the keel men,[18] by way of friendly society, for the maintenance of the poor of their fraternity, and which, had it not met with discouragements from those who ought rather to have assisted so good a work, might have been a noble provision for that numerous and laborious people. The keel men are those who manage the lighters, which they call keels, by which the coals are taken from the steaths or wharfs, and carryed on board the ships, to load them for London.

Here are several large publick buildings also, as particularly a house of state for the mayor of the town (for the time being) to remove to, and dwell in during his year: also here is a hall for the surgeons, where they meet, where they have two skeletons of humane bodies, one a man and the other a woman, and some other rarities.

There are five or six churches in Newcastle, I mean on the town side, being north by Tine, besides meeting-houses, of which, I was told, there are also five or six, (including the Quakers) some of which are throng'd with multitudes of people, the place, as has been said, being exceeding populous. It is not only enriched by the coal trade; but there are also very considerable merchants in it, who carry on foreign trade to divers parts of the world, especially to Holland, Hamburgh, Norway, and the Baltick.

They build ships here to perfection, I mean as to strength, and firmness, and to bear the sea; and as the coal trade occasions a demand for such strong ships, a great many are built here. This gives an addition to the merchants' business, in requiring a supply of all sorts of naval stores to fit out those ships.

Here is also a considerable manufacture of hard ware, or wrought iron, lately erected after the manner of Sheffield, which is very helpful for employing the poor, of which this town has always a prodigious number.

West of this town lies the town of Hexham, a pass upon the Tine, famous, or indeed infamous, for having the first blood drawn at it, in the war against their prince by the Scots in King Charles the First's time, and where a strong detachment of English, tho' advantageously posted, were scandalously defeated by the Scots.

210. Detail of the Keelman's Hospital and main quay from pl. 209.

I was tempted greatly here to trace the famous Picts wall, built by the Romans, or rather rebuilt by them, from hence to Carlisle; of the particulars of which, and the remains of antiquity seen upon it, all our histories are so full; and I did go to several places in the fields thro' which it passed, where I saw the remains of it, some almost lost, some plain to be seen. But antiquity not being my business in this work, I omitted the journey, and went on for the north.

Northumberland is a long coasting county, lying

211. Detail of Berwick bridge and town from an engraving of Berwick by Samuel and Nathaniel Buck (1745).

chiefly on the sea to the east, and bounded by the mountains of Stainmore and Cheviot on the west, which are in some places inaccessible, in many unpassable. Here is abundant business for an antiquary; every place shews you ruin'd castles, Roman altars, inscriptions, monuments of battles, of heroes killed, and armies routed, and the like: the towns of Morpeth, Alnwick, Warkworth, Tickill, and many others, shew their old castles, and some of them still in tolerable repair, as Alnwick in particular, and Warkworth; others, as Bambrough, Norham, Chillingham, Horton, Dunstar, Wark, and innumerable more, are sunk in their own ruins, by the meer length of time.

We had Cheviot Hills so plain in view, that we could not but enquire of the good old women every where, whether they had heard of the fight at Chevy Chace:[19] they not only told us they had heard of it, but had all the account of it at their fingers end; and, taking a guide at Wooller to shew us the road, he pointed out distinctly to us the very spot where the engagement was: here, he said, Earl Piercy was killed, and there Earl Douglas, here Sir William Withington fought upon his stumps, here the Englishmen that were slain were buried, and there the Scots.

A little way off of this, north, he shewed us the field of battle, called Flodden Field,[20] upon the banks of the Till, where James IV King of Scotland, desperately

fighting, was killed, and his whole army overthrown by the English, under the noble and gallant Earl of Surrey, in the reign of King Henry VIII, upon their perfidiously invading England, while the king was absent on his wars in France.

I must not quit Northumberland without taking notice, that the natives of this country, of the antient original race or families, are distinguished by a shibboleth upon their tongues, namely, a difficulty in pronouncing the letter r, which they cannot deliver from their tongues without a hollow jarring in the throat, by which they are plainly known, as a foreigner is, in pronouncing the th: this they call the Northumbrian r, and the natives value themselves upon that imperfection, because, forsooth, it shews the antiquity of their blood.

From hence lay a road into Scotland, by the town of Kelso, which I after pass'd thro', but at present not willing to omit seeing Berwick upon Tweed, we turn'd to the west, and visited that old frontier, where indeed there is one thing very fine, and that is, the bridge over the Tweed, built by Queen Elizabeth, a noble, stately work, consisting of sixteen arches, and joining, as may be said, the two kingdoms. As for the town itself, it is old, decay'd, and neither populous nor rich; the chief trade I found here was in corn and salmon.

I am now on the borders of Scotland, and must

284

either enter upon it now, and so mix it with other parts of England, or take up short, and call to mind that I have not yet taken the western coast of England in my way, I mean, the three north west counties of Lancaster, Westmoreland and Cumberland.

I cannot but say, that since I entred upon the view of these northern counties, I have many times repented that I so early resolved to decline the delightful view of antiquity, here being so great and so surprizing a variety, and every day more and more discovered; and abundance since the tour which the learned Mr. Cambden made this way, nay, many since his learned continuator; for as the trophies, the buildings, the religious, as well as military remains, as well of the Britains, as of the Romans, Saxons, and Normans, are but, as we may say, like wounds hastily healed up, the calous spread over them being remov'd, they appear presently; and though the earth, which naturally eats into the strongest stones, metals, or whatever substance, simple or compound, is or can be by art or nature prepared to endure it, has defaced the surface, the figures and inscriptions upon most of these things, yet they are beautiful, even in their decay, and the venerable face of antiquity has something so pleasing, so surprizing, so satisfactory in it, especially to those who have with any attention read the histories of pass'd ages, that I know nothing renders travelling more pleasant and more agreeable.

But I have condemn'd myself (unhappily) to silence upon this head, and therefore, resolving however to pay this homage to the dust of gallant men and glorious nations, I say therefore, I must submit and go on; and as I resolve once more to travel through all these northern countries upon this very errand, and to please, nay, satiate myself with a strict search into every thing that is curious in nature and antiquity. I mortify myself now with the more ease, in hopes of letting the world see, some time or other, that I have not spent those hours in a vain and barren search, or come back without a sufficient reward to all the labours of a diligent enquirer; but of this by the way. I must, for the present, make this circuit shorter than usual, and leave the description of the other three counties to my next.

I am, &c.

The End of the Ninth Letter

LETTER X

Sir,

HAVING thus finished my account of the east side of the north division of England, I put a stop here, that I may observe the exact course of my travels; for as I do not write you these letters from the observations of one single journey, so I describe things as my journies lead me, having no less than five times travelled through the north of England, and almost every time by a different rout; purposely that I might see every thing that was to be seen, and, if possible, know every thing that is to be known, though not (at least till the last general journey) knowing or resolving upon writing these accounts to you. Now as by my exact observations on all these several traverses of the country, I hope I am not the less able, so I am sure I am much the better furnished, as well to tell you wherein others have ignorantly or superficially represented things, as to give you such other and fuller accounts, as in your own intended travels you will find confirmed, and by which you will be able the better to guide your farther enquiries.

I entred Lancashire at the remotest western point of that county, having been at West-Chester upon a particular occasion, and from thence ferry'd over from the Cestrian Chersonesus, as I have already call'd it, to Liverpoole. This narrow slip of land, rich, fertile and full of inhabitants, tho' formerly, as authors say, a meer waste and desolate forest, is called Wirall, or by some Wirehall. Here is a ferry over the Mersee, which, at full sea, is more than two miles over. We land on the flat shore on the other side, and are contented to ride through the water for some length, not on horseback but on the shoulders of some honest Lancashire clown, who comes knee deep to the boat side, to truss you up,[1] and then runs away with you, as nimbly as you desire to ride, unless his trot were easier; for I was shaken by him that I had the luck to be carry'd by more than I car'd for, and much worse than a hard trotting horse would have shaken me.

Liverpoole is one of the wonders of Britain, and that more, in my opinion, than any of the wonders of the Peak; the town was, at my first visiting it, about the

212. 'West prospect of the Town of Liverpool as it appeared about the year 1680'; engraving after John Eyes.

213. 'The South West Prospect of Liverpoole in the County Palatine of Lancaster'; engraving by Samuel and Nathaniel Buck (1728).

year 1680, a large, handsome, well built and encreasing or thriving town; at my second visit, anno 1690, it was much bigger than at my first seeing it, and, by the report of the inhabitants, more than twice as big as it was twenty years before that; but, I think, I may safely say at this my third seeing it, for I was surpriz'd at the view, it was more than double what it was at the second; and, I am told, that is still visibly encreases[2] both in wealth, people, business and buildings: what it may grow to in time, I know not.

The town has now an opulent, flourishing and encreasing trade, not rivalling Bristol, in the trade to Virginia, and the English island colonies in America only, but is in a fair way to exceed and eclipse it, by encreasing every way in wealth and shipping. They trade round the whole island, send ships to Norway, to Hamburgh, and to the Baltick, as also to Holland and Flanders; so that, in a word, they are almost become like the Londoners, universal merchants.

The new church built on the north side of the town is worth observation. 'Tis a noble, large building, all of stone, well finish'd; has in it a fine font of marble placed in the body of the church, surrounded with a beautiful iron pallisado; the gift of the late Mr. Heysham, a merchant of London, but considerably concerned in trade on this side, and for many years Member of Parliament for Lancaster. There is a beautiful tower to this church, and a new ring of eight very good bells.

The town-house is a fine modern building, standing all upon pillars of free-stone; the place under it is their Tolsey[3] or exchange, for the meeting of their merchants; but they begin to want room, and talk of enlarging it or removing the exchange to the other part of the town, where the ships and the merchants' business is nearer hand.

In a word, there is no town in England, London excepted, that can equal Liverpoole for the fineness of the streets, and beauty of the buildings; many of the houses are all of free stone, and compleatly finished;

and all the rest (of the new part I mean) of brick, as handsomely built as London itself.

The sea coast affords little remarkable on the west side of this port, till we come farther north; so we left that part of the county, and going east we came to Warrington. This is a large market town upon the river Mersee, over which there is a stately stone bridge, which is the only bridge of communication for the whole county with the county of Chester; it is on the great road from London leading to Carlisle and Scotland, and, in case of war, has always been esteemed a pass of the utmost importance.

Warrington is a large, populous old built town, but rich and full of good country tradesmen. Here is particularly a weekly market for linnen, as I saw at Wrexham in Wales, a market for flannel. The linnen sold at this market, is, generally speaking, a sort of table linnen, called huk-a-back[4] or huk-a-buk; 'tis well known among the good housewives, so I need not describe it. I was told there are generally as many pieces of this linnen sold here every market day as amounts to five hundred pounds value, sometimes much more, and all made in the neighbourhood of the place.

From hence, on the road to Manchester, we pass'd the great bog or waste call'd Chatmos, the first of that kind that we see in England, from any of the south parts hither. It extends on the left-hand of the road for five or six miles east and west, and they told us it was, in some places, seven or eight miles from north to south. The nature of these mosses,[5] for we found there are many of them in this country, is this, and you will take this for a description of all the rest.

The surface, at a distance, looks black and dirty, and is indeed frightful to think of, for it will bear neither horse or man, unless in an exceeding dry season, and then not so as to be passable, or that any one should travel over them.

The substance of the surface seems to be a collection of the small roots of innumerable vegetables matted

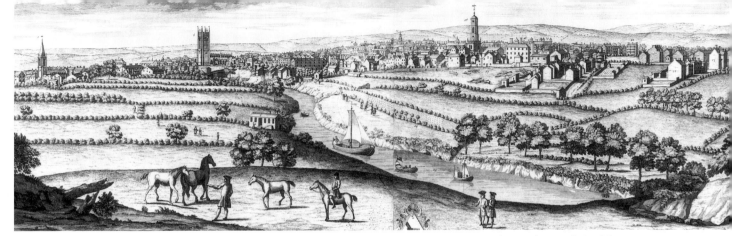

214. 'The South West prospect of Manchester and Salford'; engraving by John Harris after Robert Whitworth (1729).

together, interwoven so thick, as well the bigger roots as the smaller fibres, that it makes a substance hard enough to cut out into turf, or rather peat, which, in some places, the people cut out, and piling them up in the sun, dry them for their fewel. The roots I speak of are generally small and soft not unlike the roots of asparagus or of bearbind,[6] they have no earth among them, except what they contract from the air, and dust flying in it, but the rain keeps them, as it were always growing, though not much encreasing.

In some places the surface of this kind lies thicker, in some not very thick. We saw it in some places eight or nine foot thick, and the water that dreins from it look'd clear, but of a deep brown, like stale beer. What nature meant by such a useless production, 'tis hard to imagine; but the land is entirely waste, except, as above, for the poor cottagers' fuel, and the quantity used for that is very small.

Under this moss, or rather in the very body of it, not here only, but in several like places, and perhaps in all of them, those antient fir trees are found, of which so much dispute has been what they are or were, but especially how they should come there. Much mob-learning is sometimes expended upon these questions, which, in my weak judgment, amounts to no more than this; that nature, whose works are all directed by a superior hand, has been guided to produce trees here under ground, as she does in other places above ground; that these live rather than grow, though 'tis manifest they encrease too, otherwise they would not be found of so great a bulk; that as the trees above the surface grow erect and high, these lie prone and horizontal; those shoot forth branches and leaves; these shoot forth no branches or leaves, yet have a vegetation by methods directed by nature, and particularly to that kind; and 'tis remarkable, that as if they lie buried they will grown and encrease, so if you take them up, and plant them in the air, they will wither and die; and why should this be more strange than that a fish will strangle in the air, and a bird drown in the water, or

than that every thing lives in its proper element, and will not live, or at least not thrive out of it.

From hence we came on to **Manchester**, one of the greatest, if not really the greatest meer village in England. It is neither a wall'd town, city, or corporation; they send no members to Parliament; and the highest magistrate they have is a constable or headborough; and yet it has a collegiate church, several parishes, takes up a large space of ground, and including the suburb, or that part of the town called ———[7] over the bridge; it is said to contain above fifty thousand people; and though some people may think this strange, and that I speak by guess, and without judgment, I shall justify my opinion so well, that I believe, it will convince you my calculation is at least very probable, and much under what fame tells us is true.

The Manchester trade we all know; and all that are concerned in it know that it is, as all our other manufactures are, very much encreased within these thirty or forty years especially beyond what it was before; and as the manufacture is encreased, the people must be encreased of course. It is true, that the encrease of the manufacture may be by its extending itself farther in the country, and so more hands may be employed in the county without any encrease in the town. But I answer, that though this is possible, yet as the town and parish of Manchester is the center of the manufacture, the encrease of that manufacture would certainly encrease there first, and then the people there not being sufficient, it might spread itself further.

But the encrease of buildings at Manchester within these few years, is a confirmation of the encrease of people; for that within very few years past, here, as at Liverpoole, and as at Froom in Somersetshire, the town is extended in a surprising manner; abundance, not of new houses only, but of new streets of houses, are added, a new church also, and they talk of another, and a fine new square is at this time building; so that the town is almost double to what it was a few years

289

ago, and more than double to what it was at the time I am to mention.

The town of Manchester boasts of four extraordinary foundations, viz. a college, an hospital, a free-school, and a library, all very well supported.

I cannot doubt but this encreasing town will, some time or other, obtain some better face of government, and be incorporated, as it very well deserves to be.

About eight mile from Manchester, north west, lies **Bolton**, the town which gives title to the noble family of Powlet, Dukes of Bolton, raised to the heighth of duke by the late King William, at the same time, or near it, with the Dukes of Bedford, Devonshire, Rutland and Newcastle. We saw nothing remarkable in this town, but that the cotton manufacture reach'd hither; but the place did not, like Manchester, seem so flourishing and encreasing.

On the left hand of this town, west, even to the sea-shore, there are not many towns of note, except Wiggan, on the high post road, and Ormskirk, near which we saw Latham House, famous for its being not only gallantly defended in the times of the late fatal wars, but that it was so by a woman; for the Lady Charlotte, Countess of Derby,[8] defended the house to the last extremity against the Parliament forces; nor could she ever be brought to capitulate, but kept the hold till Prince Rupert, with a strong body of the king's army, came to her relief, and obliged the enemy to raise their siege, anno 1644: it was indeed ruin'd in a second siege, and is not yet fully recovered from the calamity of it.

In the neighbourhood of this town, that is to say, between Wiggan and Bolton, in the estate of Sir Roger Bradshaw, is found that kind of coal they call canell or candle coal, which, tho' they are found here in great plenty, and are very cheap, are yet very singular; for there are none such to be seen in Britain, or perhaps in the world besides: they so soon take fire, that, by putting a lighted candle to them, they are presently in a flame, and yet hold fire as long as any coals whatever, and more or less, as they are placed in the grate or hearth, whether flat or edg'd, whether right up and down, and polar, or level and horizontal.

They are smooth and slick when the pieces part from one another, and will polish like alabaster; then a lady may take them up in a cambrick handkerchief and they will not soil it, though they are as black as the deepest jet. They are the most pleasant agreeable fuel that can be found, but they are remote; and though some of them have been brought to London, yet they are so dear, by reason of the carriage, that few care to buy them; we saw some of them at Warrington too, but all from the same pits.

But I must now look northward. This great county, as we advance, grows narrow, and not only so, but mountainous, and not so full of towns or inhabitants as the south part, which I have been over; Preston and Lancaster are the only towns of note remaining.

Preston is a fine town, and tolerably full of people, but not like Liverpoole or Manchester; besides, we come now beyond the trading part of the county. Here's no manufacture; the town is full of attorneys,

215. 'West prospect of Preston from Penwortham Garden, August 1727'; preparatory wash and watercolour by Samuel Buck for an engraving never made.

proctors, and notaries, the process of law here being of a different nature than they are in other places, it being a dutchy[9] and county palatine, and having particular privileges of its own. The people are gay here, though not perhaps the richer for that; but it has by that obtained the name of Proud Preston. Here is a great deal of good company, but not so much, they say, as was before the late bloody action[10] with the northern rebels; not that the battle hurt many of the immediate inhabitants, but so many families there and thereabout, have been touched by the consequences of it, that it will not be recovered in a few years, and they seem to have a kind of remembrance of things upon them still.

Lancaster is the next, the county town, and situate near the mouth of the river Lone or Lune. The town is antient; it lies, as it were, in its own ruins, and has little to recommend it but a decayed castle, and a more decayed port (for no ships of any considerable burthen); the bridge is handsome and strong, but, as before, here is little or no trade, and few people. It surprized me to hear that there is not above sixty parishes in all this large county, but many of them are necessarily very large.

This part of the country seemed very strange to us, after coming out of so rich, populous and fruitful a place, as I have just now described; for here we were, as it were, lock'd in between the hills on one side high as the clouds, and prodigiously higher, and the sea on the other, and the sea itself seemed desolate and wild, for it was a sea without ships, here being no sea port or place of trade, especially for merchants; so that, except colliers passing between Ireland and Whitehaven with coals, the people told us they should not see a ship under sail for many weeks together.

Here, among the mountains, our curiosity was frequently moved to enquire what high hill this was, or that; and we soon were saluted with that old verse which I remembered to have seen in Mr. Cambden, viz.

Inglebrough, Pendle-hill and Penigent,
Are the highest hills between Scotland and Trent.

Indeed, they were, in my thoughts, monstrous high; but in a country all mountainous and full of innumerable high hills, it was not easy for a traveller to judge which was highest.

Nor were these hills high and formidable only, but they had a kind of an unhospitable terror in them. Here were no rich pleasant valleys between them, as among the Alps; no lead mines and veins of rich oar, as in the Peak; no coal pits, as in the hills about Hallifax, much less gold, as in the Andes, but all barren and

wild, of no use or advantage either to man or beast. Indeed here was formerly, as far back as Queen Elizabeth, some copper mines, and they wrought them to good advantage; but whether the vein of oar fail'd, or what else was the reason, we know not, but they are all given over long since, and this part of the country yields little or nothing at all.

But I must not forget Winander Meer, which makes the utmost northern bounds of this shire, which is famous for the char fish found here and hereabout, and no where else in England; it is found indeed in some of the rivers or lakes in Swisserland, among the Alps, and some say in north Wales; but I question the last. It is a curious fish, and, as a dainty, is potted, and sent far and near, as presents to the best friends; but the quantity they take also is not great. Mr. Cambden's continuator calls it very happily the Golden Alpine Trout.

216. Windermere char; engraving by P. Mazell after G. Wilkinson. From Thomas Pennant, *British Zoology* (1776–7; 4th edition).

Here we entred Westmoreland, a country eminent only for being the wildest, most barren and frightful of any that I have passed over in England, or even in Wales itself; the west side, which borders on Cumberland, is indeed bounded by a chain of almost unpassable mountains, which, in the language of the country, are called Fells, and these are called Fourness Fells, from the famous promontory bearing that name, and an abbey built also in antient times, and called Fourness.

But 'tis of no advantage to represent horror, as the character of a country, in the middle of all the frightful appearances to the right and left; yet here are some very pleasant, populous and manufacturing towns, and consequently populous.

Such as *Kirby Launsdale*, or Lunedale, because it stands on the river Lune, which is the boundary of the county, and leaves the hills of Mallerstang Forest, which are, in many places, unpassable. The manufac-

217. 'A view of Winander Meer, near Ambleside, a lake between Lancashire and Westmoreland'; Engraving by M. Chatelin and Müller after the painting by William Bellers (1753).

ture which the people are employed in here, are chiefly woollen cloths, at Kirkby Launsdale, and Kendal, and farther northward, a security for the continuance of the people in the place; for here is a vast concourse of people. In a word, I find no room to doubt the hills above mentioned go on to Scotland, for from some of the heighths hereabouts, they can see even into Scotland itself.

The upper, or northern part of the county, has two manufacturing towns, called Kirkby Stephen, and Appleby; the last is the capital of the county, yet neither of them offer any thing considerable to our observation, except a great manufacture of yarn stockings at the former.

When we entred at the south part of this county, I began indeed to think of Merionethshire, and the mountains of Snowden in north Wales, seeing nothing round me, in many places, but unpassable hills, whose tops, covered with snow, seemed to tell us all the pleasant part of England was at an end. The great

Winander Meer, like the Mediterranean Sea, extends itself on the west side for twelve miles and more, reckoning from North Bridge on the south, where it contracts itself again into a river up to Gresmere north, and is the boundary of the county, as I have said, on that side; and the English Appenine, as Mr. Cambden calls them, that is, the mountains of Yorkshire North Riding, lie like a wall of brass on the other; and indeed, in one sense, they are a wall of brass; for it is the opinion of the most skilful and knowing people in the country, that those mountains are full of inexhaustible mines of copper, and so rich, as not only to be called brass, copper being convertible into brass, but also to have a quantity of gold in them also: it is true, they do at this time work at some copper mines here, but they find the oar lies so deep, and is so hard to come at, that they do not seem to go cheerfully on.

But notwithstanding this terrible aspect of the hills, when having passed by Kendal, and descending the frightful mountains, we began to find the flat country show itself; we soon saw that the north and north east part of the county was pleasant, rich, fruitful, and, compared to the other part, populous. The river Eden, the last river of England on this side, as the Tyne is on the other, rises in this part out of the side of a monstrous high mountain, called Mowill Hill, or Wildbore Fell, which you please; after which, it runs through the middle of this vale, which is, as above, a very agreeable and pleasant country, or perhaps seems to be so the more, by the horror of the eastern and southern part.

In this vale, and on the bank of this river, stands Appleby, once a flourishing city, now a scattering, decayed, and half-demolished town, the fatal effects of the antient inroads of the Scots, when this being a frontier county, those invasions were frequent, and who several times were masters of this town, and at length burnt it to the ground, which blow it has not yet recovered.

Perith, or **Penrith**, is a handsome market town, populous, well built, and, for an inland town, has a very good share of trade. It was unhappily possessed by the late party of Scots Highland rebels, when they made that desperate push into England, and which ended at Preston; in the moor or heath, on the north part of this town, the militia of the county making a brave appearance, and infinitely out-numbering the Highlanders, were drawn up; yet, with all their bravery, then ran away, as soon as the Scots began to advance to charge them, and never fired a gun at them, leaving the town at their mercy. However, to do justice even to the rebels, they offered no injury to the town, only quartered in it one night, took what arms and ammunition they could find, and advanced towards Kendal.

From hence in one stage, through a country full of castles, for almost every gentleman's house is a castle, we came to **Carlisle**, a small, but well fortified city, the frontier place and key of England on the west sea, as Berwick upon Tweed is on the east; and in both which there have, for many years, I might say ages, been strong garrisons kept to check the invading Scots; from below this town the famous Picts Wall[11] began, which cross'd the whole island to Newcastle upon Tyne, where I have mentioned it already.

But before I go on to speak of this town, I must go back, as we did for our particular satisfaction, to the sea coast, which, in this northern county, is more remarkable than that of Lancashire, though the other is extended much farther in length; for here are some towns of good trade; whereas in Lancashire, Liverpoole excepted, there is nothing of trade to be seen upon the whole coast.

The cape or head land of St. Bees,[12] still preserves its name; as for the lady, like that of St. Tabbs beyond Berwick, the story is become fabulous, viz. about her procuring, by her prayers, a deep snow on Midsummer Day, her taming a wild bull that did great damage in the country; these, and the like tales, I leave where I found them, (viz.) among the rubbish of the old women and the Romish priests.

Under this shore, the navigation being secured by this cape of St. Bees, is the town of **Whitehaven**, grown up from a small place to be very considerable by the coal trade, which is encreased so considerably of late, that it is now the most eminent port in England for shipping off coals, except Newcastle and Sunderland, and even beyond the last, for they wholly supply the city of Dublin, and all the towns of Ireland on that coast; and 'tis frequent in time of war, or upon the ordinary occasion of cross winds, to have two hundred sail of ships at a time go from this place for Dublin, loaden with coals.

About ten miles from Whitehaven north east, lies Cockermouth, upon the little river Cocker, just where it falls into the Derwent. This Derwent is famous for its springing out of those hills, call'd Derwent Fells, where the ancient copper mines were found in Queen Elizabeth's time, and in which, it was said, there was a large quantity of gold. But they are discontinued since that time, for what reason, I know not; for there are several copper mines now working in this county, and which, as they told me, turn to very good account.

Some tell us, the copper mines on Derwent Fells were discontinued, because there being gold found among the oar, the Queen claimed the royalty[13] and so no body would work them; which seems to be a reason why they shou'd have been applied to the search with more vigor; but be that how it will, they are left off, and the more probable account is, what a gentleman of Penrith gave us, namely, that the charge of working them was too great for the profits.

Here are still mines of black lead found, which turn to very good account, being, for ought I have yet learned, the only place in Britain where it is to be had.

Here we saw Skiddaw, one of those high hills of which, wherever you come, the people always say, they are the highest in England. Skiddaw indeed is a very high hill, but seems the higher, because not surrounded with other mountains, as is the case in most places where the other hills are, as at Cheviot, at Penigent, and at other places. From the top of Skiddaw they see plainly into Scotland, and quite into Dumfries-shire, and farther.

Cockermouth stands upon this river Derwent, about twelve miles from the sea, but more by the windings

XXXVI (following pages). Matthias Read, *Whitehaven, Cumberland* (c.1730–35).

218. 'North West view of Cockermouth castle, in the county of Cumberland'; engraving by Samuel and Nathaniel Buck (1739).

of the river, yet vessels of good burthen may come up to it. The Duke of Somerset is chief lord of this town, in right of his lady, the only heiress of the ancient family of the Piercy's, Earls of Northumberland, and which the Duke of Somerset enjoys now in right of marriage.

The castles and great houses of this estate go every where to ruin, as indeed all the castles in this county do; for there being no more enemy to be expected here, the two kingdoms being now united into one, there is no more need of strong holds here, than in any other part of the kingdom. At Cockermouth there is a castle which belongs to the same family, and, I think they told us, the duke has no less than thirteen castles in all, here and in Northumberland.

This river Derwent is noted for very good salmon, and for a very great quantity, and trout. Hence, that is, from Workington at the mouth of this river, and from Carlisle, notwithstanding the great distance, they at this time carry salmon (fresh as they take it) quite to London. This is perform'd with horses, which, changing often, go night and day without intermission, and, as they say, very much out-go the post; so that the fish come very sweet and good to London, where the extraordinary price they yield, being often sold at two shillings and sixpence to four shillings per pound, pay very well for the carriage.

They have innumerable marks of antiquity in this county, as well as in that of Westmoreland, mentioned before; and if it was not, as I said before, that antiquity is not my search in this work, yet the number of altars, monuments, and inscriptions, is such, that it would take up a larger work than this to copy them, and record them by themselves; yet, passing these, I could

not but take notice of two or three more modern things, and which relate to our own nation: such as,

1. That of Hart-Horn Tree, where they shew'd us the head of a stag nail'd up against a tree, or rather shew'd us the tree where they said it was nail'd up, in memory of a famous chase of a stag by one single dog. It seems the dog (not a greyhound, as Mr. Cambden's continuator calls it, but a stanch buckhound, to be sure) singly chas'd a stag from this place, (Whinfield Park) as far as the Red Kirk in Scotland, which, they say, is sixty miles at least, and back again to the same place, where, being both spent, and at the last gasp, the stag strain'd all its force remaining to leap the park pales, did it, and dy'd on the inside; the hound, attempting to leap after him, had not strength to get over, but fell back, and dy'd on the outside just opposite; after which the heads of both were nail'd up upon the tree, and this distich made on them; the hound's name, it seems, was Hercules.

Hercules kill'd Hart a Greese,
And Hart a Greese kill'd Hercules.

2. Another thing they told us was in the same park, viz. three oak trees which were call'd the Three Brether, the least of which was thirteen yards about; but they own'd there was but one of them left, and only the stump of that; so we did not think it worth going to see, because it would no more confirm the wonder, than the people's affirming it by tradition only. The tree or stump left, is call'd the Three Brether Tree, that is to say, one of the three brothers, or brethren.

3. West of this Hart-horn tree, and upon the old Roman way, is the famous column, call'd the Countess

Pillar,[14] the best and most beautiful piece of its kind in Britain. It is a fine column of free-stone, finely wrought, enchas'd, and in some places painted. There is an obelisk on the top, several coats of arms, and other ornaments in proper places all over it, with dials also on every side, and a brass-plate with the following inscription upon it:

THIS PILLAR WAS ERECTED ANNO MDCLVI, BY THE RIGHT HONORABLE ANNE COUNTESS DOWAGER OF PEMBROKE, AND SOLE HEIR OF THE RIGHT HONORABLE GEORGE EARL OF CUMBERLAND, &C. FOR A MEMORIAL OF HER LAST PARTING IN THIS PLACE WITH HER GOOD AND PIOUSE MOTHER THE RIGHT HONORABLE MARGARETE COUNTESS DOWAGER OF CUMBERLAND, THE SECOUND OF APRIL, MDCXVI, IN MEMORY WHEREOF SHE ALSO LEFT AN ANNUITY OF FOUR POUNDS, TO BE DISTRIBUTED TO THE POOR WITHIN THIS PARISH OF BROUGHAM EVERY SECOND DAY OF APRIL FOR EVER UPON THE STONE TABLE HERE BY.

4. At Penrith also we saw several remarkable things, some of which I find mentioned by the right

219. The Three Brethren tree; engraving after O. Neale (published after 1750).

PILLARS IN PENRITH CHURCH YARD

220. The Giants Grave: pillars and headstones in Penrith church yard; engraving from Thomas Pennant, *A Tour in Scotland* (1769), pl. xxxvi

reverend continuator of Mr. Cambden, and which I was glad to see, so confirm'd my observation, viz. (1.) Two remarkable pillars fourteen or fifteen foot asunder, and twelve foot high the lowest of them, though they seem equal. The people told us, they were the monument of Sir Owen Cæsar,[15] the author abovenam'd calls him, Sir Ewen Cæsarius, and perhaps he may be right; but we have no inscription upon them. This Sir Owen, they tell us, was a champion of mighty strength, and of gygantick stature, and so he was, to be sure, if, as they say, he was as tall as one of the columns, and could touch both pillars with his hand at the same time.

They relate nothing but good of him, and that he exerted his mighty strength to kill robbers, such as infested the borders much in those days, others related wild boars; but the former is most probable. (2.) On the north side of the vestry of this church is erected in the wall an ancient square stone, with a memorial,

XXXVII. Anthony Devis, *View of Derwentwater and Skiddaw from Lord's Island* (*c.*1750–55).

221. 'North West view of Carlisle Castle'; engraving by Samuel and Nathaniel Buck (1739).

intimating, that in the year 1598 there was a dreadful plague in those parts, in which there dy'd;

	Persons.
In Kendal,	2500
In Penrith,	2266
In Richmond,	2200
In Carlisle,	1196
	8162

N.B. By this account it should seem that every one of those towns had separately more people that the city of Carlisle, and that Kendal, which is the only manufacturing town of them, was the most populous.

Though I am backward to dip into antiquity, yet no English man, that has any honour for the glorious memory of the greatest and truest hero of all our kings of the English or Saxon race, can go to Carlisle, and not step aside to see the monument of King Edward I[16] at Burgh upon the Sands, a little way out of the city Carlisle, where that victorious prince dy'd. Indeed I cannot wonder that two writers, both Scots, viz. Ridpath and Mr. Kay, should leave it, as it were, not worth their notice, that prince being the terror of Scotland, and the first compleat conqueror of their country, who brought away the sacred stone at Scone Abbey, on which their kings were crowned, also the regalia, and, in a word, made their whole country submit to his victorious arms.

But I return to Carlisle: the city is strong, but small, the buildings old, but the streets fair; the great church is a venerable old pile, it seems to have been built at twice, or, as it were, rebuilt, the upper part being much more modern than the lower.

King Henry VIII fortify'd this city against the Scots, and built an additional castle to it on the east side, which Mr. Cambden, though I think not justly, calls a cittadel; there is indeed another castle on the west, part of the town rounds the sea, as the wall rounds the whole, is very firm and strong. But Carlisle is strong by situation, being almost surrounded with rivers. On the east it has the river Poterell, on the north Eden, and on the south the Cande, or Canda, or Calda, which all fall into the arm of the sea, which they call the Solway, or Solway Firth.

Here is a bridge over the Eden, which soon lets you into Scotland; for the limits are not above eight miles off, or thereabout. The south part of Scotland on this side, coming at least fifty miles farther into England, than at Berwick. There is not a great deal of trade here either by sea or land, it being a meer frontier. On the other side the Eden we saw the Picts Wall, of which I have spoken already, and some remains of it are to be seen farther west, and of which I shall perhaps have occasion to speak again in my return. But being now at the utmost extent of England on this side, I conclude also my letter, and am,

Sir, &c.

The End of the Tenth Letter

LETTER XI

SIR,

I AM NOW JUST ENTER'D Scotland, and that by the ordinary way from Berwick. We tread upon Scots ground, after about three miles riding beyond Berwick; the little district between, they say, is neither in England or Scotland, and is call'd Berwickshire, as being formerly a dependant upon the town of Berwick; but we find no towns in it, only straggling farm-houses; and one sees the Tweed on one side, which fetches a reach northward, the sea on the other, and the land between lies so high, that in stormy weather 'tis very bleak and unpleasant; however, the land is good, and compar'd to our next view, we ought to think very well of it.

Mordintown lying to the west, the great road does not lie thro' it, but carries us to the brow of a very high hill, where we had a large view into Scotland: but we were welcom'd into it with such a Scots gale of wind, that, besides the steepness of the hill, it oblig'd us to quit our horses, for real apprehensions of being blown off, the wind blowing full north, and the road turning towards the north, it blew directly in our faces: And I can truly say, I never was sensible of so fierce a wind, so exceeding keen and cold, for it pierc'd our very eyes, that we could scarcely bear to hold them open.

When we came down the hill, the strength of the wind was not felt so much, and, consequently, not the cold. The first town we come to is as perfectly Scots, as if you were 100 miles north of Edinburgh; nor is there the least appearance of any thing English, either in customs, habits, usages of the people, or in their way of living, eating, dress, or behaviour; any more than if they had never heard of an English nation; nor was there an Englishman to be seen, or an English family to be found among them.

On the contrary, you have in England abundance of Scotsmen, Scots customs, words, habits, and usages, even more than becomes them; nay, even the buildings in the towns, and in the villages, imitate the Scots almost all over Northumberland; witness their building the houses with the stairs (to the second floor) going up on the outside of the house, so that one family may live below, and another above, without going in at the same door; which is the Scots way of living, and which we see in Alnwick and Warkworth, and several other towns; witness also their setting their corn up in great numbers of small stacks without doors, not making use of any barns, only a particular building, which they call a barn, but, which is itself no more than a threshing-floor, into which they take one of those small stacks at a time, and thresh it out, and then take in another; which we have great reason to believe was the usage of the antients, seeing we read of threshing-floors often; but very seldom, of a barn, except that of the rich glutton.

Being down this hill, we pass'd a bridge over the little river Eye, at the mouth of which there is a small harbour, with a town call'd Eyemouth, or, as some call it, Heymouth, which has of late been more spoken of than formerly, by giving the title of Baron to the late Duke of Marlborough, who was Duke of Marlborough, Marquiss of Blandford, and Baron of Eyemouth in Scotland; and, by virtue of this title, had a right of peerage in the Parliament of Scotland. But notwithstanding all this, I never heard that he did any thing for the town, which is, at present, just what it always was, a good fishing town, and some fishing vessels belong to it; for such it is a good harbour, and for little else.

From this bridge we enter upon a most desolate, and, in winter, a most frightful moor for travellers, especially strangers, call'd Coudingham, or, to speak properly, Coldingham Moor; upon which, for about eight miles, you see hardly a hedge, or a tree, except in one part, and that at a good distance; nor do you meet with but one house in all the way, and that no house of entertainment; which, we thought, was but a poor reception for Scotland to give her neighbours, who were strangers, at their very first entrance into her bounds.

Having pass'd this desart, which indeed, makes a stranger think Scotland a terrible place, you come down a very steep hill into the Lothains, so the counties are divided, and they are spoken of in plural; because as Yorkshire is divided into the East and

West Riding, so here is the East, and West, and Mid Lothain, or Louthain, and therefore justly call'd Lothains in the plural.

From the top of this hill you begin to see that Scotland is not all desart; and the low lands, which then show themselves, give you a prospect of a fruitful and pleasant country: As soon as we come down the hill, there is a village call'd Cockburnspeth, vulgarly Cobberspeth, where nature forms a very steep and difficult pass, and where, indeed, a thousand men well furnish'd, and boldly doing their duty, would keep out an army, if there was occasion.

The first gentleman's house we met with in Scotland was that of Dunglass, the seat of Sir James Hall; a gentleman so hospitable, so courteous to strangers, so addicted to improve and cultivate his estate, and understood it so well, that we began to see here a true representation of the gentry of Scotland; than whom, I must say, without compliment, none in Europe, understand themselves better, or better deserve the name of gentlemen. We began also to see that Scotland was not so naturally barren, as some people represent it, but, with application and judgment, in the proper methods of improving lands, might be made to equal, not England only, but even the richest, most fruitful, most pleasant, and best improv'd part of England: Nor, if I have any skill in the nature of improving lands, which I a little pretend to, or judgment of what land itself is capable of, is the county of Middlesex, or Hertfordshire, which is esteem'd the most completely improv'd part of England, and the richest soil, capable of any improvement, which this country of East Lothain is not also capable of, if they had the same methods of improvement, and the Scots were as good husbandmen as the English; and even this too might easily be brought to pass, would the gentlemen set about it, as this gentleman has, in part, already done, at their own expence.

The truth is, the soil hereabout is very good; and tho' they have not marle, or chalk, or much lime-stone to mend and manure it, yet, the sea-ware, as they call the weeds, which the sea casts up, abundantly supplies; and by laying this continually on the land, they plow every year without laying their lands fallow, as we do; and I found they had as much corn, as our plowmen express it, as could stand upon the ground.

The first town of note, from hence, is **Dunbar**, a royal burgh, so they are call'd in Scotland, which is (much what) we call a corporation in England, and which sent members to Parliament, as our corporations in England do, only that in Scotland, as is generally to be understood, they had some particular privileges separate to themselves; as that, for example, of holding a Parliament, or Convention of Burghs[1] by themselves, a method taken from the union of the Hans-Towns in the north, and not much unlike it, in which they meet and concert measures for the publick good of the town, and of their trade, and make by-laws, or acts, and declarations, which bind the whole body.

Nor have they lost this privilege by the Union with England; but it is preserved entire, and, perhaps, is now many ways more advantageous to them than it was before, as their trade is like to be, in time, more considerable than before.

222. Dunbar Castle and the Bass Rock; pen and watercolour by Francis Place (c.1701).

XXXVIII. Unknown painter, *Yester House, East Lothian* (before 1685).

This town of Dunbar is a handsome well-built town, upon the sea-shore; where they have a kind of a natural harbour, tho' in the middle of dangerous rocks.

They have here a great herring-fishery, and particularly they hang herrings here, as they do at Yarmouth in Norfolk, for the smoking them; or, to speak the ordinary dialect, they make red herrings here: I cannot say they are cur'd so well as at Yarmouth, that is to say, not for keeping and sending on long voyages, as to Venice and Leghorn, though, with a quick passage, they might hold it thither too: however, they do it very well. The herrings also themselves may a little make the difference, because they are generally larger and fatter than those at Yarmouth, which makes it more difficult to cure them, so as to keep in a hot country, and on a long voyage.

Between the town and the great road stands a little, but pleasant and agreeable seat of the Duke of Roxburgh, with a park well planted: And as the gentlemen of Scotland are now set upon planting forest trees, as well for ornament as profit, this park is, among the rest, very handsomely planted with young trees in vista's and walks, and will, when grown, add both to the value and beauty of the seat, which otherwise is but as a box. And here I would give an useful hint to the gentlemen who plant trees in Scotland, the want of which I have observ'd at several great houses and parks in that country, is the reason why they do not thrive, as they might otherwise do: the case is this.

The gentlemen, at a great expence, get quantities of forest trees, either of their own raising, or from the nursery-men, as they call them in England. Those are set at a good length, perhaps, 12 to 15 foot high, handsome bodies, and good heads; and I acknowledge they are the best siz'd trees to plant, and that when set younger they seldom stand it, or come to the like perfection: but then these trees should be all secur'd by a triangular frame to each tree; that is to say, three large stakes set about them in an equilateral triangle, and fasten'd all together by three short cross pieces at the top; and these stakes should stand from 7 to 8 foot high.

In the center of the triangle stands the planted tree; which way soever the wind blows, the body bends from it to the cross piece, which joins the stakes on that side, and which make the triangle, and then can bend no farther; by which means the root is not shaken, or the earth mov'd and loosen'd about it, and then the tree will strike root, and grow.

But for want of this, the tree being left without support, before, as we may say, it can stand alone; and the winds, especially in winter, being very strong in that country, the tree is bended every way, the earth loosen'd continually about it, the root is often stirr'd, and the tree gets no time to strike root into the earth. And this is the reason why, in many of the gentlemens' parks, I saw the trees stented and bauk'd;[2] and that, tho' they had been planted many years, they could not thrive: If this caution may be of use, as I recommend it with a desire it may, the gentlemen will not think their time lost in the reading it.

Here we turn'd out of the way to see the Marquess of Tweedal's[3] fine park, and which is, indeed, the main thing, his fine planting at Yester, or, as antiquity calls it, Zester; I say the park, because, tho' there is the design of a noble house or palace, and great part of it built; yet, as it is not yet, and perhaps, will not soon be finished, there is no giving a compleat description of it.

The old Earl of Tweedale,[4] who was a great favourite of King Charles II tho' not much concern'd in politic affairs, at least, not in England, yet took in from the King the love of managing what we call forest trees, and making fine vistas and avenues: The very first year after the restoration the King laid out, with his own hand, the planting of Greenwich and St. James's parks, and several others, and the said Earl had seen them, and was extremely delighted with the method.

This occasion'd his Lordship, as soon as he went down into Scotland, to lay out the plan and design of all those noble walks and woods of trees, or, as it might be call'd, forests of trees, which he afterwards saw planted, and of which a gentleman, whose judgment I cannot doubt, told me, that if ever those trees came to be worth but six pence a tree, they would be of more value than the fee simple of that estate; not meaning by that estate the land they grow on, but the whole paternal estate of the family: nor is it unlikely, if it be true, that his Lordship, and his immediate successor, planted above 6000 acres of land all full of firr-trees; and that, where-ever it was found that any tree fail'd, they were constantly renew'd the next year.

The park itself is said to be eight miles about, but the plantation of firr is not simply confin'd to the park, nor, indeed, to this estate; for the family of Tweedale has another seat near Musclebro, at Pinkey, where the same Lord planted also a great number of trees, as his successors have likewise done at another seat, which they have in Fife, near Aberdour.

As the success of this planting is a great encouragement to the nobility of Scotland to improve their estates by the same method, so we find abundance of gentlemen of estates do fall into it, and follow the example: And you hardly see a gentleman's house, as you pass the Louthains, towards Edinburgh, but they are distinguish'd by groves and walks of firr-trees about them; which, tho' in most places they are but young, yet they shew us, that in a few years, Scotland will not need to send to Norway for timber and deal, but will have sufficient of her own, and perhaps, be able to furnish England too with considerable quantities.

From this town of Dunbar to Edinburgh, the country may be reckon'd not only as fruitful and rich in soil, but also as pleasant and agreeable a country as any in Scotland, and, indeed, as most in England; the sea on the right hand, at a moderate distance, and the hills on the left, at a farther distance; and even those hills not extremely high, not barren, not desolate mountains, as I have given an account of some farther south, and have more to speak of farther north. But these hills are passable and habitable, and have large flocks of sheep, in many places, feeding on them, and many open roads lie over them, as from Edinburgh, and other parts towards England; as particularly to Yester, and to Duns and Coldstream on the Tweed; another way to Kelsoe, where also there is a ford and a ferry over the Tweed, and likewise by another way to Tiviotdale, to Peebles and Jedburgh, of which hereafter.

The greatest thing this country wants is more enclos'd pastures, by which the farmers would keep stocks of cattle well fodder'd in the winter, and, which again, would not only furnish good store of butter, cheese, and beef to the market, but would, by their quantity of dung, enrich their soil, according to the unanswerable maxim in grazing, that stock upon land improves land.

Two other articles would encrease and enrich them, but which they never practise.

1. Folding their sheep.

2. Fallowing their plow'd land.

The first would fatten the land, and the latter destroy the weeds: but this is going out of my way. They have, indeed, near the sea, an equivalent which assists them exceedingly, namely, the sea weed, they call it the sea ware, which the sea casts up from about November to January in great quantities, and which extremely fattens and enriches the lands, so that they are plow'd from age to age without lying fallow: But farther from the sea, and where they cannot fetch it, there they are forc'd to lay the lands down to rest; when, as we say in England, they have plow'd them out of heart, and so they get no advantage by them; whereas could they, by a stock of cattle, raise a stock of muck, or by folding sheep upon them, mend them that way, and lay them down one year in three or four, as we do in England, the lands would hold from one generation to another.

But at present, for want of enclosures, they have no winter provision for black cattle; and, for want of that winter-provision, the farmers have no dairies, no butter or cheese; that is to say, no quantity, and no heaps of dung in their yards to return upon the land for its improvement: and thus a good soil is impoverish'd for want of husbandry.

From Dunbar we pass another river Tyne, which, to distinguish it from the two Tynes in Northumberland, I call Scots Tyne, tho' not forgetting to let you know it is not so distinguish'd there, the inhabitants thereabouts scarce knowing any other. It rises in the hills near Yester, and watering part of the fine and pleasant vale I mentioned before, runs by **Haddington**, an old half ruin'd, yet remaining town; which shews the marks of decay'd beauty, for it was formerly a

223. Detail of the prospect of Haddington; engraving. From John Slezer, *Theatrum Scotiae* (1693).

224. Haddington, East Lothian; etching after a drawing by Paul Sandby (c.1750).

large, handsome, and well built town, or city rather, and esteem'd very strong.

However, Haddington is still a good town, has some handsome streets, and well built; and they have a good stone bridge over the Tyne, tho' the river is but small. The church was large, but has suffer'd in the ruin of the rest, and is but in part repair'd, tho' 'tis still large enough for the number of inhabitants; for, tho' the town is still what may be call'd populous, 'tis easy to see that it is not like what it has been. There are some monuments of the Maitlands, antient lords of this part of the country, remaining; but as the choir of the church is open and defac'd, the monuments of the dead have suffer'd with the rest.

I saw here something of a manufacture, and a face of industry; and it was the first that I had seen the least appearance of in Scotland; particularly here, was a woollen manufacture, erected by a company, or corporation, for making broad cloths, such as they call'd English cloth. And as they had English workmen employ'd, and, which was more than all, English wool, they really made very good cloth, well mix'd, and good colours: But I cannot say they made it as cheap, or could bring it so cheap to market as the English; and this was the reason, that, tho' before the late Union, the English cloth being prohibited upon severe penalties, their own cloth supplied them very well; yet, as soon as the Union was made, and by that means the English trade open'd, the clothiers from Worcester, and the counties adjoining, such as Gloucester and Wilts, brought in their goods, and underselling the Scots, those manufactories were not able to hold it.

However, as I said, here was a woollen manufacture, and the people being employ'd in spinning, dying, weaving, &c. they turn'd their hands to other things; and there is still some business going on to the advantage of the poor. Also upon the Tyne, near Haddington, we saw very good fulling-mills; whether they still have employment, I am not certain. They talk'd also of setting up a paper-mill after the Union, the French paper being not allow'd to be imported as formerly.

At the mouth of this river stands the remains of Tantallon[5] Castle, mostly bury'd in its own ruins; it was famous, in the Scots history, for being the seat of rebellion, in the reign of King James V. And hence came the old, and odd fancy among the soldiers, that the drums beating the Scots march, say, Ding down Tan-Tallon. That beat or march being invented by King James the Vth's soldiers (or, perhaps, drummers) when they march'd against the Earl of Angus, who held out Tantallon Castle against the King. But this by the way: Tantallon is now no more a fortress, or able to shelter a rebel army.

Neither is the Bass worth naming any more, which being a meer rock, standing high out of the sea, and in its situation inaccessible, was formerly made a small fortification, rather to prevent its being made a retreat for pyrates and thieves, than for any use it could be of to command the sea; for the entrance of the Forth, or Firth, is so wide, that ships would go in and out, and laugh at any thing that could be offer'd from the Bass. The most of its modern fame is contain'd in two articles, and neither of them recommend it to posterity.

1. That in the times of tyranny and cruelty, under the late King Charles II and King James II it was made a state-prison, where the poor persecuted western people, call'd, in those times, Cameronians,[6] were made close prisoners, and liv'd miserably enough, without hope or expectation of deliverance, but by death.

2. That after the Revolution a little desperate crew of people got possession of it; and, having a large boat, which they hoisted up into the rock, or let down at pleasure, committed several pyracies, took a great many vessels, and held out the last of any place in Great Britain for King James; but their boat being at last seiz'd, or otherwise lost, they were oblig'd to surrender.

The Soland geese[7] are the principal inhabitants of this island, a fowl rare as to the kind; for they are not found in any part of Britain, that I can learn, except here, and at some of the lesser islands in the Orcades, and in the island of Ailzye, in the mouth of

225. Tantallon Castle; pen and watercolour by Paul Sandby (*c.*1750)

226. 'Prospect of Bass Rock from the south shore'; engraving. From John Slezer, *Theatrum Scotiae* (1693).

the Clyde. They come as certainly at their season, as the swallows or woodcocks, with this difference, if what the people there tell us may be depended on; that they come exactly, to the very same day of the month, or, if they change it for reasons best known to themselves, then they keep exactly to the new fix'd day;

227. The Soland Goose (*anser bassanus*). From Eleazar Albin, *A Natural history of birds* (1738), pl. lxxxvi. Now better known as the gannet.

and so, upon any alteration of their time, which also is very seldom.

They feed on the herrings, and therefore 'tis observ'd they come just before, or with them, and go away with them also; tho', 'tis evident, they do not follow them, but go all away to the north, whither, as to that, none knows but themselves, and he that guides them: As they live on fish, so they eat like fish, which, together with their being so exceeding fat, makes them, in my opinion, a very coarse dish, rank, and ill relish'd, and soon gorging the stomach. But as they are look'd upon there as a dainty, I have no more to say, all countries have their several gusts and particular palates. Onions and garlick were dainties it seems, in Ægypt, and horse-flesh is so to this day in Tartary, and much more may a Soland goose be so in other places.

It is a large fowl, rather bigger than an ordinary goose; 'tis duck-footed, and swims as a goose; but the bill is long, thick, and pointed like a crane, or heron, only much thicker, and not above five inches long. Their laying but one egg, which sticks to the rock, and will not fall off, unless pull'd off by force, and then not to be stuck on again; though we thought them fictions, yet, being there at the season, we found true;

as also their hatching, by holding the egg fast in their foot. What nature meant by giving these singularities to a creature, that has nothing else in it worth notice, we cannot determine.

From hence, keeping the shore of the Firth, or Forth, due west, we find a range of large and populous villages all along the coast, almost to Leith, interspers'd, with abundance of the houses of the nobility and gentry, at a small distance from them, farther into the country.

The towns upon this coast, as I said, stand very thick, and here are two or three articles of trade which render them more populous, and more considerable than they would otherwise be.

1. There are great quantities of white fish taken and cur'd upon this coast, even within, as well as at the mouth of the Firth; and, as I had occasion to inspect this part, I took notice the fish was very well cur'd, merchantable, and fit for exportation; and there was a large ship at that time come from London, on purpose to take in a loading of that fish for Bilboa in Spain.

2. There is great plenty of coal in the hills, and so near the sea as to make the carriage not difficult; and much of that coal is carried to Edinburgh, and other towns about, for sale.

3. The coal being thus at hand, they make very good salt at almost all the towns upon the shore of the Firth; as at Seaton, Cockenny, Preston, and several others, too many to name: They have a very great trade for this salt to Norway, Hamburgh, Bremen, and the Baltick; and the number of ships loaded here yearly with salt is very considerable; nay, the Dutch and Bremers in particular, come hither on purpose to load salt, as they do on the opposite side of the Firth also, (viz.) the shore of Fife, of which I shall speak in its place.

4. They take great quantities of oysters upon this shore also, with which they not only supply the city of Edinburgh, but they carry abundance of them in large, open boats, call'd cobles, as far as Newcastle upon Tyne, from whence they generally bring back glass bottles. But there has, within a few years, a bottle-house been set up at Leith, which, for a while, work'd with success; also some furnaces were erected at Preston-Pans, one of those villages, for making flint-glass, and other glass ware: but I hear they are discontinued for want of skilful hands.

It must not be omitted, that at several of those villages there are little moles and harbours, or peers, and heads built up at considerable expence, for the securing the ships that come to them to load salt, or other goods; as at Seaton, Cokenny, at North Berwick, at Preston, and other places.

We come now to **Musclebro**, a large borough-town and populous, and may, indeed, be said to be a cluster of towns, all built together into one, namely, Musclebro, Innerask, or Inneresk, and Fisheraw; all which amount to no more than this. Musclebro, or the main or chief town of Musclebro; Inneresk, or that part of Musclebro which stands within, or on the inner side of the river Esk, and Fisheraw, or the row of houses where the fishermen usually dwell; for here is still many fishermen, and was formerly many more, when the muscle fishing was counted a valuable thing; but now 'tis given over, tho' the muscles lye on the shore, and on the shoals of sand in the mouth of this river, in vast quantities.

These three towns together make one large burrough, very populous; for here are thought to be more people than at Haddington. Here also we saw the people busy on the woollen manufacture; and as the goods they made here were an ordinary kind of stuff for poor people's wearing, we do not find they are out-done at all from England, so that the manufacture is carried on here still with success.

They call this a sea-port town; but as their river, tho' sometimes full enough of water, is not navigable; for, at low water, people ride over the mouth of it upon the sands, and even walk over it; so they do not meddle much with trading by sea.

At that part of the town call'd Inner-Esk are some handsome country houses with gardens, and the citizens of Edinburgh come out in the summer and take lodgings here for the air, as they do from London at Kensington Gravel-Pits, or at Hampstead and Highgate.

Adjoining to this part is the other fine seat of the Marquess of Tweedale, call'd Pinkey, which I mention'd before, and which the family resides at, rather than at Yester.

The house of Pinkey has a park, which they call four miles about, but, I think is not much above half so much: but the spirit of planting, which the old Earl of Tweedale so happily exerted at Yester, shew'd itself here also, and an innumerable number of fir trees are seen here in a very thriving condition, and promising, in time, to be of an inestimable value.

As the house at Yester is not finish'd, all the rich furniture, and especially pictures, of which the same Earl was a great collector, are lodg'd here; though, 'tis not doubted, they will hereafter be transpos'd and remov'd to adorn the chief palace and mansion of the family. Here are, indeed, a great many valuable pieces of painting, but the family pieces are particular, and very remarkable, some for their antiquity, and the antient dress of the age they were wrought in, and others, for the fineness of the workmanship; as especially that of the old Marquess of Tweedale, and

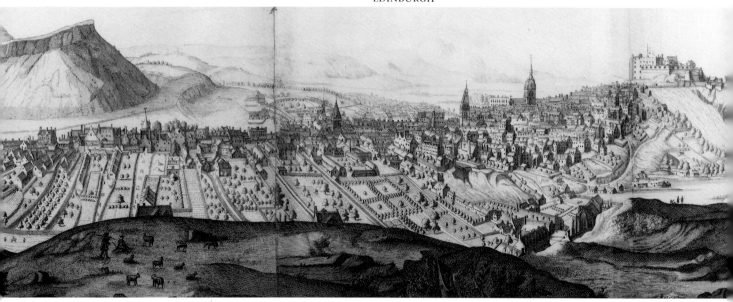

228. 'The North Prospect of the city of Edinburgh'; engraving originally sold by John Bowles but included in 1719 edition of John Slezer, *Theatrum Scotiae*.

his fifteen children, done after the manner of that of King Charles I and his royal family,[8] which formerly stood at the upper end of the long gallery, at White-hall. So this stands at the upper end of a large room, fill'd up with other family pieces, and takes up one whole square of the room.

I am now at the gates of **Edinburgh**; but before I come to describe the particulars of that city, give me leave to take it in perspective, and speak something of its situation, which will be very necessary with respect to some disadvantage which the city lyes under on that account.

When you stand at a small distance, and take a view of it from the east, you have really but a confus'd idea of the city, because the situation being in length from east to west, and the breadth but ill proportion'd to its length, you view under the greatest disadvantage possible; whereas if you turn a little to the right hand towards Leith, and so come towards the city, from the north you see a very handsome prospect of the whole city, and from the south you have yet a better view of one part, because the city is encreased on that side with new streets, which, on the north side, cannot be.

The particular situation then of the whole is thus. At the extremity of the east end of the city stands the palace or court, call'd Haly-Rood House; and you must fetch a little sweep to the right hand to leave the palace on the left, and come at the entrance, which is call'd the Water Port, and which you come at thro' a short suburb, then bearing to the left again, south, you come to the gate of the palace which faces the great street.

From the palace, west, the street goes on in almost a straight line, and for near a mile and a half in length, some say full 2 measur'd miles, thro' the whole city to the castle, including the going up the castle in the inside; this is, perhaps, the largest, longest, and finest street for buildings and number of inhabitants, not in Britain only, but in the world.

From the very palace door, which stands on a flat, and level with the lowest of the plain country, the street begins to ascend; and tho' it ascends very gradually at first, and is no where steep, yet 'tis easy to understand that continuing the ascent for so long a way, the further part must necessarily be very high; and so it is; for the castle which stands at the extremity west, as the palace does east, makes on all the three sides, that only excepted, which joins it to the city, a frightful and impassable precipice.

Together with this continued ascent, which, I think, 'tis easy to form an idea of in the mind, you are to suppose the edge or top of the ascent so narrow, that the street, and the row of houses on each side of it, take up the whole breadth; so that which way soever you turn, either to the right, or to the left, you go down hill immediately, and that so steep, as is very troublesome to those who walk in those side lanes which they call wynds, especially if their lungs are not very good: so that, in a word, the city stands upon the narrow ridge of a long ascending mountain.

On the right side, or north side of the city, and from the very west end of it, where the castle stands, is a lough, or lake of standing water; there is, indeed, a small brook runs thro' it, so that it cannot be said to be quite standing water. And we were told, that in former days there was another lough on the south side of it, which, being now fill'd up, is built into a street, tho' so much lower than the high street, or ridge, that, as I said before, the lanes or wynds between them are very steep.

It is easy to conclude, that such a situation as this could never be pick'd out for a city or town, upon any other consideration than that of strength to defend themselves from the suddain surprizes and assaults of enemies: And, tho' the building is so antient, that no history has recorded the foundation, either when, or by who, or on what occasion it was built; yet, I say, it seems most natural to conclude, that it was built for a retreat from the outrages and attempts of the Picts or Irish, or whatever other enemies they had to fear.

On the top of the ridge of a hill, an impregnable castle and precipice at one end, a lough, or lake of water on either side; so that the inhabitants had nothing to defend but the entrance at the east end, which it was easy to fortify.

If this was not the reason, what should have hinder'd them from building the city in a pleasant, delightful valley, with the sea flowing up to one side, and a fresh water river runing thro' the middle of it; such as is all that space of ground between the city, as it now stands, and the sea, or Firth, and on the south shore, whereon the town of Leith now stands?

Here they had had a noble, a pleasant, and a most useful situation, a very fine harbour for their trade, a good road in the Firth for their ships of burthen, a pleasant river, which, with small art or charge, might have been so drawn round the city as to have fill'd its ditches, and made its fortifications as impregnable as the two loughs did the city, and as the French,[9] when they fortify'd Leith, found easy to do. Or had they gone to the south side of the city, beyond the deep lough, which, they say it was, and which is now call'd the Cow-Gate, and extended the city towards Libertoun, and towards Good-Trees, where now stands the delightful seat of Sir James Stuart, late Lord Advocate of Scotland, and the antient seat of Craigmiller,[10] the seat of Sir Alexander————of Craigmiller. Here had been a plain large enough to have contain'd a second London, and water'd on the south part with a pleasant brook, sufficient, by the help of pipes, to have carried water into every street, and every house.

These things they did not foresee, or understand in those days; but, regarding immediate safety, fix'd on the place as above as a sure strength, form'd by nature, and ready at their hand. By this means the city suffers infinite disadvantages, and lies under such scandalous inconveniencies as are, by its enemies, made a subject of scorn and reproach; as if the people were not as willing to live sweet and clean as other nations, but delighted in stench and nastiness; whereas, were any other people to live under the same unhappiness, I mean as well of a rocky and mountainous situation, throng'd buildings, from seven to ten or twelve story high, a scarcity of water, and that little they have difficult to be had, and to the uppermost lodgings, far to fetch; we should find a London or a Bristol as dirty as Edinburgh, and, perhaps, less able to make their dwelling tolerable, at least in so narrow a compass; for, tho' many cities have more people in them, yet, I believe, this may be said with truth, that in no city in the world so many people live in so little room as at Edinburgh.

Having thus consider'd the city in its appearance, and in its present situation, I must look next into its inside, where we shall find it under all its discouragements and disadvantages, (and labouring with whatever inconveniencies) a large, populous, noble, rich, and even still a royal city. The main street, as above, is the most spacious, the longest, and best inhabited street in Europe; its length I have describ'd; the buildings are surprizing both for strength, for beauty, and for height; all, or the greatest part of free-stone, and so firm is every thing made, that tho' in so high a situation, and in a country where storms and violent winds are so frequent, 'tis very rare that any damage is done here. No blowing of tiles about the streets, to knock people on the head as they pass; no stacks of chimneys and gable-ends of houses falling in to bury the inhabitants in their ruins, as we often find it in London, and other of our paper built cities in England; but all is fix'd, and strong to the top, tho' you have, in that part of the city call'd the Parliament-close, houses, which, on the south side, appear to be eleven or twelve story high, and inhabited to the very top.

From the palace gate, westward, this street is call'd the Cannon-Gate, vulgarly the Canni-gate, which part, tho' a suburb, is a kind of corporation by itself, as Westminster to London; and has a toll-booth, a prison, and a town-guard by itself, tho' under the government of the provost and bailiffs of Edinburgh, as Leith itself also is. In this part of the street, tho' otherwise not so well inhabited as the city itself, are several very magnificent houses of the nobility, built for their residence when the court was in town, and on their other occasions, just as was the case in the Strand between London and Whitehall, before the encrease of the city prompted the building those fine houses into streets.

Of those the Duke of Queensberry's, the Earl of

229. Cannon-Gate; ink and watercolour drawing by Paul Sandby (1749).

Wintoun's, the Duke of Roxburg's, and the Earl of Murray's are the chief; the first and last are very magnificent, large and princely buildings, all of free-stone, large in front, and with good gardens behind them, and the other are very fine buildings, too many to be describ'd.

At the upper, or west end of this street, and where it joins to the city, is a gate which, just as Ludgate, or Temple-Bar, stands parting the city itself from the suburb, but not at all discontinuing the street, which rather widens, and is more spacious when you are thro' the gate than before. This gate, or Bow, is call'd the Nether-Bow, or, by some, the Nether-Bow Port.

Just at this Port, on the outside, turn away two streets, one goes south to a gate or Port which leads out of the city into the great road for England, by the way of Kelso, and is call'd St. Mary Wynde; and, on the right hand of it, another Port turns away west, into the low street, mention'd before, where was a lough formerly fill'd up, and is call'd the Cow-Gate, because, by this street, the cattle are driven to and from the great market-place, call'd the Grass Market, where such cattle are bought and sold, as also where

is a horse-market weekly, as in Smithfield. This street, call'd the Cow-Gate, runs parallel with the high street, but down in a bottom, as has been said. But to go back to the Nether-Bow Port, as this turning is on the left hand going into the city, so on the right hand goes another street, which they call Leith Wind, and leads down to a gate which is not in the city wall immediately, but adjoining to a church call'd the College-Kirk, and thro' which gate, a suburb runs out north, opening into the plain, leads to Leith; and all along by the road side, the road itself pav'd with stones like a street, is a broad causeway, or, as we call it, a foot way, very firm, and made by hand at least 20 foot broad, and continued to the town of Leith. This causeway is very well kept at the publick expence, and no horses suffer'd to come upon it.

We now enter the city, properly so call'd; in almost the first buildings of note on the north side of the street, the Marquess of Tweedale has a good city house, with a plantation of lime-trees behind it, instead of a garden, the place not allowing room for a large garden; adjoining to which are very good buildings, tho' in the narrow wynds and alleys, such as

312

230. Perspective view of the Parliament House and Exchequer, Edinburgh; engraving by A. Bell after a drawing by the Hon. John Elphinstone (published before 1740).

if set out in handsome streets, would have adorn'd a very noble city, but are here crouded together, as may be said, without notice.

Here the physicians have a hall, and adjoining to it a very good garden; but I saw, no simples in it of value, there being a physick garden at the palace which furnishes them sufficiently: But they have a fine Musæum, or Chamber of Rarities, which are worth seeing, and which, in some things, is not to be match'd in Europe. Dr. Balfour,[11] afterwards knighted, began the collection. Sir Robert Sibbald[12] has printed a catalogue of what was then deposited in his time. The physitians of Edinburgh have preserved the character of able, learned, and experienc'd, and have not been outdone by any of their neighbours: and the late Dr. Pitcairn,[13] who was the Ratcliff[14] of Scotland, has left large testimonies of his skill in nature and medicine to the world.

It must not be expected I can go on to describe all the buildings of the city; I shall therefore only touch at such things, and go on. From the Nether Bow, you have an open view up the high street. On the south side is the Trone Kirk, and a little farther, in the middle of the street the guard house, where the town guard does duty every night. These are in the stead of our watchmen; and the town maintains two full companies of them, cloth'd and arm'd as grenadiers.

About midway, between the Nether Bow and the Castle-Hill, is the great church, formerly it was call'd the cathedral, and was all one church, dedicated to St. Giles: but since the abolishing episcopacy, and that the Presbyterian church is now establish'd by the Union, so as never legally to suffer another change; I say never legally, because it cannot be done without dissolving the Union, which I take to be indissolvable: since this establishment, the cathedral church is divided into four parochial churches.

In one of those churches, which they call the New Church, were seats for the Parliament, High Commissioners, and the nobility, when the Parliament was assembled, tho' that occasion is now over:[15] In a room, formerly a kind of consistory room, on the south side of the church, the General Assembly[16] hold their meetings once a year, as also does the commission of the assembly in the intervals of the general meeting, as occasion requires. In the great tower of this church they have a set of bells, which are not rung out as in England, for that way of ringing is not known here; but they are play'd upon with keys, and by a man's hand, like a harpsicord; the person playing has great strong wooden cases to his fingers, by which he is able to strike with the more force, and he plays several tunes very musically, tho' they are heard much better at a distance than near at hand; the man plays

GOOD EATING DOWN THIS CLOSS 1751

231. High Street, Edinburgh; pen and watercolour drawing by Paul Sandby (dated 1751).

every day, Sunday and fast days excepted, at twelve a clock, and has a yearly salary for doing it, and very well he earns the money.

On the south side of this church is a square of very fine buildings, which is call'd by the name of the Parliament Close; the west side of the square, and part of the south, is taken up with the Parliament House, and the several courts of justice, the Council-Chamber, the Treasury, the publick offices, registers, the publick library, &c. The court for the meeting of the royal buroughs, and several offices needful, when the independency of Scotland was in being, but now not so much in use. But as the Session, or College of Justice, the Exchequer, and the Justiciary, or courts for criminal causes still exist, the usual places for their assembling are still preserved. These buildings are very fine, all of free-stone, well finish'd, and very magnificent. The great church makes up the north side of the square, and the east remaining part of the south side is built into private dwellings very stately, lofty, and strong, being seven story high to the front of the square, and the hill they stand on giving so sudden a descent, they are eleven or twelve story high backward.

The great opening into the high street, being the only passage into it for coaches, is at the north east corner, between the south east corner of the High

Kirk, and the opposite high buildings, and a little from the opening is the market-cross, where all their proclamations and publick acts are read and publish'd by sound of trumpet. Here is the great parade, where, every day, the gentlemen meet for business or news, as at an exchange, the usual time of meeting is from eleven to one. Here is also another passage at the north west corner, which goes into the Land-market, and another passage down innumerable stone stairs, on the south side, leading into the Cowgate.

On the west end of the great church, but in a different building, is the Tolbooth, or common prison, as well for criminals as debtors, and a miserable hole it is, to say no worse of it; tho', for those that can pay for it, there are some apartments tolerable enough, and persons of quality are sometimes confin'd here.

The great church and this prison also standing in the middle of the street, the breadth and beauty of it is for some time interrupted, and the way is contracted for so far as those buildings reach on the north side.

But those buildings past, the street opens again to a breadth rather wider than before, and this is call'd the Land-market,[17] but for what reason I know not. This part is also nobly built, and extends west to the Castle Hill, or rather to a narrower street which leads up to the castle.

At the upper end of this Land-market is a stone

314

building, appropriated to several publick offices of lesser value, and is call'd the Weigh-house; for below stairs are warehouses, with publick weights and scales for heavy goods.

Here the high street ends, and parting into two streets, one goes away south west, and descending gradually, leads by the West Bow, as 'tis call'd, to the Grass-market. This street, which is call'd the Bow, is generally full of wholesale traders, and those very considerable dealers in iron, pitch, tar, oyl, hemp, flax, linseed, painters colours, dyers, drugs and woods, and such like heavy goods, and supplies country shop-keepers, as our wholesale dealers in England do: and here I may say, is a visible face of trade, most of them have also warehouses in Leith, where they lay up the heavier goods, and bring them hither, or sell them by patterns and samples, as they have occasion.

There are large gates in the city which they call ports, including those to the Cannon Gate.

1. The Water-Gate, which is the east gate by the palace, leading out of the city towards Berwick, and is the great post road to England.

2. The South Port, mention'd before, leading like-wise into the road to Soutra Hill, and so to England by way of Kelso.

3. The Cowgate Port, at the east end of the Cow-gate, and entring from the street leading to the South Port.

4. The College Port, or the gate going south by the wall of Harriot's Hospital.

5. The West-Bow Port, spoken of before in the middle of the street, mention'd above where the wholsale dealers dwell.

6. The North Port, a gate leading from the but-chery, or flesh-market, over the end of the lough.

7. The Nether-Bow Port, spoken of at large, leading into the city from the Cannon Gate.

8. The College-Kirk Port, at the bottom or foot of Leith Wynd.

9. The West Port, which is the only gate in the west end of the city, and leads out to all the west and north parts of Scotland, and especially to Glasgow, to Sterling, and to the Queens Ferry, the two last being the principal passages into the north.

The markets in Edinburgh are not in the open street, except that in the high street, where there is every morning an herb and fruit market, which yet abates before noon, and what remains then is no grievance. Besides this, there are several distinct market places wall'd in, and reserv'd for the particular things they are appointed for, and very well regulated by the magistrates, and well supplies also; as

1. The Meal-Market.
2. The Flesh-Market.
3. The Poultry-Market.
4. The Butter-Market.
5. The Grass-Market. ⎱ Kept open, and in the
6. The Horse-Market. ⎰ same street just within the West Port, with several others. There is also, in the street call'd the Land-market, a weekly market for all

232. Horsefair on Bruntsfield Links; pen and watercolour drawing by Paul Sandby (dated 1750).

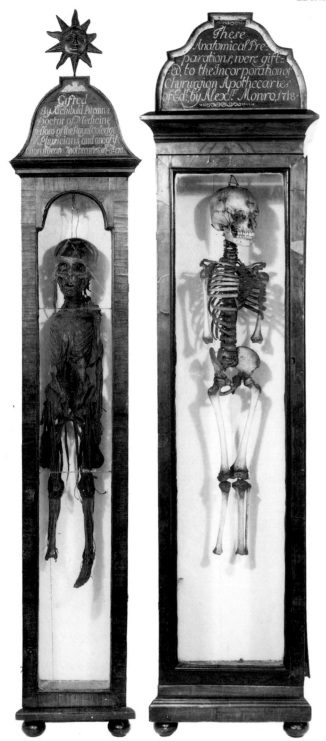

On the cases (as inscribed):

Left case: *Gifted By Archibald Pitcairne Doctor of Medicine fellow of the Royal Colledge of Physicians and one of the Chyrurgeon Apothecaries of Ed.*

Right case: *These Anatomical Preparations were gifted to the Incorporation of Chyrurgion Apothecaries of Ed. by Alexd.r Monro 1718.*

233. Dissections by Archibald Pitcairne (1702) and Alexander Monro (1718); part of the 'Chamber of Rarities' in the Royal College of Surgeons, Edinburgh.

sorts of woollen manufactures, and some mercery and drapery goods, and also for linnen cloth.

But I must not omit the seminaries of learning, and the attendants upon them, nor the surgeons and apothecaries, with the great hospital, all which stand on the south side of the city; the first of them is the surgeons hall, or surgeon-apothecaries, for here they make but one profession. They have set up a large building all at their own charge, in which is their great hall, hung round with the pictures of all the surgeons of the city, that are, or have been since the building was erected, as also the pictures of Duke Hamilton and the late Lord Chancellor.

They have also a Chamber of Rarities, a theatre for dissections, and the finest bagnio[18] in Britain; 'tis perfectly well contriv'd, and exactly well finish'd, no expence being spar'd to make it both convenient and effectually useful.

In their Chamber of Rarities they have several skeletons of strange creatures, a mummy, and other curious things, too many to be particular in them here.

The Humanity school is kept in the same part, which is reckon'd as a part of the University, as being employ'd in the finishing youth for the college. West of these is the college itself, they call it the university: but as it consists of but one college, I call it no more. However, here are all the usual methods of academick learning in their full perfection. The Principal, or Master, has a handsome dwelling-house and garden in the college: there are, besides a Professor of Divinity, four Regents, or Professors of Greek, another of Hebrew, another of History, of the Mathematicks, and of the Civil Law.

The college has a very handsome publick library; and, though not famous for number of books, is yet so for its being a valuable collection of antiquity, and has some very good manuscripts. The late Act of Parliament[19] for settling the right of copies, has made provision for a constant supply of modern books, especially such as are printed in England; so the library is like to encrease, in time, to a great one.

Here was formerly a mint, but that is now laid aside, the Union having made one and the same coinage common to the whole island.

The churches in this populous city are but ten, (viz.)

1. The Cannon Gate Church.
2. The College Kirk.
3. The Trone Kirk.
4. The New Kirk.
5. The Old Kirk.
6. The Tolbooth Kirk.
7. The Haddocks Hole Kirk.
8. The Lady Yester's Kirk.

234. Perspective view of the front of the Tron Kirk; engraving by Parr after a drawing by the Hon. John Elphinstone (published before 1740).

9. The Gray Friars Kirk.

10. The West Kirk.

There are also many meeting-houses of the Episcopal party who call themselves Church of England, though they do not all use the English Common-Prayer. These are the Dissenters in Scotland, as the Presbyterians are Dissenters in England.

There are also two churches at Leith, and very large and very full they are, and so indeed are all the churches in the city, for the people of Scotland do not wander about on the Sabbath-days, as in England; and even those who may have no more religion than enough, yet custom has made it almost natural to them, they all go to the kirk.

They have also one very good custom as to their behaviour in the church, which I wish were practis'd here, namely, that after the sermon is over, and the blessing given, they all look round upon their friends, and especially to persons of distinction, and make their civilities and bows as we do here, for, by the way, the Scots do not want manners. But if any person come in when the worship is begun, he takes notice of no body, nor any body of him; whereas here we make our bows and our cringes in the middle of our very prayers.

I have now done with the city, the palace only, and the castle remain to be mention'd; the last is strong by situation, not much better'd by art, and far from being impregnable, as has been prov'd more than once. It is now of little use, unless for salutes, and firing guns upon festivals, and in some cases to lay up a magazine of arms and ammunition, and to receive prisoners of state.

The Governor has very good apartments, and so has the Lieutenant Governor, as also the Fort-Major, and some other officers, and there are deep vaults in the rock, which they say are bomb-proof, and I doubt not but they are so, for they go down into them by a great number of steps. There is also a well of very good water in the castle, and it is carefully kept, but it is a prodigious depth. Here are not a great many guns planted, neither, indeed, is there room to place many guns, or use for them where they can be plac'd, the works being so very high.

The palace is a handsome building, rather convenient than large. The entrance is majestick, and over the gate a large apartment, which the Duke of Hamilton claims as House-keeper, or rather Gate-keeper of the Palace; within this is a large, irregular court, where, I must needs say, are very improperly plac'd the coach-houses and stables, which should much rather have been farther off, either in the park, or without the out-gate:

317

235. 'Prospect of Leith from the East'; detail from Greenvile Collins, *Great Britain's Coasting Pilot* (1693).

and, if here had been a barrack, or guard-house, like the Horse-Guards at Whitehall, it would have look'd much more like a royal palace for the king. On either side of this court are gardens, yards the Scots call them, whereof one is like our apothecaries' garden at Chelsea, call'd a physick garden, and is tolerably well stor'd with simples, and some exoticks of value; and, particularly I was told, there was a rhubarb tree, or plant, and which throve very well. In this garden stands Queen Mary's Dial,[20] which is a very curious one, but neglected.

Antiquity claims the fee-simple[21] here, and tells us that the church is still ground landlord; for, before the Reformation, this was a monastery; and, tho' it was converted into a palace before the suppression of religious houses, yet, that till then the monks had a fair apartment, and was therefore call'd Haly-Rood House, and they did but entertain the kings and queens in the other as a kind of guest mates, or, as we call them, lodgers.

The old Chapel Royal, or church of the convent, stands in its *disshabile*, ruin'd and decay'd, and must fall down. In King James IId's time, the old council-chamber was consecrated for a chapel, instead of the antient fabrick; and there the Roman priests officiated for some time, promising themselves not only to restore the great antient chapel, but even to seize upon the palace itself in the right of the church, and make a noble monastery of it, which it must be confess'd might have been done with very little charge: but their reign was too short for the undertaking.

On the side of the park was a part set out for fine gardens, and they are still call'd St. Ann's Yards, that is Gardens; but they have never been planted or form'd.

I must now visit **Leith**, the sea-port of Edinburgh, as it is properly call'd: it is a large and populous town, or rather two towns, for the river or harbour parts them, and they are join'd by a good stone bridge, about half a mile, or more, from the mouth of the river.

Up to this bridge ships of burthen may come, and, at high water, lay their sides close to the shore; but at low water people pass over on foot, even without the pier; but the water flows in the Firth near three fathom right up and down.

Here is a very fine key well wharf'd up with stone, and fenc'd with piles, able to discharge much more business than the place can supply, tho' the trade is far from being inconsiderable too. At the mouth of the harbour is a very long and well built pier, or head, which runs out beyond the land a great way, and which defends the entrance into the harbour from filling up with sand, as, upon hard gales of wind at north east, would be very likely: there are also ranges of piles, or break-waters, as the seamen call them, on the other side the harbour, all which are kept in good repair; and by this means the harbour is preserv'd, and kept open in spight of a flat shore, and a large swell of the sea.

On the other side the bridge is the remains of a strong castle, built by Oliver Cromwell to command the port, but demolish'd; yet not so much, but that a little expence and a few hands would soon restore it. Here the late rebel Highlanders[22] made a bold stop, and took possession of it for one night; but not finding their friends in the city in any condition to join them; and the troops preparing to attack them, they quitted it in the night, and march'd off to the Earl of Winton's house.

From Leith, the Firth, which is there, at least, two leagues over, holds that breadth for five or six miles, and then narrows a little beyond Cramond; and again at the Queens-Ferry it is reduc'd to two miles breadth, and an island in the middle also.

There is also a ferry at Leith, the boats going from

Leith to Burnt-Island, or, as the Scots call it, Bruntillian; but as 'tis no less than seven miles, and that sometimes they meet with bad weather: the passengers are so often frighted, that I knew several gentlemen that would always choose to go round to the Queens-Ferry, rather than venture over at Leith; this, I suppose, gave beginning to that homely piece of proverb poetry, that

There is never a Laird in Fife,
But once a year he would give his estate for his life.

Queens-Ferry is not a passage over the water only, but a very good town also, and a corporation. And here I must take notice of a thing which was to me surprising, I mean as to the quantity of herrings taken, and that might be taken in those seas. There was, at that time, a fleet of between seven and eight hundred sail of Dutch busses[23] come into the Firth, loaden with herrings, and their convoy with them, for it was in the time of the late wars; the Scots themselves had taken a vast quantity, for they said they had had a very good fishery all along upon the coast of Fife, and of Aberdeen, and the Dunbar men, and the Firth boats, were every day taking more; and yet the water of the Firth was so full of fish, that passing at the Queens-Ferry in a little Norway yawl, or boat, row'd by two boys, the boys toss'd the fish out of the water into the boat with their naked hands only: but I shall have occasion to mention this again.

Between Edinburgh and this town the Marquess of Annandale[24] has a small, but very pleasant house: and here I observ'd his Lordship was making bricks, in order to build walls round his garden; a thing hardly to be seen in Scotland, except there. On the other hand, it is for want of brick walls that the wall-fruit in Scotland does not thrive so well there as it would otherwise do: and whereas they have no peaches or nectarines, or but very few, it is evident, had they brick-walls they might have both; but the stone will not do it. The reflexion of the sun is not equally nourishing, nor does the stone hold the warmth of the sun, after it is gone, as the bricks do.

All the country, between Edinburgh and this place, is throng'd with gentlemen's houses, also as it was observ'd to be on the other side: but the beauty of all this part is Hopton House, built upon a delightful plain, and yet upon the edge, as we may say, of a high precipice; from whence you, as it were, look down upon the ships as they sail by, for you stand above the top-mast heads of them.

From hence the Firth widens again, and soon after is three or four miles wide, and makes a safe and deep road, with good anchor ground; and if there was a trade to answer it, here might ride a thousand sail of ships of any burthen.

On the south-shore, upon a narrow slip or point of land, running far into the water, lyes Blackness Castle,[25] in former times infamous for the cruel confining state-prisoners, and especially such as were taken up for religious differences, where many perished, either by the unhealthiness of the place, or want of conveniences, or something worse. It might be of use, if the harbour, as I have said, was frequented; but as it is, there seems to be no occasion at all for it.

Farther west is **Boristown Ness**, a long town, of one street, and no more, extended along the shore, close to the water. It has been, and still is, a town of the greatest trade to Holland and France, before the Union, of any in Scotland, except Edinburgh; and, for shipping, it has more ships belong to it than to Edinburgh and Leith put together; yet their trade is declin'd of late by the Dutch trade, being carry'd on so much by way of England: but, as they tell us, the Glasgow merchants are resolving to settle a trade to Holland and Hamburgh in the Firth, by bringing their foreign goods, (viz.) their sugars and tobacco by land to Alloway, and from thence export them as they see occasion. I say, in this case, which is very probable, the Borristoun Ness men will come into business again; for as they have the most shipping, so they are the best seamen in the Firth; and particularly they are not sailors only, but even pilots for the coast of Holland, they are so acquainted with it, and so with the Baltick, and the coast of Norway also.

As I resolve to go through my account of the south part of Scotland first, I shall not pass the Firth at all, till giving you an account of the western part, I come back to Sterling Bridge, and there I suppose I may finish my next letter; mean time

I am, &c.

The End of the Eleventh Letter

LETTER XII

Sir,

As I enter'd the east side of Scotland from Berwick upon Tweed, and have carry'd on my accounts through the Louthians, which are deservedly call'd the best and most pleasant, as well as most fruitful part of Scotland; and therein have also given you my observations of the capital city and port of the kingdom, I mean Edinburgh and Leith: so the west part having been travell'd over by me at another particular journey from England; and that I went from England by another road, I shall give you my account of it also by itself.

Passing the river Eden, or, (as it is ordinarily call'd) the Solway Firth at Carlisle, we enter'd upon Scotland, on the side of Dumfries shire, the southmost shire of the west of Scotland. The division of this county into Eskdale, Nithsdale, and Annandale, is but the ordinary marking out the rivers Esk, Annan, and Nid, as I observ'd of the rivers in the north of England, Tweedale, Tyndale, Swale Dale, and others; for the whole province makes but one Dumfries-shire, and as such you will understand it as I go on.

The Esk is a tolerable large river, and gives name to the south east part of this county; but we saw little worth notice but Kirsop, a small market town on a river of the same name, which afterwards falls into Esk, and is famous for being the place where, by a treaty, after the battle of Pinkey,[1] the limits of borders of the two kingdoms were settled; though the borderers observ'd it no longer than serv'd for their purpose, robbing and plundering one another upon all occasions, as opportunity offer'd.

This river soon after leaves Scotland, and runs into the English border, leaving nothing behind it worth my trouble of remarking, or yours of reading, only to tell you it empties itself into the Solway Firth, which indeed receives all the rivers on this part of the island, as well from England as from Scotland.

The first place of note we came to in Scotland was Annand, or as some call it, **Annandale**, as they do the county, though, I think, improperly. It was a town of note, and a sea-port, and having a good river and harbour, was esteem'd a town of good trade; but it was not situated for strength; and the English took it so often, and specially the last time burnt it to the ground, in that war so fatal to the Scots, in the reign of Edw. VI that it never recover'd. Here was a good salmon fishery, and a trade to the Isle of Man, and by that to Ireland: but as the face of trade is alter'd since that time, and by the ruins of the place the merchants, and men of substance, remov'd to Dumfries, the town continues, to all appearance, in a state of irrevocable decay.

It was but a dull welcome into Scotland to see, not only by this town, that the remains of the old devastations, committed in the time of the hostilities between the two nations, were so visible, so unrepair'd, and, as we might say, so likely to continue unrepair'd; whereas, tho' there are remains also on the English side, yet, not so plain, and in many places things much restor'd, and in a way to be more so: but the poverty of the common people, and the indolence of the gentry, will fully account for the difference. The bridge over the river at Annand, is very firm and good, and there is a tolerable good market.

From hence, keeping the sea as close as we could on our left, we went on due west to **Dumfries**, a sea-port town at the mouth of the river Nid, or Nith, which gives name to the third division of the county call'd Nithsdale; but the town is justly the capital of the whole shire, and indeed, of all the south west part of Scotland.

Here, indeed, as in some other ports on this side the island, the benefits of commerce, obtain'd to Scotland by the Union, appear visible; and that much more than on the east side, where they seem to be little, if any thing mended, I mean in their trade.

Dumfries was always a good town, and full of merchants. By merchants, here I mean, in the sense that word is taken and understood in England (viz.) not mercers and drapers, shop-keepers, &c. but merchant-adventurers, who trade to foreign parts, and employ a considerable number of ships. But if this was so before, it is much more so now; and as they have (with success) embark'd in trade, as well to England as to the English

321

236. High Street and Midsteeple, Dumfries; pencil sketch by G.H. Johnson (1823). The Midsteeple is almost certainly the town-hall mentioned by Defoe and had changed little since its construction in 1707, retaining even its original door.

XXXIX. Paul Sandby, *Panorama of Nithsdale with Drumlanrig.*

plantations, they apparently encrease both in shipping and people; for as it almost every where appears, where trade increases, people must and will increase; that is, they flock to the place by the necessary consequences of the trade, and, in return, where the people increase, the trade will increase, because the necessary consumption of provisions, cloaths, furniture, &c. necessarily increases, and with them the trade.

This town is situated also for an increase of commerce on the river Nid, for tho' it stands near two leagues from the sea, yet the tide flows up to the town, and ships of burthen come close up to the key; but at about four miles below the town the largest merchant-ships in Britain might come up, and ride in safety.

There is a very fine stone bridge here over the river Nid; as also a castle, tho' of old work, yet still good and strong enough; also an exchange for the merchants, and a Tolbooth, or town-hall for the use of the magistrates. They had formerly a woollen manufacture here: but as the Union has, in some manner, suppress'd those things in Scotland, the English supplying them fully, both better and cheaper; so they have more than an equivalent by an open trade to all the English plantations, and to England itself.

The river Nid here parts the two counties of Galloway and Dumfries shire; and there is a gate in the middle of the bridge which is the limit between them: and this neighbourhood of Galloway, which is a great and rich province, promotes the trade of Dumfries very much.

We could not pass Dumfries without going out of the way upwards of a day, to see the castle of Drumlanrig,[2] the fine palace of the Duke of Queensberry, which stands at twelve miles distance, upon the same river; the vale on either side the river is pleasant, and tolerably good: but when these rapid rivers overflow their banks, they do not, like Nile, or even like the Thames, and other southern streams, fatten and enrich the soil; on the contrary, they lodge so much sand and splinters of stone upon the surface of the earth, and among the roots of the grass, that spoils and beggars the soil; and the water is hurried on with such force also, as that in a good light soil it washes the best part of the earth away with it, leaving the sand and stones behind it.

Drumlanrig, like Chatsworth in Darbyshire, is like a fine picture in a dirty grotto, or like an equestrian statue set up in a barn; 'tis environ'd with mountains, and that of the wildest and most hideous aspect in all the south of Scotland; as particularly that of Enterkin, the frightfullest pass, and most dangerous that I met with, between that and Penmenmuir in North Wales; but of that in its place.

We were not so surpriz'd with the height of the mountains, and the barrenness of the country beyond them, as we were with the humour of the people, who are not in this part, by many degrees, so populous, or so polish'd, as in the other parts of Scotland. But that which was more surprising than all the rest, was to see a palace so glorious, gardens so fine, and every thing so truly magnificent, and all in a wild, mountainous country, the like we had not seen before.

As you come to the palace from the road of Edinburgh, which is by the said pass of Enterkin, you come first to the river Nid, which is just there both broad and exceeding deep, over which there is a stately stone-bridge, built by the noble founder of the castle, I mean the first Duke of Queensberry,[3] who built the house.

The building is four-square, with roundels in the inner angles of the court, in every one of which is a stair-case, and a kind of a tower on the top. This way of building, 'tis confess'd, does not seem so modern as the rest of the building; but as 'tis not seen in the front, 'tis well enough.

The house stands on the top of a rising ground, which, at its first building, lay with a steep and uncouth descent to the river, and which made the lookers on wonder what the Duke meant to build in such a disproportion'd place: but he best understood his own design; for the house once laid out, all that unequal descent is so beautifully levell'd and lay'd out in slopes and terrasses, that nothing can be better design'd, or, indeed, better perform'd than the gardens are, which take up the whole south and west sides of the house; and, when the whole design will be done, the rest will

237. James Douglas, Second Duke of Queensberry and Dover (1662–1711); painting by Sir Godfrey Kneller (*c.*1692).

be more easy, the ground being a plain the other way, and the park and avenues compleatly planted with trees.

At the extent of the gardens there are pavillions and banquetting-houses, exactly answering to one another, and the greens trimm'd, spaliers and hedges are in perfection.

The inside is answerable to the outside, the apartments finely plac'd and richly furnish'd: and the gallery may well be call'd a gallery of beauties, itself's a beauty. And being fill'd from end to end, the whole length of one side of the building, with the family-pieces of the Duke's ancestors, most of them at full length, and in their robes of state, or of office, as their history directed. They were first ennobled for the real merit of their services, in the person of the first Lord of Drumlanrig, ann. 1640. And King Charles I made the then Lord of Drumlanrig Earl of Queensberry; a title taken from Queensberry hill, a high, round hill, in a particular lordship of the estate, and in view of the house. After the Restoration, the grandson of the earl was created Marquess and Duke by King Charles II.

This was the person who built the noble palace I am speaking of, who, every way, merited the honours which the prince rather loaded him with, than bestow'd on him: he lyes buried in the parish church of Disdier or Didier, with a fine monument over him; but not like that lately erected for his son the late Duke.[4]

This last mention'd Duke would require a history rather than a bare mention, in a work of this kind: but I have forbid myself entring far into the characters of persons and families; and therefore, tho' I think myself bound to honour the merit of so great a person, I shall sum it up all in this; that as I had the honour to be known to his grace, so I had the opportunity to see and read by his permission, several letters written to him by the late King William, with his own hand, and several more by Queen Anne, written also by her majesty's own hand; with such expressions of their satisfaction in his fidelity and affection to their majesties' service, his ability and extraordinary judgment in the affairs entrusted to him; his knowledge of, and zeal for the true interest of his country, and their dependance upon his councils and conduct, that no minister of state in Europe could desire greater testimonies of his services, or a better character from his sovereign, and this from differing princes, and at the distance of several years from one another, and, to be sure, without any manner of corresponding one with the other.

That this noble person was Lord Commissioner at the time of the Union, sat in the throne at the last Parliament of Scotland, and touch'd with the scepter the Act of Parliament, which put an end to Parliaments for ever in that part of Great Britain, will always be matter of history to the end of time; whether the Scots will remember it to the advantage of the Duke's character, in their opinion, that must be as their several opinions guide them.

But I dwell too long here. While I was at Drumlanrig, being desir'd by the late Duke to make some observations on his grace's estate there, which is very great, in order to some English improvement, I, in particular, view'd some of the hills to the north of the castle, and having a Darbyshire gentleman with us, who was thoroughly acquainted with those things, we discover'd in several places evident tokens of lead-mines, such as in Darbyshire, and in Somersetshire, are said never to fail; and to confirm our opinions in it, we took up several small pieces of oar in the gulls and holes, which the rains had made in the sides of the mountains, and also of a plain sparr, such as is not found any where without the oar: but the Duke's death put an end to these enquiries, as also to several other improvements then in view.

Here we were surpriz'd with a sight, which is not now so frequent in Scotland as it has been formerly, I mean one of their field meetings, where one Mr. John Hepburn,[5] an old Cameronian, preach'd to an auditory of near 7000 people, all sitting in rows on the steep side of a green hill, and the preacher in a little pulpit made under a tent at the foot of the hill; he held his auditory, with not above an intermission of half an hour, almost seven hours; and many of the poor people had come fifteen or sixteen miles to hear him, and had all the way to go home again on foot. I shall say nothing to it, for my business is not to make remarks on such things; only this I may add, that if there was an equal zeal to this in our part of the world, and for that worship which we acknowledge to be true, and of a sacred institution, our churches would be more throng'd, and our ale-houses and fields less throng'd on the Sabbath-day than they are now. But that also by the way.

From Drumlanrig I took a turn to see the famous pass of Enterkin, or Introkin Hill: it is, indeed, not easy to describe; but by telling you that it ascends through a winding bottom for near half a mile, and a stranger sees nothing terrible, but vast high mountains on either hand, tho' all green, and with sheep feeding on them to the very top; when, on a suddain, turning short to the left, and crossing a rill of water in the bottom, you mount the side of one of those hills, while, as you go on, the bottom in which that water runs down from between the hills, keeping its level on your right, begins to look very deep, till at length it is

a precipice horrible and terrifying; on the left the hill rises almost perpendicular, like a wall; till being come about half way, you have a steep, unpassable height on the left, and a monstrous casm or ditch on your right; deep, almost as the Monument is high, and the path, or way, just broad enough for you to lead your horse on it, and, if his foot slips, you have nothing to do but let go the bridle, least he pulls you with him, and then you will have the satisfaction of seeing him dash'd to pieces, and lye at the bottom with his four shoes uppermost. I pass'd twice this hill after this, but the weather was good, and the way dry, which made it safe; but one of our company was so frighted with it, that in a kind of an extasy, when he got to the bottom, he look'd back, and swore heartily that he would never come that way again.

Indeed, there were several things this last time we pass'd it, which render'd it more frightful to a stranger: one was, that there had been, a few days before, a suddain frost, with a great deal of snow; and though, a little before the snow, I pass'd it, and there was nothing to be seen; yet then I look'd down the fright-ful precipice, and saw no less than five horses in several places, lying at the bottom with their skins off, which had, by the slipperiness of the snow, lost their feet, and fallen irrecoverably to the bottom, where the mountaineers, who make light of the place, had found means to come at them, and get their hides off.

But I must go back to Dumfries again, for this was but an excursion from thence, as I observ'd there: I resolv'd, before I quitted the west coast, to see all that was worth seeing on that side, and the next trip we made was into Galloway: and here, I must confess, I could not but look with grief and concern upon the country, and indeed upon the people.

Galloway, as I hinted before, begins even from the middle of the bridge of Dumfries; the first town on the coast, of any note, is **Kirkubright**, or, as vulgarly call'd, Kirkubry. It must be acknowledg'd this very place is a surprize to a stranger, and especially one whose business is observation, as mine was.

Here is a pleasant situation, and yet nothing pleasant to be seen. Here is a harbour without ships, a port without trade, a fishery without nets, a people without business; and, that which is worse than all, they do not seem to desire business, much less do they understand it. I believe they are very good Christians at Kirkubry, for they are in the very letter of it, they obey the text,[6] and *are contented with such things as they have.* They have all the materials for trade, but no genius to it; all the opportunities for trade, but no inclination to it. In a word, they have no notion of being rich and populous, and thriving by commerce. They have a fine river, navigable for the greatest ships to the town-key; a haven, deep as a well, safe as a mill-pond; 'tis a meer wet dock, for the little island of Ross lyes in the very entrance, and keeps off the west and north west winds, and breaks the surge of the sea; so that when it is rough without, 'tis always smooth within. But, alas! there is not a vessel, that deserves the name of a ship, belongs to it; and, though here is an extraordinary salmon fishing, the salmon come and offer themselves, and go again, and cannot obtain the privilege of being made useful to mankind; for they take very few of them. They have also white fish, but cure none; and herrings, but pickle none. In a word, it is to me the wonder of all the towns of North-Britain; especially, being so near England, that it has all the invitations to trade that nature can give them, but they take no notice of it. A man might say of them, that they have the Indies at their door, and will not dip into the wealth of them; a gold mine at their door, and will not dig it.

It is true, the reason is in part evident, namely, poverty; no money to build vessels, hire seamen, buy nets and materials for fishing, to cure the fish when it is catch'd, or to carry it to market when it is cur'd; and this discourages the mind, checks industry, and prevents all manner of application.

Again, as the people have no hands (that is, no stock) to work, so the gentry have no genius to trade; 'tis a mechanism which they scorn; tho' their estates are not able to feed them, they will not turn their hands to business or improvement; they had rather see their sons made foot soldiers, (than which, as officers treat them now there is not a more abject thing on earth), than see them apply to trade, nay, to merchandize, or to the sea, because those things are not (forsooth) fit for gentlemen.

In a word, the common people all over this country, not only are poor, but look poor; they appear dejected and discourag'd, as if they had given over all hopes of ever being otherwise than what they are. They are, indeed, a sober, grave, religious people, and that more, ordinarily speaking, than in any other part of Scotland, far from what it is in England; conversation is generally sober, and grave; I assure you, they have no assemblies here, or balls; and far from what it is in England, you hear no oaths, or prophane words in the streets; and, if a mean boy, such as we call shoe-blackers, or black-guard boys, should be heard to swear, the next gentleman in the street, if any happen'd to be near him, would cane him, and correct him; whereas, in England, nothing is more frequent, or less regarded now, than the most horrid oaths and blasphemies in the open streets, and that by the little children that hardly know what an oath means.

The country of Galloway lies due west from Dumfries, and, as that they call the Upper Galloway, runs out farther than the rest, into the Irish Seas; all that bay or sea, on the south side of it may be reckoned part of Solway-Firth, as all on the north side is called the Firth of Clyde.

The wester Galloway, which is also call'd the shire of Wigtoun, from the town of Wigtoun, its capital, runs out with a peninsula, so far into the sea, that from the utmost shores, you see the coast of Ireland very plain, as you see Calais from Dover; and here is the town of Port Patrick, which is the ordinary place for the ferry or passage to Belfast or other ports in Ireland. It has a tolerable good harbour, and a safe road; but there is very little use for it, for the packet boat, and a few fishing vessels are the sum of the navigation; it is true, the passage or ferry is wide, and the boats very indifferent, without the least convenience or accommodation; and yet, which is strange, they very rarely, if ever miscarry; nay, they told us there, they had never lost one in the memory of the oldest man in the town, except one full of cattle; which, heeling to one side more than ordinary, all the cattle run to that side, and as it were, slid out into the sea; but the loading being out, the boat came to rights again, and was brought safe into the port, and none but the four-footed passengers were drown'd.

The people of Galloway do not starve; tho' they do not fish, build ships, trade abroad, &c. yet they have other business, that is to say, they are meer cultivaters of the earth, and in particular, breeders of cattle, such as sheep, the number of which I may say is infinite, that is to say, innumerable; and black cattle, of which they send to England, if fame lies not, 50 or 60000 every year, the very toll of which before the Union, was a little estate to some gentlemen upon the borders; and particularly the Earl of Carlisle had a very good income by it.

Besides the great number of sheep and runts, as we call them in England, which they breed here; they have the best breed of strong low horses in Britain, if not in Europe, which we call pads, and from whence we call all small truss-strong riding horses Galloways: these horses are remarkable for being good pacers, strong, easy goers, hardy, gentle, well broke, and above all, that they never tire, and they are very much bought up in England on that account.

By these three articles, the country of Galloway is far from being esteemed a poor country; for the wooll, as well as the sheep, is a very great fund of yearly wealth to them, and the black cattle and horses are hardly to be valued: the gentlemen generally take their rents in cattle, and some of them have so great

238. 'The Prospect of the Town of Aire from the East'; engraving. From John Slezer, *Theatrum Scotiae* (1693).

a quantity, that they go to England with their droves, and take the money themselves. It is no uncommon thing for a Galloway nobleman to send 4000 sheep, and 4000 head of black cattle to England in a year, and sometimes much more. Going from the lower Galloway hither, we were like all to be driven down the stream of a river, tho' a countryman went before for our guide, the water swelling upon us as we pass'd, the stream was very strong, so that I was oblig'd to turn my horse's head to the current, and so sloping over edg'd near the shore by degrees, whereas, if my horse had stood directly cross the stream, he could not have kept his feet.

We now enter'd the shire of Air, full north from the Mull of Galloway, and as before, we coasted the south bay or Firth of Solway, parting England from Scotland; now we coasted the Firth or sea of Clyde, which, for above sixty miles lies on the west side the shore, standing away north east from the point of the Mull, or north point of Galloway: the shire of Air is divided into three parts, Carrick, Kyle, and Cunningham.

Coming to the north bounds of Carrick, we pass'd the river Dun, upon a bridge of one arch, the largest I ever saw, much larger than the Rialto at Venice, or the middle arch of the great bridge at York. This bridge led us into the county of Kyle. Kyle is much better inhabited than Carrick, as Carrick is better than Galloway; and as the soil here is better, and the country plainer and leveller, so on the banks of the river, here are abundance of gentlemen's seats, some of them well planted, tho' most of the houses are old built, that is, castle-wise, because of enemies. But now that fear is over they begin to plant, and enclose after the manner of England; and the soil is also encouraging, for the land is fruitful.

The capital of this country is **Air**, a sea-port, and as they tell us, was formerly a large city, had a good harbour, and a great trade: I must acknowledge to you, that tho' I believe it never was a city, yet it has certainly been a good town, and much bigger than it is now: at present like an old beauty, it shews the ruins of a good face. What the reason of the decay of trade here was, or when it first began to decay, is hard to determine; nor are the people free to tell, and, perhaps, do not know themselves. There is a good river here, and a handsome stone bridge of four arches.

The town is well situated, has a very large antient church, and has still a very good market for all sorts of provision. But nothing will save it from death, if trade does not revive, which the townsmen say it begins to do since the Union.

From Air, keeping still north, we came to **Irwin**, upon a river of the same name; there is a port, but barr'd and difficult, and not very good, when you are in; and yet, here is more trade by a great deal than at Air; nay, than at all the ports between it and Dumfries, exclusive of the last; particularly here is a considerable trade for Scots coal, of which they have plenty in the neighbouring hills, and which they carry by sea to Ireland, to Belfast, to Carickfergus, and to Dublin itself, and the commerce occasioned by this navigation between the two countries is very considerable, and much to the advantage of the town of Irwin.

As the town is better employ'd in trade than the other parts I have been speaking of, so it is better built: here are two handsome streets, a good key, and not only room in the harbour for a great many ships, but a great many ships in it also; and, in a word, a face of thriving appears every where among them.

As is the town, so is the country in which it is situated; for when we came hither, we thought ourselves in

239. A view of Greenock; engraving by Robert Paul (1768).

England again. Here we saw no more a Galloway, where you have neither hedge or tree, but about the gentlemen's houses; whereas here you have beautiful enclosures, pleasant pastures, and grass grounds, and consequently store of cattle well fed and provided.

A little from Irwin is Kilmarnock Castle, the seat of the family of Boy'd, Earl of Kilmarnock; and on the other side the Castle of Eglington, the seat of the family of Montgomery, Earl of Eglington, an antient house; and the present Earl is one of the richest peers in Scotland. Just upon the borders of this county, north east, and where it joins to Clydsdale, is the Castle of Loudon, the family-seat of the Earl of Loudon, of the family of Campbell, formerly Secretary of State to Queen Anne; it is a noble and beautiful seat.

With the division of Cunningham I quitted the shire of Ayre, and the pleasantest country in Scotland, without exception: joining to it north, and bordering

240. 'A view of the Banks of Clyde taken from York Hill on the East side of the River Kelvin'; engraving by Robert Paul (1758).

241. 'Prospect of Glasgow from the South'; engraving. From John Slezer, *Theatrum Scotiae* (1693).

on the Clyde itself, I mean the river, lyes the little shire of Renfrew, or rather a barony, or a sheriffdom, call it as you will.

It is a pleasant, rich, and populous, tho' small country, lying on the south bank of the Clyde; the soil is not thought to be so good as in Cunningham: but that is abundantly supply'd by the many good towns, the neighbourhood of Glasgow, and of the Clyde, and great commerce of both. We kept our rout as near along the coast as we could, from Irwin; so that we saw all the coast of the Firth of Clyde, and the very opening of the Clyde itself, which is just at the west point, or corner of this county, for it comes to a narrow point just in that place. There are some villages and fishing towns within the mouth of the Clyde, which have more business than large port towns in Galloway and Carrick: but the first town of note is call'd **Greenock**; 'tis not an antient place, but seems to be grown up in later years, only by being a good road for ships, and where the ships ride that come into, and go out from Glasgow, just as the ships for London do in the downs. It has a castle to command the road, and the town is well built, and has many rich trading families in it. It is the chief town on the west of Scotland for the herring fishing; and the merchants of Glasgow, who are concern'd in the fishery, employ the Greenock vessels for the catching and curing the fish, and for several parts of their other trades, as well as carrying them afterwards abroad to market.

Their being ready on all hands to go to sea, makes the Glasgow merchants often leave their ships to the care of those Greenock men; and why not? for they are sensible they are their best seamen; they are also excellent pilots for those difficult seas.

The country between Pasely and Glasgow, on the bank of Clyde, I take to be one of the most agreeable places in Scotland, take its situation, its fertility, healthiness, the nearness of Glasgow, the neighbourhood of the sea, and altogether, at least, I may say, I saw none like it.

I am now come to the bank of Clyde: the Clyde and the Tweed may be said to cross Scotland in the south, their sources being not many miles asunder; and the two Firths, from the Firth of Clyde to the Firth of Forth, have not an interval of above twelve or fourteen miles. Nor can I refrain mentioning how easy a work it would be to form a navigation, I mean a navigation of art[7] from the Forth to the Clyde, and so join the two seas, as the King of France has done in a place five times as far, and five hundred times as difficult, namely from Thouloze to Narbonne. What an advantage in commerce would this be, opening the Irish trade to the merchants of Glasgow, making a communication between the west coast of Scotland, and the east coast of England, and even to London itself; nay, several ports of England, on the Irish Sea, from Liverpool northward, would all trade with London by such a canal.

I am now cross'd the Clyde to **Glasgow**, and I went over dry-footed without the bridge; on which occasion I cannot but observe how differing a face the river presented itself in, at those two several times when only I was there; at the first, being in the month of June, the river was so low, that not the horses and carts only pass'd it just above the bridge, but the children and boys playing about, went every where, as if there was no river, only some little spreading brook, or wash, like such as we have at Enfield-Wash, or Chelston-Wash in Middlesex. But my next journey satisfy'd me, when coming into Glasgow from the east side, I found

329

242. 'A view of the Trongate of Glasgow from the East;' engraving by William Buchanan after Robert Paul (*c*.1770). The Tolbooth is on the right hand side and the buildings reflect the prosperity that came in the wake of the increase in trade Defoe predicts.

the river not only had fill'd up all the arches of the bridge, but, running about the end of it, had fill'd the streets of all that part of the city next the bridge, to the infinite damage of the inhabitants, besides putting them into the greatest consternation imaginable, for fear of their houses being driven away by the violence of the water, and the whole city was not without apprehensions that their bridge would have given way too, which would have been a terrible loss to them, for 'tis as fine a bridge as most in Scotland.

Glasgow is, indeed, a very fine city; the four principal streets are the fairest for breadth, and the finest built that I have ever seen in one city together. The houses are all of stone, and generally equal and uniform in height, as well as in front; the lower story generally stands on vast square Dorick columns, not round pillars, and arches between give passage into the shops, adding to the strength as well as beauty of the building; in a word, 'tis the cleanest and beautifullest, and best built city in Britain, London excepted.

It stands on the side of a hill, sloping to the river, with this exception, that the part next the river is flat, as is said above, for near one third part of the city, and that expos'd it to the water, upon the extraordinary flood mention'd just now.

Where the streets meet, the crossing makes a spacious

market-place by the nature of the thing, because the streets are so large of themselves. As you come down the hill, from the north gate to the said cross, the Tolbooth, with the Stadhouse, or Guild-Hall, make the north east angle, or, in English, the right-hand corner of the street, the building very noble and very strong, ascending by large stone steps, with an iron balustrade. Here the town-council sit, and the magistrates try causes, such as come within their cognizance, and do all their publick business.

On the left-hand of the same street is the university, the building is the best of any in Scotland of the kind; it was founded by Bishop Turnbull, ann. 1454, but has been much enlarg'd since, and the fabrick almost all new built. It is a very spacious building, contains two large squares, or courts, and the lodgings for the scholars, and for the professors, are very handsome; the whole building is of freestone, very high and very august. Here is a Principal, with Regents and Professors in every science, as there is at Edinburgh, and the scholars wear gowns, which they do not at Edinburgh. Their gowns here are red, but the Masters of Arts, and Professors, wear black gowns, with a large cape of velvet to distinguish them.

The cathedral is an antient building, and has a square tower in the middle of the cross, with a very handsome spire upon it, the highest that I saw in Scotland, and, indeed, the only one that is to be call'd high. This, like St. Giles's at Edinburgh, is divided now, and makes three churches, and, I suppose, there is four or five more in the city, besides a meeting or two: but there are very few of the Episcopal Dissenters here; and the mob fell upon one of their meetings so often,

that they were oblig'd to lay it down, or, if they do meet, 'tis very privately.

The Duke of Montross has so great an interest here, and in the country round, that he is, in a civil sense, governor of this city, as he is legally of their university.

Glasgow is a city of business; here is the face of trade, as well foreign as home trade; and, I may say, 'tis the only city in Scotland, at this time, that apparently encreases and improves in both. The Union has answer'd its end to them more than to any other part of Scotland, for their trade is new form'd by it; and, as the Union open'd the door to the Scots in our American colonies, the Glasgow merchants presently fell in with the opportunity; and tho', when the Union was making, the rabble of Glasgow made the most formidable attempt to prevent it, yet, now they know better, for they have the greatest addition to their trade by it imaginable; and I am assur'd, that they send near fifty sail of ships every year to Virginia, New England, and other English colonies in America, and are every year increasing.

Could this city but have a communication with the Firth of Forth, so as to send their tobacco and sugar by water to Alloway, below Sterling, as they might from thence again to London, Holland, Hambrough, and the Baltick, they would, (for ought I know that should hinder it) in a few years double their trade, and send 100 sail, or more.

I have not time here to enlarge upon the home trade of this city, which is very considerable in many things, I shall only touch at some parts of them (viz.)

1. Here is one or two very handsome sugar-baking

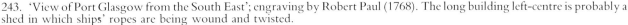

243. 'View of Port Glasgow from the South East'; engraving by Robert Paul (1768). The long building left-centre is probably a shed in which ships' ropes are being wound and twisted.

houses, carried on by skilful persons, with large stocks, and to a very great degree: I had the curiosity to view one of the houses, and I think it equal to, if not exceeding most in London. Also there is a large distillery for distilling spirits from the molasses drawn from the sugars, and which they call'd Glasgow Brandy, and in which they enjoy'd a vast advantage for a time, by a reserv'd article in the Union, freeing them from the English duties, I say for a time.

2. Here is a manufacture of plaiding[8] a stuff cross-strip'd with yellow and red, and other mixtures for the plaids or vails,[9] which the ladies in Scotland wear, and which is a habit peculiar to the country.

3. Here is a manufacture of muslins, and, perhaps, the only manufacture of its kind in Britain, if not in Europe; and they make them so good and so fine, that great quantities of them are sent into England, and sold there at a good price; they are generally strip'd, and are very much used for aprons by the ladies, and sometimes in head-clothes by the English women of a meaner sort, and many of them are sent to the British plantations.

4. Here is also a linnen manufacture; but as that is in common with all parts of Scotland, I do not insist so much upon it here, though they make a very great quantity of it, and send it to the plantations also as a principal merchandise.

Nor are the Scots without a supply of goods for sorting their cargoes to the English colonies, even without sending to England for them.

1. They have several woollen manufactures which they send of their own making; such as the Sterling serges, Musclebrow stuffs, Aberdeen stockings, Edinburgh shalloons, blankets, &c. So that they are not quite destitute in the woollen manufacture, tho' that is the principal thing in which England can outdo them.

2. The trade with England being open, they have now, all the Manchester wares, Sheffield wares, and Newcastle hard wares; as also the cloths, kerseys, half-thicks, duffels, stockings, and coarse manufactures of the north of England, as cheap brought to them by horse-packs as they can be carried to London; nor is the carriage farther, and, in some articles, not so far by much.

3. They have linnens of most kinds, especially diapers and table-linnen, damasks, and many other sorts not known in England, cheaper than England, because made at their own doors.

4. What linnens they want from Holland, or Hamburgh, they import from thence as cheap as can be done in England; and for muslins, their own are very acceptable, and cheaper than in England.

5. Gloves they make better and cheaper than in England, for they send great quantities thither.

6. Another article, which is very considerable here, is servants,[10] and these they have in greater plenty, and upon better terms than the English; without the scandalous art of kidnapping, making drunk, wheedling, betraying, and the like; the poor people offering themselves fast enough, and thinking it their advantage to go; as indeed it is, to those who go with sober resolutions, namely, to serve out their times, and then become diligent planters for themselves; and this would be a much wiser course in England than to turn thieves, and worse, and then be sent over by force, and as a pretence of mercy to save them from the gallows.

This may be given as a reason, and, I believe, is the only reason why so many more of the Scots servants, which go over to Virginia, settle and thrive there, than of the English, which is so certainly true, that if it goes on for many years more, Virginia may be rather call'd a Scots than an English plantation.

I was here in some doubt, whether I should take the south or the north in the next part of my progress; that is to say, whether to follow up the Clyde, and so into, and through Clydsdale, and then crossing east, view the shire of Peebles, the country on the banks of Tweed and Tivyot, or keeping to the north, go on for the Forth; and after a short debate we concluded on the latter. So we turn'd to the left for Sterling-shire, and passing the Clyde we came to Kilsyth, a good plain country burgh, tolerably well built, but not large.

From Kilsyth we mounted the hills black and frightful as they were, to find the road over the moors and mountains to Sterling, and being directed by our guides, came to the river Carron: the channel of a river appear'd, indeed, and running between horrid precipices of rocks, as if cut by hand, on purpose for the river to make its way; but not a drop of water was to be seen. Great stones, square and form'd, as if cut out by hand, of a prodigious size, some of them at least a ton, or ton and half in weight, lay scatter'd, and confusedly, as it were, jumbled together in the very course of the river, which the fury of the water, at other times, I doubt not, had hurried down from the mountains, and tumbled them thus over one another.

From hence, descending on the north side, we had a view of the Firth, or Forth, on our right, the castle of Sterling on the left; and in going to the latter we pass'd the famous water, for river it is not, of Bannock Bourn,[11] famous, in the Scots history for the great battle fought here between King Rob. de Bruce and the English army, commanded by King Edw. II in person, in which the English were utterly overthrown; and that with so terrible a slaughter, that of the great-

244. 'The Prospect of their Majesties Castle of Sterling'; engraving. From John Slezer, *Theatrum Scotiae* (1693).

est army that every march'd from England into Scotland, very few escap'd; and King Edw. II with much ado, sav'd himself by flight.

Sterling was our next stage, an antient city, or town rather, and an important pass, which, with Dunbarton, is indeed the defence of the Lowlands against the Highlands; and, as one very knowingly said, Dunbarton is the lock of the Highlands, and Sterling-castle keeps the key. The town is situated as like Edinburgh as almost can be describ'd, being on the ridge of a hill, sloping down on both sides, and the street ascending from the east gradually to the castle, which is at the west end; the street is large and well built, but antient, and the buildings not unlike Edinburgh, either for beauty or sight.

They who built the castle, without doubt built it, as the Scots express it, to continue *aye*, and till somebody else should build another there, which, in our language, would be *for ever and a day after*: the walls, and all the outer works are firm, and if no force is us'd to demolish them, may continue inconceivably long, at least we have reason to believe they will; for though the other buildings grow old, the castle seems as firm and fair, as if it had been but lately built.

The palace and royal apartments are very magnificent, but all in decay, and must be so: were the materials of any use, we thought it would be much better to pull them down than to let such noble buildings sink into their own rubbish, by the meer injury of time: but it is at present the fate of all the royal houses in Scotland; Haly-Rood at Edinburgh excepted.

In the park, adjoining to the castle, were formerly large gardens, how fine they were I cannot say; the figure of the walks and grass-plats remains plain to be

seen, they are very old fashion'd; but I suppose the gardens might be thought fine, as gardens were then; particularly they had not then the usage of adorning their gardens with ever-greens, trimm'd and shap'd; trees espalier'd into hedges and such-like, as now: they had, indeed, statues and busts, vasa, and fountains, flowers and fruit; but we make gardens fine now many ways, which those ages had no genius for; as by scrouls, embroidery,[12] pavillions, terrasses and slopes, pyramids and high espaliers, and a thousand ornaments, which they had no notion of.

The park here is large and wall'd about, as all the parks in Scotland are, but little or no wood in it. The Earl of Mar, of the name of Ereskin, who claims to be hereditary keeper of the king's children, as also hereditary keeper of the castle, has a house at the upper end of the town, and very finely situated for prospect.

The governor's lady (who was the Countess Dowager of Marr, when we were there, and mother of the late exil'd Earl of Marr[13]), had a very pretty little flower-garden, upon the body of one of the bastions, or towers of the castle, the ambrusiers[14] serving for a dwarf-wall round the most part of it; and they walk'd to it from her ladyship's apartment upon a level, along the castle-wall.

As this little, but very pleasant spot, was on the north side of the castle, we had from thence a most agreeable prospect indeed over the valley and the river; as it is truly beautiful, so it is what the people of Sterling justly boast of, and, indeed, seldom forget it, I mean the meanders, or reaches of the river Forth. They are so spacious, and return so near themselves, with so regular and exact a sweep, that, I think, the like is not to be seen in Britain, if it is in Europe, especially where the river is so large also.

I was, indeed, curious to enquire into the course of this river, as I had been before into that of the Clyde as to the possibility of their waters being united for an inland navigation; because I had observ'd that the charts and plans of the country brought them almost to meet; but when I came more critically to survey the ground, I found the map-makers greatly mistaken, and that they had not only given the situation and courses of the rivers wrong, but the distances also. However, upon the whole, I brought it to this; that notwithstanding several circumstances which might obstruct it, and cause the workmen to fetch some winding turns out of the way, yet, that in the whole, a canal of about eight miles in length would fairly join the rivers, and make a clear navigation from the Irish to the German Sea; and that this would be done without any considerable obstruction; so that there would not need above four sluices in the whole way, and those only to head a bason, or receptacle, to contain a flash, or flush of water to push on the vessels this way or that, as occasion requir'd, not to stop them to raise or let fall, as in the case of locks in other rivers.

There is a very considerable manufacture at Sterling, for what they call Sterling serges,[15] which are in English, shalloons; and they both make them and dye them there very well; nor has the English manufacture of shalloons broke in so much upon them by the late Union, as it was fear'd they would. This manufacture employs the poor very comfortably here, and is a great part of the support of the town as to trade, showing what Scotland might soon be brought to by the help of trade and manufactures; for the people are as willing to work here as in England, if they had the same encouragement, that is, if they could be constantly employ'd and paid for it too, as they are there.

But our business was not to the north yet; still having a part of the border to view. So we went from Sterling, first east and then south-east, over some of the same hills, which we pass'd at our coming hither, though not by the same road. The Duke of Argyle has a small house, which the family call'd the Lowland House, I suppose in distinction from the many fine seats and strong castles which they were always possess'd of in the Highlands: this seat was formerly belonging to the Earls of Sterling; and the country round it, south of the Forth, is call'd Sterlingshire, or Strivelingshire, and sends a member to Parliament, as a shire or county. The family of the Earls of Sterling is extinct, at least, if there are any of the name, as is alledg'd, they live obscurely in England. They make great complaint at Sterling, which they derive from the Papists, that the old Earl of Marr, who built the family-house under the castle, as I have just now said, was a clergy-man and prior, or abbot of the famous monastery of Cambuskeneth, a religious house, of the order of the Augustines, which stood not far off.

That upon the Reformation the said abbot turn'd Protestant and married, and was created Earl of Marr:

245. Stirling Bridge; drawing by Paul Sandby (c.1748). From Thomas Pennant, *A Tour in Scotland* (1769–72 (large set).

246. 'Prospect of Their Majesties palace of Linlithgow'; engraving. From John Slezer, *Theatrum Scotiae* (1693).

that he was so zealous afterwards for the change of religion, that he set his hand to the demolishing his own monastery; and that he brought away the stones of it to Sterling, and built this fine house with them; upon which the Romanists branded him with sacrilege and avarice together, and gave him their curse, which is not unusual in Scotland.

This clamour, however, did not hinder him from going on with his house, which he finish'd, as you see; but 'tis suppos'd those reproaches occasion'd his setting up several inscriptions, as well without the house as within; some of them are worn out with time, others are legible; whereof this distich in a Scots dialect, I think, points at the case.

> Speak forth, and spare nocht,
> Consider well, I care nocht.

There is nothing remarkable between Sterling and Lithgow but Bannockbourn, which I have mention'd already, and some private gentlemen's seats, too many to repeat.

Lithgow is a large town, well built, and antiently famous for the noble palace[16] of the kings of Scotland, where King James VI and his queen kept their court in great magnificence. This court, though decaying with the rest, is yet less decay'd, because much later repair'd than others; for King James repair'd, or rather rebuilt some of it: and his two sons, Prince Henry, and Prince Charles, afterwards king of England, had apartments here; and there are the Prince of Wales's arms, over those, call'd the Prince's lodgings to this day.

At Lithgow there is a very great linnen manufacture, as there is at Glasgow; and the water of the lough, or lake here, is esteem'd with the best in Scotland for bleaching or whitening of linnen cloth: so that a great deal of linnen, made in other parts of the country, is brought either to be bleach'd or whiten'd.

This lough is situate on the north west side of the town, just by the palace; and there were formerly fine walks planted on both sides, with bordures and flowers from the house to the water's edge, which must be very delightful.

The church of St. Michael makes a part of the royal building, and is the wing on the right hand of the first court, as all the proper offices of the court made the left: but the inner court is the beauty of the building, was very spacious, and, in those days, was thought glorious. There is a large fountain in the middle of the court, which had then abundance of fine things about it, whereof some of the carvings and ornaments remain still.

Here the kings of Scotland, for some ages, kept their courts on occasion of any extraordinary ceremony. And here King James V reinstituted, or rather restor'd the Order of the Knights of St. Andrew,[17] as the Order of Knights of the Bath were lately restor'd in

335

THE LINEN INDUSTRY

247a–e. Some illustrations of processes in the Linen industry; engravings (published by William Hincks, 1783). Although the examples are from Ireland, they illustrate general principles of techniques employed before the industrial revolution.

a. Beetling (beating with cylindrical beetle), scutching (beating with a scutching blade) to separate fibres, followed by hackling (drawing across the pins of the hackle board) to separate out the flax fibres and make them lie in a single direction.

b. Boiling, spinning and reeling the yarn.

c. Winding, warping and weaving.

d. Bleach mill where the textile is boiled, wrung out, soaped, put through a wash mill, passed between rubbing boards and sent under pressure through the beetling engine to glaze the cloth.

e. Lapping room where the cloth is measured, checked for flaws and converted from folded or lapped cloth into a roll and compressed.

England. Here he erected stalls, and a throne for them in St. Michael's Church, and made it the Chapel of the Order, according to the usage at Windsor.

Lithgow is a pleasant, handsome, well built town; the Tolbooth is a good building, and not old, kept in good repair, and the streets clean: the people look here as if they were busy, and had something to do, whereas in many towns we pass'd through they seem'd as if they look'd disconsolate for want of employment: the whole green, fronting the lough or lake, was cover'd with linnen-cloth, it being the bleaching season, and, I believe, a thousand women and children, and not less, tending and managing the bleaching business; the town is serv'd with water by one very large bason, or fountain, to which the water is brought from the same spring which serv'd the royal palace.

From Lithgow we turn'd to the right, as I said above, into the shire of Clydsdale: some business also calling us this way, and following the Clyde upwards, from a little above Hamilton, where we were before, we came to Lanerk, which is about eight miles from it due south.

From Lithgow, by this way to Lanerk, is thirty long miles; and some of the road over the wildest country we had yet seen. Lanerk is the capital indeed of the country, otherwise it is but a very indifferent place; it is eminent for the assembling of the Bothwell-Bridge rebellion,[18] and several other little disturbances of the Whigs in those days; for Whigs then were all Presbyterians, and Cameronian Presbyterians too, which, at that time, was as much as to say rebels.

A little below Lanerk the river Douglass falls into the Clyde, giving the same kind of usual surname to the lands about it, as I have observ'd other rivers do, namely Douglassdale, as the Clyde does that of Clydsdale, the Tweed that of Tweedale; and so of the rest.

In this dull vale stands the antient, paternal estate and castle, which gives name (and title too) to the great family of Douglass. The castle is very ill adapted to the glory of the family; but as it is the antient inheritance, the heads or chief of the name have always endeavour'd to keep up the old mansion, and have consequently, made frequent additions to the building, which have made it a wild, irregular mass; yet there are noble apartments in it, and the house seems, at a distance, rather a little town than one whole fabrick. The park is very large; the garden, or yards, as they call them, not set out with fine plants or greens, or divided into flower-gardens, parters, wildernesses, kitchin-gardens, &c. as is the modern usage. In short, 'tis an antient, magnificent pile, great, but not gay; its grandeur, in most parts, consists in its antiquity,

and being the mansion of one of the greatest families in Scotland above 1000 years.

From Lanerk we left the wild place call'd Crawford Muir on the right, the business that brought us round this way being finish'd, and went away west into the shire of Peebles, and so into Tweedale; the first town we came to of any note upon the Tweed, is the town of Peebles, capital of the country. The town is small, and but indifferently built or inhabited, yet the high street has some good houses on it. There is a handsome stone-bridge over the Tweed, which is not a great river here, though the current is sometimes indeed very violent.

The country is hilly, as in the rest of Tweedale, and those hills cover'd with sheep, which is, indeed, a principal part of the estates of the gentlemen; and the overplus quantity of the sheep, as also their wool, is mostly sent to England, to the irreparable damage of the poor; who, were they employ'd to manufacture their own wool, would live much better than they do, and find the benefit of the Union in a different manner, from what they have yet done.

Before the Union this wool, and more with it, brought by stealth out of England, went all away to France, still (as I say) to the great loss of the poor, who, had they but spun it into yarn, and sent the yarn into France, would have had some benefit by it; but the Union bringing with it a prohibition of the exportation, upon the severest penalties, the gentlemen of the southern countries complain'd of the loss, at the time that affair was transacted in Parliament; to make them amends for which, a large sum of money was appointed to them as an equivalent,[19] and to encourage them to set the poor to work, as appears by the Act of Union; this money, I say, was appropriated by the Act to be employ'd in setting hands to work in Scotland, to manufacture their own wool by their own people: how much of the money has been so employ'd, I desire not to examine, I leave it to them whose proper business it is.

Here are two monuments in this country, all Scotland not affording the like, of the vanity of worldly glory. The one is in the foundation of a royal palace, or seat of a nobleman, once the first man in Scotland, next the king: it is a prodigious building, too great for a subject, begun by the Earl of Morton, whose head being afterwards lay'd in the dust, his design perish'd; and the building has not been carry'd on, and, I suppose never will.

The other is in the palace of Traquair, built and finish'd by the late Earl of Traquair,[20] for some years Lord High Treasurer of Scotland, and a person in the highest posts, both of honour and profit in the king-

248. 'The Ruines of the Abbie of Melross'; engraving. From John Slezer, *Theatrum Scotiae* (1693).

dom, who yet fell from it all, by the adversity of the times; for his conduct under his majesty King Charles I being generally censur'd, and himself universally hated, he sunk into the most abject and lowest part of human life, even to want bread, and to take alms, and in that miserable circumstance died, and never saw the turn of the times, I mean the Restoration, which happen'd but a year after his death.

Here we saw the ruins of the once famous abbey of Mailross,[21] the greatness of which may be a little judg'd of by its vastly extended remains, which are of a very great circuit: the building is not so entirely demolish'd but that we may distinguish many places and parts of it one from another; as particularly the great church or chapel of the monastery, which is as large as some cathedrals, the choir of which is visible, and measures 140 foot in length, besides what may have been pull'd down at the east end; by the thickness of the foundations there must have been a large and strong tower or steeple in the center of the church, but of what form or height, that no guess can be made at: there are several fragments of the house itself, and of the particular offices belonging to it; the court, the cloyster, and other buildings are so visible, as that 'tis easy to know it was a most magnificent place in those days. But the Reformation has triumph'd over all these

things, and the pomp and glory of Popery is sunk now into the primitive simplicity of the true Christian profession; nor can any Protestant mourn the loss of these seminaries of superstition, upon any principles that agree, either with his own profession, or with the Christian pattern prescrib'd in the Scriptures.

The country next this, south east, is call'd Tiviotdale, or otherwise the shire of Roxburgh; and the Duke of Roxburgh has several fine seats in it, as well as a very great estate; indeed most of the country belongs to the family: his house call'd Floors[22] is an antient seat, but begins to wear a new face; and those who view'd it fifteen or sixteen years ago, will scarce know it again, if they should come a few years hence, when the present Duke may have finished the additions and embellishments, which he is now making, and has been a considerable time upon. Nor will the very face of the country appear the same, except it be that the river Tweed may, perhaps, run in the same channel: but the land before, lying open and wild, he will find enclos'd, cultivated and improv'd, rows, and even woods of trees covering the champaign country, and the house surrounded with large grown vistas, and well planted avenues, such as were never seen there before.

From hence we came to ***Kelsoe***, a handsome market-town upon the bank of the Tweed. Here is a

249. 'The Prospect of the Town of Kelso'; engraving. From John Slezer, *Theatrum Scotiae* (1693).

very large antient church,[23] being built in the place of an old monastery of fryars, the ruins of which are yet to be seen: the church now standing seems to have been the real chapel of the monastery, not a new one erected; only modell'd from the old one; for though it is itself a great building, yet it has certainly been much larger. Its antiquity argues this, for by the building it must have been much antienter than the Reformation.

Kelsoe, as it stands on the Tweed, and so near the English border, is a considerable thorough-fair to England, one of the great roads from Edinburgh to Newcastle lying through this town, and a nearer way by far than the road through Berwick.

They only want a good bridge over the Tweed: at present they have a ferry just at the town, and a good ford through the river, a little below it.

From Kelso we went north, where we pass'd through Lauderdale, a long valley on both sides the little river Lauder, from whence the house of Maitland, Earls first, and at last Duke of Lauderdale, took their title.

The country is good here, tho' fenc'd with hills on both sides; the river Lauder runs in the middle of it, keeping its course north, and the family-seat of Lauder, stands about the middle of the valley: 'tis an antient house, and not large; nor did it receive any additions

from Duke Lauderdale,[24] who found ways to dispose of his fortunes another way.

From hence we kept the great road over a high ridge of mountains, from whence we had a plain view of that part of the country call'd Mid-Lothian, and where we also saw the city of Edinburgh at the distance of about twelve or fourteen miles. We pass'd these mountains at a place which they call Soutra-Hill, and which gives the title of Laird of Soutra to a branch of the family of Maitland, the elder brother of which house was Lieutenant-General Maitland,[25] a gentleman of great merit, and who rais'd himself by the sword: he lost one of his hands at the great battle of Treves in Germany, where the French army, under the Mareschal De Crequi, was defeated by the Germans, commanded by the old Duke of Zell; he supply'd the want of his hand with one of steel, from which he was call'd Handy Maitland.

I could not pass this way to Edinburgh without going off a little to the right, to see two very fine seats, one belonging to the Marquess of Louthian, of the antient name of Ker, a younger branch of the house of Roxburgh, at Newbattle[26] or Newbottle. 'Tis an old building, but finely situated among the most agreeable walks and rows of trees, all full grown, and is particularly to be mention'd for the nicest, and best chosen collection of pictures of any house I have seen in Scotland: the particulars are too many to enter into a description of them. The statues and busts are also very fine; and there are the most pictures of particular families and persons, as well of the royal families of France and England, as of Scotland also, that are, I believe, not only in England, but in any palace in Europe.

Not two miles from hence is the Dutchess of Bucclugh's house at Dalkeith,[27] the finest and largest new built house in Scotland; the Dutchess, relict of the late Duke of Monmouth, has built it, as I may say, from the foundation, or as some say, upon the foundation of the old castle of Dalkeith, which was the estate of the great Earl of Morton, Regent of Scotland, who was beheaded by King James VI that is, of England, James I, the same that brought the engine[28] to behead humane bodies from Hallifax in Yorkshire, and set it up in Scotland, and had his own head cut off with it, the first it was try'd upon.

The palace of Dalkeith is, indeed, a magnificent building, and the inside answerable to the grandeur of the family. It stands on a rising ground on the edge of the river Esk; the side to the river is a precipice, from whence it overlooks the plain with a majesty, like that of Windsor, on the bank of the Thames, with necessary allowance for the difference of the country, and of the two rivers, which bear, indeed, no proportion. The park is very large, and there are fine avenues, some already made and planted, others design'd, but not yet finish'd; also there are to be water-works, *jette d'eaus*, and a canal, but these are not yet laid out; nor are the gardens finish'd, or the terrasses, which will be very spacious, if done according to the design. There are many fine paintings, especially of the ladies of the English court, and some royal originals; but we must not speak of pictures where Newbottle is so nigh.

The town of ***Dalkeith*** is just without the park, and is a pretty large market-town, and the better market for being so near Edinburgh; for there comes great quantities of provisions hither from the southern countries, which are bought up here to be carried to Edinburgh market again, and sold there. The town is spacious, and well built, and is the better, no doubt, for the neighbourhood of so many noblemen's and gentlemen's houses of such eminence in its neighbourhood.

This brought us to the very sight of the city of Edinburgh, where we rested a few days, having thus finished our circuit over the whole south of Scotland, on this side of the river Forth, and on the south side of the Firth of Clyde. So I shall conclude this letter,

And am, &c.

The End of the Twelfth Letter

LETTER XIII

Sir,

I AM NOW TO ENTER the true and real Caledonia, for the country on the north of the Firth is alone call'd by that name, and was antiently known by no other.

I went over the Firth at the Queens-Ferry, a place mention'd before, seven miles west of Edinburgh; and, as he that gives an account of the country of Fife, must necessarily go round the coast, the most considerable places being to be seen on the seaside, or near it; so I took that method, and began at the Queens-Ferry. A mile from hence, or something more, is the burrough of Innerkeithin, an antient wall'd town, with a spacious harbour, opening from the east part of the town into the Firth of Forth; the mouth of the harbour has a good depth of water, and ships of burthen may ride there with safety; but as there is not any great trade here, and consequently no use for shipping of burthen, the harbour has been much neglected: however, small vessels may come up to the key, such as are sufficient for their business.

The town is large, and is still populous, but decay'd, as to what it has formerly been; yet the market for linnen not only remains, but is rather more considerable than formerly, by reason of the increase of that manufacture since the Union. The market for provisions is also very considerable here, the country round being very fruitful, and the families of gentlemen being also numerous in the neighbourhood.

Near Innerkeithin, a little within the land, stands the antient town of **Dumfermling**, as I may say, in my Lord Rochester's words,[1] in its full perfection of decay; nay, the decay is threefold.

1. Here is a decay'd monastery; for before the Reformation here was a very large and famous abbey, but demolish'd at the Revolution; and saving, that part of the church was turn'd into a parochial church, the rest, and greatest part of that also lyes in ruins, and with it the monuments of several kings and queens of Scotland; particularly that of Malcolm III who founded the monastery, as does also the cloister and apartments for the religious people of the house, great part of

which are yet so plain to be seen, as to be distinguish'd one from another.

2. Here is a decay'd court or royal palace[2] of the kings of Scotland. They do not tell us who built this palace, but we may tell them who suffers it to fall down; for it is now (as it was observ'd before all the royal houses are) sinking into its own ruins; the windows are gone, the roof fallen in, and part of the very walls moulder'd away by the injury of time, and of the times. In this palace almost all King James the VIth's children were born; as particularly King Charles I and the Princess Elizabeth, afterwards Queen of Bohemia; and their mother, which was Queen Ann daughter of the Queen of Denmark, made this place her particular residence, which was also settled upon her as her dower of jointure; here she built herself an apartment, consisting of eight rooms over the arch of the great gate, which were her particular retirement, having a gallery reaching from that apartment to the royal lodgings.

The figure of the house remains, but as for the lodgings they are all, as I have said, in their decay, and we may now call it the monument of a court.

3. Here is a decay'd town, and we need go no farther for that part than the decay of the palace, which is irrecoverable; there might be something said here of what was done at this town, upon receiving and crowning King Charles II, by the Covenanters,[3] &c. and which might, perhaps, contribute to entail a disgust upon the house, and even upon the place; and if it did so, I see no reason to blame the King on that account, for the memory of the place could not be pleasant to his majesty for many reasons: But this is matter of history, and besides, it seems to have something in it that is not, perhaps, so well to be remember'd as to be forgot.

The people hereabout are poor, but would be much poorer, if they had not the manufacture of linnen for their support, which is here, and in most of the towns about, carry'd on with more hands than ordinary, especially for diaper,[4] and the better sort of linnen: the

343

250. 'Prospect of the town and abbey of Dunfermling'; engraving. From John Slezer, *Theatrum Scotiae* (1693).

Marquess of Tweedale has a good estate in these parts, and is hereditary House-keeper, or Porter of the Royal House, and, in effect, Lord Chamberlain.

From hence, turning east, we see many seats of private gentlemen, and some of noblemen, as particularly one belonging to the said Marquess of Tweedale at Aberdour. It was formerly one of the many noble mansion houses of the great Earl Mortoun, Regent; but with his fall the estates found new masters, as that of Dalkeith has in the house of Bucclugh, and this of Aberdour in the house of Yester, or Tweedale. The house is old, but magnificent, and the lands about it, as all must do, that come into the managing hands of the family of Tweedale, have been infinitely improv'd by planting and enclosing.

This house of Aberdour fronts the Firth to the south, and the grounds belonging to it reach down to the shores of it. From this part of the Firth, to the mouth of Innerkeithen harbour, is a very good road for ships, the water being deep and the ground good; but the western part, which they call St. Margaret's Bay, is a steep shore, and rocky, there being twenty fathom water within a ship's length of the rocks: so that in case of a south east wind, and if it blow hard, it may be dangerous riding too near. But a south east wind

blows so seldom, that the ships often venture it; and I have seen large ships ride there.

Having seen Aberdour, I took a turn, at a friend's invitation, to Lessly; but by the way stopp'd at **Kinross**, where we had a view of two things worth noting. 1. The famous lake or lough, call'd Lough Leven, where, in an island, stands the old castle where Queen Mary, commonly known in England by the name of Queen of Scots, was confin'd by the first Reformers, after she had quitted, or been forc'd to quit her favourite Bothwel, and put herself into the hands of her subjects. One would have thought this castle, standing as it were in the middle of the sea, for so it is in its kind, should have been sufficient to have held her, but she made shift to get out of their hands, whether by a silver key, or without a key, I believe is not fully known to this day.

The Lough itself is worth seeing; 'tis very large, being above ten miles about, and in some places deep, famous for fish. Formerly it had good salmon, but now chiefly trouts, and other small fish; out of it flows the river Leven, which runs from thence to Lessly.

At the west end of the lake, and the gardens reaching down to the very water's edge, stands the most beautiful and regular piece of architecture, (for a private

344

gentleman's seat) in all Scotland, perhaps, in all Britain, I mean the house of Kinross.[5] The town lies at a little distance from it, so as not to annoy the house, and yet so as to make it the more sociable; and at the town is a very good market, and the street tolerably well built.

The house is a picture, 'tis all beauty; the stone is white and fine, the order regular, the contrivance elegant, the workmanship exquisite.

Sir William Bruce, the skilful builder, was the Surveyor-General of the Works, as we call it in England, or the Royal Architect, as in Scotland.

The situation of this house of Kinross would be disliked by some for its being so very near the water, and that sometimes when the lake is swelled by winter rains and melted snows, the water comes into, or at least unto the very gardens; but as the country round is dry, free from stagnated boggs, and unhealthy marshes; this little mediterranean sea gives them very little inconvenience, if any. Sir William, according to the new and laudable method of all the Scots gentlemen, has planted innumerable numbers of firr-trees upon the estate round his house, and the present pos-

sessor Mr. Bruce, is as careful to improve as his predecessor: posterity will find the sweet of this passion for planting, which is so happily spread among the people of the south-parts of Scotland, and which, if it goes on, will in time make Scotland a second Norway for firr; for the Low-lands, as well as the Highlands, will be overspread with timber.

From Kinross, I came to **Lessley**, where I had a full view of the palace of Rothess, both inside and outside, as I had before of that of Bruce. The magnificence of the inside at Lessly is unusually great; but what is very particular, is the long gallery, which is the full length of one side of the building, and is fill'd with paintings, but especially (as at Drumlanrig) of the great ancestors of the house of Rothes or Lessly at full lengths, and in their robes of office or habits of ceremony; particularly the late Duke of Rothess, who built the house, and who was Lord High Chancellor of Scotland.

This house was built for the Duke mentioned above, in the reign of King Charles II by that man of art and master of building Sir William Bruce mentioned there also, so that the building is wholly modern. It is a square, and the fronts every way are plain, that is,

251. Kinross House; engraving by Richard Cooper from a drawing by John Borlach (one of the draughtsmen used by James Gibbs). From *Vitruvius Scoticus* (1810) pl. 62.

without wings, and make a square court within: here it was King James II lodged, most part of the time, when he was oblig'd by his brother, King Charles II to retire into Scotland while he was Duke of York; and his apartments are marked in the house and call'd the Duke of York's lodgings to this day. They had a communication with the long gallery, and with the great staircase at the other end.

The town of Lessly is at a small distance west from the house or a little north-west. There is a good market, but otherwise it is not considerable. The house is the glory of the place, and indeed of the whole province of Fife.

From Lessly, we turn'd away south to the coast, and came to **Bruntisland**; this is a port upon the Firth or Forth, and lies opposite to Leith, so that there is a fair prospect as well of the road of Leith, and the ships riding there, as of the city and castle of Edinburgh. There is a very good harbour which enters as if it had been made by hand into the center of the town; for the town is as it were built round it, and the ships lay their broad sides to the very houses. There is water enough at spring-tides, for ships of good burthen to come into the basin; but at low-water some of the ships lye a-ground: But want of trade renders all this useless; for what is the best harbour in the world without ships? And whence should ships be expected without a commerce to employ them; it is true, the ships of several other towns on the coast frequently put into this harbour, to lay up, as we call it, and to lye by in the winter: but this does not so much better the town as to make it be call'd a trading town; so that, indeed, the place is unhappy, and must decay yet farther, unless the trade revive, which, I confess, I do not yet foresee.

Here is, however, a manufacture of linnen, as there is upon all the coast of Fife, and especially for that they call green-cloth, which is now in great demand in England for the printing-trade, in the room of callicoes, which were lately prohibited.

Next to this is **Kinghorn** upon the same coast, where, not the sea, but the manufacture upon the land may be said to maintain the place; for here is a thread manufacture, which they make very good, and bleach or whiten it themselves. The women, indeed, chiefly carry on this trade, and the men are generally seamen upon all this coast, as high as the Queens-Ferry. Where I observ'd the men carry'd on an odd kind of trade, or sport rather (viz.) of shooting of porpoises, of which very great numbers are seen almost constantly in the Firth; when they catch them thus, they bring them on shore, and boil the fat of them as they do of whales, into train oil, and the like they do with

several other great fish, which sometimes they find in the sea there; and sometimes they have grampusses, finn fish, and several species of the small whale kind which come up there, and which they always make the best of, if they can take them. One year in particular there came several such fish on shore, which they could find no name for; there was eight or nine of them, which I saw lying on the shore of Fife, from Kinghorn to the Easter Weems, some of which were twenty foot long and upward.

East of this town is **Kirkcaldy**, a larger, more populous, and better built town than the other, and indeed than any on this coast. Its situation is in length, in one street running along the shore, from east to west, for a long mile, and very well built, the streets clean and well pav'd; there are some small by streets or lanes, and it has some considerable merchants in it, I mean in the true sense of the word merchant. There are also several good ships belonging to the town: also as Fife is a good corn country, here are some that deal very largely in corn, and export great quantities both to England and Holland. Here are great quantities of linnen shipp'd off for England; and as these ships return freighted either from England or Holland, they bring all needful supplies of foreign goods; so that the traders in Kirkcaldy have really a very considerable traffick, both at home and abroad.

There are several coal-pits here, not only in the neighbourhood, but even close to the very sea, at the west end of the town, and where, one would think, the tide should make it impossible to work them. At the east end of the town is a convenient yard for building and repairing of ships, and farther east than that several salt-pans for the boyling and making of salt.

Kirkcaldy is a member of the Royal Burroughs,[6] as are also Bruntisland, Kinghorn, and Dysert, tho' almost all of them together are not equal to this town: so that here are no less than four Royal Burroughs in the riding of five miles.

Dysert is next, a town that gives the title of noble or Baron to the Lord Dysert,[7] who resides in England, tho' the property both of the town and the lands adjoining, belong to the Lord Sinclare or St. Clare: but be the estate whose it will, the town, though a Royal Burgh, is, as I said before of Dumfermling, in the full perfection of decay, and is, indeed, a most lamentable object of a miserable, dying corporation; the only support which, I think, preserves the name of a town to it, is, that here is, in the lands adjoining, an excellent vein of Scots coal, and the Lord Dysert, the landlord, has a good salt-work in the town; close to the sea there is a small peer or wharf for ships, to come and load both the salt and the coal: and this, I think, may be said to be the whole trade of the town, except some nailers and hard-ware workers, and they are but few.

I take the decay of all these sea-port towns, which 'tis evident have made a much better figure in former times, to be owing to the removing of the court and nobility of Scotland to England; for it is most certain, when the court was at home, they had a confluence of strangers, residence of foreign ministers, being of armies, &c. and consequently the nobility dwelt at home, spent the income of their estates, and the product of their country among their neighbours. The return of their coal and salt, and corn and fish, brought them in goods from abroad, and, perhaps, money; they sent their linnen and other goods to England, and receiv'd the returns in money; they made their own manufactures, and though not so good and cheap as from England, yet they were cheaper to the publick stock, because their own poor were employ'd. Their wool, which they had over and above, went to France, and return'd ready money. Their lead went to Holland, and their cattle and sheep to England, and brought back in that one article above 100,000 l. sterling per ann.

Then it was the sea-port towns had a trade, their court was magnificent, their nobility built fine houses and palaces which were richly furnish'd, and nobly finish'd within and without. They had infinitely more value went out than came back in goods, and therefore the balance was evidently on their side; whereas, now their court is gone, their nobility and gentry spend their time, and consequently their estates in England; the Union opens the door to all English manufactures, and suppresses their own, prohibits their wool going abroad, and yet scarcely takes it off at home; if the cattle goes to England, the money is spent there too. The troops rais'd there are in English service, and Scotland receives no *premio* for the levies, as she might have done abroad, and as the Swiss and other nations do at this time.

The decay'd burghs being pass'd, we came to a village call'd the Weems, or by way of distinction, the Wester Weems, or Wemys. This is a small town, and no burrough, belonging to the Earl of Weemys, whose house stands a little farther east, on the top of a high cliff, looking down upon the sea, as Dover Castle looks down upon the Strait, between it and Calais, tho' not so high.

The account given lately of this noble castle of the Weemys[8] is very romantick, and must necessarily be laugh'd at by the family itself who know the house. It is a very good house, and has one large front to the sea, but without any Windsor-like terrass between the house and it, as is represented. At the west end,

upon the same cliff, is a small plain, where had been a bowling-green, and where the late Earl, being Admiral, had some small field-pieces planted to answer salutes. Behind the house is a small and irregular court-yard, with two wings of building, being offices to the house on one side, and stables on the other. Nor is there any gardens, or room for any, much less a spacious park, on the north side of the house; but the road from the Wester Weemys to the Easter passing between, there is a large, well planted orchard, and it is no other, nor otherwise intended; and as to a spacious park, there is nothing like it. There is a piece of wast ground planted with firr-trees, at the east end of the house, but they do not thrive; nor would any man call it a park, especially for a nobleman too, that had seen what a park means in England; but, indeed, in Scotland they call all enclos'd grounds parks, whether for grass or corn: and so they call all gardens yards; as St. Ann's Yards, at the palace of Haly-Rood House, and the like in other places.

From hence you pass through the East Weemys to another village, call'd **Buckhaven**, inhabited chiefly, if not only, by fishermen, whose business is wholly to catch fresh fish every day in the Firth, and carry them to Leith and Edinburgh Markets. And though this town be a miserable row of cottage-like buildings, and people altogether meer fishermen, as I have said, yet there is scarce a poor man in the town, and in general the town is rich.

Here we saw the shore of the sea cover'd with shrimps, like the ground cover'd with a thin snow; and as you rode among them they would rise like a kind of dust, being scar'd by the footing of the horse, and hopping like grasshoppers.

The fishermen of this town have a great many boats of all sorts and sizes, and some larger, which lye upon the beach unrigg'd, which every year they fit out for the herring season, in which they have a very great share.

Beyond this is the **Methuel**, a little town, but a very safe and good harbour, firmly built of stone, almost like the Cobb at Lime, though not wholly projecting into the sea, but standing within the land, and built out with two heads, and walls of thick strong stone: it stands a little on the west side of the mouth of the river Leven; the salmon of this river are esteem'd the best in this part of Scotland.

Here my Lord Weemys brings his coal, which he digs above two miles off, on the banks of the river Leven, and here it is sold or shipp'd off; as also what salt he can make, which is not a great deal. Nor is the estate his Lordship makes from the said coal-works equal to what it has been, the water having, after an immense charge to throw it off, broken in upon the works, and hinder'd their going on, at least to any considerable advantage.

The people who work in the coal mines in this country, what with the dejected countenances of the men, occasion'd by their poverty and hard labour, and what with the colour or discolouring, which comes from the coal, both to their clothes and complexions, are well describ'd by their own countryman Samuel Colvil,[9] in his famous macaronick poem, call'd, *Polemo Midinia*; thus,

Cole-hewers Nigri, Girnantes more Divelli.
Pol. Mid.

They are, indeed, frightful fellows at first sight: But I return to my progress from the Methuel; we have several small towns on the coast, as Criel or Crail, Pitten-Weem, Anstruther or Anster, as 'tis usually call'd: these are all royal burghs, and send members to Parliament, even still upon the new establishment, in consequence only that now they join three or four towns together to choose one or two members, whereas they chose every town for itself.

Over against this shore, and in the mouth of the Forth, opposite to the Isle of the Bass, lyes the Isle of May, known to mariners by having a light-house upon it; the only constant inhabitant, is said to be the man maintain'd there by the Government, to take care of the fire in the light-house.

Here (you may observe) the French fleet[10] lay with some assurance, when the Pretender was on board: and here the English four a-clock gun, on board their approaching squadron, unhappily gave them the alarm; so that they immediately weigh'd, got under sail, and made the best of their way, the English pursuing them in vain, except only that they took the *Salisbury*, which was a considerable way behind the fleet, and could not come up with the rest; the story is well known, so I need not repeat it.

The shore of the Firth or Frith ends here, and the æstuarium or mouth opening, the land of Fife falls off the north, making a promontory of land, which the seamen call Fife-Ness, looking east to the German Ocean, after which the coast trends away north, and the first town we saw there was **St. Andrew's**, an antient city, the seat of an archbishop, and an university.

Here it was, that old limb of St. Lucifer, Cardinal Beaton,[11] massacred and murther'd that famous sufferer and martyr of the Scots Church, Mr. William Wishart,[12] whom he caus'd to be burnt in the parade of the castle, he himself sitting in his balcony to feed and glut his eyes with the sight of it.

The old church here was a noble structure; it was longer than St. Paul's in London by a considerable deal, I think, by six yards, or by twenty-five foot. This building is now sunk into a simple parish church, though there are many plain discoveries of what it has been, and a great deal of project and fancy may be employ'd to find out the antient shape of it.

The city is not large, nor is it contemptibly small; there are some very good buildings in it, and the remains of many more: The colleges are handsome buildings, and well supply'd with men of learning in all sciences, and who govern the youth they instruct with reputation; the students wear gowns here of a scarlet-like colour, but not in grain, and are very numerous.

There are three colleges in all; the most antient, and which, they say, was the publick school so long before, is call'd St. Salvadore. The building is antient, but appears to have been very magnificent considering the times it was erected in, which was 1456. The gate is large, and has a handsome spire over it all of stone. In the first court, on the right side as you go in, is the chapel of the college, not extraordinary large, but sufficient. There is an antient monument of the Archbishop the founder, who lyes buried in the church of his own building. Beyond the chapel is the cloister, after the antient manner, not unlike that in Canterbury, but not so large. Opposite to this are offices, and proper buildings for the necessary use of the colleges. In the second court are the schools of the college, on the same spot where stood the antient Grammar School, mention'd above, if that part is to be depended upon. Over these schools is a very large hall for the publick exercises, as is usual in other universities; but this is a most spacious building, and far larger than there is any occasion for.

In the same court are the apartments for the Masters, Professors, and Regents, which, (as our Fellows) are in sallary, and are tutors and governors to the several students; were this college supported by additional bounties and donations, as has been the case in England; and were sufficient funds appointed to repair and keep up the buildings, there would few colleges in England go beyond it for magnificence: but want of this, and other encouragements, causes the whole building to seem as if it was in its declining state, and looking into its grave: the truth is, the college wants nothing but a good fund to be honestly apply'd for the repair of the building, finishing the first design, and encouraging the scholars. Dr. Skeen, Principal of this college, shew'd the way to posterity to do this, and laid out great sums in repairs, especially of the churches, and founded a library for the use of the house.

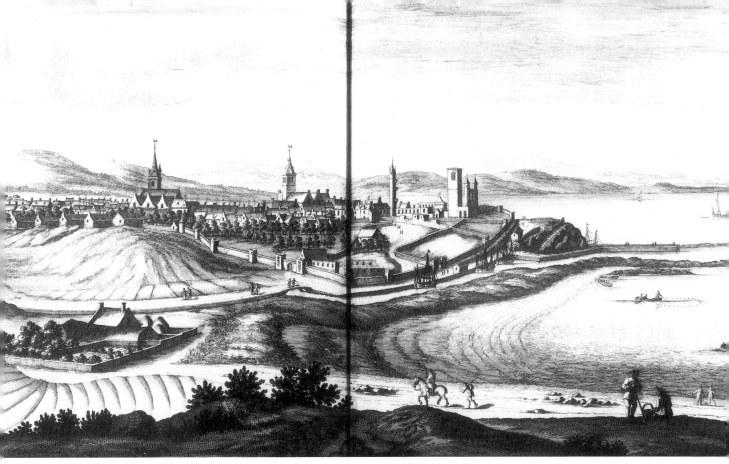

252. 'Prospect of the Town of St Andrews'; engraving. From John Slezer, *Theatrum Scotiae* (1693).

In the second college, which is call'd St. Leonard's, is a Principal, who must be a Doctor of Divinity by the foundation; but the present church government insisting upon the parity of the clergy, are pleas'd to dispense with that part: There are also four Professors of Philosophy, to whom the late Sir John Scot,[13] a bountiful benefactor to this College, has added a Professor of Philology, and has settled a very handsome stipend upon the Professor: also the same gentleman augmented the college library with several valuable books to a very considerable sum. And since that Sir John Wedderburn,[14] a gentleman of a very antient family, and a great lover of learning, has given a whole library, being a great and choice collection of books, to be added to the library of this college.

The revenue of this college is larger than that of the old college; it has also more students. It was founded and endow'd by the Earl of Lenox, being before that a religious house, of the Order of St. Benedict, as appears by the register and charter of the foundation.

It is not so large and magnificent as St. Salvador originally was; but 'tis kept in much better repair. It has but one court or square, but it is very large. The old building of the monastery remains entire, and makes the south side, and the old cells of the monks make now the chambers for the students: the chapel takes up the north side, and a large side of more modern apartments on the west, which are nevertheless old enough to be falling down; but they are now repairing them, and adding a great pile of building to compleat the square, and join that side to the north where the chapel stands.

This college has large yards, as they call them, that is to say gardens, or rather orchards, well planted, and good walks in them as well as good fruit.

The new college, call'd St. Mary's, was founded by Cardinal Beaton Archbishop of St. Andrew's, and is very singular in its reserv'd and limited laws. Here are no scholars at all; but all those scholars who have pass'd their first studies, and gone through a course of philosophy in any of the other colleges, may enter themselves here to study Hebrew and the mathematicks, history, or other parts of science.

It was in this college King Charles I held a Parliament; the place is call'd the Parliament room to this day, and is a very large, spacious room, able to receive 400 people, plac'd on seats to sit down; the form is reserv'd very plain, and the place, where the tables for the clarks and other officers were set, is to be seen.

They shew among other remains of antiquity the apartments of the palace where Cardinal Beaton stood, or sat in state to see the martyrdom of Mr. Wishart,

349

who, at the stake, call'd aloud to him, and cited him to appear at the bar of God's justice within such a certain time, within which time he was murther'd by the famous Norman Lessley,[15] thrown into the square of the court, and his body dragged to the very spot where the good man was burn'd at the stake, and also they shew us the window where they threw him out; which particular part of the building seems to have been spar'd, as if on purpose to commemorate the fact, of which, no doubt, divine justice had the principal direction.

From St. Andrew's we came to Cowper, the shire town, (as it would be call'd in England) where the publick business of the country is all done. Here are two very agreeable seats belonging to the present Earl of Leven; one is call'd Melvil, and the other Balgony. Melvil is a regular and beautiful building, after the model of Sir William Bruce's House at Kinross, describ'd before. Balgony is an antient seat, formerly belong'd to the family of Lessly, and if not built, was enlarg'd and repair'd by the great General Lessly, who was so fam'd in Germany, serving under that glorious king of soldiers Gustavus Adolphus.

The river Leven runs just under the walls, as I may say, of the house, and makes the situation very pleasant; the park is large, but not well planted, nor do the avenues that are planted thrive, for the very reason which I have mention'd already.

From hence we went north to Cowper above-nam'd, and where, as I said, the Sheriff keeps his court. The Earl of Rothess is hereditary Sheriff of the shire of Fife, and the Duke of Athol was Chancellor of the University of St. Andrew's, in the times of the episcopal government; but that dignity seems now to be laid aside.

We now went away to the north east part of the county, to see the ruins of the famous monastery of Balmerinoch, of which Mr. Cambden takes notice; but we saw nothing worth our trouble, the very ruins being almost eaten up by time: the Lord Balmerinoch, of the family of Elphingston, takes his title from the place, the land being also in his possession; the monastery was founded by Queen Ermengred, wife of King William of Scotland.

Hence we came to the bank of another Firth or Frith, call'd the Firth of Tay, which, opening to a large breadth at its entrance, as the Firth of Edinburgh does, draws in afterwards as that does at the Queens-Ferry, and makes a ferry over at the breadth of two miles to the town of Dundee; and then the Firth widening again just as that of the Forth does also, continues its breadth as four to six miles, till it comes almost to Perth, as the other does to Sterling.

This river Tay is, without exception, the greatest river in Scotland, and of the longest course, for it rises out of the mountains, on the edge of Argyle shire; and running first north into the shire of Bradalbin, there receiving many other rivers, it spreads itself into a large lake, which is call'd Lough Tay, extending for forty miles in length, and traversing the very heart of Scotland, comes into the sea near this place: Now, as I design to keep in this part of my work to the east coast of the country, I must for the present quit the Tay itself, keeping a little on the hither side of it, and go back to that part of the country which lies to the south, and yet east of Dunbarton and Lenox shires; so drawing an imaginary line from Sterling Bridge, due north, through the heart of the country to Inverness, which I take to lye almost due north and south.

In this course then I mov'd from the ferry, mention'd above, to **Perth**, lying upon the same river Tay, but on the hither bank. It was formerly call'd St. Johnston, or St. John's Town, from an old church, dedicated to the evangelist, St. John, part of which is still remaining, and is yet big enough to make two parochial churches, and serve the whole town for their publick worship.

The chief business of this town is in the linnen manufacture; and it is so considerable here, all the neighbouring country being employ'd in it, that it is a wealth to the whole place. The Tay is navigable up to the town for ships of good burthen; and they ship off here so great a quantity of linnen, (all for England) that all the rest of Scotland is said not to ship off so much more.

This town was unhappily for some time, the seat of the late Rebellion;[16] but I cannot say it was unhappy for the town: for the townsmen got so much money by both parties, that they are evidently enrich'd by it; and it appears not only by the particular families and persons in the town, but by their publick and private buildings which they have rais'd since that; as particularly a new Tolbooth or Town-hall.

It seems a little enigmatick to us in the south, how a Rebellion should enrich any place; but a few words will explain it. First, I must premise, that the Pretender and his troops lay near, or in this place a considerable time; now the bare consumption of victuals and drink, is a very considerable advantage in Scotland, and therefore 'tis frequent in Scotland for towns to petition the Government to have regiments of soldiers quarter'd upon them, which in England would look monstrous, nothing being more terrible and uneasy to our towns in England.

Again, as the Pretender and his troops lay in the neighbourhood, namely at Scone, so a very great

XL. Attributed to James Norie and Jan Griffier II, *Panorama of Taymouth Castle and Loch Tay* (detail) (?1733–1739).

253. 'Prospect of the Town of Perth'; engraving. From John Slezer, *Theatrum Scotiae* (1693).

confluence of the nobility, clergy, and gentry, how–ever fatally, as to themselves, gather'd about him, and appear'd here also; making their court to him in person, and waiting the issue of his fortunes, till they found the storm gathering from the south, and no probable means to resist it, all relief from abroad being every where disappointed, and then they shifted off as they could.

While they resided here, their expence of money was exceeding great; lodgings in the town of Perth let for such a rate, as was never known in the place before; trade was a kind of a hurry, provision dear: in a word, the people, not of the town only, but of all the country round, were enrich'd; and had it lasted two or three months longer, it would have made all the towns rich.

When this cloud was dispers'd, and all the party fled and gone, the victors enter'd, the general officers and the loyal gentlemen succeeded the abdicated and routed party; but here was still the head quarters, and afterwards the Dutch troops[17] continued here most part of the winter; all this while the money flow'd in, and the town made their market on both sides; for they gain'd, by the royal army's being on that side of the country, and by the foreigners being quarter'd there, almost as much, tho' not in so little time as by the other.

The town was well built before, but now has almost a new face; (for as I said) here are abundance of new houses, and more of old houses new fitted and repair'd, which look like new. The linnen trade too, which is their main business, has mightily increas'd since the late Act of Parliament[18] in England, for the suppressing the use and wearing of printed callicoes; so that the manufacture is greatly increased here, espec-ially of so that the manufacture is greatly increased here, especially of that kind of cloth which they buy here and send to England to be printed, and which is so much us'd in England in the room of the callicoes, that the worsted and silk weavers in London seem to have very little benefit by the bill, but that the linnen of Scotland and Ireland are, as it were, constituted in the room of the callicoes.

From Perth to Sterling there lyes a vale which they call Strathmore, and which is a fine level country, though surrounded with hills, and is esteem'd the most fruitful in corn of all that part of the country: it lies extended on both sides the Tay, and is said to reach to Brechin north east, and almost to Sterling south west. Here are, as in all such pleasant soils you will find, a great many gentlemen's seats; though on the north side of the Tay, and here in particular is the noble palace of Glames,[19] the hereditary seat of the family of Lyon, Earls of Strathmore; and as the heir in reversion now enjoys the title and estate, so it very narrowly escap'd being forfeited; for the elder brother, Earl of Strathmore, having entertain'd the Pretender magnificently in this fine palace, and join'd his forces in person, and with all his interest, lost his life in that service, being kill'd at the battle of Sheriff-Moor; by his fall, the estate being entail'd, descended to the second son, or younger brother, who is now Earl of Strathmore.

Glames is, indeed, one of the finest old built palaces in Scotland, and by far the largest; and this makes me speak of it here, because I am naming the Pretender and his affairs, though a little out of place; when you see it at a distance it is so full of turrets and lofty buildings, spires and towers, some plain, others shining with gilded tops, that it looks not like a town, but a city; and the noble appearance seen through the long vistas of the park are so differing, that it does not appear like the same place any two way together.

The great avenue is a full half mile, planted on either side with several rows of trees; when you come to the outer gate you are surpriz'd with the beauty and the variety of the statues, busts, some of stone, some of brass, some gilded, some plain. The statues in brass are four, one of King James VI; one of King Charles I booted and spurr'd, as if going to take horse at the head of his army; one of Charles II habited *à la héro*, which the world knows he had nothing of about him; and one of King James VII after the pattern of that at Whitehall.[20]

When the Pretender lodg'd here, for the Earl of Strathmore entertain'd him in his first passage to Perth with great magnificence: there were told three and forty furnish'd rooms on the first floor of the house; some beds, perhaps, were put up for the occasion, for they made eighty eight beds for them, and the whole retinue of the Pretender was receiv'd, the house being able to receive the court of a real reigning prince.

It would be endless to go about to describe the magnificent furniture, the family pictures, the gallery, the fine collection of original paintings, and the nobly painted cielings of the chapel, where is an organ for the service after the manner of the Church of England. In a

254. Glamms House; engraving. From John Slezer, *Theatrum Scotiae* (1719 edition).

353

XLII (*above right*). Attributed to Richard Waitt, *Andrew MacPherson of Cluny, chief of the Clan Chattan*. The tartans of the jacket, plaid and trews are of three different patterns. 'The gentry leading the commons or vassals, as they are call'd, to dwell within the respective bounds of their several clans, where they are, as we may say, little monarchs, reigning in their own dominions' (p. 366).

XLI (*above left*). Thomas Murray, *John Murray, First Duke of Atholl (1659–1724)* (1708). The Duke of Atholl is dressed in the robes of the Order of the Thistle and one of his mansions, Dunkeld House, is visible in the distance. 'The Duke of Athol is lord, I was almost going to say king of this country' (p. 371).

XLIII (*left*). Richard Waitt, *Alastair Grant the Champion* (1714). This portrait depicts arms, dress and tartan unlike those of any modern clan. 'The people also dress in the plaid and the trouse, go naked below the knee, wear the durk . . . and the targ or target at their shoulder' (p. 375).

255. *Prospect of the Battle of Sheriff-Muir 1715*; painting in the style of Jan Wyck.

word, the house is as nobly furnish'd as most palaces in Scotland; but, as I said, it was at the brink of destruction; for had the Earl not been kill'd, 'tis odds but it had been gutted by the army, which presently spread all the country; but it was enough, the Earl lost his life, and the present Earl enjoys it peaceably.

From hence I came away south west, and crossing the Tay below Perth, but above Dundee, came to Dumblain, a name made famous by the late battle fought between the army of King George, under the command of the Duke of Argyle, and the Pretender's forces under the Earl of Marr, which was fought on Sheriff-Moor,[21] between Sterling and Dumblain: the town is pleasantly situated, and tolerably well built, but out of all manner of trade; so that there is neither present prosperity upon it, or prospect of future.

Going from hence we took a full view of the field of battle, call'd Sheriff-Muir, and had time to contemplate how it was possible, that a rabble of Highlanders, arm'd in haste, appearing in rebellion, and headed by a person never in arms before, nor of the least experience, should come so near to the overthrowing an army of regular, disciplin'd troops, and led on by experienc'd officers, and so great a general: But when the mistake appear'd also, we bless'd the good protector of Great Britain, who, under a piece of the most mistaken conduct in the world, to say no worse of it, gave that important victory to King George's troops, and prevented the ruin of Scotland from an army of Highlanders.

From this place of reflection I came forward in sight of Sterling Bridge, but leaving it on the right hand,

turn'd away east to **Alloway**, where the Earl of Marr has a noble seat, I should have said had a noble seat, and where the navigation of the Firth of Forth begins. This is, as I hinted before, within four miles of Sterling by land, and scarcely within twenty by water, occasion'd by those uncommon meanders and reaches in the river, which gives so beautiful a prospect from the Castle of Sterling.

This fine seat was formerly call'd the castle of Alloway, but is now so beautify'd, the buildings, and especially the gardens, so compleat and compleatly modern, that no appearance of a castle can be said to remain. There is a harbour for shipping, and ships of burthen may come safely up to it: and this is the place where the Glasgow merchants are, as I am told, erecting magazines or warehouses, to which they propose to bring their tobacco and sugars by land, and then to ship them for Holland or Hamburgh, or the Baltick, or England, as they find opportunity, or a market; and I doubt not but they will find their advantage in it.

The gardens of Alloway House, indeed, well deserve a description; they are, by much, the finest in Scotland, and not outdone by many in England; the gardens, singly describ'd, take up above forty acres of ground, and the adjoining wood, which is adapted to the house in avenues and vistas, above three times as much.

The town is pleasant, well built, and full of trade; for the whole country has some business or other with them, and they have a better navigation than most of the towns on the Firth, for a ship of 300 ton may lye also at the very wharf; so that at Alloway a merchant may trade to all parts of the world, as well as at Leith or at Glasgow.

The High Street of Alloway reaches down to this harbour, and is a very spacious, well built street, with rows of trees finely planted all the way. Here are several testimonies of the goodness of their trade, as particularly a large deal-yard, or place for laying up all sorts of Norway goods, which shews they have a commerce thither. They have large warehouses of naval stores; such as pitch, tar, hemp, flax, two saw mills for cutting or slitting of deals, and a rope-walk for making all sorts of ropes and cables for rigging and fitting of ships, with several other things, which convinces us they are no strangers to other trades, as well by sea as by land.

From Alloway, east, the country is call'd the shire of Clackmannan, and is known for yielding the best of coal, and the greatest quantity of it of any country in Scotland; so that it is carry'd, not to Edinburgh only, but to England, to Holland, and to France; and they tell us of new pits, or mines of coal now discover'd, which will yield such quantities, and so easy to come at, as are never to be exhausted; tho' such great quantities should be sent to England, as the York-Buildings company[22] boast of, namely, twenty thousand ton a year; which, however, I take it as it is, for a boast, or rather a pretence to persuade the world they have a demand for such a quantity; whereas, while the freight from Scotland is, as we know, so dear, and the tax in England continues so heavy, the price of these coals will always be so high at London, as will not fail to restrain the consumption; nor is it the interest of Scotland to send away so great a quantity of coal as shall either make a scarcity, or raise the price of them at home.

On this shore of the Firth, farther down, stands the town **Culross**, a neat and agreeable town, lying in length by the water side, like Kirkcaldy, and being likewise a trading town, as trade must be understood in Scotland. Here is a pretty market, a plentiful country behind it, and the navigable Firth before it; the coal and the linnen manufacture, and plenty of corn, such exportations will always keep something of trade alive upon this whole coast.

The two Lomons in this province are two remarkable mountains, which particularly seem to promise metal in their bowels, if they were thoroughly search'd. They rise up like two sugar-loaves in the middle of a plain country, not far from Falkland, and give a view of the Firth of Edinburgh south, and the Firth of Tay north, and are seen from Edinburgh very plain.

Having made this little excursion to the south from Perth, you may suppose me now return'd northward again; and having given you my account of Perth, and its present circumstances, I now proceed that way, taking things as well in their ordinary situation as I can; we could not be at Perth and not have a desire to see that antient seat of royal ceremony, for the Scots kings, I mean of Scone, where all the kings of Scotland were crown'd.

Scone lyes on the other side of the Tay, about a mile north west from Perth; it was famous for the old chair in which the kings of Scotland were crown'd, and which Edw. I King of England, having pierc'd through the whole kingdom, and nothing being able

256. 'Prospect of the House and of the Town of Alloua'; engraving. From John Slezer, *Theatrum Scotiae* (1693).

257. South view of Culross; drawing by Paul Sandby (1748). From Thomas Pennant, *A Tour in Scotland* (1769–72 (large set)).

to withstand him, brought away with him. It is now deposited in Westminster, and the kings of Scotland are still crown'd in it, according to an old Scots prophecy, which they say, (mark it: I do but tell you they say so) was cut in the stone, which is enclos'd in the lower part of the wooden chair in which the kings are crown'd.

> Ni fallat fatum, Scoti quocunque locatum
> Inveniunt Lapidem, regnare tenentur ibidem.

Englished thus;

Or Fates deceived, and Heaven decrees in vain,
Or where this Stone is found, the Scots shall reign.

The palace of Scoon, though antient, is not so much decay'd as those I have already spoken of; and the Pretender found it very well in repair for his use: here he liv'd and kept his court, a fatal court to the nobility and gentry of Scotland, who were deluded to appear for him.

The building is very large, the front above 200 foot in breadth, and has two extraordinary fine square courts, besides others, which contain the offices, outhouses, &c. The royal apartments are spacious and large, but the building, the wainscotting, the chimney-pieces, &c. all after the old fashion.

Among the pictures there, the Pretender had the satisfaction to see his mother's picture, an original, done in Italy, when she was Princess of Modena only, and was marry'd by proxy, in the name of King James VII then Duke of York, represented by the Earl of Peterborough. Here is the longest gallery in Scotland, and the cieling painted, but the painting exceeding old.

Mr. Cambden tells us, that the Firth of Tay was the utmost bounds of the Roman Empire in Britain. But our English Cæsars have outgone the Romans; for Edw. I as is said, pass'd the Tay, for he rifled the abbey at Scoon; and, if we may believe history, penetrated into the remotest parts, which, however, I take to be only the remotest parts of what was then known to the English; for as to the Highlands, the mountains of Loquhaber, Ross, Murray, Sutherland, and Caithness, we read nothing of them: and from these retreats the Scots always return'd, Antæus[23] like, with double strength after every defeat, till in the next reign they overthrew his successor Edw. II at Bannockbourn, and drove the English out of the whole country; nay, and follow'd them over Tweed into England, ravaging the countries of Northumberland and Cumberland, and paying them in their own kind with interest.

Oliver Cromwell, indeed (according to the motto of a noble house in Scotland, (viz.) *Ride through*) rode through; he penetrated to the remotest part of the island, and that he might rule them with a rod of iron in the very letter of it, he built citadels and forts in all the angles and extremes, where he found it needful to place his stationary legions, just as the Romans did; as at Leith, at St. Andrew's, at Inverness, Irwin, Innerlochy, and several other places: and just now we find King George's forces marching to the remotest corners, nay, ferrying over into the western, and northwestern islands; but then this is not as a foreigner and conqueror, but as a sovereign, a lawful governor and father of the country, to deliver from, not entangle her in the chains of tyranny and usurpation.

But where armies have march'd, private travellers may certainly pass; and with that assurance we chearfully pass'd the Tay, trusting very much to that natural, known civility, which the Scots, in the remotest parts, always shew to strangers.

We left Strathern therefore, with the little country of Menteith, for our return, and went down into Angus, on the northern banks of Tay to **Dundee**, a pleasant, large, populous city, and well deserves the title of Bonny Dundee, so often given it in discourse, as well as in song (bonny, in Scots, signifying beautiful).

As it stands well for trade, so it is one of the best trading towns in Scotland, and that as well in foreign business as in manufacture and home trade. It has but an indifferent harbour, but the Tay is a large, safe, and good road, and there is deep water and very good anchor-hold almost all over it.

It is exceedingly populous, full of stately houses, and large handsome streets; particularly it has four very good streets, with a large market-place in the middle, the largest and fairest in Scotland, except only that of Aberdeen. The Tolbooth, or Town-hall is an old, but large and convenient building.

The inhabitants here appear like gentlemen, as well as men of business, and yet are real merchants too, and make good what we see so eminently in England, that true bred merchants are the best of gentlemen. They have a very good large correspondence here with England, and ship off a great deal of linnen thither, also a great quantity of corn is sent from hence, as well to England as to Holland. They have likewise a good share of the Norway trade; and as they are concern'd in the herring-fishery, they consequently have some east country trade, viz. to Dantzick, Koningsberg, Riga, and the neighbouring parts. They send ships also to Sweden, and import iron, copper, tar, pitch, deals, &c. from the several trading ports of that kingdom.

These several trades occasion a concourse of shipping at the port; and there are not a few ships belonging to the place. The country behind them call'd the Carse, or the Carse of Gowry, with the vale mention'd above of Strathmoor; for Strath, in their dialect, signifies a vale, or level country; I say, all that country abounds in corn, and the port of Dundee ships off great quantities, when a plentiful crop allows it, to the great advantage of the gentlemen as well as farmers; for as the gentlemen receive all their rents in kind, they would find a great difficulty sometimes to dispose of it, if the merchant here did not ship it off, either for London or Amsterdam.

The town of Dundee stands at a little distance from the Tay, but they are join'd by a causeway or walk, well pav'd with flat freestone, such as the side-ways in Cheapside and Cornhil, and rows of trees are planted on either side the walk, which make it very agreeable. On one part of this walk are very good warehouses for merchandises, especially for heavy goods; and also granaries for corn, of which sometimes they have a vast quantity laid up here; and these being near the harbour are convenient, as well for the housing of goods, when landed, as for the easy shipping off what lies for exportation.

The great church was formerly collegiate, being the cathedral of the place, and was a very large building; but part of it was demolish'd in the Civil War; the remainder is divided, like as others are at Edinburgh, Glasgow, &c. into three churches for the present use of the citizens.

They have also a meeting-house or two for the Episcopal worship; for you are to take it once for all, that north by Tay, there are far more of the Episcopal perswasion than are to be found in the south; and the farther north, the more so, as we shall see in its order.

The tower upon the great church here is a handsome square building, large, and antient, but very high, and is a good ornament to the city; it resembles the great tower upon the cathedral of Canterbury, but not quite so high.

It is twenty Scots miles from Dundee to Montrose, the way pleasant, the country fruitful and bespangl'd, as the sky in a clear night with stars of the biggest magnitude, with gentlemen's houses, thick as they can be suppos'd to stand with pleasure and conveniency. Among these is the noble palace of Penmure, forfeited in the late rebellion by the unfortunate Earl of Penmure, who was himself wounded in the fight near Dumblain, and with that action ruin'd a noble and antient family, and a fine estate. The surname of the family is Maul and Maulsburgh, a small port near Montross, bears the name still to posterity.

The town and port of **Montrose**, vulgarly, but ignorantly, call'd Montross, was our next stage, standing upon the eastmost shore of Angus, open to the German, or, if you please now, the Caledonian

258. 'Prospect of the town of Dundee'; engraving. From John Slezer, *Theatrum Scotiae* (1693).

ocean, and at the mouth of the little river south Esk, which makes the harbour.

We did not find so kind a reception among the common people of Angus, and the other shires on this side the country, as the Scots usually give to strangers: But we found it was because we were English men; and we found that their aversion did not lye so much against us on account of the late successes at, and after the Rebellion, and the forfeiture of the many noblemen and gentlemen's estates among them as fell on that occasion, though that might add to the disgust: but it was on account of the Union, which they almost universally exclaim'd against, tho' sometimes against all manner of just reasoning.

This town of Montrose is a sea-port, and, in proportion to its number of inhabitants, has a considerable trade, and is tolerably well built, and capable of being made strong, only that it extends too far in length.

The French fleet[24] first made land at this port, when they had the Pretender on board, in the reign of Queen Ann, having overshot the mouth of the Firth so far, whither they had first design'd: but this mistake, which some thought a misfortune, was certainly a deliverance to them; for as this mistake gave time to the English fleet to come up with them, before they could enter the Firth, so it left them time and room also to make their escape, which, if they had been gone up the Firth, they could never have done, but must inevitably have been all burnt and destroy'd, or taken by the British fleet under Sir George Bing, which was superior to them in force.

From Montrose the shore lies due north to Aberdeen: By the way is the Castle of Dunnoter, a strong fortification, upon a high precipice of a rock, looking down on the sea as on a thing infinitely below it. The castle is wall'd about with invincible walls, said the honest Scots man that shew'd us the road to it, having towers at proper distances, after the old way of fortifying towns.

This was chiefly made use of as a prison for state-prisoners; and I have seen a black account of the cruel usage the unhappy prisoners have met with there; but those times are over with Scotland.

From hence there is nothing remarkable till we come to **Aberdeen**, a place so eminent, that it commands some stay upon it; yet, I shall contract its description as much as possible, the compass of my work being so great, and the room I have for it so small.

Aberdeen is divided into two towns or cities, and stands at the mouth of two rivers; the towns are the New and the Old Aberdeen, about a mile distant from one another, one situate on the river Don or Dune, the other on the river Dee, from whence it is suppos'd to take its name; for Aber, in the old British language, signifies a mouth, or opening of a river, the same which in Scotland is understood by a Frith or Firth: so that both these towns are describ'd in the name, (viz.) Aberdee, the mouth of the river Dee, and Aberdeen, the mouth of the river Don. So in the south-west part of the shores of Britain, and in Wales, we have Aberconway, the mouth of the river Conway, Aberistwith, and several others.

The Old Aberdeen, on the bank of the Don, must, without doubt, be very antient; for they tell us the New Aberdeen is suppos'd to be upwards of 1200 years old. Nor do any of their registers tell us the particular time of its being built, or by whom. The cities are equally situated for trade, being upon the very edge of the sea; and 'tis the common opinion, that part of the old city was wash'd down by the sea; so that it obliged the citizens to build farther off: this part was that they call'd the monastery, and this may give rise to that opinion, that there-upon they went and built the New Aberdeen upon the bank of the other river, and which, 'tis evident, is built upon a piece of hilly ground, or upon three hills: but this is all con-jecture, and has only probability to support it, not any thing of history.

Old Aberdeen is also on one side the county, and New Aberdeen on another, though both in that which is call'd in general the county of Marr. The extra-ordinaries of Aberdeen, take both the cities together, are

   I. The cathedral.
  II. The two colleges.
 III. The great market-place.
 IV. The bridges, particularly that of one arch.
  V. The commerce.
 VI. The fishery.

1. The cathedral dedicated to St. Machar, tho' none knows who that saint was, is a large and antient building; the building majestick, rather than curious, and yet not without its beauty in architecture; it appears to have been built at several times, and, perhaps, at the distance of many years, one part from another. The columns on which the great steeple stands are very artful, and the contrivance shews great judgement in the builder or director of the work. This church has been divided into several parts since the abolishing of Episcopacy, as a government in the church; (for it is not abolished in Aberdeen, as a principle, to this day) abundance of the people are still Episcopal. in their opinion; and they have, by the gentle government they live under, so much liberty still, as that they have a chapel for the publick exercise of their worship, after the manner of the Church of England, besides several meetings for the Episcopal Dissenters, which are not so publick.

2. The two colleges; one of these are in the Old City, and the other in the New. That in the Old City is also the oldest college, being founded anno 1500 by the famous Bishop Elphingstone, who lies buried in the chapel or college church, under a very magnificent and curious monument. The steeple of this church was the most artificial that I have seen in Scotland.

3. The third article is the great market-place, which, indeed, is very beautiful and spacious; and the streets adjoining are very handsome and well built, the houses lofty and high; but not so as to be inconvenient, as in Edinburgh; or low, to be contemptible, as in most other places. But the generality of the citizens' houses are built of stone four story high, handsome sash-windows, and are very well furnish'd within, the citizens here being as gay, as genteel, and, perhaps, as rich, as in any city in Scotland.

4. The bridges; particularly that at Old Aberdeen,

259. 'Prospect of Dunotter Castle'; engraving. From John Slezer, *Theatrum Scotiae* (1963).

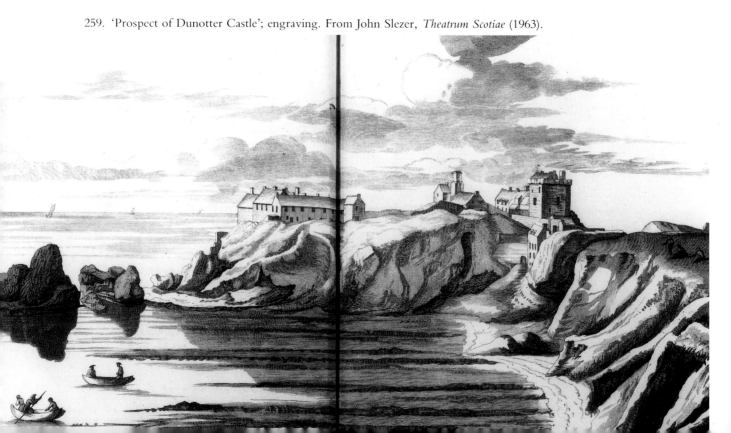

260. 'Prospect of Old Aberdien'; engraving. From John Slezer, *Theatrum Scotiae* (1693).

over the Don: it consists of one immense arch of
stone, sprung from two rocks, one on each side,
which serve as a buttment to the arch, so that it may be
said to have no foundation, nor to need any. The
workmanship is artful, and so firm, that it may possibly end with the conflagration only. The other bridge
is upon the river Dee, about a mile west above New
Aberdeen, and has seven very stately fine arches.

5. and 6. The commerce and fishery.

The fishery is very particular; the salmon is a surprising thing, the quantity that is taken in both rivers,
but especially in the Dee, is a kind of prodigy; the
fishing, or property, is erected into a company, and
divided into shares, and no person can enjoy above one
share at a time; the profits are very considerable, for
the quantity of fish taken is exceeding great, and they
are sent abroad into several parts of the world, particularly into France, England, the Baltick, and several
other parts.

The herring-fishing is a common blessing to all this
shore of Scotland, and is like the Indies at their door;
the merchants of Aberdeen cannot omit the benefit,
and with this they are able to carry on their trade
to Dantzick, and Koningsberg, Riga and Narva,
Wybourgh and Stockholm, to the more advantage.

They have a very good manufacture of linnen, and

261. Perspective view of New Aberdeen from the blockhouse; engraving based on a drawing by John Slezer (1693).
From *The Complete English Traveller*. Old Aberdeen is
located to the right, just beyond the edge of this view.

also of worsted stockings, which they send to England in great quantities, and of which they make some so fine, that I have seen them sold for fourteen, and twenty shillings a pair. They also send them over to Holland, and into the north and east seas in large quantities.

They have also a particular export here of pork, pickl'd and pack'd up in barrels, which they chiefly sell to the Dutch for the victualling their East-India ships and their men of war, the Aberdeen pork having the reputation of being the best cur'd, for keeping on very long voyages, of any in Europe.

They export also corn and meal, but they generally bring it from the Firth of Murray, or Cromarty, the corn coming from about Inverness, where they have great quantities.

In a word, the people of Aberdeen are universal merchants, so far as the trade of the northern part of the world will extend. They drive a very great trade to Holland, to France, to Hambrough, to Norway, to Gottenburgh, and to the Baltick; and it may, in a word, be esteem'd as the third city in Scotland, that is to say, next after Edinburgh and Glasgow.

From Aberdeen the coast goes on to a point of land, which is the farthest north-east part of Britain, and is call'd by the sailors Buchanness, being in the shire or county of Buchan.

Upon this part are several good towns; as particularly Peter-Head; a good market-town, and a port with a small harbour for fishing vessels, but no considerable trade, Aberdeen being so near.

This country, however remote, is full of nobility and gentry, and their seats are seen even to the extremest shores: the family of Frazer carrys its name to Fraserburgh, on the very northermost point of the county. Ereskines Earls of Marr, have their family seat at Kildrummy, in the county of Marr, a little south of this part of the country, where the late unhappy Earl first set up his standard of the Pretender. The Hayes, Earls of Errol, are in Buchan; and the family of Forbes, Lord Forbes, and Forbes Lord Pitsligo, are still farther, and the latter on the very shore of the Caledonian ocean.

Nor does the remote situation hinder, but these gentlemen have the politest and brightest education and genius of any people so far north, perhaps, in the world, being always bred in travel abroad, and in the universities at home. The Lord Pitsligo,[25] just mention'd, though unhappily drawn into the snare of the late insurrection, and forfeiting his estate with the rest, yet carries abroad with him, where-ever he goes, a bright genius, a head as full of learning and sound judgment, and a behaviour as polite, courtly, and full

of all the good qualities that adorn a noble birth, as most persons of quality I ever saw.

From hence, the east shore of Scotland being at an end, the land trends away due west; and the shire of Bamf beginning, you see the towns of Bamf, Elgin, and the famous monastery of Kinloss, where the murther'd body of King Duff was, after many years, dug up, and discover'd to be the same by some tokens, which, it seems, were undoubted.

From this point of the land, I mean Buchan-Ness, the ships take their distances, or accounts, for their several voyages; and what they call their departure: as in England, they do from Winterton-Ness, on the north-east part of Norfolk, or in the downs of the voyages to the southward.

This point of land, call'd Buchan-Ness, is generally the first land of Great Britain, which the ships make in their voyages home from Arch-Angel in Russia, or from their whale-fishing-voyages to Greenland and Spits-Berghen in the north seas; and near this point, namely, at Pitsligo, a great ship was cast away in Queen Elizabeth's time, bound home from Arch-Angel, in which was the first ambassador, which the great Duke of Muscovy sent to any of the Christian princes of Europe, and who was commission'd to treat with Queen Elizabeth for a league of peace and commerce; and on board which was a most valuable present to the Queen of rich and costly furrs; such as sables, ermine, black fox skins, and such like, being in those days esteem'd inestimable. The ambassadors, it seems, were sav'd and brought on shore by the help of the people of Pitsligo; but the ship and all the goods, and among them the rich furrs, intended for the Queen, were all lost, to her majesty's great disappointment; for the Queen valued such fine things exceedingly.

At the town of **Peter-Head** there is a small harbour with two small piers; but it is all dry at low-water: so that the smallest ships lye a-ground, and can only go in and out at high-water, and then only small vessels.

From this point of easterly land all that great bay, or inlet of the sea, reaching quite to the north of Scotland, is call'd Murray Firth; and the northermost point is Dungsby Head, which is the east point of Caithness, and opens to Pentland Firth. By Pentland Firth you are to understand the passage of the sea beyond Caithness, that is to say between Scotland and the Isles of Orkney. This bay, call'd Murray-firth, is not in the nature of a firth, as that of Edinburgh or Tay, being the mouths of rivers; as the Humber, or the mouth of Thames in England: but it is an open gulph or bay in the sea; as the Bay of Biscay, or the Gulph of Mexico are, and such-like: and though it may receive several rivers into it, as indeed it does, and as those bays do; yet itself is an open sea, and reaches from, as I have said, Peter-Head to Dungsby Head, opposite to the Orkneys; the distance upon the sea twenty-six leagues one mile, or seventy-nine miles; but it is almost twice as far by land, because of the depth of that bay, which obliges us to travel from Pitsligo, west, near seventy miles, till we come to Inverness.

This country of Buchan is, indeed, more to be taken notice of from what is to be seen on the sea-shore than in the land; for the country is mountainous, poor, and more barren than its neighbours; but as we coasted along west, we came into a much better country, particularly the shires of Bamff, Elgin, and the country of Murray, from whence the bay, I just now mention'd, is called Murray Firth.

Murray is, indeed, a pleasant country, the soil fruitful, water'd with fine rivers, and full of good towns, but especially of gentlemen's seats, more and more remarkable than could, indeed, be expected by a stranger in so remote a part of the country.

All the country, on the west side of the Spey, is surprisingly agreeable, being a flat, level country, the land rich and fruitful, well peopled, and full of gentlemen's seats. This country is a testimony how much the situation of the land is concern'd in the goodness of the climate; for here the land being level and plain, for between twenty and thirty miles together, the soil is not only fruitful and rich, but the temperature of the air is soften'd, and made mild and suitable to the fruitfulness of the earth; for the harvest in this counry, and in the vale of Strath-Bogy, and all the country to Inverness, is not only forward and early, as well as rich and strong; but 'tis more early than in Northumberland, nay, than it is in Darbyshire, and even than in some parts of the most southerly counties in England; as particularly in the east of Kent.

As a confirmation of this, I affirm that I have seen the new wheat of this country and Innerness brought to market to Edinburgh, before the wheat at Edinburgh has been fit to reap; and yet the harvest about Edinburgh is thought to be as forward as in most parts, even of England itself. In a word, it is usual for them to begin their harvest, in Murray and the country about it, in the month of July, and it is not very unusual to have new corn fully ripe and thresh'd out, shipp'd off, and brought to Edinburgh to sale, within the month of August.

As the country is rich and pleasant, so here are a great many rich inhabitants, and in the town of Elgin in particular; for the gentlemen, as if this was the Edinburgh, or the court, for this part of the island, leave their highland habitations in the winter and come and live here for the diversion of the place and plenty of provisions; and there is, on this account, a great variety of gentlemen for society, and that of all parties and of all opinions. This makes Elgin a very agreeable place to live in, notwithstanding its distance, being above 450 measur'd miles from London, and more, if we must go by Edinburgh.

This rich country continues with very little intermission, till we come to Strath-Nairn, that is the valley of Nairn, where it extends a little farther in breadth towards the mountains. Nor is Strath-Nairn behind any of the other in fruitfulness: From the western part of this country you may observe that the land goes away again to the north; and, as if you were to enter into another island beyond Britain, you find a large lake or inlet from the sea of Murray, mention'd above, going on west, as if it were to cut through the island, for we could see no end of it; nor could some of the country people tell us how far it went but that it reach'd to Loquabre: so that we thought, till our maps and farther inquiries inform'd us, it had join'd to the western ocean.

After we had travell'd about twelve miles, and descended from a rising ground, which we were then upon, we perceived the lake contracted in one particular place to the ordinary size of a river, as if design'd by nature to give passage to the inhabitants to converse with the northern part; and then, as if that part had been sufficiently perform'd, it open'd again to its former breadth, and continued in the form of a large lake, as before, for many more miles than we could see; being in the whole, according to Mr. Cambden, twenty-three miles long; but if it be taken on both sides the pass, 'tis above thirty-five miles in length.

This situation must necessarily make the narrow part be a most important pass, from the south part of Scotland to the northern countries, which are beyond it.

In the narrow pass (mention'd above over the lake) stands the town and fortress of *Inner-Ness*, that is a town on the inner bank of the river Ness. The situation of it, as I have said before, intimates that it is a place for strength; and accordingly it has a castle, founded in antient times to command the pass: and some authors write that it was antiently a royal house for the kings of Scotland. Be that as it will, Oliver Cromwel thought it a place of such importance, that he built a strong citadel here, and kept a stated garrison always in it, and sometimes more than a garrison, finding it needful to have a large body of his old veteran troops posted here to preserve the peace of the country, and keep the Highlands in awe, which they did effectually all his time.

262. 'Prospect of the town of Innerness'; engraving. From John Slezer, *Theatrum Scotiae* (1693).

Here it is observ'd, that at the end of those trouble-some days, when the troops on all sides came to be disbanded, and the men dispers'd, abundance of the English soldiers settled in this fruitful and cheap part of the country, and two things are observ'd from it as the consequence.

1. That the English falling to husbandry, and cultivation of the earth after their own manner, were instrumental, with the help of a rich and fruitful soil, to bring all that part of the country into so good a method and management, as is observ'd to outdo all the rest of Scotland to this day; and this not a little contributes to the harvest being so early, and the corn so good, as is said above; for as they reap early, so they sow early, and manure and help the soil by all the regular arts of husbandry, as is practis'd in England, and which, as they learnt it from England, and by English men, so they preserve the knowledge of it, and also the industry attending it, and requir'd for it to this day.

2. As Cromwell's soldiers initiated them thus into the arts and industry of the husbandman, so they left them the English accent upon their tongues, and they preserve it also to this day; for they speak perfect English, even much better than in the most southerly provinces of Scotland; nay, some will say that they speak it as well as at London; though I do not grant that neither. It is certain they keep the southern accent very well and speak very good English.

They have also much of the English way of living among them, as well in their manner of dress and customs, as also of their eating and drinking, and even of their dressing and cookery, which we found here much more agreeable to English stomachs than in other parts of Scotland; all which, and several other usages and customs, they retain from the settling of three regiments of English soldiers here, after they were disbanded, and who had, at least many of them, their wives and children with them.

The fort, which was then built, and since demolish'd, has been restor'd since the Revolution; and a garrison was always kept here by King William, for the better regulating the Highlands; and this post was of singular importance in the time of the late insurrection of the Lord Marr for the Pretender; when though his party took it, they were driven out again by the country, with the assistance of the Earl of Sutherland, and several other of the nobility and gentry, who stood fast to the King's interest.

Here is a stately stone bridge of seven large arches over the river Ness, where, as I said above, it grows narrow between the sea and the lake; small vessels may come up to the town, but larger ships, when such come thither, as they often do for corn, lye at some distance east from the town.

When you are over this bridge you enter that which we truly call the north of Scotland, and others the north Highlands; in which are several distinct shires, but cannot call for a distinct description, because it is all one undistinguish'd range of mountains and woods, overspread with vast, and almost uninhabited rocks and steeps fill'd with deer innumerable, and of a

364

great many kinds; among which are some of those the antients call'd harts and roebucks, with vast over-grown stags and hinds of the red deer kind, and with fallow-deer also.

And here, before I describe this frightful country, it is needful to observe that Scotland may be thus divided into four districts, or distinct quarters, which, how-ever, I have not seen any of our geographers do before me, yet, I believe, may not be an improper measure-ment for such as would form a due idea of the whole in their minds, as follows:

1. The South Land, or that part of Scotland south of the river Tay, drawing a line from the Tay, about Perth, to Loch-Lomond, and down again to Dumbar-ton, and the bank of Clyde.

2. The Middle, or Midland, being all the country from the Tay and the Lough-Lomon, north to the Lake of Ness and the Aber, including a long slope to the south, taking in the western Highlands of Argyle and Lorn, and the Isles of Isla and Jura.

3. The North Land, being all the country beyond Innerness, and the Lough, or river Ness, north, drawing the line over the narrow space of Glengary, between the Ness and the Aber, and bounded by them both from the eastern to the western sea.

4. The Islands, being all the western and northern islands (viz.) the Hebrides, the Skye, the Orkneys, and the Isles of Shetland.

Upon the foot of this division I am now, having passed the bridge over the Ness, entered upon the third division of Scotland call'd the North Land; and it is of this country that, as I am saying, the mountains are so full of deer, harts, roe-bucks, &c.

Here are also a great number of eagles which breed in the woods, and which prey upon the young fawns when they first fall. Some of these eagles are of a mighty large kind, such as are not to be seen again in those parts of the world.

Here are also the best hawks of all the kinds for sport which are in the kingdom, and which the nobility and gentry of Scotland make great use of; for not this part of Scotland only, but all the rest of the country abounds with wild-fowl.

The rivers and lakes also in all this country are pro-digiously full of salmon; it is hardly credible what the people relate of the quantity of salmon taken in these rivers, especially in the Spey, the Nairn, the Ness, and other rivers thereabout.

Innerness is a pleasant, clean, and well built town: there are some merchants in it, and some good share of

263. 'View of Fort George and the town of Inverness as it was in the year 1744'; engraving by T. Cook after a drawing by Paul Sandby.

264. Berrydale, Sutherland; aquatint by William Daniell.

trade. It consists of two parishes, and two large, handsome streets, but no publick buildings of any note, except as above, the old castle and the bridge.

North of the mouth of this river is the famous Cromarty Bay, or Cromarty Firth, noted for being the finest harbour, with the least business, of, perhaps, any in Britain; 'tis, doubtless, a harbour or port, able to receive the Royal Navy of Great Britain, and, like Milford-Haven in Wales, both the going in and out safe and secure: but as there is very little shipping employ'd in these parts, and little or no trade, except for corn, and in the season of it some fishing, so this noble harbour is left intirely useless in the world.

All the country beyond this river, and the Loch flowing into it, is call'd Caithness, and extends to the northermost land in Scotland.

Here are few towns, but the people live dispers'd, the gentry leading the commons or vassals, as they are call'd, to dwell within the respective bounds of their several clans, where they are, as we may say, little monarchs, reigning in their own dominions; nor do the people know any other sovereign, at least many of them do not.

This occasions the people to live dispers'd among the hills without any settled towns. Their employment is chiefly hunting, which is, as we may say, for their food; though they do also breed large quantities of black cattle, with which they pay their lairds or leaders the rent of the lands: and these are the cattle which, even from the remotest parts, as well as from other in the west and south, are driven annually to England to be sold, and are brought up even to London, especially into the countries of Norfolk, Suffolk, and Essex.

Having thus, as I say, few or no towns to describe north of Innerness, it must suffice, that I thus give a just description of the country in general: for example,

366

it is surrounded with the sea, and those two great inlets of water, mention'd above, call'd the Ness and the Abre: so that except a small part, or neck of land, reaching from one to the other, and which is not above six miles, I mean that country which Mr. Cambden calls the Garrow, or Glengarrough, others Glengary; I say, this neck of land excepted, the whole division, as form'd above under the head of the North Land, would be a distinct island, separated from all the rest of Great Britain, as effectually as the Orkneys or the Isle of Skey is separated from this.

In a word, the great Northern Ocean surrounds this whole part of Scotland; that part of it to the east, mention'd just now, lyes open to the sea without any cover; the west and north parts are, as it were, surrounded with out-works as defences, to break off the raging ocean from the north; for the western islands on one side, and the Orkneys on the other, lye as so many advanc'd fortifications or redoubts, to combat that enemy at a distance. I shall view them in their course.

The land thus extended as above, lyes north and south to Dungsby-Head, which is the utmost extent of the land on the east side of Britain, north, and is distant from Cromarty eighteen leagues north. This point of Dingsby, or Dungsby-Head, is in the north part, as I observ'd of Buchan and Winterton before; 'tis the place from whence the sailors take their distances and keep their accounts in their going farther north.

I am now to observe that we are here at the extremest end or point of the island of Great Britain; and that here the land bears away west, leaving a large strait or sea, which they call Pentland Firth, and which divides, between the island of Great Britain, and the Isles of the Orkneys; a passage broad and fair, for 'tis not less than five leagues over, and with a great depth of water; so that any ships, or fleets of ships may go thro' it: but the tides are so fierce, so uncertain, and the gusts and suddain squals of wind so frequent, that very few merchants-ship care to venture thro' it; and the Dutch East-India ships, which come north about, (as 'tis call'd) in their return from India, keep all further off, and choose to come by Fair Isle, that is to say, in the passage between the islands of Orkney and Shetland. And here the Dutch send their squadron of men of war generally to meet them, because, as if it were in a narrow lane, they are sure to meet with them there.

Here the passage is not only broader; for it is at least nine leagues from north Ranalsha, the farthest island of the Orkneys, to Fair Isle, and five more from Fair Isle to Shetland: so that they have a passage of fourteen leagues between the Orkneys and Shetland, with only a small island in the way, which has nothing dangerous about it; also the mountainous country being now all

out of reach; the sea is open and calm, as in other places; nor is there any dangerous current or shoals to disturb them.

As Dingsby-Head is the most northerly land of Great Britain, 'tis worth observing to you that here, in the month of June, we had so clear an uninterrupted day, that, though indeed the sun does set, that is to say, the horizon covers its whole body for some hours, yet you might see to read the smallest print, and to write distinctly, without the help of a candle, or any other light, and that all night long.

No wonder the antient mariners, be they Phœnician or Carthaginian, or what else you please, who in those days knew nothing of the motion of the heavenly bodies, when they were driven thus far, were surpris'd at finding they had lost the steady rotation of day and night, which they thought had spread over the whole globe.

No wonder they talked much of their *Ultima Thule*, and that the *Elysian Fields* must lye this way; when they found that they were already come to everlasting day, they could no longer doubt but heaven lay that way, or at least that this was the high way to it; and accordingly, when they came home, and were to give an account of these things among their neighbours, they fill'd them with astonishment; and 'twas wonderful they did not really fit out ships for the discovery; for who would ever have gone so near heaven, and not ventur'd a little farther to see whether they could find it or no?

From hence west we go along the shore of the firth or passage, which they call Pentland; and here is the house so famous, call'd John a Grot's house, where we set our horses feet into the sea, on the most northerly land, as the people say, of Britain, though, I think, Dungsby-Head is as far north.

Here we found, however mountainous and wild the country appear'd, the people were extremely well furnish'd with provisions; and especially they had four sorts of provisions in great plenty; and with a supply of which 'tis reasonable to say they could suffer no dangerous want.

1. Very good bread, as well oat bread as wheat, though the last not so cheap as the first.

2. Venison exceeding plentiful, and at all seasons, young or old, which they kill with their guns wherever they find it; for there is no restraint, but 'tis every man's own that can kill it. By which means the highlanders not only have all of them fire-arms, but they are all excellent marksmen.

3. Salmon in such plenty as is scarce credible, and so cheap, that to those who have any substance to buy with, it is not worth their while to catch it themselves.

265. Market Cross in a highland township; engraving. From Edward Burt, *Letters from a Gentleman in the North of Scotland to his friend in London* (1754).

This they eat fresh in the season, and for other times they cure it by drying it in the sun, by which they preserve it all the year.

They have no want of cows and sheep, but the latter are so wild, that sometimes were they not, by their own disposition, used to flock together, they would be much harder to kill than the deer.

From hence to the west point of the passage to Orkney is near twenty miles, being what may be call'd the end of the island of Britain; and this part faces directly to the North Pole; the land, as it were, looking forward just against the Pole Star, and the Pole so elevated, that the tail of the Ursa Major, or the Great Bear, is seen just in the zenith, or over your head; and the day is said to be eighteen hours long, that is to say, the sun is so long above the horizon: but the rest of the light is so far beyond a twilight, by reason of the

smalness of the arch of that circle, which the sun makes beneath the horizon, that it is clear and perfect day almost all the times; not forgetting withal, that the dark nights take their turn with them in their season, and it is just as long night in the winter.

Yet it is observable here, that they have more temperate winters here generally speaking, than we have to the most southerly part of the island, and particularly the water in some of the rivers as in the Ness, for example, never freezes, nor are their frosts ordinarily so lasting as they are in the most southerly climates, which is accounted for from the nearness of the sea, which filling the air with moist vapours, thickens the fluids and causes that they are not so easily penetrated by the severity of the cold.

On this account the snows also are not so deep, neither do they lie so long upon the ground, as in other

266. Houses in a highland township; engraving. From Edward Burt, *Letters from a Gentleman in the North of Scotland to his friend in London* (1754).

places, except it be on some of the high hills, in the upper and innermost part of the country, where the tops, or summits of the hills are continually cover'd with snow, and perhaps have been so for many ages, so that here if any place of the world they may justly add to the description of their country,

—Vast wat'ry lakes, which spread below,
And mountains cover'd with eternal snow.

On the most inland parts of this country, especially in the shire of Ross, they have vast woods of firr trees, not planted and set by men's hands, as I have described in the southern part of Scotland; but growing wild and undirected, otherwise than as nature planted and nourished them up, by the additional help of time, nay of ages. Here are woods reaching from ten, to fifteen, and twenty miles in length, and proportioned in breadth, in which there are firrs, if we may believe the inhabitants, large enough to make masts for the biggest ships in the Navy Royal, and which are rendered of no use, meerly for want of convenience of water carriage to bring them away; also they assure us there are a sufficient quantity of other timber for a supply to all Britain.

We find no manufactures among the people here, except it be what the women call their thrift, namely, spinning of woollen, or linnen for their own uses, and indeed not much of that; perhaps, the time may come, when they may be better and more profitably employ'd that way; for if as I have observ'd, they should once come to work the mines, which there is reason to believe are to be found there, and to search the bowels of the earth, for iron and copper, the people would soon learn to stay at home, and the women would find work as well as the men; but this must be left to time and posterity.

We were now in the particular county called Strathnaver, or the vale on the Naver, the remotest part of all the island, though not the most barren or unfruitful; for here as well as on the eastern shore is good corn produced, and sufficient of it at least for the inhabitants; perhaps they do not send much abroad, though sometimes also they send it over to the Orkneys, and also to Shetland. This county belongs to the Earl of Sutherland whose eldest son bears the title of Lord Strathnaver.

And now leaving the northern prospect we pass the opposite point west from Dingsby-head, and which the people call Farrohead.

From hence the vast western ocean appears, what name to give it the geographers themselves do not seem to agree, but it certainly makes a part of the great

267. Strathnaver; aquatint by William Daniell.

Atlantick Sea, and is to be called by no other name, for it has no land or country to derive from.

And now we were to turn our faces S. for the islands of this sea, which make the fourth division of Scotland as mentioned before. I may if I have room give as just a description of them as I can from authentick relations; for being on horse-back and no convenience of shipping presenting itself here, I am to own that we did not go over to those islands personally, neither was it likely any person whose business was meer curiosity and diversion, should either be at the expence, or run the risque of such a hazardous passage where there was so little worth observation to be found.

We therefore turned our faces to the south, and with great satisfaction after so long and fateaguing a journey; and unless we had been assisted by the gentlemen of the country, and with very good guides, it had been next to an impossibility to have pass'd over this part of the country. I do confess if I was to recommend to any men whose curiosity tempted them to travel over this country, the best method for their journeying, it should be neither to seek towns, for it would be impossible to find such in proper stages for their journey; nor to make themselves always burthensome to the high-land chiefs, tho' there I can assure them they would always meet with good treatment, and great hospitality.

But I would propose travelling with some company, and carrying tents with them, and so encamping every night as it they were an army.

It is true they would do well to have the countenance of the gentlemen, and chiefs as above, and to be recommended to them from their friends from one to another, as well for guides as for safety, otherwise I would not answer for what might happen: but if they are first well recommended as strangers, and have letters from one gentleman to another, they would want neither guides nor guards, nor indeed would any man touch them; but rather protect them if there was occasion in all places; and by this method they might in the summer time lodge, when, and wherever they pleased, with safety and pleasure; travelling no farther at a time, than they thought fit; and as for their provisions, they might supply themselves by their guns, with very great plenty of wild fowl, and their attendants and guides would find convenient places to furnish other things sufficient to carry with them.

Indeed in our attempt to come down to the southward by the coast of Tain, and the shire of Ross, we should have been extreamly disappointed, and perhaps have been obliged to get a ship or bark, to have carry'd us round the Isle of Skye into Loquhaber, had it not been for the extraordinary courtesie of some of the gentlemen of the country.

On the other hand we unexpectedly met here some English men, who were employ'd by merchants in the S. (whether at London or Edinburgh I do not now remember) to take and cure a large quantity of white fish, and afterwards of herrings, on account of trade. Here we had not only the civility of their assistance and accommodation in our journey, but we had the pleasure of seeing what progress they made in their undertaking.

As for herrings indeed the quantity was prodigious, and we had the pleasure of seeing something of the prodigy, for I can call it no other; the shoal was as I might say beginning to come, or had sent their vant-couriers before them, when we first came to the head of Pentland Firth, and in a fortnight's time more, the body of their numberless armies began to appear; but before we left the coast you would have ventur'd to say of the sea, as they do of the river Tibiscus,[26] or Theisse in Hungary, that it was one third water, and two thirds fish; the operation of taking them, could hardly be call'd fishing, for they did little more than dip for them into the water and take them up.

As to the quantity, I make no scruple to say, that if there had been ten thousand ships there to have loaded with them, they might all have been filled and none of them mist; nor did the fish seem to stay, but pass'd on to the south, that they might supply other parts, and make way also for those innumerable shoals which were to come after.

Had the quantity of white fish been any way proportion'd to the undertaking as the herring was, there

would no doubt have been such encouragement to the merchant, that they would never have given it over, but they found it would not fully answer: not but there were great quantities of cod, and the fish very sizeable and good, but not so great a quantity as to make that dispatch in taking them (as they are taken with hook and line) sufficient for loading of ships, or laying up a large quantity in the season; and this I doubt discouraged the undertaking, the merchants finding the expence to exceed the return.

Here we found the town of **Tain**, and some other villages tollerably well inhabited, and some trade also, occasioned principally by the communication with the western islands, and also by the herring fishing, the fishing boats from other parts often putting into these ports; for all their coast is full of loughs and rivers, and other openings which make very good harbours of shipping; and that which is remarkable, some of those loughs, are infinitely full of herrings, even where, as they tell us, they have no communication with the sea, so that they must have in all probability been put into them alive by some particular hands, and have multiplied there as we find at this time.

We could understand nothing on this side of what the people said, any more than if we had been in Morocco; and all the remedy we had was, that we found most of the gentlemen spoke French, and some few spoke broad Scots; we found it also much for our convenience to make the common people believe we were French.

Should we go about here to give you an account of the religion of the people in this country, it would be an unpleasant work, and perhaps scarce seem to deserve credit; you would hardly believe that in a Christian island, as this is said to be, there should be people found who know so little of religion, or of the custom of Christians, as not to know a Sunday, or Sabbath, from a working day, or the worship of God from an ordinary meeting, for conversation: I do not affirm that it is so, and I shall say no more of it here, because I would not publish what it is to be hoped may in time find redress; but I cannot but say that his majesty's gift of 1000 l. annually to the Assembly of Scotland, for sending ministers or missionaries for the propagating Christian knowledge in the Highlands, is certainly one of the most needful charities that could have been thought of, worthy of a king, and well suited to that occasion; and if prudently apply'd, as there is reason to believe it will be, may in time break in upon this horrible ignorance, that has so far spread over this unhappy part of the country.

On the other hand, what shall we say to the neglect, which for so many years past has been the occasion of

268. Fort William; drawing by Paul Sandby (*c*.1749). From Thomas Pennant, *A Tour in Scotland* (1769–72 (large set)).

this surprizing darkness among the people, when the poor abandon'd creatures have not so much as had the common instruction of Christianity, so much as to know whether there was any such thing as a God or no, much less how to worship him; and if at any time any glympse of light had been infus'd into them, and they had been taught any knowledge of superior things, it has been by the diligence of the Popish clergy, who to do them justice, have shewn more charity, and taken more pains that way, than some whose work it had been, and who it might much more have been expected from?

On this coast is the Isle of Skye, lying from the west north west, to the east south east, and bearing upon the main island, only separated by a narrow strait of water; something like as the Isle of Wight is separated from the county of Southampton. We left this on our right, and crossing the mountains, came with as little stay as we could to the Lough of Abre, that is, the water which as I said above, assists with Lough Ness, or Loch Ness, to separate the north land of Scotland, from the middle part.

From this river or water of Abre, all that mountainous barren and frightful country, which lies south of the water of Abre is call'd Loquabre, or the country bordering on Loch Abre. It is indeed a frightful country full of hidious desart mountains and unpassable, except to the Highlanders who possess the precipices. Here in spight of the most vigorous pursuit, the Highland robbers, such as the famous Rob Roy[27] in the late disturbances, find such retreats as none can pretend to follow them into, nor could he be ever taken.

On this water of Abre, just at the entrance of the Loch, was anciently a fort built, to curb the Highlanders, on either side; it was so situated, that tho' it might indeed be block'd up by land and be distress'd by a siege, the troops besieging being masters of the field, yet as it was open to the sea, it might always receive supplies by shipping, the government being supposed to be always master of the sea, or at least 'tis very probable they will be so.

At this place we take our leave of the third division, which I call the North Land of Scotland, for this fort being on the south side of the Loch Abre is therefore called inner Lochy, as the other for the like reason was called inner Ness.

We have nothing now remaining for a full survey of Scotland, but the western part, of the Middle Part, or division of Scotland, and this though a large country, yet affords not an equal variety with the eastern part of the same division.

To traverse the remaining part of this country, I must begin upon the upper Tay, as we may justly call it, where I left off when I turn'd away east; and here we have in especial manner the country of Brechin, the Blair as 'tis called of Athol, and the country of Bradalbin: this is a hilly country indeed, but as it is water'd by the Tay, and many other pleasant rivers which fall into it, there are also several fruitful valleys, intersperst among the hill; nor are even the Highlands themselves, or the Highlanders the inhabitants any thing so wild, untaught, or untractable, as those whom I have been a describing in the north-land division, that is to say, in Strath-Naver, Ross, Tain, &c.

The Duke of Athol[28] is lord, I was almost going to say king of this country, and has the greatest interest, or if you please, the greatest share of vassalage of any

269. The Earl of Breadalbane's seat at Killing; engraving by W. Walker and W. Angus after an earlier drawing by Paul Sandby (published 1779).

270. Dupplin House; engraving by P. Mazell after a drawing by Moses Griffith.

nobleman in this part of Scotland; if I had said in all Scotland, I believe I should have been supported by others that know both his person and his interest as well as most people do.

As I have said something of this country of Bradalbin, it will be needfull to say something more, seeing some other authors have said so much: it is seated as near the center of Scotland, as any part of it can be well fixt, and that which is particular, is, that it is alledg'd, it is the highest ground of all Scotland, for that the rivers which rise here, are said to run every way from this part, some into the eastern, and some into the western seas.

The Grampian mountains, which are here said to cut through Scotland, as the Muscovites say of their Riphæan Hills,[29] that they are the girdle of the world. As is the country, so are the inhabitants, a fierce fighting and furious kind of men; but I must add that they are much chang'd, and civiliz'd from what they were formerly, if Mr. Cambden's account of them is just. I mean of the Highlanders of Bradalbin only; tho' I include the country of Loquhabre, and Athol, as adjoyning to it.

It is indeed a very bitter character, and possibly they might deserve it in those days; but I must insist that they are quite another people now: and tho' the country is the same, and the mountains as wild and desolate as ever, yet the people, by the good conduct of their chiefs and heads of clans, are much more civilized than they were in former times.

As the men have the same vigour and spirit; but are under a better regulation of their manners, and more under government; so they make excellent soldiers, when they come abroad, or are listed in regular and disciplin'd troops.

The Duke of Athol, though he has not an estate equal to some of the nobility, yet he is master of more of these superiorities, as they are called there, than many of those who have twice his estate; and I have been told, that he can bring a body of above 6000 men together in arms at very little warning.

The pomp and state in which this noble person lives, is not to be imitated in Great Britain; for he is served like a prince, and maintains a greater equipage and retinue then five times his estate would support in another country.

The Duke has also another seat in Strathearn, which is called Tullibardin, and which gives title at this time to the eldest son of the house of Athol, for the time being. At the lower part of this country, the river Earn falls into Tay, and greatly increases its waters. This river rises far west, on the frontiers of the western Highlands near Glengyl, and running through that pleasant country called Strathearn, falls into Tay, below St. Johnstons.

Soon after its first coming out from the mountains, the Earn spreads it selfe into a loch, as most of those rivers do; this is called Loch Earn, soon after which it runs by Duplin Castle,[30] the seat of the Earl of Kinnowl, whose eldest son is known in England, by the title of Lord Duplin, taking it from the name of this castle. The late Earl of Kinnowl's Son, the Lord Duplin, was marry'd to the daughter of the late Earl of Oxford, then Lord High Treasurer of England, and who was on that occasion made a peer of Great Britain.

The ancient seat is situated in a good soil, and a pleasant country, near the banks of the river Earn, and the Earl has a very good estate; but not loaded with vassals, and highland superiorities, as the Duke of Athol is said to be.

The house is now under a new decoration, two new wings being lately added for offices as well as ornament.

The old building is spacious, the rooms are large, and the cielings lofty, and which is more than all the appearance of the buildings, 'tis all magnificently finished, and furnished within; there are also abundance of very fine paintings, and some of great value, especially court pieces, and family pieces, of which it would take up a book to write the particulars; but I must not omit the fine picture of King Charles the First, with a letter in his hand, which he holds out to his son the Duke of York, afterwards King James the Second, which they say he was to carry to France; also a statue in brass of the same King Charles the First on horseback; there are also two pictures of a contrary sort, namely, one of Oliver Cromwell, and one of the then General Monk, both from the life.

Also there is a whole length of that Earl of Kinnoul, who was Lord Chancellor of Scotland, in the reign of King James the Sixth, with several other peices of Italian masters of great value.

From this place we went to Brechin, an ancient town with a castle finely situate; but the ancient grandour of it not supported; the family of Penmure, to whom it belong'd, having been in no extraordinary circumstances for some time past, and now their misfortunes being finished, it is under forfeiture, and sold among the spoils of the late rebellion.

We were now as it were landed again, being after a long mountain-ramble, come down to the low lands, and into a pleasant and agreeable country; but as we had yet another journey to take west, we had a like prospect of a rude and wild part of Scotland to go through.

271. 'Prospect of the towne of Brechin'; engraving. From John Slezer, *Theatrum Scotiae* (1693).

The Highlands of Scotland are divided into two parts, and known so as two separate countries, (viz.) the West Highlands, and the North Highlands; the last, of which I have spoken at large, contain the countries or provinces of

Bradalbin,	Sutherland,	
Athol,	Ross,	together with
Lochaber,	Strathnaver,	the Isle of Skye.
Buchan,	Caithness,	
Mar,		

The West Highlands, contain the shires or counties of

Dunbritton or Dunbarton,	
Lenox.	Argyle,
Bute,	Lorn and Cantyre.

On the bank of this river Earn lies a very pleasant vale, which continues from the Tay, where it receives the river quite up to the Highlands; this is called according to the usage of Scotland Strath Earn, or the Strath or Vale of Earn, 'tis an agreeable country, and has many gentlemen's seats on both sides the river; but it is near the Highlands, and has often suffered by the depredations of those wild folk in former times.

The family of Montrose, whose chief was sacrificed for the interest of King Charles the First, had a strong castle here called Kincardin; but it was ruin'd and demolished in those wars, and is not rebuilt. The castle of Drummond is almost in the same condition, or at least is like soon to be so, the Earl of Perth, to whom it belongs, being in exile, as his father was before him,

by their adhering to the late King James the Seventh, and to the present Pretender. King James the Seventh made the father a duke, and knight of the garter, and governor to his son the Pretender. His eldest son who should have succeeded to the honours and titles dy'd in France, and three other sons still remaining are all abroad, either following the ruin'd fortunes of the Pretender, or in other service in foreign courts; where, we know not, nor is it material to our present purpose.

The western Highlands are the only remaining part of Scotland, which as yet I have not toucht upon. This is that particular country, which a late great man in King James the Second's time, called the Kingdom of Argyle; and upon which occasion it was a compliment upon King James, that he had conquer'd two kings, when he suppress'd the rebellion of the Whigs; namely, the Duke of Monmouth, whom in derision they called the little King of Lime, and the Earl of Argyle whom they called with much more propriety, the great King of the Highlands.

It is true that the greatest part of these western Highlands, may be said to be subject, or in some respect to belong to the house of Argyle, or to speak more properly, to the family or clan of the Campbells, of whom the Duke of Argyle is the chief; but then it should be noted too, that those western gentlemen are not so blindly to be led, or guided by their chiefs as those in the north; nor when led on, are they so apt for mischief and violence. But as many of them are toucht with the Cameronian Whig, or at least the English Whig principles, they would venture to enquire what they were to do, and whom to fight against, at least before they dipt far in any hazardous undertaking.

Though the people of these countries are something more civiliz'd than those of their bretheren montaineers in the north, yet the countries seem to be so near a kin that no strangers could know them asunder, nor is there any breach in the similitude that I could observe, except it be that in the north Highlands, there are such great woods of fir-trees, which I have taken notice of there, and which we do not see the like of here: nor did we see so many or so large eagles in these western mountains as in the north, tho' the people assure us there are such too.

The quantity of deer are much the same, and the kinds too, and the black cattle are of the same kind, and rather more numerous; the people also dress after the same manner, in the plaid and the trouse,[31] go naked from below the knee to the mid thighs, wear the durk and the pistol at their girdle, and the targ or target at their shoulder.

Some reckon the shire of Braidalbin to belong to these western Highlands, not that it is west in its situation, for it is rather north, and as I have mention'd, is said to be the center of Scotland; and the highest land, being in the very body of those they call the Grampian Mountains; all the reason that I could find they give for reckoning this country among the western Highlands, is because they say one part of it is

272. Roadbuilders in the Scottish Highlands; watercolour by Paul Sandby (c.1750).

273. Highlanders wearing the plaid in different ways; engraving. From Edward Burt, *Letters from a Gentleman in the North of Scotland to his friend in London* (1754).

inhabited by the Campbells, whose clan, as I have observed, generally possesses all the west High-lands.

But if they will claim the country, they must claim the people too, who are, if I may give my opinion, some of the worst, most barbarous, and ill governed of all the Highlands of Scotland; they are desperate in fight, cruel in victory, fierce even in conversation, apt to quarrel, mischievous, and even murderers in their passion.

I am now to return to our progress. Leaving the country of Brechin, and the low lands of Strathearn, we went away west; but were presently interrupted by a vast inland sea, rather than a lake called Loch Lomond. It is indeed a sea, and look'd like it from the hills from whence we first descry'd it; and its being a tempestuous day, I assure you it appear'd all in a

274. View near Dumbarton, towards Ben Lomond; drawing by Paul Sandby (*c.*1750). From Thomas Pennant, *A Tour in Scotland* (1769–72 (large set)).

breach, rough and raging, like the sea in a storm. There are several islands in it, which from the hills we could plainly perceive were islands, but that they are a-drift, and float about the lake, that I take as I find it, for a story, namely, a story call'd a f ——[32] as I do also that of the water of this loch, turning wood into stone.

This lake or loch is, without comparison, the greatest in Scotland, no other can be call'd half so big; for it is more than twenty miles long, and generally eight miles in breadth, though at the north end of it, 'tis not so broad by far. It receives many rivers into it, but empties itself into the Firth of Clyde, at one mouth; near the entrance of it into Clyde, stands the famous Dunbarton Castle, the most antient, as well as the most important castle in Scotland; and the gate, as 'tis call'd of the Highlands. It is now not much regarded, the whole country being, as it were, buried in peace, yet there is a garrison maintain'd in it; and the pass would be still of great import, were there any occasion of arms in time to come; 'tis exceeding strong by situation, being secur'd by the river on one side, the Firth of Clyde on the other, by an unpassable morass on the third side, and the fourth is a precipice.

Passing from Dunbarton Castle, we enter the terri-

275. 'Prospect of the castle of Dumbritton [Dumbarton] from the east'; engraving. From John Slezer, *Theatrum Scotiae* (1693).

276. Crag of Ailsa; engraving by P. Mazell after a drawing by Moses Griffith. From Thomas Pennant, *A Tour in Scotland and Voyage to the Hebrides* (1772).

tory of Argyle. As to the county of Lenox, the paternal estate and property of the Stuarts, it lyes extended from both sides the Levin, that is, the river, which (as I said before) empties the Loch-Lomon into the Clyde. On this side, or eastward, Lenox joins to Monteith, and runs up for some length on the east side of the Loch, and on the west side it extends to the edge of the Loch-Loing, and a great way north, almost to the mountains of Loquhabre.

Beyond this Loch-Loing begins the large extended country of Argyle, or the western Highlands, whose extent takes in the shire or county of Lorn to the north, and Cantyre to the south, all possess'd by the Campbells, and vulgarly understood by the country of Argyle; for as for Cantyre, which is a *chersonese*, or peninsula, it belongs mostly, if not wholly to the Campbell's; and as to Lorn, 'tis the title of the eldest son of the house of Argyle to this day.

The west side of this country lyes extended along the Irish Sea for a very great length, at least eighty miles (viz.) from the Mull of Cantyre to Dunstaffnage, and the Isle of Stackar and Listnoc, in the water of Loquhaber. On all this shore there is no town eminent for trade, no port or harbour, at least none made use of for shipping; nor are there any ships to require them, except fishing-barks and boats, which are in the season employ'd for catching herrings, of which the shoals that are found upon this coast in the season are incredible, especially in the Clyde, in Loch-Finn, and about the Isle of Arran, which lyes in the mouth of Clyde.

From the Mull of Cantyre they see Ireland very plain, it being not above fifteen or sixteen miles from the point of land, which they call the Mull to the Fair Foreland, on the coast of Colrain, on the north of Ireland. In the mouth of this sea of Clyde lyes a rock, somewhat like the Bass in the Firth of Forth, or of Edinburgh, not for shape, but for this particular, that here, as at the Bass, the Soland geese are pleas'd to come in the season of the fishery, and to breed and inhabit as they do at the Bass, and to go away and come again just at the same seasons, as at the Bass: this island is call'd the Ailze. Here are also the islands of Arran and of Bute; the first giving title of earl to the family of Hamilton, and the other the title of Duke of Rothsay to the eldest son of the crown of Scotland, who is call'd Duke of Rothsay, from the castle of Rothsay in this island; nor is there any thing else considerable to be said of either of the islands; for as for their present condition, which is what is my particular business in this book, they have nothing considerable in or about them, except it be a tumultuous and dangerous sea for sailors, especially when a south-west wind blows hard, which brings the sea rowling in upon them in a frightful manner. However, there is one good harbour on the north side of the island, call'd Lamlach, which is their safety in such cases.

Off of the western shore of Argyle and Lorn there are abundance of islands, which all belong to the family of Argyle, or at least to its jurisdiction; as Isla, Jura, Tyrry, Mull, Lysmore, Coll, and several others of less note.

The End of the Thirteenth and Last Letter

FINIS

NOTES

Notes to Introduction

1. The original title of the *Review* was *A Review of the Affairs of France: Purg'd from the Errors and Partiality of News-Writers and Petty-Statesmen, of all Sides*. It later became *A Review of the State of the British Nation*.
2. In the Preface to volume VIII of the *Review*, 1712.
3. See Letter IV below, p. 109. Subsequent references to the *Tour* are given in parentheses in the text.
4. James Sutherland, *Defoe* (1937), p. 263.
5. Pat Rogers, 'Defoe at Work: The Making of *A Tour thro' Great Britain*, Volume I', *Bulletin of the New York Public Library*, 78 (1975), pp. 431–50. See also his later article, 'The Making of Defoe's *A Tour thro' Great Britain*, Volumes II and III', *Prose Studies*, 3 (1980), pp. 109–37.
6. *The Complete English Tradesman* (1726 [for 1725]), vol. I, pp. 402–4.
7. Ibid., vol. II, part 2, p. 140.
8. Ibid., vol. I, chapter 22, *passim*.
9. Ibid., vol. I, pp. 375–6.
10. John McVeagh, 'Defoe and the Romance of Trade', *Durham University Journal*, 70 (1978), pp. 141–7.
11. *The Complete English Tradesman*, vol. I, pp. 381–3.
12. Pat Rogers, 'Defoe and Virgil: The Georgic Element in *A Tour Thro' Great Britain*', *English Miscellany*, 22 (1971), pp. 93–106.
13. Cited in Raymond Carr, *English Fox Hunting* (1976), p. 54.
14. See the Preface to volume II of the *Review*, 1711.
15. *The Letters of Daniel Defoe*, ed. George Harris Healey (Oxford, 1955), pp. 158–9.

Notes to Defoe's Tour

ABBREVIATIONS

Andrews	J.H. Andrews, 'Defoe and the Sources of his "Tour"', *Geographical Journal*, 126 (1960), pp. 268–77.
Camden	William Camden, *Britannia*, translated and edited by Edmund Gibson, 2 vols (1695; fourth edition, 1772)
Kerridge	Eric Kerridge, *Textile Manufactures in Early Modern England* (1985)
Macky	John Macky, *A Journey Through England in Familiar Letters*, 3 vols (1714–23) [the third volume being in fact entitled *A Journey Through Scotland*]
Rogers	Defoe, *A Tour Through the Whole Island of Great Britain*, edited by Pat Rogers (Penguin Books, 1971)

PREFACE

1. *the learned writers on the subject of antiquity*: see Introduction above, pp. ix, xii.
2. *The preparations for this work*. Andrews (p. 268) points out that, according to later volumes, some of the tours listed here by Defoe had not then taken place.
3. *Israelitish spies*. An allusion to the spies sent into Canaan by Moses; see Numbers 13.32.

LETTER I

1. *fish-pools*. Sir Richard Steele formed a company to promote a Fish Pool, or Company for Importing Live Fish, in 1720.
2. *tenders*. A tender is a ship or boat attendant on a larger one.
3. *Calais, St. Maloes*. They were bombarded by the British fleet during the War of the Protestant Succession.
4. *penny-worths*: bargains.
5. *breach*. The Thames burst its banks in 1707 and was not finally dammed till 1720.
6. *Captain Perry*. John Perry (1670–1732), engineer. He published *An Account of the Stopping of the Daggenham Breach* (1721).
7. *Dutch war*. England was at war with the Dutch in 1652–4, 1665–7, and 1672–4.
8. *good farm*: i.e., a profitable investment.
9. *Lord Viscount Barrington*. John Shute (1678–1734), first Viscount Barrington, third son of Benjamin Shute, a London merchant. He was an influential spokesman in the Presbyterian interest.
10. *Sir Josiah Child*. The famous financier (1630–99), who became chairman of the East India Company.
11. *a severe seige*: Colchester was besieged by the Parliamentary army in 1648. Defoe reproduced a lengthy contemporary account of the siege, omitted here.
12. *Sir Charles Lucas, and Sir George Lisle*: noted royalist officers, shot after a court martial on 28 August 1648 for their part in the Kentish insurrection and the defence of Colchester.
13. *culverine*: a long cannon.
14. *hoys and small barks*. A hoy was a small vessel, usually rigged as a sloop, used for short coastal voyages.
15. *bays*: (i.e., baize) 'a plain weave, with a woollen weft that was about four times as heavy as the

warp and crammed enough to hide it' (Kerridge).

16. *new sea mark*. This was erected in 1720.

17. *blind*. Defoe is referring, perhaps, to a horse's blinker.

18. *Sir Peter Parker, and Humphrey Parsons, Esq*. They were elected in 1722.

19. *chaldron*: a dry measure of 32 or 36 bushels.

20. *flyboats*. Small flat-bottomed boats, of Dutch origin.

21. *caption*: capture.

22. *the Revolution*: i.e., the 'Glorious Revolution' of 1688 which placed William and Mary on the throne.

23. *late calamities of stocks and bubbles*: the South Sea Bubble of 1720, i.e., the collapse of the South Sea company and others, which led to widespread financial ruin.

24. *Rowland Taylor*. Archdeacon and Protestant martyr, burnt on Aldham Common, near Hadleigh, on 9 February 1555, for opposition to Queen Mary's religious policy.

25. *detestable conspiracy of the Papists*: Bishop Atterbury's Jacobite conspiracy, discovered in the summer of 1723.

26. *says*: 'A distinct two-and-two twill with a single weft and a warp twisted from two or three threads' (Kerridge).

27. *perpetuana's*. Perpetuanas were a white pinnion serge finished in a manner invented in the late sixteenth century in the West country and a very popular export in the ensuing century: a light, smooth, inexpensive fabric (Kerridge).

28. *the Montpelier of Suffolk*. Macky calls Bury 'the Montpellier of England'.

29. *act of barbarity*. The murderers were executed at the end of March 1722.

30. *the Coventry Act*: statute of 1670, 22 and 23 Car.2, c.1. The name commemorates Sir John Coventry, who was set upon by ruffians and had his nose slit, in revenge for a speech in the House of Commons.

31. *old poet*. Professor W.S. Watt notes a close resemblance to Rutilius Claudius Namatianus, *De reditu suo* (*c*.AD 417) 1. 413f.: *non indignemur mortalia corpora solvi:/ cernimus exemplis oppida posse mori*.

32. *turnips*. Viscount Townshend (see note 43 below) promoted the ex-tended culture of turnips, an important agricultural improvement, at his estate at Rainham.

33. *voiture*: carriage.

34. *perch*: the centre pole running underneath some four-wheeled vehicles.

35. *twisting-mills*. Strictly speaking, a twisting-mill is a mechanical device for twisting yarn: here extended to refer to a workshop.

36. *Duke of Norfolk*. Thomas Howard, thirteenth Duke of Norfolk (1683–1732) came under suspicion of involvement in a Jacobite conspiracy in 1722.

37. *Sir Tho. Brown*. Sir Thomas Browne's *Posthumous Works* (1712) include *Repertorium: or, the Antiquities of the Cathedral Church of Norwich*.

38. *gross*: great majority.

39. *key*: quay.

40. *head-fasts*. A headfast is a rope or chain at the head of a vessel, to make her fast to a quay.

41. *camblets*: i.e., camlets, a worsted with a 'watered' pattern imitating a costly eastern fabric.

42. *prescription right*: i.e., prescriptive right, or right by customary law.

43. *Lord Viscount Townshend*: Charles, 2nd Viscount Townshend (1674–1736), Secretary of State and brother-in-law and political associate of Walpole.

44. *Robert Walpole*. Sir Robert Walpole, 1st Earl of Orford (1676–1745) became Chancellor of the Exchequer in 1721.

45. *statue of King William on horseback*. Andrews (p. 276) notes that, as was noticed by a tourist in 1735, the statue was actually of James II. The tourist added: 'This is not the only lie in that author's [i.e., Defoe's] book'. He might have added that, as the drawing shows, the statue is not equestrian.

46. *moorish*: boggy.

47. *sharping*: cheating.

48. *horse-coursers in Smithfield*: jobbing dealers in horses at London's meat-market and horse-fair in Smithfield.

49. *biting*: fraudulently deceiving.

50. *Mr. Frampton*. Tregonwell Frampton (1641–1727), keeper of the king's horses.

51. *Sir R— Fagg*: Sir Robert Fagg, third Baronet (1673–1736).

52. *Blackwell-Hall*: the great London cloth-market, adjoining the Guildhall.

53. *pennistons*. Penistones were a coarse cloth originally from the Penistone, Wakefield and Barnsley district. 'Ordinary penistones, otherwise "forest whites", were heavily milled broadcloths, mostly dozens' (Kerridge).

54. *serges*: 'a very durable twilled cloth of worsted, or with the warp of worsted and the woof of wool' (*OED*).

55. *du-roys*: a lightweight worsted material used chiefly for men's wear.

56. *druggets*: a loosely-woven plain cloth. 'Before pressing, a drugget had a face rather like baize, but when hot-pressed it acquired a smooth and flannelly finish' (Kerridge).

57. *shalloons*: says woven from line yarns. 'They were often glazed and hot-pressed to a smooth finish for the linings of suits, coats and other garments. The shalloon's original name was *serge de Chalons*' (Kerridge).

58. *cantaloons*: coarse striped worsteds made in a variety of bright colours, often including medley yarns. The name derives from 'Catalonia'.

59. *kersies*. Kersey: 'A kind of coarse narrow cloth, woven from long wool, and usually ribbed' (*OED*).

60. *toy-shops*: shops selling trinkets, small ornaments and such like.

61. *Pye-Powder courts*: courts of summary jurisdiction at fairs, so-called after 'Piepowders' (Fr. *pieds poudreux*), a term for itinerant merchants.

62. *The Antiquities of Cambridge*: probably referring to John Caius, *De antiquitate Cantabrigiensis Academiae* (1574).

63. *Audley End*. The great mansion built by Sir Thomas Audley in the sixteenth century was partly demolished in 1721.

64. *noble family of Petre*. The family was first lent distinction by Sir William Petre (1505?–72), a statesman in the employ of Queen Mary and Queen Elizabeth. His estate at Ingatestone was confiscated monastic property.

65. *great battle in Sussex*: the battle of Hastings, 14 October 1066.

66. *palace of the Lord Castlemain*. Wanstead House was built between

1715 and 1720 by Richard Child, who in 1718 became Viscount Castlemain.

LETTER II

1. *Royal Hospital for Seamen*. The building of the Royal Naval Hospital, designed by Wren, Hawksmoor and Vanbrugh and incorporating a portion of Charles II's new palace, continued through much of the eighteenth century.

2. *Queen's House*. A palace in the style of an Italian villa designed by Inigo Jones for James I's Queen, Anne of Denmark, 1616, later enlarged for Queen Henrietta Maria.

3. *Flamstead House*. It was built in 1675–6 and named after John Flamstead (1646–1719), the first Astronomer Royal.

4. *Horn-Fair*: a fair held annually at Charlton on St. Luke's day, 18 October. It involved a procession with ram's horns, in allusion to St. Luke's ox and to cuckoldry.

5. *rope-walk*: a stretch of ground devoted to rope-making.

6. *bavin*. According to the *OED* a bavin is 'a bundle of brushwood etc., bound with only one withe'.

7. *tilt-boat*: a large rowing-boat covered with an awning or tilt.

8. *coquets*. A coquet was a sealed document certifying that duty had been paid.

9. *that dreadful tempest of 1703*. The great storm that began on 27 November 1703 was celebrated by Defoe in his book *The Storm*. It lasted seven days and was altogether more violent than the one in 1987.

10. *doggers*: two-masted fishing vessels used in the North Sea.

11. *escape into France*. The King's first, abortive attempt to flee the country took place on 11 December 1688.

12. *glass-houses*: glass-factories.

13. *writing sand*: presumably the sand used for blotting ink.

14. *the Three Cranes*. Rogers locates this as near today's Cannon Street station.

15. *the yeomen of Kent*. The 'men of Kent' enjoyed a reputation for sturdy independence dating back to 1066 when they went to meet the Conqueror, carrying green boughs, and were confirmed by him in their ancient privileges.

16. — *miles*: about six miles.

17. *champian*: i.e., champaign, meaning level and open.

18. *Owlers*. 'Owling' or nocturnal smuggling was the response to the prohibition of wool exports, enacted in 1662.

19. *physically*: i.e., for medicinal purposes.

20. *Bright Helmstone*: better known as Brighton.

21. *the Streights*: i.e., the Straits of Gibraltar.

22. *Cowley*. The poet Abraham Cowley (1618–67) was much inclined to hymn the praises of retirement, and eventually, in 1665, his patrons enabled him to acquire a country residence near Chertsey. He died of a cold caught while admiring the beauties of nature, or, according to another account, from coming home drunk from a dinner-party and spending the night under a hedge.

23. *cottagers*. A cottager or cottar was a (sometimes landless) peasant who occupied a cottage belonging to a farm, for which he had to provide labour on the farm, at a fixed rate, when required.

24. *Sir Tho. Bludworth*: (d. 1682), Lord Mayor in 1665–6.

25. *Mr. Howard*. Rogers identifies him as Charles Howard (d. 1720), of Deepden, whose son became the 15th Duke of Norfolk. ·

26. *Sir Adam Brown*. Frank Bastian (*Defoe's Early Life* (1981), p. 38) refers to Sir Adam Browne as 'joint Lord of the Manor of Dorking and Knight of the Shire for Surrey, a strong royalist described a few years later as "a vassal to the Duke of York"'.

27. *Sir John Parsons*. He was a member of a brewing family and was Lord Mayor in 1703–4. His son Humphrey was Lord Mayor in 1730–1, having held the offices of alderman and sheriff in 1721 and 1722.

28. *late Earl of Jersey*: Edward Villiers (1656–1711), 1st Earl.

29. *stink-pots*: hand-thrown missiles which emitted a thick smoke, used by assailants when boarding a ship.

30. *unhappy stock jobbing year*: 1720, the year of the South Sea Bubble.

31. *raffling shops*. Raffling shops were gambling establishments apparently combining dicing and 'raffling' in the modern sense, i.e., a

lottery for some prize. They were a recent development in Defoe's time (see the *Tatler*, 25 August 1709, no. 59) and were particularly associated with spas.

32. *higglers*: itinerant dealers who bought up poultry and dairy produce in exchange for commodities from shops in towns.

33. *rattle*: chatter.

34. *the Prince's court*. During the summer the Prince held court at Richmond Lodge.

35. *masslapatam chints*. Chintz, a species of painted or printed calico (see note 37 below), was popularised in the 1650s by the East India company. 'Masslapatam' is presumably Masulipatam.

36. *atlasses*. Johnson's Dictionary defines 'atlas' as 'a rich kind of silk or stuff made for women's clothes'.

37. *painted callicoes*. In 1701 the importation of Asian coloured calicoes and wrought silks was prohibited, and in 1720, with effect from 1722, the use of all calicoes other than all-blue ones.

38. *scrutores*: escritoires.

39. *Roan*: Rouen.

40. *Loign*: the river Loign, which joins the Seine in the vicinity of Fontainebleau.

41. *capital messuages*: i.e., the 'great house' of an estate.

42. *Bastides*: the name given to little summer residences in the environs of Marseilles.

43. *Sir Josiah Child*. See note 10 above, p. 378.

44. *Sir John Lethulier*: (d. 1719). He was a wealthy Levant merchant.

45. *Sir James Bateman*: (d. 1718), Lord Mayor 1716–17 and a director of the East India company.

46. *Sir Robert Clayton*: (1629–1707), merchant and politician. He made a very large fortune, which helped him play an influential role in the Whig interest in City, and national, politics. Defoe, who was friendly with him, introduced him into his novel *Roxana* (1724).

47. *Sir William Scawen*: knighted 1692; died 1722.

48. *the Mint*: a place of privilege in Southwark, near the King's Prison, where people sheltered from justice on the pretext that it was an ancient royal palace. It was also known as Suffolk Place. It was suppressed in 1723.

49. *bills of mortallity*: weekly and annual

records of baptisms and burials kept by parish clerks in the City of London and Westminster, hence by extension those areas of London.

LETTER III

1. *marriage of old Isis*. The gender of the rivers Isis and Thame (or Thames) varies in legend. Michael Drayton, in *Polyolbion* (Song the Fifteenth) speaks of the marriage of 'the lovely Tame' ('old Chiltern's son') to his bride Isis ('Cotswold's heir'). Isis is also sometimes represented as Thame's mother.

2. *chints bed*: bed with chintz hangings.

3. *cartoons*. Defoe is referring to the celebrated cartoons (actually seven) by Raphael, bought by Charles I in 1632 and now in the Victoria and Albert Museum. The tapestries now hanging in their place, in Hampton Court, were made in the seventeenth century.

4. *sudden and surprizing fire*. It happened in 1689.

5. *batter'deau*. The modern French spelling is *batardeau*.

6. *Bishop Morley*: George Morley (1597–1684), Bishop of Winchester from 1660.

7. *Sir William Waller*. The Parliamentary general Sir William Waller (1597–1668) was the originator of the New Model Army, the soldiers of which sometimes broke into churches, tore up prayerbooks and surplices and burned the communion-rails.

8. *Monasticon*: Sir William Dugdale's *Monasticon Anglicanum*, an account of English monastic houses, published in 1655–73.

9. *William of Wickham*: William of Wykeham (1324–1404), Bishop of Winchester and Chancellor of England. He obtained a papal bull for the founding of Winchester College in 1378.

10. *Quietist*: a member of a devotional and mystical movement founded by Miguel Molinos in the 1670s, prescribing passive contemplation and extinction of the will.

11. *Bishop Fox*: Richard Foxe (*c.*1448–1528), Bishop of Winchester from 1501.

12. *statues of King James, and his son*. The statues, now against the west wall of the nave, are by Le Sueur

and come from Inigo Jones's rood screen.

13. *Bishop Mew*: Peter Mew (1619–1706), Bishop of Winchester from 1684.

14. *piece of an old monastry*. Hyde House, in Hyde Street, was given a curious brick front and Dutch gable around 1660–70.

15. *hospital*: the hospital of St. Cross, founded *c.*1136 by Cardinal Beaufort, see next note.

16. *Cardinal Beaufort*: Henry Beaufort (*c.*1377–1447), Chancellor of England under Henry IV. He was made a cardinal in 1426 and was sent as papal legate in a crusade against the Hussites.

17. *Salisbury whites*. 'Whites' were undressed and undyed fabrics.

18. *Earl of Pembroke*: Thomas Herbert, 8th Earl of Pembroke (*c.*1656–1733).

19. *chamber of rarieties at Munick*. The Elector of Bavaria, Maximilian I, built up an important collection of art-works, subsequently enlarged by the Elector Max Emmanuel, who in 1684 built a new *Schloss* to house it at Schleissheim, three miles north of Munich.

20. *gallery of Luxemburg*: the gallery of the Palais du Luxembourg in Paris, built in 1615–20 by Marie de Médicis.

21. *family peice of King Charles I*. The painting by Van Dyck (1633) is now in the Royal Collection.

22. *Mr. Jones*. See Inigo Jones's *The Most Notable Antiquity of Great Britain, Vulgarly Called Stonehenge*, published by Webb in 1655.

23. *Mr. Aubury*: John Aubrey (1626–97), who included much research on Stonehenge in his posthumously published *Natural History of Wiltshire*.

24. *barrows*. Neolithic and bronze-age barrows are found near Stonehenge.

25. *Godolphin*: Sydney, 1st Earl of Godolphin (1645–1717), Lord High Treasurer 1702–10. Defoe worked for him as a pamphleteer.

26. *inhabitants of the Palatinate*. In 1709 there was a mass exodus of German Protestants from the Rhineland to England. The emigrants, numbering some 13,000 or 14,000, came as a result of religious persecution and their sufferings at the hands of the French invaders, and also of encouragement from Eng-

lish trading companies, in search of settlers for the American colonies. For some months they lived in tents on the outskirts of London, being received there with much hostility. Defoe, in his *Review*, argued eloquently for giving them permanent asylum in Britain, and in the present Letter he goes on to describe in some detail the remarkable plan he submitted to Godolphin for a settlement for the Germans in the New Forest.

27. *— miles*: about nineteen miles.

28. *riffe*: reef. This is now known as Chesil Beach.

29. *half-pay officers*. The half-pay system for army officers originated in a temporary measure passed by Parliament early in 1698, granting officers half pay as a retaining fee, until arrears of pay could be met in full. During the ensuing running-down of the peacetime army the 'half-pay officer' became a regular feature.

30. *knitting-stocking engine*. See note 22 below, p. 386.

31. *jouring*. Possibly the same word as *jowing* (to *jower*), a West-country expression meaning grumbling.

32. *a relation's house*. We have not been able to identify this relation of Defoe.

33. *powdering-tub*: a tub in which meat was 'powdered', i.e., salted and pickled.

34. *salmon peal*: young salmon, or salmon of a smaller species.

35. *great dispute about the doctrine of the Trinity*. Disputes about Arianism among the Dissenting ministry in Exeter threatened to cause a schism in the Dissenting community, and a conference was convened in Salter's Hall in London to restore harmony.

36. *Mr. Winstanley*: Henry Winstanley (1644–1703).

37. *engineers*: designers and constructors of military engines or works.

38. *setting up the English packets*: this was a result of the Methuen Treaty of December 1703 for trade with Portugal.

39. *circle of great stones*: the Boscawen-un circle in the parish of Buryan, four and a half miles west of Penzance. It is elliptical in shape, comprising a ring of nineteen stones with a monolith in the middle.

40. *Sir Cloudesly Shovel*: (*c.*1650–1707),

the famous admiral, whose ship was lost with all hands off the Scilly isles on 27 October 1707 on its return from a raid on Toulon.

41. *diving engine*. Projects for rescuing treasure from sunken ships by diving-engines became a craze after a successful salvage-feat by Sir William Phipps in 1687. Defoe himself in 1692 took shares in a diving-engine company formed to rescue silver from ships wrecked off the Lizard. (He also became its treasurer.) His irony may thus be partly aimed at himself. (See F. Bastian, *Defoe's Early Life* (1981), pp. 168–9.)

42. *cherosonese*: more usually spelt 'chersonese'; meaning peninsula.

LETTER IV

1. *Agricola*. The governorship of Britain by Gnaius Julius Agricola in AD 77–84 saw the consolidation of the Roman conquest of the country.

2. *coinage towns*. The number of towns furnished with a royal mint varied considerably from reign to reign. Charles I set up several small provincial mints, and for the great re-coinage of William III short-lived ones were established in York, Bristol, Norwich, Chester and Exeter.

3. *The Hurlers*: a group of three stone circles, on the south-west of Cheesewring Hill, in the parishes of Linkinhorne and St. Cleer, five miles north of Liskeard. Camden says that there was a local legend that they were men changed into stones because they had profaned the Lord's Day by throwing a ball.

4. *hurlers*: i.e., hurling, a Cornish game akin to handball.

5. *whirlbats*. The name 'whirlbat' (corruption of 'Hurbat') was used to translate the Latin *caestus*, a sporting weapon with plummets of lead.

6. *Richard, Earl of Cornwall*: second son of King John, 1209–72, also entitled King of the Romans. He was given the earldom of Cornwall in 1225.

7. *Bartlet*. Three generations of Bartlets served as minister of the meeting-house at Bideford, beginning with William (d. 1682). It is uncertain which Defoe is referring to.

8. *Peter Blundel*: 1520–1601. Blundell's School, which still exists, was opened in 1604.

9. *sagathies*: says made with silk.

10. *not a child in the town*. Cf. the enthusiastic report of a clothier in Defoe's *A Plan of the English Commerce* (1728), p. 92: 'We have 1100 looms . . . in this town, and the villages about it, and not one of them want work; and there is not a poor child in the town of above four years old, but can earn his own bread.'

11. *Potwalloners*: more usually known as 'potwallers' or 'potwallopers'. The franchise survived until the Reform Act of 1832.

12. *Jeffries*: George Jeffreys, 1st Baron Jeffreys (1644–89), the judge notorious for his brutality at the 'Bloody Assizes' following Monmouth's rebellion.

13. *Warren*: Matthew Warren (1642/3–1706). He was an ejected minister who later had charge of the St. Paul's meeting in Taunton.

14. *Admiral Blake*. Robert Blake (1599–1657), admiral of the Commonwealth navy and victor over Van Tromp and De Witt in the First Dutch War.

15. *the Toleration*. By the Toleration Act of 1689, Protestant nonconformists who subcribed to the doctrine of the Trinity were allowed to have their own meeting-house and ministers.

16. *Spanish medley cloths*. The clothiers of this area 'dyed their wools in various colours, rolled, teased, carded and scribbled them into delicate blends' (Kerridge).

17. *deep, frightful chasm*: the Cheddar gorge.

18. *broad-cloth*: cloth made on the horizontal broad loom, an invention dating back to the thirteenth century in Flanders and adopted in England in the following century.

19. *fulling*: the cleansing and thickening of cloth by beating and washing.

20. *dyed in grain*: dyed in the fibre, with a fast colour.

21. *carpet ground*. Defoe seems to use the term to mean smooth-turfed ground. Cf. Pope, *Epistle IV*, 95: 'One boundless green, or flourish'd carpet views.'

22. *late severe Acts*. An Act of 1689 restricted the sale of wool within fifteen miles of the coast in

Kent and Sussex.

23. *fell-wooll*: an inferior wool taken from the undersides of sheep.

24. *Jack of Newbery*: John Winchcombe (d. 1520), a wealthy clothier of the reign of Henry VII, said to have had a hundred looms in his own house in Newbury. He was a hero of Deloney's novel *Jack of Newbury*. Defoe is in error in associating him with the reign of King James.

25. *Mr. Kenrick*. Details of the many benefactions of 'Mr. John Kendrick, Draper, who departed December 3d, 1674' are given in Stow's *Survey of London*, ed. J. Strype (1720), Book 1, p. 276.

26. *Sir Owen Buckingham*: (d. 1713). He was a salter and was Lord Mayor of London 1704–5.

27. *Sir John Lanier*: (d. 1692), army commander who served under the Duke of Monmouth and James II. He declared for William III and led his regiment at the Battle of the Boyne.

28. *lapis caliminaris*. From early times brass was made by a cementation process with calamine (*lapis calaminaris*) and charcoal.

29. *fellies*: felloes, i.e., wheel-rims.

30. *billet wood*: sawn logs, for fires.

31. *flat, or half pace*. A half-pace or *haut-pas* is a high step.

32. *painted upon the wall*. Sir Godfrey Kneller did a semi-illusionist wall-painting in St. George's Hall *c*.1695–1700, completing the decoration of the room initiated by Charles II. There were five steps of real marble going up to the painting continued by five more fictitious ones in the painting itself. A fragment of the painting still survives; see plate 99, p. 129.

LETTER V

1. *Tot-Hill Fields*: site of the present Tothill Street, in Westminster.

2. *Peterburgh House*: an ancient house in Millbank built by the Earls of Peterborough and bought from them by the Grosvenor family in the early eighteenth century, being known thereafter as Grosvenor House. It was, because of its situation, sometimes referred to as 'the last house in London'.

3. *Montague House*. See note 17 below.

4. *fine new church*: St. Paul's, in Deptford High Street, designed by

Thomas Archer, built 1712–30.

5. *the Burrough*: i.e., the Borough.

6. *St. George's Fields*: an extensive open space between Southwark and Lambeth. It was used as a training ground for soldiers and for large gatherings, e.g., on visits from foreign potentates. It was a favourite Sunday resort for Londoners.

7. *privileges*. The Court of the Marshalsea, originally held before the Steward and the Marshal of the royal household, was empowered to administer justice between the sovereign's domestic servants within the verge (i.e., within twelve miles) of the royal residence. For the Mint, see note 48 above, p. 380.

8. *Stow*: John Stow's *A Survey of London* (1598 and 1603). There were continuations of this important work by Anthony Munday in 1618 and Strype in 1720.

9. *by treachery*. It was rumoured that the fire of London had been deliberately started by Roman Catholics. The inscription on the Monument making this accusation was erased under James II, re-cut under William III and erased again under William IV in 1831.

10. *the Savoy*: originally a palace built for the Earl of Savoy in 1245, then a royal hospital, and by Defoe's time a warren of lodgings with right of sanctuary for debtors.

11. *Hatton-House*. This was the gatehouse of Ely House in Holborn, named after Elizabeth's favourite Sir Christopher Hatton, who acquired it in 1581. It was pulled down during the Civil War.

12. *New Convent Garden*: i.e., Covent Garden. The area takes its name from being a produce garden for Westminster Abbey in the middle ages. In the seventeenth century it became the first great square laid out in London, to the design of Inigo Jones. The scheme was promoted in 1630 by the Duke of Bedford.

13. *Lord Brook's house*. Brooke Street in London EC1 is the site of the house of Sir Fulke Greville, Lord Brooke, adviser to Queen Elizabeth and James I and patron of Ben Jonson. It was demolished about 1680.

14. *Goodman's Fields*. Stow notes that there was a farm attached to the nunnery of Saint Clare ('The Minories'), which was cultivated by Rowland Goodman and at which Stow himself used to buy milk. The land was let out by Goodman's son as garden plots.

15. *D— of Powis's House*. William Herbert (d. 1745), 2nd Marquis and titular Duke of Powis built Powis House in Great Ormond Street and was living there in 1708. The building became the French embassy. It was burned down in 1713 and rebuilt at the expense of the French government. It was demolished near the end of the eighteenth century.

16. *St. George's Chapel*: in Queen Square. It was founded in 1706 as a chapel-of-ease for St. Andrew's, Holborn and was consecrated in 1723.

17. *Montague House*. This was built by the 1st Duke of Montagu (1638?–1709), ambassador to France, as his London house. The original building, by Robert Hook, was erected 1674–80 and rebuilt after a fire. It was purchased to house the British Museum in the 1750s.

18. *the Monument*. It was designed by Wren. According to Macky its form is meant to represent a candle.

19. *Royal Exchange*. Gresham's Exchange, begun 1566, was burnt in the Great Fire, and a new Royal Exchange, designed by Edward Jarman, was opened in 1669 (being itself burnt in 1838).

20. *Bedlam*. Bedlam, or Bethlem Hospital, was moved to Moorfields in 1676.

21. *Custom-House*. It was rebuilt by Thomas Ripley between 1718 and the early 1720s.

22. *new church in the Strand*: St. Mary-le-Strand, designed by James Gibbs, built 1714–17.

23. *excellent lines*. Lines 17–19 of Dryden's 'To My Dear Friend, Mr. Congreve, on his Comedy called the Double-Dealer', more correctly as follows:

Firm Dorique pillars found your
    solid Base,
The fair Corinthian crowns the
    higher Space;
Thus all below is Strength, and all
    above is Grace.

24. *shutting up the Exchequer*. On 2 January 1662 Charles II placed a stop on the Exchequer, freezing the assets of the goldsmith-bankers of Lombard Street.

25. *bringing a quo warranto*. In 1683, as part of a campaign against the Whiggish tendency of city corporations, Charles II forced the surrender of the City of London's charter by a writ of *quo warranto*. It was not restored till the last year of James II's reign.

26. *the Bank*. It was founded in 1684 by William Paterson, to help finance William III's wars.

27. *the additional penny upon the letters*: i.e., from the Penny Post set up in 1683 for letters and packets within the City of London. See notes 29 and 30 below.

28. *Sir Robert Viner*. See note 39 below.

29. *William Dockraw*. William Dockwray or Dockwra (d. 1702?), a London merchant, set up a penny postal system in the City in 1683. There were six large offices, and a receiving house in every principal street.

30. *General Post-Office*. Originally known as the General Letter Office, it was moved from the Black Swan in Bishopsgate to Lombard Street about 1678.

31. *Exchange Alley*: where financial dealings took place.

32. *higglary goods*: goods sold by hucksters; see note 32 above, p. 380.

33. *communibus annis*: taking one year with another.

34. *meeters*: measurers.

35. *gabel*: i.e., *gabelle*. There was a famous salt-tax of this name in France.

36. *bilanders and schoots*. A bilander was a kind of hoy with a trapezoidal mainsail. A schuit was a Dutch flat-bottomed river boat.

37. *kennel*: gutter.

38. *New River*. It was constructed 1609–13.

39. *equestrian statue of King Charles II*. Sir Robert Viner (1631–88), Lord Mayor of London in 1674 and Charles II's friend and principal banker, decided to set up a monument to Charles in Stocks Market, on the site of the present Mansion House. For this purpose he acquired an equestrian statue of John Sobieski, King of Poland, trampling a Turk underfoot, the two figures being made to do duty for Charles and Oliver Cromwell. The effect was somewhat spoiled by the Turk's turban.

40. *D—ss of Portsmouth*: King Charles II's mistress Louise de Kéroualle (1649–1734) who became Duchess of Portsmouth in 1673.

41. *pillion*: saddle.

42. *City train'd bands*. 'Train-bands' (or 'trained bands') was a name given to the militia in the sixteenth century. By an Act of 1662 the system of train-bands was discontinued in the counties, but the City train-bands survived until 1794.

43. *Temple-Bar*. The Temple Bar, designed by Wren, was removed to Waltham Cross in 1878 and replaced by a monument.

44. *Whitehall*. Wolsey's palace of Yorke Place fell into the hands of Henry VIII who made it, as Whitehall, his main London palace. It was destroyed by fire in 1698.

45. *King's old palace*. Westminster Palace was the main residence of the Norman kings and of subsequent monarchs till the time of the Henry VIII, who removed his court to Whitehall.

46. *Westminster-Hall*. It housed many important government offices and courts of law. Macky describes it thus: 'On your left as you enter this Hall, a large pair of stairs leads you to the office of the Exchequer . . . and on the right, another pair of stairs from the Hall leads you to the Court where the barons of the Exchequer sit on all causes relating to the revenue. As likewise to Equity, as in Chancery. Near the middle of the Hall, on the right as you enter, sits a Court called the Court of Common-Pleas . . . at the upper and of the Hall are kept the Court of Chancery on the right, and the King's Bench on the left.'

47. *Stephen Lobb*: nonconformist divine (d. 1699). He was a leading Independent and controversialist but accused of Jacobitism because of his eagerness to treat with James II at the time of the latter's proposals for a toleration.

48. *Locket's*. Probably Locket's coffee-house in Spring Garden, Charing Cross. It is mentioned in Congreve's *Love for Love* (1695).

49. *Man's coffee-house*: a famous establishment near Charing Cross, founded by Alexander Man in 1666.

50. *equestrian statue of King Charles*. See note 39 above.

51. *Northumberland-House*: in the Strand, built in the early seventeenth century for the Earl of Northampton. It passed by marriage into the Percy family, when it became known as Northumberland House. It was demolished in 1874 to make way for Northumberland Avenue.

52. *new theatre*. Rogers identifies this as Vanbrugh's Opera House, built in 1704.

53. *Blue-coat Hospital*. Christ's Hospital, founded in 1552, was originally a hospital for foundlings but quickly became a school. It is named the Blue Coat School after the boys' dress of long blue coat, yellow stockings, white bands, leather girdle and buckled shoes.

54. *Dr. Ridley*: Nicholas Ridley (c.1500–55), Protestant martyr. He became Bishop of London in 1550. Condemned for heresy, he was burned at Oxford in 1555.

55. *Mr. Thomas Guy*: (c.1645–1724), wealthy bookseller and shrewd investor, who actually managed to increase his fortune during the disaster of the South Sea Bubble.

56. *Charter House*. The building of the old Carthusian monastery was bought in 1611 by Thomas Sutton, a rich military man, who left an endowment of £200,000 for a hospital for 'decayed gentlemen' and a Free School.

57. *St. Martin's in the Fields*: designed by James Gibbs, built 1722–6.

58. *fifty churches*. An act was passed in 1711 for the building of fifty new churches, to be financed from a tax on coal.

59. *Figg's Theatre*. A famous boxing-booth, off the Tyburn Road, opened by James Figg about 1721.

60. *Sir William Petty*: (1623–87), the famous statistician and political economist.

Letter VI

1. *Sir William Ashurst*. He became Lord Mayor of London in 1694 and died in 1720.

2. *waters*. Hampstead became much frequented in the early eighteenth century for its medicinal springs.

3. *Bellsize*. The 'projector', named Howell, took Belsize House in 1720 and fitted it out as a gambling resort. It soon became fashionable, and the Prince and Princess of Wales came there in the summer of 1721. In May 1722 the Middlesex justices ordered the High Constable of Holborn to clamp down on it.

4. *Duke of Chandos*. The Duke of Chandos (1673–1744) had, as James Brydges, been Paymaster-General during the War of the Spanish Succession and made a fortune in the process. He appointed Handel his music-master and modelled the music in the chapel at Cannons on that of the Chapel Royal. Cannons was demolished in 1744–48.

5. *Pargotti . . . Paolucci*. According to Rogers these names are Defoe's errors for Artari and Bellucci, Italian stuccadors employed by the Duke of Chandos. They also worked, singly or as a pair, on several other great houses and on St. Martin's in the Fields.

6. *New-Hall*. New Hall was the seat of the Radcliffes, Earls of Sussex, having previously belonged to Sir Thomas Boleyn and to Henry VIII.

7. *hospital*. The Royal Hospital in Chelsea, designed by Wren, was built in imitation of Louis XIV's Hôtel des Invalides, as a refuge for invalided soldiers and veterans. Building began in 1622, and the first inmates took up residence in 1689.

8. *Sir Stephen Fox*. Fox (1627–1716) assisted Charles II over his private finances, during his exile and after, and in 1661 he was appointed Paymaster-General, an exceedingly lucrative office. He bought his estate in Chiswick in 1685.

9. *Mr. Guy*. Henry Guy (1631–1710). He was Secretary to the Treasury 1679–88 and 1691–5. He built a mansion at Great Tring, to designs by Wren.

10. *affair of Magdalen College*. In 1687 James II took it upon himself to have the newly elected President of Magdalen College, Oxford, removed and replaced by his own Roman Catholic candidate; and in anger at the resistance of the Fellows, he had almost the whole of the governing body expelled, turning the college into a Catholic seminary.

11. *Archbishop Sheldon*. Gilbert Sheldon

(1598–1677) became Archbishop of Canterbury in 1663.

12. *Mr. Speed.* See the *Historie of Great Britaine* (1611) by John Speed, the historian and cartographer.

13. *Sir Thomas Bodley*: (1545–1613). He was England's representative at the Hague 1588–96 before founding the Bodleian Library, which opened in 1602.

14. *Dr. Radcliff.* John Radcliffe (1650–1714) made a fortune as physician to royalty and from the sale of patent medicines. The Radcliffe Camera, the reading-room of the Bodleian described by Defoe as in progress, was opened in 1749.

15. *fate of the fair Rosamond.* According to legend, King Henry built her a house in the shape of a labyrinth, so that no one could come near her, but Queen Eleanor traced her by a clue of thread and murdered her.

16. *Blenheim.* In 1705 it was enacted that the Duke of Marlborough, victorious at Blenheim, should be rewarded with the royal manor of Woodstock and a palace to be built there at the nation's expense. Vanbrugh was the chief designer, in close collaboration with Hawksmoor. Work stopped in 1712, when the Duke was dismissed by the Tories, but was resumed in 1715 at Marlborough's own expense.

17. *Croprady Bridge.* The battle took place on 6 June 1644.

18. *Edge-Hill.* The battle took place on 23 October 1642.

19. *Roll-Richt-Stones.* The stone circle stands between the villages of Great and Little Roll-Right. It consists of a King Stone, a circle of about 70 stones known as the King's Men, and a few others called the Whispering Knights.

20. *a Mop*: annual hiring- or statute-fair, at which domestic and agricultural servants would offer themselves for employment, carrying a broom, mop, etc., to indicate their line of work.

21. *ways and manners of servants.* Defoe published some 'Familiar Letters' on 'The Insolence and Unsufferable Behaviour of Servants' under the title *The Great Law of Subordination Consider'd* (1724).

22. *Gulielmus Malmsburiensis.* William of Malmesbury (*c*.1095–1143), the first major writer of history in

England after Bede, produced a history of England from 449 to 1120 and an ecclesiastical history of England from 597 to 1125.

23. *King Bladud*: legendary British king, supposed to have reigned about 900 BC; said to have been the father of King Lear.

24. *I have myself drank the waters of the Bath.* Defoe may mean that he drank bottled Bath water in London.

25. *Badminton.* The oldest part of this grand mansion was built by Henry Somerset, Marquis of Worcester who became 1st Duke of Beaufort in 1682. It was enlarged for the 3rd Duke by William Kent.

26. *Berkley-Castle.* Berkeley Castle was built in 1153 and is the oldest inhabited castle in England.

27. *last battle.* The battle took place on 4 May 1471.

28. *Stroud-Water.* According to John Aubrey it was running through deposits of iron that made the Stroudwater so good for dyeing red with.

29. *Monmouth cups.* Bewley was an important centre for pewterers at this period, so Monmouth cups may have been pewter drinking vessels.

30. *lindsey woolseys.* A species of linen-union cloth with linen warp and woollen weft, akin to tartan.

31. *a tour into Wales.* F. Bastian's verdict in 'Defoe's *Tour* and the Historian', *History Today*, 17 (1967), pp. 845–51, is that 'Defoe's account of Wales is almost entirely secondhand, except for Wrexham (which he is known to have visited in 1705) and for Conway and a number of ports in the south-west.'

32. *castle of Ludlow.* A pre-Conquest Norman castle, founded *c*.1050 by Richard le Scrob, one of the nobles brought over from France by Edward the Confessor.

33. *Brampton-Brian*: seat of the Harley family since 1309, when Sir Robert de Harley married Margaret Brampton. It was he who built the great gatehouse. Defoe's employer, Sir Robert Harley, spent his youth here.

34. *Wigmore-Castle.* The ruined castle dates back to the twelfth century. It was the centre of the Mortimer family's power.

35. *Jeoffrey of Monmouth.* Geoffrey of

Monmouth (d. 1155) produced a famous *Historia Regum Britanniae*, purportedly drawing on an 'ancient book in the British tongue' and contributing much to the popularity of the Arthurian legends.

36. *called —.* The 'hill' must form part of the Bernese Alps.

37. *Glendower*: Owen Glendower (1359–1415), last champion of Welsh independence against the English kings.

38. *Vortigern*: legendary fifth-century king of Britain who was said to have enlisted Hengist and Horsa against his former allies the Picts, thus bringing about the Anglo-Saxon conquest. The story is related by Geoffrey of Monmouth.

39. *Roger of Mortimer.* Roger de Mortimer, 1st Earl of March (1287?–1330) was one of the greatest landowners in Britain, with territories in the Welsh border country and Ireland. As lover of Edward II's queen Isabel he became for a time the effective ruler of England, till seized by supporters of the young Edward III and executed.

40. *Pelagian heresy.* Pelagius, the latinized form of the name of a British monk Morghan of the 4th and 5th century, denied the doctrine of original sin and held that the human will was capable of good without the assistance of grace.

41. *Lord Mansel*: Thomas Mansell of Margan (1668–1723), created Baron of Margan in 1711 or 1712.

42. *famous monument.* See Camden: 'on the top of a hill called Mynydd Margan is a pillar of exceeding hard stone, erected for a sepulchral monument ... with an inscription, which whoever happens to read, the ignorant common-people of that neighbourhood affirm that he shall die soon after'.

43. *Kily-Maen Ibwyd.* See Camden: 'But Buarth Arthur, or Meinee Gwyr, on a mountain near Kil y maen lhwyd, is one of that kind of circular stone monuments which our English historians ascribe to the Danes'.

44. *beavers.* F. Bastian ('Defoe's *Tour* and the Historian', p. 847), refers to the 'calm effrontery' with which Defoe, who 'cribs' his account of Cardiganshire entirely from Camden, invents this incident of country people speaking

to him about beavers on the Tivy.

45. *Enterkin*: a long, V-shaped defile leading to Leadhills (in Dumfriesshire). See also p. 324.

46. *Holly-well*. St. Winifred, the patron saint of North Wales, was supposedly the daughter of a Welsh chieftain and instructed by St. Beuno. When Prince Caradoc attempted to rape her, she fled to the church, but he pursued here there and cut off her head, whereupon it was replaced on her body by St. Beuno. She died for the second time about the year 600. According to Macky, her Chapel eventually became a Protestant school, though Catholics erected pilgrim chapels in all the nearby inns.

LETTER VII

1. *fire and vinegar*. Hannibal, during his crossing of the Alps, is said to have split boulders by lighting fires under them and then pouring sour wine over the hot rocks.

2. *prisoners taken at Preston*. During the Jacobite rising of 1715 an Anglo-Scottish force led by Thomas Forster and the Lords Derwenwater and Widdrington was compelled to capitulate at Preston (13 November), some 1,600 prisoners being taken.

3. *formerly at this city*. Frank Bastian speculates that Defoe visited Chester in 1690 on his return from a trading voyage to Belfast. (See *Defoe's Early Life*, p. 151.)

4. *County Palatine*: 'a county of which the earl or lord had originally royal privileges with exclusive civil and criminal jurisdiction' (*OED*).

5. *Talbot, first Earl of Shrewsbury*: John Talbot (*c.*1388–1453), a daring warrior who played a large part in subduing the Irish and in the French wars.

6. *Pelagius*. See note 40 above, p. 385.

7. *Lord Chancellor Jefferies*. See note 12 above, p. 382. He was appointed Chancellor in 1685.

8. *the great Lewellin*. He was Prince of North Wales and married an illegitimate daughter of King John. During the reign of Henry III he was frequently attacked by the English, and he was finally forced

to acknowledge Henry's suzerainty in 1237.

9. *White Ladies*. Whiteladies, and the nearby Boscobel House, gave Charles II refuge in 1651 after the battle of Worcester. The house of Whiteladies is built near the ruins of a twelfth-century nunnery.

10. *Ingestre*. The south front of Ingestre Hall, built by Sir Walter Chetwynd (d. 1638) is, according to Pevsner, 'the foremost display of Jacobean grandeur in the county'.

11. *little lake*. Lichfield has in fact two large mill pools, dating back to the early middle ages: Minster Pool, to the south of the cathedral, and Stowe Pool to the east of it. Defoe would no doubt have traversed Lichfield by the north–south road and to the west of the Cathedral, so would have seen only the Minster Pool. The causeways were later replaced by a bridge in Bird Street.

12. *when I first came to this city*. This was perhaps on the occasion of the general election that followed the unexpected dissolution of Parliament on 6 February 1690. Coventry was noted for unruly behaviour at election time.

13. *tammies*. 'A stammet or tammy yarn was one that had been shrunk and smoothed by scouring, and a tammy was a cloth woven thereof' (Kerridge).

14. *Guy Earl of Warwick*: a famous English hero of romance, whose exploits were chronicled by an Anglo-Norman poet in the twelfth century.

15. *terrible fire*. This happened in 1694.

16. *Mr. Dugdale*: Sir William Dugdale (1605–86), antiquary, author of *The Antiquities of Warwickshire* (1656) and of *Monasticon Anglicanum* (1655–73).

17. *burnt down*. This was in 1675.

18. *Holmby*. Holdenby or Homby House was Elizabethan and was where the Scots 'sold' Charles I to the Parliamentary Commissioners in 1647.

19. *Althorp*. The house was begun in the early sixteenth century by John Spencer and enlarged in 1573. The great staircase was begun in 1666. John Evelyn, in 1688, referred to the place as a 'palace'.

20. *Boughton*. The estate, with substantial remains of a sixteenth-century house, was inherited in

1663 by the 1st Duke of Montagu, who added the great north facade.

21. *stades*. 'Stade' is the anglicized form of 'stadium', meaning a measure, or a stage in a process.

22. *weaving of stockings by frames*. The iron knitting-machine or stocking-frame, a remarkable piece of pre-industrial revolution technology, was invented in 1589 by William Lee, curate of Calverton near Nottingham. It was not completely automatic and depended on a human operator both for power and for the co-ordination of its parts. Colbert introduced it into France, and it was still widely used on a commercial basis in England and France in the eighteenth century.

23. *famous castle*. Newark castle was built by Alexander, Bishop of Lincoln, about 1133. It stood on a cliff above the river, commanding the crossing from northern England.

24. *the Adventurers*. Thirteen 'Adventurers' joined with the 4th Duke of Bedford in the early 1630s in a project to drain the Fens. They employed a Dutchman, Cornelius Vermuyden, as chief engineer.

25. *hemp*: for sails and cordage.

26. *Gilbertine nuns*: a medieval religious order, founded in England by Gilbert of Sempringham. The Gilbertines controlled some twenty-five houses, of monks and nuns, when they were dissolved by Henry VIII.

27. *Varrio*: i.e., Antonio Verrio (1639–1707), the famous Italian ceiling-painter.

28. *Stilton*. Frank Bastian notes that Defoe was the first writer to mention Stilton cheese ('Defoe's *Tour* and the Historian', p. 850).

29. *famous drum*. This well was reputed to give out a drumming sound on the eve of great events. Baxter in his *World of Spirits*, tells of hearing it, as a schoolboy at Oundle, when the Scots were about invade. (See J. Brand, *Faiths and Folklore*, ed. W.C. Hazlitt (1905).)

30. *a terrible fire*. It took place in June 1724.

31. *Wooburn Abbey*. Woburn Abbey is built on the site of a Cistercian abbey, dissolved at the Reformation. In the early seventeenth century the 4th Duke of Bedford, the creator of the park and estate, com-

missioned further building from Henry Flitcroft.

32. *Bruces Earls of Ailesbury*. Houghton House, near Ampthill, built originally for Mary, Countess of Pembroke, was bought at her death in 1630 by Thomas Bruce, 1st Earl of Elgin, whose son became the 1st Earl of Ailesbury.

LETTER VIII

1. *the castle*. The castle was frequently damaged and rebuilt over the years. It was bought from Charles II by William Cavendish, 1st Duke of Newcastle, who erected a palace on the site, completed in 1679.

2. *Count Tallard*. Camille, Comte de Tallard (1652–1728), French ambassador to England and later Marshal of France, was captured in 1704 by Marlborough's troops and kept prisoner for some years, under very relaxed conditions, near Nottingham.

3. *increase of tea-drinking*. Despite heavy taxes, the price of tea dropped to twenty shillings a pound by 1689. It did not really become a cheap and popular drink, however, until a decade or two after Defoe's death.

4. *Woollaton Hall*: built 1580–8 by Robert Smythson for Sir Francis Willoughby, a great colliery magnate.

5. *Peace of Ryswick*: the treaty, signed in 1697, that brought to an end 'King William's War'.

6. *Prado at Mexico*: the central square in Mexico City.

7. *Paulinus*. Paulinus (d. *c*.644), Bishop or Archbishop of York, was a Roman sent by Pope Gregory the Great to join Augustine in England.

8. *Welbeck*. Originally a twelfth-century Premonstratensian abbey, it was bought by Sir Charles Cavendish, son of Bess of Hardwick, in 1607, and he had it rebuilt on a vast scale by the architect Robert Smythson.

9. *throwster's mill*. Silk-throwing machinery was introduced at Derby, and patented by John and Thomas Lombe, some fifty years before Arkwright's first cotton-mill.

10. *Soracole*: George Sorocold, an engineer and associate of the Lombe brothers in the development of silk-throwing machinery.

11. *Cotton's Wonders of the Peak*. P.N. Hartle, in an article 'Defoe and *The Wonders of the Peake*: the place of Cotton's poem in *A Tour Thro' the Whole Island of Great Britain*,', *English Studies*, 67 (1986), pp. 420–31, points out that, although Defoe draws heavily on Charles Cotton's poem *Wonders of the Peake* (1681), which is a mixture of picturesque description and burlesque, he is unjust in representing Cotton as merely gullible, reserving the credit for amused scepticism for himself.

12. *Barmoot court*. The Great Barmote Court and Small Barmote Court still exist to administer the mineral laws and customs relating to lead-mining in the Peak district.

13. *Mr. Hobbes*. Thomas Hobbes published a Latin poem *De Mirabilibus Pecci* ('The Wonders of the Peak') in 1636. It was frequently reprinted after the Restoration.

14. *common-shore*: common sewer.

15. *ab inferis*: from the infernal regions.

16. *Duke of Devonshire*. The Devonshires had from the late sixteenth century been lords of the manor of Buxton. At the time that Defoe was writing the reigning duke was William Cavendish, 3rd Duke.

17. *Mr. Burnet's theory*. See Book I, chapter 6 of Thomas Burnet's *Sacred Theory of the Earth*: '. . . Moses saith, the great Abysse was broken open at the Deluge. Let us suppose, that at a time appointed by Divine Providence, and from Causes made ready to do that great execution upon a sinful World, that this Abysse was open'd, and that the frame of the Earth broke and fell down into the Great Abysse.'

18. *Dr. Leigh*: Charles Leigh (1662–1701), physician and naturalist who published *The Natural History of Lancashire, Cheshire and the Peak in Derbyshire* (Oxford, 1700).

19. *deceptio visus*: optical illusion.

20. *Chatsworth*. The building of Chatsworth, to designs by Talman, took place between 1687 and 1710.

21. *Cavendo tutus*: i.e., 'by being cautious one is safe,' with a pun on 'Cavendish'.

22. *Whittl-making*. 'Whittle' was the name for various sorts of large knife.

23. *Geoffry Chaucer*. The relevant line from Chaucer's 'Reeve's Tale',

garbled in Defoe's doggerel version, is given in F.N. Robinson's edition of Chaucer as: 'A Sheffeld thwitel baar he in his hose.'

24. *Hallamshire*: an ancient lordship in the West Riding, South Yorkshire. It includes Sheffield.

25. *Tankersly*. The Earl of Strafford's house was built about 1630. (By 1723 building had in fact begun on the Marquess of Rockingham's great mansion of Wentworth Woodhouse, on the same site.)

26. *Yorkshire kersies*. Kersey cloth was manufactured in England from the thirteenth century onwards. Kersey yarns were spun in large gauges from inferior grades of carded wool and were used to make 'warp-backed cloths woven in twill order on kersey looms' (Kerridge). It was a humble type of cloth, and north-country kersies had the reputation of being smelly.

27. *cross-post*. Rogers explains: 'This was a postal route running from one major route to another; as opposed to bye-posts, which followed major roads which did not run to or from London.'

28. *half-thicks*. Kerridge notes that by 1606 a lighter and thinner kersey had been introduced, known as 'washer', 'wash-white', 'half-thick' and 'quarter-thick'.

29. *Blackstone Edge*. Rogers notes the affinity of this vivid passage with the description of a journey over Blackstone Edge in *Memoirs of a Cavalier* (1720). (See 'The Making of Defoe's *A Tour thro' Great Britain*, Volumes II and III', p. 128.)

30. *tenter*. 'A wooden framework on which cloth is stretched after being milled, so that it may set or dry evenly and without shrinking' (*OED*).

31. *Seven Dials*. Seven Streets, meeting in a star-shaped pattern around a Doric pillar. It was a speculative development begun in 1693 by Thomas Neale, Master of the Mint, and though intended as a fashionable district, to rival Covent Garden, it soon degenerated into a notorious 'rookery'.

32. *scouring-shops*. Woven cloth was cleansed and scoured, before fulling, with soap, potash or fuller's clay.

33. *Popish army*. Charles Neville, 6th Earl of Westmoreland, was one of the leaders of the rebellion of

the northern earls, in November 1569–February 1570, which was intended to re-establish the Catholic religion and to secure the succession of Mary Queen of Scots.

34. *Frith Borges.* Defoe seems to be referring to the Frithbogh, otherwise known as frankpledge, an association of ten people into which, about the time of the Conquest, all men were bound, as sureties for one another's good behaviour. His etymology seems to be erroneous: the Anglo-Saxon terms *friborh* and *frithborh* meant, literally, pledge or surety for peace.

35. *from Hell, Hull and Hallifax.* John Taylor, known as 'the Water-Poet' (1580–1653), quotes this as a beggars' or vagabonds' prayer. Hull was to be avoided because beggars there were made to work for their keep.

36. *engine*: Celia Fiennes writes of the 'Engine' at Halifax ('to behead their criminalls at one stroake with a pully') as having been destroyed, 'since theire Charter or Liberty was lost or taken from them'. This occurred about 1650. The Halifax 'engine' was the model for the Scottish 'Maiden', from which in turn Dr. Guillotin borrowed the idea of the guillotine. (See *Journeys of Celia Fiennes*, ed. C. Morris (1949), p. 221 and fn.)

37. *handsell'd*: i.e., been used for the first time.

38. *Some years ago*: in 1699.

39. *stately beautiful seat.* 'Northward from Knaresborough is a most noble hall built by Sir Edward Blacket, with delicate gardens, adorned with statues' (Camden).

40. *barbs*: Barbary horses.

41. *jennets*: a type of small Spanish horse.

42. *Fleeter*: i.e. (presumably) a shady individual such as would be likely to be found in the Fleet prison and its 'liberties'.

43. *the late war*: the War of the Spanish Succession, 1702–1713.

LETTER IX

1. *Dr. Oglethorp*: (d. 1559). He was appointed Bishop of Carlisle by Mary Tudor in 1557. At the accession of Queen Elizabeth, the see of Canterbury was vacant, and the Archbishop of York, for religious reasons, refused to crown her;

thus, despite his Roman Catholic allegiances, Oglethorpe agreed to officiate, a decision which troubled his conscience afterwards.

2. *the old Bale.* The fortifications on the Old Baile probably go back to Roman times.

3. *Ut rosa, etc*: 'As the rose is the flower of all flowers, so is this house the flower of all houses.'

4. *half-pay men.* See note 29 above, p. 381.

5. *entertain King Charles I.* In the spring of 1642 Charles, in the face of determined opposition in the capital, set up his court in York and began to assemble an armed force around him.

6. *Castle Howard.* Castle Howard, the architect Vanbrugh's masterpiece, was designed between 1699 and 1726 for the 3rd Earl of Carlisle.

7. *Earl of Burlington's.* Londesborough Hall, near Hull, was the ancient seat of the earls of Burlington, and the architect Earl (Richard Boyle, 3rd Earl) spent much time there and is buried in the chapel. The house was pulled down in 1819.

8. *John a Beverley.* St John of Beverley (d. 721) was for thirty-three years Archbishop of York and was tutor to the Venerable Bede. He founded a college for secular priests at Beverley.

9. *freed stool*: a seat, otherwise known as a frith-stool, placed near the altar in a church, affording sanctuary.

10. *our author.* In an article 'A case of plagiarism in Defoe's *Tour*' in *Notes & Queries*, n.s. 6 (1959), p. 399, J.H. Andrews points out that in his account of Beverley Defoe lifted about a thousand words almost verbatim from Edmund Gibson's description of the East Riding published in the 1695 edition of Camden's *Britannia*, inserting it rather awkwardly within his own narrative and inadvertently carrying over Gibson's reference to 'our Author', meaning Camden. We have made heavy cuts in the present edition.

11. *bone-lace.* Lace made by knitting upon a pattern with bobbins, originally made from bone. The art of bone-lace making was introduced by Flemish immigrants in the sixteenth century.

12. *Leland*: John Leland (1506?–52), an early authority on British antiquities, whose *Itinerary* in nine volumes was first published in 1710.

13. *northern fisherman.* The Eskimo figure in his kayak is still to be seen at Hull Trinity House; it dates from a venturing voyage in 1613 by Andrew Barker.

14. *Trinity House.* It was one of the five maritime societies, set up in the sixteenth century, to manage the interests of seamen, of which Trinity House in London, now the principal pilotage authority of the U.K., is the best known.

15. *Hell Kettles.* Cf. Camden: 'In a field belonging to this place there are three wells of great depth, commonly called Hell-kettles, or the kettles of hell; because the water by an anti-peristasis (or reverberation of the cold air) is heated in them. The more thinking sort reckon them to have been sunk by an earthquake.'

16. *Zouch.* William de la Zouche or Zouch (d. 1352) became Archbishop of York in 1342; in 1346 Edward III appointed him Warden of the Scottish Marches, and he took a prominent part in repelling Scottish invasions.

17. *Lumley Castle.* Sir Ralph Lumley began building the castle in 1389. Alterations were made in 1570–80, and at about the time that Defoe was writing the Earl of Scarborough was employing Vanbrugh to undertake a large-scale remodelling.

18. *keel men.* Defoe writes to Harley 14 February 1711/12 offering to submit an 'abstract' of the Newcastle keelmen's grievances. The House of Lords upheld the keelmen on 29 March. (See *Letters of Daniel Defoe*, ed. G. Healey (1955), p. 369.)

19. *Chevy Chace.* The name refers to the vow of Percy, Earl of Northumberland, to hunt for three days across the Scottish border (i.e., across the Cheviots) in defiance of the Earl Douglas.

20. *Flodden Field.* The battle took place on 9 September 1513.

LETTER X

1. *truss you up*: gather you up in a bundle.

2. *encreases*: the population of Liver-

pool increased from 4,000 to about 10,000 between 1680 and 1760.

3. *Tolsey*: otherwise toll-booth.

4. *Huk-a-back*. Kerridge observes that 'by the 1720s Warrington had a market in huckaback napkins and tablecloths whose familiar hucklebacked squares were formed by criss-crossing warp and weft floats.'

5. *mosses*. 'Moss' was a current name for a bog, swamp or morass and is so still in Scotland and Ireland.

6. *bearbind*: bearbine or bearbind is the lesser convolvulus.

7. —. Salford. The population figure given by Defoe for Manchester and Salford is now regarded as somewhat inflated.

8. *Charlotte, Countess of Derby*. She married the 16th Earl of Derby and died in 1664. The siege of Latham House was raised on 27 May 1644.

9. *dutchy*: (duchy), a territory once ruled by a duke or duchess.

10. *late bloody action*. See note 2 above, p. 386.

11. *famous Picts wall*: i.e., Hadrian's Wall, designed to keep out the Picts and Scots.

12. *St. Bees*. St. Bee (otherwise Begh or Bega) was an Irish maiden who founded a nunnery at St. Bees Head in Cumberland. She died in 681.

13. *the royalty*. The Crown, by virtue of statutes of 1688 and 1693, has a right of pre-emption of any gold or silver found in mines of copper, tin, iron or lead.

14. *Countess Pillar*. Anne, Baroness Clifford (*c*.1590–1676), married the 4th Earl of Pembroke.

15. *Sir Owen Caesar*. See Camden: 'In the churchyard at Penrith, on the north side of the church, are erected two large pillars of about four yards in height each, and about five yards distant one from the other; it is said, that they were set in memory of one Sir Ewen Caesarius, knight, in old time a famous warrior of great strength and stature, who lived in these parts, and killed wild boars in the forest of Inglewood, which much infested the country. He was buried here, they say, and was of such a prodigious stature, as to reach from one pillar to the other.'

16. *King Edward I*. He died in 1307 on his way to attack Robert Bruce,

who had seized the crown of Scotland.

LETTER XI

1. *Convention of Burghs*. Royal burghs in Scotland were first created in the twelfth century. The king's dealings with them were conducted through his chamberlain, who visited each burgh to see that the king's dues were paid and presided over the meetings of the Convention of Royal Burghs (a powerful burghal 'parliament').

2. *stented and bauk'd*: stinted (i.e., checked) and balked.

3. *Marquess of Tweedale*: John Hay, 4th Marquess of Tweeddale (*c*.1695–1762), Scottish representative peer who went on to become Principal Secretary of State for Scotland 1742–6.

4. *old Earl of Tweedale*: John Hay, 2nd Earl and 1st Marquess of Tweeddale, Lord High Chancellor of Scotland.

5. *Tantallon*. Tantallon Castle, picturesquely situated on a rocky promontory, dates back to the later fourteenth century and was a stronghold of the Douglases. It was captured from the Scots by General Monk in 1651 and never afterwards ranked as a fortress.

6. *Cameronians*. In 1680 Presbyterian rebels in south-west Scotland formed a sect known as 'the Society People' or (after their leader Richard Cameron) as 'Cameronians': its members publicly disavowed allegiance to Charles II and would ambush government agents. They were hunted down with great severity.

7. *Soland geese*: otherwise known as gannets. They live on the ocean except in the breeding season; and the present pattern, not necessarily that of Defoe's day, is for there to be a great and sudden influx of them on the Bass Rock early in the second half of January.

8. *Charles I and his royal family*. See note 21 above, p. 381.

9. *the French*. On the invasion of Scotland in 1547 by the Protector Somerset, the Scots called in French aid, and in May 1548 a force from France, under the Sieur d'Esse, landed in Leith.

10. *Craigmiller*. The ruined castle of Craigmiller was built by the

Preston family in the fourteenth century, and the property was bought in 1660 by Sir John Gilmour, later President of the Court of Session. The Gilmours continued to live there till the late eighteenth century.

11. *Dr. Balfour*. Sir Andrew Balfour (1630–94) helped found the Botanic Gardens in Edinburgh about 1680. He left his curiosities and manuscripts to Sir Robert Sibbald (see next note).

12. *Sir Robert Sibbald*: (1641–1722), Scottish physician and antiquary. He was instrumental in founding the Royal College of Physicians in Edinburgh, and in 1692 he presented his natural history collection to Edinburgh university.

13. *Dr. Pitcairn*: Archibald Pitcairne (1652–1713), a celebrated Scottish physician, involved in bitter medical controversies and a great mocker of the kirk. He endowed many charities.

14. *Ratcliff*: i.e., Radcliffe, see note 14 above, p. 385.

15. *that occasion is now over*. By the Act of Union the Scots lost their Parliament.

16. *General Assembly*: the General Assembly of the Church of Scotland.

17. *Land-market*. It is now known as the Lawnmarket.

18. *bagnio*: a bathing-house with facilities for sweating and cupping.

19. *late Act of Parliament*. The Copyright Act of 1709 required nine copies of every book published to be delivered to Stationers' Hall, for the benefit of the Royal Library, the two English and four Scottish universities, Sion College and the Advocates' Library in Edinburgh. It was evaded on a large scale.

20. *Queen Mary's dial*. This sundial was in fact named after Henrietta Maria, Queen to Charles I.

21. *fee-simple*: absolute ownership in law.

22. *late rebel highlanders*. A rebel force crossed the Forth in fishing boats and occupied Leith for the night of 15–16 October 1715.

23. *busses*. A buss was a two- or three-masted vessel, of the type used by Dutch herring-fishers.

24. *Marquess of Annandale*: William Johnstone, 3rd Earl of Annandale and 1st Marquess of Annandale (d. 1721). He was pensioned for

his services to the Glencoe inquiry and created Marquess in 1701. He was Lord High Commissioner to the General Assembly 1701 and 1711.

25. *Blackness Castle.* The present tower was built in the fifteenth century and was one of Scotland's most important fortresses, becoming one of the four that, by the terms of the Act of Union in 1707, were to be maintained at full military strength. It was used as a prison for Covenanters.

LETTER XII

1. *battle of Pinkey*: the first engagement in the Protector Somerset's attempt to subdue Scotland in 1547. It took place near Musselburgh on 10 September, the English being victorious.

2. *castle of Drumlanrig.* It was built in 1689 for the 1st Duke of Queensberry, who however disliked it and only spent a single night there.

3. *first Duke of Queensberry*: William Douglas, 3rd Earl and 1st Duke of Queensberry (1637–95). He was made Lord High Treasurer of Scotland in 1682 and received his dukedom in 1684.

4. *his son the late Duke*: James Douglas (1662–1711), 2nd Duke of Queensberry. He headed the Scottish Ministry as High Commissioner at the time of the Union. Defoe, who knew him personally, dedicated his *History of the Union* to him and to Queen Anne.

5. *John Hepburn.* John Hepburn (d. 1723) was a turbulent Cameronian minister who opposed the Union, as all Cameronians did, but was suspected of secretly revealing his associates' plans to Government agents. The description here of his field meeting was actually based by Defoe on a report given him by his agent in Scotland, James Pierce, eighteen years earlier. (See Defoe's letter to Harley 26 December 1706, in *Letters of Daniel Defoe*, ed. G.H. Healey (1955), pp. 180–1.)

6. *the text*: Hebrews 13:5.

7. *navigation of art.* The project of a canal to join the Clyde and the Firth of Forth was taken up some thirty years after Defoe was writing and was completed, with government assistance, in 1790.

8. *plaiding*: cloth of tartan pattern.

9. *vails*: veils.

10. *servants.* It was common in Defoe's day for the poor of either sex to sell themselves into indentured service in the American colonies, to pay for their passage. They were known as 'redemptioners', and their term of service was normally five years. In Virginia and Maryland they outnumbered negro slaves until the end of the seventeenth century.

11. *Bannock Bourn*: the great battle of Bannockburn, at which Robert Bruce inflicted a crushing defeat on the English under Edward II, was fought on 24 June 1314.

12. *embroidery.* 'Parterres de broderie (embroidered parterres) with flowing plant-like designs were pioneered by the Mollet family in France [in the seventeenth century]. They were made of box against a background of coloured earth, sometimes with bands of turf.' (*Oxford Companion to Gardens*)

13. *late exil'd Earl of Marr*: John Erskine, 6th or 11th Earl of Mar, of the Erskine line (1675–1732), nicknamed 'Bobbing John'. He was Secretary of State for Scotland under Queen Anne but became a Jacobite at the accession of George I and led the 1715 rebellion. He fled to France in 1716 and was attainted and had his title and estates confiscated in the same year.

14. *ambrusiers*: perhaps Defoe's spelling of 'embrasures'.

15. *Sterling serges.* By the early eighteenth century Stirling was making jersey serges.

16. *noble palace.* The oldest part of the palace is the tower built by Edward I in 1302. James I planned large extensions from 1425 onwards, and there were further additions in the mid-sixteenth century.

17. *Order of the Knights of St. Andrew.* The Order of the Thistle, sometimes known as the Order of St. Andrew, was founded by James II in 1687. In his royal warrant James declared it to be revival of an Order originally founded by his predecessor Achaius, King of the Scots, in commemoration of a victory over Athelstan, King of the Saxons.

18. *Bothwell-Bridge rebellion.* On 2 July 1679 the Scottish Covenanters, holding Bothwell Brig on the banks of the Clyde, were heavily defeated by a force of loyalist militia under the Duke of Monmouth.

19. *equivalent.* As part of the terms of the Union, Scotland was to be paid the sum of £398,085 as an 'equivalent' for the share of the National Debt that it would have to shoulder.

20. *Earl of Traquair*: Sir John Stewart (d. 1659), 1st Earl of Traquair (cr. 1633). He was Lord High Treasurer of Scotland and was employed by Charles I to treat with the Covenanters but came under the suspicion of double-dealing and ended his career in semi-disgrace.

21. *abbey of Mailross.* Melrose Abbey, a famous Cistercian house, was founded by David I about 1136. It was partly destroyed by Edward II (1322) and Richard II (1385) and was wrecked during Hereford's expedition of 1545.

22. *Floors.* Floors Castle, the seat of the Duke of Roxbrughe, was built to designs by Vanbrugh in 1718.

23. *large antient church.* Kelsoe Abbey was founded in 1128.

24. *Duke Lauderdale.* Defoe is referring to John Maitland, 1st Duke of Lauderdale (1616–82), famous for his part in the 'Cabal' and for his ruthless administration as Secretary of State for Scotland under Charles II.

25. *Lieutenant-General Maitland.* Rogers suggests that this refers to James Maitland, brigadier in 1696, lieutenant-general in 1709.

26. *Newbattle.* Newbattle Abbey was a twelfth-century Cistercian foundation which after the Reformation became the family seat of the Kerrs, later Marquesses of Lothian.

27. *Dalkeith.* Dalkeith House was built by Vanbrugh for the Duchess of Buccleuch in 1700 around the older castle and in imitation, on a smaller scale, of the Dutch royal palace at Loo.

28. *engine.* See note 36 above, p. 388.

LETTER XIII

1. *Lord Rochester's words.* Rogers notes that the phrase 'full perfection of decay' is not to be found

in modern editions of Rochester's poems and perhaps belongs to his extensive apocrypha.

2. *royal palace.* Malcolm Canmore built a palace, and also a priory, in Dunfermline in the eleventh century. The palace remained a favourite with succeeding kings, and the priory became their burial-place.

3. *by the Covenanters.* He was crowned at Scone on 1 January 1651, being made to swear to the Solemn League and Covenant.

4. *diaper.* Diaper looms, introduced by Flemish linen-weavers, were used to create intricate geometrical patterns.

5. *house of Kinross.* Kinross House was designed for himself 1685–90 by the courtier-architect Sir William Bruce (d. 1710).

6. *Royal Burroughs.* See note 1 above, p. 389.

7. *Lord Dysert:* Lionel Tollemache, 3rd Earl of Dysart (1649–1727).

8. *castle of the Weemys.* Near east Wemyss stands Wemyss Castle, the ancient seat of the family. It was here that Mary Queen of Scots first met Lord Darnley. The 'account lately given' is evidently the one by Macky in his *Journey Through Scotland*, where he writes: 'This Palace is above 200 Foot front to the South, with a Terrace on the top of the Rock, as at Windsor.'

9. *Samuel Colvil.* Colvil is best known for his burlesque poem *The Scotch Hudibras* (1681). We have been unable to trace a poem by him with the title *Polemo Midinia*. The line of macaronic verse may be rendered: 'Black coal-hewers looking savage ['girnantes' from the Scotch to 'girn'] in the manner of the Devil'.

10. *French fleet.* In 1708 the Old Pretender, with some 4,000 troops and a small French naval escort, made an abortive attempt to land in Scotland. The British fleet closed in on them as they were waiting the tide to enter the Firth of Forth, and they were forced to move off northward, losing one ship. The French admiral then refused to set the Prince on shore, and the survivors returned to Dunkirk reporting total failure.

11. *Cardinal Beaton.* David Beaton, born 1494, made Cardinal in 1538 and Archbishop of St. Andrews in 1539, was the champion of Roman Catholicism and of the French interest in Scotland. He was murdered in his own castle of St. Andrews on 29 May 1546–an act of Protestant vengeance.

12. *William Wishart.* Actually George Wishart (1513?–1546), a fiery Reformist preacher and Protestant martyr. He was arrested in 1545 and delivered into the hands of Cardinal Beaton, who imprisoned him in his castle of St. Andrews. He was convicted of heresy and burned 1 March 1546. Beaton watched the execution from the tower near the gate.

13. *Sir John Scot* (1585–1670). He was a Lord of Session and was knighted by James I and VI. He established a chair of Latin at St. Andrew's.

14. *Sir John Wedderburn* (1599–1679). He was a very successful physician, knighted and given a pension by Charles I, the pension being continued by Charles II. He left his library to St. Leonard's College at St. Andrew's university.

15. *Norman Lessley:* (or Leslie; d. 1556). He was the eldest son of George, 4th Earl of Rothes, and leader of the party that assassinated Cardinal Beaton.

16. *seat of the late rebellion.* The Jacobite leader the Earl of Mar raised the standard of revolt at Perth on 6 September 1715, and the Pretender joined his followers there in late December. There is a striking description of the progressive disillusionment of the rebels in the pamphlet *A True Account of the Proceedings at Perth* (1716), which has been attributed to Defoe.

17. *Dutch troops.* In December 1715 the government's forces in Scotland, under the Duke of Argyll, were reinforced by 6,000 Dutch troops, in fulfilment of the Barrier Treaty of 1713.

18. *late Act of Parliament.* See note 37 above, p. 380.

19. *Glames.* The original structure of Glamis castle dates back to the eleventh century, and several early Scots kings used it as an occasional residence. Its present form belongs mainly to the seventeenth century.

20. *that at Whitehall:* the bronze statue of James II in Roman costume, from the factory of Grinling Gibbons, erected in Whitehall Palace in 1686 and now standing in front of the National Gallery.

21. *Sheriff-Moor.* The indecisive battle at Sheriffmuir took place on 13 November 1715. It proved the end of the Earl of Mar's activities.

22. *York-Buildings company.* The company was set up to manage a waterworks near Villiers Street. It extended its operations into various speculative enterprises and was always in financial trouble.

23. *Antaeus:* in Greek mythology a giant wrestler who became stronger every time he touched the earth.

24. *French fleet.* See note 10 above.

25. *Lord Pitsligo.* Alexander Forbes, 4th and last Lord Forbes of Pitsligo (1678–1762) took part in the Jacobite rebellion of 1715 and had to flee to the Continent. He returned to Scotland in 1720, conducting a correspondence with the French Quietists, but took arms again in the rebellion of 1745 and in 1748 his estates were seized.

26. *river Tibiscus.* The river Theiss (Hungarian *Tisza*) is a tributary of the Danube and drains the eastern part of Hungary and much of Transylvania.

27. *Rob Roy:* nickname, meaning 'Robert the Red', of Robert McGregor (1671–1734), a Scottish outlaw and freebooter, sometimes described as the Robin Hood of Scotland.

28. *Duke of Athol:* John Murray, 1st Duke (1660–1724). He died in November 1724, nearly two years before Defoe is supposedly writing.

29. *Riphaean Hills:* fabled mountains in the extreme north, often referred to by the classical poets, later identified with real mountains in Scythia.

30. *Duplin Castle.* Dupplin Castle, on the bank of the Ern, was once the seat of the barons Oliphant and was bought by Sir George Hay, created Earl of Kinnoul by Charles I in 1633. It was burnt down in 1827. The estate now belongs to the Dewar trust.

31. *plaid and the trouse.* According to Hugh Trevor-Roper, in an essay 'The Highland Tradition of Scotland' in *The Invention of Tradition*, ed. E. Hobsbawm and T. Ranger (1983), the ordinary dress of the Highlanders was a long shirt, a

tunic and a cloak or plaid, probably of tartan. 'Besides this normal dress, chieftains and great men who had contact with the more sophisticated inhabitants of the Lowlands might wear trews: a combination of breeches and stockings. Trews could only be worn out of doors in the Highlands by men who had attendants to protect or carry them: they were therefore a mark of social distinction.'

32. *f*—. Defoe perhaps means 'fib'.

ARTISTS' BIOGRAPHIES

Some of the principal artists with work represented in this edition are listed below, together with brief biographical notes.

Pieter Angillis *(1685–1734)*

Born in Dunkirk. Lived in Covent Garden from 1716 to 1728 and was a popular painter of landscape, low life and conversation pieces in a style based on Teniers and Watteau. Travelled and worked extensively in Europe after 1728, dying in Rennes.

Thomas Bowles

Draughtsman and line engraver of topographical views working in London towards the middle of the eighteenth century, often with John Bowles, publishing their own prints as well as those commissioned from others.

Samuel Buck *(1696–1779)*

Born in Richmond. Actively encouraged by the Yorkshire antiquary Ralph Thoresby and later William Stukeley and the Society of Antiquaries of London, he developed a profitable business (based initially on subscription) drawing and engraving castles, monasteries, palaces and historical remains as well as large town prospects on a systematic county-by-county basis. From 1711 to 1742 his work normally followed a pattern–spring and summer spent on drawing expeditions in particular counties, with winters devoted to engraving plates for publication in sets the following spring. Up to the end of 1726 he acted as his own draughtsman and engraver with his younger brother Nathaniel joining him as full partner in 1727 until his death in 1756. Well over four hundred views of abbeys, castles and other historical remains and eighty-six large town prospects were produced. They were collected into three very large volumes titled *Buck's Antiquities*, published by Robert Sayer in 1774.

Greenvile Collins *(fl.1679–93)*

Naval captain who began, in 1681, a survey of the coast of Britain, a project that created one of the earliest reliable hydrographical surveys, published in 1693 as *Great Britain's Coasting Pilot* and republished several times in the following century.

Jan Griffier the Elder *(c.1645/52–1718)*

Born in Amsterdam, probably coming to London in the 1660s and specialising in painting ruins, river scenes and some bird's-eye views of cities in a dramatic fashion. His son

Robert (1688–1750) and probably his grandson Jan Griffier Jr or II (*fl.*1738–73) were also topographical and landscape painters.

Moses Griffith *(1747–1819)*

Welsh topographical draughtsman and engraver. Taken into service about 1769 by the traveller and naturalist Thomas Pennant (1726–98). He accompanied Pennant on most of his tours in the British Isles, providing engravings for the published accounts.

John Harris *(fl.1722–59)*

Topographical painter and probably engraver of his own work as well as of architectural and topographical work by many of his contemporaries. His father, also John Harris (*c.*1686–1749), was a topographical engraver, friend of Thomas Badeslade (*fl.* 1715–50) and Johannes Kip, contributing plates to *Britannia Illustrata*.

Johannes Kip *(1653–1719)*

Born in Amsterdam, came to England in 1697. Developed a successful practice composing and engraving topographical views. Active collaboration with the influential landscape painter Leonard Knyff (1650–1720) depicting estates and country seats, leading to the publication of *Britannia Illustrata or Views of Several of the Queens Palaces also of the Principal Seats of the Nobility and Gentry of Great Britain* in 1707 (with editions in 1709, 1715 and later) and the much larger selection *Nouveau Théâtre de la Grande Bretagne* after 1715.

George Lambert *(1710–65)*

Pupil of John Wootton and a friend of Hogarth and Samuel Scott, specialised in topographical and imaginary landscape painting as well as theatrical scenery.

Herman Moll *(d.1732)*

Of Dutch origins, Moll came to England in 1698. Became an 'old acquaintance' of Stukeley and built a considerable reputation for his composition and publication of many maps and geographical expositions.

Sutton Nicholls

Early eighteenth-century draughtsman and engraver of architectural and antiquarian subjects, working extensively for London booksellers.

Francis Place *(1647–1728)*

Personal friend of Wenceslaus Hollar and acquainted with an extensive circle of artists and antiquarians (including Robert Thoresby and Thomas Lodge) centred on York, where he lived for forty years. Undertook several fishing and drawing expeditions with Lodge through England, Wales and Ireland, which provided the basis of a number of engraved plates used in publications by his friends.

Edmund Prideaux *(1653–1745)*

Born in East Anglia, Prideaux developed a keen interest in travel and in drawing scenery and houses, especially those associated with his family. Undertook three main itineraries: two in Devon and Cornwall in 1716 and 1727, and one in East Anglia probably in 1725. Inherited and moved to Prideaux Place, Padstow, in 1728.

Paul Sandby *(1725–1809)*

From a post in the military-drawing department at the Tower of London, Sandby was appointed official draughtsman to the survey of the new line of the road to Fort George and the northern and western Highlands under the direction of Col. David Watson in 1747. Travelled and drew extensively all over Scotland before leaving in 1751 to join his brother Thomas at Windsor. Throughout the rest of his long and succesful career he undertook many sketching expeditions and landscape-painting commissions. Pioneered the use of aquatint in 1775.

Samuel Scott *(c.1702–72)*

From an early career concentrating on naval and shipping scenes, developed a considerable reputation for shore and river scenes, some enlivened by figures added by his friend Hogarth. His Thameside paintings earned him the nickname of the English Canaletto, even though some of his work almost certainly predates Canaletto's arrival in London in 1746.

Jan Siberechts *(1627–c.1703)*

Born in Antwerp where he built a considerable practice before settling in England c.1672 and developing some important commissions, specialising in portraits of country houses, bird's-eye estate views and panoramic paintings of river valleys.

John Slezer *(d.1714)*

Military engineer and later artillery officer, initially attached to the House of Orange. Settled in Scotland about 1669, beginning a project, *Scotia Illustrata*, in 1678 'to make a book of figures, and draughts... of all the King's Castles, Pallaces, towns and other notable places in the kingdom belonging to private subjects'. Encouraged by Charles II,

James II and William III, the first volume, *Theatrum Scotiae*, was published by royal authority in 1693. It failed to cover its costs by a wide margin but, in response to Slezer's petition in 1695, the Scottish parliament granted a proportion of a special tax on goods exported by sea to cover the costs and finance further publication. In the event very little was ever paid to Slezer who died in penury hiding from his creditors in 1714. Editions of the only volume ever published appeared with various selections of plates in 1693, 1710, 1718, 1719, 1797, 1814 and 1874.

William Stukeley *(1687–1765)*

Trained as a physician, Stukeley was a founding member of the Society of Antiquaries of London in January 1718 and its secretary for nine years. The surviving drawings and the published *Itinerarium Curiosum* (1724) document his long summer excursions in the years 1721–5 partly to satisfy a passionate interest in antiquities of all sorts and partly to help alleviate gout. Extensive work and writing on Avebury, Stonehenge and the Druids followed. In 1730 became vicar of All Saints, Stamford.

Peter Tillemans *(1684–1734)*

Born in Antwerp, brought to England in 1708 and employed as a copyist of old-master paintings. Developed a lucrative practice as a painter of country seats and landscapes with sporting subjects. Lived in Richmond on Thames for many years. Retained by John Bridges (1666–1724), author of *History of Northamptonshire*, for whom he produced over 500 drawings.

George Vertue *(1684–1756)*

Eminent antiquary and engraver. First draughtsman and engraver to the Society of Antiquaries of London. Much of his later work concentrated on archaeological material. His posthumous *Anecdotes of Painting in England* and *Notebooks* are prime sources of reliable information on his contemporaries.

Richard Wilson *(1713–82)*

Born and died in Wales. Developed reputation as portrait and landscape painter before going to Venice in 1750 and spending considerable part of his career in Italy, returning to English and Welsh landscape much later.

John Wootton *(1678–1765)*

First came to prominence at Newmarket where he painted all the best known racehorses of the day and for fifty years was the most esteemed horse painter for the aristocracy. He also developed a considerable reputation as a painter of dogs, hunting scenes and battles, as well as for some late classical landscapes.

ILLUSTRATIONS

General Acknowledgements

The assistance of suppliers of photographs and copyright holders is noted in the credits listed below. However, visual research for this book would not have been possible without the active and generous help of many more people. To identify them all would fill a fairly large volume, and so I hope that they will accept this broad note of thanks. I received all kinds of thoughtful local and detailed assistance by letter and telephone from individuals in local-studies libraries, record offices, museums, local societies and history groups, as well as from individuals in the departments of the national collections of England, Scotland and Wales. Help making rare and unusual documents available came from many different and sometimes unusual directions. In this respect my fellow editors and I are particularly grateful for the assistance provided by the staffs of the Bodleian Library, British Library, London Library, Guildhall Library, Paul Mellon Centre for Studies in British Art, British Museum Department of Prints and Drawings, Witt Library of the Courtauld Institute, Museum of English Rural Life, National Library of Scotland and National Library of Wales.

Finally, I wish to record special thanks to my colleagues at the Open University Library and to my wife. Without their encouragement, patience and support none of this work would have been possible.

A.J.C.
August 1990

Black and White Plates

The maps facing the openings of Letters I–IV and VI–XIII are details taken from a map of England and Wales, from Hermann Moll, *A set of fifty new and correct maps of England and Wales* (1724), Bodleian Library, Oxford, c.17.e.2., and from a map of 'The North Part of Great Britain called Scotland', from Thomas Taylor, *England exactly described* (1715), Bodleian Library, Oxford, Gough Maps 115. The illustration facing the opening of Letter V is a detail from plate 101 (*see below*). The title-page of the 1724 edition of Defoe's *A Tour thro' the Whole Island of Great Britain* on page 1 is reproduced by permission of the British Library Board.

1. Industries: woollen manufactury, ship building, husbandry, mining, timber felling, fishery. Cartouche of Lewis Morris Chart of the Welsh Coast, 1748. Pembrokeshire Record Office, Dyfed, Archives Service. Photo: Paul Harrison.

2. Detail from pl. 101.

3a and b. Dutch sloop and a dogger. From Robert C. Leslie, *Old Sea Wings, Ways and World* (1890).

4. Dutch hoy or bilandre. From *Spectacle de la Nature* (1740). Mary Evans Picture Library.

5. Dutch schuyt. From Edward W. Hobbs, *Sailing ships at a glance* (1925).

6. 'A plan of the late breach in the levels of Havering and Dagenham', by Herman Moll (1721). Valence House Museum, London Borough of Barking and Dagenham.

7. Cattle grazing on Essex freshwater marshes near Hadleigh; painting by George Shalders. Beecroft Art Gallery, Southend on Sea Museums Services.

8. Tilbury fort; engraving, late eighteenth century. Mansell Collection.

9. 'A New and Exact Prospect of Colchester taken from ye north part'; engraving by John Pryer (1724). Colchester Museum.

10a and b. Details of castle and abbey gate from 'A New and Exact Prospect of Colchester . . .' (see pl. 9).

11. Harwich; engraving by R. Sheppard. From Silas Taylor, *History and Antiquities of Harwich and Dovercourt, topographical, dynastical and political . . . now much enlarged by Samuel Dale* (1730). Reproduced by courtesy of Harwich Society and Mr L. Weaver.

12. Detail from pl. 11.

13. 'The South-West prospect of Ipswich in the County of Suffolk'; engraving by Samuel and Nathaniel Buck (1741). Photo: Fotomas Index.

14. The Market Cross at Ipswich. From Sir James Thornhill, *Sketchbook travel journal of 1711*, p. 5. National Art Library. Reproduced by courtesy of the Board of Trustees of the Victoria and Albert Museum.

15. Bury St Edmunds. Ruins of the abbey on the north and east sides. From a sketchbook of Edmund Prideaux (c.1725). Prideaux Place, Padstow, by kind permission of Peter Prideaux-Brune.

16. Dunwich; engraving by John Kirby and I. Wood (published 1753). Bodleian Library, Oxford. Gough Maps, 41J, 40 recto.

17. 'The North East Prospect of the city of Norwich'; engraving by J. Kirkall (1724). British Library. K.T.C. XXXI.34a. Reproduced by permission of the British Library Board.

18a and b. Details of the Custom House and of some merchants' houses from pl. 19.

19. 'The West Prospect of the town of Great Yarmouth'; engraving by J. Harris after J. Corbridge (1724). Yale Center for British Art. Paul Mellon Collection B1977.14.11290 a–c.

20. Details of herring fishing (c.1720). *Top*: herring busses under sail; *bottom*: pickling and barrelling herrings. Engravings by Sieuwert van der Meulen. National Maritime Museum, London.

21. 'Tuesday Market Place. Kings Lynn'; engraving ascribed to H. Bell. Harley Collection, vol. 8, p. 57. Reproduced by kind permission of the Society of Antiquaries of London.

22. John Wootton, *Warren Hill* (c.1715). Private Collection. Photo courtesy of the Paul Mellon Centre for Studies in British Art, London.

23. 'Map of the Great Level of the Fenns, called Bedford Level' (1723). From *The History of the ancient and present state of the navigation of. . . Kings Lynn* (1724), pp. 26–7. Bodleian Library, Oxford. G.A. Eng. rivers. c.17.

24. Detail from pl. 19.

25. 'Plan of Sturbock Fair' (1725). Bodleian Library, Oxford, Gough Maps 2 fol. 10 verso.

26. A stall at Stourbridge Fair; engraving. From W. Hone, *Yearbook of Early Recreation* (1835). Cambridgeshire Collection, Cambridgeshire Libraries.

27. 'The North-East view of Cambridge Castle'; engraving by Samuel and Nathaniel Buck (1730). Photo: Fotomas Index.

28. 'A General Prospect of the Royal Palace of Audlyene seen from the Mount Garden'; engraving by Henry Winstanley and Littleby. Bodleian Library, Oxford. Gough Maps 8, fol. 10 recto.

29. Wanstead (bird's-eye view from the east); engraving by J. Kip after a drawing by L. Knyff (c.1710). Bodleian Library, Oxford. Gough Maps 8 fol. 45 verso.

30. Detail of Wanstead House: the entrance from the west; engraving by J. Rocque (c.1735). Bodleian Library, Oxford. Gough Maps 8 fol. 48 recto.

31. London from Greenwich Park; painting by Jan Griffier the Elder (c.1710–15). Brukenthalmuseum, Sibiu, Romania. Photo reproduced courtesy of Diane de Marly.

32. Detail of a lime kiln in the grounds of Ingries, Greenhythe, seat of Jonathan Smith, from an engraving by J. Kip after a drawing by Thomas Badeslade. From John Harris *The History of Kent* (1719). Reproduced courtesy of Kent County Library.

33. A wagon (1709). From a *Table of Fares issued by the Sheriffs' court*. Mary Evans Picture Library.

34. Bird's-eye view of Rochester and the Medway as far as Sheerness from the Strood side of the river; engraving by J. Kip after a drawing by Thomas Badeslade. From John Harris *The History of Kent* (1719). Reproduced courtesy of Kent County Library.

35. Detail of Rochester cathedral from the bird's-eye view of Rochester (see pl. 34).

36. 'The West prospect of His Majesty's Dockyard at Chatham'; engraving by Samuel and Nathaniel Buck (1738). National Maritime Museum, London.

37. 'View of the Downs from Wye to Ayslford. . .This is taken from the land above Aylsford.' Drawing by William Stukeley (5 June 1725). From his *Collection of prints and original drawings*, vol. 3: *Roman Prints* (c.1758), f. 9 verso. Reproduced by permission of the Society of Antiquaries of London.

38. 'The South West prospect of the city of Canterbury'; engraving by Samuel and Nathaniel Buck (1738). Photo: Fotomas Index.

39. Paul Sandby, *The West Gate, Canterbury*; gouache. Yale Center for British Art. Paul Mellon Collection B1977.14.6273.

40. 'The Description of Romney Marsh. . .with the divisions of their waterings, their heads, Arms, principall sewers and their gutts for serving of the fresh waters that fall into the same. . .with marshes adjoining;' engraving by S. Parker, from William Dugdale, *History of Imbanking and Draining*, reproduced in John Harris, *The History of Kent* (1719). Reproduced courtesy of Kent County Library.

41. Tunbridge Wells; engraving by J. Kip after a drawing by Thomas Badeslade. From John Harris, *The History of Kent* (1719). Reproduced courtesy of Kent County Library.

42. 'A Prospect of the Landport Gate and Bridge with the Ravelin before it at Portsmouth' (c.1717). Portsmouth City Records Office.

71. Steam fire engine used to provide power in tin mines; engraving. From William Pryce, *Mineralogia Cornubiensis* (1778), pl. 3. County Museum and Art Gallery. Royal Institution of Cornwall, Truro.

72. 'Pendennis and St Mawes castles, October 9, 1727'; drawing by Edmund Prideaux. Prideaux Place, Padstow. Reproduced by kind permission of Mr Peter Prideaux-Brune.

73. Falmouth; map. From Greenvile Collins, *Great Britain's Coasting Pilot* (1693). Bodleian Library, Oxford. Gough Maps 86.

74. Details of tin miners and fishermen from a cartouche of the map of Falmouth in Greenvile Collins, *Great Britain's Coasting Pilot* (1693). Bodleian Library, Oxford. Gough Maps 86.

75. 'North East Prospect of Penzance'; wash drawing by R. Scadden (1747). Bodleian Library, Oxford. Gough Maps 3 fol. 28 verso.

76. 'South West Prospect of St Michael's Mount'; engraving by Samuel and Nathaniel Buck (1739). Bodleian Library, Oxford. Gough Maps 3 fol. 30.

77. Detail from pl. 79.

78. 'Sir Cloudesly Shovel in the Association with the Eagle, Rummny and the Firebrand lost on the rocks of Scilly, October 22, 1707'; contemporary engraving. National Maritime Museum, London.

79. 'The Lands End'; engraving by E. Harding. From Richard Polwhele, *The History of Cornwall* (1803). County Museum and Art Gallery. Royal Institution of Cornwall, Truro.

80. Pentire Point and Padstow Haven; drawing by Edmund Prideaux (2 October 1727). Prideaux Place, Padstow. Reproduced by kind permission of Mr Peter Prideaux-Brune.

81. 'The Hurlers near the Cheeswring said by ye country people to be men turned into stones for hurling on a Sunday'; drawing by Edmund Prideaux (21 September 1727). Prideaux Place, Padstow. Reproduced by kind permission of Mr Peter Prideaux-Brune.

82. Launceston castle and town; drawing by Edmund Prideaux (20 September 1727). Prideaux Place, Padstow. Reproduced by kind permission of Mr Peter Prideaux-Brune.

83. Calstock on the Tamar, drawing by Edmund Prideaux. Prideaux Place, Padstow. Reproduced by kind permission of Mr Peter Prideaux-Brune.

84. Bideford Meeting House; print from the early nineteenth century before its destruction later in the century but showing its state soon after completion in 1696. North Devon Library and Record Office, Barnstaple. Photo: Baths Photographic.

85. Blundell's Free Grammar School in Tiverton; engraving by W. Thomas (1784). Tiverton Museum Society.

86. James Scott, Duke of Monmouth and Buccleuch (1649–85); painting after William Wissing. National Portrait Gallery, London.

87. Sheep and cattle; painting by Pieter Angillis (1729). Private Collection. Photo courtesy of the Paul Mellon Centre for Studies in British Art, London, and Christie's.

88. 'Prospect of the ruins of Glasenbury Abby, August 17, 1723'; engraving by E. Kirkall after William Stukeley. From William Stukeley, *Itinerarium Curiosum* (1724), pl. 36. Bodleian Library, Oxford. Gough Gen. Top. 55.

89. 'South view of Wells Palace in the county of Somerset'; engraving by Samuel and Nathaniel Buck (1733). Somerset County Library.

90. Cheesemaking; engraving from Denis Diderot, *Encyclopédie*, vol. 6: *Addition à l'Economie Rustique* (c.1760), pl. 1 (c.1760). Institute of Agricultural History and Museum of English Rural Life, University of Reading.

91. A view of Cheddar cliffs; engraving (c.1760). Somerset County Library.

92. Sheep; frontispiece to Richard Bradley, *The Gentleman and Farmer's guide for the increase and improvement of cattle* (1739). Institute of Agricultural History and Museum of English Rural Life, University of Reading.

93a–c. Three plates depicting woollen manufacture, from the *Universal Magazine of Knowledge and Pleasure*, vol. 5 (August 1749) facing p. 82; vol. 5 (October 1749) facing p. 180; vol. 7 (August 1750) facing p. 170. Bodleian Library, Oxford. Per. 2705e. 552/1.

94. Devizes; engraving after William Stukeley (1723). From his *Itinerarium Curiosum* (1724), pl. 69. Bodleian Library, Oxford. Vet. A4.c.192.

95. 'A true ground plot of Wey Hill Faire, 1683'. Hampshire Museums Service. Photo: David Robson.

96. 'South prospect of Reading in the county of Berks'; engraving for *London Magazine* (1734). Reading Central Library. Berkshire Library and Information Service.

97. Detail of a barge carrying bulk cargo, from an anonymous painting of Windsor castle seen from the Thames (c.1700). Yale Center for British Art. Paul Mellon Collection B1981.25.647.

98. Windsor Castle, from Isherwood's Brewhouse, Datchet Lane, Windsor; pen, watercolour and gouache by Paul Sandby. Royal Library, Windsor Castle. © 1990 Her Majesty the Queen.

99. Fragment of a wall painting of King William III by Sir Godfrey Kneller, from St George's Hall. Royal Collection, Windsor. Reproduced by gracious permission of Her Majesty the Queen.

100. Eton College; watercolour attributed to Paul Sandby. National Gallery of Scotland. Dept. of Prints and Drawings. D2283.

101. 'The East Prospect of London, Southwark and the Bridge . . . looking up the river'; engraving by Sutton Nicholls (1723). British Museum. Dept. of Prints and Drawings. Crace Collection II.70. Reproduced by permission of the Trustees of the British Museum.

102. Somerset House, the garden and the Folly; engraving by J. Kip after L. Knyff (1714). British Museum. Dept. of Prints and Drawings. Crace Collection VI.201. Reproduced by permission of the Trustees of the British Museum.

103. 'A view of the Savoy from the River Thames . . . as it appeared in 1736'; engraving after a plan by George Vertue (published 1750). British Museum. Dept. of Prints and Drawings. Crace Collection V.177. Reproduced by permission of the Trustees of the British Museum.

104. Powis House; engraving by H. Terasson (1714). Guildhall Library, Corporation of London. Dept. of Prints. PrH4/Gre/Orm.

105. The Monument; vignette from *A new description of England and Wales with adjacent islands . . .* (1724). Bodleian Library, Oxford. c.17.2, pl. 19.

106. Royal Exchange interior, with inset of Gresham's original building; engraving by Sutton Nicholls (1712). Guildhall Library, Corporation of London. Dept. of Prints. Pr512/Roy(2)Int.

107. Custom House as reconstructed to the designs of Ripley after the fire of 1718; engraving (published by J. Bowles, 1725). British Museum. Dept. of Prints and Drawings. Crace Collection VIII.18. Reproduced by permission of the Trustees of the British Museum.

108. North prospect of St Paul's; engraving by J. King. Guildhall Library, Corporation of London. Dept. of Prints. 460/PAU(2).

109. 'The Bubblers Medley'; engraving by Thomas Bowles (1720). British Museum. Dept. of Prints and Drawings. Crace Collection XXV.19. Reproduced by permission of the Trustees of the British Museum.

110a–d. Contemporary Firemarks displayed on buildings to denote insurance cover by particular London Insurance companies. **a.** The Sun Fire Office (1710–1959). Chartered Insurance Institute Museum. **b.** The Hand in Hand Fire Office (1696–1905). **c.** The Royal Exchange Assurance Insurance (1720–1968). **d.** The London Assurance (1720–1965). Photos for b–d courtesy of Brian Sharp.

111. The General Post Office; engraving by Sutton Nicholls (1710). British Museum. Dept. of Prints and Drawings. Crace Collection XXIII.18. Reproduced by permission of the Trustees of the British Museum.

112. 'The Butcher'; satirical engraving by George Bickham (*c.*1737). Guildhall Library, Corporation of London. Dept. of Prints. Satirical Prints 80.

113. 'The view and humours of Billingsgate'; engraving by Arnold Vanhaeken (1736). Guildhall Library, Corporation of London. Dept. of Prints. Pr71/BIL.

114. Howland Great Dock; engraving by J. Kip after Thomas Badeslade (1717). British Museum. Dept. of Prints and Drawings. Crace Collection VIII.126. Reproduced by permission of the Trustees of the British Museum.

115. 'The New Sucking Worm Fire Engine, dedicated to King George I by John Lofting.' Harley Collection, vol. 5, p. 66. Reproduced by permission of the Society of Antiquaries of London.

116. Detail of watermills and mechanism for raising water from the Thames, from an engraving of the east and west side of London Bridge by Sutton Nicholls (*c.*1720). Guildhall Library, Corporation of London. Dept. of Prints. 361/LON(1).

117. Equestrian statue of Charles II in the Stocks Market; engraving (published by Thomas Bowles, 1738). British Museum. Dept. of Prints and Drawings. Crace Collection XXI.93. Reproduced by permission of the Trustees of the British Museum.

118. The City Gates of London; engraving by Sutton Nicholls (published by John Bowles, *c.*1720). British Museum. Dept. of Prints and Drawings. Crace Collection XXXVII.21. Reproduced by permission of the Trustees of the British Museum.

119. Reception of King George I at St James's Palace on September 1714; engraving by A. Allard. British Museum. Dept. of Prints and Drawings. Crace Collection XII.1.1. Reproduced by permission of the Trustees of the British Museum.

120. Westminster Hall and adjoining buildings; anonymous watercolour (*c.*1720). British Museum. Dept. of Prints and Drawings. Crace Collection XV.71. Reproduced by permission of the Trustees of the British Museum.

121. Whitehall, view towards the King Street Gate; engraving by J. Kip (1724). British Museum. Dept. of Prints and Drawings. Crace Collection XVI.18a. Reproduced by permission of the Trustees of the British Museum.

122. 'The Coffee House Mob'; engraving. From Edward Ward, *Vulgus Britannicus, or the British Hudibras*, London (1711). London Library.

123. King's Theatre, Haymarket; watercolour by William Capon (*c.*1770). Guildhall Library, Corporation of London. Dept. of Prints. W2/HAY.

124. Guy's Hospital for Incurables with eight views of the wards and other parts of the buildings; engraving (sold by Thomas Bowles, 1725). British Museum. Dept. of Prints and Drawings. Crace Collection XXXIV.84. Reproduced by permission of the Trustees of the British Museum.

125. View of Hampstead from the top of Pond Street, engraving by J.B.C. Chatelain 1752. London Borough of Camden. Local Studies Library.

126a and b. Bellsize House and the accompanying announcement of its reopening; engravings (*c.*1724). London Borough of Camden. Local Studies Library, and British Library. K.T.C. XXX.25a. Reproduced by permission of the British Library Board.

127. South front of Cannons, seat of James, Duke of Chandos; engraving by H. Hulsbergh after a drawing by John Price (*c.*1720). British Library. K.T.C. XXX.25a. Reproduced by permission of the British Library Board.

128. Kensington Palace and Garden; engraving by T. Bowles (1724). British Museum. Dept. of Prints and Drawings. Crace Collection IX.4. Reproduced by permission of the Trustees of the British Museum.

129. View of the Vale of Aylesbury from Whitchurch (published by Byrne and Cadell, 1803). Buckinghamshire County Library. Local Collection.

130. South prospect of the city of Oxford; engraving by Sutton Nicholls (1724). Harley Collection, vol. 7, p. 26. Reproduced by permission of the Society of Antiquaries of London.

131. Unknown painter, *View of the harvesting field of James Higford's manor, Dixton, Gloucestershire* (*c.*1725–35), oil on canvas, 113 × 287 cm. Cheltenham Museum and Art Gallery.

132. 'Rowldrich Stones from the West, Sept 11 1724'; engraving by William Stukeley. From his *Abury* (1740). Ashmolean Museum Library, Oxford.

133. 'South East prospect of the city of Bath'; engraving by Samuel and Nathaniel Buck (1734). Photo: Fotomas Index.

134. Old town hall and High Street, Bath; watercolour by Edward Eyre (*c.*1776, from an earlier lost drawing), 18.5 × 25 cm. Victoria Art Gallery. Bath City Council.

135. The Cross Bath; engraving by John Fayram (1739). Bath Reference Library.

136. Hot wells, Bristol; engraving by W. Milton after S. Pye (1747). City of Bristol Museum and Art Gallery.

137. Berkeley Castle from the east; drawing by L. Knyff (*c.*1676). British Museum. Dept. of Prints and Drawings. 1948.11.26.9. Reproduced by permission of the Trustees of the British Museum.

138. The art of stocking frame work knitting. From the *Universal Magazine of Knowledge and Pleasure*, vol. 7 (1750), facing p. 49. British Library. P.P. 5439. Reproduced by permission of the British Library Board.

139. East prospect of the city of Worcester (1742). Coleraine Collection, vol. 7, p. 24. Reproduced by permission of the Society of Antiquaries of London.

140. Cidermaking using a handpress. From John Worlidge, *Vinetum Britannicum, or a treatise of cider* (1691). Museum of Cider, Hereford.

141. Chepstow castle and bridge; engraving by J. Kip (1705). Bodleian Library, Oxford. Gough Maps 37 fol. 1 verso.

142. Brecknock Mere; engraving by Thomas Jones of Pencerrig. From his *Six views after nature in South Wales* (1775). National Library of Wales.

143. Coal mine and horse gin near Neath; engraving (*c.*1778). Welsh Industrial and Maritime Museum. National Museum of Wales.

144. 'South East view of Carmarthen'; engraving by Samuel and Nathaniel Buck (1745). Carmarthen Museum.

145. Tenby; drawing by Francis Place (1678). National Museum of Wales.

146. 'A map of that part of Cardiganshire wherin are the mines belonging to the Governor and company of Mine Adventurers of England'. From William Waller, *Report on lead and silver mines* (1709). Bodleian Library, Oxford. Gough Wales 31(4).

147. Merionethshire girl; aquatint by Paul Sandby (published 1776). British Museum. Dept. of Prints and Drawings. 1904.8.19.699. Reproduced by permission of the Trustees of the British Museum.

148. Caernarvon castle; painting by Richard Wilson (*c.*1745–50). Yale Center for British Art. Paul Mellon Collection B1976.7.174.

149. Holyhead; drawing by Francis Place (1699). National Museum of Wales.

150. Conway castle; painting by Paul Sandby (1789). Yale Center for British Art. Paul Mellon Collection B1977.14.4405.

151. An inside view of the Rows, Chester; engraving by J. Landseer after J. Webster (1810). Reproduced by permission of the Chester Archeological Society from originals in Chester City Record Office.

152. Chester and the Roodee; engraving after Peter Tillemans, from 'The South West Prospect of Chester' (1725). Reproduced by permission of the Chester Archeological Society from originals in Chester City Record Office.

153. Refining common salt, from William Brownrigg *The Art of making common salt* (1748). Salt Museum, Northwich. Cheshire Museums Service.

154. 'West view of Wrexham steeple, July 1712'; drawing by William Stukeley. From his *Pocket Sketchbook*. Bodleian Library, Oxford. MS Top. Gen. e.61. fol. 19 recto.

155. 'Prospect of South side of Shrewsbury taken from Coney Green'; engraved by J. Kip (*c*.1715). Shropshire Libraries. Local Studies Dept., Shrewsbury.

156. 'East view of the cathedral church and close of Lichfield, taken from Stow pool'; engraving by John Wood after Richard Greene (1745). British Library. K.T.C. XXXVIII.45a.i. Reproduced by permission of the British Library Board.

157. 'The Ribbon weaver in his loom'; engraving. From the *Universal Magazine* (July 1747) facing p. 83. Bodleian Library, Oxford. Per. 2705.e.552/1.

158. 'North-West prospect of All Saints church, Northampton, 28 June 1711'; drawing by William Stukeley. From his *Pocket Sketchbook*. Bodleian Library, Oxford. MS Top. Gen. e.61. fol. 14 verso.

159. Detail from 'South West prospect of Northampton'; engraving by Samuel and Nathaniel Buck (1731). Photo: Fotomas Index.

160. Ruins of Holdenby, 25 April 1709; drawing by William Stukeley. From his *Pocket Sketchbook*. Bodleian Library, Oxford. MS Top. Gen. e.61. fol. 19 recto.

161. 'The Town of Leicester from the South, July 30, 1724'; drawing by Samuel Buck. From his *Sketchbook* (1724). Bodleian Library, Oxford. Gough Linc. 15, p. 90.

162. 'South view of the Antient city of Lincoln taken from Mr Dickinson's Summer House at Canwick'; engraving by Samuel Buck (*c*.1724–5). Usher Art Gallery, Lincoln. Lincolnshire County Council, Recreation Services.

163. Boston (29 August 1722); engraving by Thornton after William Stukeley. From William Stukeley *Itinerarium Curiosum* (1724), pl. 19. Bodleian Library, Oxford. Gough Gen. Top. 55.

164. 'Map of the Levels in Lincolnshire commonly called Holland, described by William Stukeley 1723'. Bodleian Library, Oxford. Gough Maps 41D fol. 10 recto.

165. The form of the decoys in Lincolnshire with a diagram of a decoy pipe into which the ducks are driven to be captured; based on a drawing by William Stukeley. (*c*.1722). Bodleian Library, Oxford. Gough Maps 16 Lincolnshire fol. 3 recto.

166. Beating hemp; engraving. From Denis Diderot *Encyclopédie*, vol. 6: *L'Economie Rustique* (*c*.1760). Mary Evans Picture Library.

167. Grantham; drawing by William Stukeley. From his *Drawings in a journey with Mr Roger Gale* (1721). Bodleian Library, Oxford. Gough Gen. Top. d.13. fol. 50 recto.

168. 'Prospect of the town of Stamford from Worthrop Warren'; engraving by Thornton (1726). Bodleian Library, Oxford. Gough Maps 16 fol. 48 verso.

169. 'South prospect of Burleigh House'; engraving by J. Caldwall after P. Tillemans (*c*.1720). Photo by permission from the Burghley House Collection.

170. Verrio's ceiling decoration in the second George room, Burghley House (1688–98). Photo by permission from the Burghley House Collection.

171. Buckden Palace; engraving. From the *Ladies Magazine* (1749–53). Mary Evans Picture Library.

172. Two people carrying bundles; drawing by Samuel Buck. From his *Sketchbook* (1724), p. 122. Bodleian Library, Oxford, Gough Linc. 15 fol. 53 verso.

173. 'South prospect of the town of Nottingham'; engraving. From George C. Deering, *Nottinghamia Vetus et Nova* (1750). Local Studies Library. Nottinghamshire Country Library.

174. Pierrepont House, Nottingham; painting by unknown artist (*c*.1708–13). Yale Center for British Art. Paul Mellon Collection B1976.7.125.

175. Detail from 'East prospect of Derby'; engraving by Samuel and Nathaniel Buck (1728). Photo: Fotomas Index.

176. Derby silk mill; engraving by Walker and Storer after an earlier drawing by J. Nixon (published 1798). Derby Industrial Museum.

177. Diagrams of basic manual operations of winding and twisting (or doubling) silk. From the *Universal Magazine*, vol. 1 (July 1747), facing p. 135. Bodleian Library, Oxford. Per. 2705.e.552/1.

178. Diagram of the basic waterpowered silk mill mechanism adapted by Thomas and John Lombe from Italian precedents and modified by George Sorocold for use in their mill. From Vittorio Zonca, *Novo Teatro di Machine et Edificii* (1607).

179. Cliff on one side of the castle above Castleton; drawing by Sir James Thornhill. From his *Sketchbook* (1699–1718). British Museum. Dept. of Prints and Drawings. 201.6.8. Photo courtesy of the Paul Mellon Centre for Studies in British Art, London.

180. Matlock Bath; engraving by John Boydell (1749). Bodleian Library, Oxford. Gough Maps 4 fol. 27 verso.

181. Pennine leadminer, from a lost painting of 'Old Curly', an old gang worthy (*c*.1760). Photograph in Backhouse MSS Swaledale 39. Leeds City Libraries.

182. Harborough Cave, suggested by local mining historians as a possible location for Defoe's miner's cave near Brassington. Photo courtesy of Roy Paulson and Peak District Mines Historical Society.

183. Buxton Bath; drawing by William Stukeley (July 1712). From his *Pocket sketchbook*. Bodleian Library, Oxford. MS Top. Gen. e.61. fol. 14 recto.

184. The entrance to Pool's Hole in Derbyshire with the doorkeeper, Alice Needham (3 July 1727); watercolour by an unknown artist. Bodleian Library, Oxford. Gough Maps 4 fol. 39 verso.

185. Pool's Hole or cave and Elden Hole. From *The Genuine Poetical Works of Charles Cotton* (1741). British Library. 1488.de.24. Reproduced by permission of the British Library Board.

186. Mam Tor; drawing by Sir James Thornhill. From his *Sketchbook* (1699–1718). British Museum. Dept. of Prints and Drawings. 201.6.8 Photo courtesy of the Paul Mellon Centre for Studies in British Art, London.

187. The Devil's Arse. From *The Genuine Poetical Works of Charles Cotton* (1741). British Library. 1488.de.24. Reproduced by permission of the British Library Board.

188. Chatsworth, house of the Duke of Devonshire; engraving by J. Kip after L. Knyff (*c.*1707). British Library. K.T.C. XI.12a. Reproduced by permission of the British Library Board.

189. Sheffield; engraving by Thomas Outerbridge (1736). Sheffield Industrial Museum.

190. 'Wakefield as it appears from London Road'; engraving by William Lodge (1680). Wakefield Art Gallery. Wakefield Metropolitan District Council Leisure Services.

191. Tenters, detail from 'East prospect of the town of Leeds'; engraving by I. Harris after a drawing by Samuel Buck (1720). Reproduced by permission of the Society of Antiquaries of London.

192. Early bell-shaped coal pits with horse- and hand-powered windlasses to remove coal and miners; engraving. Salford Mining Museum.

193. Eighteenth-century miner working underground; engraving. Salford Mining Museum.

194. 'Execution according to Halifax Law'; vignette from *A New description of England and Wales with adjacent islands . . .*, London (1724). Bodleian Library, Oxford, c.17.2. pl. 42.

195. *A New and exact plan of the town of Leeds*; engraved by J. Cossins (1725). Leeds City Libraries.

196. 'South East prospect of Rippon'; engraving by Samuel and Nathaniel Buck (1745). Yale Center for British Art. Paul Mellon Collection B1977.14.9664.

197. Dropping Well, Knaresborough; drawing by Francis Place (1711). British Museum. Dept of Prints and Drawings. 1850.2.23.822. Reproduced by permission of the Trustees of the British Museum.

198. 'Knaresborough Spa'; engraving of the building located at the Sweet Spa, Harrogate (probably early eighteenth century). Royal Pump Room Museum, Harrogate.

199. 'South West prospect of Richmond'; engraving by Samuel and Nathaniel Buck (1749). Photo: Fotomas Index.

200. The great fall of the Tees, County Durham; painting by George Lambert (1761). R.G. Cave Collection. Photo courtesy of the Paul Mellon Centre for Studies in British Art, London.

201. 'A Prospect . . . on the Foss, September 7, 1722' (the banks of the Trent near Nottingham going North); engraving by E. Kirkall after a drawing by William Stukeley. From William Stukeley, *Itinerarium Curiosum* (1724), pl. 90. Bodleian Library, Oxford. Gough Gen. Top. 55.

202. 'The South East Prospect of the city of York'; engraving by Samuel and Nathaniel Buck, 1745. Photo: Fotomas Index.

203. 'Prospect of a noble terras walk . . . York'; engraving by C. Grignion after a drawing by Nathan Drake (1756). York City Art Gallery.

204. 'Bonny Black' at Hambleton race course York; painting by John Wootton (*c.*1725). Private Collection. Photo courtesy of Christie's.

205. 'South East prospect of Kingston upon Hull'; engraving by Samuel and Nathaniel Buck (1745). Photo: Fotomas Index.

206. View of Scarborough Well and Governor Dicky's house; drawing by George Vertue (*c.*1720–30). Bodleian Library, Oxford. MS Gough Drawings a.1.

207. Durham cathedral and castle; painting attributed to George Lambert. Yale Center for British Art. Paul Mellon Collection B1976.7.126.

208. 'Elevation of an engine for raising coal and ore invented by Thomas Hunt . . . inscribed to the gentlemen who are proprietors of the collieries in the environs of Newcastle upon Tyne'; engraving (*c.*1735). Bodleian Library, Oxford. Gough Maps 25 fol. 55.

209. 'South East prospect of Newcastle upon Tyne'; engraving by Samuel and Nathaniel Buck (1743). Photo: Fotomas Index.

210. Detail from pl. 209.

211. Detail of Berwick bridge and town from an engraving of Berwick by Samuel and Nathaniel Buck (1745). Borough Museum, Berwick-upon-Tweed.

212. 'West prospect of the Town of Liverpool as it appeared about the year 1680'; engraving after John Eyes. Liverpool Record Office.

213. 'The South West Prospect of Liverpoole in the County Palatine of Lancaster'; engraving by Samuel and Nathaniel Buck (1728). Photo: Fotomas Index.

214. 'The South West prospect of Manchester and Salford'; engraving by John Harris after Robert Whitworth (1729). Yale Center for British Art. Paul Mellon Collection B.1977.14.9671.

215. 'West prospect of Preston from Penwortham Garden, August 1727'; preparatory wash and watercolour by Samuel Buck for an engraving never made. The engraving of Preston published in 1728 by Buck brothers was from the south. Bodleian Library, Oxford. Gough Maps 12, 20.

216. Windermere char; engraving by P. Mazell after G. Wilkinson. From Thomas Pennant, *British Zoology* (1776–7; 4th edition). Reproduced by permission of the Natural History Museum, London.

217. 'A view of Winander Meer, near Ambleside, a lake between Lancashire and Westmoreland'; engraving by M. Chatelin and Müller after the painting by William Bellers (1753). British Library. K.T.C. XLIII.16.6.1. Reproduced by permission of the British Library Board.

218. 'North West view of Cockermouth castle, in the county of Cumberland'; engraving by Samuel and Nathaniel Buck (1739). Photo: Fotomas Index.

219. The Three Brethren tree; engraving after O. Neale (published after 1750). Hothfield Muniments, on deposit at Cumbria Record Office, Kendal.

220. The Giants Grave: pillars and headstones in Penrith church yard; engraving from Thomas Pennant, *A Tour in Scotland* (1769), pl. xxxvi. Carlisle Library. Cumbria Library Service.

221. 'North West view of Carlisle Castle'; engraving by Samuel and Nathaniel Buck (1739). Carlisle Library. Cumbria Library Service.

222. Dunbar Castle and the Bass Rock; pen and watercolour by Francis Place (*c*.1701). Glasgow Art Gallery and Museums.

223. Detail of the prospect of Haddington; engraving. From John Slezer, *Theatrum Scotiae* (1693). National Library of Scotland.

224. Haddington, East Lothian; etching after a drawing by Paul Sandby (*c*.1750). National Galleries of Scotland. Dept. of Prints and Drawings.

225. Tantallon Castle; pen and watercolour by Paul Sandby (*c*.1750). National Galleries of Scotland. Dept. of Prints and Drawings.

226. 'Prospect of Bass Rock from the south shore'; engraving. From John Slezer, *Theatrum Scotiae* (1693). National Library of Scotland.

227. The Soland Goose (*anser bassanus*). From Eleazar Albin, *A Natural history of birds* (1738), pl. lxxxvi. Bodleian Library, Oxford. R.R.x.57(1).

228. 'The North Prospect of the city of Edinburgh'; engraving originally sold by John Bowles but included in 1719 edition of John Slezer, *Theatrum Scotiae*. National Library of Scotland.

229. Cannon-Gate; ink and watercolour drawing by Paul Sandby (1749), 26 × 34.29 cm. City of Edinburgh Art Centre.

230. Perspective view of the Parliament House and Exchequer, Edinburgh; engraving by A. Bell after a drawing by the Hon. John Elphinstone (published before 1740). National Galleries of Scotland. Dept. of Prints and Drawings.

231. High Street, Edinburgh; pen and watercolour drawing by Paul Sandby (dated 1751). British Museum. Dept. of Prints and Drawings. LB 80c. Royal vol. 36.

232. Horsefair on Bruntsfield Links; pen and watercolour drawing by Paul Sandby (dated 1750). National Galleries of Scotland. Dept. of Prints and Drawings.

233. Dissections by Archibald Pitcairne (1702) and Alexander Monro (1718); part of the 'Chamber of Rarities' in the Royal College of Surgeons, Edinburgh. Reproduced courtesy of the Royal College of Surgeons, Edinburgh.

234. Perspective view of the front of the Tron Kirk; engraving by Parr after a drawing by the Hon. John Elphinstone (published before 1740). National Galleries of Scotland. Dept of Prints and Drawings.

235. 'Prospect of Leith from the East'; detail from Greenvile Collins, *Great Britain's Coasting Pilot* (1693). Bodleian Library, Oxford. Gough Maps 86.

236. High Street and Midsteeple, Dumfries; pencil sketch by G.H. Johnson (1823). Dumfries Museum.

237. James Douglas, Second Duke of Queensberry and Dover (1662–1711); painting by Sir Godfrey Kneller (*c*.1692). Devonshire Collection, Chatsworth. Reproduced by permission of the Chatsworth Settlement Trustees. Photo courtesy of the Courtauld Institute of Art, University of London.

238. 'The Prospect of the Town of Aire from the East'; engraving. From John Slezer, *Theatrum Scotiae* (1693). National Library of Scotland.

239. A view of Greenock; engraving by Robert Paul (1768). Glasgow Collection, Mitchell Library, Glasgow.

240. 'A view of the Banks of Clyde taken from York Hill on the East side of the River Kelvin'; engraving by Robert Paul (1758). Glasgow Collection, Mitchell Library, Glasgow.

241. 'Prospect of Glasgow from the South'; engraving. From John Slezer, *Theatrum Scotiae* (1693). National Library of Scotland.

242. 'A view of the Trongate of Glasgow from the East'; engraving by William Buchanan after Robert Paul (*c.*1770). Glasgow Collection, Mitchell Library, Glasgow.

243. 'View of Port Glasgow from the South East'; engraving by Robert Paul (1768). Glasgow Collection, Mitchell Library, Glasgow.

244. 'The Prospect of their Majesties Castle of Sterling'; engraving. From John Slezer, *Theatrum Scotiae* (1693). National Library of Scotland.

245. Stirling Bridge; drawing by Paul Sandby (*c.*1748). From Thomas Pennant, *A Tour in Scotland* (1769–72 (large set)). National Library of Wales.

246. 'Prospect of Their Majesties palace of Linlithgow'; engraving. From John Slezer, *Theatrum Scotiae* (1693). National Library of Scotland.

247a–e. Processes in the linen industry; engravings (published by William Hincks, 1783). Ulster Folk and Transport Museum.

248. 'The Ruines of the Abbie of Melross'; engraving. From John Slezer, *Theatrum Scotiae* (1693). National Library of Scotland.

249. 'The Prospect of the Town of Kelso'; engraving. From John Slezer, *Theatrum Scotiae* (1693). National Library of Scotland.

250. 'Prospect of the town and abbey of Dunfermling'; engraving. From John Slezer, *Theatrum Scotiae* (1693). National Library of Scotland.

251. Kinross House; engraving by Richard Cooper from a drawing by John Borlach. From *Vitruvius Scoticus* (1810) pl. 62. Royal Commission on Ancient and Historical Monuments, Scotland.

252. 'Prospect of the Town of St Andrews'; engraving. From John Slezer, *Theatrum Scotiae* (1693). National Library of Scotland.

253. 'Prospect of the Town of Perth'; engraving. From John Slezer, *Theatrum Scotiae* (1693). National Library of Scotland.

254. Glamms House; engraving. From John Slezer, *Theatrum Scotiae* (1719 edition). National Library of Scotland.

255. *Prospect of the Battle of Sheriff-Muir 1715*; painting in the style of Jan Wyck. Private Collection. Photo courtesy of Oscar and Peter Johnson Ltd.

256. 'Prospect of the House and of the Town of Alloua'; engraving. From John Slezer, *Theatrum Scotiae* (1693). National Library of Scotland.

257 South view of Culross; drawing by Paul Sandby (1748). From Thomas Pennant, *A Tour in Scotland* (1769–72 (large set)). National Library of Wales.

258. 'Prospect of the town of Dundee'; engraving. From John Slezer, *Theatrum Scotiae* (1693). National Library of Scotland.

259. 'Prospect of Dunotter Castle'; engraving. From John Slezer, *Theatrum Scotiae* (1693). National Library of Scotland.

260. 'Prospect of Old Aberdien'; engraving. From John Slezer, *Theatrum Scotiae* (1693). National Library of Scotland.

261. Perspective view of New Aberdeen from the blockhouse; engraving based on a drawing by John Slezer (1693). From *The Complete English Traveller*. Aberdeen City Arts Department. Art Gallery and Museum.

262. 'Prospect of the town of Innerness'; engraving. From John Slezer, *Theatrum Scotiae* (1693). National Library of Scotland.

263. 'View of Fort George and the town of Inverness as it was in the year 1744'; engraving by T. Cook after a drawing by Paul Sandby. Courtauld Institute of Art, University of London. Witt Print Collection.

264. Berrydale, Sutherland; aquatint by William Daniell. Aberdeen City Arts Department. Art Gallery and Museum.

265. Market Cross in a highland township; engraving. From Edward Burt, *Letters from a Gentleman in the North of Scotland to his friend in London* (1754), facing p. 60. Bodleian Library, Oxford. Douce SS 297.

266. Houses in a highland township; engraving. From Edward Burt, *Letters from a Gentleman in the North of Scotland to his friend in London* (1754), facing p. 120. Bodleian Library, Oxford. Douce SS 297.

267. Strathnaver; aquatint by William Daniell. Aberdeen City Arts Department. Art Gallery and Museum.

268. Fort William; drawing by Paul Sandby (*c.*1749). From Thomas Pennant, *A Tour in Scotland* (1769–72 (large set)). National Library of Wales.

269. The Earl of Breadalbane's seat at Killing; engraving by W. Walker and W. Angus after an earlier drawing by Paul Sandby (published 1779). Courtauld Institute of Art, University of London. Witt Print Collection.

270. Dupplin House; engraving by P. Mazell after a drawing by Moses Griffith. Royal Commission on Ancient and Historical Monuments, Scotland. PTD 144/1.

271. 'Prospect of the towne of Brechin'; engraving. From John Slezer, *Theatrum Scotiae* (1693). National Library of Scotland.

272. Roadbuilders in the Scottish Highlands; watercolour by Paul Sandby (*c*.1750). National Galleries of Scotland. Dept. of Prints. D2343.

273. Highlanders wearing the plaid in different ways; engraving. From Edward Burt, *Letters from a Gentleman in the North of Scotland to his friend in London* (1754), facing p. 113. British Library. 10370.bbb.25. Reproduced by permission of the British Library Board.

274. View near Dumbarton, towards Ben Lomond; drawing by Paul Sandby (*c*.1750). From Thomas Pennant, *A Tour in Scotland* (1769–72 (large set)). National Library of Wales.

275. 'Prospect of the castle of Dumbritton [Dumbarton] from the east'; engraving. From John Slezer, *Theatrum Scotiae* (1693). National Library of Scotland.

276. Crag of Ailsa; engraving by P. Mazell after a drawing by Moses Griffith. From Thomas Pennant, *A Tour in Scotland and Voyage to the Hebrides* (1772), facing p. 190. London Library.

Colour Plates

I. Detail from pl. XXXI.

II. Detail from pl. XXI.

III. Peter Tillemans, *From my Turit in Blackfriers Lambeth* (after 1708). Watercolour, 19.8 × 36.9 cm. Ashmolean Museum, Oxford.

IV. Unknown painter, *Market square, Bury St Edmunds* (*c*.1700). Oil on board, 66 × 91.4 cm. Clock Museum. Borough of St. Edmundsbury Leisure Services (Museums).

V. John Wootton, *Newmarket scene* (1737). Oil on canvas, 88.9 × 127 cm. Reproduced by permission of the Marquess of Bath, Longleat House, Warminster, Wiltshire.

VI. Samuel Scott, *Greenwich Hospital* (*c*.1750). Oil on canvas, 102.9 × 186.7 cm. Collection of The Rt. Hon. Lord Carrington P.C. Photo: A.C. Cooper.

VII. Unknown painter, *Rochester Bridge* (probably early eighteenth century). Oil on canvas, 78.7 × 190 cm. Bridge Chamber, Rochester. Reproduced courtesy of the Wardens and Assistants of the Rochester Bridge Trust. Photo: Dudley Studios.

VIII. Richard Wilson, *Dover* (*c*.1746–7). Oil on canvas, 43.18 × 54.61 cm. Yale Center for British Art. Paul Mellon Collection B1976.7.173.

IX. Unknown painter, *Castle Street, Farnham, Surrey* (1761). Watercolour, 43.18 × 30.5 cm. Reproduced courtesy of Ray Tindle and Tindle Newspapers Limited.

X. John Wootton, *Landscape from Box Hill, Surrey* (1716). Oil on canvas, 62.23 × 106.68 cm. Private Collection.

XI. Peter Tillemans, *The Thames from Richmond Hill (The Thames between Twickenham and Ham)* (1720–23). Oil on canvas, 279.4 × 584.2 cm. Government Art Collection.

XII. Peter Tillemans, *The Thames at Twickenham* (1720–25). Oil on canvas, 167.64 × 391.16 cm. Private Collection. Photo courtesy of Sotheby's.

XIII. After Jan Griffier the Elder, *The Thames at Horseferry, with Lambeth Palace and a distant view of the city* (*c*.1706–10). Oil on canvas, 61.59 × 110.49 cm. Museum of London.

XIV. Leonard Knyff, *Hampton Court Palace, Middlesex, Bird's-eye view from the east* (*c*.1702). Oil on canvas, 153 × 216 cm. Royal Collection, Hampton Court Palace. Reproduced by gracious permission of Her Majesty the Queen.

XV. Painted wooden panel depicting the expulsion of Adam and Eve, Abraham and Isaac, and an angel, by an unknown artist of the sixteenth century. 68 × 53 cm. Museum of South Somerset, Yeovil.

XVI. George Lambert with, traditionally, William Hogarth, *Landscape with haymakers* (*c*.1730–40). Oil on canvas, 101.6 × 127 cm. Yale Center for British Art. Paul Mellon Collection B1981.25.356.

XVII. *The Cornish Chough.* From Eleazar Albin, *A Natural History of Birds* (1738). Colour engraving, 24 × 20 cm. Bodleian Library, Oxford. RR.X.57(2).

XVIII. Unknown painter, possibly Edmund Prideaux, *Padstow harbour and Prideaux Place* (*c*.1730). Oil on canvas, 65.4 × 56.5 cm. Prideaux Place, Padstow. Photo: Barrie Aughton Studio. Reproduced by permission of Mr Peter Prideaux-Brune.

XIX. Leonard Knyff, *Windsor Castle. Prospect from the north* (*c*.1704–5). Oil on canvas, 150 × 216 cm. Royal Collection, Windsor. Reproduced by gracious permission of Her Majesty the Queen.

XX. William Grimbaldson, *Hermes House, Islington, London. View from the garden with a prospect of London* (*c*.1725). Oil on canvas, 58.5 × 137.2 cm. Collection of Wiggins Teape, Basingstoke. Photo: Rod Clarke.

XXI. Pieter Angillis, *Covent Garden* (*c*.1726). Oil on copper, 47.78 × 63.02 cm. Yale Center for British Art. Paul Mellon Collection B1976.7.91.

XXII. Samuel Scott, *The So-called Custom House Quay* (*c.*1757). Oil on canvas, 137.16 × 129.54 cm. The Worshipful Company of Fishmongers, London. Photo: Bridgeman Art Library.

XXIII. Joseph Nickolls, *A view of Charing Cross and Northumberland House* (1746). Oil on canvas, 50.8 × 76.2 cm. National Westminster Bank p.l.c.

XXIV. Peter Tillemans, *The Thames with Chelsea Hospital* (*c.*1725). Oil on canvas, 309.9 × 541 cm. Reproduced by kind permission of the Commissioners of the Royal Hospital, Chelsea. Photo: Bridgeman Art Library.

XXVa, b, c. Unknown painter, *Views of the harvesting field of James Higford's manor, Dixton, Gloucestershire* (*c.*1725–35). Oil on canvas, 113 × 287 cm. Cheltenham Art Gallery and Museums. Photo: Bridgeman Art Library.

XXVI. Unknown painter, *Broad Quay, Bristol* (early eighteenth century). Oil on canvas, 64.14 × 77.15 cm. City of Bristol Museum and Art Gallery.

XXVII. Peter Tempest after Francis Place, *St Winefrid's Well, called Holy Well, near Flint* (*c.*1735). Hand-coloured engraving, 29.3 × 41.7 cm. Clwyd Record Office, 1009.

XXVIII. *Painted notice of the names of the Grand Jury called to try rioters after disturbances in 1705.* Oil on wood, 45 × 30 cm. Herbert Art Gallery and Museum, Coventry.

XXIX. Francis Barlow, *The Decoy* (*c.*1680). Oil on panel, 254 × 345.5 cm. Clandon Park, Surrey. Photo: National Trust Photographic Library/J. Whitaker.

XXX. George Lambert, *Landscape near Woburn Abbey, Bedfordshire* (1733). Oil on canvas, 35.75 × 72.5 cm. Tate Gallery, London.

XXXI. Jan Siberechts, *Wollaton Hall and Park, Nottinghamshire* (1695). Oil on canvas, 210.8 × 304.8 cm. Collection of the Honourable Michael Willoughby.

XXXII. Jan Siberechts, *Crossing the Ford, Wollaton* (1695). Oil on canvas, 105.4 × 142.2 cm. Collection of the Honourable Michael Willoughby.

XXXIII. (?)John Harris II, *Derbyshire landscape: view of Dovedale with figures fishing and cattle.* Oil on canvas, 114.3 × 106.7 cm. Dunham Massey, Cheshire. National Trust Photographic Library/Angelo Hornak.

XXXIV. Jan Siberechts, *View of Nottingham and the Trent* (1695). Oil on canvas, 109.2 × 146 cm. Collection of the Honourable Michael Willoughby.

XXXV. Unknown painter, *Whitby harbour* (after 1750). Watercolour, 31.75 × 49.53 cm. Whitby Museum. Reproduced by permission of the Literary and Philosophical Society.

XXXVI. Matthias Read, *Whitehaven, Cumberland* (*c.*1730–35). Oil on canvas, 101.6 × 182.88 cm. Yale Center for British Art. Paul Mellon Collection B1981.25.514.

XXXVII. Anthony Devis, *View of Derwentwater and Skiddaw from Lord's Island* (*c.*1750–55). Oil on canvas, 114.3 × 138.43 cm. Abbot Hall Art Gallery, Kendal.

XXXVIII. Unknown painter, *Yester House, East Lothian* (before 1685). Oil on canvas, 123.2 × 96 cm. Scottish National Portait Gallery, Edinburgh.

XXXIX. Paul Sandby, *Panorama of Nithsdale with Drumlanrig* (1751). Pen and watercolour, 15 × 41 cm. British Library. K.T.C. XLIX.54.I.c.

XL. Attributed to James Norie and Jan Griffier II, *Panorama of Taymouth Castle and Loch Tay* (detail) (?1733–1739). Oil on canvas, 66 × 133 cm. Scottish National Portrait Gallery, Edinburgh.

XLI. Richard Waitt, *Alastair Grant the Champion* (1714). Oil on canvas, 218.4 × 161.3 cm. Private Collection. Photo courtesy of the Scottish National Portrait Gallery, Edinburgh.

XLII. Attributed to Richard Waitt, *Andrew MacPherson of Cluny, chief of the Clan Chattan* (after 1720). Oil on canvas, 76.2 × 64 cm. Scottish National Portrait Gallery, Edinburgh.

XLIII. Thomas Murray, *John Murray, First Duke of Atholl (1659–1724)* (1708). Oil on canvas, 238.8 × 137.2 cm. From his Grace the Duke of Atholl's Collection at Blair Castle, Perthshire.

INDEX

Entries in the Index follow Defoe's spellings. Cross-references are normally made only when alphabetisation is seriously affected.

Names in **bold** type are those given prominence in the text. Figures in *italic* indicate pages with illustrations.

Abberforth, 267
Abbotsbury, 86, *86*
Aberdeen, 358, 359–62, *361*
Aberdour, 304, 344
Abington, 124
Abre, river, 367, 371
Abrystwyth, 195
Ackerman's Street, 179
Addison, Joseph, xii
Admiralty Office, London, 160, 165
African Company, London, 144, 146
Agricola, viii, 109
Ailesbury, earls of (Bruce family), 227
Ailsa Crag, *377*
Ailzye island, Clyde, 307, 377
Air (Ayr), 327, *327*
Air shire, 327–8
Aire, river, 254, 261, 264, 272, 274, 277
Albro' (Aldeburgh), 21
Aldborough, 267
Aldeburgh *see* Albro'
Aldersgate, London, 156, *156*
Alderton Hill, *176*
Aldgate, London, 156, *156*
Alloa *see* Alloway
Alloway (Alloa), 319, 331, 355–6, *356*
Alloway House, 355, *356*
Alnwick, 284, 301
Alresford, 74
Althorp (house), 213
Alton, 57, 74
Amesbury, 80
Ampthill, 227
Anabaptists, 18
Ancaster South, 216; *see also* Ankaster
Andover, 74, 124–5
Anglesea, or Mona, isle of, 195–7
Angus, 359
Angus, Archibald Douglas, 6th Earl of, 307
Ankaster, 222; *see also* Ancaster South
Anker, river, 214
Annan, river, 321
Annandale, Annand, 321
Annandale, William Johnstone, 1st Marquess of, 319
Anne, Queen, vii, 159, 160, 172, 192, 324, 343

Anstruther, or Anster, 348
Antipoedo Baptists, 18, 165
Appleby, 292–3
Arch-Angel, Russia, 362
Argyle, 374, 377–8
Argyle, Archibald Campbell, 9th Earl of, 374
Argyle, Archibald Campbell, 1st Duke of, 334, 355, 374
Arran, Isle of, 377
Arthur, King, 116, 192
Artillery Ground, London, 155, 165
Arun, river, 55
Arundel, 55, 62
Ashbourn, 240
Ashburton, 91
Ashdown Forest, 62
Ashurst, Sir William, 167
assemblies, 87–8
Athelstan, King, 276
Atherstone, 213
Athol, Blair, 371, 373–4
Athol, John Murray, 1st Duke of, 350, *354*, 371
Attleboro', 24
Aubury (Aubrey), John, 81
Audley End, 39, *39*
Augustine, St, 50
Aumont, Duc d', 138
Aust, 184
Avon, river (Warwickshire), 185, 209, 211
Avon, river (Wiltshire), 82, 122, 181, 184
Avon, Vale of, 185
Aylesbury, 173
Aylesbury, Vale of, 173, *173*
Aylesford, *49*
Ayr *see* Air

Badminton, 181
Bagshot-Heath, 58, *58*, 60, 74
Balfour, Sir Andrew, 313
Balgony (house), 350
Baliol College, Oxford, 113
Balmerinoch monastery, 350
Balmerinoch, John Elphingston, 4th Baron, 350
Bambrough, 284
Bamff (Banff), 362–3
Bampton, 91
Banbury, 178
Banff *see* Bamff
Bangor, Caernarvonshire, 197
Bangor Bridge, 205
Bank, London, 144, 147
Bannock Bourn, 332, 335, 357

Banqueting House, Whitehall, 160
Banstead Downs, 62
Barford-Bridge, 31
Barking, 8, 10
Barmoot Court (the Peak), 241
Barnard Castle, 269
Barnsley, or Black Barnsley, 253–4, 264
Barnstable hundred, Essex, 11
Barnstable, or Barnstaple, Devon, 112–14
Barnstable Water, 112–13
Barrington, John, Viscount (*formerly* Shute), 11
barrows and ancient monuments, 81, 124
Bartlet, ?William, 112
Barton on Humber, 216
Barton-Mills, 31
Basing, 74
Basingstoke, 74
Bass Rock, 102, *302*, 307, *308*
Bateman, Sir James, 68
Bath, or Achmanster, 115, 123, 179–81, *180*, *181*
Battersea, 65
Baumaris (Beaumaris) castle, 197
Bautry (Bawtry), 252, 277
Bear Key Market, London, 148, 150
Beaton, Cardinal David, Archbishop of St Andrews, 348–9
Beaufort, Cardinal Henry, 76
Beaufort, Dukes of, 181
Beaumaris *see* Baumaris
Beckenham, 62
Beckman, Sir Martin, 9
Bedal, Yorkshire, 267–8
Bedford, 31, 225, 227
Bedford, Dukes of, 227
Bedford Level, *34*
Bellsize (Belsize), 169
Bellsize House, *169*
Belvoir, Vale of, 214
Beminster, 119
Bere, 119
Berkley Castle, *184*, 185
Berrydale, *366*
Berwick upon Tweed, 284, *284*, 301
Bethlehem, or Bedlam hospital, London, 141, 157, 163, 165
Beverley, 218, 276
Bewdley, or Beawdly, 187–8
Biddiford (Bideford), 112–13, *112*
Biggleswood, 227
Billingsgate, London, 8, 148, *151*
Bing (Byng), Admiral Sir George, 359
Birmingham, 187
Bishopsgate, London, 156, *156*
Blacket, Sir Edward, 266–7